A Chanticleer Press Edition

EASTERN FORESTS

By Ann Sutton and Myron Sutton

Birds
John Bull, Field Associate, The American Museum of Natural History; and John Farrand, Jr., Editor, *American Birds,* National Audubon Society

Butterflies
Robert Michael Pyle, Consulting Lepidopterist, International Union for Conservation of Nature and Natural Resources

Insects and Spiders
Lorus Milne and Margery Milne, Lecturers, University of New Hampshire

Mammals
John O. Whitaker, Jr., Professor of Life Sciences, Indiana State University

Mushrooms
Peter Katsaros, Mycologist

Reptiles and Amphibians
John L. Behler, Curator of Herpetology, New York Zoological Society; and F. Wayne King, Director, Florida State Museum

Trees
Elbert L. Little, Jr., former Chief Dendrologist, U.S. Forest Service

Wildflowers
William A. Niering, Professor of Botany, Connecticut College, New London; and Nancy C. Olmstead, former Research Associate, Connecticut Arboretum

Alfred A. Knopf, New York

COPYRIGHT

Prepared and produced by
Chanticleer Press, Inc., New York.

Printed and bound by Dai Nippon, Tokyo, Japan.
Typeset in Garamond by Dix Type Inc., Syracuse, New York.

First Published March 1985
Reprinted Three Times
Fifth Printing, May 1988

Library of Congress Cataloging in Publication Data
Sutton, Ann, 1923–
The Audubon Society nature guides. Eastern forests.
Includes index.
1. Natural history–United States–Handbooks, manuals, etc.
2. Forest ecology–United States–Handbooks, manuals, etc.
3. Zoology–United States–Handbooks, manuals, etc.
4. Botany–United States–Handbooks, manuals, etc.
5. Forest fauna–United States–Identification. 6. Forest flora–
United States–Identification.
I Sutton, Myron, 1925–   II. National Audubon Society. III.
Title. IV. Title: Eastern forests.
QH104.S88   1986   574.5′2642′0978   84-48671
ISBN 0-394-73126-3 (pbk.)

Cover photograph: Autumn brings a blaze of color to the
mixed forest of Vermont's Green Mountains.

CONTENTS

ACKNOWLEDGMENTS

The authors wish to extend their deep appreciation to the many field specialists who contributed over a number of years the ecological data upon which this book is based. Especially helpful have been personnel associated with national parks, forests, and wildlife refuges; state parks and forests; The Appalachian Trail Conference; national and state Audubon societies; The Nature Conservancy; and private organizations devoted to field training in forest ecology.
Stanley G. Canter of Great Smoky Mountains National Park, U.S. Department of the Interior, provided key data and information, as did Connie Light Dickard of the Forest Service, U.S. Department of Agriculture, Tallahassee, Florida. Others that provided assistance include Buddy Corbett, Ozark National Forest; Grette Herrick, Mark Twain National Forest; David Dunitchik and Dianne Siegfried, Big Thicket National Preserve; Dennis Carter, Shenandoah National Park; Robert Rothe, Acadia National Park; Frank Ackermann, Cape Cod National Seashore; and the staff of Aransas National Wildlife Refuge.
We are grateful to Professor Peter Marks of Cornell University for his comprehensive review and suggestions, and to Laurence R. Sutton for data on pinelands ecology and for reviewing the manuscript.
To the editorial staff of Chanticleer Press, we express our thanks and admiration. Susan Costello, Mary Beth Brewer, Ann Whitman, Marian Appellof, David Allen, and Constance Mersel served with keen professionalism and worked long hours.
Ann Sutton
Myron Sutton

Ann Sutton and Myron Sutton
Collaborators for the past thirty years, Ann and Myron Sutton have written more than twenty books on natural history, including *Wildlife of the Forests, The Audubon Society Book of Trees,* and *Yellowstone: A Century of the Wilderness Idea.* Myron Sutton graduated from Northern Arizona University in Flagstaff where he majored in botany. After graduation he served for thirty-two years in the National Park Service as ranger, naturalist, museum specialist, and international conservation expert. Ann Sutton graduated from the University of Illinois in Urbana, majoring in geology. She later worked at the U.S. Geological Survey in Washington, D.C., and taught geology at the University of Kentucky in Lexington. The Suttons continue to travel widely and to write, photograph, and lecture about natural history and conservation.

HOW TO USE THIS GUIDE

This guide is designed for use both at home and in the field. Its clear arrangement in four parts—habitat essays, color plates, species descriptions, and appendices—puts information at your fingertips that would otherwise only be accessible through a small library of field guides.

The habitat essays enable you to discover the many kinds of forest habitats, the relationships among the plants and animals there, and highlights not to be missed. The color plates feature woodland and forest scenes and over 600 photographs of different plant and animal species. The species descriptions cover the most important information about a plant or animal, including a description, the range, specific habitat, and comments. Finally, the appendices include a bibliography, a glossary, and a comprehensive index.

Using This Guide at Home

Before planning an outing, you will want to know what you can expect to see in an eastern forest.

1. Begin by leafing through the color plates for a preview of eastern forests.

2. Read the habitat section. For quick reference, at the end of each chapter you will find a list of some of the most common plants and animals found in that habitat.

3. Look at the color plates of some of the animals and plants so that you will be able to recognize them later in the field. The table called How to Use the Color Plates provides a visual table of contents to the color section, explains the arrangement of the plates, and tells the caption information provided. The habitats where you are likely to encounter the species are listed in blue type so that you can easily refer to the correct habitat chapter. The page number for the full species description is also included in the caption.

4. Turn to the species descriptions to learn more about the plants and animals that interest you. A range map or drawing appears in the margin for birds, mammals, reptiles, and amphibians, and for many of the trees and wildflowers. Poisonous mushrooms and reptiles are indicated by the danger symbol ⊗ next to the species name.

5. Consult the appendices for definitions of technical terms and suggestions for further reading.

Using This Guide in the Field

When you are out in the field, you will want to find information quickly and easily.

1. Turn to the color plates to locate the plant or animal you have seen. At a glance the captions will help you narrow down the possibilities. First, verify the habitat by checking the blue type information to the left of the color plate. Next, look for important field marks, which are also indicated in blue type— for example, how and where a mushroom grows, an insect's food, or a caterpillar's host plants. To find out whether a bird, mammal, reptile, or amphibian is in your area, check the range map next to the color plate.

2. Now turn to the species description to confirm your identification and to learn more about the species.

First frontispiece. Black Bear cub sitting in a Red Spruce tree, Great Smoky Mountains National Park, Tennessee.

Second frontispiece. View of a hardwood forest from a mountaintop, Great Smoky Mountains National Park, Tennessee.

Third frontispiece. Male birch catkins open in early spring in the Green Mountains of Vermont.

Fourth frontispiece. A stream running through a transition forest in autumn, Taconic Mountains, New York.

Fifth frontispiece. Tiger swallowtails congregate near a stream in a hardwood forest, Great Smoky Mountains National Park, Tennessee.

PREFACE

The forests of eastern North America have a special allure.
They are a sanctuary for millions of people accustomed to
urban and suburban living, offering solitude, clean air, and
pure water, and beckoning persons who dote on the double
challenges of discovery and identification.

Among the most compelling attractions of eastern forests—
and they are world famous for this—is the color of leaves in
autumn. The brilliant reds, oranges, and purples of the dying
leaves are a magnificent sight, one that draws visitors from
around the world. Spring flowering is a close second in its
kaleidoscope of beauty in bloom.

There are many more marvels than color, however. Chief
among them are the sheer number and variety of billions of
plants and animals and the remarkable ways they operate in
cooperation or conflict with each other.

Entering the forests is an introduction into a new world of
adventure, surprise, delight, and discovery. There are puzzles,
too, and this book holds clues to solving them.

Crucial to a clear understanding of forest systems is an
approach that corresponds with the forest's own natural
division into different habitats—spruce woods, deciduous
woods, pine woods, and so forth.

Some habitats, like the boreal and mixed deciduous forests,
cover thousands of square miles and are generally composed of
the same life forms throughout. Other habitats, by contrast,
are relatively small; places such as the Pine Barrens of New
Jersey and the scrub and hammock forests of Florida are self-
contained systems of life.

The habitat approach that we have used in this guide is
designed to provide a picture of a visitor's actual experience in
a given kind of forest. There, the visitor is surrounded by the
many elements of an ecosystem—plants, animals, soils, rocks,
moisture, and climate. As one moves from place to place in
the habitat, the combination of elements may change subtly,
resulting in a change in the kinds of plants and animals.

When you witness action in a forest, there are many ways to
determine what is going on. Perhaps the most obvious activity
observed is the search of animals for food—birds and
mammals are most often discovered eating or hunting.
Sometimes there is drama—small tracks in the snow ending
abruptly in a flurry of wingtip impressions, suggesting that a
hawk swooped down to pick up its prey.

Such activities are easy to trace. More complex
interrelationships can be deciphered as visitors increase their
skills of observation and add personal experience to the
revelations in this book. In due course, the advanced naturalist
will be able to tell at a glance why certain trees have died or
where moose and deer are likely to be seen.

Such themes—not only what we see but why—are the
principal focus of this book: functional ecology (what is
happening) rather than simple descriptions of what is there.
This book stresses details of habitat ecology: the principal
plants and animals that live there, what they do, and how they
coexist.

Discovering all this, a little at a time, results in personal excitement and adventure that are renewed every time one enters the forest. Surprise is also an enriching experience, and encountering the unexpected is a delightful and remarkably frequent occurrence. For while nature is usually stable and predictable over millions of years, one is wise to keep in mind words attributed to the ancient Greek philosopher, Arcesilaus: "Nothing is certain, not even that."

Outdoor Equipment and Advice

Any excursion into the out-of-doors, whether just a short day-hike or a two-week camping trip, can be more enjoyable if planned in advance. Even for a stroll in the nearby woods, useful equipment might include a pair of binoculars, a field guide or two, and a sweater or rain gear as the local weather dictates. A camera, note pad, and pencil will help you to record what is seen. It is always smart to make a note of the weather, time of day, and the plants and animals that you encounter. The more complete a record you keep, the more useful and evocative these notes will be later.

Sunglasses, suntan lotion, and a hat are also often useful. All of this gear can be carried in a lightweight backpack.

If a hike in unfamiliar forests is planned—even just a short hike—you should carry a map and compass, and someone should be informed of your plans. Hiking in a group is safer than going it alone. If you hike in an area where poisonous snakes are common, bring along a small snake-bite kit. Wear broken-in walking shoes or boots. Comfort should be your paramount consideration here, as good footwear can mean the difference between enjoyment and misery.

For a longer camping trip, advance planning is very necessary. Learn about what kind of weather you can expect, because this will determine what clothes you bring. Aside from adequate food, clothing, and camping gear, you can often make reservations in overnight campgrounds.

Use maps of the area to select your route carefully; trail maps of many areas are available, and these can be invaluable. Remember that distances on maps can be deceiving: A mile of climbing is much more strenuous than a mile of walking on the level.

Much information can be obtained by writing to the authorities in national parks, forests, wildlife refuges, state parks and forests, and even local chambers of commerce. Most natural areas have strict regulations about litter and about the use of soaps near or in water supplies. They also have strictly enforced regulations regarding the removal, defacement, or destruction of plant and animal life, although fish are usually governed by special guidelines. It is the responsibility of the visitor to be aware of and to follow the existing regulations.

New discoveries await the patient and careful observer around each bend in the trail. There is a never-ending fascination in observing the complex interactions of wild plants and animals as they exist without human interference.

INTRODUCTION

The eastern forests support mighty trees of record dimensions, unbroken forests that stretch for hundreds of miles, thousands of species of trees, shrubs, and herbs, and a wide variety of wildlife ranging from microorganisms to the imposing Black Bear—all coexisting with human settlements in one of the most heavily populated regions on the globe.

Today very little remains of what Miles Standish, John Smith, or Hernando De Soto saw in the sixteenth and seventeenth centuries. Despite periodic setbacks, however, the same laws function now as then, particularly the laws of change. The forests are composed of a multitude of healthy, working natural systems, both small and large, that are flexible enough to absorb a high degree of impact. Each forest type is characterized by a combination of variables that makes it ecologically distinct from all the others.

Tundra to Tropics: Forest Types

Over their north-south range of 2000 miles, the forests of eastern North America extend from the southern shores of Hudson Bay to Florida. They change from near-arctic to near-tropical, and are part of every habitat, from seashore to mountaintop.

The coldest and slowest-growing forest—the boreal—is the largest in the area, partly because there is more land in northern North America than in southern. The boreal forest is circumpolar, composed of the same genera of trees, if not the same species, around the world. In North America it extends from the Atlantic Ocean to Alaska, and from Hudson Bay to the Canadian border. The conifer species that dominate the boreal forest are adapted to withstand below-zero temperatures for long periods of time. These trees are equipped to reproduce quickly in a short summer growing season, and to come back, albeit slowly, from the ravages of fire.

In the northern United States and portions of southern Canada, the boreal forest mixes with the deciduous to form the transition forest. This zone is scarcely 150 miles wide from north to south, but reaches from Minnesota to the Maritime Provinces. Much of it, like the boreal forest, is filled with a system of large lakes, but in New England and New York it is also carried to high elevations on the summits of rounded mountains and ridges. In the transition zone, the Sugar Maple reigns supreme wherever it can crowd out spruce, fir, pine, and hemlock. But usually Sugar Maple associates with such deciduous trees as Yellow Birch, poplars, and basswoods.

From the Great Lakes to the beginnings of the Deep South, the mixed deciduous forest spreads like a green blanket. Here there is an explosion in the number of species. Whereas the boreal forest contains a limited number of conifers and hardwoods, the deciduous forest has well over a hundred species. The Sugar Maple no longer dominates but rather joins with dozens of other species, among them Yellow-poplar, sycamores, Sweetgum, oaks, Yellow Birch, and magnolias. In the north-central portion of the mixed deciduous forest, Sugar Maple and American Beech dominate. In the northwest portion Sugar Maple associates primarily with American Basswood. And while oaks and hickories occur over most of the deciduous forest, the dominant concentration is found in the Ozark Highlands west of the Mississippi River.

From Virginia to Tennessee, along the Blue Ridge Mountains and the southern Appalachians, the deciduous forest achieves its peak in age, maturity, number of species, size of individuals, and area preserved in virgin state. The cove hardwood (untouched) forests of mountain ravines are the most impressive; remote and undisturbed, they express the destiny of a deciduous forest after millions of years of evolutionary development.

Along the eastern and southern borders of the mixed deciduous forest lie mile after mile of pines, their roots in sand, clay, or gravel, and their crowns vulnerable to fire. Some of these pine areas are called barrens, a term that indicates more or less treeless tracts, land covered with stunted forests, or land with poor soil. The New Jersey Pine Barrens is the most distinctive such area, and it is one of the best places in North America to study the impact of fire upon vegetation. From New Jersey along the Atlantic and Gulf coastal plains stretch the southern pinelands, great expanses of Longleaf, Loblolly, and Slash pines periodically singed by fires that cut back competing oaks, hickories, and other deciduous trees. Huge live oaks, often draped with Spanish Moss, are abundant in certain localities.

On the Florida peninsula the temperate and tropical forests meet. Ironically, the region with the longest growing season contains some of the scrubbiest forests. The pines retain their dominance, but extensive "islands" of deciduous hardwoods appear, as do groves of palms and palmettos. From Lake Okeechobee south to the southern tip of Florida, the vegetation becomes almost entirely tropical, as though West Indian forests had been transported across the Caribbean Sea. The "islands" of trees here are tropical hardwood hammocks, rich collections of trees where none (except possibly the mahogany) dominates.

Geological History and Soils

The nature and distribution of soils have determined what trees grow where. These factors, in turn, are the result of the physical evolution of the earth and the erosion of its surface. Fifteen thousand years ago, the polar ice cap extended over more than half of North America, and there were scarcely any forests whatever north of what is today the Ohio River. Immense continental ice sheets, 1000 to 2000 feet thick, accumulated across the northern part of the globe; moisture evaporating from the sea was deposited as rain or snow, which added to the depth of the ice. These events lowered sea level, broadening the coastal plains along the Atlantic Ocean and Gulf of Mexico and more than doubling the size of the exposed peninsula of Florida.

South of the range of the glaciers were forests. These were undoubtedly much colder then, but they still harbored representatives of the species that once grew on glaciated lands. After the glaciers melted and retreated, wind, birds, and mammals transported seeds to the north, repopulating the recently uncovered areas with species from the southern forests. Glaciers never reached south of the Ohio and Missouri rivers, so most temperate forests have been able to evolve under comparatively stable conditions for millions of years. During interglacial periods, they have served as seed sources— fountains of replenishment for glaciated areas.

Much of the debris scraped up by glaciers was subsequently released; today it constitutes a variety of soils, many of them rich and highly supportive of dense forest growth. By contrast, some rocky uplands, such as those of the various rock assemblages of the Canadian shield, were scraped clean. Only after the glaciers melted away and exposed this barren rock could soil begin to form. In the 10,000 years that have elapsed since the end of the last ice age there has not been time for deep, rich soils to develop. That is why the northern coniferous forests must obtain many of their nutrients from sources other than soils.

From a geological point of view, eastern North America has been comparatively quiet since the upheavals of the Precambrian and Paleozoic eras: no volcanoes, relatively few earthquakes, no uplifts, and only a slow coastal submergence. This geological repose has allowed erosion to dissect the ridges and plateaus and permitted disintegration of rock to continue undisturbed over large areas of land for long periods of time. That, together with all the more recent soil-making activities, has created a region of the earth's crust with extremely mature and varied soil resources.

The soils that support dense deciduous forests receive annual enrichment from fallen leaves and decaying debris. This litter forms a layer on the forest floor, where it is decomposed by microscopic fungi, microorganisms, and animals, its nutrients eventually released to support further plant growth.

With the help of gravity and running water, some soil from higher elevations is deposited at successively lower levels until part of it reaches floodplains beside streams and rivers and eventually forms deltas at the edge of the sea. Accordingly, some of the richest loams in eastern North America are located in bottomlands and broad valleys.

As a result of better drainage and more leaching of nutrients during runoff, some upland soils may be less fertile, although the difference is usually small. Soils in the southern Appalachians, for example, are exceptionally fertile, and they support some of the richest forests on the continent. Great expanses of jagged cliffs or naked rocky plateaus do not exist among the forests of eastern North America.

Barren sand, however, is another matter. One of the most abundant and widespread soil types in this region, sand has a vastly lower mineral content than loamy topsoil. Therefore, the vegetation growing on sand must be adapted to get the bulk of needed nutrients from sources other than the soil. The trouble with sand is twofold: It does not hold water well, and it does not contain many nutrients. Sands and gravels, being porous, are notorious for their inability to retain water; rain that falls on them quickly passes the roots of plants on the way to the subterranean water table, and what the plants get is only what they can capture during and immediately after a storm. This situation offers too much stress for delicate plants that need more sustained supplies of moisture; hence forests adapted to sand are of necessity also adapted to aridity. The chemical nature of the soil also exercises a controlling factor over the components of each habitat. Some soils, including sands, are very nearly chemically neutral. Those based on limestone are alkaline and support such trees as basswood, Blue Ash, and Chinkapin Oak. The forest itself contributes to the chemical nature of the soil, especially where there has been accumulation of decomposed material and debris. Such soils may be acidic. Many kinds of plants, such as the heaths (which include blueberries, azaleas, and rhododendrons) are notable for their occurrence on acid soils.

The Role of Fire
Although the forests of eastern North America normally receive more than adequate precipitation, all of them periodically suffer some degree of drought. Consequently, every forest is vulnerable to one of the most powerful of forces, fire. Indeed, fires have been a factor in forest development for millions of years.

Every treetop is an effective point of discharge for lightning, which, with a current of 250,000 amperes, can explode a tree, deform it, split it, or leave a scar that remains for the rest of the tree's natural life. One electrical storm can touch off scores of fires; in very dry woods with a great deal of accumulated litter and downed debris, such fires may coalesce and reach high temperatures. Heavy wind can make a fire so intense that the trees and resident wildlife are nearly obliterated. In places like the pinelands, however, where fires are frequent, debris does not have much chance to accumulate; in such places, ground and crown fires are slow-moving and relatively cool. Fires are pervasive over much of eastern North America, and fire-adapted forest communities have developed from Canada to Florida and as far west as Texas. Deciduous forests do not burn often, because their rich growth has a high moisture content. The coniferous forests of the North are also moist and the cold environments keep fire temperatures lower; hence fire is not as destructive a factor there as elsewhere. Nonetheless, the boreal forest does burn occasionally—and catastrophically. The truly fire-prone forests are the pine barrens, southern pinelands, flatwoods, scrub, and sandhill forests. In these areas, pines dominate because they are well insulated from heat and can survive all but the hottest fires. They are adapted to grow best in open sunlight and therefore, along with aspens in the North, spring up before other trees in areas disturbed by fire. In the course of events, hardwoods begin to grow among the pines, shading them, hampering their growth, and crowding them out. In some localities hardwoods eventually assume dominance, but in most places they are eventually burned back, and the pines once again take over.

In every forest that burns regularly, fires provide significant benefits. They stimulate the cycle of death and renewal and release nutrients into the soil. They also create additional types of habitats favored by different species of plants and animals, thus promoting natural diversity. The notable disadvantage of fires is the occasional removal of vegetation that holds soil in place, and the consequent exposure of the forest floor to erosion by heavy water runoff.

Climate

Temperatures in eastern North America vary from extremely cold and dry in the North to hot (but not extremely hot) and humid in the South. Rain provides a steady flow of moisture throughout the year from boreal forests to the southern pinelands; in Florida the precipitation falls chiefly in the summer months, when plants need water most.

Atmospheric conflicts can bring severe storms during the growing season. Because there are no protective mountain ranges to moderate the flow of cold air from the north or hot, humid air from the tropics, masses of air move across the eastern part of the continent without interruption. As a result, the forests of eastern North America lie directly in the path of air movements from both the north and the south.

Hurricanes are massive tropical storm systems, generated at sea, that cover thousands of square miles and, when they move inland, can devastate forests from the Gulf all the way to New England. They bring heavy rainfall that often results in severe flooding, and their high winds push seawater into low-elevation coastal forests. Although trees are flexible and adapted to sway with the wind, it is impossible for even the hardiest ones to spring back after extremely severe storms.

The smallest but most devastating storms are tornadoes, which break the trunks of trees and hurl limbs at speeds of 200 miles an hour across the countryside. Tornadoes occur from the central Great Plains states eastward; they are most common in the prairie states, but every state in eastern North America has experienced them.

In coastal areas the sea moderates environmental extremes. Atlantic and Gulf coastal forests can be lashed by gales, flooded with salt water, and subjected to continuous winds. As a result, whole sections of shoreline shift their contours and the trees are pruned as though sculpted by human hands.

High winds carry salt spray for long distances inland—as, for example, in Massachusetts, where even the hardy Pitch Pines on Cape Cod have suffered salt-spray damage. Cold air masses from the interior sweep along the coasts and occasionally reach far enough south to kill even the sturdy mangroves on Florida's southern shores.

The Flow of Water

Nothing is more vital to the growth of vegetation than moisture. The external sources of moisture include not only rain, snow, and the subterranean flow of groundwater to the roots of plants, but also dew and vapor in the air. Under the right conditions, trees "comb" moisture from clouds and fog, and the condensation drips to the ground like rain. High forests in the Adirondacks and in the Green and White mountains collect an impressive amount of water in this way. Spruces and firs have countless small needles and twiggy branches that make up a combined surface of perhaps fourteen million square yards per forested acre. These surfaces trap water droplets from low-lying clouds or fog, making at least five inches of water each year available to the plants.

On its way down to the soil, water is absorbed and stored in considerable quantity by mosses, leaf litter, and air plants, or epiphytes. This process helps to maintain atmospheric humidity, which protects against fire and the effects of climatic extremes. After reaching the soil, water either flows out of the forest system or is absorbed by plant roots. In the latter case, the water works its way back up through the plant, and part of it is finally released to the atmosphere through transpiration.

The presence of water supports photosynthesis, the movement of nutrients, respiration, cell turgidity, osmosis, and other physiological functions. Water also has the important role of collecting minute particles of dust from the air and debris from stem flow to form a dilute solution of nutrients. This is one means whereby forests can develop on relatively sterile soil; it is especially important to southern pineland and scrub forests that grow in sand.

The Nutrient Cycle

Plants, like animals, require nutrition, which comes in the form of various elements present in soil, water, and air. The capture and retention of these raw materials becomes all-important, especially in those ecosystems, such as sandhill forests, where there are precious few nutrients to begin with, and fewer still introduced on a daily basis.

As rainfall filters through vegetation, some nutrients are intercepted and stored, some dissolved and carried down to the millions of small rootlets that absorb minerals. As water evaporates from the leaves above, more moisture and minerals are drawn from the soil upward through the tree and into the leaves for use in photosynthesis. With the inflow of carbon dioxide from the air, the materials are all in place for the production of carbohydrates.

Where soils are really poor in nutrients, as in parts of Florida, some plants receive aid from saprophytic fungi that are attached to plant roots by a filamentlike structure known as hyphae. These fungi decompose dead matter, thus freeing nutrients for the use of other plants.

The components of a mature and well-developed ecosystem are adapted to conserve existing nutrient stock; thus the nutrient cycle is tightly organized and few nutrients escape. Forests that grow on floodplains, for example, are able to draw nutrients directly from the water, because of the nutritionally rich muds and other deposits that collect there.

No matter how sterile or rich the soil is, nutrient supplies must be continuously accessible to plants. If there is prolonged stoppage at any point, the system's functions could cease. Therefore, to keep the system healthy, the sources of nutrients —decomposers, rain, runoff, fire, and recycling organisms— must be maintained.

The Limits of Tolerance

A species can grow when a certain 'range of conditions affecting its growth is met. The geographical range of each of the forests of eastern North America is dictated by the limits of tolerance possessed by its components. Many deciduous trees, for example, could spread much farther to the west were the climate less arid. Sugar Maple and Eastern Cottonwood are able to range west because they are vigorous competitors for moist soil in bottomlands along streams. Oaks and hickories are able to live in drier climates, but where they venture out on the prairies they become shrubby.

Unlike pines, which have thick insulating bark, deciduous trees burn easily and therefore are not successful in the pine barrens and southern pinelands, where fire is a common occurrence. Some broad-leaved trees will survive a fire, and there are places in the New Jersey Pine Barrens and throughout the southern pinelands where oaks and other hardwood species dominate. But even where they grow in swamps, these species are still at the mercy of fire.

Most deciduous trees cannot endure extreme cold and therefore cannot compete effectively with the hardy spruce and firs of the North and of high elevations. Deciduous trees do their best on loam with fertile humus that supplies the abundance of nutrients they need. They grow poorly or not at all in sterile, sandy soils, but fare well on soils enriched by centuries of plant growth and litter deposition. In comparatively poor soils, then, they are no match for pines, which survive with fewer nutrients.

Most trees are desiccated by salt spray in the air; only mangroves, pines, Yaupon (a kind of holly), and a few other trees can tolerate a saline environment. Just beyond such salt-tolerant species, however, oaks, White Cedars, and palms become established in protected places, resulting in maritime forests of remarkable density. Likewise, some trees tolerate flooding and some do not. On the lower Mississippi River, for example, certain hardwood forests stand for months with their lower trunks submerged in floodwaters.

Thus the presence of different types of forests, composed of different groups of species, is dictated by the limits of tolerance that each of its components possesses.

Competition and Succession

There are times when an ecosystem such as a lake or pond becomes overenriched and fills with mud, roots, and other debris that eventually become soil. The resultant meadow is covered first by moisture-tolerant grasses, then small trees such as pines, which do well in open spaces, and then hardwoods. This process of growth, called succession, is

neither random nor simple. It is governed by the requirements
of each plant for moisture, soil acidity, or shade. And the
growth of one type of vegetation will either preclude or make
possible the growth of the next, or successive, species.
Over time, different areas will display different characteristic
patterns of succession. The change from pond to hardwood
forest is described briefly above. In burned-over areas of the
boreal or transition forest, hardy lichens and mosses are usually
the pioneer species, followed shortly by grasses and magenta-
flowered fireweeds. An open, sunny environment is ideal for
aspen trees, and so groves of them spring up out of the grass
and fireweed and grow rapidly during the long summer days.
But the aspens do not tolerate shade and are vulnerable to
being crowded out by certain conifers, which get their start in
the shelter of aspens. The group that ultimately takes over in
the absence of further disturbance is a climax community; it
represents the culmination of a forest's development.
As the climax forest ages, branches drop to form a clutter of
flammable debris beneath, and the community becomes
vulnerable to lightning and fire, along with disease, wind, and
other external influences. When a forest is destroyed, the way
is once again opened for the succession from pioneer species to
climax growth to begin again.
For thousands of square miles, the boreal forest is dominated
by a spruce-fir climax. The deciduous forest and the tropical
hardwood hammock forest are climax communities with many
dominant species. Without the frequent disruption of fire, the
pinelands and pine barrens would have a hardwood climax
community. Hardwoods have taken over in a few places, such
as oak groves in the pine barrens and hardwood hammocks in
the scrub country of north-central Florida.

Forest Communities

Trees adjusted to particular types of soils, dry or moist
environments, and climatic situations tend to grow together in
associations; for example, maple and basswood often grow
together, forming the maple-basswood association. It is now
more usual to refer to the entire grouping of shrubs, herbs,
mosses, as well as trees, as a community: the maple-basswood
community, for example. More comprehensive yet is a
designation that includes every living and nonliving thing in
the community. This requires a full consideration of animals
along with plants, soils, and climate. Every part of a
community has some influence on every other part; the whole
is referred to as a system of ecological relationships, or
ecosystem, for short. In this sense, the organic and inorganic
components constitute the structure of the ecosystem, while
the constant crosscurrents of productivity, consumption,
competition, and cooperation are the functional components.
In nearly all forests, and especially in deciduous forests, several
layers of life can be seen to work together harmoniously.
Layering—from beneath the soil to the treetops—enables
different species to occupy virtually the same space without
competing with one another.

The lowest layer is the soil. It is home to billions of organisms, large and small, and provides shelter for many burrowing animals, such as gophers, Woodchucks, armadillos, and moles. Earthworms and other invertebrates constantly churn the soil, enriching it as they pass it through their bodies, aerating it, and loosening it for better plant growth. Burrowing animals bring soil to the surface in an effective program of nutrient recycling.

The next layer above the soil is the forest floor, which is carpeted with herbaceous plants, such as Wood Sorrel and blueberries, that grow from discarded, decaying leaves, needles, feathers, feces, and other organic remains. In most forests, this is a dimly lighted environment because the trees form a tight umbrella of limbs and leaves. Some plants that thrive here, like ferns and mosses, are adapted to shade, while others, like wild flowers, bloom and reproduce in early spring before the leaves on the trees grow out and filter the sunlight for the rest of the summer. Certain forests, like the oak-hickory, are somewhat open and illuminated, but in other places the leaves form an impenetrable layer, and little grows on the forest floor. In the open pineland forests much sunlight reaches the ground, but the understory vegetation must contend with the sterility of sandy soils and the repeated occurrence of fire.

Certain animals live on the forest floor and never venture higher; among these are shrews, mice, salamanders, and many reptiles. Birds like Bobwhites, Turkeys, and Ovenbirds nest on the forest floor. Others are well adapted to the next higher level, which in the East consists of shrubs and thickets of palmetto, or of rhododendron, spicebush, huckleberry, or thimbleberry.

In many places, there is an understory between the shrub layer and the canopy. This includes such small trees as dogwood, redbud, and witch hazel. Beginning at this level, the warblers and woodpeckers search for insects and the squirrels gather acorns.

The highest forest layer is the canopy, where the tallest trees lift their leaves to the sun. In eastern forests, some of the most commonly encountered giants of the forest are oaks, maples, Beeches, Yellow-poplars, hemlocks, basswoods, hickories, and in the tropical forests, the Gumbo-limbo and mahogany. It is a place where eagles, hawks, and owls perch to scrutinize the land below for food, where bats and flycatchers search for insects, and where migratory species sometimes pause to rest.

Layering is not clearly defined in every forest community. Where there is a pure stand of Longleaf Pine on the coastal plain, the understory may be only an occasional oak. But even there, certain animals keep to separate levels of the forest, and can therefore live in close association with a minimum of conflict. From the point of view of an entire ecosystem, this arrangement provides a built-in redundancy. If one component is reduced or impaired, its function in the system is assumed by others with overlapping or similar functions, thus reducing stress on the overall system.

Producers

No matter how complex the forests of eastern North America seem, their inhabitants may be readily divided into two groups: those that produce and those that consume. It is a balanced division most of the time, but there are times when one group outnumbers the other.

The trees and other plants make up the greatest amount of living matter, called biomass. The tree itself is one of the most remarkable and durable of self-sustaining life forms, able to absorb all kinds of environmental punishment and still produce great quantities of wood, leaves, and seeds. Inside the bark is the sapwood, where food is stored and through which water and nutrients move upward to the leaves and down to the roots. As a tree grows, the sapwood at the very center is no longer used to transport fluids; this material is transformed into heartwood, and gives the tree its strength and stability.

Green plants are the producers. Through photosynthesis, they use solar energy to make carbohydrates from carbon dioxide and water. From this fundamental process of photosynthesis, the plant's principal engine of life, all living creatures meet their energy requirements. The sugars formed in photosynthesis store energy until it is needed by the plant or those organisms that consume the plant. At that time, the sugar is broken down and the energy is used in the normal metabolic processes of the consuming organisms.

The food sources provided by the forest take many forms. One of the most widespread and useful products is the acorn, but hickories, walnuts, and pecans are also plentiful. A vigorous oak tree can produce as many as 28,000 acorns in a single year. There are fleshy fruits, such as plums and persimmons, numerous berries, pine seeds, capsules, balls, and beans. Leaves themselves constitute a fleshy produce. To this is added a huge variety of herbs and bulbs, bark, and the products of secondary producers such as saprophytic fungi.

Consumers

Eventually, all this material is broken down and used in one way or another. Thus each ecosystem is regularly renewed through the process of production and consumption.

The consumers are animals and other organisms, such as certain fungi and parasites that do not have the ability to produce foods through photosynthesis. They obtain energy from the chemical compounds they consume. The consumers can be conveniently divided according to what they eat. Microbes on the forest floor decompose the discarded material that falls within their reach. Parasites feed on living hosts, weakening them and helping to control their populations. Scavengers, such as vultures, feed on carrion and partially decayed material. Herbivores—such as rabbits, deer, a variety of birds, and many destructive forest insects—consume vegetation. Carnivores eat other consumers, and omnivores can eat almost anything.

Most of what consumers eat is discharged back into the ecosystem. These materials decompose and provide nutrients to the soil, which in turn provides sustenance for the primary producers—the plants.

Interruptions or dislocations at any point affect the whole food-making process of an ecosystem. The health of all consumers is linked to the success of food production, but the forests of eastern North America are filled with periodic dislocations and disruptions.

Seed production, for example, varies tremendously from year to year. A successful crop requires mature, vigorous trees, adequate rainfall, moderate temperature, lack of severe weather, good dispersal of pollen, timely seed germination, and low consumption by animals. Many trees produce crops in cycles, with prolific crops in one year, then little or nothing for several years.

All ecosystems are constantly under some degree of stress brought about by disruptions in balances between supply and demand. Far from being in precise equilibrium, the forest's components exist at various stages of recovery from one or another event.

Animal populations also often outgrow the capability of the forest community to support them. Deer populations, notorious for this, sometimes graze so vigorously that they eliminate certain favorite trees.

Eventually these large populations will outgrow available food supplies. Weakened, they grow fewer through starvation, disease, or predation. Such imbalances as supply and demand might not occur at all if the deer's natural predators, including Mountain Lions and wolves, existed in numbers sufficient to keep the deer population culled. Predation is a natural procedure for maintaining populations of strong, energetic individuals in numbers proportional to their habitat.

The Flow of Energy

In every forest the transfer of food is the most observable natural activity. It is seen in browsing deer, foraging squirrels, darting flycatchers. As one organism consumes another, there soon is established a direct line of consumption—for instance, from seeds to mouse, to hawk, to decomposer. This line is known as a food chain. It is a biological pathway along which energy originally manufactured by primary producers is passed along to successive consumers.

In the forest multiple food chains form an intricate network, called a food web. Since the amount of stored energy is reduced each time it is consumed and passed on, the energy at any one level is always less than that at the level below, and much more food must be produced than is consumed. That is why one commonly sees the plant producers—oak trees, for instance—but rarely encounters the animals at the top of the food chain, such as bears and owls.

The chain of production and consumption does not end with these predators, however, for the forests are filled with organisms that consume dead and discarded plant material as well as animals that feed on decayed organic matter. Invertebrates living in the soil break down litter with the assistance of fungi and bacteria. This enriches the tiny particles in the soil with protein and makes them an energy-rich food source for lower-layer organisms.

Adaptations to Stress

Every ecosystem, from boreal forests to tropical hammocks, suffers naturally from a variety of stresses. These include bad weather, temperature extremes, strong winds, drought, flood, low fertility of the soils, overconsumption by animals, underproduction of foods, or human intervention. An ecosystem continues at its best only as long as it withstands these stressful influences.

But these stresses require some kind of expenditure of energy to overcome, and plants and animals at risk may lack reserves of strength—especially those living at the edge of survival in a marginal habitat.

When the temperature rises above about 90° F, the amount of energy a plant must expend to overcome excessive heat exceeds the energy output of photosynthesis. Growth decreases and the stored energy in the biomass must be consumed as a defense against excessive heat, resulting in decreased productivity.

Some organisms are so often beset with certain types of stress that they have become specialized to cope with it. For example, the ability of pines to withstand fire is a function of their insulating bark, quick recovery, and regrowth in open, disturbed areas. One of the most common adaptations is the ability to conserve water. The needles of spruce, fir, hemlock, and pine are leaves that have become reduced not only to expose less area to cold but also to lose less moisture through transpiration.

Some trees, such as the Southern Magnolia, have heavily cutinized, or waxed, leaves to retard evaporation from their surfaces. The Turkey Oak turns its leaves at midday so that the edges, rather than the flat area, are toward the sun, thus exposing less surface area.

Often the result of too much stress is a reduction in the number of species. This is well illustrated in the boreal forest, which has fewer species of plants and animals than more southerly forests because of the low temperature and short growing season. Spruces have little competition from hardwoods because few hardwoods are adapted to withstand subarctic climates. In the same way, few conifers are adapted to cope with subtropical heat.

When all these adaptations are added up, it becomes clear that it is not just individual trees, shrubs, and animals that are adapted to withstand stress, but whole ecosystems as well. The components of an ecosystem are linked, so that if extended drought, for example, arrests the development of one group of organisms, others continue to survive.

Because a forest is a collection of communities, one kind of stress may not affect all communities at once. Trees may die, but not the understory shrubs and herbs. And in the end, the parts of the community grow back or reassemble, bit by bit, piece by piece, individual by individual.

THE BOREAL FOREST

The northernmost forest in North America—and the largest forest by far—is known as the boreal forest. The boreal forest can be divided roughly into three bands: 1) a pine and hemlock zone in the south; 2) a central belt of spruce-fir climax forest in the center; and 3) a northern zone of taiga, where the spruces and firs become increasingly dwarfed in more northerly latitudes, until they are replaced by tundra. The boreal forest forms a continent-wide band that extends northwestward in a wide arc from Newfoundland to Alaska. Over most of the area between the Cordillera and the Atlantic Ocean the landscape is uninterrupted by mountains, and the forest virtually unbroken. Within this area is one of the world's most extensive systems of rivers and lakes.

The great ice sheets that sprawled across this region from 500,000 to 10,000 years ago left a random series of channels and basins. Some of the lakes seem somewhat aligned in a northeast-southwest trend, but whatever drainage patterns existed in preglacial times have been distorted and otherwise deranged into a system that seems to make little sense. The glaciers picked up giant boulders and transported them, then melted to deposit random hills of till (glacial drift) and to fill up valleys on a less than systematic basis.

A typical summer day in the boreal forest begins calmly, the ponds placid, the waters overhung with mist. By midmorning, wind blows the fog away, clouds race over the tips of the spruces, and rain squalls blot out the forest. The rest of the day is likely to be cool and cloudy, with light breezes. There are few roads, trails, or settlements over most of the boreal forest, and the principal means of access is by canoe. A canoeist gliding along the placid water's surface, stepping out on a point of land, or entering the forest experiences a feeling of water everywhere. In roving through this wilderness during summer, the traveler encounters water continuously.

Conifers

The woods are broken by light brown outcrops of granite and other ancient rocks that underlie the forest, or by huge boulders, called erratics, that were dropped as the glaciers melted. Nearly every geological feature is obscured by forest, which is dominated by Balsam Fir, Black and White spruces, and Red, White, and Jack pines.

The Red Pine is a handsome species that grows as high as one hundred feet. The Jack Pine presents a ragged, stunted appearance and seldom exceeds sixty feet in height, but it covers thousands of square miles; pioneering mostly on relatively sterile soils that few other trees inhabit, it shelters the seedlings of Red Pines for a time, yielding to their dominance as the trees mature.

As for the White Pine, no other tree in northern North America was as important to early settlers. It has been called the most generally useful wood our country has ever possessed. Soft and lightweight yet strong, it was ideal for the masts of ships, among other uses, and was therefore so widely and extensively employed that the tree was nearly removed from

Balsam Fir
Abies balsamea
33, 172

Black Spruce
Picea mariana
30, 169

White Spruce
Picea glauca
29, 170

Red Pine
Pinus resinosa
22

Eastern White Pine
Pinus strobus
19

Jack Pine
Pinus banksiana
28

Quaking Aspen
Populus tremuloides
64

Paper Birch
Betula papyrifera
67, 239

Balsam Poplar
Populus balsamifera
101

Bigtooth Aspen
Populus grandidentata
66, 222

Common Spatterdock
Nuphar advena

Wild Rice
Zizania aquatica

Labrador Tea
Ledum groenlandicum

Mountain Maple
Acer spicatum

Showy Mountain-ash
Sorbus decora

Northern White-cedar
Thuja occidentalis
37

Tamarack
Larix laricina
35

Bur Oak
Quercus macrocarpa
110, 205

Northern Red Oak
Quercus rubra
118, 209

Harebell
Campanula rotundifolia
498

the greater part of its range. No other tree grew so large in eastern forests; many specimens in primeval forests are thought to have been more than 250 feet tall (although some experts question this). It was also one of the most widespread species in northern woods. By 1900, however, the virgin White Pines had nearly all been eliminated from the North, and less useful trees such as spruce and fir took over much of their range. Today White Pines are slowly returning.

The White Spruce, more common on drier soils, is a taller and more shapely tree than the Black Spruce, which is well adapted to moist and poorly drained soils. Because of their disparate habitat requirements, these two species are among the most abundant and widely distributed of North American conifers. The Balsam Fir also reproduces and spreads vigorously because of its plentiful winged seeds, adaptability, and speed of growth.

The boreal forest is not made up entirely of coniferous trees. Stands of white-barked Quaking Aspen mingle with the conifers, and in wetter places the Paper Birch sinks its roots into shallow, sandy loam. Balsam Poplar and Big-toothed Aspen also occur.

Bogs
Occasionally the canoe glides over a mucklike "soup," which contrasts sharply with the pure clean lakes and crystal-clear rivers of the region. This means that the traveler has entered a bog. A bog can be virtually any size, shape, or depth, but its existence usually signifies that the area is in some stage of transition from lake to meadow to forest. The presence of aquatic plants—Common Spatterdock, water lilies, pondweed, sedges, and the like—indicates that vegetation and soil are moving in and taking over.

Farther on, there are bogs in which the aquatic species are crowded out by sphagnum moss, ferns, Wild Rice, Labrador Tea, equisetum, and shrubs such as blueberry, Mountain Maple, and Showy Mountain-ash. Where sunlight reaches the water's edge, there is likely to be an abundance of willows, Northern White-cedar, and Tamarack. It is only a matter of time until spruce and fir become established on the developing meadow and eventually dominate, as they do across the granite uplands. Uphill, away from the bogs, the soil is well drained and Bur and Northern Red oaks have become established, at least tentatively.

Fires do occur in the boreal forest, but they are less frequent than in drier forests such as the southern pinelands. Although precipitation falls rather uniformly throughout the year, there are times in summer and autumn when the woods dry out and are ignited by lightning. Wide areas of the vast boreal forest may be burned, but the lakes and streams act as firebreaks.

Sunlight
Within the forest, sunlight is reduced to a minimum by the year-round canopy of interlaced evergreen branches, so wild flowers are scarce and hard to find. Harebells often grow next to waterfalls, where sunlight can reach them. In places

Fireweed
Epilobium angustifolium
480

Spotted Touch-me-not
Impatiens capensis

Red Baneberry
Actaea rubra
429, 504

Bunchberry
Cornus canadensis
445, 506

Thimbleberry
Rubus parviflorus

American Elder
("Elderberry")
Sambucus canadensis

where conifers are removed by fire and temporarily displaced by aspen, birch, and blueberry, the canopy is more open, and there are more extensive displays of flowers on the forest floor, including the magenta Fireweed and yellow Spotted Touch-me-not. Late in summer, more color is added to the forest in areas where the showy red fruits of Red Baneberry, Bunchberry, Thimbleberry, and Elderberry are produced. In autumn, the pockets of broad-leaved woods become patches of brilliant colors. For most of the year, however, these deciduous stands are leafless and gray. The boreal forest is dark and cold, its constituent species of plants and animals adapted to survive long months of winter when lands and lakes are frozen and the sun appears above the horizon for only a few hours each day.

Range
The boreal forest extends 4000 miles between Newfoundland and Alaska, and ranges from the boundary of the United States north through southern Canada to the shores of Hudson Bay. Extensions of this forest type occur in suitably cool environments along the high ridges of the Appalachian Mountains as far south as Georgia. The largest expanse of boreal forest in the lower forty-eight states is found around the shores of Lake Superior in northern Minnesota, stretching from Lake Itasca State Park to the Boundary Waters Canoe Area There are also a few boreal stands in the Upper Peninsula of Michigan, the northern tip of lower Michigan, and in a few localities in Wisconsin.

Physical Features
The boreal forest is locked in ice and buried in snow for perhaps eight months of each year. The elevation of the forest is never greater than 2500 feet. Consequently, the forest does not ordinarily receive the very heavy accumulations of snow— more than fifteen feet a year—that characterize mountain forests. In eastern North America, precipitation throughout the boreal forest ranges from twenty to fifty inches annually, with higher amounts falling near the Great Lakes and the Atlantic Ocean. The average temperature in January is 0° to −20° F, with extremes of −60° F. The average July temperature is 50° to 70° F, but may reach as high as 100° F. Evaporation is normally slow in cool humid environments, and more precipitation falls than can be removed by sluggish streams in random drainage patterns. These factors help account for the exceptionally moist environment of the boreal forest.
The rocks underlying parts of the boreal forest are Precambrian, some of them among the oldest on earth. They form a complex collection of granite and metamorphic rocks that in the billions of years since their formation have been contorted and deeply eroded. In many places, little or no soil has accumulated above the bedrock, and the granite and granite-gneiss are exposed at the surface.
For more than 500,000 years, as glaciers advanced and retreated, these rocky surfaces were scraped clean, chiseled,

Beaver
Castor canadensis
597

and channeled. Evidence indicates that with each melting of the glaciers, ancient forests that had retreated to the south advanced and covered the northern landscapes again. These forests were inhabited by mammals such as mastodons, Beavers, and wolves. The last glacial retreat occurred roughly 10,000 years ago; at this time, the ancestors of our modern forests began to grow back, and it is likely that the ancestors of present-day mammals also moved north at that time.

After the last ice age, the wide distribution of lakes in the boreal forest helped to keep the climate cool and the atmosphere humid. Any soils that formed as a thin veneer on the barren rock remained largely sterile. Consequently, the boreal forest is young in terms of the development of its soils and life forms.

Considering the adverse conditions under which it grows, it may seem surprising that so dense a forest can grow successfully and spread for thousands of miles from coast to coast. One explanation is that there has been much less human intervention in this forest than in others. European settlers tried to introduce agriculture in the more southerly parts of the forest, but they succeeded only marginally. Increased commercial trade had a strong impact on forest ecosystems. Rivers were used as avenues of transport by fur trappers, and railroads made wood products accessible. The boreal forest was extensively exploited in the nineteenth century; White Pine was particularly in demand. The consequences of these activities on slow-growing forests were, in places, significant, but the intense fires that swept over the area had the most devastating effect on White Pine forests. The current impact of human intervention appears to be from sulfur dioxide in the air and the consequent effects of acid rain.

Plant Life

Despite the limitations imposed by climate, the boreal forest harbors a rich variety of life. At first glance, it appears to be composed of Black Spruce, White Spruce, and Balsam Fir for as far as the eye can see, but there are other types of vegetative associations in addition to the dominant conifers. These include glades, meadows, sedge marshes, swamps, bogs, deciduous woods, and communities along the shores of lakes and streams. The variety of plant communities creates diverse environments for animals. However, because of environmental limitations, particularly climatic ones, there is less diversity than in other forests. In fact, only the tundra to the north has a less varied flora and fauna.

The acidic soil offers some limits, too. Spruce and fir grow in moister areas; Jack Pine inhabits drier areas, becoming established after fires. The cones of Jack Pine are serotinous, opening when heated; hence the seeds are most likely to be scattered at opportune times—when competing vegetation has been burned away, the shade removed, and needed mineral soil exposed.

The three principal broad-leaved trees in the boreal forest occupy not only sites opened by fire but also other types of clearings or disturbed soil. The Quaking Aspen is especially widespread throughout North America, partly because it can reproduce vegetatively and partly because its tiny seeds can be blown great distances by the wind. The Paper Birch does well in northern latitudes because it has a corklike bark that protects it, at least to some degree, from the extreme cold of winter. The Balsam Poplar—our northernmost hardwood— grows to be the tallest broad-leaved tree in the boreal forest, reaching a height of eighty feet and a diameter of three feet. The perennial shrubs and herbs of the boreal forest are nearly all low-lying, weighted down much of the year by winter snows. But the protective blanket of snow enables them to survive the harsh winters and the drying effects of cold air.

Bearberry
Arctostaphylos uva-ursi
507

Nodding Trillium
Trillium cernuum

One-sided Pyrola
Pyrola secunda

Northern White Violet
Viola pallens

Twinflower
Linnaea borealis
472

Starflower
Trientalis borealis
443

Bluebead Lily
Clintonia borealis
455, 509

There is a considerable understory of blueberries, Bearberry, rhododendrons, and cassiope, together with a carpet of sphagnum moss, mushrooms, and lichens. Also common are Nodding Trillium, One-sided Pyrola, Northern White Violet, Twinflower, Bunchberry, Starflower, and the Bluebead Lily. It is curious that the forest floor of the cold coniferous forest is in places more heavily vegetated than parts of the oak-hickory forest a few hundred miles to the south.

Ecology

The key to such seeming anomalies is the presence of nutrients —chiefly carbon, oxygen, hydrogen, and nitrogen—in the soil. Nitrogen is especially important because it is a chief constituent of proteins. Cold slows the rate of decay, and often little nitrogen is released.

In the boreal forest, however, there is some fixation of nitrogen in the soil, especially by alders (which are nonetheless scarce in comparison to conifers). Nitrogen fixation is a process whereby certain bacteria in the soil convert atmospheric nitrogen into nitrogen compounds that plants can use. The spruce and fir succeed because they seem able to make more efficient use of nutrients. Being evergreen, they do not have to use energy to sprout new growth as systematically as deciduous trees. Moreover, they have a longer time to use what nutrients they do obtain. Some plants have time to transfer valuable minerals from old leaves to new before shedding the old leaves, thus keeping the minerals at work within the plant. All conifers except the Tamarack keep their needles year-round and continue to grow even when the temperature is low.

Perhaps this is one reason that so much other vegetation in the boreal forest is also evergreen: Evolutionary processes have favored those plants that are thrifty with what they have and can make efficient use of it.

In addition to the recycling process, plants get nutrients from other sources, such as mosses. Sphagnum mosses abound where sufficient moisture exists—on tree trunks, tipped-over trees, rocks, and litter. If their roots don't penetrate deep into the duff in order to draw up water, the mosses have to depend to a considerable extent on water that falls through the branches of trees above. Fallout from occasional showers, on passing down through the limbs from the canopy overhead, becomes a dilute solution of minerals by the time it reaches the forest floor. Even with that, nitrogen is still scarce and must be obtained from every possible source.

Scarcity of nutrients makes organic growth tenuous, and competition is vigorous. There is evidence that the germination, growth, and development of Jack Pine seedlings is inhibited by several things, among them the goldenrods that share the vicinity. It is believed that there may be a transfer of chemicals in the soil that limits the growth of plants that would compete with one another.

Among the deciduous trees found in the boreal forest, supple branches are the norm. Aspen and birch branches can bend almost double without breaking under the weight of snow. This suppleness has a distinct advantage for forest animals: It brings tree buds within their reach as food. The birch also has tough waterproof bark that can withstand cold, desiccating winds. All life here is adapted to survive the cold. These adaptations include a heavy coat of fur for mammals and feathers for birds that insulate them from the cold and permit them to remain more or less active all winter. Less hardy animals hibernate or remain within the relative warmth of burrows under the snow or in the ground.

Although extremes of temperature do limit the range and habits of animal life, they are not the most crucial factors governing northern forest ecology. More important to forest life is the length of the growing season, which averages three or four months in the boreal forest. The brevity of the summer is somewhat balanced by long midsummer days of close to twenty-two hours with uninterruptedly warm temperatures. So despite the severity of winter, the boreal forest in summer becomes an enormous engine of productivity.

The moist forest floor furnishes an ideal habitat for mushrooms and other fungi. Generally, only the larger, more colorful kinds are seen, but hundreds of species grow here in all sizes, shapes, and colors. The Clustered Blue Chanterelle and the bright orange Hemlock Varnish Shelf form bright spots in the shade. Some species, like the Clustered Coral, may resemble undersea corals, whereas the russulas and boletes have the more common stalked mushroom shape. All serve important functions in the forest. Many fungi provide food for various animals, and those that grow on dead or dying wood aid in the process of decomposition and thus help return nutrients to the soil.

Clustered Blue Chanterelle
Polyozellus multiplex

Hemlock Varnish Shelf
Ganoderma tsugae

Clustered Coral
Ramaria botrytis

Yellow-bellied Flycatcher
Empidonax flaviventris

Olive-sided Flycatcher
Contopus borealis
282

Tree Swallow
Iridoprocne bicolor

Northern Parula
Parula americana
296

Wildlife

The insect populations provide an important base in the boreal food chain for the next echelon of consumers, the insectivores, which include bats and millions of migratory birds that arrive in summer to find plentiful food supplies. Some of the most common birds are the Yellow-bellied and Olive-sided flycatchers, Tree Swallows, and warblers such as the Northern Parula. Warblers, which are abundant and breed in the boreal forest, form an extensive consumer population.

Cape May Warbler
Dendroica tigrina
303

Blackburnian Warbler
Dendroica fusca
304

Black-throated Green
Warbler
Dendroica virens
291

Magnolia Warbler
Dendroica magnolia
298

Ovenbird
Seiurus aurocapillus
346

Ruby-crowned Kinglet
Regulus calendula
326

Golden-crowned Kinglet
Regulus satrapa
337

Black-capped Chickadee
Parus atricapillus
333

Moose
Alces alces
618

Caribou
Rangifer tarandus
619

Red Squirrel
Tamiasciurus hudsonicus
586

Several species of nesting warblers have worked out a way to share the food resources in the tall spruces and firs of the boreal forest: They have specialized through evolution. Cape May Warblers nest and hunt insects in the treetops. Just below them are Blackburnian Warblers, while Black-throated Green Warblers are found as low as fifteen feet above the ground. At the lowest level of trees and shrubs live Magnolia Warblers. Sometimes this layering of animal life is completed when an Ovenbird nests on the forest floor.

Many species of birds make their summer homes in the boreal forest. Herring Gulls, Broad-winged Hawks, and Bald Eagles are commonly observed overhead; Three-toed Woodpeckers, Ruby-crowned and Golden-crowned kinglets, and Black-capped and Boreal chickadees inhabit the coniferous trees. Lincoln's Sparrows and American Redstarts live in alders by the bogs; and Common Loons and the Common, Hooded, and Red-breasted mergansers keep to the water. Some birds are easily heard but seldom seen: Ovenbirds and Solitary Vireos sing from the trees, and the distant song of the Hermit and Swainson's thrushes are heard in the early morning or evening. The Gray Jay is nearly everywhere. The voices of White-throated Sparrows and Song Sparrows are mixed with the hammering of various woodpeckers and the chatter of chickadees. Pine Siskins slip through the shrubbery. Cedar Waxwings move in flocks higher up in the trees. As the afternoon wanes, the evening is heralded by Common Nighthawks, which dive and buzz above the waters in their quest for insects. Sunset is characterized by the calls and answers of loons across the lakes.

Boreal Mammals

Mammals exist in modest numbers in the boreal forest, but many are shy or nocturnal and seldom seen by human visitors. Trails of the River Otter pass through mud or weeded surfaces, and the presence of the Porcupine is evidenced by the gnawed bark of pines. Muskrats and Beavers inhabit the bogs, and beaver lodges are often seen in streams and lakes. Fast-swimming minks make their homes in chambers of sphagnum moss. The largest mammal—and the one most apt to be observed—is the Moose, which often stands in water near a willow thicket. But sightings of Lynx, Snowshoe Hares, Wolverine, Black Bear, Gray Wolf, or Caribou are likely to depend on some additional knowledge of population distribution as well as species behavior.

Many mammals of the boreal forest are herbivorous. Moose usually seek out willows; Caribou, also herbivores, may have to subsist for long winter periods on lichens. Red Squirrels extract the seeds from cones of spruce and pine and also eat and store fruits and berries.

Interactions among animals are common, complex, and often unseen by travelers in the boreal forest. For example, parasites and their effect on other animals are seldom noticed except by biologists, but they influence the survival of the host populations. What is only a harmless lungworm in the white-tailed Deer can, when it infests a Moose, become a deadly brain worm.

Other biological interactions are more obvious; namely, those between predator and prey. Martens hunt birds and squirrels in the trees, and Ermines prowl for mice. Wolverines gorge on meat, dead or alive. Wolves hunt Moose, Caribou, and other mammals.

Bears are omnivorous; it can almost be said that they stop at nothing. They hunt small mammals and fish, rip open bees' nests for honey, and eat berries, twigs, buds, and roots. Large animals such as bears have a substantial demand for food that restricts the number of consumers in a given area; individuals usually occupy larger ranges than do smaller animals.

The Arctic and subarctic are well known for cyclical population explosions. The best-known interrelationship is that surrounding the ubiquitous Snowshoe Hare. Brown in summer, white in winter, and camouflaged with splotches in between, this herbivore subsists on such vegetation as buds, bark, and seeds. Heavy fur helps it to survive cold weather, and powerful muscles allow it to escape from predators. Its huge hind feet enable it to move rapidly over deep powdery snow. But it does not always escape; virtually every carnivore in the forest pursues this hare whenever it gets the chance. Consequently, the hare reproduces abundantly.

Chief among its pursuers is the Lynx, which may lie in wait in a tree or chase its prey on the forest floor. Like its prey, the Lynx has feet that are huge and heavily furred, well adapted to fast speed in deep snow. The Fisher—another fierce predator—will launch nearly the same kind of attack, and Bobcats also depend to a considerable extent on the Snowshoe Hare. When the hares are abundant and times are good, such predators increase in numbers.

However, for reasons not fully understood, Snowshoe Hare populations experience drastic attrition about every eleven years. The populations of the predators, which increase enormously as the hare's numbers increase, cannot survive the reduction of the prey population; the Lynxes, Bobcats, and their competitors begin to starve as the Snowshoe Hare population declines.

The hares that survive and begin to rebuild the population have something of an ideal situation for a while: The Bobcats, Lynxes, and other predators are few in number. But that sort of situation seldom endures under the natural laws that govern an ecosystem. In due course, the predator populations approach an equilibrium with their food supply, increasing enough to help stabilize the numbers of hunted. For a while, the populations live more or less in balance. But in time, the cycle of feast and famine begins again.

Such changes are normal in other wooded regions where one group of organisms is dependent on another. But changes are dramatic and extreme in the boreal forest, where life forms must survive the lowest temperatures and the shortest growing season in the forests of eastern North America.

THE BOREAL FOREST: PLANTS AND ANIMALS

Trees
American Elm 86
American Mountain-
ash 130, 194
Balsam Fir 172
Balsam Poplar 101
Bigtooth Aspen 66, 222
Black Spruce 30, 169
Buttonbush 60, 163
Jack Pine 28
Northern White Cedar 37
Paper Birch 67, 238
Pin Cherry 84, 152, 189,
218
Quaking Aspen 64
Red Maple 120, 180, 228
Red-osier Dogwood 51
Smooth Sumac 142, 197
Tamarack 35
White Spruce 29, 170

Birds
American Redstart 306
American Robin 307
American Woodcock 520
Barred Owl 244
Bay-breasted Warbler 310
Black-and-white
Warbler 336
Black-backed
Woodpecker 279
Black-capped
Chickadee 333
Black-throated Blue
Warbler 322
Black-throated Green
Warbler 291
Blackburnian Warbler 304
Blackpoll 335
Blue Jay 324
Broad-winged Hawk 257
Brown Creeper 348
Brown Thrasher 341
Canada Warbler 295
Cape May Warbler 303
Cedar Waxwing 311
Chestnut-sided Warbler 302
Common Crow 266
Common Loon 263
Common Raven 264
Cooper's Hawk 254
Dark eyed Junco 267
Downy Woodpecker 275
Eastern Wood-Pewee 281

Evening Grosbeak 305
Fox Sparrow 340
Golden-crowned
Kinglet 337
Gray Jay 330
Great Gray Owl 245
Great Horned Owl 242
Hairy Woodpecker 276
Hermit Thrush 344
Long eared Owl 243
Magnolia Warbler 298
Mourning Dove 270
Northern Flicker 277
Northern Saw-whet
Owl 246
Northern Goshawk 255
Northern Shrike 331
Olive-sided Flycatcher 282
Ovenbird 346
Pileated Woodpecker 271
Pine Grosbeak 314
Pine Siskin 339
Purple Finch 313
Red-breasted Nuthatch 297
Red Crossbill 312
Red-eyed Vireo 283
Red-tailed Hawk 258
Rose-breasted Grosbeak 316
Ruby-crowned Kinglet 326
Ruby-throated
Hummingbird 321
Ruffed Grouse 247
Sharp-shinned Hawk 253
Solitary Vireo 289
Spruce Grouse 248
Swainson's Thrush 345
Tennessee Warbler 288
White-throated
Sparrow 338
White-winged Crossbill 315
Winter Wren 347
Wood Duck 262
Yellow-bellied
Sapsucker 274
Yellow-rumped
Warbler 301

Butterflies and Moths
Large Wood Nymph 362
Little Wood Satyr 361
Mourning Cloak 369
Red Admiral 367
Spicebush Swallowtail 368
Spring Azure 375

THE TRANSITION FOREST

Between the pure coniferous woodlands of the boreal forest and the mixed deciduous woodlands of temperate North America lies a transition zone of forests that combines both types. Conifers mingle with deciduous trees as far south, and deciduous trees mix with conifers as far north, as their evolutionary adaptations enable them. As a result, there is a curving band of mixed forest types, ranging from 100 to 500 miles wide, in which this transition occurs, from Minnesota to New England and the Canadian Maritime Provinces.

The transition forest differs from the boreal forest in a number of ways. It is warmer, with a longer growing season. In winter, the snowfall may be heavy, but it does not remain on the ground as long. The forest canopy is patchier, and the woods are therefore more open, more filled with sunlight, with a richer understory and herbaceous layer. In the transition forest, moisture evaporates at a faster rate; consequently the woods are less damp and the soils less saturated.

In some ways, however, the transition forest resembles the boreal forest. For example, it has numerous lakes, especially in northern Wisconsin and northern Minnesota, and bogs are common across the northern tier of states. Where temperatures are cooler and the ground is moist, as on the northern sides and summits of mountain ranges, there are forests that are actually southern extensions of the boreal forest.

If that sounds complex enough, be assured that the transition region is regarded, in the eyes of ecologists, as having many more individual forest types and associations. The best way to study in depth the numerous forest communities in this region —or in any other, for that matter—is to visit state and national parks or forests where the details of forest populations and ecology are provided in signs, folders, and booklets. In this habitat guidebook, the emphasis is on describing how the transition forest appears generally to a person entering portions of it from the east or west. Included are areas of mountaintop boreal forest and of pine forests that are often encountered by visitors exploring the transition forest, although these areas technically do not form part of the transition forest.

The transition forest is more open and accessible than the boreal. Although the virgin forests of New England have been reduced from ninety-five percent of the landscape to five percent, enough time has elapsed since widespread lumbering operations took place that the forests are beginning to regain a semblance of their primeval character, especially in protected areas.

There the transition forest has recovered so well that parts of it resemble a Gothic cathedral, with massive pillars of Yellow Birch and Sugar Maple rising up to a canopy of leaves that permits sprinklings of sunlight to illuminate the oxalis leaves, ferns, and beds of maple saplings on the forest floor. The moisture is sufficient to support rich growths of mosses and lichen over the trunks and gnarled roots of giant beeches. The woods are redolent with the scent of Balsam Fir and Balsam Poplar. The forests are frequently spotted with Eastern

Hemlock, an evergreen that appears in deciduous forests from the northern tier of states to the southern. The forest floor is padded with the needles and cones of this hemlock.

Mushrooms are usually mixed with the debris, and shelf fungi cling to fallen trunks. As in virtually every forest of North America, there is some member of the heath family present—most often small blueberries—especially where the soil is acidic. Waterleaf is also common.

Because the transition forest occurs mostly on relatively low land, its general character is maintained over thousands of square miles. But within the broad outlines of mixed conifers and deciduous trees, the constituent species tend to collect in specific communities, according to such factors as soil composition, temperature gradients, moisture, and the stage of contemporary distribution patterns.

Dominant Tree Types in the Midwest

For example, the Eastern Hemlock is lacking in most of Minnesota. Yellow Birch and Eastern White Pine are also diminished there, whereas Red, White, and Bur oaks are more abundant than in other parts of the transition forest. The most common species is White Pine, sometimes growing in pure stands or with scattered Sugar Maple and American Basswood. But to the south, as environmental conditions moderate, Sugar Maple and Basswood become more dominant.

In northern Wisconsin the picture is similar, except that Eastern Hemlock is more apparent, though it is at the western edge of its range. Sugar Maple continues to be prominent, though American Basswood dominates from place to place. White Pine, Red Spruce, and Balsam Fir mingle with the hardwoods, and among the bogs and lakes are communities of various pines and Quaking Aspen. The aspen springs up thickly wherever conditions are just right: open places recently burned or cultivated, scattered sunny spots within the woods, around the edges of lakes and bogs, or along streambanks. Quaking Aspen is not a sturdy tree, will not tolerate much crowding, and is merely a temporary growth that eventually gives way to climax conifers or more hardy deciduous trees. But it is a major factor in forests at these latitudes from the Atlantic Ocean to Alaska. The Bigtooth Aspen is less widespread, but its role in transition forests is similar to that of the Quaking Aspen.

In the northern parts of Michigan, there is much more Eastern Hemlock, with maple, American Beech, and Eastern Hophornbeam in the understory. The western part of the transition forest has a considerable understory, although some places may support little shrubby or herbaceous growth except saplings of maples and beeches. The small tree layer is usually made up of young individuals of dominant species, especially beeches and maples. But there are also other small trees, such as American Mountain-ash and Mountain Maple. The shrubs include Elderberry, Thimbleberry, Beaked Hazel, and Bush Honeysuckle. Numerous ferns grow in transition woods; some, like the Maidenhair, occupy very moist sites.

Eastern White Pine
Pinus strobus
19

Northern Red Oak
Quercus rubra
118, 209

White Oak
Quercus alba
109, 206

Bur Oak
Quercus macrocarpa
110, 205

American Basswood
Tilia americana
72, 239

Red Spruce
Picea rubens
31, 171

Quaking Aspen
Populus tremuloides
64

Bigtooth Aspen
Populus grandidentata
66, 222

American Beech
Fagus grandifolia
88, 204, 215, 236

Eastern Hophornbeam
Ostrya virginiana
75, 167, 176, 234

American Mountain-ash
Sorbus americana
130, 194

Gray Birch
Betula populifolia

Yellow-poplar
("Tuliptree")
Liriodendron tulipifera
123, 162, 229

Paper Birch
Betula papyrifera
67, 238

Red Pine
Pinus resinosa
22

White Birch
Betula populifolia

Pitch Pine
Pinus rigida
25, 173

Fraser Fir
Abies fraseri
32

Dominant Tree Types in the East

From Pennsylvania northward to eastern Canada is a region of moderate relief with occasional glacial features and low mountain complexes. The forests vary from mixed deciduous in the Allegheny Mountains to boreal in eastern Canada. Red Spruce and Gray Birch assume important roles. The character of the transition forest changes with rises in elevation: The higher Catskill Mountains are covered with spruce and fir, beneath which are transition areas, and finally deciduous forests of Sugar Maple, Beech, and Yellow Birch mixed with spruce and fir, while the lower elevations support Eastern Hemlock mixed with oak and hickory.

New York State lies squarely in the midst of the transition zone. Southern species—intrusions from the more southerly mixed deciduous woodlands as well as of pinelands or pine barrens—are found around New York City and on Long Island. Up the Hudson River valley, oaks, hickories, and Yellow-poplars ("Tuliptrees") grow. Over the greater part of the state are communities of Sugar Maple, Beech, Yellow Birch, White Pine, and Eastern Hemlock. On the uplands and in the northern part of the state are coniferous forests with Paper Birch. The Adirondacks, with their pronounced relief and peaks of over a mile high, support a mixture of forests: swamp, hardwood, spruce, and stunted communities—mostly of Balsam Fir—at tree line.

In New England, where most of the virgin forests were removed, the recovering species are primarily birch, a few White Pines, Red Pines, and Red Oak. The hardwood remnants—largely Beech, Sugar Maple, and American Basswood—mix with hemlock, as do White Birch and aspens. Toward the coast are white-cedar and Pitch Pine. To the far north, the transition forest meets the boreal on the Gaspé Peninsula, in southeastern Quebec.

New England forests are exceptional for their autumn color, especially that of the Sugar Maple. There is, of course, a fair amount of fall color throughout the transition forest; on high ground in New York and New England, it is possible to view wide panoramas painted with nearly every shade of red, orange, and yellow. At such times, the mosaic nature of the transition forest is clearly revealed, because the patches of red, yellow, or orange contrast with the dark green pockets of coniferous forests.

The autumn mixture of colors demonstrates that the shift from boreal to deciduous forest is gradual. No sudden line delineates the change; it is instead marked by a gentle transition between two large forests of markedly different characteristics.

The spruces and firs extend all the way through the transition forest and down the Appalachian Mountains to Georgia as spruce-fir "islands" in a sea of deciduous trees. In a sense, they are outliers of the boreal forest and follow the climate to which they have adapted. Red Spruce is distributed uninterruptedly between Nova Scotia and northern New York, but only in isolated ridgetop localities from there south. Fraser Fir

replaces Balsam Fir, but the overall appearance of the forest is the same. On the low points and saddles, where spruce and fir fail to grow, pure stands of American Beech are often found, because Beech has a wide tolerance and can inhabit near-boreal climatic conditions.

Range

The transition forest stretches across the northern portions of the Great Lakes states and nearly all of New England, southern Ontario, part of Quebec, and the lower portions of the Canadian Maritime Provinces, where the deciduous forest associates with spruce, fir, and hemlock. Included are most of Minnesota, Wisconsin, Michigan, and New York, and all of Vermont, New Hampshire, and Maine. Outliers of boreal and transition forests occur southward along ridges of the Appalachian Mountains, wherever the elevation is high enough and cool enough to sustain a mixture of northern conifers and middle-latitude hardwoods.

Climate

South of the boreal forest, the growing season becomes longer and solar radiation more intense. The amount of rainfall increases along with the rate of evaporation, and the ground has a chance to dry out now and then. When drenched in fog, the transition forest can be soaking wet with dew; moisture of that sort supports a luxuriant vegetation.

Across the transition forest, precipitation is a fairly uniform thirty to forty inches a year, reaching greater amounts only in northern Maine and parts of the Canadian Maritime Provinces, where the influence of atmospheric moisture from the sea is greater. The precipitation decreases to around twenty-two inches in the western part of the transition forest, a relative aridity that favors growth of grasslands more than woodlands.

The transition forest endures severe temperature extremes, from $-60°$ F to more than $110°$ F. The average temperature in winter months is below $32°$ F, and the snowfall is heavy. The transition forest generally has good weather and a growing season of four or five months; as a result, a considerable number of temperate deciduous trees, such as hickories, most oaks, and the American Beech, reach the northern limit of their range here. But this forest is also vulnerable to severe storms, which generally move from west to east, with freezing polar air masses occasionally descending southward from the northern interior of the continent. Around the Great Lakes it is not uncommon for shores and islands to be shrouded in fog, awash with drizzle, or battered by gales. It is also colder in such localities, which makes the growing season a little shorter. The mountains experience rough storms as well. From time to time the weather is exceptionally violent. In 1977, a squall line advanced across Wisconsin and leveled or severely damaged 850,000 acres of forest, and a 1939 hurricane felled a million Sugar Maples in Vermont. High winds prune the trees and thin the woods, opening up patches of the forest and affecting the whole community of life.

Geology and Soils

The Canadian shield, which underlies much of the boreal forest, also underlies the western third of the transition forest as far east as the Upper Peninsula of Michigan. This extremely old Precambrian bedrock of granite, gneiss, schist, and basalt is exposed in some of the uplands and shore features around Lake Superior. Younger sandstones and dolomite protrude on cliffs on the edge of Lake Superior, whereas sandy soils occur locally around parts of the lakes.

Most soils have developed on bedrock or on glacial deposits, and their fertility depends on the nature of the underlying rock, the richness of transported materials, and the length of time humus has accumulated since glacial retreat. Generally, soils that develop on granites and metamorphic rocks are less fertile than those formed on sedimentary formations; soils on limestone tend to be richest because of the high carbonate content of the limestones. Where mixed deciduous forest has reached a climax, the soils are likely to be deep and fertile.

The Great Lakes themselves are a product of the scouring and gouging effects of glaciers. Some of the bedrock polished by these continental ice sheets has not yet been covered by rich soil. But as the ice melted, it also deposited a considerable load of sediment, or till, that had been scooped up in its advance. The huge blocks of ice contained in the glacial debris melted, creating small lakes. Some of these lakes still exist as far east as Cape Cod; others filled in to become bogs, marshes, or swamps.

In the eastern part of the transition forest lies a concentration of high mountains that carry a tundra flora on their summits. The northern peaks of the Appalachian Mountains wind through Quebec and New England, between the Atlantic Coast and the Adirondacks.

Westward to the Great Lakes the landscape is less mountainous, composed of basalt ridges, sand hills, and valleys filled with rich alluvial soil. The mountains and ridges, though seemingly indestructible, have been no match for the persistent eroding forces of running water and freezing ice over thousands of years. The legacy is a base of rock and soil on which primitive forests began to develop perhaps as long ago as 60 million years.

The transition forest has little of the disordered maze of lakes and ponds characteristic of the drainage system of the boreal forest. Northern Minnesota and Wisconsin do have large numbers of lakes, but most other localities in the transition region are drained by streams arranged in the more common patterns of trunks and branches, in a process called dendritic drainage. In the center of the transition forest, the Great Lakes drain northeastward into the Saint Lawrence River and thence to the Atlantic Ocean.

Competition

Because the transition forest is a geographic region where plants from one type of forest environment meet and compete with plants from another type, there inevitably are conflicts.

This is true at the outer fringes of nearly every community. Changes in water, soil, and weather guarantee to each community a limit of its expansion. Boundary changes are usually gradual, not only in the transition zone but also where the boreal forest turns into taiga and tundra in the far North, and where the transition forest dwindles on the western prairies. Competition is a limiting factor, and many trees compete for space even in severe environments.

In New England's mountains, for example, one can observe what happens to trees that try to grow in climates or regions that are outside their normal range. The weather is windy, cold, or snowy for extended periods. Ridges of nearly barren rock possess low amounts of soil and nutrients to nourish organisms of any size. But herbaceous plants and trees cling to life with notable tenacity and for surprisingly long times. How this happens is not fully understood, though certain adaptations are obvious: Reduced size of leaves cuts down exposure and helps prevent excessive loss of moisture; a thickened epidermis protects against weather extremes; large subterranean parts and smaller aerial parts make a plant less vulnerable to its environment; and the rooting of branches lying prostrate against the slope facilitates the spread of the trees. The climate near the ground can be markedly milder than that a few feet above it. The three principal trees that reach high altitudes in New England are Balsam Fir, Black Spruce, and Paper Birch.

Trees

With well-distributed rainfall in summer, and weather extremes less severe than in the boreal forest, the productivity of the transition forest is remarkable. Left undisturbed, the trees reach immense proportions. But they do so only under tension, a constant competition among trees for available sunlight, minerals, and moisture. Usually the Sugar Maple and Yellow Birch dominate the forest; any fir, spruce, or other plant that manages to get started in the understory must compete with thousands of maple seedlings and saplings. The Yellow Birch is not always successful when competing with Sugar Maple, but in places the Beech holds its own quite well. There are pure stands in which Sugar Maple shares its dominance with no other tree. Usually, though, the giants of the forest join in codominance (maple-beech, maple-birch, maple-basswood) with an understory of those species in association with Red Maple, Red Spruce, White Ash, and Black Cherry.

In the transition forest, the Paper Birch grows at considerable distances south of its boreal forest home, but it more commonly grows on cooler north-facing slopes than on slopes with warm southern exposures. This habitat selection may be partly due to the prominence of Bronze Birch Borers on southerly slopes.

In any forest, the tree with the greatest ability to withstand a wide variety of conditions is the one most likely to dominate. Sugar Maple, the most abundant tree in New York State, has

Black Spruce
Picea mariana
30, 169

Red Maple
Acer rubrum
120, 180, 228

White Ash
Fraxinus americana
134, 178

Black Cherry
Prunus serotina
153

Bronze Birch Borer
Agrilus anxius

Eastern White Pine
("White Pine")
Pinus strobus
19

a wide tolerance for many kinds of weather; it can also tolerate vigorously growing neighbors and shaded conditions, under which it grows to maturity. It is flexible, able to share dominance from place to place, and long-lived (up to 400 years). ·

White Pines thrive in areas disturbed by fire, although aspens are likely to spring up and cast some growth-inhibiting shade. In the transition forest, White Pines do better than other conifers because they grow faster and root deeper.

One conifer that competes most successfully with hardwoods is the Eastern Hemlock. It ranges into the boreal forest, but it is better adapted to environments that are cool rather than cold. Because it tolerates shade, it can grow well in dense forests that would choke out pines and larches. Eastern Hemlock thrives on the moisture and high humidity prevalent in lake country and along river bottoms. It does well individually and in shady groves on ridge tops farther south, in Virginia, North Carolina, and Tennessee, where it reaches near-record proportions. It can even germinate on decaying logs. This ubiquitous species, easily recognized by its drooping tip and soft, dark-green foliage, has exceptional environmental tolerance and tenacity.

The Red Spruce has similar characteristics; it tolerates cold a bit better than hemlock, and so has become the master species in the Adirondack Mountains and along the summits of the Appalachians. Within the past decade, however, its growth has stopped in certain localities, and the trees are dying. Forest experts are trying to find out why this is happening, focusing on the possibility of long-range damage by pollutants in the air.

The softwoods compete vigorously, although they are limited by climatic conditions. Both Quaking and Bigtooth aspens, which range widely in the boreal forest, come down into the transition forest but are found no farther south. Where fire or wind levels an old forest, aspen springs up vigorously. Eventually, though, it commits a kind of suicide: Maturing trees shade the seedlings, and shade is something that an aspen cannot tolerate.

When aspen invades fire-wracked terrain, it often competes with Paper Birch, which outdoes it in places. The Yellow Birch can also compete aggressively in transition forests, and it tolerates harsher conditions than either aspen or Paper Birch. Yellow Birch mingles with conifers and hardwoods alike, from New England to the southern Appalachians. Nevertheless, it remains sensitive to change, and it withers and dies when disturbed by fire, logging, and the like.

One tough and durable tree from the South has managed to compete well with northern species and to extend its range into colder climates. Northern Red Oak is the only widespread oak in the transition forest; it usually grows along rivers in association with basswood and elm.

Basswoods, commonly known as lindens, are popular, well-known, and widely planted. American Basswood thrives in the wild, especially in the rich moist soil of lowlands, and the

White Basswood
Tilia heterophylla
71

American Elm
Ulmus americana
86

Slippery Elm
Ulmus rubra
177

Wild Sarsaparilla
Aralia nudicaulis
427

Starflower
Trientalis borealis
443

Pipsissewa
Chimaphila umbellata

Rose Twisted-stalk
Streptopus roseus

Round-leaved Orchis
Orchis spectabilis

Hepatica
Hepatica americana

Wood Lily
Lilium philadelphicum
462

Twinflower
Linnaea borealis
472

Wood Anemone
Anemone quinquefolia
441

Canada Mayflower
Maianthemum canadense
452

Wild Currant
Ribes americanum

Tamarack
Larix laricina
35

trees reach large dimensions—100 feet tall and 3 feet in diameter. Its flowers are markedly fragrant and highly attractive to bees. The American Basswood of transition forests differs from the White Basswood of mixed deciduous forests in being larger and more northerly in range.

American Elms thrive from subtropical to boreal habitats. But they are vulnerable to Dutch elm disease, which, in the last half century, has much reduced their populations. The Slippery Elm occupies the same moist environment but is a bit less widespread.

For the most part, the floor of the transition forest is a veritable botanic garden of hundreds of species of herbaceous plants. Among the most common are Wild Sarsaparilla, Starflower, milkworts, Pipsissewa, Rose Twisted-stalk, Round-leaved Orchis, Hepatica, Wood Lily, Twinflower, and various species of baneberry, violet, trillium, and clematis. The herbaceous layer on the forest floor endures overwhelming competition from the massive trees above, especially the deciduous woods whose canopy fills with leaves each spring and shuts out much of the sunlight. The evolutionary trick here is that these plants bloom before the leaves of trees appear. Hence they accomplish the bulk of their reproduction by the time they are shaded. As a consequence, early spring in transition deciduous forests is characterized by thick carpets of wild flowers on the forest floor. In the Great Lakes region, the progression includes Wood Anemones first, followed by Canada Mayflower, trillium, lilies, and others.

Diseases and Pests
Like most vegetation, trees are subject to attack by insects and blights. Among the most notable is the White Pine Blister Rust, a fungus introduced from the Old World. It has caused extensive damage to North American trees, which have little or no resistance to this exotic fungus. In addition to infecting White Pine, this rust damages Wild Currant, which is often eradicated in control programs in order to save the pine.

The principal insect damage in the transition forest is done by the Spruce Budworm, a leaf-chewer with specialized mouthparts adapted to biting and chewing on spruces, firs, Tamarack, hemlocks, and pines. The arrangement is quite efficient. The adult, a moth, lays eggs on the needles of a host tree, and the eggs hatch in summer. The larvae immediately hibernate in a sheltered spot, encased in a silken web. The following spring the caterpillars emerge and begin to munch on the nearest available food supply—tender budding needles. If the supply of needle-eaters is excessive, and if the tree is repeatedly attacked over several years, death results.

The depredations of native insects are part of the scheme of things, and their existence is not without long-range benefits to the ecosystem. When tree limbs, laden with ice and snow, snap and fall, the openings are attacked by fungi, carpenter ants, and woodpeckers. That is only one of an almost infinite number of food chains, most of which are well hidden from human observation.

Balsam Woolly Aphid
Chermes piceae

Gypsy Moth
Lymantria dispar
354

American Chestnut
Castanea dentata
85

Along with exotic fungi, North American trees have fallen victim to the invasion of introduced insect species, against which no defense has evolved. The Balsam Fir, for example, seems to be losing its battle with the Balsam Woolly Aphid. This Old World insect, which sucks the sap from beneath the bark of twigs, limbs, and tree trunks, injects a saliva into the fir that stimulates enlargement of plant tissues, resulting in gall-like growths and contorted twigs and stems. The insect is now found between eastern Canada and North Carolina.

Hordes of voracious Gypsy Moth caterpillars, another introduced pest, have now spread into every state in which the transition forest grows, from Minnesota through New York to Maine and Canada. Indeed, most of this area is where the Gypsy Moth outbreaks are at their most severe. The caterpillars are partial to oak, Beech, pine, and hemlock, but they will also consume leaves of at least 400 other species of trees and shrubs. A single Gypsy Moth egg can produce more than 1000 larvae; and because these larvae go through five or six stages of caterpillar growth, the potential for damage to trees is awesome. Some entomologists fear that the White Oak may be exterminated by the Gypsy Moth and follow the American Chestnut and American Elm toward oblivion.

Adaptations and Human Intervention
With all the periodic alterations that go on in each forest, it is not surprising that nature has evolved residents flexible and adaptable to changing conditions. That capacity was especially useful when human beings arrived and began to make large-scale changes.

From the times of earliest settlement by Europeans, portions of the transition forest have been deliberately burned to open the woods for passage, provide places where berries and domestic crops could be grown, and release to the soil the nutrients locked in vegetation. Although the transition forest evolved in the presence of lightning and is naturally adapted to occasional fires—even fires of long duration and wide extent —the forest has become discontinuous in the presence of man. The virgin forests were removed to support human settlement and industry and further modified by post-logging fires. Less than five percent of the original forest remains undisturbed. As a consequence, most of the transition forest is composed of secondary or tertiary growth. Only in the higher, hard-to-get-to places, and in specially protected reserves, do remnants of original forests remain.

As the environments changed over the years, the ranges and populations of forest animals changed also. White-tailed Deer moved into forest-edge environments where food and shelter were available, then moved on as replacement forests began to grow in burned-over sites and abandoned fields. By contrast, animals adapted to deeper forests—the Black Bear, for example—moved into areas that had newly grown over. Certain mammals retreated permanently from areas of intensive habitat modification and are no longer found in the transition forest; the last Wolverines had left Minnesota by

White-tailed Deer
Odocoileus virginianus
616

Black Bear
Ursus americanus
609

Wolverine
Gulo gulo
608

Beaver
Castor canadensis
597

Mink
Mustela vison

Muskrat
Ondatra zibethicus

Fisher
Martes pennanti
603

Raccoon
Procyon lotor
607

Virginia Opossum
Didelphis virginiana
600

1918. Beavers suffered, as did Marten and Lynx populations, which were reduced by trapping and lumbering, but they are now making a comeback. Other animals were less adversely affected; Mink and Muskrat, though heavily trapped, maintained comparatively stable populations.

In northern Wisconsin, Coyotes, Gray Wolves, Red Foxes, Bobcats, and Lynxes were once abundant. The Wolverine, Mountain Lion, and woodland Caribou have disappeared from that area, although the Moose remains. The Black Bear is still relatively numerous.

Beavers were once so widely pursued that they may well have disappeared for a time from such places as the White Mountains, but they have made a recovery along forest streams. The Fisher has also recovered well. In places, the foxes, skunks, and Raccoons seem immortal. The limits of distribution are changing too. Virginia Opossums, so familiar in warmer forests throughout the South, have extended their range northward into the transition forest.

As human settlements expanded, the larger animals—such as the Gray Wolf and the Moose—sometimes suffered most, because they normally require large areas in which to sustain themselves and could not compete with humans for available space. Some large mammals cannot support crowded conditions in the wilderness either, and when aggressive species compete for the same territory, there are further reductions. The Gray Wolf, once the principal predator in northern regions, has been largely eliminated, along with the Mountain Lion. Woodland Caribou have been so crowded out that there are few, if any, south of the Saint Lawrence River.

Wildlife and the Food Chain
The most active stream of life in the transition forest is that of the billions of microorganisms in the soil. They digest fallen plant debris and convert it into nutrients required for forest growth. These microscopic consumers are preyed upon by tiny predators, and so on up the scale of size in a complex web of food production and consumption.

Gray Squirrel
Sciurus carolinensis
588

Red Squirrel
Tamiasciurus hudsonicus
586

Canada Yew
Taxus canadensis

Above the forest floor, the staple of life is vegetation, and the principal food products are seeds and leaves, often gathered before they have a chance to fall. Squirrels are among the best-known seed gatherers and storers; the Gray Squirrel is adapted mostly to deciduous portions of the transition forest, and the Red Squirrel to coniferous woods. Grosbeaks, finches, buntings, towhees, siskins, juncos, and sparrows also consume large quantities of seeds.

The most widespread leaf consumer is the White-tailed Deer. Where deer populations are high, overbrowsing can modify the distribution of trees. Hemlock, White and Yellow Birch, and Canada Yew are especially favored and therefore almost removed from certain habitats, largely because there are more deer than the trees will support. Deer nibble available saplings so severely that they cut off reproduction. This allows competing trees such as Balsam Fir to enter, and because the deer have little liking for fir, they have effectively altered the

Porcupine
Erethizon dorsatum

Snowshoe Hare
Lepus americanus
592

Cedar Waxwing
Bombycilla cedrorum
311

Ruffed Grouse
Bonasa umbellus
247

Ruby-crowned Kinglet
Regulus calendula
326

Golden-crowned Kinglet
Regulus satrapa
337

Black-capped Chickadee
Parus atricapillus
333

Boreal Chickadee
Parus hudsonicus

White-breasted Nuthatch
Sitta carolinensis
334

Red-breasted Nuthatch
Sitta canadensis
297

Northern Oriole
Icterus galbula
309

Scarlet Tanager
Piranga olivacea
317

Brown Creeper
Certhia americana
348

Gray Wolf
("Timber Wolf")
Canis lupus
610

makeup of the community by allowing these trees to spread unchecked by browsing. In the long run, of course, the deer diminish their own food source, so they themselves diminish in numbers or move on, not to be restored until their customary food trees are reestablished.

Porcupines will consume nearly every part of a conifer and are well known for occasionally killing a tree by girdling it. Snowshoe Hares also munch on conifer bark but seldom kill the trees. Cedar Waxwings flock to sources of fruits. Ruffed Grouse browse on fruits, catkins, and tree buds.

Herbivores occupy all levels of the forest, from ground to treetop, because their food is found at all levels. Carnivores, too, penetrate every level of the forest. Insects, for example, are found from the ground to the canopy, and they become a food source for a wide variety of animal life. The most abundant insectivores are birds, from the tiny Ruby-crowned and Golden-crowned kinglets to multiple species of warblers, Black-capped and Boreal chickadees, White-breasted and Red-breasted nuthatches, Northern Orioles, Scarlet Tanagers, and Brown Creepers, most of which get their principal sustenance from insects associated with trees. The same is true of flickers and other woodpeckers. Insects in the open air are captured by aerial feeders such as bats and flycatchers. On the forest floor the invertebrate fauna is consumed by robins, thrushes, thrashers, and woodcocks, as well as by snakes and frogs.

Dominating these animals—hunted and hunter alike—are the large carnivores. Hovering over all in the transition forest are two dozen species of raptors, including eagles, owls, and hawks. These birds trim the populations of fish, snakes, birds, and small mammals. In the upper story, Porcupines are preyed on by Fishers, and squirrels are taken by Martens.

The top of the food chain is occupied by the largest consumers, which take the largest animals. The Timber Wolf, for example, preys upon Moose as well as other animals; the Coyote consumes deer; and the Lynx and Bobcat, hares. The largest of the carnivores is the Black Bear, although its all-encompassing diet qualifies it as an omnivore.

Many of these food chains continue southward into the mixed deciduous forest, though the farther south one goes the less evidence there is of boreal forest elements, except on ridgetops. Eventually the climate becomes so warm that most boreal species give way to competitive species better adapted to warm weather and a long growing season. But where the elements of both boreal and deciduous forests mingle, one finds interesting competition, adaptation, and food chains with characteristics of both. Clearly the transition forest is a busy middle ground between two worlds, where the life of the North meets the life of the South.

THE TRANSITION FOREST: PLANTS AND ANIMALS

THE MIXED DECIDUOUS FOREST

From the Potomac to the Mississippi, down the Ohio River valley, across the mountains and plateaus of West Virginia, Kentucky, and Tennessee, and to the fringes of the Old South, the deciduous forest reigns supreme. Every spring, the warm sun and abundant rain convert the heartland of eastern North America from a gray landscape of barren trunks and leafless branches to a rich and productive green forest. Every autumn, uncounted millions of trees shed their leaves in an unparalleled, almost unbroken display of color, heralding another six months of dormancy. The mixed deciduous forest of North America is an immense nursery, food-storage center, water-catchment complex, and engine of productivity.

Unlike the boreal and transition forests, the mixed deciduous woods have a preponderance of broad-leaved trees; pines, hemlocks, and magnolias represent the minority evergreens. And unlike the spruce-fir forests, in which only a few major trees stand out, three dozen species are prominent here, all competing for light and space, nutrients and water. The trees are diverse and crowded; so are the understory trees and shrubs and the organisms on the forest floor and in the soil.

On a typical walk through a rocky patch of deciduous woodland in early morning, much of the wildlife is visible and vociferous. Patches of moss drape the gray limestones and carpet the forest floor. Old stumps, eaten and rotted almost to the ground, sport speckles of lichen. Across the forest floor, new growths burst from the dank, fragrant litter: clumps of mushrooms, quadruplet leaves of oak, triplets of hickory, clumps of burgeoning dogwood, tiny Eastern Redbuds with heart-shaped leaves, and fountains of tiny locust leaves reaching tall above the rest. The maples have fresh new leaves of the brightest green and stems of a vivid red.

Springs emerge from black mossy banks; their waters tumble over carpeted boulders and fall from pool to pool. Watercress grows in the ripples or gathers on flats beside eddies.

There is continuous movement here. Some animals are silent, such as the six-foot-long black Racer that moves along logs, then into the water, and across streams as it explores crevices, shrubs, and the layer of leaves on the forest floor.

Silver-spotted Skippers land on moss beside miniature waterfalls and fly back and forth above the creeks. Bees visit the flowers of Queen Anne's Lace. Cardinals flit from shrub to shrub. Whippoorwills and thrushes call from within the woods, wood-pewees and vireos from up in the higher branches.

Seldom is the growth in the mixed deciduous forest as dense as that in the boreal forest. There are fewer large animals here than in boreal or transition forests—deer and bear are the principal ones—but small life abounds: snakes, birds, butterflies, and the lesser mammals such as Raccoons, foxes, and skunks.

From summit balds, the traveler can have unobstructed views of a tumble of rolling hills and plunging valleys for as far as the eye can see. In spring and summer, the mixed deciduous forest is a uniform and mist-covered mass of green, but it appears most spectacular in October. Millions of splotches of color convert the solid green of spring and summer into the multiple hues of autumn. The air is sharper then, and colder. At no other time is the mixture of trees so apparent. Each type of tree assumes its own distinctive color. The giant Yellow-poplar, which bears such large yellow flowers in spring that it earns the nickname "Tuliptree," has leaves of the brightest yellow in the forest, and it is possible from one vantage point to discern dozens or hundreds of these trees scattered along lower slopes and valley bottoms. The scarlet leaves of oaks, the maroon of dogwoods, the purple of Sweetgum, the cinnamon-orange of Sassafras, the ivory of beech—all contribute to a magnificent display of color.

The trees shut down for the season by growing a corky layer of cells, the abscission layer, between leaf stems and twigs. Because water and minerals to the leaf are cut off, chlorophyll production ceases, and the green fades to reveal orange, yellow, and red pigments, as well as purples and browns. The first leaves of the next spring have already been manufactured; they wait at the edges of twigs as buds, tightly wrapped and protectively encased to withstand the extremes of winter.

Plant Life

The composition of the mixed deciduous forest varies as a result of selective climatic, soil, and topographical factors, together with the history of fire and cultivation. Generally, the richness of soil and the favorable climate produce conditions for a diversity of plant life. This is most evident in the understory trees. Whereas the transition forest has few understory trees, and the boreal forest even fewer, the mixed deciduous understory is thickly populated with dogwoods, Redbud, American Holly, Striped Maple, Hophornbeam, and various members of the magnolia family. Beneath those are shrubs of Spicebush, Witch Hazel, Pawpaw, Wild Hydrangea, Mountain Pepperbush, and Hercules'-club. The forest floor, celebrated for its surpassing variety of wild flowers, supports hundreds of species, many with showy blossoms: Trout Lily, Yellow Lady's Slipper, Bloodroot, Wood Poppy, larkspur, Phacelia, Spring Beauty, trillium, and various violets and mints.

Range and Geological Heritage

In an overall sense, a deciduous forest exists wherever there are broad-leaved trees that lose their leaves more or less in unison every fall. But the mixed deciduous forest lies in the heart of eastern North America: along the foothills of the Blue Ridge and southern Appalachians in Virginia and North Carolina, across the Cumberland Mountains of Kentucky and Tennessee, in the ridge and valley country from New York and Pennsylvania southward, across much of Ohio and Indiana, and into Illinois. The mixed deciduous forest may seem homogeneous, but there are many variations, outliers, and intrusions. These woods reach up the sides of mountains, mingle with pines on the coastal plains, and extend their range westward and southwestward. They reach their

Yellow-poplar
("Tuliptree")
Liriodendron tulipifera
123, 162, 229

Sweetgum
Liquidambar styraciflua
122, 182, 226, 230

American Holly
Ilex opaca
105, 193

Eastern Hophornbeam
Ostrya virginiana
75, 167, 176, 234

Spicebush
Lindera benzoin
467

Witch-hazel
Hamamelis virginiana
95, 165, 203, 237

Pawpaw
Asimina triloba
59, 184

Sugar Maple
Acer saccharum
121, 227

White Oak
Quercus alba
109, 206

Canada Mayapple
Podophyllum peltatum

Wild Sarsaparilla
Aralia nudicaulis
427

American Basswood
Tilia americana
72, 239

American Elder
("Elderberry")
Sambucus canadensis

Maidenhair
Adiantum pedatum

Rattlesnake
Botrychium virginianum

Silvery Spleenwort
Athyrium thelypteroides

Jack-in-the-pulpit
Arisaema triphyllum
456, 503

Wild Ginger
Asarum canadense
459

Rue Anemone
Anemonella thalictroides

Hepatica
Hepatica americana

Lopseed
Phryma leptostachya

Spikenard
Aralia racemosa

Large-flowered Trillium
Trillium grandiflorum
446

optimum development in the central uplands, plateaus, ridges and valleys, and across unplowed flatlands.

Pollen evidence shows that following the retreat of the last glaciers 10,000 years ago, much of the northern part of the mixed deciduous area was spruce-fir forest. Undoubtedly the freshly exposed land remained cold and moist for centuries, suitable only for the establishment of boreal forest. But as the continent warmed, the hardwoods slowly spread northward and finally established climax communities that replaced the conifers. The speed of this transformation depended on how rapidly a suitable soil horizon was built up. In geological terms, 10,000 years is only a short time; the process of soil building and climax adjustment has not yet finished, at least not to the degree of maturity found in forests of the southern Appalachians that were never glaciated.

Hence, the northern tier of the mixed deciduous forest is ecologically young, characterized by two dominant species of trees, the Beech and the Sugar Maple. It is located on what is left of the young glacial deposits of the Wisconsin ice sheet, except in places where the moraines and other ridges are too sandy, gravelly, or dry, in which case oaks and hickories are dominant. Generally, maples and Beeches form a nearly pure community around the southern portion of the Great Lakes, in southern Ontario, and in northern Ohio and Indiana and western Pennsylvania.

Conspicuous Trees and Shrubs

Although the two climax trees form an almost exclusive canopy, other trees, chiefly White Oak and Yellow-poplar, do associate. The understory is mostly composed of young maples and Beeches, and the forest floor is covered with ferns, Canada Mayapple, and Wild Sarsaparilla.

In the northwestern part of the mixed deciduous forest, mainly in southern Minnesota, southwestern Wisconsin, and northwestern Illinois, another shared dominance has evolved, that of Sugar Maple with American Basswood. This dominance is persistent; if birches and aspens grow in open or burned areas, they are soon crowded out by maples and basswoods. The chief shrub is Elderberry. In the rich soil of the forest floor are Maidenhair, Rattlesnake, Interrupted, and Silvery Spleenwort ferns, Jack-in-the-pulpit, Wild Ginger, Rue Anemone, Hepatica, Bloodroot, violets, Lopseed, Spikenard, and Large-flowered Trillium.

The rest of the mixed deciduous forest occupies landscapes from the Mississippi River to the Blue Ridge, an east-west distance of more than 600 miles. The northern limits of this part of the forest, which was never covered by glaciers, are along the latitude of southern Pennsylvania; on the south, the deciduous woods merge with the southern pinelands at the northern edge of the Gulf coastal plain, a north-south distance of about 400 miles. This is the heart of the eastern forests, a landlocked interior.

However, there are modest uplands at the center of the mixed deciduous forest in the Cumberland Mountains and parts of

White Basswood
Tilia heterophylla
71

Yellow Buckeye
("Sweet Buckeye")
Aesculus octandra
131, 202

Northern Red Oak
Quercus rubra
118, 209

White Ash
Fraxinus americana
134, 178, 213

Black Cherry
Prunus serotina
91, 153

the Allegheny and Cumberland plateaus. The principal characteristic of these uplands, except for the northern fringes, is that there is not a single dominant tree, as in a pure maple grove, or two dominant trees, as in the maple-beech community, but many. The climax is undifferentiated, formed from three dozen species of trees, among them Beech, White Basswood, Sugar Maple, Yellow-poplar, Sweet Buckeye, Red and White oak, hickory, magnolia, birch, White Ash, and Black Cherry—a roll call of the most notable and abundant deciduous trees in North America. The principal exception is the hickories, and although these occur sparsely in mixed deciduous forests, they are more dominant to the west, beyond the Mississippi River; they are discussed in the chapter on the oak-hickory forest.

Climate

The mixed deciduous forest has four distinct seasons, all more or less the same length. Winter usually arrives on schedule in the middle of December, and the next three months of uninterrupted cold winds from the north bring snow, ice storms, glaze, sleet, and sometimes weeks of temperatures below freezing. This season is usually relatively mild, but occasionally there are days of bitter cold and heavy snow. When spring arrives, cold air masses from the Arctic collide with warm and moist air from the Gulf of Mexico. This collision usually produces unsettled weather, including electrical storms, fast-moving squalls, heavy downpours, and tornadoes. Nonetheless, April can be dry, which may lead to desiccated woods and wildfires.

Sunshine and precipitation are usually adequate and uniformly distributed throughout the seasons, despite rare dry spells in August; the average annual precipitation is approximately thirty-seven inches. Average summer temperatures in the Ohio Valley are around 79° F; in January, the average temperature ranges between 22° F and 46° F. If the air masses that provide precipitation slow down, stop, and become stagnant, then the humidity builds up, the temperature rises, and a hot, muggy spell sets in. At such times, the sky becomes hazy and the concentration of atmospheric pollutants increases. Even the forest itself contributes water vapor; each day in summer, evaporation is estimated to return as much as 2500 gallons of water to the air from each acre of forest.

Geology and Soils

Variations in weather are to some degree modified by variations in the landscape. Uplands exist in profusion—and, some would say, confusion. Flat plains are rarities, for this part of the continent has been uplifted, folded, tilted, and broken many times; in the North, the land has been glaciated and deglaciated, and erosion has been at work for a long period. As a result, there is nearly every topographic feature imaginable. A few plateaus are relatively flat on top; others are broken into canyons, ravines, cliffs, gorges, or crags. Ridges may extend for hundreds of miles, accompanied by smoothly eroded valleys on each side. There are abundant streams, from mountain brooks to major rivers: the James, Potomac, Shenandoah, Ohio, Tennessee, Mississippi, and Missouri rivers all run through the mixed deciduous forest. Bottomlands, floodplains, and alluvial valleys are filled with accumulations of rich soils. Springs and seeps as well as underground rivers provide evidence of immense subterranean reservoirs.

On the eastern side of the Blue Ridge is the Piedmont, the least mountainous of the Appalachian uplifts. It lies between the coastal plain and the Appalachians from New York to Alabama and is characterized by rolling hills of granite, gneiss, and other durable rocks.

To the west of the Appalachians, beyond the ridge and valley region, lie the Cumberland and Allegheny plateaus and other highlands that extend from New York southwestward through Pennsylvania, West Virginia, Kentucky, and Tennessee to Alabama. These plateaus have not been subject to the intensity of compression that folded the ridge and valley country. They are made up of comparatively horizontal strata, though the landscape is rugged because streams and rivers have deeply dissected the sandstones, shales, and conglomerate masses of rock. Some of the uplands in the Catskills and Alleghenies of New York State were glaciated, but the rest of the plateaus were not. In fact, the Cumberland and Allegheny plateaus have existed for so long, and their forests are so old, that the ancestral trees most likely helped supply seeds with which glaciated lands were reforested when the ice masses melted.

The central lowlands of Ohio, Indiana, Illinois, Missouri, and Iowa all give testimony to the leveling effect of continental glaciation, which filled low places in gently rolling terrain. When glaciers began to melt, a considerable outflow of water into "sluiceways" formed the ancestral channels of the Ohio, Wabash, Illinois, Mississippi, and Missouri rivers. Therefore, much of the debris in those valleys represents an outflow of sediments captured in the old glaciers.

The direct legacy of all this glaciation, uplifting, folding, and rearrangement of the earth's surface is a variety of landscapes and a diversity of soils. With the passage of time, sandstones at the surface have disintegrated into sands, shales into silt, limestones into calcareous soils, granites and schists into loam. In most places, the soils have built up to the point where they can support one of the richest forests on earth.

Plants are generally concentrated on soils and terrain to which they are best adapted—alders along streams, for example, Yellow-poplars in lowlands and on mountain slopes, hemlocks in ravines, and oaks on ridgetops. Adequate drainage carries away the vast inflow of precipitation. Water-loving vegetation thrives in the few swamps found in the region.

Human Intervention
The rich and productive mixed deciduous forests have long invited human settlement. In historic times, most of the mature trees grew well over 100 feet in height and became a resource widely used by early settlers. Man's greatest influence

Passenger Pigeon
Ectopistes migratorius

on the mixed deciduous forest, however, was not logging or
fire but agriculture. If the forest burned or was cut, regrowth
healed the wounds, and new woods grew on the site of the
old. But on cultivated land, such regrowth was extremely
limited.

Today, forest is more prevalent in mountain country than in
Ohio, where scarcely fifteen percent of the forest remains. In a
few places, atmospheric pollutants have had a more severe
effect than agriculture, eliminating all life on the surrounding
hills.

The impact of human settlement on wildlife distribution has
been pronounced, owing especially to excess hunting and
removal of habitat. The Passenger Pigeon was so dependent
upon a single species of tree, the Beech, that when the tree
was extensively cut, populations of the pigeon diminished
sharply. Some flights of Passenger Pigeons in North America
were reported to be 300 miles long and a mile wide, requiring
more than fourteen hours to pass a given point. One such
flight was estimated to contain four billion birds. The pigeons
disappeared, first by the millions, then by the hundreds, then
one by one, until the last survivor died in a Cincinnati zoo
in 1914.

Ecology

The mixed deciduous forest comprises numerous microhabitats
—cool shady ravines and north-facing slopes for organisms
requiring lower temperatures, and open areas, ridgetops, and
south-facing slopes for the sun-loving species. It is complex
because it is old geologically and biologically, and evolution
has been at work, relatively uninterrupted, for millions of
years. The trees compete vigorously for space in which to raise
their leaves to the sunlight.

This growth translates into an abundance of food for
herbivores, and although the animal life in the woods is not
nearly as conspicuous as the showy wild flowers, it is there in
great numbers. Bees make direct use of the nectar of the
flowers and in so doing transfer pollen from plant to plant.
Bears eat the honey produced by bees. Other insects are
attracted to flowers, and so there are flycatchers in the
deciduous forests, including wood-pewees, phoebes, and
kingbirds. Hummingbirds fly from flower to flower, as do
butterflies and moths. Flowers are clearly hubs of activity in
the deciduous forest but of course are just one aspect of the
food chain.

The deciduous forest is rich in species not only because of the
cycling of nutrients but also because of numerous organisms
that can coexist in virtually the same space. All trees and
understory plants need sunlight. The herbaceous layer
blossoms in early spring and completes a large portion of its
reproductive process before the leaves of canopy trees shade the
forest floor. Such adaptation allows a host of species, including
Bloodroot and various trilliums and violets, to share the same
ground as the trees.

Such adaptations are not necessary in the case of phlox, which spreads over exposed and rocky slopes and hence is seldom shaded as spring progresses. Sumac and blackberries are also pioneers on open and disturbed ground, often at the edge of the forest. Other plants, such as goldenrods and asters, bloom later and tend to do best on meadows or at the forest edge, where more sunlight is available. Some understory plants, including wild grape, Virginia creeper, and clematis, are adapted to climb up away from the forest floor and secure more sunlight while clinging to tree trunks and rock faces. Every leaf is a source of nutrients, and the search for food is universal, as indicated by the work of leaf-chewing insects, twig borers, cambium eaters, wood eaters, sapsucking insects, seed eaters, and gall makers. All of this action, including both production and consumption, requires energy. One scientist has estimated that the total energy used by plants and animals on an acre of beech-maple forest every year is equal to that needed to supply an average home with electricity for nearly half a century.

Inhabitants of the Forest Floor

It has been estimated that each year up to ten million leaves fall on an acre of a productive deciduous forest. Limbs also fall, as do twigs, bark, whole tree trunks, and animal carcasses. All this amounts to thousands of pounds of biomass, and were it not decomposed and used up, the forest would suffocate beneath its own debris.

Decomposition is the work of a silent majority beneath the layer of leaves, a horde of hundreds of billions of decomposers, mostly bacteria and microscopic fungi, with a smaller number of protozoans. Their role in the normal working of an ecosystem is to recycle nutrients into the food chain so that plants will continue to thrive. They also aerate and loosen the soil, making the penetration and growth of roots easier. Some fungi take food directly from the roots and in return supply those roots with water, minerals, and nutrients.

The fungi and bacteria that first attack fallen materials possess enzymes in their cells that induce chemical actions. Some substances are broken down more slowly than others, and different species of decomposers combine to break down different categories of materials. Earthworms feed principally on the leaves of aspens, White Ash, and basswoods. Fungi, mainly *Polyporus* and *Fomes,* grow in woody material and soften —that is, rot—the tissues. These tissues are then invaded by scarabaeid beetle larvae, millipedes, and isopods, which in turn are consumed by such predators as Daddy Longlegs and pseudoscorpions. Wood-eating termites and carpenter ants move in. Many insects arrive to consume the fungi. Eyed click beetles prey upon the larvae. These organisms work mostly in a stable environment, although their activities, especially the rate of decomposition they cause, are controlled by changes in temperature and moisture.

Above the insects in size are mice and shrews, the mice consuming vegetation, the shrews invertebrates as well as mice. That under-the-leaves environment, insulated against

Virginia Creeper
Parthenocissus quinquefolia

Earthworm
Lumbricus terrestris

Eastern Daddy-long-legs
Leiobunum spp.
421

Eastern Eyed Click Beetle
Alaus oculatus
507

Dusky Salamander
Desmognathus fuscus
548

Red-backed Salamander
Plethodon cinereus

Green Salamander
Aneides aeneus

Cheat Mountain
Salamander
Phethodon nettingi nettingi

Grandfather Mountain
Salamander
Plethodon welleri

Scarlet Snake
Cemophora coccinea

Worm Snake
Carphophis amoenus

Milk Snake
Lampropeltis triangulum
533

Copperhead
Agkistrodon contortrix
530

Timber Rattlesnake
Crotalus horridus
529

Rat Snake
Elaphe obsoleta
524

Kentucky Warbler
Oporornis formosus
287

Tree Sparrow
Spizella arborea

Broad-winged Hawk
Buteo platypterus
257

drying out and therefore partially protected from weather-related variables, also attracts salamanders. In the mixed deciduous forest live more species and larger populations of these amphibians than in any other forest in the world. Some are difficult to discern, especially those camouflaged in a remarkable match of their environment; others are red, green, yellow, blue, spotted, marbled, striped. Because of their long and relatively undisturbed evolution here, salamanders have become increasingly specialized. For example, the Dusky Salamander lives near streams; the Red-backed Salamander occupies drier woodlands under logs and rocks; Green Salamanders inhabit caves and wet sandstone cliffs; other species, notably the Cheat Mountain and Grandfather Mountain salamanders, occur in relatively isolated places. Salamanders and their close relatives, the newts, chiefly consume worms, larvae, and ground-dwelling invertebrates. Frogs, toads, and salamanders occupy similar ecological niches. Their principal predators are snakes, skunks, and Raccoons, which inhabit the same level of the forest floor and prowl about at night.

The mixed deciduous forest floor is ideal for ground-dwelling reptiles and amphibians because of ample shelter and available food. As aggressive carnivores, the snakes cull populations of ground-dwelling insects, birds, mammals, amphibians, and other reptiles. They are in turn preyed upon by hawks, foxes, Raccoons, and other snakes. Most, such as the Scarlet, Worm, and Milk snakes, the Racer, Copperhead, and Timber Rattlesnake, seek their prey on the forest floor. Others, like the Rat Snake, will climb trees when necessary. The Copperhead and Timber Rattlesnake are, like some others, effectively patterned to match the colors and designs of the forest floor.

Birds

Because the climate varies from cold in winter to hot in summer, and because the mixed deciduous forest is well supplied with food and shelter, this region is a biological crossroads. Many species of birds that nest in transition or boreal forests migrate through these woods in spring, just as insects and larvae emerge, and then pass through again on the return trip in autumn. Other species, such as the Kentucky Warbler, fly only as far north as the deciduous forest to breed. Some species, such as the Tree Sparrow, breed in the North and winter in the deciduous forest. And dozens of species, such as juncos, are resident year-round. If they migrate at all, it is only to the top of the nearest ridge to reproduce in summer, returning to the valley for the winter.

The migratory flights of autumn are characterized by large numbers of birds, especially warblers, passing through the forest canopy or high above it. The most spectacular migratory flights are those of hawks, notably the Broad-winged, which make use of strong updrafts above Appalachian ridges.

In contrast with the long-range movements of most birds, other animals of the mixed deciduous woods are short-range travelers. Their peregrinations cover only short distances from their places of birth. Their ranges overlap without conflict if feeding habits differ, or if the animals are "layered"—that is, if they occupy the same territory but at different levels in the forest. For example, the Gray Squirrel gathers most of its seeds from the forest canopy and seldom competes with the Ruffed Grouse, which feeds on the forest floor.

The Ruffed Grouse has a unique adaptation to winter. Each autumn, special cuticular appendages, called pectinations, grow on the outer edges of each toe. These serve as "snowshoes," holding the bird up in all but the softest snow.

Gray Squirrel
Sciurus carolinensis
588

Ruffed Grouse
Bonasa umbellus
247

Mammals

Animals without such adaptations must be prepared to withstand temperature extremes or avoid them altogether. The Woodchuck is characteristic of burrowing animals that avoid extremes by retreating underground. No other animal in the deciduous forest digs so many dens, with such extended use. A den in New York State was found to contain both a Woodchuck and an Eastern Cottontail; later a skunk moved in, followed by a Raccoon, and then a Red Fox that gave birth to its young there. Woodchucks' shelters are also shared by Ring-necked Pheasants, weasels, Gray Foxes, and other animals. In digging its shelters, the Woodchuck also moves, mixes, and aerates the soil; one estimate credits Woodchucks with moving more than one and a half million tons of New York State soil to the surface every year.

White-tailed Deer make modest contributions, too, by returning certain nutrients back to the environment. Their antlers, which are shed in the autumn, are eaten by mice and other rodents; these animals obtain from them a supply of calcium and phosphorus. In producing such nutrients, the deer browse mainly on twigs, buds, leaves, and such seeds as acorns and hazelnuts.

Elk were once abundant in the mixed deciduous woods, but they are no longer, although attempts have been made to reintroduce them. Bison lived in the woods and on grasslands of eastern North America, but disappeared about 1800. Black Bears became scarce during the lumbering era but are now coming back, especially where human activities are largely excluded, as in Shenandoah National Park, Virginia. There the Black Bears, once absent altogether, are finding larger trees with more places to den than in the days when the mountains were freshly logged.

Thus, despite the loss of much of the mixed deciduous forest that once covered the heart of the continent south of the Great Lakes, the habitat is recovering in many places. There the ecological functions of the habitat remain mostly intact, which demonstrates the remarkable resilience and durability of the broad-leaved forest.

Woodchuck
Marmota monax
595

Eastern Cottontail
Sylvilagus floridanus
596

Red Fox
Vulpes vulpes
612

Ring-necked Pheasant
Phasianus colchicus

Gray Fox
Urocyon cinereoargenteus
611

White-tailed Deer
Odocoileus virginianus
616

Elk
Cervus elaphus

Bison
Bison bison

Black Bear
Ursus americanus
609

THE MIXED DECIDUOUS FOREST: PLANTS AND ANIMALS

Trees

Birds

THE OAK-HICKORY FOREST

Excepting the riparian forests of the prairies, the oak-hickory forest of the Ozark Highlands represents the western limit of North America's deciduous forests. In the Ozark, Boston, and Ouachita mountains of Missouri, Arkansas, and Oklahoma, the oak-hickory forest has attained dominance. In these regions, climate—in particular the decrease of precipitation from east to west—is a controlling factor in the distribution of hardwood species. So, although oaks and hickories grow in nearly every deciduous forest of North America, these trees are preponderant in this region, in a climate and on terrain less suited to the growth of other hardwood species, which dominate the forests to the east and north.

Oaks and hickories favor comparatively dry, well-drained habitats. These trees appear among pines on the Piedmont uplands and coastal plains from Connecticut to Texas, and grow in isolated or outlying communities up the Mississippi River valley to Wisconsin and Minnesota. Much of Illinois and parts of Indiana and Ohio are also dominated by oak-hickory forest. But the principal concentration occurs in the Ozark Highlands, where dissected plateaus, ridges, and otherwise broken terrain provide an ideal setting for the growth of this forest type.

Diversity

Like the mixed deciduous forests to the east, the oak-hickory region in the Ozark Highlands is exceptionally diverse in habitat. Variations in soil, moisture, and exposure create favorable environments for many kinds of trees here, despite the predominance of oaks and hickories.

One reason for the diversity is the area's location in the center of North America, which makes the Ozarks a biological crossroads. There is a touch of the boreal forest in the presence of mosses and Harebells; elements of western prairie flora, such as primrose, Indian Paintbrush, and Prickly Pear Cactus; various species of pine, Water Tupelo, and Sweetgum, all typical of coastal plain flora to the south; and floristic connections to the Appalachian plateaus and ridges, among them Beech and magnolias. Trees with widely different requirements are found in suitable habitats: cool and shady or warm and sunny; wet or dry; with level, sloping, or vertical surfaces; and with acidic, alkaline, or sandy soil.

The oaks and hickories are themselves selective. In places they congregate on north- and east-facing slopes as well as in ravines and small valleys. There the dominant oaks are White, Black, Bur, Northern Red, and Chinkapin; the hickories are Shagbark, Mockernut, and Bitternut. Now and then a Red or Sugar maple intrudes. Black Tupelo and White Ash mix among the dominants. Black Walnut, Black Cherry, American Beech, and Basswood associate in limited numbers. On the ridge tops and the drier south- and west-facing slopes that are primarily derived from sandstone outcroppings, the composition changes. It is still an oak-hickory forest, but in this instance the community is dominated by Southern Red, Black, Post, and Blackjack oaks, together with an assortment

White Oak
Quercus alba
109, 206

Black Oak
Quercus velutina
113, 208, 225

Bur Oak
Quercus macrocarpa
110, 205

Northern Red Oak
Quercus rubra
118, 209

Chinkapin Oak
Quercus muehlenbergii
106, 210

Shagbark Hickory
Carya ovata
132, 232, 233

Mockernut Hickory
Carya tomentosa
137

Bitternut Hickory
Carya cordiformis
135

Overcup Oak
Quercus lyrata
108

Pecan
Carya illinoensis
139

River Birch
Betula nigra
69

Sycamore
Platanus occidentalis
124, 183

Eastern Redcedar
Juniperus virginiana
38

of hickories, Red Maple, Common Persimmon, and Sassafras. On these dry sites the Shortleaf Pine competes so well that portions of the habitat are oak-pine forest.

By contrast, a few species of oaks and hickories have become adapted to lower and wetter habitats. Among them are Water Oak, Overcup Oak, Water Hickory, Nutmeg Hickory, and Pecan.

Owing in part to greater aridity, there is not such a dense understory of medium-sized trees in the oak-hickory forest as in the mixed deciduous woods; Flowering Dogwood is a common middle-layer tree. As usual, blueberries predominate in the shrub layer. Spicebush, Witch-Hazel, ceanothus, and Fragrant Sumac are also characteristic, as are a number of vines: various grapes, Woodbine, Common Greenbrier, Trumpet Creeper, Rattan, and Poison Ivy.

In the thick layers of leaves on the forest floor, the roots of seedlings must sometimes grow relatively long distances to find soil. Where they succeed, there will be wild gardens of Dittany, Tick Trefoil, Goat's Rue, St. Andrew's Cross, Pencil Flower, Snakeroot, Sensitive Pea, and the familiar bush clovers, well liked by White-tailed Deer, Turkey, and Bobwhite.

On soils derived from limestone the prevailing forest is markedly different: Sugar Maple, Black Walnut, basswoods, Blue Ash, and Chinkapin Oak. Among the understory on limestone and dolomite glades are Umbrella Plant (a buckwheat), larkspurs, asters, goldenrods, bedstraws, and plants typical of the American West: Prairie Spurge, acacias, and penstemons.

Along the streams grow concentrations of River Birch, Sweetgum, Black Tupelo, willow, and—largest of all along these streams—Sycamore, a tree larger than the oaks and hickories. Cool, moist cliffs, some as high as 500 feet, are festooned with moss and lichen. Occasional Eastern Redcedars secure precarious rootholds on nearly vertical slopes. Moreover, close observation reveals that bald knobs, deep ravines, springs, and sinkholes have specific plant and animal associations. In some cases, the species are specialized and rare because they have adapted to continuously wet environments, deep shade, or relatively cool spots.

From the vantage point of a river or a lookout on top of a hill, the impression of this forest may be one of continuous high density. The openness of the oak-hickory forest, however, separates it from other deciduous associations, for it is not nearly as thick as the mixed deciduous woods to the east or the coniferous boreal forests to the north. The tree trunks are thinner, the canopy less dense. Close observation, however, calls for deliberate caution: Cottonmouths, Copperheads, and rattlesnakes, all venomous, find ideal habitats in the wetlands and woodlands. And not only is the Poison Ivy ubiquitous, but the woods are also replete with ticks and chiggers.

The seasons are distinctive and the colors showy. Beginning with the Flowering Dogwood's vivid display at the earliest hint of spring there is a succession of wild flowers in the

Black Locust
Robinia pseudoacacia
129, 157

understory and on the forest floor, lasting through spring and summer—at least where the density of oaks and hickories permits. There is red in the forest in April as well as in October. During spring the maples put forth a new growth of reddish leaves. In autumn, the Overcup Oak, at lower elevations, is principally responsible for the blaze of yellow, orange, and scarlet that the Ozarks are famous for. Sumac, Sweetgum, Black Locust, and Flowering Dogwood also contribute rich colors. All through the winter, Post Oaks retain their withered brown leaves on the twigs.

Since no part of the mountains rises above 3000 feet, there is only a limited altitudinal diversity, without the abrupt transitions from one forest type to another found in regions with higher mountains. The composition of the forest changes in response to the type of soil, the amount of moisture, and location with respect to the sun.

Physical Features
This area, the western section of North America's extensive deciduous forests, lies close to the geographic center of the continent. It is vulnerable to icy winds from the north, unobstructed as they blow down across the prairies. These winds are met by warm, moist winds that move up from the south, producing turbulence. Floods occur along the lower reaches of tributaries of the Mississippi and other large rivers. At certain times of year, excess runoff inundates the forests, and the trees may stand in water for long periods of time. Because of the dampness in the woods and the high humidity, winter may appear to be exceptionally cold, and, indeed, temperatures sometimes fall as low as 0° F. But on the whole the temperatures are moderately low. Average July temperatures in the Ozarks range between 64° F. and 92° F. In January, the range is between 29° F. and 50° F. Snow is seldom a problem; four to eight inches a year is the norm, though twenty-inch snowfalls have been recorded at upper elevations. Once or twice a year, freezing rain may cause the limbs of trees and shrubs to break. But overall, winters are comparatively mild and relatively short.

The growing season lasts for seven months in the oak-hickory forest. In summer, the heat rises markedly, reaching highs of 100° F. Heavy storms and destructive tornadoes periodically devastate portions of the land: Among the states, Oklahoma, Arkansas, and Missouri are ranked third, fifth, and sixth, respectively, in frequency of tornadoes. Severe droughts are more widely destructive than tornadoes, however, causing extreme stress and mortality in certain species of oak.

Cold, steady rains keep the forest damp for extended periods. The annual precipitation varies between forty and sixty inches, and while this is a great deal of moisture, the region is warm for much of the year, and there is considerable evaporation as well as heavy runoff. Thunderstorms are frequent and may contribute as much as six inches of rain in twenty-four hours. This not only helps to replenish subterranean water reserves, but also sustains a diversity of plants in more moist soil locations. Because most Ozark streams have steep gradients, the runoff is usually rapid. Generally there is less humidity and moisture in the oak-hickory forest than in the mixed deciduous regions; indeed, the semiarid prairie is not far away. In a sense, then, the area is a transition zone between humid and arid regions. Storms from the Gulf of Mexico carry moisture-laden masses of air northeastward to the Appalachians, usually bypassing the region. Nevertheless, if air masses stagnate in summer, the humidity increases and the temperature rises, resulting in a hazy atmosphere.

Geology and Soils
Although the Ouachita Mountains exhibit folding and faulting, the Ozarks consist primarily of uplifted sedimentary deposits, the layers remaining essentially horizontal. The result is a tableland that has been gradually dissected by erosion into plateaus, ridges, ravines, hollows, sinkholes, caverns, pedestal rocks, and natural bridges.
The surface rocks today are mainly limestone, dolomite, chert, and sandstone. Because the land has been elevated, and because the rock layers are often porous, stream systems are well developed and drainage is good—the kind of dry terrain to which oaks, hickories, and pines are best adapted. Once water drains from the upper slopes and reaches the lowlands, it slows and saturates the soils, attracting vegetation adapted to moist environments.

Ecology
The adaptations of forest organisms to specific environmental limitations is nicely illustrated in the oak-hickory forest. Each plant grows only where its limits of tolerance are not exceeded, and where there are conditions to which it has, over thousands or millions of years, become best adapted.
White Oaks, for example, tend to grow on cooler, moister north-facing slopes, where the soil is less exposed to the sun. Such variations of condition also affect the distribution of other vegetation. Where soil moisture increases, there are woodlands as luxuriant as those of mixed deciduous forests, except that in the more arid oak-hickory forest the tree canopy is not usually as dense, allowing more sunlight to penetrate to the forest floor.

Eastern Redbud
Cercis canadensis
63, 146

Juniper
Juniperus ashei

Smoke-tree
Cotinus obovatus

Western Soapberry
Sapindus drummondii

Fringetree
Chionanthus virginicus

Another environmental variable that influences forest growth is the soil. Limestone-based soils in the Ozark Highlands are ideal for Redbuds and Sugar Maples. On rocky patches, cliffs, and talus slopes, other communities become established. Dominant among these is the Eastern Redcedar, or Juniper, well known for its ability to spring up in abandoned farmlands, fire-devastated areas, and poor soil sites. The Redcedar is a pioneer species. Over the years, it shelters a growing community of plants—including currants, acacias, Smoke-tree, Western Soapberry, and Fringetree—that may eventually yield to a climax of oaks and hickories.
West of the Ozarks, where precipitation is less than abundant and the soils are coarser, the forest dwindles and the trees become more modest in size, even shrubby. As the

environmental limitations approach those of the semiarid West, as in Oklahoma, the contrast between forest types becomes sharper. On the one hand, there are stretches of oak-hickory forest with little understory; but at springs and seeps or in ravines and gorges, dense vegetation reminiscent of the southern Appalachians exists.

Beyond this zone, as they intrude on the prairies and plains, the deciduous forests change to an oak-hickory savanna. In increasingly arid climate, the oaks and hickories become shrubby and finally thin out. Sugar Maples are about the only other hardwood pioneers that can tolerate these conditions, and they grow only in deep canyons or similar environments where there is more moisture and less heat than on the open prairie. Botanical history suggests that deciduous forests once extended farther west than they do now. Remnants of those woods are known as relict, or genetically isolated, forests, and they survive in pockets where conditions resemble those of the forests of origin.

South of the Ozarks, the oaks and hickories merge with pinelands on the coastal plain of eastern Texas, and associate with pines on the rest of the coastal plain. But like other hardwoods, they have limited tolerance to fire and for the most part are unable to overcome the pines, which easily tolerate frequent fires. Given several centuries without fire, oaks and hickories might manage to become dominant. But the frequency of fire along the coastal plain, which promotes the growth of pines at the expense of hardwoods, makes this possibility very unlikely.

Just as pines manage to dominate coastal areas, oaks and hickories themselves often crowd out competing plants in other localities. In mixed deciduous forests, abundant showy plants grow on the forest floor. There the understory plants depend on the nutrients from fallen leaves and debris from trees, and are kept alive by decomposition of plant material. Oaks compete successfully with other trees in soil that is somewhat acid and relatively poor in nutrients. But such moderate conditions seldom obtain where oaks and hickories dominate. Fallen oak leaves are particularly poor in nutrients because the nutrients in them are withdrawn into the branches before the leaves die. Thus, most of the nutrients in the oak-hickory forest are locked in the trees themselves, and what little nutrient material escapes into the soil is quickly retrieved by the roots.

Because the leaves of oaks and hickories often form an almost impenetrable layer on the forest floor, the trees have evolved large seeds capable of producing a stout root when they germinate; this root is able to penetrate the leaf litter and maintain the dominance of oaks and hickories. The large seed also provides nutrients to the seedling during its early growth in the poor soil.

The Effects of Human Intervention
Once a hunting area for the Osage Indians, the oak-hickory forest provided settlers from the East with timber for many

kinds of construction, including the building of railroads. And as early as 1541, Hernando de Soto and his group of explorers had found another important commercial aspect of the hickory forest—the Pecan. Early explorers cut down entire trees to reach the seeds more easily, with the predictable result that the Pecan tree began to become rare. Today the species has been hybridized and commercialized, and is no longer in danger of extinction. Protected forests also keep the wild pecan alive and well.

Past abuses, such as indiscriminate burning, overgrazing, and "cut-and-run" logging, have largely ended. The Ozark Highlands were never heavily settled; more often than not, farms remained individual plots, hemmed in by cliffs and further isolated by tortuous roads. As a result, much of the oak-hickory forest still stands, and some is recovering from inroads made in the past.

Wildlife of the Ozarks

The abundant seeds produced in the oak-hickory forest are a rich food source for animals—one that requires a smaller expenditure of energy on their part than is needed in other forests to harvest the small seeds of birches and hemlocks. In addition to hard mast (the nuts of trees and shrubs, including oaks, hickories, and walnuts), this forest also produces many kinds of fruit, among them persimmons, blueberries, wild grapes, and prickly pear, that are a source of food for the wildlife. A host of animals makes use of this supply, including birds, mammals, and insects. Because the nuts are produced only in the autumn, some nut-eating animals store them for use at other seasons, caching them in hollow trees or burying them in the ground.

In one year, large numbers of acorns or hickory nuts may be produced, while in the next, the crop may be very small. In years of scarcity, the population of nut-eating animals drops significantly, so that when there is another bumper crop, only a few of these animals will have survived and the number of nuts they can take is relatively small. When the acorn crop is reduced, there is usually a large southward migration of Blue Jays, while in years of really acute scarcity, even the squirrels are forced to leave. In any particular area, the oaks and hickories often produce bumper crops in synchrony; in a lean year, no single species produces enough seeds to sustain the entire population of nut-eating animals.

As in all ecosystems, there are numerous interrelated food chains in the oak-hickory forest. Flycatchers, gnatcatchers, and woodpeckers, for example, are here because of the insect populations. Hawks and owls prey on mice and other small mammals. Raccoons search the wet places for food. Squirrels and chipmunks feed on nuts, but have to watch for weasels, hawks, and Bobcats. And the hickories themselves are a staple in the diet of many insects.

Among the scores of other native mammals are White-tailed Deer, Black Bear, Red and Gray foxes, Gray and Fox squirrels, cottontails, Virginia Opossum, and Woodchucks.

Blue Jay
Cyanocitta cristata
324

Raccoon
Procyon lotor
607

Bobcat
Felis rufus
613

White-tailed Deer
Odocoileus virginianus
616

Black Bear
Ursus americanus
609

Red Fox
Vulpes vulpes
612

Gray Fox
Urocyon cinereoargenteus
611

Gray Squirrel
Sciurus carolinensis
588

Red Squirrel
Tamiasciurus hudsonicus
586

Virginia Opossum
Didelphis virginiana
600

Woodchuck
Marmota monax
595

Corn Snake
Elaphe guttata
531

Rat Snake
Elaphe obsoleta
524

Prairie Kingsnake
Lampropeltis calligaster

Milk Snake
Lampropeltis triangulum
533

Coachwhip
Masticophis flagellum
523

Timber Rattlesnake
Crotalus horridus
529

Red-tailed Hawk
Buteo jamaicensis
258

Great Horned Owl
Bubo virginianus
242

Red-shouldered Hawk
Buteo lineatus
256

Barred Owl
Strix varia
244

Hackberry
Celtis occidentalis
77, 188

Coyote
Canis latrans

The region is good snake country, with more than two dozen species occupying uplands and lowlands. These include the Corn and Rat snakes, which are tree climbers when need be, the Prairie Kingsnake, Milk Snake, Coachwhip, Copperhead, and Timber Rattlesnake.

Diurnal or nocturnal, reptiles and small mammals alike are vulnerable to predation—by the Red-tailed Hawk in the day, or Great Horned Owl at night. Because of their complementary hunting styles, these two large predatory birds are capable of occupying the same territory with minimal competition. The owls often appropriate the large, bulky nests of the hawks, which simply move on and build a new nest.

The Red-tailed Hawk uses trees primarily as a perch to observe shrews, moles, chipmunks, mice, rabbits, and other prey. A bird of this size needs a considerable food supply and therefore a sizeable area of wild forest in which to hunt.

Both the Red-tailed Hawk and the Great Horned Owl prefer to hunt in dry upland territory. Conversely, the Red-shouldered Hawk and Barred Owl are adapted to seeking food in moist, wooded lowlands. Despite their territorial preferences, because large predatory birds such as these can shift from one food source to another, they can avoid starvation when certain animal populations diminish.

The Wild Turkey

No animal in the oak-hickory forest is more involved in the feasts and famines of the area than the Wild Turkey. Its principal reason for being here, of course, is the abundance of its favorite foods, acorns and hickory nuts. Indeed, the Turkey may well reach its largest populations in oak-hickory forests. However, since acorns are not a consistently dependable crop, the Turkey has become adapted to consuming other items available in its habitat: insects, spiders, crustaceans, salamanders, toads, lizards, and even small snakes. Wild Turkeys also consume wild grapes, Hackberry fruits, and rose hips. If there is a scarcity of all else, the Turkey will partake of the buds of ashes, oaks, and birches.

On occasion the Turkey's food is covered by snow, but the bird takes advantage of the deer's pawing of snow to open up feeding areas during the winter.

The Turkey itself is also liable to predation, and Raccoons, skunks, opossums, snakes, and crows prowl for Turkey eggs. And because Turkeys feed on the ground, they are vulnerable to surprise attacks by Coyotes, foxes and Bobcats—one reason why Turkeys roost in trees at night.

The Turkey's most effective predator has been man. Early records tell of flocks numbering in the thousands, but countless numbers of birds have been slaughtered. But the Turkey is coming back, even though—with all its enemies—the nesting success may be scarcely thirty-five percent. The bird is also vulnerable to diseases, parasites, and severe cold. At sunset the turkey finds its way to a tree for a night's roost, rounding out a day in the life of a creature which, perhaps more than any other, depends upon the oak-hickory forest.

THE OAK-HICKORY FOREST: PLANTS AND ANIMALS

THE SOUTHERN APPALACHIANS

The forest types of the Southern Appalachian Mountains deserve special treatment. This relatively small region contains such a rare and remarkable overlapping of forest habitats, reaching what might be called a zenith of development, that we can only do them justice by focusing a separate chapter on them. The Blue Ridge Parkway and Great Smoky Mountains National Park are among the most heavily visited parts of the national park system, and by the simple expedient of riding in a bus or automobile, more than fifteen million visitors annually can travel through this multiplicity of habitats in a relatively short time.

It is logical, then, to guide the reader through this premier collection of eastern forest types, because the public focuses on it as much as it does on any other grouping of forest habitats. To be sure, there are mixed deciduous woods here, as well as boreal and transition forests in the high country, oaks and hickories scattered about, and pines in the lower regions. These diverse habitats are treated individually in other chapters. But because so many visitors probe the wonders of this superlative region, they will be served by an objective review of how and why so many forest habitats merge and flourish here.

At the southern end of the Appalachian Mountains, the ridges rise to a maximum of 6684 feet, the highest in eastern North America. Between these summits and the surrounding lowlands at less than 1000 feet there is a range of climates and environments that are as diversified as the habitats found in the area from Georgia to Newfoundland. This one mountain range encompasses almost every forest type that occurs in the eastern half of the continent.

Nearly every kind of habitat is represented, from mixed deciduous forests in the lowlands to spruce-fir summit forests, similar to the boreal forests a thousand miles to the north. To find these habitats at or near sea level would require a trip by automobile of up to three days' duration. But in the heart of the mountains, all of these habitats can be visited on a single three-hour hike. By the time one reaches the Appalachian summits, the forest is ninety-eight percent different from what it was at lower levels. Rare is the tree or shrub that can survive in all these different environments.

The southern Appalachian forest begins to appear at the southern end of the Blue Ridge Mountains in Virginia. The forest extends south into the Great Smoky Mountains, and adjacent uplands in Virginia, North Carolina, Tennessee, Georgia, and Alabama. From the hot and humid lowlands, where deciduous trees are best adapted, to the cool ridges, where spruce and fir survive, lies an exceptional collection of forest communities. The greatest number of species of trees in North America is found here, including a score of species whose representatives reach record proportions and are the oldest in North America. So dense are these woods that there are, in fact, very few places—streams and certain bald ridgetops—where trees do not grow.

The boundaries between the different types of forest in the

southern Appalachians are not always distinct; such demarcations are much more pronounced in the Rocky Mountains, where the temperature gradients are sharper. The southern highlands are bathed in humidity, and this humidity is an effective moderator of extremes. Nevertheless, there are locally wide variations in environmental factors. Some groves of trees face the sun all day; others are hidden from it for most of the year. Some vegetation grows on promontories vulnerable to fierce mountain winds; other plant associations, utterly different, gather in sheltered coves. Some locations are rocky and steep; others are in the bottoms of gentle valleys. The rarest environment is level land.

Lowland Forest

Yellow-poplar
("Tuliptree")
Liriodendron tulipifera
123, 162, 229

Sycamore
Platanus occidentalis
124, 183

Black Tupelo
Nyssa sylvatica
57

Black Locust
Robinia pseudoacacia
129

Sugar Maple
Acer saccharum
121, 227

Sourwood
Oxydendrum arboreum
93, 219

Yellow Birch
Betula alleghaniensis
68

Pignut Hickory
Carya glabra
136

Red Hickory
Carya glabra var. *odorata*

Mockernut Hickory
Carya tomentosa
137

At the lowest elevations, the forests observable today are recovering from extensive logging; these were the forests most accessible to man over the past two centuries. Groves of Pitch Pine are the first to take root on burned, cut-over, or cultivated lands, but they soon give way to the White, Chestnut, Northern Red, and Black oaks that rise to shade them out.

Where climax forest still exists, it is among the richest on the continent. It resembles the mixed deciduous woods in that there is a shared dominance: Yellow-poplar, Sycamore, Black Tupelo, Black Locust, Mountain Silverbell, Sugar Maple, Sourwood, Yellow Birch, magnolia, and three hickories— Pignut, Red, and Mockernut. The understory trees are mainly dogwoods, but Witch-hazel may be found, often along streams. The rhododendrons in these mountains are as large as small trees and are abundant at all altitudes and in nearly every habitat.

The shrubs and vines in these lowland forests are equally varied: Smooth Hydrangea, Sweetshrub, greenbrier, and Virginia creeper, among many others. The forest floor is densely overgrown with ferns, mosses, and lichens as well as a variety of wild flowers and herbs, including asters, galax, Trailing Arbutus, Yellow Violet, Foamflower, False Foxglove, pedicularis, and goldenrods. For an observer who is not on a trail, many thickets are virtually impassable.

The lowland forests are essentially closed—that is, the mature trees are so huge, so voluminous, and so closely bunched together that the canopy coalesces and shuts out a great deal of sunlight. As in many dense tropical forests, there are deep shadows within these woods.

Lower Slopes

By contrast, certain pine-oak forests on lower slopes and ridges do not form such a dense canopy and are thus more open. Scarlet, White, Chestnut, and Black oaks grow alongside various pines—Pitch, Virginia, Table Mountain, Eastern White, and Shortleaf. This more open forest has a variety of species, including Red Maple, Sassafras, and Serviceberry, along with the sproutings of a tree that once dominated all— the American Chestnut, which has been nearly obliterated by blight. The understory in these open and drier forests is

Mountain Laurel
Kalmia latifolia
44, 148

Eastern Hemlock
Tsuga canadensis
34

Yellow Buckeye
("Sweet Buckeye")
Aesculus octandra
131, 202

White Ash
Fraxinus americana
134, 178, 213

American Beech
Fagus grandifolia
88, 204, 215, 236

Black Cherry
Prunus serotina
91, 153

Cucumber Tree
Magnolia acuminata
58

difficult to penetrate because of the extensive thickets of Mountain Laurel. Many of the shrubs and herbaceous plants in lowland forests also persist at higher elevations, so the understories in these two types of forest have many species in common.

The forests become more dense the closer to water they grow —and water is abundant. It surges from springs and seeps, cascades for miles down rocky canyons, plunges over cliffs, and flows into major rivers, principally the Tennessee. In this upended, rocky landscape there is scarcely a placid pool of any size. The water is crystal clear and silt-free even after days of downpour, and although the flow removes many tons of sediment from the mountains each year, it is not evident here. The enormous biomass of trees, shrubs, mosses, ferns, and decaying vegetation thoroughly absorbs the precipitation and filters the downflowing waters; as a result, the streams are among the purest on earth.

This kind of repeated soaking has helped give the forests of the southern Appalachians their richness and variety, the record size of many of their trees, their density, and the massive spring spectacle of 200 species of wild flowers. The Eastern Hemlock thrives in cooler and wetter environments along the streams, where water cascades over massive rocks covered with mosses and lichens and an extensive population of mushrooms, slime molds, and shelf fungi—more than 2000 species of them throughout these mountains—in red, white, orange, yellow, and brown. The wetness promotes both growth and decay.

Cove Forests

It is in remote upper portions of valleys, more or less at the 4500-foot level, that one discovers a rarity in eastern North America: virgin forests. In these remote sheltered coves, logging proved difficult, so lumbering companies left these upland forests till last. But before the remaining trees could all be cut, preserves such as the Great Smoky Mountains National Park had been established.

These protected hardwood cove forests have evolved over millions of years. So sheltered are they from wind, temperature extremes, and other environmental changes that certain trees within them grow to greater size than anywhere else. Within the cove forests of the Great Smoky Mountains National Park, several species attain record or near-record size; these include basswood, Yellow-poplar, Yellow Buckeye, Mountain Silverbell, Eastern Hemlock, White Ash, Sugar Maple, Yellow Birch, American Beech, Northern Red Oak, Black Cherry, and Cucumber Tree. The Yellow-poplar grows to thirty feet in circumference; the hemlock, twenty; the Yellow Buckeye, nearly sixteen; Yellow Birch, over fourteen; and Sugar Maple, over thirteen.

Rich vegetation in such deep ravines is typical. But the exceptional examples in the southern Appalachians are not the result only of the state of ecological repose and environmental equilibrium that governs such areas. These forests have been relatively undisturbed during much of their evolution, undergoing millions of years of biological development without glaciation, ocean inundation, or other interruptions. Today, some of the individual trees are more than 500 years old—not old compared to forests in and near the Sierra Nevada, but exceptional for trees of eastern North America. Away from the coves and out along the south-facing slopes, where the terrain receives the full brunt of solar radiation, the forests dry out more rapidly than do woodlands in coves or along streams. Consequently, the forest changes from huge hemlocks adapted to shade to modest pines and oaks that thrive in the sun. With such heat the forest dries out rapidly, less water soaks into the soils, and the habitat is drier than in sheltered, mossy vales or on north-facing slopes.

Nevertheless, the environment is nowhere too dry, not even here, and there is often a dense understory of shrubs beside the trail. These are dominated throughout the southern Appalachians by one family, Ericaceae—the heaths. Numerous members of the family—which includes rhododendron, azalea, huckleberry, blueberry, dog-hobble, spotted wintergreen, sand myrtle, and trailing arbutus—are remarkably tenacious.

The Rosebay Rhododendron, which forms dense thickets in deep protected ravines, flowers with large white blossoms in July. The Catawba Rhododendron is much more conspicuous because it occupies prominent ridges and treeless summits, or balds. Roan Mountain, for example, is celebrated for its extensive thickets of rhododendron that produce showy displays of lavender flowers in summer.

Coniferous Forests

At the highest elevations, principally above 4000 feet, spreads a dense and nearly continuous forest of Red Spruce, Fraser Fir, and Yellow Birch. This is a southern extension of the great boreal forest, which fills the Canadian subarctic from Newfoundland to Alaska. It extends down the ridges of the Appalachians from New England along the Blue Ridge to the southern tip of the Appalachians, broken only where the ridges, worn down by wind and water, support beeches and other upper-elevation deciduous trees.

The species of conifers in these spruce-fir forests differ from those farther north—Red Spruce instead of Black or White, Fraser Fir instead of Balsam (although both firs are often referred to locally as Balsam). As in the boreal forest, spruces and firs grow so closely together that their limbs seem interlocked. This shuts out the light, and the forest floor becomes as dark as that of the hardwood forests below. The soil is almost peatlike, resembling brown sawdust, with decaying leaves and needles. Over it spreads a mat of delicately flowering Wood Sorrel in a kind of mosaic with ferns and mosses. On open patches in the dense summit woods are tiny bluets and tangles of blackberry.

Even on the summits of the southern Appalachians, the vegetation in the spruce-fir forest is thick. The growing season

Dog-hobble
Leucothoë catesbaei

Spotted Wintergreen
Chimaphila maculata
453

Sand Myrtle
Leiophyllum buxifolium
473

Trailing Arbutus
Epigaea repens
486

Rosebay Rhododendron
Rhododendron maximum
150

Catawba Rhododendron
Rhododendron catawbiense
147

Red Spruce
Picea rubens
31, 171

Fraser Fir
Abies fraseri
32

Common Wood Sorrel
Oxalis montana
488

is amply long at this latitude, and the temperature extremes, although severe, do not prevent forest growth. A few species grow at all elevations; the most notable is the Yellow Birch.

Climate and Geology

The Southern Appalachian Mountains are a jumble of ridges, domes, and uplands with deep ravines and valleys that are often inaccessible to motor vehicles. Steep cliffs and waterfalls are abundant, but the terrain is seldom as sheer and precipitous as that in the Sierra Nevada, where glaciers and movements of the earth have been at work in fairly recent times. The Appalachians, however, have been quietly eroding from the end of Paleozoic time, more than 200 million years ago. For all the protection against erosion afforded by dense vegetation, these mountains have worn down considerably from what, in the past, may have been Sierralike dimensions. Rainfall is abundant throughout the year, varying from fifty to eighty inches, plus a contribution from droplets of dew that form when mists and clouds roll by. The precipitation is well distributed throughout the year, and the seasons are distinct. Though summers may be hot, winters can be frigid even this far south in latitude. On the mountain summits especially, snow whitens the land, rime forms, and ice accumulates. Water seeps into crevices of rock; as it freezes, it expands and rips apart the ledges. This process of disintegration, combined with gravity and stream flow that take the debris away, slowly wears down the mountains.

As in many other parts of the temperate deciduous forests, the landscape is cooled in winter by air masses from the Arctic and warmed and drenched in summer by moist air from the Gulf of Mexico. Between these extremes, spring and autumn bring nearly any kind of weather, with sharp temperature changes between day and night.

Since Precambrian times, the Appalachians have been eroding, occasionally uplifted by earth movements less dramatic than the overturning of primeval ages. The result is that some ridges are composed of upturned layers that, when undermined by erosion and lubricated by prolonged rainfall, give way and slide down into the ravines below, taking the forests with them. Bluffs, cliffs, and granite domes are not uncommon. Broken fragments of every size, shape, and color fill the streams.

During the most recent ice ages, the continental sheets of glacial ice apparently never reached this far south, but with all the masses of ice to the north, together with frigid winds blowing from them, the southern Appalachians became a refuge for plants that could not cope with the rigors of the Arctic. After the glaciers melted, vegetation here served as a source of seeds that settled farther and farther north. Forests grew and expanded their range, repopulating the freshly exposed landscapes, just as is happening in certain parts of the subarctic today.

Millions of generations of forests have grown and died in the southern Appalachians, repeatedly enriching the soils. Today, the specific type of soil in a given locality depends on where the site is located, its degree of exposure to the sun, the presence or absence of streams and rivers, and the nature of the underlying rock. In cases where fires have burned off the humus or where landslides have exposed new rock, there is little or no soil. There will not be for quite a while; even in this region of rich soil-making resources, it takes an estimated 500 years to make one inch of topsoil.

Though existing soils are usually very moist in the southern Appalachians, swamplike conditions are rare. Because the bedrock has been folded over time, the rocky slopes provide for adequate drainage, and often the only places of supersaturation are around permanent seeps and springs. The soil serves as a medium of transport for the immense amount of precipitation that falls on the forest each year. Usually there is no problem in getting rid of the moisture, even after weeks of rain. But if the downpour is too heavy—if, for example, three inches of rain fall in an hour—then violent floods rampage down the slopes, loosening rocks and breaking them free, ripping away soil, uprooting trees, dislodging tons of debris and transporting it down to the valleys below. The jumbles of rock in Appalachian ravines illustrate that such violence has happened periodically.

Human Intervention

Although the southern Appalachians have been settled for centuries, the effects of human intervention upon the forest processes have not everywhere been pronounced. To a large degree, the southern Appalachians were so steep and covered so much area that access was difficult; human populations were limited to isolated homes and remote settlements. The southern highlanders adapted to their environment and got from it most of what they needed: timber, food, medicine, housewares. They had an impact upon natural forest communities and in places a substantial one, but the scars are healing. Where old homesites and cut-over areas were abandoned, the buildings are crumbling and the native forest is growing back. Hundreds of thousands of acres of the mountains were protected in reserves before the human populations in fragile areas of virgin forest could expand and grow larger. It is still possible to find old cabins all but rotted away, pine groves that have come up in old fields, and exotic plants such as roses, daffodils, and forsythias, which were used for ornamentation and have since gone wild.

Ecology

Like the plants, many populations of animals in the southern Appalachians have adapted to specific elevations. In the pine-oak lowland forests are found the Gray Squirrel, White-tailed Deer, chipmunks, Wild Turkey, Ovenbird, Wood Thrush, Box Turtle, and Fence Lizard.

In cove forests, Red Squirrels are more dominant because they favor groves of hemlock trees. These sheltered woods are also famed spots for salamanders, of which some two dozen species can be found. Among the characteristic birds are Carolina

Gray Squirrel
Sciurus carolinensis
588

White-tailed Deer
Odocoileus virginianus
616

Wild Turkey
Meleagris gallopavo
249

Ovenbird
Seiurus aurocapillus
346

Wood Thrush
Hylocichla mustelina
342

Eastern Box Turtle
Terrapene carolina
512

Fence Lizard
Sceloporus undulatus

Red Squirrel
Tamiasciurus hudsonicus
586

Carolina Chickadee
Parus carolinensis
332

Pileated Woodpecker
Dryocopus pileatus
271

Scarlet Tanager
Piranga olivacea
317

Barred Owl
Strix varia
244

Black-capped Chickadee
Parus atricapillus
333

Veery
Catharus fuscescens
343

Dark-eyed Junco
Junco hyemalis
267

Common Raven
Corvus corax
265

Winter Wren
Troglodytes troglodytes
347

Pygmy Shrew
Microsorex hoyi
577

Black Bear
Ursus americanus
609

Southern Pine Beetle
Dendroctonus frontalis

Chickadees, Pileated Woodpeckers, Scarlet Tanagers, and Barred Owls.

Although some animals, like bears and chipmunks, occupy several habitats, the populations on the summits differ considerably from those in the lowlands. At higher elevations, Black-capped Chickadees, for example, replace Carolina Chickadees, and Red Squirrels replace Gray Squirrels. Also in the spruce-fir forests of the highlands are Veeries, Dark-eyed Juncos, Common Ravens, and Winter Wrens.

These forests are biologically and geologically mature, with many species of trees, many kinds of shrubs, wild flowers, mammals, and invertebrates, all living in a benign environment. It is natural in such a place to find an almost infinite variety of interconnections among life forms. After all, in these mountains are found organisms from the largest trees to the smallest mammal in eastern North America, the Pygmy Shrew.

All forms are linked by food webs of enormous proportions and complexity. Life lines go out in all directions, with the Black Bear at the top, ripping up trees and logs, digging out honeycombs, eating acorns and berries, dropping scats that microorganisms use to fertilize the soil, and dropping seeds that serve to spread and perpetuate vegetation. The trees and shrubs that grow from these seeds absorb immense quantities of water, then give off tons of moisture in the process of transpiration. This thickens the already substantial atmospheric moisture, producing a smokelike haze that gives the Great Smoky Mountains their name.

The climate influences growth, which is sometimes reduced to a struggle for survival. Even in these gentle mountains, the weather is a deciding factor of life or death, especially at upper elevations. Winds raging at more than one hundred miles an hour bend, twist, break, and topple trees, opening them to attack by insects and microscopic predators. Ice and snow build up and break off limbs. Lightning splits and injures trees, and the healed-over scars may commonly be observed along the trunks from top to bottom. When extremes of cold are reached, for example, the cambium layers in trees at high elevations may freeze, rupturing the bark of Red Spruce into what are called frost cracks.

The birch seeds that fall on rotting logs germinate to produce a neatly aligned row of saplings whose roots reach down over the side of the log and through it to anchor in the soil. When the "nurse log" decays, there stands the birch with aerial roots, as though the tree were walking on stilts. Or when a birch seed lodges and starts to grow in the crotch of some limb, the host tree bears this burden, at least for a while, and becomes known as a "piggyback" tree.

Competition

No tree is free from the peril of insect attack. Southern Pine Beetle populations increase after several mild winters in a row, then decrease in cold winters. But they are a natural element of the original ecosystems here, and the pine forests survive.

Such is not the case, however, when native trees are exposed to organisms introduced from other lands, a direct if inadvertent example of human intervention. Most deadly has been the Chestnut Blight, an introduced fungus that reached southern Appalachian forests about 1920. All the giant American Chestnuts that shared dominance with oaks were killed by the late 1930s. Limbs still sprout from stumps, but spores of the blight kill the trees before seeds can be produced.

The demise of "balsam" forests of Fraser Fir is projected by government authorities unless the Balsam Woolly Aphid, another exotic insect, can be controlled or eliminated. This insect pierces the bark of living firs to draw its nourishment, thereby introducing secretions that clog the interior channels that carry water through the wood. An infected tree has two or three years to live.

European Wild Boar and Other Setbacks

Competition from aggressive introduced trees, such as the Norway Spruce, and introduced mammals, such as the nefarious Wild Boar, influences native ecosystems. The Boars that plague the southern Appalachians escaped in the 1920s from a game reserve in North Carolina and took up residence in an environment ideal for them: thick tangles of shrubbery in wooded ravines. There they satisfy their voracious appetites by eating acorns, the nuts of Beech, hickories, the tubers of wild yams, the roots of Pitch Pine, and, like pigs just about everywhere, anything they can find. In so doing, they rip up rhododendron thickets, root into hillsides, dig up sod on the grass balds, pollute streams, and compete directly with native animals for food. They eat, uproot, or trample wild flowers such as Spring Beauty, Wake-Robin, and Yellow Adder's-tongue. They damage tree roots, seedlings, and saplings, opening up land so that erosion is accelerated.

The Wild Boars are in direct competition with Black Bears for berries, acorns, and nuts. Because the crop of such seeds varies in abundance from year to year, the conflict can be serious, and the Bear's margin of survival was sometimes scant even before the Boars came.

This conflict is a classic example of the more aggressive introduced species crowding out the native species. In this case, a part of the Boar's "aggressiveness" is the ability of one female to reproduce up to twelve young at any time of the year, compared with the Bear's normal reproduction of one or two cubs every other year. If nothing checks that imbalance of reproduction, the increasing population of Boars, now in the thousands in the southern Appalachians, could reduce substantially the populations of Bears, squirrels, and other species.

An alarming development in recent years in the southern Appalachians is the failure of trees to grow at upper elevations. Large groves are dead or dying, and although investigation is under way, it is likely to be years before the underlying causes can be fully determined. One leading possibility is that injurious chemicals and particulate matter

Eastern Bluebird
Sialia sialis

Ruffed Grouse
Bonasa umbellus
247

Eastern Chipmunk
Tamias striatus
585

Raccoon
Procyon lotor
607

Crayfish
Cambarus spp.

Pilot Black Snake
Elaphe obsoleta

Racer
("Black Racer")
Coluber constrictor
521

Pine Woods Snake
Rhadinaea flavilata
522

King Snake
Lampropeltis getulus

Corn Snake
Elaphe guttata
531

Copperhead
Agkistrodon contortrix
530

Timber Rattlesnake
Crotalus horridus
529

Water Snake
Natrix spp.

Common Garter Snake
Thamnophis sirtalis
526, 527

Pygmy Salamander
Desmognathus wrighti

Hellbender
Cryptobranchus alleganiensis

are rising on air currents that flow up from human settlements below. In California, injury to coniferous trees due to pollution around the perimeter of the Los Angeles basin has been documented; in the southern Appalachians, research may verify the same cause for the death of the forests.

Adaptable Ecosystem

Despite these native and nonnative setbacks, the forests of the southern Appalachians are largely healthy, and seedlings, saplings, and new growth are widespread. The forest ecosystem adapts and changes whenever conditions are altered. The acorn has replaced the chestnut as a major food source for Turkeys, squirrels, and other animals. But the oaks that filled in the "chestnut gap" don't always produce the same bountiful harvest. During a poor year, when acorns grow scarce, the animals have to seek other sources of food.

Shelter, of course, exists in a more constant supply. The oaks offer shelter as well as food, and even the Black Bear will den in a Scarlet Oak if it can find one large enough. Birds and squirrels use wild grapevines for building nests, often in trees. Cavity-dwelling species, such as the Eastern Bluebird, will make use of trees that have been killed by insects and softened up by other insects, fungi, and bacteria.

The forest is full of predators like the Barred Owl, which launches its attack from a perch on the branch of a tree. Forest animals have different ways of avoiding external danger; some species, including many birds, flee from danger, whereas others, such as the Ruffed Grouse or the Eastern Chipmunk, rely on camouflage to protect them. And some species survive through the advantage of sheer numbers. But no creature, not even the Bear, is invulnerable; animals large and small are subject to attack by parasites.

Natural controls of one animal population by another have significant advantages, however. Insects would fill the woods to overflowing were it not for frogs and salamanders on the forest floor, or insectivorous birds at all layers of growth within the ecosystem. In turn, Raccoons hunt Crayfish and salamanders. Some two dozen species of snakes, including the Pilot Black Snake, Black Racer, Pine Snake, King Snake, Corn Snake, Copperhead, and Timber Rattlesnake, have evolved in the warm climate of the southern Appalachians. The Water Snake and Common Garter Snake are probably the most common in the area.

The mountain forests, with all their humidity, rainfall, and streams, provide a prime habitat for amphibians. More than two dozen kinds of salamanders inhabit the southern Appalachians, varying from the tiny Pygmy Salamander, which is less than two inches long at maturity, to the Hellbender, which reaches nearly thirty inches. The Pygmy Salamander is a terrestrial species, adapted to high-elevation forests; the Hellbender is characteristic of warmer, low-altitude streams.

Normally, salamanders remain hidden under leaves, bark, and rocks, where they find the invertebrate fare upon which they

Bird-foot Violet
Viola pedata
491

White Trillium
Trillium grandiflorum

Painted Trillium
Trillium undulatum
447 ˙

Fringed Phacelia
Phacelia fimbriata
496

Crested Dwarf Iris
Iris cristata
495

Wild Bleeding Heart
Dicentra eximia
477

Showy Orchid
Orchis spectabilis
448

Pink Lady's Slipper
Cypripedium acaule
470

Large Purple Fringed
Orchid
Habenaria fimbriata
481

Creeping Bluet
Houstonia serpyllifolia

Pallid Violet
Viola striata

Flame Azalea
Rhododendron calendulaceum
461

Pin Cherry (Fire Cherry)
Prunus pensylvaniea
84, 152, 189, 218

live. But during heavy rains, they will come out of hiding and pursue their prey away from shelter, becoming vulnerable to predation themselves.

Natural Economy
There is very little wasted energy in the natural economy of these mountain forests. Many giant trees, for example, have few or no limbs on the lower half of their trunks, where dense shade would make leaves inefficient. In this competitive environment, the tree's energy is applied to pushing its leaves up to and through the canopy high above in order to reach the sun's light.

This canopy, which casts a pervasive shade over practically everything underneath, is mainly absent in the winter months, because most trees in this forest are deciduous. Some plants bloom in the early spring, when sunlight comes down to them through leafless boughs above. By the time the leaves come out on the major deciduous trees, the flowering of the lower-layer dogwoods and many of the other plants is over, and they withdraw into the anonymity of summer.

The southern Appalachians are notable for their hundreds of species of wild flowers, which begin to bloom in late March while sunlight still reaches the forest floor. Some of the showy species are Bird-foot Violet, White and Painted trilliums, Fringed Phacelia, Crested Dwarf Iris, and Wild Bleeding Heart. Members of the orchid family may be a bit harder to observe; they include Showy Orchid, Pink Lady's Slipper, and Large Purple Fringed Orchid. Blooming occurs later in the high country, where Creeping Bluet, Pallid Violet, Flame Azalea, and Mountain Laurel are at their best in May and June.

At higher altitudes the blossoming period extends throughout much of the summer, depending on the persistence of flowers from species to species. Asters, goldenrods, and groundsels are typical of plants that bloom late in the summer. When all other species have ceased to flower, the Witch-hazel bursts into bloom in November.

Autumn color spreads throughout the southern Appalachians in reverse order to the altitudinal rise of spring flowering. The leaves of the Pin Cherry (also called Fire Cherry) first show red at high elevations in early October, and throughout the remainder of that month, as the frost line descends, each deciduous species turns its peculiar color; the browns of Beeches, the scarlets of oaks, the light cinnamon brown of Sassafras, and the brilliant yellow of Yellow-poplar all signal the arrival of winter.

THE SOUTHERN APPALACHIANS: PLANTS AND ANIMALS

THE PINE BARRENS

With this chapter we begin a review of the many eastern forest ecosystems dominated by pine trees. We have already briefly touched on the pinelands around the Great Lakes, but pines are ubiquitous. They exist in every eastern forest habitat from the subarctic to the subtropical, from lowlands to highlands, and wetlands to dry lands. Pines are so flexible in response to wind, salt spray, and other environmental stresses that they are among the most tenacious of trees, and are especially celebrated for their ability to recover and reproduce after forest fires.

Pines can also grow extremely well in relatively infertile sandy soil. Because huge areas of eastern North America are underlain by sand, there are immense concentrations of pines covering thousands of square miles.

In a guidebook of limited size, it is not possible to discuss all pinelands in adequate detail. There are fascinating coastal pine forests on Cape Cod in Massachusetts. The pine forests of Wisconsin, Kentucky, and those on the sand plains between Schenectady and Albany, New York, deserve more mention than is possible here. Ecologists feel that the dwarf pine plains of New Jersey are also extremely interesting.

This chapter and the next focus on two major pineland habitats, very unequal in extent. First is the relatively small pine barrens area of New Jersey, well known and more or less typical of pine barrens in eastern North America. Second is the huge area of southern pinelands from Maryland south to Florida and west to Texas.

The reader should avoid a mental picture of pineland habitats composed of pines and no other types of trees. While there are forests that are almost entirely pine, it is much more common to encounter pine-dominated forests in which deciduous trees are also present. In places, although deciduous trees may constitute the bulk of the population, the forest may still be considered "pineland," because such deciduous intruders are apt to be only transient. After the next forest fire, the more vulnerable deciduous trees will be much less in evidence.

Pine barrens occur mostly on sand, shale, and serpentine soil types in eastern North America. We will concentrate on the most extensive, which are found in central and southern New Jersey. Located thirty miles east of Philadelphia and sixty miles south of New York City, they cover nearly one and one-half million acres. This tract is bounded on the east by the Atlantic Coast and on the west by deciduous forest and urban and agricultural land.

Human Intervention

Despite their many assets, the New Jersey Pine Barrens have not been densely settled and today are a comparative wilderness in the heavily populated stretch from New York to Washington. Throughout recent history, people have made some use of the area; for example, early Indians hunted deer here, setting the woods afire to claim their quarry as it fled. There was some farming and pasturing by European settlers, but better soils existed elsewhere. Lumbering and the commercial collection of fuel wood proved short-lived industries, and for a time, cranberry cultivation centered in the bogs.

In more recent years, entrepreneurs subdivided parts of the land into homesites and small farms. Forest fires continued to be set for various purposes—by charcoal makers, for example, to render the trees unfit for other use, and by agriculturalists to clear the way for the growth of blueberries. But even though hundreds of thousands of acres were disturbed by human intervention, the forests have recovered, and much of the Pine Barrens is relatively wild today. There is no denying, however, that one of the reasons for that is that the Pine Barrens are out of the way. It is reasonable to assume that had they been located in a direct line between New York and Philadelphia, most of their natural ecological processes would not now exist.

An Ecological Mosaic

The general appearance is one of open flatlands dominated nearly everywhere by Pitch Pine. But in fact, the Pine Barrens are a mosaic of forest types, and instead of growing on a uniformly flat terrain, the forests occupy both uplands and lowlands. The difference in elevation between the two areas is not significant, but in the lowlands the underground water is much closer to the surface—hence to the roots of plants— than it is in the uplands.

Ecologists have identified six major vegetation types in the Pine Barrens: pine-oak forest; Atlantic White-cedar–Red Maple swamp; bog; marsh; stream-pond; and old field.

In the lowlands, the ground is often thoroughly saturated for most of the year. The swamplike forest that results is dominated by Red Maple, Sweetbay (Swamp Magnolia), and Black Tupelo; Pitch Pine is also present, sometimes in abundance. In other wet places grow dense stands of Atlantic White-cedar, also with pines. These communities are localized to a considerable degree, because they have developed along marshes or stream courses or near ponds. The shrubby understory consists of Highbush Blueberry, azaleas, bayberry, Fetterbush, and the ground cover of Chain Fern, sphagnum moss, Partridgeberry, bladderworts, pitcher plants, and other species characteristic of soils that are damp.

At subtly higher elevations the forest is almost continuously dominated by Pitch Pine, with occasional Shortleaf and Virginia pines. Oaks are much more prominent in the drier uplands; the most commonly encountered species are Black, Blackjack, White, Chestnut, and Post oaks. The shrubby understory also differs from the vegetation of the swampy lowlands; the major species here are Lowbush Blueberry, Black Huckleberry, and Bear Oak, which form a dominant and continuous thicket under the pines. The herbaceous layer includes goldenrods, asters, lobelias, Wild Indigo, False Foxglove, and Turkey Beard.

The pines, however, are not universally dominant; nor does the percentage of oaks per acre follow any precise pattern. The

Pitch Pine
Pinus rigida
25, 173

Atlantic White-cedar
Chamaecyparis thyoides
39

Red Maple
Acer rubrum
120, 180, 228

Sweetbay (Swamp Magnolia)
Magnolia virginiana
45, 159

Black Tupelo
Nyssa sylvatica
57

Shortleaf Pine
Pinus echinata
23, 174

Virginia Pine
Pinus virginiana
27

Black Oak
Quercus velutina
113, 208, 225

Blackjack Oak
Quercus marilandica
117, 223

White Oak
Quercus alba
109, 206

Chestnut Oak
Quercus prinus
107

Post Oak
Quercus stellata
111

presence of certain trees in certain areas is most likely the result of the repeated action of fire over the centuries. Severe forest fires have a profound capacity to thin out forests, and the Pine Barrens are a good place to observe how different vegetative associations develop in response to natural burning. A large portion of the Pine Barrens is currently composed of Pitch Pines averaging twenty-five feet in height; these associate with Blackjack Oaks less than twenty feet high. Small patches of Pitch Pine grow with Post Oak, and at other sites there are Pitch Pines with a Sprinkling of Black, Scarlet, and Red oaks.

There are also patches of woods that demonstrate how oaks have managed to gain some dominance. In these, the Black, Chestnut, White, and Scarlet oaks are slightly more abundant than pines, and in a few places, the oaks form ninety percent or more of the canopy. In others, Pitch Pine becomes a minor component of the community, and Shortleaf Pine becomes more abundant.

Because there are many ecological variables in the coastal plain environment, the tree mosaics in these two floristic complexes of the Pine Barrens—wet lowlands and dry uplands—are much less stable than those of such forests as the southern Appalachians, which are characterized by ecological repose.

There is no lack of animal life, as abundant footprints in the sands of old roads suggest: For herbivores, the Pine Barrens are a gourmet's paradise. In places the undergrowth is so thick that a human traveler must plow through densely interlocked shrubs and head-high Bracken Fern, both of which provide good shelter for birds and small mammals. On the forest floor, animal life is sustained in an environment of Club Moss, large clumps of Reindeer Lichen, Trailing Arbutus, and mats of pine needles through which grasses grow. The water-loving plants found in ponds, bogs, and swamps—such as alders, cranberries, rushes, and sedges—attract wild herbivores, which in turn bring carnivores.

Nine different kinds of salamanders live in the Pine Barrens, three kinds of lizards, eighteen kinds of snakes, ten kinds of turtles, and thirteen kinds of frogs and toads. Scores of species of birds live or pass through these woods, and seventy species breed here.

Human observers need to watch for Timber Rattlesnakes, and sometimes the presence of skunks is strongly indicated. The sounds of flickers and woodpeckers drilling in trees, the songs of doves and wrens, and the music of warblers can all be heard in season. Among the most common birds are the Rufous-sided Towhee, Turkey Vulture, American Kestrel, Common Crow, Fish Crow, Mourning Dove, Carolina Chickadee, Blue Jay, Carolina Wren, Northern Mockingbird, Common Nighthawk, and Whip-poor-will. The Pine Barrens possess a unique invertebrate fauna, including abundant populations of moths, gall wasps, tiger beetles, velvet ants, and antlions. Wood ticks are common, as are Daddy-long-legs. But earthworms are rare, probably owing to the acid nature of the soils.

Climate
Based on available evidence from ancient pollens in coastal
plain sediments, the pines, cedars, oaks, heaths, magnolias,
and other genera that dominate the Pine Barrens today have
occupied this region intermittently since upper Cretaceous
times, 100 million years ago. There are extensive interruptions
in the record, owing to long climatic changes and inundations
by the sea. During glacial ages, this area was almost certainly
covered by tundra and arctic forests of spruce and fir. The
habitat as now constituted appears to have developed about
10,000 years ago, and today survives under the influence of
climate, soils, fire, and humans.
Every form of life in the Pine Barrens must be adaptable to
extremes of weather. There are no protective mountain ranges
to keep out storms or to moderate very extreme temperatures,
although the area's proximity to the Atlantic Ocean does have
a moderating effect on the weather patterns. Cold air masses
repeatedly surge southeastward from the interior of the
continent, bringing snow, ice, freezing rain, and subfreezing
temperatures. Ordinarily such cold causes few problems in the
Pine Barrens, where vegetation and animal life have adapted
to withstand it. Occasional long winters, however, with low
temperatures that coincide with the beginning of the growing
season, may wreak havoc on new plants.
In summer, warm air masses from the Gulf of Mexico or the
Caribbean bring high humidity, afternoon and evening
thundershowers, and temperatures that exceed 100° F. Most
weather patterns are fairly uniform from one year to the next.
The average annual precipitation ranges around forty-four
inches, but prolonged droughts now and then may persist for
years. At the other extreme are the tropical storms that
occasionally advance northward along the Pine Barrens, with
winds reaching hurricane intensity and carrying with them
torrential rains. Although such excesses are rare, they loom as
limiting factors; only those life forms that can withstand
occasional deep snow, high winds, and floods may survive.

Geology
During the ice ages, the southern terminus of the continental
ice sheet came very near to the Pine Barrens, stopping less
than a dozen miles to the north. The icy north winds that
blew from the nearby glaciers profoundly influenced the
vegetation.
For millions of years the ocean rose and fell in response to the
melting and refreezing of glacial ice; on several occasions it
covered the coastal plain of eastern North America. Since the
last retreat of the Atlantic, the present vegetation has
developed. Sea-level fluctuations during the glacial and
interglacial periods left the coastal plain geologically a product
of the sea and the land, a place where incoming streams from
the continental side mixed their muddy sediments with the
sands at the shore. The result is sedimentation typical of
deltas, beaches, and floodplains. The gravels, sands, silts, and
clay that make up the soil of the Pine Barrens form a substrate

of loose and unconsolidated particles with little water-retaining capacity. The frequent thundershowers that come in spring and summer—when plants need moisture most—make it possible for roots to find enough moisture to survive. The water flows rapidly away, however, leaching nutrients from the soil. The remaining substrate is effectively described in one word: impoverished. It is sterile and acidic, largely poor in nutrients. How any vegetation can sustain itself seems at first a remarkable puzzle. But soils like these typify the coastal plain from Massachusetts to Mexico, and a great deal of vegetation does grow.

An exceptional characteristic of the New Jersey Pine Barrens is the extent of groundwater. Some precipitation is intercepted by vegetation and some runs off, but the rest drains into an underground reservoir so vast that it could furnish a billion gallons of water daily to New Jersey cities without endangering the supply.

Ecology

Forest ecology is dictated by a number of circumstances. Climate determines patterns of forest distribution, and the abundance of water influences forest growth. Soils determine what grows where, and human and wildlife settlement can have significant impact. Yet there is one factor that overrides all others. In the Pine Barrens, as much as anywhere in North America, fire has been the dominant force in determining the makeup of the vegetation. In most places in the Pine Barrens, fires have seared the forest every dozen years or so. During the last few years, there has been an average of nearly 2000 fires annually.

How the forest recovers each time and grows anew attests to the resilience and tenacity of the vegetation. For one thing, not all fires are alike. Some burn quickly, sweeping rapidly and lightly through the woods; others are extremely hot and burn slowly, destroying vegetation down to the ground. When the woods are wet or humid, fires make little headway and do little more than smolder. If there is copious dry undergrowth, a fire can be intense, long-lasting, and destructive; flames fanned by wind can devastate thousands of acres. Controlled fires, deliberately set by land-managing agencies, are used to manage the ecosystem.

After a fire occurs, the natural processes of recovery and succession begin. Grasses and sedges appear first, then seedlings of pine, which must begin to grow in open places with ample sunlight; they soon tower above everything else. In their shade other plants grow slowly and new generations of pines hardly at all. The oaks, however, which can do quite well in shade, grow slowly but steadily among the pines. Under ordinary circumstances, the oaks would likely join with hickories to form a climax forest. But fire, wind, disease, or human action fells the trees before the oaks can reach maturity and choke the pines in shade. Oaks are more susceptible than pines to fire, especially in the seedling and sapling stages, and cannot recover as rapidly; in a fire-prone forest such as this, the pines retain mastery. It is only a matter of a few years until the pines, germinating from seeds or sprouting from stumps, have covered the old burn site.

There are variations in this process. Some pines with especially thick bark may not be killed by fire. Winter fires may also prove less destructive than summer ones, because the prevailing temperature is lower. Such factors help determine whether a tree is killed outright or merely wounded. The degree of destruction of a forest depends on whether a burn is a ground fire or a crown fire, how fast the fire moves, and how intense it is. There is always something left behind to be decomposed.

The Pitch Pine may not be as tall and graceful as other pines or as commercially in demand, but few trees rival it in the ability to survive. Its greatest strength is its adaptability. Evolution has prepared it to grow successfully in sterile soils, to recover from fire, and to withstand attacks by sawflies, webworms, needle miners, beetles, moths, and loopers. Many individual trees are serotinous, opening their cones and casting out seeds when heated. When a fire has eliminated some or all of the competing vegetation, such as oaks, the seeds can sprout and grow in the clearings that have been created. However, seedlings can be eliminated by deer, drought, or competition from overshadowing hardwoods. But despite these inroads the Pitch Pine reproduces in sufficient numbers to assure survival. On the outer reaches of its range, the Pitch Pine even hybridizes with other pines to produce genetically improved trees.

Not every plant that gets a start in this environment succeeds, especially when the margin of survival is narrowed by human intervention. The Pine Barrens contain a large proportion of rare or endangered plants, including species of sedge, orchid, lily, lobelia, and bladderwort. More than seventy plant species are considered to be in jeopardy.

Animal Life

The abundance and variety of vegetation in the Pine Barrens guarantees an abundance and variety of animal life. On a summer morning, the American crow is heard first, loud and clear, before the sun has washed the trees with orange light. A White-breasted Nuthatch is vociferous as it zigzags up, around, and down the trunk of a tree, then over to another to repeat its exploration. Robins join in with their warning notes, followed by the Blue Jay with its explosive calls. A Red Squirrel climbs into a Shortleaf Pine, always, it seems, warning someone away from its favorite food, the pine seeds. A Whip-poor-will sings its last notes of the night, flying up into the limbs or treetops. Towhees flit through the shrubbery and scratch in the leaves for acorns. A Ruffed Grouse swoops by with its tail fanned, moving to a quiet locality to peck among the leaves and shrubs for insects and buds. White-tailed Deer raise their bright tails and leap off through the pines to browse somewhere else. Another flash of white—and a cottontail zips across a glade to settle down and feed on

American Crow
Corvus brachyrhynchos
266

White-breasted Nuthatch
Sitta carolinensis
334

American Robin
Turdus migratorius
307

Red Squirrel
Tamiasciurus hudsonicus
586

Ruffed Grouse
Bonasa umbellus
247

White-tailed Deer
Odocoileus virginianus
616

Brown Thrasher
Toxostoma rufum
341

Raccoon
Procyon lotor
607

Woodchuck
Marmota monax
595

Gray Fox
Urocyon cinereoargenteus
611

Mountain Lion
Felis concolor

Gray Wolf
Canis lupus
610

Black Bear
Ursus americanus
609

grasses. A Brown Thrasher slips unobtrusively among the bracken ferns, little more than a shadow as it chases insects or digs in the soft ground for larvae.

Shrews and mice are less easy to hear or to observe, but the chances of seeing Raccoons, weasels, Woodchucks, Gray Foxes, and deer are very good. Mountain Lions, Gray Wolves, and Black Bears once lived here as well.

The streams, tinted with tannin from the decaying vegetation, are populated with enough fishes to support kingfishers, which perch on limbs overhanging the water. From that vantage point they either dive into the water with a dramatic splash or drop from the tree and glide above the surface of the stream. The moisture here and in wet spots throughout the woods provides a medium for the breeding of insects, and the activity of phoebes, flycatchers, kingbirds, bats, and other insect eaters indicates a plentiful food supply.

Despite the thickets of Bear and Blackjack oaks, much of the forest is relatively open pineland, thanks to the dominance of Pitch Pines. Sunlight usually falls into these woods with little obstruction. If there is no moderating sea breeze, the midday heat can be stifling. From midmorning to midafternoon, the animals quiet down to avoid the heat.

By evening the woods are noisy again. As darkness descends, the jays and crows subside, bats and nighthawks begin their nocturnal flights, and Whip-poor-wills resume their calls. A high-pitched hum of crickets rises, and the constant scratching cadence of katydids fills the woods.

The Food Chain

There are complex ecological relations here, the most obvious of which have to do with food. White-tailed Deer browse on sprouts of pines and oaks, which are usually in abundance in fire-prone forests. But in some years, the deer feed so heavily that certain groups of trees are cut back and replaced by less palatable growth. As would be expected, pine seeds are a staple in the diet of numerous inhabitants, including Carolina Chickadees, Dark-eyed Juncos, Ruffed Grouse, Bobwhites, squirrels, and white-footed mice.

Dark-eyed Junco
Junco hyemalis
267

Bobwhite
Colinus virginianus

Vegetation is the key to survival at all levels of animal life, not the least among insects. In the Pine Barrens, one of the most common indicators of the insect-plant relationship is the galls of gall wasps. These insects lay their eggs in a twig or on a leaf of an oak, after which abnormal growths arise to protect the tree and shelter the new larvae.

The caterpillars of moths feed heavily on oaks and almost any other vegetation in the Pine Barrens, and none is so all-consuming as Gypsy Moth larvae. Leaf-cutting ants are less destructive; they carry portions of needles and other leaves into their subterranean chambers to assist in the production of fungal foods. Insect predators keep these and other insect consumers in check. A leaf canopy may be stripped occasionally and the forest appear bedraggled, but it recovers during the absence of those insects in later years, and thus whole forests are not decimated.

Gypsy Moth
Lymantria dispar
354

Honey Bee
Apis mellifera
404

Ladybird Beetle
Hippodamia convergens

Wild Turkey
Meleagris gallopavo
249

Not all insects are destructive, of course. Honey Bees, bumble bees, and butterflies pollinate some of the trees and shrubs. Ladybird beetles prey on aphids, scale insects, and other organisms injurious to vegetation.

Whereas grasshoppers, locusts, walking sticks, and beetles associate with vegetation, some invertebrates have adapted to animals—including human beings. The most common of these are wood ticks, mites, chiggers, mosquitoes, and black flies.

The enormous insect population of the Pine Barrens draws large numbers of insectivorous animals. Shrews are the most voracious, celebrated for their capacity to consume each day an amount of food nearly equivalent to their own body weight. Moles likewise consume insects at the lower levels of the forest, whereas bats and such birds as flycatchers, Whip-poor-wills, and Common Nighthawks take insects on the wing. Insect meals are not always supplied in the same quantities each year. Population explosions of locusts produce a superabundance one year followed by a dearth the next. But the hundreds of species of insects provide alternate choices to keep insectivores supplied.

The largest birds and mammals of the Pine Barrens focus to a considerable degree not on the pines but on the oaks, where White-tailed Deer, Wild Turkeys, Blue Jays, and squirrels congregate in search of acorns. Oaks are also the preferred nesting sites for hawks and owls.

The smaller herbivores, such as voles and mice, provide fundamental sources of food for predators. But food supplies can be erratic from year to year, and competition is often stiff, so most of the carnivores indulge in eclectic diets, consuming just about anything that comes their way. In the Pine Barrens, foxes catch not only the smaller mammals but will dine on insects, birds, eggs, fruit, and acorns. Raccoons are almost omnivorous; their diet takes in the usual terrestrial fare in addition to streamside creatures such as frogs, salamanders, and crayfish.

Decomposers at Work

In some areas untouched by fire for years, debris accumulates and decays as organisms die and fall to the forest floor. These areas are rich in decomposing organic matter and are another important source of nutrition in the forest.

Ants and beetles go to work on fallen logs. Fungi, algae, and bacteria assemble to decompose available plant and animal tissues. Mites and springtails attack the decomposers. And higher-order predators consume the mites and springtails. These decomposing realms are organized in complex food webs of their own. The decomposition communities go largely unnoticed by human visitors but are necessary to process and release the nutrients locked up in the falling biomass.

Studies show that although fires have an impact on the wildlife of the Pine Barrens at every level down to the decomposers, the impact is not as profound as might be expected. Any population reductions resulting from fire will in all probability be only temporary. Some plants and animals recover more rapidly than others. The greatest obliteration of life appears to occur among ants and spiders, which live just under the fallen leaves on the forest floor.

In the long run, natural communities respond favorably to the cleaning out of undergrowth by fire. Moreover, the renewal of successional changes in life forms increases the diversity of species. A burned-over area, after all, is attractive to such organisms as the pines, which do their best in sunlight. Bluebirds and sparrows, adapted to getting their food in open spaces, increase. Towhees and thrashers, which spend their lives primarily in thickets, move to places where fires have not removed the underbrush.

Life often depends on how frequently fires sweep through the pines and oaks. Fire-ravaged plant and animal communities need time to recover, and if fires burn any woodland more than once every two or three years, recovery is difficult and populations are apt to be severely cut back, if not eliminated.

THE PINE BARRENS: PLANTS AND ANIMALS

THE SOUTHERN PINELANDS

Every natural habitat has both biological and geographical limits. The southern pinelands are bounded on one side by the ocean and on the other by uplands. Situated on the coastal plains of the Atlantic Ocean and the Gulf of Mexico, they extend roughly from the southern limit of the New Jersey Pine Barrens south to Florida, west to the Big Thicket of Texas, and southwestward intermittently to the mouth of the Rio Grande. These forests are also found upstream along the Mississippi River and its tributaries as far as Missouri.

Inland, the principal biological boundary of the southern pinelands is the mixed deciduous forests, but the delineation between the two is not sharp. Especially along the Mississippi River, deciduous forest intrudes so far down into the pinelands that the pines become scarce indeed. Yet this massive sweep of pine country along most of the eastern and southern coasts of the United States has ecological continuity as well as remarkable diversity.

The pinelands are not one kind of forest, but hundreds: pure groves of Longleaf Pine; groves of Loblolly Pine mixed with oaks and hickories, or with White and Post oaks; Shortleaf Pine with oak and hickory; Slash Pine in the southernmost regions and Sand Pine on sterile sites; Spruce Pine, Virginia Pine, and Pond Pine.

The southern pinelands contain representatives of nearly every biological community typical of warm temperate climates. There are maritime forests on sand dunes, hammock forests, scrub forests, oak mottes, swamp forests, bogs, bays, bayous, and broad-leaved forests.

The pinelands call up images of great arms of Live Oaks draped with Spanish Moss, red clay hills sparsely covered with scraggly oaks and pines, and brooding swamps filled with Alligators and Cottonmouths. The southern pinelands provide all these scenes, but are dominated virtually throughout by a diversity of pines. The pines are interrupted in certain places by the oaks that take over on coastal islands and the Baldcypresses that command the wetlands. But nowhere in this vast region, which covers more than 3000 miles of temperate North American coastal plain, is a traveler very far from some member of the pine family. Stately, straight-trunked Longleaf Pines, the most widespread species and the leading commercial tree, grow in pure stands. Loblolly Pines root successfully in wetter soils. Slash Pine is the only pine that extends its range into the deep subtropics.

Seldom do these dominant species grow in pure associations. Oaks, magnolias, hickories, Sweetgums, and dozens of other hardwoods compete, but cannot thrive in the face of the constant fires that sweep the hardwoods back and favor the pines. Very little of the southern pinelands is climax forest because of the immaturity of soils and the action of fires.

The Longleaf, or "Southern Yellow," Pine tolerates infertile and well-drained soil better than most other species, and has become established on elevated sandy ground from the Carolinas to Texas. These drier habitats are shared principally by two broad-leaved evergreens, Eastern Live Oak and

Southern Magnolia
Magnolia grandiflora
40, 161

Eastern Redcedar
Juniperus virginiana
38

Sycamore
Platanus occidentalis
124, 183

Pitch Pine
Pinus rigida
25, 173

American Holly
Ilex opaca
105, 193

Black Tupelo
Nyssa sylvatica
57

Red Maple
Acer rubrum
120, 180, 228

Chestnut Oak
Quercus prinus
107

Ground-pine
Lycopodium clavatum

Virginia Creeper
Parthenocissus quinquefolia

Mayapple
Podophyllum peltatum
439

Southern Magnolia. The oaks hug the coast, often advancing out onto the dunes.

Because of mild winters and long growing seasons, the pinelands constitute a kind of transition zone between the temperate deciduous forest and the subtropical forest. The southern edge of this forest marks the boundary of a number of trees, such as White Oak, Eastern Redcedar, and Sycamore.

A Journey Through Pine Country

Strictly speaking, the southern pinelands are a pine-dominated forest. But as a practical matter, other forest types are widespread and often encountered by travelers in the region. A less strict interpretation of the term "pinelands" lets us identify the whole of what we observe on the coastal plain from Maryland southward.

Despite the prevalence of pines over such a large segment of eastern North America, there is little monotony in these southern woodlands. In state and national parks and forests where the canopy and understory are reasonably intact in a more or less natural condition, random walks in the pinelands reveal numerous contrasts and parallels.

No one natural area is identical to the others: The pinelands of Virginia differ from the pinelands of Georgia or Mississippi. Pines are a unifying element of the overall ecosystem, but differences in precipitation, soil, and drainage produce significant modifications in the natural forest distribution. Moreover, it is virtually impossible to find an acre of pinelands that has not been affected by human intervention since Captain John Smith came ashore in Virginia in 1607.

The contemporary pinelands are characterized by pronounced variety. In the northern part, especially Virginia and Maryland, the forest contains elements of the mixed deciduous forest and the New Jersey Pine Barrens, but the Pitch Pine is replaced by Virginia Pine, and the forest is almost entirely second growth. A traveler can observe the natural scene as it has come to restore itself in certain localities: pines, White Oaks, American Holly, and occasional Black Tupelos and Sweetgums.

Pinelands of Maryland and Virginia

In Maryland and Virginia, the pineland forest covers rolling hills with occasional bluffs and cliffs. In places, streams gush vigorously beneath blankets of herbaceous vegetation, and along them the Red Maple dips its leaves into the waters, and Chestnut Oaks spread their limbs. Overall, however, the pinelands of the eastern Atlantic region are not as luxuriant as the forests of the Appalachian uplands, even though they receive almost as much precipitation—an annual average of forty-five to sixty-two inches.

The sandy soil makes for very efficient drainage: the forest seems to absorb rain like a sponge. The moisture softens and swells the fallen leaves on the forest floor, turning them reddish. Moss appears to puff out with new life. The thick herbaceous cover of fern, Ground-pine, Virginia Creeper, and Mayapple holds the rainwater for a while, then transfers it to

the sands, where it sinks and disappears. The length of time in which water is available to the roots of plants is fairly short, and the rapid water flow translates into reduced availability for plant growth. There would, in fact, be a coastal plain desert here as in southern Florida were it not for the relatively even distribution of rainfall throughout the year. Because the pinelands are not subject to periodic extremes, they maintain a relatively rich association of plant and animal species. Although the pinelands are drab in winter, there is a great deal of color and activity in spring. Typically, the spring woods of the coastal plains of Maryland and Virginia have an understory of Flowering Dogwoods, whose showy white or pink blossoms come apart at maturity, scattering the petals. Blueberries, also with whitish flowers, grow in abundance, while the Pinxter Flower, an azalea, produces showy pink blossoms with delicate stamens. The forest floor is covered with flowering Bluets and Partridgeberries, the latter with white tubular flowers, scarlet fruits, and dark green leaves. There are numerous species of mushrooms, including the delectible Chanterelle and Chicken mushroom, and row after row of shelf fungi lined up on fallen logs. Among the notable rare species of flowers is the Pink Lady's Slipper orchid, which raises its delicate flower on a slender stalk ten inches above the layer of leaves.

Near open water—for example, along the shores of the Chesapeake Bay, largest of American estuaries—the forest soils become rich and black, covered with Wild Geranium and Goosegrass Bedstraw. Black Locust trees, their branches heavy with pendant clusters of white blossoms, mingle with the pines. The pine forest proceeds to the edges of marshes before its extensive range is halted; but along the coastal lowlands, pines cross semiarid sand flats where Prickly Pear Cactus grows in abundance. In bayside thickets, Poison Ivy, marked by its shiny leaves, is a conspicuous component, and the introduced Japanese Honeysuckle weaves through the undergrowth, its flowers emitting a powerful fragrance.

Pinelands from the Deep South to the Big Thicket
In North Carolina, the first hints of the tropics appear in the form of an occasional Cabbage Palmetto near the shore. The hardiest of southern shrubs, the Yaupon, grows here too; this holly hugs the shore tenaciously in the face of salt spray, shifting sands, and raging winds.

In some areas, the sands extend fifty to one hundred miles inland. In such spots the forest is dominated by Longleaf Pine and a variety of such scrub oaks as Turkey, Bluejack, Blackjack, and Sand Post oak. In places the sand is so widespread that the milieu is almost semiarid, despite regular and plentiful precipitation. Carolina sand hills are sometimes called "deserts in the rain."

Huge swamps occur in parts of the South, where the pines, Sycamores, oaks, and Sweetgums seem to have walked right into the water to join the Baldcypresses. One of the best examples is Georgia's Okefenokee Swamp.

Turkey Oak
Quercus laevis

Bluejack Oak
Quercus incana

Blackjack Oak
Quercus marilandica
117, 223

Sand Post Oak
Quercus stellata margaretta

The pinelands sweep around through Georgia and Alabama, over sand hills, black hills, and red hills, to the heart of the continent. The primary aspect of these southern forests is their layered quality—with every vertical niche occupied in a manner reminiscent of a tropical rain forest.

Along the lower Mississippi River, the coastal plain broadens considerably, reaching a width of up to 500 miles. This area is an ancient embayment that reaches north into the heart of the continent, and its lowlands are subject to repeated inundation. The flooding disrupts the continuity of pines, although they are present, and increases the incidence of hardwoods. These woods are in many ways similar to the Maryland woods a thousand miles away. The aroma of honeysuckle is common.

Yellow-poplar
("Tuliptree")
Liriodendron tulipifera
123, 162, 229

The forest floor is strewn with the pastel orange petals from Tuliptrees. Masses of Mayapples associate with banks of ferns. And giant beech trees, ancient and split, with little vital force remaining, typify the antiquity of individual trees and illustrate the continuous process of death, decay and rebirth.

A visitor walking through the mixed pines and hardwoods of the Mississippi lowlands may find it necessary to duck under hanging grapevines and push through spider webs. Here one encounters Black Walnut, Southern Bayberry, magnolia, Water Oak, and Persimmon—the latter with orange fruits and distinctively plated gray bark. The forest floor is covered with patches of Fire Pink, phlox, Common Groundsel, and clusters of daisies.

Black Walnut
Juglans nigra
140

Southern Bayberry
Myrica cerifera
100

Water Oak
Quercus nigra

Common Persimmon
Diospyros virginiana
56, 185

Fire Pink
Silene virginica

Common Groundsel
Senecio aureus

West of Mississippi, the coastal pinelands extend through the bayou country, through remnants of the legendary Big Thicket of eastern Texas, and eventually give out among the oak mottes, or thickets, and dune grasses along the shore of the Gulf of Mexico. Finally, before the acacia deserts of Mexico have fully replaced this habitat, there is the lower valley of the Rio Grande, with an abundance of pines and plamettos draped with Spanish Moss, and hundreds of species of birds and plants, many more typical of Mexico than of the United States.

Geology and Soils

The coastal plain is composed primarily of loosely consolidated sediments—some marine, some terrestrial—formed during the Cretaceous Period, less than 130 million years ago. It is characterized nearly throughout by terraces, either fashioned by marine activity or laid down by streams bringing sediments from the interior of the continent. While no glaciers reached farther south than New Jersey along the Atlantic coastal plain, on several occasions a vast amount of water was locked up in the continental ice sheets, with the result that sea level dropped worldwide, then later rose as the glaciers melted. These advances and retreats created the terraces at various places throughout the coastal plain; some are still submerged beneath the sea.

For the most part, as a result of this geologic activity, the coastal plain is level or rolling, and covered with sand, silt, gravel, and other materials laid down over the millennia by the action of incoming streams. The coastal plain largely lacks such distinct topographic features as deep canyons and high mountains.

One mysterious feature of the landscape is the presence of half a million shallow, pondlike, elliptical Carolina "bays," named probably for the presence in them of evergreen bay trees. They are scattered across the Southeast between Virginia and Georgia in a pattern that resembles ink spattered diagonally across a piece of paper. Speculation has risen that they may be the result of a shower of meteorites hitting the earth hundreds of thousands of years ago. Other theories hold that the bays are extinct lagoons or a system of ancient artesian springs, but there appears to be insufficient evidence to support any of these theories conclusively.

The Atlantic coastal plain is in places submerged, so that the portion above sea level is relatively narrow or absent, as at Washington, D.C., where the distance from the Piedmont uplands to the sea is negligible. Between there and Georgia, the coastal plain—and consequently the region of southern pinelands—varies in width from 20 to 150 miles.

Along the Gulf of Mexico, where there is no system of Piedmont uplands, the coastal plain is broader, ranging from 150 to 300 miles wide. The sedimentary deposits are thicker (up to 30,000 feet) than along the Atlantic Coast (where they vary from a thin veneer one hundred feet thick to thicknesses of several thousand feet). The rich soils have long supported heavy agricultural use. Along the lower floodplains of the Mississippi River and on the delta there have been many centuries of deposition of rich sediments from the North American heartlands, and these floodplains overlie the marine deposits.

Some of the soils are not as nutrient-rich, however, on parts of the coastal plain. Longer warm seasons speed decomposition and slow the buildup of humus. Furthermore, most precipitation falls as rain, which washes through the forest and leaches away soil nutrients. Oxides of iron and aluminum accumulate, forming red clays and yellow soils. Certain "black belt" soils, on the other hand, have developed by the weathering of the Cretaceous Selma formation. All of this points up the varied assortment of soils on which coastal plain forests have grown.

The southwestern extreme of the coastal plain, across Louisiana, Arkansas, and Texas, is widest of all, bounded by cuestas, or escarpments, formed by the more resistant rock faces inland. Many streams crossed the coastal plain to reach the Gulf of Mexico, transported sediments and deposited them where stream velocities were reduced. In such places, the finer particles of alluvial soils are characteristically more fertile than the larger particles that make up marine-deposited sands, clays, silts, and gravels, which trap fewer nutrients. In addition, marine terrace soils, churned for centuries by relentless waves along ancient shorelines, contain minerals that are more weathered, and therefore less rich in nutrients, than those of alluvial soils.

Climate

Because of the region's low elevation and proximity to the sea, the coastal plain experiences high humidity in both summer and winter. The precipitation is normally well distributed throughout the year. Dry seasons sometimes occur in spring, but these spells do not bring the kind of prolonged drought one experiences in true deserts. Periods of exceptional precipitation and unaccustomed drought do occur, but by and large seldom limit plant growth seriously.

While such intense storms are usually of short duration, the heat waves are not. It is possible for maximum daily temperatures in the shade to approach 100° F for weeks at a time. The heat of the Gulf Coast, when invaded by the cold of air masses pouring out of the Arctic, stimulates intense storms that generally move to the east and northeast.

The Gulf of Mexico and Caribbean Sea also spawn a variety of weather-related disturbances, from brief and gentle showers dropping less than an inch of rain to full-force tropical storms. Hurricanes have the most influence of any weather phenomenon on the plants and animals of the pinelands. The winds do terrific damage, as do the coastal inundations of wind-propelled seawater and the heavy rains, which cause widespread floods. Rolling walls of water ten feet high are not unknown. These floods lift animals out of the forest and swirl them among the flooded precincts of civilization.

It is often difficult to track the loss of wild animals, but the impact on forests is more readily apparent. The near-total destruction wrought by tornadoes is seldom experienced during hurricanes, but saplings may be uprooted or buried in gravel, individual trees battered by floating debris, and whole groves felled by extraordinary surges of water or wind. The forests grow back, of course, and become repopulated with animal life, but the community structure and population distribution are altered for a time.

During the winter, snow and ice are not customary, but rainfall may be steady and prolonged. This causes many rivers, such as the Pearl, Leaf, and Bouie, in Mississippi, to rise over their banks and flow out through the adjoining pinelands. Where certain rivers join, as in Arkansas and Louisiana, the floods rise the highest and endure the longest, depositing rich soil on which extensive hardwood forests have developed.

Human Intervention

In their occupation, humans have altered or eliminated portions of the forests simply by replacing these ecosystems with domestic crops, houses, cities, and roads. Large portions of forest have been cut, burned, flooded, polluted with oil or salt water, or modified by introduced plant species. In the process, millions of acres of forest have been eliminated. In the Big Thicket, for example—a remarkable series of forest communities and a biological crossroads in eastern Texas—the native forest was logged and cleared for petroleum production and thereby reduced by ninety percent.

Under such competition, those animal residents unable to cope fled to protected or less disturbed forests, and it is in these spots that relatively intact and naturally integrated forest communities may be best observed today.

Fire

The success of the pines—of the Longleaf more than any other —lies in the resistance of their seedlings and saplings to fire. Certainly they are more resistant than the young of deciduous trees. Pine bark is thick and porous, its insulative qualities protecting the inner tissues from excessive heat. That is why pine forests are sometimes referred to as "fireproof." Lightning, of course, is the principal natural means of ignition, but fires are helped along when there is a good fuel source such as tinder-dry debris on the forest floor and by the relatively few times when the environment is not damp from rains or covered with dew. A dry lightning storm over areas of continuous fuel supply, when there is a high wind and low humidity, provides ideal conditions for an extensive burn. It might be expected that the flammable pines, with their generous content of resin, would be thorougly consumed in a forest fire. Indeed, if the fire is intense enough, they are. But in many, if not most, cases, the very frequency of fires has cleaned out the underbrush and prevented an accumulation of the flammable materials that support intense fires. As a result, the fires that occur move rapidly, fed mostly by a few years' accumulation of dead grasses. Such fires do not build up high temperatures, and though they may fatally injure certain saplings, they only scorch the trunks of mature trees. The effect of fires upon animal life in the pinelands varies from severe to helpful. Much depends not only on how successfully an animal can escape the flames but also on what happens to the environment in which each animal has evolved. Two southern woodpeckers offer a classic illustration. Red-bellied Woodpeckers nest in dead trees, usually standing snags, and Red-cockaded Woodpeckers nest in living pines, usually Longleaf and Loblolly. For that reason there is no direct competition between these two birds for nesting sites. However, where territories overlap, there is competition for food and space, with the larger Red-bellied Woodpecker having the upper hand. In the past, fire ran through southern pine forests regularly, and because of the nature of the fuel, fast-spreading fires burned only the litter and the dry or dead trees. This resulted in vast tracts of land containing only live trees, prime habitat for the Red-cockaded Woodpecker. For years, however, natural fires have been suppressed by man, so certain forests now have a greater percentage of trees that have died but not been burned. They remain standing, allowing the relatively aggressive Red-bellied Woodpeckers to move in, colonize new areas and push out the Red-cockaded. To reverse the decline of the Red-cockaded, some forests within its range must be artificially burned from time to time, or else be permitted to burn naturally.

Maritime Forests

At the edge of the sea, survival is seldom a simple matter. The winds blow steadily and furiously much of the time, waves lash the shore, sand dunes bury forests, and salt spray devastates living organisms. In certain places, such as the Outer Banks of North Carolina, there is no extensive forest. But on sea islands off the coasts of South Carolina and Georgia, southern pines and hardwoods manage to establish themselves and survive.

The key to success is an anchorage of woody plants amidst the dunes to shelter other plants from the full force of the wind or the drenching salt spray. Both broad-leaved and coniferous plants tolerate a little salt spray, providing it is soon washed off.

Given two years or so of protection from wind and salt, herbaceous plants such as grasses, sunflowers, and morning-glory vines sprout on the lee side of dunes. In exposed places, Sea Oats grow over the dunes and anchor the sand, interrupting the air flow and causing wind-blown sand to form dunelets. Slowly, dry thickets are established and the hardy Yaupon screens out some of the more severe environmental extremes so that oaks can grow.

The brackish water present in some of the hollows behind the dunes is gradually filtered and becomes fresh. This process produces a swamp microhabitat that finally dries out a bit; over enough time, the vegetation changes from wet thicket to maritime forest.

By the time it matures, the maritime forest represents a kind of oasis at the edge of the sea. It is sheltered, stable, and densely constructed. One such forest occurs on Shackelford Bank, North Carolina, where the three most important dominants are Live Oak, Redcedar, and American Holly. With relatively moderate humidity, moisture, and temperature, the woods begin to resemble a tropical jungle.

Birds

The Southern Pinelands are among the most active and noisy of American forests. Ovenbirds and Wood Thrushes, characteristic inhabitants of the pinelands, sing almost incessantly. Carolina Chickadees traveling in flocks chatter continually as well; Cardinals sing from the trees; and wrens, from somewhere within a tangle of brush, join the chorus. Along the coast, the habitat echoes with the repetitive notes of Yellowthroats and Song Sparrows in thickets, of Yellow Warblers in the trees, and with the calls of Red-winged Blackbirds. Brown Thrashers flit in and out of thickets, and as a reminder that the pinelands are never very far from the sea, it is only necessary to look above the trees and see Laughing Gulls sailing overhead.

Coastal Live Oak forests, in association with pine, provide nesting habitats for such birds as Chickadees, wrens, nuthatches, thrashers, Cardinals, towhees and Pine Warblers. One common factor, apart from the abundance of vegetable foods and insects in these forests, is Spanish Moss. This air plant spreads over the oaks and other vegetation, reducing the amount of sunlight filtering to the forest floor.

Sea Oats
Uniola paniculata

Ovenbird
Seiurus aurocapillus
346

Wood Thrush
Hylocichla mustelina
342

Carolina Chickadee
Parus carolinensis
332

Northern Cardinal
Cardinalis cardinalis
319

Yellowthroat
Geothlypis trichas

Song Sparrow
Melospiza melodia

Yellow Warbler
Dendroica petechia

Red-winged Blackbird
Agelaius phoeniceus

Brown Thrasher
Toxostoma rufum
341

Laughing Gull
Larus atricilla

Pine Warbler
Dendroica pinus
292

Northern Parula
Parula americana
296

Painted Bunting
Passerina ciris
320

Cumberland Island Pocket
Gopher
Geomys pinetis

St. Simon Island Raccoon
Procyon lotor littoreus

Anastasia Island Cotton
Mouse
*Peromyscus gossypinus
anastasiae*

Blackbeard Island Deer
*Odocoileus virginianus
nigribarbis*

Black Bear
Ursus americanus
609

Wood Duck
Aix sponsa
262

Raccoon
Procyon lotor
607

Rat Snake
Elaphe obsoleta
524

Starling
Sturnus vulgaris

Southern Pine Beetle
Dendroctonus frontalis

Black-horned Pine Borer
Callidium antennatum
381

But it also provides nesting material for such birds as the
Northern Parula and Yellow-throated warblers, and the
Painted Bunting. Bats use the fronds for nest-building
materials. Many invertebrates find the plant an important
element in their existence: more than 160 species of
arthropods are associated with Spanish Moss.

Maritime islands are heavily populated with animals—some
recent arrivals, others that have been established for
generations. Such islands are small, and there is limited
interaction between island and mainland animals; because of
this circumstance, some species tend to inbreed and produce
populations with recognizable genetic differences. The
Cumberland Island Pocket Gopher, the St. Simon Island
Raccoon, the Anastasia Island Cotton Mouse, and the
Blackbeard Island Deer are good illustrations.

Considerable numbers of Black Bears live in the pinelands,
although they are largely limited to protected reserves. Bears
do best in the larger refuges because they roam widely in
search of food.

One species of waterfowl that has become well adapted to the
pineland ecosystems is the Wood Duck, which nests in hollow
cavities in the trunks of trees. The dozen or so ducklings must
climb up out of the nest, which is often as much as six feet
below the entrance in the tree trunk. Young are outfitted with
sharp hooked claws to do this, but they are ill-equipped to fly,
so they tumble out, even if the ground is sixty feet below the
opening to the nest. The Wood Duck can fly through dense
woods at high speed, threading its way among the limbs and
trunks of trees, cane thickets, and tangles of vines.

Raccoons and Rat Snakes seek Wood Duck eggs at nesting
time, and aggressive birds, especially Starlings, compete for
nesting cavities. The gravest danger has come from hunting
pressure and habitat modification by humans, and the bird
approached extinction at the beginning of the twentieth
century.

Insects

The numerous insect species of the pinelands include many
forest pests. The most injurious is the Southern Pine Beetle,
which generally moves in after a group of pines has been
weakened by wind or drought. Its larvae feed beneath the
bark, where the intricate tunnels they bore may coalesce and
kill the tree.

An interesting reversal of roles can be seen in the moister areas
of the pinelands, which tend to be more complex than the
surrounding pine-dominated woodlands. On the forest floor
grow rare pitcher-plants, sundews, and Venus Fly-traps, all
with mechanisms for attracting, trapping, and digesting
insects.

The pinelands provide an ideal habitat for other insects as
well. The Black-horned Pine Borer favors felled trees and, like
wood eaters generally, is equipped with strong biting and
chewing mouthparts that enable it to eat away extensive
passageways. This insect, however, is only one of a host of

organisms that attack the wood of fallen trees. After the larvae, mites, and beetles move in, and fungi begin to disintegrate the sapwood, burrows are formed in the rotting wood. Next, termites and ants arrive, together with tiny predators, millipedes, snails, and slugs. When at last a log is hollowed out, it can be taken over by bees, birds, mammals, or any other forest organism needing shelter.

Frogs and Toads

Pine Woods Treefrog
Hyla femoralis
538

Green Treefrog
Hyla cinerea
535

Oak Toad
Bufo quercicus

Insects harbored by the pinelands form a critical food base for a wide variety of animals, including large populations of frogs and toads. The Pine Woods Treefrog, Green Treefrog, and Oak Toad are three examples of predators linked to trees. The nocturnal Pine Woods Treefrog is most common in treetops. The Green Treefrog occasionally sleeps in the daytime on the underside of a large leaf. Toads dine primarily on insects and worms, but will capture virtually anything that moves. Treefrogs feast on grasshoppers, katydids, and other invertebrates.

Mammals

Virginia Opossum
Didelphis virginiana
600

Another insect-eater is the Virginia Opossum, North America's only marsupial. But its diet is not altogether insectivorous, for the Opossum is nothing if not an opportunist. There are times when the bulk of its diet consists of beetles, crickets, grasshoppers, frogs, snakes, and salamanders. But when the right fruits ripen in spring, it becomes a nearly full-time herbivore. It has a particular fondness for the fruit of the Persimmon tree.

Gray Squirrel
Sciurus carolinensis
588

The Gray Squirrel feeds at all levels of the forest, from canopy to below the ground. The nuts abundantly produced in the pinelands are so eagerly sought by so many forms of life that they seldom remain very long on the trees. When the nut supply diminishes, squirrels and other animals must get through the balance of the winter by subsisting on such things as caterpillars, which they dig from crevices in trees. In spring, squirrels feed on the catkins of beeches and oaks. Like many other forest animals, the Gray Squirrel carries around something of an ecosystem of its own: fleas, mites, and ticks ride along in the fur. In addition, squirrel nests contain mites, ticks, spiders, and centipedes.

Eastern Diamondback
Rattlesnake
Crotalus adamanteus
528

Timber Rattlesnake
Crotalus horridus
529

Red-tailed Hawk
Buteo jamaicensis
258

Great Horned Owl
Bubo virginianus
242

Young squirrels are preyed upon by Eastern Diamondback and Timber rattlesnakes, Red-tailed Hawks, Great Horned Owls, foxes, skunks, and Raccoons. Because the pine forests are often more open and parklike than a deciduous grove with its dense understory, the underbrush being kept at a minimum by periodic fires, there is not much shelter for small animals. In appearing at the edge of a burrow or in crossing an open glade, an animal risks aerial attack by hawks and owls or pursuit by foxes. Red-tailed Hawks are among the most formidable of predators, owing to their keen eyesight and ability to dive at a speed of 120 miles an hour. They also consume nearly anything that moves, including insects, birds, bats, mice, voles, ground squirrels, and rabbits.

The pine forests of the South may appear to be rather static, uneventful spots on the evidence of a short visit. But, in fact, they are dynamic habitats and there is a constant interchange of organisms from one environment to another. Because of the frequent burning, the forest is perpetually in some stage of recovery in the natural process of succession. Trees advance on meadows as one group of plants replaces another on the way to the culminating stage of pines or oaks.

Grasshoppers move into meadows opened by fire. For as long as three years, an open area may host nothing but a scrub grass community—an ideal habitat for rabbits, sparrows, and voles. Pine seeds germinate, and during the next twenty years or so, pine seedlings become a young pine forest—a habitat preferred by foxes and skunks. In another thirty years, the pine forest matures. The area now shelters hardwoods, and provides all or most of the requirements of squirrels, hawks, shrews, and a multitude of other forest animals.

These changes are constantly in progress, and while the human visitor on a short trip may not see them occurring, it is possible to note what stage of succession each section of a forest has attained.

The Mississippi Embayment

No coastal plain forests are as mature and rich as those in sections of the lowlands along the Mississippi River. While Longleaf, Shortleaf, Loblolly, and Spruce pines occur, they are often in the minority. In this sense, the Mississippi Embayment is a transition zone between the southern pinelands to the east, south, and west, and the mixed deciduous and oak-hickory forest types to the north. Where the White River joins the Mississippi in Arkansas, for example, the topsoils are gleaned from far upstream and laid down over years of gentle flooding. The levels of the lower White River have been too unpredictable for human habitation—except in cabin boats. The bottomlands are subject to frequent and prolonged inundation, often to a depth of twenty-five feet, which makes them unsuitable for agriculture as well. A labyrinth of bayous and other channels connects with the major rivers, and there are 169 lakes within the White River National Wildlife Refuge alone.

Back in the more remote and undisturbed bayous, massive Baldcypress trees rise out of brown waters with a mirrorlike surface. Typical along the bayous are Water Tupelo, with its buttressed trunks; Waterlocust, a species with spiny twigs; Water-elm, or Planetree, an inconspicuous and rather uncommon member of the elm family; and the Water Hickory or Bitter Pecan. Where the land is better drained, there are associations of Pecan, oak, ash, maple, Sycamore, elm, and Sweetgum. The abundance of water and warmth of climate provide ideal conditions for plant growth. Accordingly, productivity is substantial, as indicated by one ancient Water Oak found to produce more than 28,000 acorns in just a single year.

This collection of deciduous trees constitutes a kind of natural infrastructure not only for birds but for mammals like Black

Water Tupelo
Nyssa aquatica
82

Waterlocust
Gleditsia aquatica

Water-elm
("Planetree")
Planera aquatica

Water Hickory
Carya aquatica

Overcup Oak
Quercus lyrata
108

Wild Turkey
Meleagris gallopavo
249

Common Grackle
Quiscalus quiscula

American Robin
Turdus migratorius
307

Rusty Blackbird
Euphagus carolinus

Sugar Maple
Acer saccharum
121, 227

Bloodroot
Sanguinaria canadensis
440

Eastern Redbud
Cercis canadensis
63, 146

Elliott's Blueberry
Vaccinium elliottii

Tree Sparkleberry
Vaccinium arboreum

Farkleberry
Vaccinium arboreum

Cabbage Palmetto
Sabal palmetto

Swamp Cyrilla
Cyrilla racemiflora

Titi
Cyrilla racemiflora

Redbay
Persea borbonia

Gallberry Holly
Ilex coriacea

Black Hickory
Carya texana

Mountain Lion
Felis concolor

Jaguar
Felis onca

Bears, which include among their den preferences the hollow trunks of Overcup Oaks. Bears feed on Persimmon fruits, as Opossums and Raccoons do, and they dine as well on such items as acorns and pokeberries. Wild Turkeys stuff themselves on pecans, berries, grasshoppers, and beetles, and one biologist once reported that a Turkey crop he examined contained 3,000 seeds of Poison Ivy. Common Grackles, making their way through the woods and cleaning out much of the wild autumn produce, are sometimes so numerous that beneath their temporary roosting sites the guano has accumulated to a depth of six inches. Thousands of Robins and Rusty Blackbirds also roost in these woods.

The Big Thicket
The coastal plain forests of southeastern Texas were originally such a dense accumulation of plants and animals that one explorer called them "the thickest woods I ever saw." The name stuck and the Big Thicket, once 3,500,000 acres in extent, became one of the most celebrated and coveted forests of the Southern Pinelands. The trees were huge, probably a climax of beech, magnolia, and Loblolly Pine, a closed-canopy wood with Sugar Maple and White Oak underneath, little underbrush, and in spring a few trilliums, orchids, and Bloodroot. Spring in the woodlands burst forth with the blooming of dogwoods, Redbud, azalea, and Elliott's Blueberry.
Longleaf Pine, Bluejack Oak, and Tree Sparkleberry, or Farkleberry, grew on the sand hills, progressing toward an oak-hickory association in the absence of fire. There were thickets of hardwoods, Palmetto, and Swamp Cyrilla, or Titi, vine-hung swamps, pine savannas, cypress sloughs, bogs, brakes, tupelo swamps, baygalls (wet woods named after the Redbay and the Gallberry Holly), ridges of Bluejack Oak and Black Hickory, and floodplain forests along the Neches River and other streams. There were bears, wolves, Mountain Lions, Jaguars, Alligators—apparently the closest resemblance to the prevailing image of a Central American forest as one could find north of the tropics. As in the rest of the Southern Pinelands, the principal factor in segregating thicket from prairie from open woodland was fire, the various woodlands representing stages of recovery from fires.
When the railroads came to east Texas in 1876, a lumbering bonanza followed, and between 1880 and 1930 the region was crossed and recrossed by rails, with spur lines run into the forest at intervals of a few hundred yards until a section was logged, then taken up and relaid farther along. Oil derricks rose like a replacement forest. A severe hurricane flattened the forest around the turn of the century. A devastating outbreak of Southern Pine Beetles killed hundreds of acres of pine. Housing developments mushroomed, roads and cities were built, and farms and plantations spread. The original thicket was reduced by ninety percent—to 300,000 acres, of which less than thirty percent is now protected in the Big Thicket National Preserve.

Prairie Vole
Microtus ochrogaster

Hog-nosed Skunk
Conepatus mesoleucus

Red Wolf
Canis rufus

Ocelot
Felis pardalis

Roadrunner
Geococcyx californianus

Wood Thrush
Hylocichla mustelina
342

Reindeer Moss
Cladonia polycarpoides

Speckled Kingsnake
Lampropeltis getulus

Cottonmouth
Agkistrodon piscivorus

Copperhead
Agkistrodon contortrix
530

Texas Coral Snake
Micrurus fulvius tenere

That may not seem like much, and such large-scale habitat reduction over the past century would seem to have left little of nature intact. But the ability of forests to recuperate is well known, and while the Prairie Vole, Hog-nosed Skunk, Red Wolf, Black Bear, Jaguar, Mountain Lion, and Ocelot have been extirpated from the Big Thicket, more than two dozen mammals are still common there. In this extraordinary assemblage of a dozen distinctive habitats, all more or less intact, nearly 200 species of trees, shrubs, and vines have been listed in the surviving sections of the Thicket, along with 134 grasses, 551 herbaceous plants, 114 lichens, and 79 reptiles and amphibians.

These numbers illustrate the richness of the Big Thicket as well as its diversity. The Big Thicket contains subtropical ferns, orchids, and palmettos characteristic of the South; cactus, yucca, and Roadrunners from the West; rhododendrons, trillium, and the Wood Thrush of eastern forests; and Reindeer Moss and sphagnum bogs similar to those of northern forests. Much of the area is moist, the rainfall reaching one hundred inches during especially wet years. There are arid communities as well, though, a result of porous soils. Indeed, underlying the Big Thicket area are more than one hundred types of soil, which vary greatly in texture and acidity.

Under some of the pine trees there is such a fall of needles that the heavy accumulation stifles the growth of wild flowers, resulting in something of a biological desert. Not far away, in the wetlands, wild flowers abound. And deep in the woods, either hidden by dense vegetation or carried on at night when we do not see it, is an extraordinarily complex system of associations in which native animals compete with one another for food, living space, and—ultimately—survival. For species like the aggressive Speckled Kingsnake, the Big Thicket is an Elysium. Among its victims are certain reptiles poisonous to man—Cottonmouths, Copperheads, Texas Coral Snakes, and rattlesnakes—which are known to constitute more than ten percent of its diet. Because these nocturnal events are remote and little observed by visitors, they constitute an unseen ecology that people are only slowly beginning to observe in detail.

As with most ecosystems, one of the best times of day to visit the Thicket is early morning, when fog threads the Sweetgum leaves and pine needles, and the sun illuminates droplets of water like tiny diamonds when it breaks through the mist. Though little remains of the Big Thicket, with continued protection the recovering inhabitants will carry on in the future more or less as they always have.

THE SOUTHERN PINELANDS: PLANTS AND ANIMALS

THE SUBTROPICAL FOREST

The Florida Peninsula marks a transition zone between temperate and tropical forests. The northern border of Florida is deep in the southern pinelands along the coastal plain. But while the state is an extension of the coastal plain, there are significant differences. Although no part of Florida falls within the tropics, the evidence of tropical influence is everywhere, more notably toward the coasts than inland. Vegetation at the southern tip of the peninsula, which is nearly devoid of temperate influences, is almost entirely tropical, an enclave quite reminiscent of the West Indies. Florida, then, is best described as being on the threshold of the tropics.

The fundamental tropical nature of this part of Florida is determined by two overriding factors—the intensity of the light and the intensity of the heat. High intensity of light controls the ecosystem: because the efficiency of photosynthesis is greatest at low light levels, intense light inhibits growth and thereby influences productivity. Extremes of heat add two more limitations: reduced photosynthesis and increased respiratory losses. It might be tempting to think of Florida as a humid tropical jungle where plants flourish as in a greenhouse. The contradiction is that while Florida is humid and plants do flourish, it is also periodically dry—and many plants are vulnerable to drought. The forests of Florida are by necessity adapted to aridity, in many places more so than any other forest in eastern North America.

Lack of rainfall is not the sole cause of aridity. There is as much or more precipitation here—forty to seventy-six inches annually—as in the mixed deciduous forest. But the yearly dry seasons require that plants be adapted to moisture stress. The true culprit, however, in converting Florida from potential greenhouse to another "desert in the rain" is the presence of sand or limestone, both so porous that rainfall is absorbed into the ground and quickly sinks out of the reach of roots. What the roots manage to capture while the water is passing through is about all the moisture they get—not nearly enough for most deciduous trees.

Furthermore, the soils are nearly sterile in many places. In the thousands of years during which present-day Florida has been above sea level, the accumulation of fertile sod has been minimal. Many nutrients are flushed down into the sand and carried away in the hydrologic cycle, while organic material has been burned and washed away, after the repeated fires that typically swept uncontrolled across the landscape before the advent of modern civilization. Only where there were fewer fires, or where the soils were moist from streams, swamps, and high water tables, could rich soil have a chance to accumulate and remain in place. Such places are now the sites of rich and varied broad-leaved forests.

Climate

The annual rainfall in Florida exceeds fifty inches, but unlike the precipitation in other parts of eastern North America, that in Florida is not well distributed throughout the year. Florida has distinct wet and dry seasons: The wettest

months occur in midsummer, the driest are November and December. Even at its most arid, Florida is not really a desert, but some of the peninsula's vegetative associations have desert elements because the exceptional porosity or coarseness of certain soils means an inability to retain moisture.

Although the Florida peninsula is vulnerable to tornadoes and intense electrical disturbances, the more usual weather consists of frequent summer showers, usually borne on storms that move slowly across the more or less level landscape.

Surrounded on three sides by warm water, Florida has a generally mild climate, usually without sharp fluctuations of temperature—either during the course of a day or over the period of a year. Nevertheless, the temperature can rise above 100° F and fall below freezing. Frosts occur periodically in winter, and snow has fallen in Miami. Such temperature extremes are rare; nonetheless, trees must be adapted to withstand them or perish. In the ordinarily warm waters at the southern tip of the peninsula, mangroves have been killed by temperatures that remained below freezing for too long.

Since Florida is vulnerable to hurricanes, its forests have been battered by high winds and its coastal vegetation inundated by storm-driven seas. These have leveled sections of forests, and recovery takes many years or even decades. Because another storm is likely to strike before complete recovery can be achieved, the forests of Florida typically represent some stage of transition rather than a well-established climax. Lightning-ignited fires also take their toll, so that a forest that even nears a successional climax is rare. The changing nature of the Florida forests is in direct contrast to the more or less static condition of spruce-fir climax in the boreal forest of Canada or of cove hardwoods in the southern Appalachians.

Fire and Flood

From the scrub forest to the tropical hammocks, nearly all life has to be adapted to fire, low temperatures, or periodic floods. One adaptation is to grow where environmental problems can be avoided. The Slash Pine, for example, does well on limestone ridges and other elevated sites because it cannot tolerate much flooding. It is resistant to fire because the many-layered bark protects delicate inner tissues from heat damage. The associated Saw-palmetto survives fire because its storage roots are protected in rocky pockets of limestone and are capable of resprouting even after fire has burned off all the plant above ground. The pine-palmetto association therefore is virtually fireproof.

Fires in Florida can be numerous and spectacular; central and southern Florida have one of the highest incidences of lightning storms in eastern North America. Most fires here are fast-moving because their very frequency keeps the supplies of combustible material low; dry pine litter provides the primary fuel source for ground fires, which move rapidly and generate relatively little heat. One fire in Ocala National Forest in 1935 burned 35,000 acres in just four hours.

Fires in the Everglades burn in long, curving lines. They send

Slash Pine
Pinus elliottii
21

Saw-palmetto
Serenoa repens or *Paurotis wrighti*

up dramatic curtains of flame but seldom remain very long at any locality. Tropical hammocks surrounded by water are well protected; because they develop on elevated patches of limestone, they also suffer little flood damage. Furthermore, the dense forest generates enough heat to enable it to survive periodic frosts. The hammocks are unusual: They are protected against all three environmental problems.

The pine flatwoods are frequently flooded because there is no gradient to create runoff. Where water remains most of the time, as in swamps, bayheads, and cypress domes, the trees are adapted to saturated soils. Nonetheless, even these areas are burned from time to time. As the leaf litter is covered by water, aerobic decomposition slows and the leaves are stored as peat. During extended periods of low rainfall the wetlands dry out, along with the peat, and intense fires may result.

Florida is a peninsular extension of the coastal plain, and more than half of it is submerged beneath the sea. When water accumulated in continental ice masses, sea level fell as much as 300 feet, exposing more of the peninsula.

Geology and Soils

While the peninsula was covered with ocean, more sediments of calcium carbonate were deposited than could later be washed away when the seas retreated and the land lay uncovered. After millions of years of intermittent inundation and deposition, a two-mile-deep layer of limestone and other sedimentary strata was accumulated. As a result, the surface rocks are largely limestone: coralline out on the Keys, oolitic (constituted of small, rounded concretions called oolites) from Miami west across the southern tip, and in the north formed of a relatively pure calcium carbonate filled with shelled marine organisms some forty million years old. The central highlands, which extend from Lake Okeechobee to the northern boundary of the state, have long remained above sea level.

Soils derived from the basal limestones include clays, sands, and gravels; much of the Florida scrub forest is underlain by dune sands. In wet areas are found calcareous marl (limestone in the making), muck (organic materials), and peat. The limestones are splendid aquifers, having formed porous strata through a process of dissolution. Fresh water flows long distances underground through these systems before pouring forth up to 500 million gallons a day. If this abundance of fresh water in the underground water table does not approach the surface, however, then it is of little use to the roots of plants, and in such localities the vegetation must obtain what it needs from rain showers.

The drainage is rapid in some places because so much of the soil is deep, dry sand, as is the case beneath the scrub and pine-oak forests. In the flatwoods, this situation is somewhat mitigated because of the level landscape. Even so, the total amount of water available to these communities between rains is small and the forests appear dry. The water balance depends on soil texture, and the well-being of the forest is related less

Longleaf Pine
Pinus palustris
20

Turkey Oak
Quercus laevis

Baldcypress
Taxodium distichum
36

Wild Boar
("Razorback Hog")
Sus scrofa
615

to the fertility of the soils than to the amount of moisture they retain. Hence, more than any other factor, the availability of water is the controlling factor influencing the distribution of plant species and their organization into communities. Where there is a favorable moisture balance in the soil, the hardwoods become established and are seldom destroyed by fire.

With the gradual incorporation of organic materials, the soils in certain areas are improving in fertility. But this is a slow process. Despite the general lack of rich soils and the periodic inundations of parts of Florida by the sea, forests have grown for long periods on the central highlands. The scrub pine forests and the Longleaf Pine and Turkey Oak associations are of considerable antiquity, estimated to date from late Miocene times, more than thirteen million years ago.

Human Intervention

The natural character of the subtropical forests has been modified to varying degrees through the course of human history. Some forested areas have been cleared entirely to make room for citrus groves, livestock pastures, or vegetable fields. Virgin stands of pines and Baldcypress have been cut, converting the profile of many groves from stately to ragged. The introduction of aggressive animals has also had an impact. Razorback Hogs, for example, uproot and consume pine seedlings and "plow" the forest floor for acorns, and uncontrolled cattle grazing has caused some forage species to disappear from the scrub. Wild animals in general have retreated under hunting pressure; the Florida Wolf was exterminated in the 1800s.

Introduced plants, their spread unchecked in a foreign habitat, have crowded out native vegetation over wide areas. Biocides have been employed to control unwanted plant growth. Water impoundments and drainage canals have altered the water balance in natural areas, and heavy recreation use has eroded banks and contributed pollutants. Fire suppression programs have altered the natural fire regimen and allowed too large a buildup of the fuel supply. Longleaf Pine systems, as a result, bear little resemblance to their appearance before settlement of the region.

But the increase of exploitation also stimulated an increase in pressures for conservation, particularly at ecologically important sites. The entire scrub pine habitat was included within the boundaries of Ocala National Forest, which was established in 1908 as the first national forest east of the Mississippi River. Hammock forests and more than half a dozen other significant communities in southern Florida were later placed under protection in Everglades National Park and the Big Cypress National Preserve.

Loblolly Pine
Pinus taeda
24

Pond Pine
Pinus serotina

Flatwoods, Scrub and Sandhill Forests

Although the forests of northern and central Florida are composed predominantly of pine and oak, there are dozens of distinctive forest communities. The flatwoods, in the northern part of the peninsula, are the most "piney" of all, with Longleaf, Loblolly, Slash, and Pond pines.

Sand Pine
Pinus clausa

Myrtle Oak
Quercus myrtifolia
42

Chapman Oak
Quercus chapmanii

Scrub Oak
Quercus virginiana var.
maritima

Laurel Oak
Quercus laurifolia
41

Southern Magnolia
Magnolia grandiflora
40, 161

Pignut Hickory
Carya glabra
136, 199, 232

Flowering Dogwood
Cornus florida
52

The scrub forest—so named because the dominant Sand Pines look scrubby when compared to the stately Longleaf Pines—occurs in north-central Florida, thirty miles north of Orlando. Although it is not very large (less than 500 square miles in area), it is the largest of its kind and unique to Florida. The upper story is composed of Sand Pine, Myrtle, Chapman, and Scrub Live oaks; the understory of silkbay, Scrub and Saw-palmetto, Turkey Oak, and Scrub and Carolina holly. The vegetation of the forest floor here—as in every other forest of eastern North America—includes some form of heath; in this case it is Tree Sparkleberry. There are also Rosemary, Gopher Apple, lichen, cactus, sumac, and Greenbrier.

The sandhill community occurs on well-drained sand ridges in the central highlands of Florida, which reach from Lake Okeechobee to the northern boundary of the state. Normally a kind of tug-of-war goes on between Longleaf Pine on the one hand and mixed hardwood forest, led by Turkey, Bluejack, and Sand Post oaks, on the other. In the absence of fire, the pine seedlings cannot develop because too many hardwoods grow up and shade them out; moreover, they may be afflicted with brown spot fungus. But when the hardwoods have spread and have almost established dominance, fire wipes them out, kills back the fungus, and opens the canopy. Now the pine seedlings grow rapidly in a favorable environment and the oaks again commence their slow ascent toward dominance.

The flatwoods, so named because this association is usually found on level terrain, constitute one of the most common forest communities in Florida. Pines dominate: Longleaf on the dry and well-drained sites, Slash on less well-drained soils, and Pond Pine in wet or periodically flooded places. Other trees include Sweetbay, Loblolly-bay, Dahoon, waxmyrtle, Red Maple, Black Tupelo, Sweetgum, and Tree Lyonia.

Mixed Hardwood and Bayhead Communities

More than any other in upland Florida, mixed hardwood communities conform more closely to the stereotypical "jungle" image of tropical forests. They are densely populated at all layers. Some of the trees are huge: the Laurel Oak grows rapidly and reaches one hundred feet in height and four feet in diameter. The Southern Magnolia, with its showy flowers and dark evergreen leaves, is a conspicuous member of the community. Pignut Hickories thrive in the shade. The Red Maple is one of those rare trees adaptable to a variety of situations; its range is from Canada to the Florida Keys. The Flowering Dogwood is likewise a familiar tree in all but the most northerly deciduous forests. The Sweetgum reaches large dimensions in this environment. Other understory trees include American Holly, Red Mulberry, Carolina Laurelcherry, and Hackberry. Species more tropical than temperate include Scrub Palmetto, Saw-palmetto, and the shrubby Needle Palm.

Moist, wet, and partially submerged forests are also common in northern and central Florida, especially in or along swamps and along rivers. They are dominated by deciduous species,

Green Ash
Fraxinus pennsylvanica

Waterlocust
Gleditsia aquatica

American Elder
("Elderberry")
Sambucus canadensis

Pondcypress
Taxodium distichum nutans

Spanish Moss
Tillandsia usneoides
458

Greenfly Orchid
Epidendrum conopseum

Resurrection Fern
Polypodium polypodioides

Saw Grass
Cladium jamaicense

such as Baldcypress, Green Ash, Waterlocust, and American Elder. Where the swamps have become highly organic after years of accumulation of biological debris, the bay trees do best, forming associations known as bayhead communities. In other spots, Pondcypress trees collect in dome-shaped communities known as cypress domes.

Everglades and Hammocks
As one moves south, the subtropical setting becomes more evident with the increasing prevalence of air plants. Spanish Moss, of course, grows in the coastal plain and in the maritime forests farther north. So does the epiphytic Greenfly Orchid. But from here south the epiphytes pervade all woodlands, a distinctive characteristic of subtropical forests. Chief among them is the Resurrection Fern, which lines the branches of trees and gives them a bearded aspect.

In southern Florida the land flattens out and becomes covered with broad, shallow rivers—like sheets of water—emanating largely from Lake Okeechobee. Where these rivers have not been diverted by drainage canals they are thickly grown up with Saw Grass (actually a sedge), through which the waters glide imperceptibly toward Florida Bay and the Gulf of Mexico. These sedge prairies form immense, flat, watery glades. They are maintained by periodic fires, which keep back the growth of tropical hardwoods—and as a result are called Everglades. Occasionally, however, the glades are interrupted by clumps of trees: a few inches change in elevation and the protection of the surrounding water is enough to make a barrier against the ravages of most fires. The underlying limestone is pitted, pocked, and jagged, and forms irregular outcrops; where it rises above the prevailing water-covered flats it forms a bastion of more or less dry land in a sea of sedge. It is these structures that are often covered with hardwood trees. These outcrops are known as islands, reefs, keys, or hammocks; indeed they are islands, although the water that surrounds them may be almost invisible in the thick vegetation. In dry seasons the water may be absent altogether.

The important point is that each island is elevated above its surroundings. Soils here have had a chance to mature; protection from disturbances such as fire and flooding has permitted the development of a climax community. These islands of low relief are most commonly referred to as hammocks, and the dense forests on them as hammock forests. The term is widely used in eastern North America to denote an isolated, slightly elevated patch of trees. In northern Florida, drier mixed deciduous forests often occur in a pine-dominated landscape—these are often referred to as hardwood hammocks, and they appear as islands of deciduous trees in a sea of pines. In southern Florida, the hammocks become conspicuous because the dense tropical forests that grow on them are surrounded by a great expanse of grass. Hundreds of such hammocks dot the watery glades from Lake Okeechobee to the Gulf, looking like a flotilla of ships at anchor.

Redbay
Persea borbonia
48

Live Oak
Quercus virginiana
49

Passionflower
Passiflora incarnata
494

The Gumbo-limbo, with its copper-colored bark and dramatically twisted limbs, is also a familiar sight. Vines of Hippocratea ascend to the canopy, clinging to the trees by tendrils. ·
Hammocks range in size from less than an acre to many square miles. Since the forests are principally tropical, they have a characteristically undifferentiated climax, and there may be more than seventy species of trees in a single hammock. Some of the best known are Marlberry, Paurotis, Strangler Fig, Lancewood, Redbay, tamarind, stoppers, Paradise-tree, Coco-plum, Satinleaf, and Mastic. The air plants of the area are chiefly bromeliads (members of the pineapple family); the principal ferns are Sword and Resurrection. Some thirty species of orchids festoon the trees. In addition, the hammock forests are replete with vines and creepers. The Live Oak is one of the few representatives of temperate forests.

Slash Pine Forest
A ridge of limestone that extends from Fort Lauderdale southwest into the Everglades forms an ideal environment for a fire-maintained Slash Pine forest with Saw-palmetto on the floor. At first glance these pinelands do not appear very diverse, but holes and pockets in the limestone have accumulated soils over the years, and these provide a base for a variety of plants, including Coontie (a small cycad resembling a fern), Croton, Wild Poinsettia, iris, Tetrazygia, the Pine-pink Orchid, Passionflower, and Florida Fiddlewood.
Pineland forests extend out along the Florida Keys, but many of these islands as well as the southern tip of Florida are edged by mangroves, stilt-rooted trees adapted to brackish and saline environments. Since there does not seem ever to have been a land connection between Florida and the West Indies, to reach Florida the tropical vegetation must originally have floated in seed form on the prevailing currents, or have been ferried on tiny islets torn from Caribbean shores and riverbanks, or have been transported by birds or wind. Whatever the case, a West Indian vegetation has become well established in southern Florida. Along with the tropical residents of pinelands and hammock forests, there are the violently poisonous Machineel and the Florida Poisontree, two trees best avoided by human visitors.
The growing season in southern Florida is twelve months long, and flowering and fruiting continue all year. Tropical forests are usually classified as wet or dry, depending on the amount of moisture in the soil. The vegetation here is almost entirely tropical and, except for the showy Poinciana, a native of Madagascar, has emigrated primarily from the West Indies. It exhibits the characteristics of tropical vegetation. Vines, lianas, and air plants are common. It is nearly all based on limestone, and is adaptable to disturbed areas. Many trees contain a milky sap that may be poisonous to humans.
One of the most common air plants is the Resurrection Fern, which in dry periods, when its photosynthetic processes are suspended, can shrivel and appear lifeless. When its water

supply is renewed, it seems to come to life again. The bromeliads, which include Spanish Moss, are the most conspicuous epiphytes, but there are also at least two dozen epiphytic orchids.

Many air plants have evolved to attract hummingbirds; certain adaptations center on the specific manner of nectar secretion and presentation. The more successful the strategy is, and the more often the plant is visited by hummingbirds, the more assured is pollination and the perpetuation of the species.

Ecology

The anomalous fact is that Florida's extraordinary richness and diversity of plant and animal life are based not on deep humus and rich soil but on comparatively sterile sand. The adapations of organisms—indeed of whole ecosystems—to the acquisition and retention of nutrients is a marvel of evolution.

It is important to remember that even the most sterile systems provide some kind of nutrients. A fire, for example, can reduce organic material to nutrient-rich ashes. Old plants, mainly pines and hardwoods, contribute their dead twigs, fruits, leaves, and trunks to the litter on the forest floor. Animals make continual contributions in the form of feathers, feces, hair, skin, and carcasses. Even the rainfall as it works its way to the ground contains weak solutions of nutrients—absorbed from aerial dust and washed from the vegetation.

Some nutrients are intercepted by lichens, which in certain localities cover thirty percent of the forest floor. The lichens hold the nutrients in place until they can be released and distributed to producer organisms.

Nutrients are also taken up directly through root systems. The roots of Sand Pines are sites of mutually beneficial relationships. Microscopic fungi are connected to plant roots by filamentlike structures that aid in making water, carbon dioxide, and mineral nutrients available to the plant. Other fungi, called mycorrhizae, live in the roots and fix atmospheric nitrogen (that is, convert it into a compound that can be utilized in plant metabolism). The roots of an individual Sand Pine may also graft onto other Sand Pine roots, especially where young trees crowd together; this arrangement provides a channel for exchange of organic and inorganic materials, creating a large pool of potential energy for Sand Pines to draw on. This sharing of resources gives the Sand Pine an advantage over other plants.

Despite these adaptations, a considerable supply of nutrients does get away and sift through the sand, below the reach of roots, to lower levels of the soil profile. There the minerals collect at places where impermeable rock layers prevent further descent. These soil horizons, however, are the milieu of burrowing animals such as pocket gophers, ants, beetles, tortoises, and mice; these burrowers bring a great deal of nutrient-rich soil to the surface.

By actual count there are nearly 1800 animal burrow mounds on each acre of the floor of the scrub forest. Since each mound weighs about two pounds, almost two tons of earth are thus brought to the surface in one acre. Additional mounds built as time goes on may double or triple that total in a year's time, suggesting that perhaps five or six tons of soil are brought back up annually. The potential for nutrient recycling through this process is considerable.

Cooperation

Plants as well as animals have specific roles in the circulation of nutrients through the ecosystem, especially in the pine flatwoods and Saw-palmetto communities that are abundant from northern to southern Florida. Potassium, vital in the growth of new tissues, is absorbed from the leaves back into plants prior to leaf fall. Calcium, on the other hand, is retained in the cell walls of the leaf and lost to the plant when the leaf is shed. The plant must accordingly make up for this calcium loss, especially at the critical period when new cell walls are being produced.

Cabbage Palmetto
Sabal palmetto

Enter the Palmetto. This ubiquitous understory shrub collects and concentrates the calcium in the soil and returns it to the litter surface as leaf and fruit fall. This process makes calcium readily available to the surface feeder roots of other plants, which would face calcium deficiency if the calcium had drained away. The Palmetto, therefore, forms a vital link in the function of the flatwoods ecosystem, just as the Dogwood similarly serves as a calcium "pump" in hardwood ecosystems. These cooperative functional roles in the pine and hardwood systems extend beyond nutrient retrieval. Although cooperation among elements of the ecosystem is not something that each organism does deliberately, the word well describes the effect of interactions that have slowly evolved to make the functioning of the ecosystem more efficient. Oak trees, for example, produce acorns that are a basic food for many consumers, including the squirrel. In return, the squirrel helps the oaks regenerate by burying more acorns than it retrieves.

Flowering Dogwood
Cornus florida
52, 160, 190, 214

Squirrels and jays, well equipped to extract acorns from their seed coats, drop portions of the acorns. These are eaten by Northern Bobwhites, which have difficulty opening acorns themselves. Other animals consume fruits but do not digest the seeds, which are discharged in nutrient-rich feces, a good environment in which to sprout. This latter process helps propagate the host plant and also widens its range.

Bobwhite
Colinus virginianus

Because the growing season is nearly year-long, leaves are grazed virtually continually by forest animals, ranging from insects to deer. In the scrub forest this consumption seldom removes more than twelve percent of the leaf biomass, and that is accomplished by different species at different times of year. The resultant opening of the canopy in the scrub, hammock, and sandhill forests permits more sun to reach lower plant layers. Better aeration assists transpiration, which withdraws water from the leaves. This in turn helps the flow of water through the entire ecosystem.

Populations of Wildlife

The diversity of animal life in the sand pine scrub, sandhill, hammock, flatwoods, and wet forest ecosystems may be indicated by an inventory of the species of vertebrate animals known to occur in Ocala National Forest: 35 kinds of amphibians, 13 turtles, 12 lizards, 38 snakes, 238 birds, 51 mammals, 109 fishes, as well as uncounted numbers of invertebrates. The interconnections amòng all these organisms make the subtropical forests one of the ᴍost complex collections of ecosystems in eastern North America.

Wild Turkey
Meleagris gallopavo
249

Fox Squirrel
Sciurus niger
587

Deer herds are common. The largest population of Wild Turkeys east of the Mississippi River is believed to occur in Florida. Great numbers of migratory birds pass through twice a year, and other large populations are permanent residents. The largest of North American tree squirrels, the Fox Squirrel, inhabits the sand hills.

Predators
With so many food sources present, together with so many animals, predation is heavy. Insects are preyed upon by frogs. Frogs are eaten by snakes. Snakes and amphibians are consumed by hawks and falcons, which also eat rodents and rabbits. Pine Snakes enter burrows in pursuit of gophers.

Black Bear
Ursus americanus
609

Mountain Lions (called "Florida Panthers" here) prey on deer. White-tailed Deer, Black Bears, squirrels, Wild Turkeys, and feral pigs all compete for acorns and the berries from palmettos.

Bald Eagles are tertiary consumers: they fly high above the forest-water ecosystems, observing the Osprey's hunt for fish. As soon as the Osprey dives and retrieves a fish, the Eagle utters a scream and dives. The Osprey is so startled that it drops the fish, which is usually caught in midair by the Eagle. When food is scarce, the competing populations decrease until their numbers are brought in balance with the food supply.

Virginia Opossum
Didelphis virginiana
600

Because Virginia Opossums eat just about anything, they compete with most other animals. Much the same can be said about Bears, of which approximately 1000 remain in Florida. In this benign climate, shrews compete by reproducing prodigiously—four to six litters annually—but their numbers are controlled by hawks, owls, snakes, and foxes.

Nine-banded Armadillo
Dasypus novemcinctus
598

Few predators are as well adapted to the pine and palmetto country as the Nine-banded Armadillo, which forages for insects in the palmetto thickets. Without fur, the animal does not endure cold snaps very well, but it has plenty of burrows in which to seek warmth.

While nearly all the vegetation of this region of hammocks, mangroves, and coastal forests is West Indian, as are the resident water birds, insects, and lizards, there are two groups of organisms that are notable exceptions. Of all the land mammals (which include Raccoons, cottontails, Gray Foxes, Bobcats, Mountain Lions, and White-tailed Deer) and land birds (such as Barred Owls, Red-shouldered Hawks, Cardinals, towhees, and Red-bellied Woodpeckers), not one is tropical. Their presence means that they have never been crowded out by aggressive tropical immigrants, because there

Liguus Tree Snail
Liguus fasciatus

Tamarind
Tamarindus indica

Jamaica Dogwood
Piscida piscipula

has apparently never been a land connection between Florida and the West Indies. What we are left with is the anomaly of temperate land organisms consuming tropical vegetation, insects, lizards, and other foods—a situation unique among the forests of eastern North America.

One of the most colorful West Indian invertebrates is the Liguus Tree Snail, about two and a half inches in length, which occurs in southern Florida hammocks in as great a variety as do salamanders in the southern Appalachians. More than fifty color variants have been identified, each snail possessing a distinctive combination of color and banding on its shell. In the dry season the snails remain dormant, but during the wet season they move along the trunks of such trees as Tamarind and Jamaica Dogwood, slowly consuming algal and fungal growths. They feed chiefly at night, but are vulnerable to predation by rats, Raccoons, Opossums, and carnivorous birds.

The tropical forest is a constant buzz of activity—literally so. One of the most abundant insects is the mosquito, an important food for birds and fish. But in the wet season certain populations may be so dense that they are a serious menace to unprotected travelers.

Indeed, life is vigorous and prolific at all levels. Raccoons and Opossums are the most abundant of the larger mammals; thousands of wading birds, such as egrets and ibises, congregate each year in forest rookeries. Some years the rookeries fail, perhaps for want of food, perhaps on account of drought, perhaps because of a combination of causes. But here in the midst of plenty, life is relentlessly exuberant. On the threshold of the tropics, the productivity of natural ecosystems, despite occasional disruptions, is continuous, day and night, all year long.

THE SUBTROPICAL FOREST: PLANTS AND ANIMALS

1 Pine and spruce forest Near the Vermilion River, northern Minnesota

Boreal Forest

2 Jack Pine and Sugar Maple forest Hiawatha National Forest, Upper Peninsula, Michigan

Boreal Forest

3 Red Pine and Northern White-cedar Lake Superior area, Minnesota

Boreal Forest

4 Sugar Maple, Pin Cherry, and conifer forest

Lake Superior area, Ontario

Transition Forest

5 Sugar Maple and Red Spruce forest

Glen Ellis Gorge, New Hamphire

Transition Forest

6 Gray Birch and spruce forest

Acadia National Park, Mount Desert Island, Maine

Transition Forest

7 Beech and maple forest   Holmes County, Ohio

Mixed Deciduous Forest

8 Beech and maple forest   Shiller Woods, Norridge, Illinois

Mixed Deciduous Forest

9 Oak and hickory forest   Northern Illinois

Oak-Hickory Forest

10. Oak, hickory, maple and elm forest   Ozark Mountains, Richland, Arkansas

Oak-Hickory Forest

11. Oak, hickory, maple and elm forest   Ozark Mountains, Richland, Arkansas

Oak-Hickory Forest

12. Dogwood in hardwood forest   Ozark Mountains, Devil's Fork on Buffalo River, Arkansas

Oak-Hickory Forest

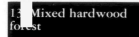

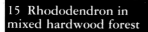

15 Rhododendron in mixed hardwood forest

Great Smoky Mountains National Park, Tennessee

Southern Appalachians

16 Pitch Pine forest   Southern New Jersey

Pine Barrens

17 Longleaf Pine forest   Okefenokee National Wildlife Refuge, southern Georgia
with Saw-palmetto

Southern Pinelands

18 Edge of a hammock   Everglades National Park, Florida

Subtropical Forest

HOW TO USE THE COLOR PLATES

The color plates on the following pages include eight major groups of plants and animals: trees, birds, butterflies and moths, insects and spiders, wildflowers, reptiles and amphibians, mushrooms, and mammals.

Table of Contents
For easy reference, a table of contents precedes the color plates. The table is divided into two sections. On the left, we list each major group of plants or animals. On the right, the major groups are usually subdivided into smaller groups, and each small group is illustrated by a symbol. For example, the large group of trees is divided into small groups based on characteristics such as leaf shape or fruit type. Similarly, the large group of reptiles and amphibians is divided into small groups made up of distinctive animals such as turtles or snakes.

Captions for the Color Plates
The black bar above each color plate contains the following information: the plate number, the common and scientific names of the plant or animal, its dimensions, and the page number of the full species description. To the left of each color plate, the habitats where you are likely to encounter the species are always indicated in blue type. Additionally, you will find either a fact helpful in field identification, such as the food that an insect eats (also in blue type), or a range map or drawing.

The chart on the facing page lists the dimensions given and the blue-type information, map, or drawing provided for each major group of plants or animals.

CAPTION INFORMATION

Dimensions	Blue Type/Art
Trees	
Leaf, leaflet, or needle length; flower width or length; fruit length, width, or diameter	Winter tree silhouette
Birds	
Length, usually of adult male, from tip of bill to tail	Range map showing breeding, winter, and/or permanent range
Butterflies and Moths	
Wingspan of fully spread adult	Caterpillar's host plants
Insects and Spiders	
Length of adult, excluding antennae and appendages	Major food
Wildflowers	
Plant height and flower length or width	Drawing of plant or flower
Reptiles and Amphibians	
Maximum length of adult	Range map
Mushrooms	
Approximate size of mature mushroom: height of stalked mushroom; width of round, cup-shaped, or unusually shaped mushroom	Specific habitat
Mammals	
Length of adult	Range map

Trees

Needle-leaf and Scale-leaf Conifers

19–39

Simple Leaves

40–126

Compound Leaves

127–143

Palmetto

144

Flowers

145–168

Cones

169–176

Keys

177–180

Capsules and Balls

181–183.

Fleshy Fruit

184–186

Berrylike Fruit

187–198

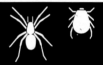

Rabbits

592–594

Woodchuck and Beaver

595, 597

Bat

596

Armadillo

598

Weasel-like Mammals

599, 601–604

Opossum, Skunks, Raccoon, and Wolverine

600, 605–608

Bear

609

Gray Wolf and Foxes

610–612

Bobcat and Lynx

613–614

Boar and Deer

615–618

19 Eastern White Pine   *Pinus strobus*   Needle length: 2½–5"
p. 355

Transition and Mixed
Deciduous forests;
Southern Appalachians

20 Longleaf Pine   *Pinus palustris*   Needle length: 10–15"
p. 355

Subtropical Forest and
Southern Pinelands

21 Slash Pine   *Pinus elliottii*   Needle length: 7–10"
p. 356

Subtropical Forest and
Southern Pinelands

22 Red Pine *Pinus resinosa* Needle length: 4¼–6½"
p. 356

Transition Forest

23 Shortleaf Pine *Pinus echinata* Needle length: 2¾–4½"
p. 357

Mixed Deciduous and Oak-
hickory forests; Southern
Appalachians; Pine
Barrens; and Southern
Pinelands

24 Loblolly Pine *Pinus taeda* Needle length: 5–9"
p. 357

Subtropical Forest and
Southern Pinelands

25 Pitch Pine *Pinus rigida* Needle length: 3–5″
p. 358

Southern Appalachians and
Pine Barrens

26 Table Mountain Pine *Pinus pungens* Needle length: 1¼–2½″
p. 359

Southern Appalachians

27 Virginia Pine *Pinus virginiana* Needle length: 1½–3″
p. 359

Pine Barrens and Southern
Pinelands

28 Jack Pine *Pinus banksiana* Needle length: ¾–1½"
p. 360

Boreal and Transition forests

29 White Spruce *Picea glauca* Needle length: ½–¾"
p. 360

Boreal Forest

30 Black Spruce *Picea mariana* Needle length: ¼–⅝"
p. 361

Boreal and Transition forests

31 Red Spruce

Picea rubens
p. 362

Needle length: ½–⅝″

Transition Forest and
Southern Appalachians

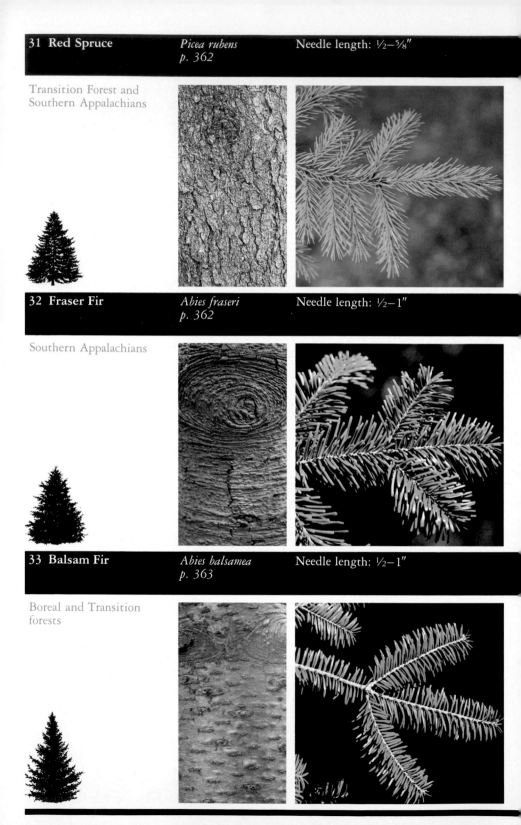

32 Fraser Fir

Abies fraseri
p. 362

Needle length: ½–1″

Southern Appalachians

33 Balsam Fir

Abies balsamea
p. 363

Needle length: ½–1″

Boreal and Transition
forests

| **34 Eastern Hemlock** | *Tsuga canadensis*
 p. 364 | Needle length: ⅜–⅝″ |

Transition and Mixed
Deciduous forests;
Southern Appalachians

| **35 Tamarack** | *Larix laricina*
 p. 364 | Needle length: ¾–1″ |

Boreal, Transition, and
Mixed Deciduous forests

| **36 Baldcypress** | *Taxodium distichum*
 p. 365 | Needle length: ⅜–¾″ |

Subtropical Forest and
Southern Pinelands

37 Northern White-cedar

Thuja occidentalis
p. 366

Leaf length: $1/16-1/8''$

Boreal and Transition forests

38 Eastern Redcedar

Juniperus virginiana
p. 366

Leaf length: $1/16''$

Transition, Mixed Deciduous, and Oak-hickory forests; Southern Appalachians; Pine Barrens; and Southern Pinelands

39 Atlantic White-cedar

Chamaecyparis thyoides
p. 367

Leaf length: $1/16-1/8''$

Pine Barrens and Southern Pinelands

40 Southern Magnolia *Magnolia grandiflora* Leaf length: 5–8"
p. 367

Subtropical Forest and
Southern Pinelands

41 Laurel Oak *Quercus laurifolia* Leaf length: 2–5½"
p. 368

Subtropical Forest and
Southern Pinelands

42 Myrtle Oak *Quercus myrtifolia* Leaf length: ¾–2"
p. 369

Subtropical Forest

43 Catawba Rhododendron
Rhododendron catawbiense
p. 369

Leaf length: 3–6"

Mixed Deciduous Forest and Southern Appalachians

44 Mountain-laurel
Kalmia latifolia
p. 370

Leaf length: 2½–4"

Mixed Deciduous Forest, Southern Appalachians, Pine Barrens, and Southern Pinelands

45 Sweetbay
Magnolia virginiana
p. 371

Leaf length: 3–6"

Subtropical Forest, Pine Barrens, and Southern Pinelands

46 Myrtle Dahoon

Ilex myrtifolia
p. 371

Leaf length: ½–1¼"

Subtropical Forest and
Southern Pinelands

47 Rosebay Rhododendron

Rhododendron maximum
p. 372

Leaf length: 4–10"

Mixed Deciduous Forest
and Southern Appalachians

48 Redbay

Persea borbonia
p. 373

Leaf length: 3–6"

Subtropical Forest and
Southern Pinelands

49 Live Oak
Quercus virginiana
p. 373
Leaf length: 1½–4″

Subtropical Forest and
Southern Pinelands

50 Dahoon
Ilex cassine
p. 374
Leaf length: 1½–3½″

Subtropical Forest

51 Red-osier Dogwood
Cornus stolonifera
p. 374
Leaf length: 1½–3½″

Boreal, Transition, and
Mixed Deciduous forests

52 Flowering Dogwood — *Cornus florida* — Leaf length: 2½–5″
p. 375

Transition, Mixed Deciduous, and Oak-hickory forests; Southern Appalachians; and Southern Pinelands

53 Bigleaf Magnolia — *Magnolia macrophylla* — Leaf length: 15–30″
p. 376

Mixed Deciduous Forest, Southern Appalachians, and Southern Pinelands

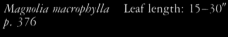

54 Umbrella Magnolia — *Magnolia tripetala* — Leaf length: 10–20″
p. 376

Mixed Deciduous Forest and Southern Appalachians

55 Fraser Magnolia

Magnolia fraseri
p. 377

Leaf length: 8–18"

Southern Appalachians

56 Common Persimmon

Diospyros virginiana
p. 377

Leaf length: 2½–6"

Mixed Deciduous, Oak-
hickory, and Subtropical
forests; Southern
Appalachians; and
Southern Pinelands

57 Black Tupelo

Nyssa sylvatica
p. 378

Leaf length: 2–5"

Mixed Deciduous, Oak-
hickory, and Subtropical
forests; Southern
Appalachians; Pine
Barrens; and Southern
Pinelands

58 Cucumbertree

Magnolia acuminata
p. 379

Leaf length: 5–10″

Mixed Deciduous and Oak-hickory forests; Southern Appalachians; and Southern Pinelands

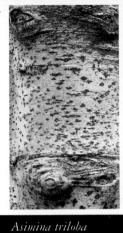

59 Pawpaw

Asimina triloba
p. 379

Leaf length: 7–10″

Mixed Deciduous and Oak-hickory forests; Southern Appalachians

60 Buttonbush

Cephalanthus occidentalis
p. 380

Leaf length: 2½–6″

All eastern forests

61 Northern Catalpa

Catalpa speciosa
p. 381

Leaf length: 6–12″

Mixed Deciduous Forest

62 Southern Catalpa

Catalpa bignonioides
p. 381

Leaf length: 5–10″

Southern Pinelands

63 Eastern Redbud

Cercis canadensis
p. 382

Leaf length: 2½–4½″

Mixed Deciduous, Oak-hickory, and Subtropical forests; Southern Appalachians; and Southern Pinelands

64 Quaking Aspen

Populus tremuloides
p. 383

Leaf length: 1¼–3"

Boreal and Transition
forests

65 Eastern Cottonwood

Populus deltoides
p. 384

Leaf length: 3–7"

Mixed Deciduous and Oak-
hickory forests; Southern
Pinelands

66 Bigtooth Aspen

Populus grandidentata
p. 384

Leaf length: 2½–4"

Boreal, Transition, and
Mixed Deciduous forests

67 Paper Birch

Betula papyrifera
p. 385

Leaf length: 2–4"

Boreal and Transition
forests

68 Yellow Birch

Betula alleghaniensis
p. 386

Leaf length: 3–5"

Transition Forest and
Southern Appalachians

69 River Birch

Betula nigra
p. 386

Leaf length: 1½–3"

Mixed Deciduous and Oak-
hickory forests; Southern
Appalachians; and
Southern Pinelands

70 Red Mulberry   *Morus rubra*   Leaf length: 4–7″
p. 387

Mixed Deciduous, Oak-hickory and Subtropical forests; Southern Appalachians; and Southern Pinelands

71 White Basswood   *Tilia heterophylla*   Leaf length: 3–7″
p. 388

Mixed Deciduous and Oak-hickory forests; Southern Appalachians

72 American Basswood   *Tilia americana*   Leaf length: 3–6″
p. 388

Transition, Mixed Deciduous and Oak-hickory forests; Southern Appalachians

73 Green Hawthorn   *Crataegus viridis*   Leaf length: 1–2½″
p. 389

Mixed Deciduous and Oak-hickory forests; Southern Pinelands

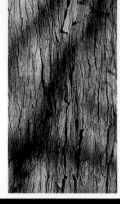

74 Downy Hawthorn   *Crataegus mollis*   Leaf length: 3–4″
p. 389

Mixed Deciduous and Oak-hickory forests

75 Eastern Hophornbeam   *Ostrya virginiana*   Leaf length: 2–5″
p. 390

Transition, Mixed Deciduous, and Oak-hickory forests; Southern Appalachians; and Southern Pinelands

76 Sweet Birch | *Betula lenta* | Leaf length: 2½–5″
p. 391

Mixed Deciduous Forest
and Southern Appalachians

77 Hackberry | *Celtis occidentalis* | Leaf length: 2–5″
p. 391

Mixed Deciduous and Oak-
hickory forests

78 Sugarberry | *Celtis laevigata* | Leaf length: 2½–4″
p. 392

Mixed Deciduous, Oak-
hickory and Subtropical
forests; Southern Pinelands

79 Downy Serviceberry
Amelanchier arborea
p. 393
Leaf length: 1½–4"

Transition, Mixed Deciduous, and Oak-hickory forests; Southern Appalachians

80 Nannyberry
Viburnum lentago
p. 393
Leaf length: 2½–4"

Transition and Mixed Deciduous forests

81 Eastern Burningbush
Euonymus atropurpureus
p. 394
Leaf length: 2–4½"

Mixed Deciduous and Oak-hickory forests

82 Water Tupelo *Nyssa aquatica* Leaf length: 5–8"
p. 394

Oak-hickory Forest and
Southern Pinelands

83 American Plum *Prunus americana* Leaf length: 2½–4"
p. 395

Mixed Deciduous and Oak-
hickory forests; Southern
Appalachians

84 Pin Cherry *Prunus pensylvanica* Leaf length: 2½–4½"
p. 396

Boreal and Transition
forests; Southern
Appalachians

85 American Chestnut
Castanea dentata
p. 396
Leaf length: 5–9"

Transition, Mixed
Deciduous, and Oak-
hickory forests; Southern
Appalachians

86 American Elm
Ulmus americana
p. 397
Leaf length: 3–6"

All eastern forests

87 Ozark Chinkapin
Castanea ozarkensis
p. 398
Leaf length: 5–8"

Oak-hickory Forest

88 American Beech · *Fagus grandifolia* p. 398 · Leaf length: 2½–5″

Transition, Mixed Deciduous, and Oak-hickory forests; Southern Appalachians; and Southern Pinelands

89 American Hornbeam · *Carpinus caroliniana* p. 399 · Leaf length: 2–4½″

Transition, Mixed Deciduous, Oak-hickory, and Subtropical forests; Southern Appalachians; and Southern Pinelands

90 Allegheny Chinkapin · *Castanea pumila* p. 400 · Leaf length: 3–6″

Mixed Deciduous Forest, Southern Appalachians, and Southern Pinelands

91 Black Cherry

Prunus serotina
p. 400

Leaf length: 2–5″

Transition, Mixed
Deciduous, and Oak-
hickory forests; Southern
Appalachians; Pine
Barrens; and Southern
Pinelands

92 Carolina Silverbell

Halesia carolina
p. 401

Leaf length: 3–6″

Mixed Deciduous Forest
and Southern Appalachians

93 Sourwood

Oxydendrum arboreum
p. 402

Leaf length: 4–7″

Mixed Deciduous Forest
and Southern Appalachians

94 Slippery Elm
Ulmus rubra
p. 402
Leaf length: 4–7"

Transition, Mixed
Deciduous, and Oak-
hickory forests

95 Witch-hazel
Hamamelis virginiana
p. 403
Leaf length: 3–5"

Transition, Mixed
Deciduous, Oak-hickory
and Subtropical forests;
Southern Appalachians;
and Southern Pinelands

96 Arrowwood
Viburnum dentatum
p. 404
Leaf length: 1½–4"

Mixed Deciduous Forest,
Southern Appalachians,
and Southern Pinelands

Mixed Deciduous and Oak-
hickory forests; Southern
Pinelands, and Subtropical
Forest

Transition, Mixed
Deciduous, and Oak-
hickory forests; Southern
Appalachians; Pine
Barrens; and Southern
Pinelands

Subtropical Forest and
Southern Pinelands

| 100 Southern Bayberry | *Myrica cerifera*
p. 406 | Leaf length: 1½–3½" |

Subtropical Forest and
Southern Pinelands

| 101 Balsam Poplar | *Populus balsamifera*
p. 407 | Leaf length: 3–5" |

Boreal and Transition
forests

| 102 Cockspur Hawthorn | *Crataegus crus-galli*
p. 407 | Leaf length: 1–4" |

Mixed Deciduous and Oak-
hickory forests; Southern
Pinelands

103 Blackhaw

Viburnum prunifolium
p. 408

Leaf length: 1½–3"

Mixed Deciduous and Oak-hickory forests

104 Yaupon

Ilex vomitoria
p. 409

Leaf length: ¾–1¼"

Subtropical Forest and Southern Pinelands

105 American Holly

Ilex opaca
p. 409

Leaf length: 2–4"

Mixed Deciduous and Subtropical forests; Southern Appalachians; and Southern Pinelands

106 Chinkapin Oak

Quercus muehlenbergii
p. 410

Leaf length: 4–6″

Mixed Deciduous and
Oak-hickory forests

107 Chestnut Oak

Quercus prinus
p. 411

Leaf length: 4–8″

Mixed Deciduous Forest,
Southern Appalachians,
and Pine Barrens

108 Overcup Oak

Quercus lyrata
p. 411

Leaf length: 5–8″

Oak-hickory Forest and
Southern Pinelands

109 White Oak

Quercus alba
p. 412

Leaf length: 4–9″

Mixed Deciduous and Oak-
hickory forests; Southern
Appalachians; and Pine
Barrens

110 Bur Oak

Quercus macrocarpa
p. 412

Leaf length: 4–10″

Transition, Mixed
Deciduous, and Oak-
hickory forests

111 Post Oak

Quercus stellata
p. 413

Leaf length: 3¼–6″

Mixed Deciduous and Oak-
hickory forests; Southern
Appalachians; and
Southern Pinelands

112 Southern Red Oak — Quercus falcata
p. 413 — Leaf length: 4–8"

Mixed Deciduous and Oak-hickory forests; Southern Appalachians; and Southern Pinelands

113 Black Oak — Quercus velutina
p. 414 — Leaf length: 4–9"

Mixed Deciduous and Oak-hickory forests; Southern Appalachians; Pine Barrens; and Southern Pinelands

114 Shumard Oak — Quercus shumardii
p. 415 — Leaf length: 3–7"

Mixed Deciduous and Oak-hickory forests; Southern Pinelands

115 Scarlet Oak   *Quercus coccinea*   Leaf length: 3–7"
p. 415

Transition, Mixed
Deciduous, and Oak-
hickory forests; Southern
Appalachians; and Pine
Barrens

116 Pin Oak   *Quercus palustris*   Leaf length: 3–5"
p. 416

Mixed Deciduous and Oak-
hickory forests; Southern
Appalachians

117 Blackjack Oak   *Quercus marilandica*   Leaf length: 2½–5"
p. 416

Mixed Deciduous and Oak-
hickory forests; Southern
Appalachians; Pine
Barrens; and Southern
Pinelands

118 Northern Red Oak   *Quercus rubra*
   p. 417   Leaf length: 4–9″

Transition, Mixed
Deciduous, and Oak-
hickory forests; Southern
Appalachians

119 Silver Maple   *Acer saccharinum*
   p. 417   Leaf length: 4–6″

Transition, Mixed
Deciduous, and Oak-
hickory forests; Southern
Appalachians

120 Red Maple   *Acer rubrum*
   p. 418   Leaf length: 2½–4″

All eastern forests

| 121 Sugar Maple | *Acer saccharum*
p. 419 | Leaf length: 3½–5½" |

| 122 Sweetgum | *Liquidambar*
styraciflua
p. 420 | Leaf length: 3–6" |

Transition, Mixed
Deciduous, and Oak-
hickory forests; Southern
Appalachians

Mixed Deciduous and Oak-
hickory forests; Southern
Appalachians; and
Southern Pinelands

| 123 Yellow-poplar | *Liriodendron tulipifera*
p. 420 | Leaf length: 3–6" |

Mixed Deciduous Forest,
Southern Appalachians;
and Southern Pinelands

124 Sycamore

Platanus occidentalis
p. 421

Leaf length: 4–8″

Mixed Deciduous and Oak-hickory forests; Southern Appalachians; and Southern Pinelands

125 White Mulberry

Morus alba
p. 422

Leaf length: 2½–7″

Widely cultivated in parks and gardens

126 Sassafras

Sassafras albidum
p. 422

Leaf length: 3–5″

Mixed Deciduous, Oak-hickory, and Subtropical forests; Southern Appalachians; Pine Barrens; and Southern Pinelands

127 Southeastern Coralbean

Erythrina herbacea
p. 423

Leaflet length: 1½–3″

Subtropical Forest

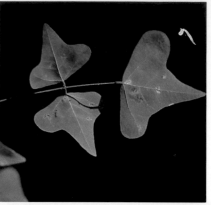

128 Lime Prickly-ash

Zanthoxylum fagara
p. 424

Leaflet length: ⅜–1″

Subtropical Forest

129 Black Locust

Robinia pseudoacacia
p. 424

Leaflet length: 1–1¾″

Mixed Deciduous and Oak-hickory forests; Southern Appalachians

130 American Mountain-ash

Sorbus americana
p. 425

Leaflet length: 1½–4″

Boreal and Transition forests; Southern Appalachians

131 Yellow Buckeye

Aesculus octandra
p. 426

Leaflet length: 4–8″

Mixed Deciduous Forest and Southern Appalachians

132 Shagbark Hickory

Carya ovata
p. 426

Leaflet length: 3–7″

Mixed Deciduous and Oak-hickory forests; Southern Appalachians; and Pine Barrens

133 Boxelder

Acer negundo
p. 427

Leaflet length: 2–4"

Transition, Mixed
Deciduous, and Oak-
hickory forests; Southern
Appalachians

134 White Ash

Fraxinus americana
p. 428

Leaflet length: 2½–5"

Transition, Mixed
Deciduous, and Oak-
hickory forests; Southern
Appalachians; and
Southern Pinelands

135 Bitternut Hickory

Carya cordiformis
p. 428

Leaflet length: 2–6"

Transition, Mixed
Deciduous, and Oak-
hickory forests; Southern
Appalachians; Pine
Barrens; and Southern
Pinelands

Mixed Deciduous, Oak-
hickory, and Subtropical
forests; Southern
Appalachians; Pine
Barrens; and Southern
Pinelands

Mixed Deciduous and Oak-
hickory forests; Southern
Appalachians, and
Southern Pinelands

Transition, Mixed
Deciduous, and Oak-
hickory forests; Southern
Appalachians

139 Pecan   *Carya illinoensis*   Leaflet length: 2–7"
p. 431

Oak-hickory Forest and
Southern Pinelands

140 Black Walnut   *Juglans nigra*   Leaflet length: 2½–5"
p. 432

Mixed Deciduous and Oak-
hickory forests; Southern
Appalachians

141 Shining Sumac   *Rhus copallina*   Leaflet length: 1–3¼"
p. 433

Mixed Deciduous, Oak-
hickory, and Subtropical
forests; Southern
Appalachians; Pine
Barrens; and Southern
Pinelands

142 Smooth Sumac *Rhus glabra* Leaflet length: 2–4″
p. 433

All eastern forests except
Subtropical

143 Staghorn Sumac *Rhus typhina* Leaflet length: 2–4″
p. 434

Transition and Mixed
Deciduous forests

144 Cabbage Palmetto *Sabal palmetto* Leaf length: 4–7′
p. 435

Subtropical Forest

| 145 Southeastern Coralbean | *Erythrina herbacea* p. 423 | Flower length: 2″ |

Subtropical Forest

| 146 Eastern Redbud | *Cercis canadensis* p. 382 | Flower length: ½″ |

Mixed Deciduous, Oak-hickory, and Subtropical forests; Southern Appalachians; and Southern Pinelands

| 147 Catawba Rhododendron | *Rhododendron catawbiense* p. 369 | Flower width: 2¼″ |

Mixed Deciduous Forest and Southern Appalachians

148 Mountain-laurel
Kalmia latifolia
p. 370
Flower width: ¾–1″

Mixed Deciduous Forest,
Southern Appalachians;
Pine Barrens; and Southern
Pinelands

149 Northern Catalpa
Catalpa speciosa
p. 381
Flower length: 2–2¼″

Mixed Deciduous Forest

150 Rosebay Rhododendron
Rhododendron maximum
p. 372
Flower width: 1½″

Mixed Deciduous Forest
and Southern Appalachians

151 American Plum   *Prunus americana*   Flower width: ¾–1″
                         p. 395

Mixed Deciduous and Oak-
hickory forests; Southern
Appalachians

152 Pin Cherry   *Prunus pensylvanica*   Flower width: ½″
                         p. 396

Boreal and Transition
forests; Southern
Appalachians

153 Black Cherry   *Prunus serotina*   Flower width: ⅜″
                         p. 400

Transition, Mixed
Deciduous, and Oak-
hickory forests; Southern
Appalachians; Pine
Barrens; and Southern
Pinelands

154 Nannyberry   *Viburnum lentago*   Flower width: ¼"
p. 393

Transition and Mixed
Deciduous forests

155 Downy Hawthorn   *Crataegus mollis*   Flower width: to 1"
p. 389

Mixed Deciduous and Oak-
hickory forests

156 Carolina Silverbell   *Halesia carolina*   Flower length: ½–1"
p. 401

Mixed Deciduous Forest
and Southern Appalachians

157 Black Locust

Robinia pseudoacacia
p. 424

Flower length: ¾"

Mixed Deciduous and Oak-hickory forests; Southern Appalachians

158 Downy Serviceberry

Amelanchier arborea
p. 393

Flower width: 1¼"

Transition, Mixed Deciduous, and Oak-hickory forests; Southern Appalachians

159 Sweetbay

Magnolia virginiana
p. 371

Flower width: 2–2½"

Subtropical Forest, Pine Barrens, and Southern Pinelands

Transitional, Mixed
Deciduous, and Oak-
hickory forests; Southern
Appalachians; and
Southern Pinelands

Subtropical Forest and
Southern Pinelands

Mixed Deciduous Forest,
Southern Appalachians,
and Southern Pinelands

163 Buttonbush

Cephalanthus occidentalis
p. 380

Flower length: ⅝"

All eastern forests

164 Huisache

Acacia farnesiana
p. 435

Flower length: ³⁄₁₆"

Southern Pinelands

165 Witch-hazel

Hamamelis virginiana
p. 403

Flower width: 1"

Transition, Mixed
Deciduous, Oak-hickory,
and Subtropical forests;
Southern Appalachians;
and Southern Pinelands

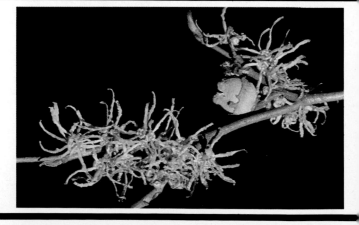

166 Sweet Birch   *Betula lenta*   Flowers: tiny, in catkins 3–4″
                     p. 391

Mixed Deciduous Forest
and Southern Appalachians

167 Eastern Hophornbeam   *Ostrya virginiana*   Flowers: tiny, in clusters to 2½″
                     p. 390

Transition, Mixed
Deciduous, and Oak-
hickory forests; Southern
Appalachians; and
Southern Pinelands

168 Shining Sumac   *Rhus copallina*   Flower width: ⅛″
                     p. 433

Mixed Deciduous, Oak-
hickory, and Subtropical
forests; Southern
Appalachians; Pine
Barrens; and Southern
Pinelands

169 Black Spruce

Picea mariana
p. 361

Cone length: ⅝–1¼"

Boreal and Transition
forests

170 White Spruce

Picea glauca
p. 360

Cone length: 1¼–2½"

Boreal Forest

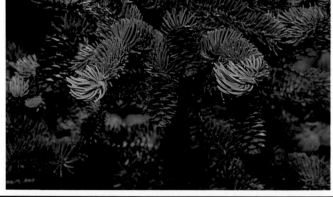

171 Red Spruce

Picea rubens
p. 362

Cone length: 1¼–1½"

Transition Forest and
Southern Appalachians

172 Balsam Fir   *Abies balsamea*   Cone length: 2–3¼"
                        p. 363

Boreal and Transition
forests

173 Pitch Pine   *Pinus rigida*   Cone length: 1¼–2¾"
                        p. 358

Southern Appalachians and
Pine Barrens

174 Shortleaf Pine   *Pinus echinata*   Cone length: 1½–2½"
                            p. 357

Mixed Deciduous and Oak-
hickory forests; Southern
Appalachians; Pine
Barrens; and Southern
Pinelands

175 Eastern White Pine
Pinus strobus
p. 355

Cone length: 4–8"

Transition and Mixed
Deciduous forests;
Southern Appalachians

176 Eastern Hophornbeam
Ostrya virginiana
p. 390

Fruit length: 1½–2"

Transition, Mixed
Deciduous, and Oak-
hickory forests; Southern
Appalachians; and
Southern Pinelands

177 Slippery Elm
Ulmus rubra
p. 402

Fruit length: ½–¾"

Transition, Mixed
Deciduous, and Oak-
hickory forests

178 White Ash

Fraxinus americana
p. 428

Fruit length: 1–2″

Transition, Mixed
Deciduous, and Oak-
hickory forests; Southern
Appalachians; and
Southern Pinelands

179 Silver Maple

Acer saccharinum
p. 417

Fruit length: 1½–2½″

Transition, Mixed
Deciduous, and Oak-
hickory forests; Southern
Appalachians

180 Red Maple

Acer rubrum
p. 418

Fruit length: ¾–1″

All eastern forests

Mixed Deciduous and Oak-
hickory forests; Southern
Pinelands

182 Sweetgum *Liquidambar styraciflua* Fruit diameter: 1–1¹⁄₄″
p. 420

Mixed Deciduous and Oak-
hickory forests; Southern
Appalachians; and
Southern Pinelands

183 Sycamore *Platanus occidentalis* Fruit diameter: 1″
p. 421

Mixed Deciduous and Oak-
hickory forests; Southern
Appalachians; and
Southern Pinelands

184 Pawpaw

Asimina triloba
p. 379

Fruit length: 3–5"

Mixed Deciduous and Oak-
hickory forests; Southern
Appalachians

185 Common Persimmon

Diospyros virginiana
p. 377

Fruit diameter: ¾–1½"

Mixed Deciduous, Oak-
hickory, and Subtropical
forests; Southern
Appalachians and Southern
Pinelands

186 American Plum

Prunus americana
p. 395

Fruit diameter: ¾–1"

Mixed Deciduous and Oak-
hickory forests; Southern
Appalachians

187 Eastern Burningbush

Euonymus atropurpureus
p. 394

Fruit width: ⅝″

Mixed Deciduous and Oak-hickory forests

188 Hackberry

Celtis occidentalis
p. 391

Fruit diameter: ¼–⅜″

Mixed Deciduous and Oak-hickory forests

189 Pin Cherry

Prunus pensylvanica
p. 396

Fruit diameter: ¼″

Boreal and Transition forests; Southern Appalachians

190 Flowering Dogwood
Cornus florida
p. 375

Fruit length: ⅜–⅝″

Transition, Mixed
Deciduous, and Oak-
hickory forests; Southern
Appalachians; and
Southern Pinelands

191 Yaupon
Ilex vomitoria
p. 409

Fruit diameter: ¼″

Subtropical Forest and
Southern Pinelands

192 Winterberry
Ilex decidua
p. 436

Fruit diameter: ¼″

Oak-hickory Forest and
Southern Pinelands

Mixed Deciduous and
Subtropical forests;
Southern Appalachians;
and Southern Pinelands

Boreal and Transition
forests; Southern
Appalachians

Transition and Mixed
Deciduous forests

1　5　Arrowwood　　*Viburnum dentatum*　　Fruit length: ¼–⅜″
　　　　　　　　　　　　p. 404

Mixed Deciduous Forest,
Southern Appalachians,
and Southern Pinelands

197　Smooth Sumac　　*Rhus glabra*　　Fruit diameter: ⅛″
　　　　　　　　　　　　p. 433

All eastern forests except
Subtropical

198　Staghorn Sumac　　*Rhus typhina*　　Fruit diameter: ³⁄₁₆″
　　　　　　　　　　　　p. 434

Transition and Mixed
Deciduous forests

199 Pignut Hickory

Carya glabra
p. 429

Fruit length: 1–2"

Mixed Deciduous, Oak-hickory, and Subtropical forests; Southern Appalachians; Pine Barrens; and Southern Pinelands

200 Butternut

Juglans cinerea
p. 430

Fruit length: 1½–2½"

Transition, Mixed Deciduous, and Oak-hickory forests; Southern Appalachians

201 Black Walnut

Juglans nigra
p. 432

Fruit diameter: 1½–2½"

Mixed Deciduous and Oak-hickory forests; Southern Appalachians

Mixed Deciduous Forest
and Southern Appalachians

Transition, Mixed
Deciduous, Oak-hickory,
and Subtropical forests;
Southern Appalachians;
and Southern Pinelands

Transition, Mixed
Deciduous, and Oak-
hickory forests; Southern
Appalachians; and
Southern Pinelands

Transition, Mixed
Deciduous, and Oak-
hickory forests

206 **White Oak**   *Quercus alba*   Acorn length: ⅜–1¼"
                     p. 412

Mixed Deciduous and Oak-
hickory forests; Southern
Appalachians; and Pine
Barrens

207 **Scarlet Oak**   *Quercus coccinea*   Acorn length: ½–1"
                       p. 415

Transition, Mixed
Deciduous, and Oak-
hickory forests; Southern
Appalachians; and Pine
Barrens

208 Black Oak

Quercus velutina
p. 414

Acorn length: ⅝–¾″

Mixed Deciduous and Oak-hickory forests; Southern Appalachians; Pine Barrens; and Southern Pinelands

209 Northern Red Oak

Quercus rubra
p. 417

Acorn length: ⅝–1⅛″

Transition, Mixed Deciduous, and Oak-hickory forests; Southern Appalachians

210 Chinkapin Oak

Quercus muehlenbergii
p. 410

Acorn length: ½–1″

Mixed Deciduous and Oak-hickory forests

Mixed Deciduous, Oak-hickory, and Subtropical forests; Southern Appalachians; Pine Barrens; and Southern Pinelands

Transition and Mixed Deciduous forests

Transition, Mixed Deciduous, and Oak-hickory forests; Southern Appalachians; and Southern Pinelands

214 Flowering Dogwood *Cornus florida* p. 375 Leaf length: 2½–5″

Transition, Mixed Deciduous, and Oak-hickory forests; Southern Appalachians; and Southern Pinelands

215 American Beech *Fagus grandifolia* p. 398 Leaf length: 2½–5″

Transition, Mixed Deciduous, and Oak-hickory forests; Southern Appalachians; and Southern Pinelands

216 American Hornbeam *Carpinus caroliniana* p. 399 Leaf length: 2–4½″

Transition, Mixed Deciduous, Oak-hickory, and Subtropical forests; Southern Appalachians; and Southern Pinelands

217 Nannyberry

Viburnum lentago
p. 393

Leaf length: 2½–4"

Transition and Mixed
Deciduous forests

218 Pin Cherry

Prunus pensylvanica
p. 396

Leaf length: 2½–4½"

Boreal and Transition
forests; Southern
Appalachians

219 Sourwood

Oxydendrum arboreum
p. 402

Leaf length: 4–7"

Mixed Deciduous Forest
and Southern Appalachians

220 Eastern Burningbush

Euonymus atropurpureus
p. 394

Leaf length: 2–4½"

Mixed Deciduous and Oak-hickory forests

221 Downy Serviceberry

Amelanchier arborea
p. 393

Leaf length: 1½–4"

Transition, Mixed Deciduous, and Oak-hickory forests; Southern Appalachians

222 Bigtooth Aspen

Populus grandidentata
p. 384

Leaf length: 2½–4"

Boreal, Transition, and Mixed Deciduous forests

Mixed Deciduous and Oak-hickory forests; Southern Appalachians, Pine Barrens; and Southern Pinelands

Transition, Mixed Deciduous, and Oak-hickory forests; Southern Appalachians; and Pine Barrens

Mixed Deciduous and Oak-hickory forests; Southern Appalachians; Pine Barrens; and Southern Pinelands

226 Sweetgum

Liquidambar styraciflua p. 420

Leaf length: 3–6"

Mixed Deciduous and Oak-hickory forests; Southern Appalachians; and Southern Pinelands

227 Sugar Maple

Acer saccharum p. 419

Leaf length: 3½–5½"

Transition, Mixed Deciduous, and Oak-hickory forests; Southern Appalachians

228 Red Maple

Acer rubrum p. 418

Leaf length: 2½–4"

All eastern forests

229 Yellow-poplar
Liriodendron tulipifera Leaf length: 3–6"
p. 420

Mixed Deciduous Forest,
Southern Appalachians,
and Southern Pinelands

230 Sweetgum
Liquidambar styraciflua Leaf length: 3–6"
p. 420

Mixed Deciduous and Oak-
hickory forests, Southern
Appalachians, and
Southern Pinelands

231 Sassafras
Sassafras albidum Leaf length: 3–5"
p. 422

Mixed Deciduous, Oak-
hickory, and Subtropical
forests; Southern
Appalachians; Pine
Barrens; and Southern
Pinelands

232 Pignut Hickory
Carya glabra
p. 429
Leaflet length: 3–6″

Mixed Deciduous, Oak-
hickory, and Subtropical
forests; Southern
Appalachians; Pine
Barrens; and Southern
Pinelands

233 Shagbark Hickory
Carya ovata
p. 426
Leaflet length: 3–7″

Mixed Deciduous and Oak-
hickory forests; Southern
Appalachians; and Pine
Barrens

234 Eastern Hophornbeam
Ostrya virginiana
p. 390
Leaf length: 2–5″

Transition, Mixed
Deciduous, and Oak-
hickory forests; Southern
Appalachians; and
Southern Pinelands

235 Sweet Birch

Betula lenta
p. 391

Leaf length: 2½–5″

Mixed Deciduous Forest
and Southern Appalachians

236 American Beech

Fagus grandifolia
p. 398

Leaf length: 2½–5″

Transition, Mixed
Deciduous, and Oak-
hickory forests; Southern
Appalachians; and
Southern Pinelands

237 Witch-hazel

Hamamelis virginiana
p. 403

Leaf length: 3–5″

Transition, Mixed
Deciduous, Oak-hickory,
and Subtropical forests;
Southern Appalachians;
and Southern Pinelands

238 Paper Birch *Betula papyrifera* Leaf length: 2–4"
p. 385

Boreal and Transition
forests

239 American Basswood *Tilia americana* Leaf length: 3–6"
p. 388

Transition, Mixed
Deciduous, and Oak-
hickory forests; Southern
Appalachians

240 Eastern Cottonwood *Populus deltoides* Leaf length: 3–7"
p. 384

Mixed Deciduous and Oak-
hickory forests; Southern
Pinelands

241 Eastern Screech-Owl *Otus asio*   Length: 10"
p. 438

All eastern forests except
Boreal

242 Great Horned Owl *Bubo virginianus*   Length: 25"
p. 438

All eastern forests

243 Long-eared Owl *Asio otus*   Length: 15"
p. 438

Boreal, Mixed Deciduous,
and Oak-hickory forests

244 Barred Owl | *Strix varia* p. 439 | Length: 20″

All eastern forests

245 Great Gray Owl | *Strix nebulosa* p. 439 | Length: 24–33″

Boreal Forest

246 Northern Saw-whet Owl | *Aegolius acadicus* p. 440 | Length: 7″

Boreal, Transition, and Mixed Deciduous forests; Pine Barrens

247 Ruffed Grouse
Bonasa umbellus
p. 440
Length: 16–19"

Boreal and Transition forests; Southern Appalachians; and Pine Barrens

248 Spruce Grouse
Dendragapus canadensis
p. 441
Length: 15–17"

Boreal Forest

249 Wild Turkey
Meleagris gallopavo
p. 441
Length: males 48"; females 36"

Mixed Deciduous, Oak-hickory, and Subtropical forests; Southern Appalachians; Pine Barrens; Southern Pinelands

250 American Woodcock
Scolopax minor
p. 442
Length: 11″

All eastern forests

251 Chuck-will's-widow
Caprimulgus carolinensis
p. 442
Length: 12″

Oak-hickory and
Subtropical forests;
Southern Appalachians;
Pine Barrens; Southern
Pinelands

252 Whip-poor-will
Caprimulgus vociferus
p. 443
Length: 10″

Transition, Mixed
Deciduous, and Oak-
hickory forests; Pine
Barrens

253 Sharp-shinned Hawk
Accipiter striatus
p. 443

Length: 10–14"

All eastern forests except Subtropical

254 Cooper's Hawk
Accipiter cooperii
p. 443

Length: 14–20"

All eastern forests

255 Northern Goshawk
Accipiter gentilis
p. 444

Length: 20–26"

Boreal Forest

| 256 Red-shouldered Hawk | *Buteo lineatus* p. 445 | Length: 16–24" |

Transition, Mixed Deciduous, Oak-hickory, and Subtropical forests; Southern Appalachians; Southern Pinelands

| 257 Broad-winged Hawk | *Buteo platypterus* p. 445 | Length: 13–15" |

All eastern forests except Subtropical

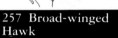

| 258 Red-tailed Hawk | *Buteo jamaicensis* p. 445 | Length: 18–25" |

All eastern forests

259 American Swallow-tailed Kite
Elanoides forficatus
p. 446
Length: 22–24"

Southern Pinelands and
Subtropical Forest

260 Mississippi Kite
Ictinia mississippiensis
p. 446
Length: 12–14"

Oak-hickory Forest and
Southern Pinelands

261 Wood Stork
Mycteria americana
p. 447
Length: 40–44"

Southern Pinelands and
Subtropical Forest

262 Wood Duck
Aix sponsa
p. 447
Length: 17–20"

All eastern forests

263 Common Loon
Gavia immer
p. 448
Length: 28–36"

Boreal and Transition
forests

264 Anhinga
Anhinga anhinga
p. 448
Length: 34–36"

Southern Pinelands and
Subtropical Forest

265 Common Raven
Corvus corax
p. 449
Length: 21–27"

Boreal Forest and Southern
Appalachians

266 American Crow
Corvus brachyrhynchos
p. 449
Length: 17–21"

All eastern forests

267 Dark-eyed Junco
Junco hyemalis
p. 450
Length: 5–6½"

Boreal and Transition
forests

268 Black-billed Cuckoo *Coccyzus*   Length: 12"
                              erythropthalmus
                              p. 450

Transition, Mixed
Deciduous, and Oak-
hickory forests

269 White-crowned *Columba leucocephala* Length: 13"
Pigeon   *p. 451*

Subtropical Forest

270 Mourning Dove *Zenaida macroura* Length: 12"
                        p. 451

All eastern forests

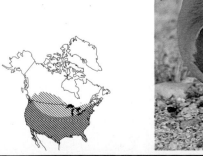

| 271 Pileated Woodpecker | *Dryocopus pileatus* p. 451 | Length: 17″ |

All eastern forests

| 272 Red-headed Woodpecker | *Melanerpes erythrocephalus* p. 452 | Length: 10″ |

All eastern forests

| 273 Red-bellied Woodpecker | *Melanerpes carolinus* p. 452 | Length: 10″ |

Mixed Deciduous, Oak-hickory, and Subtropical forests; Southern Appalachians; and Southern Pinelands

274 Yellow-bellied Sapsucker *Sphyrapicus varius* Length: 8½"
p. 453

Boreal and Transition forests

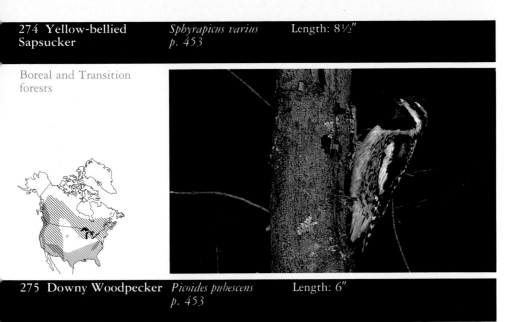

275 Downy Woodpecker *Picoides pubescens* Length: 6"
p. 453

All eastern forests

276 Hairy Woodpecker *Picoides villosus* Length: 9"
p. 454

All eastern forests

277 Northern Flicker

Colaptes auratus
p. 454

Length: 12″

All eastern forests

278 Red-cockaded Woodpecker

Picoides borealis
p. 455

Length: 8″

Mixed Deciduous and Subtropical forests, Southern Appalachians; and Southern Pinelands

279 Black-backed Woodpecker

Picoides arcticus
p. 455

Length: 9″

Boreal Forest

280 Gray Kingbird

Tyrannus dominicensis   Length: 9"
p. 455

Southern Pinelands and
Subtropical Forest

28. Eastern Wood-Pewee

Contopus virens   Length: 6½"
p. 456

All eastern forests

28. Olive-sided Flycatcher

Contopus borealis   Length: 7½"
p. 456

Boreal and Transition
forests

283 Red-eyed Vireo
Vireo olivaceus
p. 457
Length: 5½–6½"

All eastern forests

284 Worm-eating Warbler
Helmitheros vermivorus
p. 457
Length: 5½"

Mixed Deciduous and Oak-hickory forests; Southern Appalachians

285 White-eyed Vireo
Vireo griseus
p. 457
Length: 5"

Mixed Deciduous, Oak-hickory, and Subtropical forests; Southern Appalachians; Pine Barrens; Southern Pinelands

286 Hooded Warbler *Wilsonia citrina* Length: 5½"
p. 458

Mixed Deciduous and Oak-hickory forests; Southern Appalachians; Pine Barrens; Southern Pinelands

287 Kentucky Warbler *Oporornis formosus* Length: 5½"
p. 458

Mixed Deciduous and Oak-hickory forests; Southern Appalachians; and Southern Pinelands

288 Tennessee Warbler *Vermivora peregrina* Length: 5"
p. 459

Boreal Forest

| **289 Solitary Vireo** | *Vireo solitarius*
p. 459 | Length: 5–6" |

Boreal and Transition
forests; Southern
Appalachians

| **290 Yellow-throated**
Vireo | *Vireo flavifrons*
p. 460 | Length: 6" |

Transition, Mixed
Deciduous, and Oak-
hickory forests; Southern
Appalachians; Pine
Barrens; Southern
Pinelands

| **291 Black-throated**
Green Warbler | *Dendroica virens*
p. 460 | Length: 5" |

Boreal and Transition
forests; Southern
Appalachians

292 Pine Warbler

Dendroica pinus
p. 460

Length: 5½"

Transition, Mixed Deciduous, and Subtropical forests; Southern Appalachians; Pine Barrens; Southern Pinelands

293 Prairie Warbler

Dendroica discolor
p. 461

Length: 5"

All eastern forests except Boreal

294 Yellow-breasted Chat

Icteria virens
p. 461

Length: 6½–7½"

Mixed Deciduous and Oak-hickory forests; Southern Appalachians; Pine Barrens; Southern Pinelands

295 Canada Warbler
Wilsonia canadensis
p. 462
Length: 5"

Boreal and Transition
forests

296 Northern Parula
Parula americana
p. 462
Length: 4½"

All eastern forests except
Boreal

297 Red-breasted Nuthatch
Sitta canadensis
p. 463
Length: 4½–4¾"

Boreal and Transition
forests; Southern
Appalachians

| 298 Magnolia Warbler | *Dendroica magnolia* p. 463 | Length: 5″ |

Boreal and Transition forests

| 299 Yellow-throated Warbler | *Dendroica dominica* p. 463 | Length: 5″ |

Mixed Deciduous and Oak-hickory forests; Southern Appalachians; and Southern Pinelands

| 300 Kirtland's Warbler | *Dendroica kirtlandii* p. 464 | Length: 6″ |

Transition Forest

301 Yellow-rumped Warbler *Dendroica coronata* Length: 5–6"
p. 464

Boreal and Transition
forests

302 Chestnut-sided Warbler *Dendroica pensylvanica* Length: 5"
p. 465

Boreal and Transition
forests; Southern
Appalachians

303 Cape May Warbler *Dendroica tigrina* Length: 5"
p. 465

Boreal Forest

304 Blackburnian Warbler

Dendroica fusca
p. 466

Length: 5"

Boreal and Transition forests; Southern Appalachians

305 Evening Grosbeak

Coccothraustes vespertinus
p. 466

Length: 7½–8½"

Boreal Forest

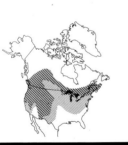

306 American Redstart

Setophaga ruticilla
p. 467

Length: 4½–5½"

Boreal, Transition, Mixed Deciduous, and Oak-hickory forests; Southern Appalachians; Pine Barrens

307 American Robin
Turdus migratorius
p. 467
Length: 9–11"

All eastern forests except
Subtropical

308 Rufous-sided Towhee
Pipilo erythrophthalmus
p. 468
Length: 7–9½"

All eastern forests except
Boreal

309 Northern Oriole
Icterus galbula
p. 468
Length: 7–8½"

Transition, Mixed
Deciduous, and Oak-
hickory forests; Southern
Appalachians

310 Bay-breasted Warbler
Dendroica castanea
p. 469
Length: 5½"

Boreal Forest

311 Cedar Waxwing
Bombycilla cedrorum
p. 469
Length: 6½–8"

Boreal, Transition, and Mixed Deciduous forests

312 Red Crossbill
Loxia curvirostra
p. 470
Length: 5¼–6½"

Boreal and Transition forests; Pine Barrens

313 Purple Finch

Carpodacus purpureus
p. 470

Length: 5½–6½"

Boreal and Transition
forests

314 Pine Grosbeak

Pinicola enucleator
p. 471

Length: 8–10"

Boreal Forest

315 White-winged Crossbill

Loxia leucoptera
p. 471

Length: 6–6½"

Boreal Forest

316 Rose-breasted Grosbeak
Pheucticus ludovicianus   Length: 8"
p. 471

Boreal, Transition, and
Mixed Deciduous forests;
Southern Appalachians

317 Scarlet Tanager
Piranga olivacea   Length: 7½"
p. 472

Transition, Mixed
Dedicuous, and Oak-
hickory forests; Southern
Appalachians

318 Summer Tanager
Piranga rubra   Length: 7–8"
p. 472

Mixed Deciduous, Oak-
hickory and Subtropical
forests; Southern
Appalachians; and
Southern Pinelands

319 Northern Cardinal
Cardinalis cardinalis Length: 8–9"
p. 473

Northern Transition, Mixed Deciduous, Oak-hickory, and Subtropical forests; Southern Appalachians; Pine Barrens; Southern Pinelands

320 Painted Bunting
Passerina ciris Length: 5½"
p. 473

Southern Pinelands and Subtropical Forest

321 Ruby-throated Hummingbird
Archilochus colubris Length: 3½"
p. 474

All eastern forests

Boreal and Transition forests; Southern Appalachians

Subtropical Forest

All eastern forests

325 Blue-gray Gnatcatcher
Polioptila caerulea
p. 476
Length: 4½–5″

Mixed Deciduous, Oak-hickory, and Subtropical forests; Southern Appalachians; Southern Pinelands

326 Ruby-crowned Kinglet
Regulus calendula
p. 476
Length: 3¾–4½″

Boreal Forest

327 Acadian Flycatcher
Empidonax virescens
p. 477
Length: 6″

Mixed Deciduous and Oak-hickory forests; Southern Appalachians; and Southern Pinelands

328 Brown-headed Nuthatch
Sitta pusilla
p. 477
Length: 4–5"

Southern Pinelands and Subtropical Forest

329 Tufted Titmouse
Parus bicolor
p. 477
Length: 6"

Transition, Mixed Deciduous, and Oak-hickory forests; Southern Appalachians; Pine Barrens; Southern Pinelands

330 Gray Jay
Perisoreus canadensis
p. 478
Length: 10–13"

Boreal Forest

331 Northern Shrike   *Lanius excubitor*   Length: 9–10½"
p. 478

Boreal Forest

332 Carolina Chickadee   *Parus carolinensis*   Length: 4–5"
p. 479

Mixed Deciduous and Oak-
hickory forests; Southern
Appalachians; Pine
Barrens; Southern
Pinelands

**333 Black-capped
Chickadee**   *Parus atricapillus*   Length: 4¾–5¾"
p. 479

Boreal and Transition
forests

334 White-breasted Nuthatch

Sitta carolinensis
p. 480

Length: 5–6"

Transition, Mixed Deciduous, and Oak-hickory forests; Southern Appalachians; Pine Barrens; Southern Pinelands

335 Blackpoll Warbler

Dendroica striata
p. 480

Length: 5½"

Boreal Forest

336 Black-and-white Warbler

Mniotilta varia
p. 481

Length: 5"

Boreal, Transition, Mixed Deciduous, and Oak-hickory forests; Southern Appalachians; Pine Barrens

Boreal and Transition
forests; Southern
Appalachians

Boreal and Transition
forests; Pine Barrens

Boreal and Transition
forests

Boreal Forest

All eastern forests

All eastern forests except
Boreal

343 Veery
Catharus fuscescens
p. 484
Length: 6½–7¼"

Transition Forest and
Southern Appalachians

344 Hermit Thrush
Catharus guttatus
p. 484
Length: 6½–7½"

Boreal and Transition
forests

345 Swainson's Thrush
Catharus ustulatus
p. 485
Length: 6½–7¾"

Boreal Forest

346 Ovenbird
Seiurus aurocapillus
p. 485
Length: 6"

Boreal, Transition, and
Mixed Deciduous forests;
Pine Barrens

347 Winter Wren
Troglodytes troglodytes
p. 485
Length: 4–4½"

Boreal and Transition
forests

348 Brown Creeper
Certhia americana
p. 486
Length: 5–5¾"

Boreal and Transition
forests; Pine Barrens

349 Luna Moth
Actias luna
p. 488
Wingspan: 3⅛–4½"

Transition, Mixed
Deciduous, and Oak-
hickory forests; Southern
Appalachians

Host Plants
Foliage of hickory (*Carya*),
walnut (*Juglans*),
sweetgum (*Liquidambar*),
persimmon (*Diospyros*),
birch (*Betula*), and others

350 Veined White
Artogeia napi
p. 488
Wingspan: 1½–1⅝"

Boreal and Transition
forests

Host Plants
Cresses (*Thlaspi, Arabis,*
and *Barbarea*) and
toothwarts (*Dentaria*)

351 Rosy Maple Moth
Dryocampa rubicunda
p. 489
Wingspan: 1⅛–2"

Transition, Mixed
Deciduous, and Oak-
hickory forests; Southern
Appalachians

Host Plants
Foliage of red and silver
maples (*Acer rubrum* and *A.
saccharinum*)

352 Florida White

Appias drusilla
p. 489

Wingspan: 1⅝–2⅛"

Subtropical Forest

Host Plants
Capers (*Capparis*) and
Guiana plum (*Drypetes
lateriflora*)

353 Falcate Orangetip

Anthocharis midea
p. 490

Wingspan: 1⅜–1½"

Transition, Mixed
Deciduous, and Oak-
hickory forests; Southern
Appalachians; Pine
Barrens; and Southern
Pinelands

Host Plants
Various cresses (*Arabis,
Cardamine,* and *Barbarea*),
hedge mustard
(*Sisymbrium*), and
shepherd's purse (*Capsella
bursapastoris*)

354 Gypsy Moth

Lymantria dispar
p. 490

Wingspan: ¾" (males); 1⅛–2¾"
(females)

Transition, Mixed
Deciduous, and Oak-
hickory forests; Pine
Barrens

Host Plants
Deciduous and evergreen
trees including oak
(*Quercus*), pine (*Pinus*), and
hemlock (*Tsuga*)

355 Spotted Tiger Moth
Halisidota maculata
p. 491
Wingspan: 1⅜–2″

Transition, Mixed Deciduous, and Oak-hickory forests; Southern Appalachians

Host Plants
Foliage of poplar (*Populus*), maple (*Acer*), and other trees

356 Pepper-and-salt Skipper
Amblyscirtes hegon
p. 491
Wingspan: ⅞–1″

Transition Forest and Southern Appalachians

Host Plants
Indian grass (*Sarghastrum nutans*, *S. secundum*) and Kentucky bluegrass (*Poa pratensis*)

357 White-marked Tussock Moth
Orgyia leucostigma
p. 492
Wingspan: 1⅛–1¼″ (males); ½–⅝″ (females, wingless body)

Mixed Deciduous and Oak-hickory forests; Southern Appalachians

Host Plants
Foliage of a great variety of trees and shrubs

358 Promethea Moth
Callosamia promethea
p. 492
Wingspan: 2¾–4″

Transition, Mixed
Deciduous, and Oak-
hickory forests

Host Plants
Variety of trees and shrubs
including spicebush
(*Lindera benzoin*), wild
cherry (*Prunus serotina*), and
sassafras (*Sassafras albidum*)

359 Carolina Satyr
Hermeuptychia sosybius
p. 493
Wingspan: 1⅛–1⅝″

Southern Pinelands and
Subtropical Forest

Host Plants
Various grasses (Poaceae)

360 Polyphemus Moth
Antheraea polyphemus
p. 493
Wingspan: 3½–5½″

Mixed Deciduous and
Subtropical forests;
Southern Pinelands

Host Plants
Leaves of many trees
including alder (*Alnus*),
basswood (*Tilia*), birch
(*Betula*), chestnut
(*Castanea*), elm (*Ulmus*),
hickory (*Carya*), maple
(*Acer*), poplar (*Populus*), and
sycamore (*Platanus*)

361 Little Wood Satyr   *Megisto cymela*   Wingspan: 1¾–1⅞"
p. 494

All eastern forests

Host Plants
Grasses (Poaceae) and
possibly sedges
(Cyperaceae)

362 Large Wood Nymph   *Cercyonis pegala*   Wingspan: 2–2⅞"
p. 495

All eastern forests

Host Plants
Various grasses (Poaceae)

363 Palmetto Skipper   *Euphyes arpa*   Wingspan: 1⅜–1¾"
p. 496

Southern Pinelands and
Subtropical Forest

Host Plant
Saw palmetto (*Serenoa
repens*)

364 Hobomok Skipper
Poanes hobomok
p. 496
Wingspan: 1–1⅜"

Transition, Mixed
Deciduous, and Oak-
hickory forests; Southern
Appalachians

Host Plants
Grasses (Poaceae)

365 Leonardus Skipper
Hesperia leonardus
p. 497
Wingspan: ⅞–1⅜"

Transition, Mixed
Deciduous, and Oak-
hickory forests; Southern
Appalachians; Pine
Barrens; and Southern
Pinelands

Host Plants
Bent grass (*Agrostis*), panic
grass (*Panicum*), and
tumble grass (*Eragrostis*)

366 Hackberry Butterfly
Asterocampa celtis
p. 497
Wingspan: 1¾–2¼"

Transition and Mixed
Deciduous forests;
Southern Appalachians;
and Southern Pinelands

Host Plant
Hackberry trees (*Celtis*)
only

All eastern forests

Host Plants
Nettles (*Urtica*) best known, but other species in family Urticaceae such as pelletories (*Partetaria*), false nettles (*Boehmeria*), and hops (*Humulus*)

All eastern forests

Host Plants
Include spicebush (*Lindera benzoin*), sassafras (*Sassafras albidum*), and various bays (*Persea*)

All eastern forests

Host Plants
Many broadleaf deciduous plants including willow (*Salix*), elm (*Ulmus*), hackberry (*Celtis*), and cottonwood (*Populus*)

All eastern forests

Host Plants
Favorites include willows
and cottonwoods
(Salicaceae), birches
(Betulaceae), ashes
(*Fraxinus*), many cherries
(*Prunus*), and tulip-poplars
(*Liriodendron tulipifera*)

Southern Pinelands and
Subtropical Forest

Host Plants
Passionflowers (*Passiflora*)

Southern Pinelands

Host Plants
Red bay (*Persea borbonia*),
sassafras (*Sassafras albidum*),
and sweet bay (*Magnolia
virginiana*)

373 Hammock Skipper   *Polygonus leo*   Wingspan: 1¾–2″
p. 502

Subtropical Forest

Host Plants
Jamaica dogwood
(*Ichthyomethia*) and pongam
(*Pongamia*)

374 Florida Purplewing   *Eunica tatila*   Wingspan: 1⅝–2″
p. 502

Subtropical Forest

Host Plants
Unknown

375 Spring Azure   *Celastrina ladon*   Wingspan: ¾–1¼″
p. 503

All eastern forests

Host Plants
Many flowers, especially
dogwoods (*Cornus*),
viburnum (*Viburnum*),
ceanothus (*Ceanothus*),
blueberries (*Vaccinium*),
black snakeroot (*Cimicifuga
racemosa*), and
meadowsweets (*Spiraea*)

376 Banded Hairstreak
Satyrium calanus
p. 503
Wingspan: 1–1¼"

Mixed Deciduous Forest
and Southern Pinelands

Host Plants
Vary regionally, including
walnuts (*Juglans*),
hickories (*Carya*), and oaks
(*Quercus*); shagbark hickory
(*Carya ovata*) preferred in
Connecticut

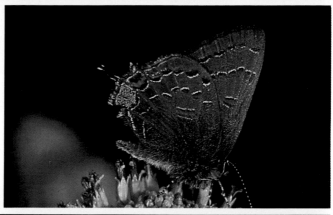

377 Big Poplar Sphinx
Pachysphinx modesta
p. 504
Wingspan: 3½–5½"

Transition, Mixed
Deciduous, and Oak-
hickory forests; Southern
Appalachians and Southern
Pinelands

Host Plants
Foliage of poplar (*Populus*)
and willows (*Salix*)

378 Hickory Hairstreak
Satyrium caryaevorus
p. 505
Wingspan: 1–1¼"

Transition and Mixed
Deciduous forests

Host Plants
Hickories (*Carya*), also
reported on ashes
(*Fraxinus*); perhaps other
broadleaf trees

379 Eastern Eyed Click Beetle
Alaus oculatus
p. 507
Length: 1–1¾″

Mixed Deciduous and Oak-hickory forests

Food
Roots of various plants; small animals in soil

380 Common Black Ground Beetles
Pterostichus spp.
p. 507
Length: ½–⅝″

All eastern forests

Food
Caterpillars and other soft insects

381 Black-horned Pine Borer
Callidium antennatum
p. 507
Length: ⅜–½″

All eastern forests

Food
Sapwood of pines (*Pinus*), spruce (*Picea*), and other conifers

382 Horned Fungus Beetle

Bolitotherus cornutus
p. 508

Length: ⅜–½″

Transition, Mixed Deciduous, Oak-hickory, and Subtropical forests; Southern Appalachians; Pine Barrens; and Southern Pinelands

Food
Fungus tissue, particularly woody bracket type on dead tree trunks

383 Elephant Stag Beetle

Lucanus elephus
p. 508

Length: 1¾–2⅜″ (males); 1⅛–1⅜″ (females)

Mixed Deciduous and Oak-hickory forests; Southern Appalachians

Food
Plant juices; honeydew produced by aphids (Aphididae); wet decaying wood

384 Bark Beetles

Scolytus spp.
p. 509

Length: ⅛–¼″

All eastern forests and pinelands

Food
Inner bark of various trees including hickory and pecan (*Carya*) and walnut (*Juglans*)

385 Divergent Metallic Wood Borer

Dicerca divaricata
p. 509

Length: ⅜–⅞″

Boreal, Transition, Mixed Deciduous, and Oak-hickory forests; Southern Appalachians

Food
Many kinds of dying and dead trees

386 Twig Pruners

Elaphidionoides spp.
p. 509

Length: ⅜–⅝″

Transition, Mixed Deciduous, and Oak-hickory forests; Southern Appalachians

Food
Tender wood of twigs

387 Slender Checkered Beetles

Cymatodera spp.
p. 510

Length: ¼–⅜″

Transition, Mixed Deciduous, Oak-hickory, and Subtropical forests; Southern Appalachians; Pine Barrens; and Southern Pinelands

Food
Gall wasps (Cynipidae) and their larvae

388 Red Flat Bark Beetle

Cucujus clavipes
p. 510

Length: ³⁄₈–¹⁄₂″

All eastern forests

Food
Larvae of bark beetles
(*Scolytus*) and wood borers
(Bostrichidae)

389 Oak Timberworm Beetle

Arrhenodes minutus
p. 511

Length: ¹⁄₄–1¹⁄₈″

Transition, Mixed
Deciduous, and Oak-
hickory forests; Southern
Appalachians

Food
Fungi, other insects, wood,
and liquid exuded by wood

390 Cylindrical Hardwood Borer

Neoclytus acuminatus
p. 511

Length: ¹⁄₄–³⁄₄″

All eastern forests

Food
Oak (*Quercus*), hickory
(*Carya*), ash (*Fraxinus*),
other hardwoods, and
unseasoned lumber

391 American Carrion Beetle

Silpha americana
p. 512

Length: ⅝–⅞″

Transition, Mixed Deciduous, Oak-hickory, and Subtropical forests; Southern Appalachians; Pine Barrens; and Southern Pinelands

Food
Drying carrion, rat-size and larger; larvae of flies (Diptera), and small larvae of other beetles (Coleoptera)

392 Pennsylvania Firefly

Photuris pennsylvanicus
p. 512

Length: ⅜–⅝″

Transition, Mixed Deciduous, Oak-hickory, and Subtropical forests; Southern Appalachians; Pine Barrens; and Southern Pinelands

Food
Soft-bodied insects, snails, slugs, mites

393 Pine and Spruce Engraver Beetles

Ips spp.
p. 512

Length: ⅛–¼″

All eastern forests and pinelands

Food
Cambium and phloem tissues of inner bark

394 Goldsmith Beetle *Cotalpa lanigera* Length: ¾–1″
  p. 513

Transition, Mixed
Deciduous, Oak-hickory,
and Subtropical forests;
Southern Appalachians;
Pine Barrens; and Southern
Pinelands

Food
Foliage and roots,
especially poplar (*Populus*)

395 Dogwood *Calligrapha* Length: ⅜″
Calligrapha *philadelphica*
  p. 513

Transition, Mixed
Deciduous, and Oak-
hickory forests; Southern
Appalachians

Food
Foliage of dogwood
(*Cornus*), basswood (*Tilia*),
elm (*Ulmus*), and other
trees

396 Eastern Black Oak *Curculio baculi* Length: ¼″
Acorn Weevil *p. 514*

Mixed Deciduous and Oak-
hickory forests; Southern
Appalachians

Food
Acorns of black oak
(*Quercus velutina*) and other
oaks

397 Florida Hunting Wasp

Palmodes dimidiatus
p. 514

Length: ¾–⅞"

All eastern forests

Food
Nectar; camel crickets
(Gryllacrididae) and long-
horned grasshoppers
(Tettigoniidae)

398 Giant Ichneumons

Megarhyssa spp.
p. 514

Length: 1–1½" (males); 1⅜–3"
(females)

All eastern forests

Food
Larvae of Pigeon Horntail
(*Tremex columba*) and related
borers

399 Tree-hole Mosquito

Aedes triseriatus
p. 515

Length: ¼–⅜"

All eastern forests

Food
Plant juices, blood of
mammals and birds;
microscopic aquatic plants
and algae

400 Pigeon Horntail

Tremex columba
p. 515

Length: 1–1½"

Transition, Mixed
Deciduous, and Oak-
hickory forests; Southern
Appalachians; and
Southern Pinelands

Food
Nectar; fungus-infected
wood of elm (*Ulmus*), beech
(*Fagus*), maple (*Acer*), oak
(*Quercus*), and other
deciduous trees

401 Yellow Jackets

Vespula spp.
p. 516

Length: ½–⅝"

All eastern forests and
pinelands

Food
Nectar; insects

402 Cicada Killer

Sphecius speciosus
p. 516

Length: 1⅛–1⅝"

All eastern forests

Food
Nectar; cicadas (Cicadidae)

403 Giant Hornet
Vespa crabro germana
p. 517
Length: ¾–1⅛"

Transition and Mixed
Deciduous forests;
Southern Appalachians

Food
Nectar; other insects

404 Honey Bee
Apis mellifera
p. 517
Length: ⅝" (male drones); ¾" (queen);
⅜–⅝" (sterile female workers)

All eastern forests

Food
Nectar; honey; royal jelly
secreted by workers

405 Red-tailed Bumble Bee
Bombus ternarius
p. 518
Length: ⅜–½" (male drones); ⅜–½"
(workers); ½–¾" (spring queen)

Transition and Mixed
Deciduous forests;
Southern Appalachians

Food
Nectar; honey

406 Black Flies
Simulium spp.
p. 519
Length: 1/16–1/8"

All eastern forests and
pinelands except
Subtropical Forest

Food
Nectar; blood of birds and
mammals; diatoms and
bacteria

407 Deer Flies
Chrysops spp.
p. 519
Length: 3/8–5/8"

All eastern forests and
pinelands

Food
Plant juices; blood of
mammals; small aquatic
insects

408 Mason Bees
Osmia spp.
p. 520
Length: 3/8–1/2"

All eastern forests

Food
Nectar; pollen

409 Oak Lace Bug
Corythuca arcuata
p. 520
Length: ⅛"

Transition, Mixed Deciduous, Oak-hickory, and Subtropical forests; Southern Appalachians; Pine Barrens; and Southern Pinelands

Food
Sap from foliage and young stems of oaks (*Quercus*) and other trees

410 Black Pine Sawyer
Monochamus scutellatus
p. 521
Length: ⅝–1"

Boreal and Transition forests; Pine Barrens; and Southern Pinelands

Food
Bark of small twigs; inner wood of pine (*Pinus*)

411 Fungus Gnats
Mycetophila spp.
p. 521
Length: ⅛–¼"

All eastern forests

Food
Flowers, fungi, decaying wood, and other wet plant matter

412 Buffalo Treehoppers
Stictocephala spp.
p. 522

Length: ⅜″

All eastern forests

Food
Alfalfa (*Medicago sativa*) and low succulent plants; also willow (*Salix*), elm (*Ulmus*), cherry (*Prunus*), locust (*Robinia*), and orchard trees; sometimes potato (*Solanum tuberosum*), tomato (*Lycopersicon*), clover (Fabaceae), goldenrod (*Solidago*), and aster (*Aster*)

413 True Katydid
Pterophylla camellifolia
p. 522

Length: 1¾–2⅛″

Transition, Mixed Deciduous, Oak-hickory, and Subtropical forests; Southern Appalachians; Pine Barrens; and Southern Pinelands

Food
Foliage of deciduous trees

414 Black-horned Tree Cricket
Oecanthus nigricornis
p. 522

Length: ½″

Transition, Mixed Deciduous, and Oak-hickory forests; Southern Appalachians

Food
Aphids (Aphididae), caterpillars; leaves, flowers, young fruit

415 Dogday Harvestfly

Tibicen canicularis
p. 523

Length: 1⅛–1¼"

Transition Forest

Food
Root juices, especially pine
(*Pinus*)

416 Periodical Cicadas

Magicicada spp.
p. 523

Length: 1⅛"

Transition, Mixed
Deciduous, and Oak-
hickory forests; Southern
Appalachians

Food
Sap of tree roots

417 Carolina Mantid

Stagmomantis carolina
p. 524

Length: 2⅜"

Mixed Deciduous Forest
and Southern Pinelands

Food
Butterflies and moths
(Lepidoptera), flies
(Diptera), small wasps and
bees (Hymenoptera), true
bugs (Hemiptera), and
caterpillars

418 Northern Walkingstick

Diapheromera femòrata
p. 524

Length: 3″ (males); 3¾″ (females)

Southern Pinelands

Food
Foliage of deciduous trees and shrubs, especially oaks (*Quercus*) and hazelnuts (*Corylus*)

419 Oyster Shell Scale

Lepidosaphes ulmi
p. 525

Length: ⅛″

Transition and Mixed Deciduous forests; Southern Appalachians

Food
Juices of woody vegetation including vines, and apple (*Malus*), pear (*Pyrus*), plum (*Prunus*), ash (*Fraxinus*), elm (*Ulmus*), and maple (*Acer*) trees

420 American Tent Caterpillar

Malacosoma americanum
p. 525

Length: 2″

All eastern forests and pinelands

Food
Foliage of cherry and plum (*Prunus*), apple (*Malus*), hawthorn (*Crataegus*), and other trees

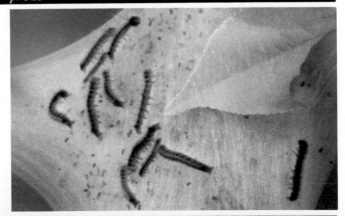

421 Eastern Daddy-long-legs   *Leiobunum* spp.   Length: ¼–⅜″
p. 526

All eastern forests

Food
Minute insects, mites, and plant juices

422 Golden-silk Spider   *Nephila clavipes*   Length: ⅛″ (males); ⅞–1″ (females)
p. 526

Subtropical Forest and Southern Pinelands

Food
Flying insects

423 Eastern Wood Ticks   *Dermacentor* spp.   Length: ⅛″
p. 527

All eastern forests and pinelands

Food
Larger animals and blood of mammals, especially deer (Cervidae); rodents (Rodentia)

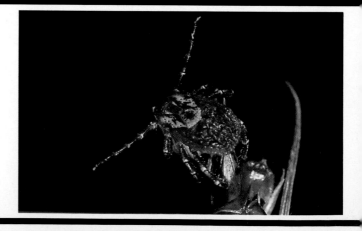

424 Wandering Spiders *Ctenus* spp. Length: ¼–⅞″ (males); ⅜–1″
                           p. 527 (females)

Southern Pinelands

Food
Insects

425 Forest Wolf Spider *Lycosa gulosa* Length: ⅜″ (males); ⅜–½″ (females)
                            p. 528

Transition, Mixed
Deciduous, and Oak-
hickory forests; Southern
Appalachians

Food
Small insects

426 Metaphid Jumping *Metaphidippus* spp. Length: ⅛–¼″ (males); ⅛–¼″
Spiders   *p. 528* (females)

All eastern forests

Food
Small insects

| 427 Wild Sarsaparilla | *Aralia nudicaulis*
p. 530 | Plant height: 8–15"
Flower width: 1½–2" |

Boreal, Transition, Mixed
Deciduous, and Oak-
hickory forests; Southern
Appalachians

| 428 White Baneberry | *Actaea pachypoda*
p. 530 | Plant height: 1–2'
Flower width: about ¼" |

Transition Forest, Southern
Appalachians, and
Southern Pinelands

| 429 Red Baneberry | *Actaea rubra*
p. 530 | Plant height: 1–2'
Flower width: about ¼" |

Boreal and Transition
forests

| 430 Foamflower | *Tiarella cordifolia* | Plant height: 6–12″ |
| | *p. 531* | Flower width: ¼″ |

Transition and Mixed
Deciduous forests;
Southern Appalachians

| 431 Devil's Bit | *Chamaelirium luteum* | Plant height: 1–4′ |
| | *p. 531* | Flower length: about ⅛″ |

Transition and Mixed
Deciduous forests;
Southern Appalachians

| 432 False Solomon's Seal | *Smilacina racemosa* | Plant height: 1–3′ |
| | *p. 532* | Flower length: ⅛″ |

Transition, Mixed
Deciduous, and Oak-
hickory forests

433 Poison Ivy

Rhus radicans
p. 532

Vine
Flower width: ⅛"

All eastern forests

434 Early Meadow Rue

Thalictrum dioicum
p. 533

Plant height: 8–30"
Flower width: about ¼"

Transition, Mixed Deciduous, and Oak-hickory forests; Southern Appalachians

435 Goldthread

Coptis groenlandica
p. 533

Plant height: 3–6"
Flower width: ½"

Boreal and Transition forests

| 436 Mountain Laurel | *Kalmia latifolia*
p. 533 | Plant height: 3–15'
Flower width: ³⁄₄–1" |

Transition and Mixed
Deciduous forests;
Southern Appalachians;
Pine Barrens; and Southern
Pinelands

| 437 Great Laurel | *Rhododendron*
maximum
p. 534 | Plant height: 5–35'
Flower width: 1½–2" |

Transition and Mixed
Deciduous forests;
Southern Appalachians

| 438 Highbush Blueberry | *Vaccinium corymbosum*
p. 534 | Plant height: 5–15'
Flower length: ¹⁄₄–½" |

Transition and Mixed
Deciduous forests;
Southern Appalachians;
and Pine Barrens

439 Mayapple

Podophyllum peltatum
p. 535

Plant height: 12–18"
Flower width: 2"

All eastern forests

440 Bloodroot

Sanguinaria canadensis
p. 535

Plant height: to 10"
Flower width: to 1½"

Boreal, Transition, and
Subtropical forests;
Southern Pinelands

441 Wood Anemone

Anemone quinquefolia
p. 536

Plant height: 4–8"
Flower width: 1"

Transition and Mixed
Deciduous forests;
Southern Appalachians

| 442 **Sweet White Violet** | *Viola blanda*
p. 536 | Plant height: 3–5″
Flower width: about ½″ |

Transition and Mixed
Deciduous forests;
Southern Appalachians

| 443 **Starflower** | *Trientalis borealis*
p. 536 | Plant height: 4–8″
Flower width: about ½″ |

Boreal, Transition, and
Mixed Deciduous forests

| 444 **Partridgeberry** | *Mitchella repens*
p. 537 | Creeper
Flower length: ½–⅔″ |

All eastern forests

| 445 **Bunchberry** | *Cornus canadensis* p. 537 | Plant height: 3–8″ Flower width: about 1½″ |

Boreal, Transition, and
Mixed Deciduous forests

| 446 **Large-flowered Trillium** | *Trillium grandiflorum* p. 538 | Plant height: 8–18″ Flower width: 2–4″ |

Transition and Mixed
Deciduous forests;
Southern Appalachians

| 447 **Painted Trillium** | *Trillium undulatum* p. 538 | Plant height: 8–20″ Flower width: 2–2½″ |

Transition Forest and
Southern Appalachians

448 Showy Orchis	*Orchis spectabilis* p. 539	Plant height: 5–12″ Flower length: 1″

Transition, Mixed
Deciduous and Oak-
hickory forests; Southern
Appalachians

449 Indian Pipe	*Monotropa uniflora* p. 539	Plant height: 3–9″ Flower length: ½–1″

All eastern forests

450 Dutchman's Breeches	*Dicentra cucullaria* p. 539	Plant height: 4–12″ Flower length: ¾″

Transition, Mixed
Deciduous, and Oak-
hickory forests; and
Southern Appalachians

451 Shinleaf	*Pyrola elliptica* *p. 540*	Plant height: 5–10" Flower width: about ⅔"

Boreal and Transition
forests

452 Canada Mayflower	*Maianthemum* *canadense* *p. 540*	Plant height: 2–6" Flower length: about ⅙"

Boreal and Transition
forests; Southern
Appalachians

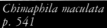

453 Spotted Wintergreen	*Chimaphila maculata* *p. 541*	Plant height: 3–9" Flower width: about ⅔"

Transition and Mixed
Deciduous forests;
Southern Appalachians;
and Pine Barrens

| 454 Indian Cucumber Root | *Medeola virginiana* p. 541 | Plant height: 1–2½″ Flower length: ½″ |

Transition, Mixed Deciduous, and Oak-hickory forests; Southern Appalachians; Southern Pinelands

| 455 Bluebead Lily | *Clintonia borealis* p. 542 | Plant height: 6–15″ Flower length: ¾–1″ |

Boreal, Transition, and Mixed Deciduous forests; Southern Appalachians

| 456 Jack-in-the-pulpit | *Arisaema triphyllum* p. 542 | Plant height: 1–3′ Flower length: 2–3″ |

Mixed Deciduous and Oak-hickory forests; Southern Appalachians; and Southern Pinelands

| 457 Dutchman's Pipe | *Aristolochia durior*
p. 543 | Vine
Flower length: 2″ |

Mixed Deciduous Forest
and Southern Appalachians

| 458 Spanish Moss | *Tillandsia usneoides*
p. 543 | Epiphyte
Flower length: ½–¾″ |

Subtropical Forest and
Southern Pinelands

| 459 Wild Ginger | *Asarum canadense*
p. 543 | Plant height: 6–12″
Flower width: 1½″ |

Transition, Mixed
Deciduous, and Oak-
hickory forests

| 460 Purple Trillium | *Trillium erectum*
p. 544 | Plant height: 8–16″
Flower width: about 2½″ |

Transition and Mixed
Deciduous forests;
Southern Appalachians

| 461 Flame Azalea | *Rhododendron*
calendulaceum
p. 544 | Plant height: to 15′
Flower width: 1½–2″ |

Mixed Deciduous Forest
and Southern Appalachians

| 462 Wood Lily | *Lilium philadelphicum*
p. 544 | Plant height: 1–3′
Flower width: 2″ |

Transition Forest and
Southern Appalachians

| 463 Trout Lily | *Erythronium* *americanum* p. 545 | Plant height: 4–10" Flower width: 1" |

Transition, Mixed Deciduous, and Oak-hickory forests; Southern Appalachians; and Southern Pinelands

| 464 Woodland Sunflower | *Helianthus strumosus* p. 545 | Plant height: 3–7' Flower width: 2½–3½" |

Transition, Mixed Deciduous, and Oak-hickory forests

| 465 Sessile Bellwort | *Uvularia sessifolia* p. 546 | Plant height: 6–12" Flower length: about 1" |

Transition, Mixed Deciduous, and Oak-hickory forests; Southern Appalachians

466 Downy False Foxglove

Aureolaria virginica
p. 546

Plant height: 1–5′
Flower width: 1″

Transition and Mixed
Deciduous forests;
Southern Pinelands

467 Spicebush

Lindera benzoin
p. 547

Plant height: 6–17′
Flower width: ⅛″

Transition, Mixed
Deciduous, Oak-hickory,
and Subtropical forests;
Southern Pinelands

468 Yellow Lady's Slipper

Cypripedium calceolus
p. 547

Plant height: 4–28″
Flower length: lip about 2″

Boreal, Transition, Mixed
Deciduous, and Oak-
hickory forests; Southern
Appalachians

469 Pinesap

Monotropa hypopitys
p. 547

Plant height: 4–16"
Flower length: about ½"

All eastern forests

470 Pink Lady's Slipper

Cypripedium acaule
p. 548

Plant height: 6–15"
Flower length: lip about 2½"

Boreal, Transition, and
Mixed Deciduous forests;
Southern Appalachians;
and Southern Pinelands

471 Calypso

Calypso bulbosa
p. 548

Plant height: 3–8"
Flower length: 1½–2"

Boreal and Transition
forests

| 472 Twinflower | *Linnaea borealis* p. 549 | Creeper Flower length: ½" |

Boreal, Transition, and
Mixed Deciduous forests

| 473 Sand Myrtle | *Leiophyllum buxifolium* p. 549 | Plant height: 4–20" Flower width: about ¼" |

Southern Appalachians,
Pine Barrens, and Southern
Pinelands

| 474 Wild Columbine | *Aquilegia canadensis* p. 550 | Plant height: 1–2' Flower length: 1–2" |

Transition and Mixed
Deciduous forests;
Southern Appalachians

475 Fringed Polygala

Polygala paucifolia
p. 550

Plant height: 3–7"
Flower length: ¾"

Transition and Mixed
Deciduous forests;
Southern Appalachians

476 Shooting Star

Dodecatheon meadia
p. 551

Plant height: 8–20"
Flower length: 1"

Transition, Mixed
Deciduous, and Oak-
hickory forests; Southern
Appalachians

477 Wild Bleeding Heart

Dicentra eximia
p. 551

Plant height: 10–18"
Flower length: ¾"

Transition Forest and
Southern Appalachians

478 Lousewort

Pedicularis canadensis
p. 551

Plant height: 6–18″
Flower length: ¼″

Transition, Mixed Deciduous, Oak-hickory, and Subtropical forests; Southern Pinelands; and Southern Appalachians

479 Wood Sage

Teucrium canadense
p. 552

Plant height: 1–3′
Flower length: ¼″

Transition and Oak-hickory forests; Southern Pinelands

480 Fireweed

Epilobium angustifolium
p. 552

Plant height: 2–6′
Flower width: 1″

Boreal and Transition forests; Southern Appalachians

481 Large Purple Fringed Orchid *Habenaria fimbriata* Plant height: 2–4'
p. 553 Flower length: 1"

Boreal, Transition, and Mixed Deciduous forests; Southern Appalachians

482 Pinxter Flower *Rhododendron nudiflorum* Plant height: 2–6'
p. 553 Flower width: 1½–2"

Mixed Deciduous Forest, Southern Appalachians, and Southern Pinelands

483 Wild Bergamot *Monarda fistulosa* Plant height: 2–4'
p. 553 Flower length: 1"

Transition, Mixed Deciduous, and Oak-hickory forests; Southern Appalachians

484 Mountain Laurel
Kalmia latifolia
p. 533
Plant height: 3–15'
Flower width: ¾–1"

Transition and Mixed
Deciduous forests;
Southern Appalachians;
Pine Barrens; and Southern
Pinelands

485 Purple-flowering Raspberry
Rubus odoratus
p. 554
Plant height: 3–6'
Flower width: 1–2"

Transition and Mixed
Deciduous forests;
Southern Appalachians

486 Trailing Arbutus
Epigaea repens
p. 554
Creeper
Flower width: about ½"

Boreal and Transition
forests; Southern
Appalachians; and Pine
Barrens

487 Round-lobed Hepatica   *Hepatica americana*   Plant height: 4–6″
p. 555   Flower width: ½–1″

Transition, Mixed
Deciduous, Oak-hickory,
and Subtropical forests;
Southern Appalachians;
and Southern Pinelands

488 Common Wood Sorrel   *Oxalis montana*   Plant height: 3–6″
p. 555   Flower width: ¾″

Boreal and Transition
forests; Southern
Appalachians

489 Spring Beauty   *Claytonia virginica*   Plant height: 6–12″
p. 555   Flower width: ½–¾″

Transition, Mixed
Deciduous, and Oak-
hickory forests; Southern
Appalachians; and
Southern Pinelands

490 Bluets

Houstonia caerulea
p. 556

Plant height: 3–6″
Flower width: about ½″

Transition, Mixed
Deciduous, and Oak-
hickory forests; Southern
Appalachians

491 Bird-foot Violet

Viola pedata
p. 556

Plant height: 4–10″
Flower width: often 1½″

Transition, Mixed
Deciduous, and Oak-
hickory forests; Southern
Appalachians; and
Southern Pinelands

492 Common Blue Violet

Viola papilionacea
p. 557

Plant height: 3–8″
Flower width: ½–¾″

All eastern forests

493 Spring Larkspur | *Delphinium tricorne* p. 557 | Plant height: 4–24″ Flower width: ¾″

Mixed Deciduous and Oak-hickory forests; Southern Appalachians

494 Passionflower | *Passiflora incarnata* p. 558 | Vine Flower width: 1½–2½″

Mixed Deciduous and Subtropical forests; Southern Pinelands

495 Crested Dwarf Iris | *Iris cristata* p. 558 | Plant height: 4–9″ Flower width: about 2½″

Mixed Deciduous and Oak-hickory forests; Southern Appalachians; and Southern Pinelands

496 Fringed Phacelia   *Phacelia fimbriata*   Plant height: 8–16"
p. 559   Flower width: ½"

Southern Appalachians

497 Virginia Bluebells   *Mertensia virginica*   Plant height: 8–24"
p. 559   Flower length: about 1"

Transition, Mixed
Deciduous, and Oak-
hickory forests; Southern
Appalachians

498 Harebell   *Campanula*   Plant height: 6–20"
                   rotundifolia   Flower length: ¾"
                   p. 559

Boreal, Transition, Mixed
Deciduous, and Oak-
hickory forests

499 Mistletoe

*Phoradendron
serotinum*
p. 560

Plant height: 1'
Flower width: about ⅛"

Mixed Deciduous and Oak-
hickory forests; Southern
Pinelands

500 Winterberry

Ilex verticillata
p. 560

Plant height: 3–10'
Flower width: ¼–½"

Transition, Mixed
Deciduous, and Oak-
hickory forests; Southern
Appalachians; and Pine
Barrens

501 White Baneberry

Actaea pachypoda
p. 530

Plant height: 1–2'
Flower width: about ¼"

Transition Forest, Southern
Appalachians, and
Southern Pinelands

502 Winged Sumac *Rhus copallina* Plant height: 3–30′
                       p. 561   Flower length: cluster to 6″

Transition, Mixed
Deciduous, Oak-hickory,
and Subtropical forests;
Southern Appalachians;
Pine Barrens; and Southern
Pinelands

503 Jack-in-the-pulpit *Arisaema triphyllum* Plant height: 1–3′
                            p. 542   Flower length: 2–3″

Mixed Deciduous and Oak-
hickory forests; Southern
Appalachians; and
Southern Pinelands

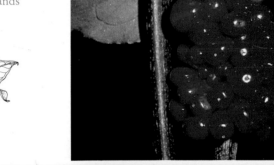

504 Red Baneberry *Actaea rubra* Plant height: 1–2′
                       p. 530   Flower width: about ¼″

Boreal and Transition
forests

Transition, Mixed
Deciduous, and Oak-
hickory forests; Southern
Appalachians; and Pine
Barrens

Boreal, Transition, and
Mixed Deciduous forests

Boreal, Transition, and
Mixed Deciduous forests;
Pine Barrens

| 508 **Partridgeberry** | *Mitchella repens*
p. 537 | Creeper
Flower length: ½–⅔″ |

All eastern forests

| 509 **Bluebead Lily** | *Clintonia borealis*
p. 542 | Plant height: 6–15″
Flower length: ¾–1″ |

Boreal, Transition, and
Mixed Deciduous forests;
Southern Appalachians

| 510 **Highbush Blueberry** | *Vaccinium corymbosum*
p. 534 | Plant height: 5–15′
Flower length: ¼–½″ |

Transition and Mixed
Deciduous forests;
Southern Appalachians;
and Pine Barrens

511 Painted Turtle
Chrysemys picta
p. 563
Length: 4–9⅞"

Transition, Mixed Deciduous, and Oak-hickory forests; Southern Appalachians; Pine Barrens; and Southern Pinelands

512 Eastern Box Turtle
Terrapene carolina
p. 563
Length: 4–8½"

Mixed Deciduous, Oak-hickory, and Subtropical forests; Southern Appalachians; Pine Barrens; and Southern Pinelands

513 Wood Turtle
Clemmys insculpta
p. 563
Length: 5–9"

Transition and Mixed Deciduous forests; Pine Barrens

Transition, Mixed
Deciduous, and Oak-
hickory forests; Southern
Appalachians; Pine
Barrens; and Southern
Pinelands

Mixed Deciduous and Oak-
hickory forests; Southern
Appalachians; Southern
Pinelands

Subtropical Forest and
Southern Pinelands

517 Ground Skink
Scincella lateralis
p. 565
Length: 3–5⅛"

Mixed Deciduous, Oak-hickory, and Subtropical forests; Southern Appalachians; Pine Barrens; and Southern Pinelands

518 Broadheaded Skink
Eumeces laticeps
p. 565
Length: 6½–12¾"

Mixed Deciduous and Oak-hickory forests; Southern Appalachians; Southern Pinelands

519 Green Anole
Anolis carolinensis
p. 566
Length: 5–8"

Subtropical Forest

520 Rough Green Snake   *Opheodrys aestivus*   Length: 20–45⅝"
p. 566

Subtropical Forest, Pine
Barrens, and Southern
Pinelands

521 Racer   *Coluber constrictor*   Length: 34–77"
p. 566

All eastern forests and
pinelands except Boreal
Forest

522 Pine Woods Snake   *Rhadinaea flavilata*   Length: 10–15⅞"
p. 567

Subtropical Forest and
Southern Pinelands

523 Coachwhip
Masticophis flagellum
p. 567
Length: 36–102"

Subtropical Forest and
Southern Pinelands

524 Rat Snake
Elaphe obsoleta
p. 568
Length: 34–101"

Mixed Deciduous, Oak-
hickory, and Subtropical
forests; Southern
Appalachians; Pine
Barrens; and Southern
Pinelands

525 Common Kingsnake
Lampropeltis getulus
p. 568
Length: 36–82"

Mixed Deciduous and
Subtropical forests;
Southern Appalachians;
Southern Pinelands

| **526 Common Garter Snake** | *Thamnophis sirtalis* p. 569 | Length: 18–51⅝″ |

All eastern forests and pinelands

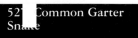

| **52█ Common Garter Snake** | *Thamnophis sirtalis* p. 569 | Length: 18–51⅝″ |

All eastern forests and pinelands

| **528 Eastern Diamondback Rattlesnake** | *Crotalus adamanteus* p. 569 | Length: 36–96″ | ⊗ |

Subtropical Forest and Southern Pinelands

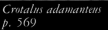

529 Timber Rattlesnake *Crotalus horridus* Length: 35–74½"
p. 570

Mixed Deciduous and Oak-
hickory forests; Southern
Appalachians; Pine
Barrens; and Southern
Pinelands

530 Copperhead *Agkistrodon contortrix* Length: 22–53"
p. 570

Mixed Deciduous and Oak-
hickory forests; Southern
Appalachians; Pine
Barrens; and Southern
Pinelands

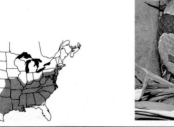

531 Corn Snake *Elaphe guttata* Length: 24–72"
p. 571

Mixed Deciduous, Oak-
hickory, and Subtropical
forests; Southern
Appalachians; Pine
Barrens; and Southern
Pinelands

532 Pigmy Rattlesnake *Sistrurus miliarius* Length: 15–30⅞"
p. 571

Subtropical Forest and
Southern Pinelands

533 Milk Snake *Lampropeltis triangulum* Length: 14–78¼"
p. 572

All eastern forests and
pinelands except Boreal
Forest

534 Eastern Coral Snake *Micrurus fulvius* Length: 22–47½"
p. 572

Subtropical Forest and
Southern Pinelands

| 535 Green Treefrog | *Hyla cinerea*
p. 572 | Length: 1¼–2½" |

Subtropical Forest and
Southern Pinelands

| 536 Carpenter Frog | *Rana virgatipes*
p. 573 | Length: 1⅝–2⅝" |

Pine Barrens and Southern
Pinelands

| 537 Southern Leopard
Frog | *Rana sphenocephala* ♂
p. 573 | Length: 2–5" |

Mixed Deciduous, Oak-
hickory, and Subtropical
forests; Southern Pinelands

Subtropical Forest and
Southern Pinelands

Mixed Deciduous and Oak-
hickory forests; Southern
Appalachians

Transition, Mixed
Deciduous, and Oak-
hickory forests; Southern
Appalachians, Pine
Barrens, and Southern
Pinelands

Pseudacris nigrita
p. 575

Length: ¾–1¼"

Subtropical Forest and
Southern Pinelands

Rana sylvatica
p. 575

Length: 1⅜–3¼"

Boreal, Transition, and
Mixed Deciduous forests;
Pine Barrens

Rana palustris
p. 576

Length: 1¾–3⁷⁄₁₆"

Boreal, Transition, and
Mixed Deciduous forests

544 American Toad *Bufo americanus*　　Length: 2–13/8″
p. 576

Boreal, Transition, Mixed
Deciduous, and Oak-
hickory forests; Southern
Appalachians

545 Southern Toad　*Bufo terrestris*　　Length: 15/8–41/2″
p. 576

Subtropical Forest and
Southern Pinelands

546 Spring Peeper　*Hyla crucifer*　　Length: 3/4–13/8″
p. 577

Boreal, Transition, Mixed
Deciduous, and Oak-
hickory forests; Southern
Appalachians; Pine
Barrens; and Southern
Pinelands

547 Eastern Newt   *Notophthalmus*   Length: 2⅜–5½"
viridescens
p. 577

All habitats

548 Mountain Dusky   *Desmognathus*   Length: 2¾–4⅜"
Salamander   *ochrophaeus*
p. 578

Mixed Deciduous Forest
and Southern Appalachians

549 Appalachian   *Plethodon jordani*   Length: 3¼–7¼"
Woodland Salamander   p. 578

Southern Appalachians

550 Eastern Newt   *Notophthalmus*   Length: 2⅝–5½"
                        viridescens
                        p. 577

All habitats

551 Eastern Tiger   *Ambystoma tigrinum*   Length: 6–13⅜"
Salamander   *tigrinum*
                         p. 579

Mixed Deciduous and Oak-
hickory forests; Southern
Pinelands

552 Marbled Salamander   *Ambystoma opacum*   Length: 3½–5"
                              p. 579

Mixed Deciduous and Oak-
hickory forests; Southern
Appalachians; and Pine
Barrens

553 Destroying Angel

Amanita virosa
p. 581

Height: 3–8"

All eastern forests and pinelands

Habitat
On the ground under hardwoods, or in mixed woods; also in grassy areas near trees

554 Tacky Green Russula

Russula aeruginea
p. 581

Height: 1⅜–2⅜"

All eastern forests and pinelands

Habitat
In deciduous and coniferous woods, particularly under oak, aspen, and lodgepole pine

555 Slimy Gomphidius

Gomphidius glutinosus
p. 581

Height: 2–4"

Boreal and Transition forests; Southern Appalachians

Habitat
On the ground under conifers, primarily spruce

556 Fawn Mushroom

Pluteus cervinus
p. 582

Height: 2–4"

All eastern forests and pinelands

Habitat
Decaying wood, stumps, sawdust, buried wood

557 Brick Tops

*Naematoloma
sublateritium*
p. 582

Height: 2–4"

Transition and Mixed Deciduous forests

Habitat
Stumps and logs of deciduous trees

558 Orange Mycena

Mycena leaiana
p. 582

Height: 1¼–2¾"

Transition and Mixed Deciduous forests; Southern Appalachians

Habitat
In clusters on deciduous wood, in particular on beech

559 Jack O'Lantern
Omphalotus illudens
p. 583
Height: 3–8″

All eastern forests and
pinelands

Habitat
Clustered at the base of
hardwood stumps or buried
roots, most frequently oak

560 Chanterelle
Cantharellus cibarius
p. 583
Height: 1–3″

All eastern forests and
pinelands

Habitat
Mixed woods, or under
conifers or oaks

561 Two-colored Bolete
Boletus bicolor
p. 583
Height: 2–4″

Transition and Mixed
Deciduous forests;
Southern Appalachians

Habitat
Primarily under oaks

562 King Bolete

Boletus edulis
p. 584

Height: 4–10″

Transition and Mixed
Deciduous forests

Habitat
Under conifers, and under
birch and aspen

563 Dotted-stalk Suillus

Suillus granulatus
p. 584

Height: 1⅝–3¼″

Transition Forest and
Southern Appalachians

Habitat
Under various conifers

564 Old Man of the Woods

Strobilomyces floccopus
p. 584

Cap width: 1⅝–6″

Transition and Mixed
Deciduous forests;
Southern Appalachians;
Pine Barrens; and Southern
Pinelands

Habitat
Under hardwoods, conifers,
or in mixed woods

565 Scaly Tooth

Hydnum imbricatum
p. 584

Cap width: 2–8"

All eastern forests and
pinelands

Habitat
In coniferous, deciduous,
and mixed woods

566 Thick-maze Oak Polypore

Daedalea quercina
p. 585

Cap width: 2–6"

Transition and Mixed
Deciduous forests;
Southern Appalachians

Habitat
Primarily oak stumps and
logs

567 Half-free Morel

Morchella semilibera
p. 585

Height: 3⅝–5⅝"

Transition, Mixed
Deciduous, and Oak-
hickory forests; Southern
Appalachians; and
Southern Pinelands

Habitat
Damp ground in open
deciduous woods

Transition and Mixed
Deciduous forests;
Southern Appalachians

Habitat
Near deciduous trees and
stumps

Mixed Deciduous and Oak-
hickory forests; Southern
Appalachians

Habitat
Clustered on fallen
hardwood, primarily oak

Transition, Mixed
Deciduous, and Oak-
hickory forests; Southern
Pinelands

Habitat
Hardwood debris

571 Beefsteak Polypore

Fistulina hepatica
p. 586

Cap width: 3–10″

Transition, Mixed
Deciduous, and Oak-
hickory forests; Southern
Appalachians; Southern
Pinelands

Habitat
Decaying trunks and
stumps of oak, or on base
of living oak

572 Violet Toothed Polypore

Trichaptum biformis
p. 587

Cap width: ⅜–3″

All eastern forests and
pinelands

Habitat
Decaying deciduous trees;
also rarely on coniferous
wood

573 Common Fiber Vase

Thelephora terrestris
p. 587

Cap width: 1–2″

Boreal, Transition, Mixed
Deciduous, and Oak-
hickory forests; Southern
Pinelands

Habitat
Sandy soil under pines; also
on stumps and very young
trees

Transition, Mixed
Deciduous, and Oak-
hickory forests; Southern
Appalachians

Habitat
Hardwood stumps, logs,
and sticks

All eastern forests and
pinelands

Habitat
On decaying wood; very
infrequently on dead leaves
and debris

All eastern forests and
pinelands

Habitat
Decaying wood, especially
poplar, aspen, and willow

577 Pygmy Shrew *Microsorex hoyi* Length: 3⅛–3⅞″
p. 590

Boreal and Transition
forests

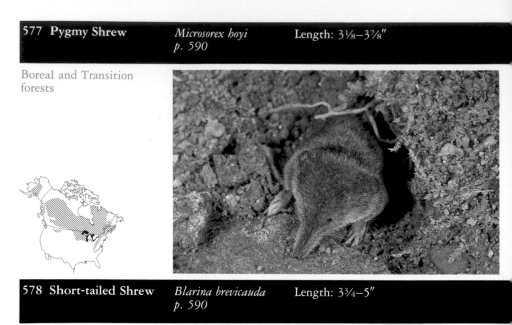

578 Short-tailed Shrew *Blarina brevicauda* Length: 3¾–5″
p. 590

Boreal, Transition, and
Mixed Deciduous forests;
Southern Appalachians

579 White-footed Mouse *Peromyscus leucopus* Length: 6⅛–8⅛″
p. 590

Transition, Mixed
Deciduous, and Oak-
hickory forests; Southern
Appalachians

Boreal, Transition, Mixed
Deciduous, and Oak-
hickory forests; Southern
Appalachians

Mixed Deciduous and
Subtropical forests;
Southern Pinelands

Mixed Deciduous and
Subtropical forests;
Southern Pinelands

583 Woodland Vole

Microtus pinetorum
p. 592

Length: 4⅛–5¾"

All eastern forests except
Boreal

584 Woodland Jumping Mouse

Napaeozapus insignis
p. 592

Length: 8–10"

Boreal and Transition
forests

585 Eastern Chipmunk

Tamias striatus
p. 592

Length: 8½–11¾"

Boreal, Transition, Mixed
Deciduous, and Oak-
hickory forests; Southern
Appalachians; Pine
Barrens; Southern
Pinelands

586 Red Squirrel

Tamiasciurus hudsonicus
p. 593

Length: 10⅝–15¼″

Boreal and Transition forests; Southern Appalachians

587 Fox Squirrel

Sciurus niger
p. 593

Length: 17⅞–27½″

All eastern forests except Boreal Forest

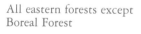

588 Gray Squirrel

Sciurus carolinensis
p. 594

Length: 16⅞–19¾″

All eastern forests except Boreal Forest

589 Southern Flying Squirrel　　*Glaucomys volans*　p. 594　　Length: 8¼–10″

All eastern forests except
Boreal Forest

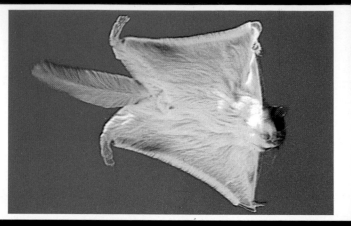

590 Southern Flying Squirrel　　*Glaucomys volans*　p. 594　　Length: 8¼–10″

All eastern forests except
Boreal Forest

591 Northern Flying Squirrel　　*Glaucomys sabrinus*　p. 595　　Length: 10⅜–14½″

Boreal and Transition
forests

| 592 Snowshoe Hare | *Lepus americanus* p. 595 | Length: 15–20½" |

Boreal and Transition
forests

| 593 New England Cottontail | *Sylvilagus transitionalis* p. 596 | Length: 14¼–19" |

Transition and Mixed
Deciduous forests;
Southern Appalachians

| 594 Eastern Cottontail | *Sylvilagus floridanus* p. 596 | Length: 14¾–18¼" |

All eastern forests except
Boreal

595 Woodchuck

Marmota monax
p. 597

Length: 16½–32¼"

Boreal, Transition, and
Mixed Deciduous forests;
Southern Appalachians

596 Hoary Bat

Lasiurus cinereus
p. 597

Length: 4–6"

All eastern forests except
Subtropical Forest

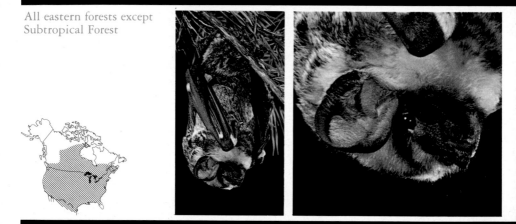

597 Beaver

Castor canadensis
p. 597

Length: 35½–46"

All eastern forests except
Subtropical Forest

598 Nine-banded Armadillo
Dasypus novemcinctus
p. 598
Length: 24¼–31½″

Subtropical Forest and Southern Pinelands

599 Marten
Martes americana
p. 598
Length: 19¼–26⅞″

Boreal and Transition forests

600 Virginia Opossum
Didelphis virginiana
p. 599
Length: 25⅜–40″

Transition, Mixed Deciduous, Oak-hickory, and Subtropical forests; Southern Appalachians; Pine Barrens; Southern Pinelands

Long-tailed Weasel *Mustela frenata* Length: 11–21¾"
p. 600

Transition, Mixed
Deciduous, and Oak-
hickory forests; Pine
Barrens; Southern
Pinelands

602 Ermine *Mustela erminea* Length: 7½–13½"
p. 600

Boreal and Transition
forests

603 Fisher *Martes pennanti* Length: 31⅛–40¾"
p. 601

Boreal and Transition
forests

604 Ermine

Mustela erminea
p. 600

Length: 7½–13½"

Boreal and Transition
forests

605 Striped Skunk

Mephitis mephitis
p. 601

Length: 20½–31½"

All eastern forests

606 Eastern Spotted Skunk

Spilogale putorius
p. 602

Length: 13½–22¼"

All eastern forests except
Boreal

607 Raccoon
Procyon lotor
p. 602
Length: 23¾–37⅜"

All eastern forests

608 Wolverine
Gulo gulo
p. 603
Length: 31½–44¼"

Boreal Forest

609 Black Bear
Ursus americanus
p. 604
Length: 4½–6¼'

Boreal, Transition, and
Subtropical forests;
Southern Appalachians

610 Gray Wolf
Canis lupus
p. 604
Length: 39½–80⅝"

Boreal Forest

611 Gray Fox
Urocyon cinereoargenteus
p. 605
Length: 31½–44¼"

All eastern forests except Boreal Forest

612 Red Fox
Vulpes vulpes
p. 605
Length: 35⅜–40⅜"

All eastern forests

613 Bobcat
Felis rufus
p. 606
Length: 28–49⅜"

Transition, Mixed
Deciduous, and Subtropical
forests; Southern
Appalachians; Southern
Pinelands

614 Lynx
Felis lynx
p. 607
Length: 29⅛–41⅞"

Boreal and Transition
forests

615 Wild Boar
Sus scrofa
p. 607
Length: 4½–6'

Southern Appalachians

616 White-tailed Deer
Odocoileus virginianus   Length: 4½–6¾'
p. 608

All eastern forests

617 Moose
Alces alces   Length: 6¾–9'
p. 609

Boreal Forest

618 Caribou
Rangifer tarandus   Length: 4½–6¾'
p. 610

Boreal Forest

TREES

At any time of the year, a walk through the eastern forests will reveal an interesting variety of trees. In the fall, the brilliant colors of maples, oaks, and other hardwoods light up the landscape; in spring, the fresh bright green of their new leaves is always a welcome sight. The stately evergreen trees of the north offer a shady retreat on a hot summer day, and look magnificent in a mantle of fresh white snow. Included here are descriptions of many of the typical trees of the East.

Eastern White Pine
Pinus strobus
19, 175

The largest northeastern conifer, a magnificent evergreen tree with straight trunk and crown of horizontal branches, 1 row added a year, becoming broad and irregular.
Height: 100' (33 m), formerly 150' (46 m) or more.
Diameter: 3–4' (0.9–1.2 m) or more.
Needles: evergreen; 2½–5" (6–13 cm) long; 5 in bundle; whorled; slender; blue-green.
Bark: gray; smooth becoming rough; thick and deeply furrowed into narrow scaly ridges.
Cones: 4–8" (10–20 cm) long; narrowly cylindrical; yellow-brown; long-stalked; cone-scales thin, rounded, flat.

Habitat
Well-drained sandy soils; sometimes in pure stands.

Range
SE. Manitoba east to Newfoundland, south to N. Georgia, and west to NE. Iowa; a variety in Mexico. From near sea level to 2000' (610 m); in the southern Appalachians to 5000' (1524 m).

Comments
The largest conifer and formerly the most valuable tree of the Northeast, Eastern White Pine is used for construction, millwork, trim, and pulpwood. Younger trees and plantations have replaced the once seemingly inexhaustible lumber supply of virgin forests. The tall straight trunks were prized for ship masts in the colonial period. It is the state tree of Maine, the Pine Tree State; the pine cone and tassel are the state's floral emblem.

Longleaf Pine
Pinus palustris
20

Large tree with the longest needles and largest cones of any eastern pine and an open, irregular crown of a few spreading branches, 1 row added each year.
Height: 80–100' (24–30 m). Diameter: 2–2½' (0.6–0.8 m).
Needles: evergreen; mostly 10–15" (25–38 cm) long, on small plants to 18" (46 cm). Densely crowded; 3 in bundle; whorled; slightly stout, flexible; spreading to drooping; dark green.
Bark: orange-brown, furrowed into scaly plates; on small trunks, gray and rough.
Twigs: dark brown; very stout, ending in large white bud.
Cones: 6–10" (15–25 cm) long; narrowly conical or cylindrical; dull brown; almost stalkless; opening and shedding at maturity; cone-scales raised, keeled, with small prickle.

Habitat
Well-drained sandy soils of flatlands and sandhills; often in pure stands.

Range
Coastal Plain from SE. Virginia to E. Florida, and west to E. Texas. Usually below 600' (183 m); to 2000' (610 m) in foothills of Piedmont.

Comments
Longleaf Pine is a leading world producer of naval stores. The trees are tapped for turpentine and resin and then logged for construction lumber, poles and pilings, and pulpwood. Frequent fires caused by man or by lightning have perpetuated subclimax, pure stands of this species. The seedlings pass through a "grass" stage for a few years, in which the stem grows in thickness rather than height and the taproot develops rapidly. Later, the elongating, unbranched stem produces very long needles.

Slash Pine
Pinus elliottii
21

Large tree with narrow, regular, pointed crown of horizontal branches and long needles.
Height: 60–100' (18–30 m). Diameter: 2–2½' (0.6–0.8 m).
Needles: evergreen; 7–10" (18–25 cm) long; 2 and 3 in bundle; whorled; stout, stiff; slightly shiny green.
Bark: purplish brown, with large, flattened, scaly plates; on small trunks, blackish gray, rough and furrowed.
Cones: 2½–6" (6–15 cm) long; narrowly egg-shaped; shiny dark brown; short-stalked; opening and shedding at maturity, leaving a few cone-scales on twig; cone-scales flat, slightly keeled, with short stout prickle.

Habitat
Low areas such as pond margins, flatwoods, swamps, or "slashes," including poorly drained sandy soils; also uplands and old fields. In pure stands after fires and in mixed forests.

Range
Coastal Plain from S. South Carolina to S. Florida, and west to SE. Louisiana; mostly near sea level, locally to 500' (152 m).

Comments
An important species both for lumber and naval stores and one of the fastest-growing southern pines, Slash Pine is extensively grown in forest plantations both in its natural range and farther north. Its beauty makes it popular as a shade and ornamental tree. A variety, South Florida Slash Pine, is a medium-sized tree of south and central Florida with needles mostly 2 in a bundle and with a grasslike seedling stage.

Red Pine
Pinus resinosa
22

A common, large tree with small cones and broad, irregular or rounded crown of spreading branches, 1 row added a year.
Height: 70–80' (21–24 m). Diameter: 1–3' (0.3–0.9 m), often larger.
Needles: evergreen; 4¼–6½" (11–16.5 cm) long; 2 in bundle; whorled; slender; dark green.
Bark: reddish brown or gray; with broad, flat, scaly plates; becoming thick.
Cones: 1½–2¼" (4–6 cm) long; egg-shaped; shiny light brown; almost stalkless; opening and shedding soon after maturity; cone-scales slightly thickened, keeled, without prickle.

Habitat
Well-drained soils; particularly sand plains; usually in mixed forests.

Range
SE. Manitoba east to Nova Scotia, south to Pennsylvania, and west to Minnesota. Local in Newfoundland, N. Illinois and E. West Virginia. At 700–1400′ (213–427 m) northward; to 2700′ (823 m) in Adirondacks; and at 3800–4300′ (1158–1311 m) in West Virginia.

Comments
This New World species is also misleadingly called Norway Pine, perhaps because early English explorers confused it with Norway Spruce. Another explanation is that the name comes from the tree's occurrence near Norway, Maine, founded in 1797. Because the name was in usage before this time, the former explanation is more likely.

Shortleaf Pine
Pinus echinata
23, 174

The most widely distributed of the southern yellow pines; a large tree with broad, open crown.
Height: 70–100′ (21–30 m). Diameter: 1½–3′ (0.5–0.9 m).
Needles: evergreen; 2¾–4½″ (7–11 cm) long; 2 or sometimes 3 in bundle; whorled; slender, flexible; dark blue-green.
Bark: reddish brown, with large, irregular, flat, scaly plates.
Cones: 1½–2½″ (4–6 cm) long; conical or narrowly egg-shaped, dull brown; short-stalked; opening at maturity but remaining attached; cone-scales thin, keeled, with small prickle.

Habitat
From dry rocky mountain ridges to sandy loams and silt loams of floodplains, and in old fields; often in pure stands or with other pines and oaks.

Range
Extreme SE. New York and New Jersey south to N. Florida, west to E. Texas, and north to S. Missouri; to 3300′ (1006 m).

Comments
Also called "Southern Yellow Pine," Shortleaf Pine is native in 21 eastern and southeastern states. An important timber species, producing lumber for construction, millwork, and many other uses, as well as plywood and veneer for containers. This and other southern pines are the major native pulpwoods and leading woods in the production of barrels. Seedlings and small trees will sprout after fire damage or injury.

Loblolly Pine
Pinus taeda
24

The principal commercial southern pine, a large, resinous, and fragrant tree with rounded crown of spreading branches.
Height: 80–100′ (24–30 m). Diameter: 2–3′ (0.6–0.9 m).
Needles: evergreen; 5–9″ (13–23 cm) long; 3 in bundle; whorled; stout, stiff, often twisted; green.
Bark: blackish gray; thick, deeply furrowed into scaly ridges

exposing brown inner layers.
Cones: 3–5" (7.5–13 cm) long; conical; dull brown; almost
stalkless; opening at maturity but remaining attached; cone-
scales raised, keeled, with short stout spine.

Habitat
From deep, poorly drained floodplains to well-drained slopes
of rolling, hilly uplands. Forms pure stands, often on
abandoned farmland.

Range
S. New Jersey south to central Florida, west to E. Texas,
north to extreme SE. Oklahoma; to 1500–2000'
(457–610 m).

Comments
Loblolly Pine is native in 15 southeastern states. Among the
fastest-growing southern pines, it is extensively cultivated in
forest plantations for pulpwood and lumber. One of the
meanings of the word *loblolly* is "mud puddle," where these
pines often grow. It is also called Bull Pine, from the giant
size, and Rosemary Pine, from the fragrant resinous foliage.

Pitch Pine
Pinus rigida
25, 173

Medium-sized tree often bearing tufts of needles on trunk,
with a broad, rounded or irregular crown of horizontal
branches.
Height: 50–60' (15–18 m). Diameter: 1–2' (0.3–0.6 m).
Needles: evergreen; 3–5" (7.5–13 cm) long; 3 in bundle;
more or less whorled; stout, stiff, often twisted; yellow-green.
Bark: dark gray; thick, rough, deeply furrowed into broad
scaly ridges, exposing brown inner layers.
Cones: 1¼–2¾" (3–7 cm) long; egg-shaped; yellow-brown;
opening at maturity but remaining attached; cone-scales raised
and keeled, with slender sharp prickle.

Habitat
Shallow sands and gravels on steep slopes and ridges, also in
river valleys and swamps. Forms temporary pure stands,
gradually replaced by hardwoods; also in mixed forests.

Range
S. Maine west to New York and southwest mostly in
mountains to N. Georgia; local in extreme S. Quebec and
extreme SE. Ontario. From sea level in Coastal Plain to about
2000' (610 m) in north; 1400–4500' (427–1372 m) in upper
Piedmont and southern mountains.

Comments
Now used principally for lumber and pulpwood, Pitch Pine
was once a source of resin. Colonists produced turpentine and
tar used for axle grease from this species before naval stores
were developed from the southern pines. Pine knots, when
fastened to a pole, served as torches at night. The common
name refers to the high resin content of the knotty wood.
Pitch Pine is suitable for planting on dry rocky soil that other
trees cannot tolerate, becoming open and irregular in shape in

exposed situations. This hardy species is resistant to fire and injury, forming sprouts from roots and stumps. It is the pine at Cape Cod; and large areas of the New Jersey Pine Barrens are composed of dwarf sprouts of Pitch Pine that grow following repeated fires.

Table Mountain Pine
Pinus pungens
26

Tree with rounded or irregular crown of stout, horizontal branches and abundant spiny cones in clusters along branches.
Height: 20–40' (6–12 m). Diameter: 1–2' (0.3–0.6 m).
Needles: evergreen; 1¼–2½" (3–6 cm) long; 2 in bundle (sometimes 3); stout, stiff, usually twisted; whorled; dark green.
Bark: dark brown; thick, furrowed into scaly plates.
Cones: 2–3½" (5–9 cm) long; egg-shaped; shiny light brown; usually in clusters of 3–4; stalkless; pointing backward or downward; opening partly at maturity but remaining attached many years; cone-scales thickened and keeled, with stout curved spine.

Habitat
Dry gravelly and rocky slopes and ridges of mountains with other pines, sometimes in pure stands.

Range
Appalachian region from Pennsylvania south to NE. Georgia and E. Tennessee, local in New Jersey, Delaware, and District of Columbia. To 4000' (1219 m); rarely down almost to sea level.

Comments
Easily seen at Shenandoah and Great Smoky Mountains National Parks, this tree of mountain ridges is the only pine restricted to the Appalachian Mountains. It is also called Hickory Pine because of the very tough, hickorylike branches.

Virginia Pine
Pinus virginiana
27

Short-needled tree with open, broad, irregular crown of long spreading branches; often a shrub.
Height: 30–60' (9–18 m). Diameter: 1–1½' (0.3–0.5 m).
Needles: evergreen; 1½–3" (4–7.5 cm) long; 2 in bundle; more or less whorled; stout, slightly flattened and twisted; dull green.
Bark: brownish gray, thin, with narrow scaly ridges, becoming shaggy; on small trunks, smoothish, peeling off in flakes.
Cones: 1½–2¾" (4–7 cm) long; narrowly egg-shaped, shiny reddish brown; almost stalkless; opening at maturity but remaining attached; cone-scales slightly raised and keeled, with long slender prickle.

Habitat
Clay, loam, and sandy loam on well-drained sites. Forms pure stands, especially on old fields or abandoned farmland, even in poor soil or severely eroded soil. Also found in mixed forest types.

Range
SE. New York (Long Island) south to NE. Mississippi, and
north to S. Indiana; at 100–2500′ (30–762 m).

Comments
Used principally for pulpwood and lumber, it is hardier than
most pines and suitable for planting in poor dry sites. Also
called Scrub Pine, this species is common in old fields as a
pioneer after grasses on hills of the Piedmont, growing rapidly
and forming thickets. Later this pine is replaced by taller,
more valuable hardwoods.

Jack Pine
Pinus banksiana
28

Open-crowned tree with spreading branches and very short
needles; sometimes a shrub.
Height: 30–70′ (9–21 m). Diameter: 1′ (0.3 m).
Needles: evergreen; more or less opposite; ¾–1½″ (2–4 cm)
long; 2 in bundle; stout, slightly flattened and twisted, widely
forking; shiny green.
Bark: gray-brown or dark brown; thin, with narrow scaly
ridges.
Cones: 1¼–2″ (3–5 cm) long; narrow, long-pointed, and
curved upward; shiny light yellow; usually remaining closed
on tree many years; cone-scales slightly raised and rounded,
keeled, mostly without prickle.

Habitat
Sandy soils, dunes, and on rock outcrops; often in extensive
pure stands.

Range
Mackenzie and Alberta, east to central Quebec and Nova
Scotia, southwest to New Hampshire, and west to N. Indiana
and Minnesota; to about 2000′ (610 m).

Comments
Jack Pine is a pioneer after fires and logging, although it is
damaged or killed by fires. The cones usually remain closed for
many years until opened by heat of fires or exposure after
cutting. The northernmost New World pine, it extends
beyond 65° northern latitude in Mackenzie and nearly to the
limit of trees eastward. Kirtland's warbler is dependent upon
Jack Pine; this rare bird breeds only in north-central
Michigan, where it is confined to dense stands of young pines
following forest fires. The needles are an important food source
for the spruce grouse.

White Spruce
Picea glauca
29, 170

Tree with rows of horizontal branches forming a conical
crown; smaller and shrubby at tree line.
Height: 40–100′ (12–30 m). Diameter: 1–2′ (0.3–0.6 m).
Needles: evergreen; ½–¾″ (12–19 mm) long. Stiff, 4-angled,
sharp-pointed; somewhat spiraled, spreading mainly on upper
side of twig, from very short leafstalks. Blue-green, with
whitish lines; exuding skunklike odor when crushed.
Bark: gray or brown; thin; smooth or scaly; cut surface of

inner bark whitish.

Twigs: orange-brown; slender, hairless, rough with peglike bases.

Cones: 1¼–2½" (3–6 cm) long; cylindrical; shiny light brown; hanging at end of twigs; falling at maturity; cone-scales thin and flexible, margins nearly straight and without teeth; paired brown long-winged seeds.

Habitat
Many soil types in conifer forests; sometimes in pure stands.

Range
Across northern North America near northern limit of trees from Alaska and British Columbia east to Labrador, south to Maine, and west to Minnesota; local in NW. Montana, South Dakota, and Wyoming; from near sea level to timberline at 2000–5000' (610–1524 m).

Comments
The foremost pulpwood and generally the most important commercial tree species of Canada. As well as providing lumber for construction, the wood is valued for piano sounding boards, violins, and other musical instruments. White Spruce and Black Spruce are the most widely distributed conifers in North America after Common Juniper, which rarely reaches tree size. Various kinds of wildlife, including deer, rabbits, and grouse, browse spruce foliage in winter. Also known as Canadian Spruce and Skunk Spruce.

Black Spruce
Picea mariana
30, 169

Tree with open, irregular, conical crown of short, horizontal or slightly drooping branches; a prostrate shrub at timberline. Height: 20–60' (6–18 m). Diameter: 4–12" (0.1–0.3 m). Needles: evergreen; ¼–⅝" (6–15 mm) long. Stiff, 4-angled, sharp-pointed; somewhat spiraled, spreading on all sides of twig from very short leafstalks. Ashy blue-green with whitish lines.

Bark: gray or blackish, thin, scaly; brown beneath; cut surface of inner bark yellowish.

Twigs: brown; slender, hairy, rough, with peglike bases.

Cones: ⅝–1¼" (1.5–3 cm) long; egg-shaped or rounded; dull gray; curved downward on short stalk and remaining attached, often clustered near top of crown; cone-scales stiff and brittle, rounded and finely toothed; paired brown long-winged seeds.

Habitat
Wet soils and bogs including peats, clays, and loams; in coniferous forests; often in pure stands.

Range
Across northern North America near northern limit of trees from Alaska and British Columbia east to Labrador, south to N. New Jersey, and west to Minnesota; at 2000–5000' (610–1524 m).

Comments
Black Spruce is one of the most widely distributed conifers in

North America. Uses are similar to those of White Spruce; however, the small size limits lumber production. The lowest branches take root by layering when deep snows bend them to the ground, forming a ring of small trees around a large one. Spruce gum and spruce beer were made from this species and Red Spruce.

Red Spruce
Picea rubens
31, 171

The only spruce southward in eastern mountains, a handsome tree with broad or narrow, conical crown.
Height: 50–80′ (15–24 m). Diameter: 1–2′ (0.3–0.6 m).
Needles: evergreen; ½–⅝″ (12–15 mm) long. Stiff, 4-angled, sharp-pointed; somewhat spiraled, spreading on all sides of twig from very short leafstalks. Shiny green, with whitish lines.
Bark: reddish brown; thin, scaly.
Twigs: brown; slender, finely hairy, rough with peglike bases.
Cones: 1¼–1½″ (3–4 cm) long; cylindrical; reddish brown; hanging down on short, straight stalk; falling at maturity; cone-scales stiff, rounded, often finely toothed; paired brown long-winged seeds.

Habitat
Rocky mountain soils; often in pure stands.

Range
Ontario east to Nova Scotia; from New England south in mountains to W. North Carolina and E. Tennessee; to 4500–6500′ (1372–1981 m) in south.

Comments
Extensive virgin spruce-fir forests are preserved in Great Smoky Mountains National Park. This species is a handsome ornamental; the wood has uses similar to White Spruce. Spruce gum, a forerunner of modern chewing gum made from chicle (gum from a tropical American tree), was obtained commercially from resin of both Red and Black spruce trunks. The young leafy twigs were boiled with flavoring and sugar to prepare spruce beer. Where the ranges overlap, Black Spruce is distinguishable from Red by its smaller dull gray cones curved downward on short stalks and remaining attached.

Fraser Fir
Abies fraseri
32

The only native southeastern fir, a handsome tree with pointed crown of silvery white aromatic foliage.
Height: 30–50′ (9–15 m). Diameter: 1–2′ (0.3–0.6 m).
Needles: evergreen; ½–1″ (1.2–2.5 cm) long. Spreading almost at right angles in 2 rows on slender hairy twigs, crowded and curved upward on upper twigs; flat, with tip usually rounded. Shiny dark green above, 2 broad silvery-white bands beneath.
Bark: gray or brown; thin, smooth, with many resin blisters, becoming scaly.
Cones: 1½–2½″ (4–6 cm) long; cylindrical; dark purple; upright on topmost twigs; cone-scales finely hairy, partly

covered by yellow-green pointed and toothed bracts; paired long-winged seeds.

Habitat
Coniferous forests with Red Spruce in high mountains.

Range
Appalachian Mountains in SW. Virginia, W. North Carolina, and E. Tennessee; at 4000–6600' (1219–2012 m).

Comments
Also known as "Balsam," Fraser Fir is common in Great Smoky Mountains National Park in virgin spruce-fir forests and at Mount Mitchell, North Carolina. With its silvery and green foliage, this species is grown for Christmas trees and ornament. This tree is known locally as "She-balsam," apparently because of the resin produced in the bark. In contrast, Red Spruce in the same forest but without resin blisters is often called "He-balsam." John Fraser (1750–1811), the Scottish explorer, discovered this fir and introduced it and many other plants to Europe.

Balsam Fir
Abies balsamea
33, 172

The only fir native to the Northeast, with narrow, pointed, spirelike crown of spreading branches and aromatic foliage.
Height: 40–60' (12–18 m). Diameter: 1–1½' (0.3–0.5 m).
Needles: evergreen; ½–1" (1.2–2.5 cm) long. Spreading almost at right angles in 2 rows on hairy twigs, curved upward on upper twigs; somewhat spiraled; flat, with rounded tip (sometimes notched or short-pointed). Shiny dark green above, with 2 narrow whitish bands beneath.
Bark: brown, thin, smooth, with many resin blisters, becoming scaly.
Cones: 2–3¼" (5–8 cm) long; cylindrical; dark purple; upright on topmost twigs; cone-scales finely hairy, bracts mostly short and hidden; paired long-winged seeds.

Habitat
Coniferous forests; often in pure stands.

Range
Alberta east to Labrador and south to Pennsylvania, west to Minnesota and NE. Iowa; local in West Virginia and Virginia; to timberline in north and above 4000' (1219 m) in south.

Comments
A major pulpwood species. Interior knotty pine paneling is a special product; Christmas trees, wreaths, and balsam pillows utilize the aromatic foliage. Canada balsam, an aromatic oleoresin obtained from swellings or resin blisters in the bark, is used for mounting microscopic specimens and for optical cement. Deer and moose browse the foliage of Balsam Fir in winter.

Eastern Hemlock
Tsuga canadensis
34

Evergreen tree with conical crown of long, slender, horizontal branches often drooping down to the ground, and a slender, curved, and drooping leader.
Height: 60–70′ (18–21 m). Diameter: 2–3′ (0.6–0.9 m).
Needles: evergreen; ⅜–⅝″ (10–15 mm) long. Flat, flexible, rounded at tip; spreading in 2 rows from very short leafstalks. Shiny dark green above, with 2 narrow whitish bands beneath and green edges often minutely toothed.
Bark: cinnamon-brown; thick, deeply furrowed into broad scaly ridges.
Twigs: yellow-brown; very slender, finely hairy, rough with peglike bases.
Cones: ⅝–¾″ (15–19 mm) long; elliptical; brown; short-stalked; hanging down at ends of twigs; composed of numerous rounded cone-scales; paired, light brown, long-winged seeds.

Habitat
Acid soils; often in pure stands. Characteristic of moist cool valleys and ravines; also rock outcrops, especially north-facing bluffs.

Range

S. Ontario east to Cape Breton Island, south in mountains to N. Alabama, and west to E. Minnesota. To 3000′ (914 m) in north; at 2000–5000′ (610–1524 m) in south.

Comments
The bark was once a commercial source of tannin in the production of leather. Pioneers made tea from leafy twigs and brooms from the branches. A graceful shade tree and ornamental, it can also be trimmed into hedges. Its needles are a preferred food of the white-tailed deer.

Tamarack
Larix laricina
35

Deciduous tree with straight, tapering trunk and thin, open, conical crown of horizontal branches; a shrub at timberline.
Height: 40–80′ (12–24 m). Diameter: 1–2′ (0.3–0.6 m).
Needles: deciduous; ¾–1″ (2–2.5 cm) long, ¹⁄₃₂″ (1 mm) wide. Soft, very slender, 3-angled; crowded in cluster on spur twigs, also scattered and alternate on leader twigs. Light blue-green, turning yellow in autumn before shedding.
Bark: reddish brown; scaly, thin.
Twigs: orange-brown; stout, hairless, with many spurs or short side twigs.
Cones: ½–¾″ (12–19 mm) long; elliptical; rose red turning brown; upright, stalkless; falling in second year; several overlapping rounded cone-scales; paired brown long-winged seeds.

Habitat
Wet peaty soils of bogs and swamps; also in drier upland loamy soils; often in pure stands.

Range
Across northern North America near northern limit of trees

from Alaska east to Labrador, south to N. New Jersey, and
west to Minnesota; local in N. West Virginia and W.
Maryland; from near sea level to 1700–4000' (518–1219 m)
southward.

Comments
One of the northernmost trees, the hardy Tamarack is useful as
an ornamental in very cold climates. Indians used the slender
roots to sew together strips of birch bark for their canoes.
Roots bent at right angles served the colonists as "knees" in
small ships, joining the ribs to deck timbers. The durable
lumber is used as framing for houses, railroad cross-ties, poles,
and pulpwood. The larch sawfly defoliates stands in infrequent
years, causing damage or death.

Baldcypress
Taxodium distichum
36

Large, needle-leaf, aquatic, deciduous tree often with cone-
shaped "knees" projecting from submerged roots, with trunks
enlarged at base and spreading into ridges or buttresses, and
with a crown of widely spreading branches, flattened at top.
Height: 100–120' (30–37 m) or more. Diameter: 3–5' (0.9–
1.5 m), rarely 10' (3 m) or more.
Needles: deciduous; ⅜–¾" (10–19 mm) long. Borne singly
in 2 rows on slender green twigs, crowded and featherlike;
flat, soft, and flexible. Dull light green above, whitish
beneath; turning brown and shedding with twig in fall.
Bark: brown or gray; with long fibrous or scaly ridges, peeling
off in strips.
Cones: ¾–1" (2–2.5 cm) in diameter; round; gray; 1–2 at
end of twig; several flattened, 4-angled, hard cone-scales shed
at maturity in autumn; 2 brown, 3-angled seeds nearly ¼" (6
mm) long, under cone-scale. Tiny pollen cones in narrow
drooping cluster 4" (10 cm) long.

Habitat
Very wet, swampy soils of riverbanks and floodplain lakes that
are sometimes submerged; often in pure stands.

Range
S. Delaware to S. Florida, west to S. Texas and north to SE.
Oklahoma and SW. Indiana. Below 500' (152 m); locally in
Texas to 1700' (518 m).

Comments
Called the "wood eternal" because of the heartwood's
resistance to decay, Baldcypress is used for heavy construction,
including docks, warehouses, boats, bridges, as well as general
millwork and interior trim. The trees are planted as
ornamentals northward in colder climates and in drier soils.
Also called Cypress and Swamp-cypress, this species is easily
seen in Big Cypress National Preserve near Naples, Florida.
Pondcypress, a variety with shorter scalelike leaves, is found in
shallow ponds and poorly drained areas from southeastern
Virginia to southeastern Louisiana below 100' (30 m).

Northern White-cedar
Thuja occidentalis
37

Resinous and aromatic evergreen tree with an angled, buttressed, often branched trunk and a narrow, conical crown of short, spreading branches.
Height: 40–70' (12–21 m). Diameter: 1–3' (0.3–0.9 m).
Leaves: evergreen; opposite in 4 rows; $\frac{1}{16}$–$\frac{1}{8}$" (1.5–3 mm) long. Scalelike; short-pointed; side pair keeled, flat pair with gland-dot. Dull yellow-green above, paler blue-green beneath.
Bark: light red-brown; thin, fibrous and shreddy, fissured into narrow connecting ridges.
Twigs: branching in horizontal plane; much flattened; jointed.
Cones: $\frac{3}{8}$" (10 mm) long; elliptical; light brown; upright from short curved stalk; with 8–10 paired, leathery, blunt-pointed cone-scales, 4 usually bearing 2 tiny narrow-winged seeds each.

Habitat
Adapted to swamps and to neutral or alkaline soils on limestone uplands; often in pure stands.

Range
SE. Manitoba east to Nova Scotia and Maine, south to New York, and west to Illinois; south locally to North Carolina; to 3000' (914 m) in south.

Comments
Probably the first North American tree introduced into Europe, the Northern White-cedar was discovered by French explorers and grown in Paris about 1536. The year before, tea prepared from the foliage and bark, now known to be high in vitamin C, saved the crew of Jacques Cartier from scurvy. It was named *arborvitae*, Latin for "tree-of-life," in 1558. The trees grow slowly and reach an age of 400 years or more. The lightweight, easily split wood was preferred for canoe frames by Indians, who also used the shredded outer bark and the soft wood to start fires.

Eastern Redcedar
Juniperus virginiana
38

Evergreen, aromatic tree with trunk often angled and buttressed at base and narrow, compact, columnar crown; sometimes becoming broad and irregular.
Height: 40–60' (12–18 m). Diameter: 1–2' (0.3–0.6 m).
Leaves: evergreen; opposite in 4 rows forming slender 4-angled twigs; $\frac{1}{16}$" (1.5 mm) long, to $\frac{3}{8}$" (10 mm) long on leaders. Scalelike, not toothed; dark green, with gland-dot.
Bark: reddish brown; thin, fibrous and shreddy.
Cones: $\frac{1}{4}$–$\frac{3}{8}$" (6–10 mm) in diameter; berrylike; dark blue with a bloom; soft, juicy, sweetish, and resinous; 1–2 seeds. Pollen cones on separate trees.

Habitat
From dry uplands, especially limestone, to floodplains and swamps; also abandoned fields and fence rows; often in scattered pure stands.

Range
S. Ontario and widespread in eastern half of United States

from Maine south to N. Florida, west to Texas, and north to North Dakota.

Comments
Also called Red Juniper. The most widely distributed eastern conifer, native in 37 states, Eastern Redcedar is resistant to extremes of drought, heat, and cold. The aromatic wood is used for fenceposts, cedar chests, cabinetwork, and carvings. First observed at Roanoke Island, Virginia, in 1564, it was prized by the colonists for building furniture, rail fences, and log cabins. Cedar oil for medicine and perfumes is obtained from the wood and leaves. The heartwood was once almost exclusively the source of wood for pencils; Incense-cedar (*Libocedrus decurrens*) is now used instead. Grown for Christmas trees, shelterbelts, and in many cultivated varieties for ornament. The juicy "berries" are consumed by many kinds of wildlife, including the cedar waxwing, which was named for this tree. Redcedar can be very injurious to apple orchards because it is an alternate host for cedar-apple rust, a fungus disease.

Atlantic White-cedar
Chamaecyparis thyoides
39

Evergreen, aromatic tree with narrow, pointed, spirelike crown and slender, horizontal branches.
Height: 50–90' (15–27 m). Diameter: 1½–2' (0.5–0.6 m).
Leaves: evergreen; opposite; 1/16–1/8" (1.5–3 mm) long. Scalelike; dull blue-green, with gland-dot.
Bark: reddish brown; thin, fibrous, with narrow connecting or forking ridges, becoming scaly and loose.
Twigs: very slender, slightly flattened or partly 4-angled, irregularly branched.
Cones: tiny, ¼" (6 mm) in diameter; bluish purple with a bloom, becoming dark red-brown; with 6 cone-scales ending in short point; maturing in 1 season; 1–2 gray-brown seeds under cone-scale.

Habitat
Wet, peaty, acid soils; forming pure stands in swamp forests.

Range
Central Maine south to N. Florida and west to Mississippi in narrow coastal belt; to 100' (30 m).

Comments
Ancient logs of the Atlantic White-cedar that were buried in swamps have been mined and found to be well preserved and suitable for lumber. Pioneers prized the durable wood for log cabins, including floors and shingles. During the Revolutionary War, the wood produced charcoal for gunpowder. One fine forest is preserved at Green Bank State Forest in southern New Jersey.

Southern Magnolia
Magnolia grandiflora
40, 161

One of the most beautiful native trees; an evergreen with straight trunk, conical crown, and very fragrant, very large, white flowers.

Height: 60–80' (18–24 m). Diameter: 2–3' (0.6–0.9 m). Leaves: evergreen; alternate; 5–8" (13–20 cm) long, 2–3" (5–7.5 cm) wide. Oblong or elliptical; thick and firm with edges slightly turned under. Shiny bright green above, pale and with rust-colored hairs beneath. Stout leafstalks with rust-colored hairs.
Bark: dark gray; smooth, becoming furrowed and scaly.
Twigs: covered with rust-colored hairs when young; with ring scars at nodes; ending in buds also covered with rust-colored hairs.
Flowers: 6–8" (15–20 cm) wide; cup-shaped; 3 white sepals and 6 or more petals; very fragrant; solitary at end of twig; in late spring and summer.
Fruit: 3–4" (7.5–10 cm) long; conelike; oblong; pink to brown; covered with rust-colored hairs; composed of many separate, short-pointed, 2-seeded fruits that split open in early autumn.

Habitat
Moist soils of valleys and low uplands with various other hardwoods.

Range
E. North Carolina to central Florida and west to E. Texas; to 400' (122 m).

Comments
Planted around the world in warm temperate and subtropical regions, the Southern Magnolia is a popular ornamental and shade tree, hardy north as far as Philadelphia. Several horticultural varieties have been developed.

Laurel Oak
Quercus laurifolia
41

Large, nearly evergreen tree with dense, broad, rounded crown.
Height: 60–80' (18–24 m). Diameter: 1–2½' (0.3–0.8 m). Leaves: alternate; 2–5½" (5–14 cm) long, ⅜–1½" (1–4 cm) wide. Narrowly oblong; diamond- or lance-shaped, often broadest near middle; bristle-tipped; edges straight (rarely, with few lobes or teeth); thin or slightly thickened; usually hairless. Shiny green or dark green above, light green and slightly shiny beneath; shedding in early spring and nearly evergreen.
Bark: brown to gray, smooth; becoming blackish, rough, and furrowed.
Acorns: ½" (12 mm) long; nearly round, a quarter or less enclosed by shallow cup of blunt hairy scales; short-stalked or nearly stalkless; becoming brown; maturing second year.

Habitat
Moist to wet well-drained sandy soil along rivers and swamps; sometimes in pure stands.

Range
SE. Virginia to S. Florida, west to SE. Texas, and north locally to S. Arkansas; to 500' (152 m).

Comments
The names refer to the resemblance of the foliage to the European Grecian Laurel (*Laurus nobilis*). A handsome shade tree, Laurel Oak is widely planted in the Southeast.

Myrtle Oak
Quercus myrtifolia
42

Evergreen, much-branched, thicket-forming shrub or small tree with short, crooked branches and rounded crown.
Height: 30' (9 m). Diameter: 1' (0.3 m).
Leaves: evergreen; alternate; ¾–2" (2–5 cm) long, ½–1" (1.2–2.5 cm) wide. Usually elliptical to obovate but varying in shape; rounded or sometimes pointed at tip, gradually narrowed to blunt or rounded base; edges turned under and sometimes wavy or toothed; thick and leathery; leafstalks very short, hairy. Shiny dark green and hairless with prominent network of veins above, dull light green beneath with tufts of hairs in vein angles.
Bark: light gray; smooth, becoming furrowed.
Acorns: ⅜–½" (10–12 mm) long; nearly round, a quarter to a third enclosed by shallow cup; becoming brown; stalkless or short-stalked; usually maturing second year.

Habitat
Dry sandy ridges and sand dunes, especially near coast and on islands; usually with other oaks and pines.

Range
S. South Carolina to S. Florida and west to S. Mississippi; near sea level.

Comments
Common and Latin species names refer to the resemblance of the leaves of those of Myrtle (*Myrtus communis*), an evergreen shrub from the Mediterranean region, introduced in Florida and California. Also called Scrub Oak.

Catawba Rhododendron
Rhododendron catawbiense
43, 147

Evergreen, thicket-forming shrub or small tree with broad, rounded crown and spectacular displays of large, purplish blossoms.
Height: 20' (6 m). Diameter: 4" (10 cm).
Leaves: evergreen; alternate; 3–6" (7.5–15 cm) long, 1½–2½" (4–6 cm) wide. Elliptical, blunt at tip, rounded at base; thick and leathery with edges often rolled under; hairless; long stout leafstalks. Shiny dark green above, whitish beneath.
Bark: brown or gray; fissured into narrow scaly ridges.
Twigs: greenish, stout.
Flowers: 2¼" (6 cm) wide; with bell-shaped corolla of 5 rounded lobes; waxy lilac-purple (sometimes pink); slender-stalked; in upright branched rounded clusters; in late spring and early summer.
Fruit: ½–⅝" (12–15 mm) long; a long-stalked, narrowly egg-shaped capsule, densely covered with reddish brown hairs; 5-celled, splitting along 5 lines; many-seeded; maturing in late summer and autumn.

Habitat
Rocky slopes and ridges in understory of mountain forests, and in shrub thickets called "heath balds" or "laurel slicks."

Range
W. Virginia south to N. Georgia and NE. Alabama, north to E. Kentucky; usually at 1500–6500′ (457–1981 m); locally down to 200′ (61 m).

Comments
Catawba or "Purple" Rhododendron is plentiful in Great Smoky Mountains National Park, attracting thousands of visitors each year. On high mountain ridges, plants usually flower in June; at lower altitudes, flowers appear earlier, although the times may vary slightly. The common and scientific names, of American Indian origin, are from the Catawba River in North Carolina. Thickets provide shelter for many species of wild animals.

Mountain-laurel
Kalmia latifolia
44, 148

Evergreen, many-stemmed, thicket-forming shrub or sometimes a small tree with short, crooked trunk; stout, spreading branches; a compact, rounded crown; and beautiful, large, pink flower clusters.
Height: 20′ (6 m). Diameter: 6″ (15 cm).
Leaves: evergreen; alternate or sometimes opposite or in 3's; 2½–4″ (6–10 cm) long, 1–1½″ (2.5–4 cm) wide. Narrowly elliptical or lance-shaped; hard whitish point at tip; without teeth; thick and stiff. Dull dark green above, yellow-green beneath.
Bark: dark reddish brown; thin, fissured into long narrow ridges and shredding.
Twigs: reddish green with sticky hairs when young; later turning reddish brown, peeling, and exposing darker layer beneath.
Flowers: ¾–1″ (2–2.5 cm) wide; saucer-shaped, with 5-lobed pink or white corolla with purple lines, from pointed deep pink buds; on long stalks covered with sticky hairs; in upright branched flat clusters 4–5″ (10–13 cm) wide; in spring.
Fruit: ¼″ (6 mm) wide; a rounded dark brown capsule; with long threadlike style at tip; covered with sticky hairs; 5-celled, splitting open along 5 lines; many tiny seeds; maturing in autumn and remaining attached.

Habitat
Dry or moist acid soils; in understory of mixed forests on upland mountain slopes and in valleys; also in shrub thickets called "heath balds" or "laurel slicks."

Range
SE. Maine south to N. Florida, west to Louisiana, and north to Indiana; to 4000′ (1219 m), higher in southern Appalachians.

Comments
Mountain-laurel is one of the most beautiful native flowering

shrubs and is well displayed as an ornamental in many parks. The stamens of the flowers have an odd, springlike mechanism that spreads pollen when tripped by a bee. The leaves, which are poisonous to livestock, are seldom browsed. Honey from the flowers is believed to be poisonous. Nonetheless, deer and ruffed grouse feed extensively on the foliage, buds, and twigs. The plant is a good source of shelter throughout the year.

Sweetbay
Magnolia virginiana
45, 159

Tree with narrow, rounded crown that sheds its leaves in winter or is almost evergreen southward, and with aromatic spicy foliage and twigs.
Height: 20–60′ (6–18 m). Diameter: 1½′ (0.5 m).
Leaves: alternate; 3–6″ (7.5–15 cm) long, 1¼–2½″ (3–6 cm) wide. Oblong, blunt at tip, without teeth, slightly thickened; short-stalked, becoming shiny green above, whitish and finely hairy beneath.
Bark: gray; smooth, thin, aromatic.
Twigs: with ring scars at nodes; ending in buds covered with whitish hairs.
Flowers: 2–2½″ (5–6 cm) wide; cup-shaped, with 9–12 white petals; fragrant; in late spring and early summer.
Fruit: 1½–2″ (4–5 cm) long; conelike; elliptical; dark red; composed of many separate pointed fruits, each with 2 red seeds; maturing in early autumn.

Habitat
Wet soils of coastal swamps and borders of streams and ponds.

Range
Long Island south to S. Florida and west to SE. Texas; local in NE. Massachusetts; to 500′ (152 m).

Comments
This attractive native ornamental is popular for its fragrant flowers borne over a long period, showy conelike fruit, handsome foliage of contrasting colors, and smooth bark. This species was called Beavertree by colonists who caught beavers in traps baited with the fleshy roots.

Myrtle Dahoon
Ilex myrtifolia
46

Evergreen shrub or small tree with broad, dense crown of many crooked branches and small, narrow leaves.
Height: 18′ (5.5 m). Diameter: 6″ (15 cm).
Leaves: evergreen; alternate; ½–1¼″ (1.2–3.2 cm) long, ⅛–⅜″ (3–10 mm) wide. Linear, bristle-tipped, short-pointed at base; thick and stiff; edges turned under and usually without teeth; with wide midvein and obscure side veins; crowded, very short-stalked; becoming nearly hairless. Dark green above, paler beneath.
Bark: whitish gray; rough and warty.
Twigs: brown, slender, stiff, hairy when young.
Flowers: ³⁄₁₆″ (5 mm) wide; with 4 rounded white petals; on short stalks at leaf bases; in spring; male and female on separate plants.

Fruit: ¼″ (6 mm) in diameter; berrylike; red (rarely orange or yellow); thin bitter pulp; 4 narrow grooved nutlets; short-stalked; maturing in autumn, remaining attached in winter.

Habitat
Wet, mostly poor or acid sandy soils, bordering ponds and swamps; in pine or Baldcypress forests.

Range
North Carolina to central Florida, west to SE. Louisiana; to 200′ (61 m).

Comments
Myrtle Dahoon, also called Myrtle-leaf Holly, is closely related to Dahoon and has been considered a variety of that species. However, the latter has larger, broader leaves and grows in richer, wet soil. The leaves resemble those of the unrelated Myrtle (*Myrtus communis*), native to the Mediterranean region.

Rosebay Rhododendron
Rhododendron maximum
47, 150

Evergreen, thicket-forming shrub or tree with short, crooked trunk, broad, rounded crown of many stout, crooked branches, and large white blossoms.
Height: 20′ (6 m). Diameter: 6″ (15 cm).
Leaves: evergreen; alternate; 4–10″ (10–25 cm) long, 1–3″ (2.5–7.5 cm) wide. Oblong or narrowly elliptical, short-pointed at both ends; thick and leathery with edges rolled under; short stout leafstalks. Shiny dark green above, whitish and covered with fine hairs beneath.
Bark: red-brown; scaly, thin.
Twigs: green with reddish gland-hairs, becoming reddish brown and scaly; stout.
Flowers: 1½″ (4 cm) wide; bell-shaped corolla of 5 rounded lobes; waxy white or sometimes light pink (rarely reddish); the largest or upper lobe with many green spots; in upright, branched, rounded clusters; in summer.
Fruit: ½″ (12 mm) long; long-stalked, narrowly egg-shaped capsule; dark reddish brown, with gland-hairs; 5-celled and splitting open along 5 lines; many seeds; maturing in autumn and remaining attached.

Habitat
Moist soils, especially along streams in understory of mountain forests, forming dense thickets.

Range
Maine southwest to W. New York and south, mostly in mountains, to N. Georgia; to 6000′ (1829 m) in southern Appalachians.

Comments
Rosebay Rhododendron is abundant in the Great Smoky Mountains National Park. Often grown as an ornamental, it is one of the hardiest and largest evergreen rhododendrons. The wood is occasionally used for tool handles, and a home remedy has been prepared from the leaves. Honey from rhododendrons is poisonous. Dense thickets offer excellent shelter for wildlife.

Redbay
Persea borbonia
48

Handsome, aromatic, evergreen tree, with dense crown.
Height: 60′ (18 m). Diameter: 2′ (0.6 m).
Leaves: evergreen; alternate; 3–6″ (7.5–15 cm) long, ¾–1½″
(2–4 cm) wide. Elliptical or lance-shaped; short-stalked; thick
and leathery, with edges slightly rolled under. Shiny green
above, pale with whitish or rust-colored hairs beneath.
Bark: dark or reddish brown; furrowed into broad scaly ridges.
Flowers: ³⁄₁₆″ (5 mm) long; light yellow; several in long-
stalked cluster at leaf base; in spring.
Fruit: ½–⅝″ (12–15 mm) long; nearly round; shiny dark
blue-black; with 6-lobed cup at base, thin pulp, and rounded
seed; maturing in autumn.

Habitat
Wet soils of valleys and swamps, also sandy uplands and
dunes, in mixed forests.

Range
S. Delaware south to S. Florida and west to S. Texas; to 400′
(122 m).

Comments
The wood, which takes a beautiful polish, is used for fine
cabinetwork and also for lumber. The spicy leaves can be used
to flavor soups and meats. Birds eat the bitter fruit.

Live Oak
Quercus virginiana
49

Medium-sized evergreen tree with short, broad trunk
buttressed at the base forking into a few nearly horizontal,
long branches, and very broad, spreading, dense crown.
Height: 40–50′ (12–15 m). Diameter: 2–4′ (0.6–1.2 m).
Leaves: evergreen; alternate; 1½–4″ (4–10 cm) long, ⅜–2″ (1–
5 cm) wide. Elliptical or oblong; thick; rounded tip
sometimes ending in tiny tooth; base short-pointed; edges
usually straight and slightly rolled under, rarely with few
spiny teeth. Shiny dark green above, gray-green and densely
hairy beneath; shedding after new leaves appear in spring.
Bark: dark brown; rough, deeply furrowed into scaly ridges.
Acorns: ⅝–1″ (1.5–2.5 cm) long; narrow and oblong, a
quarter to a half enclosed by deep cup; green becoming brown;
long-stalked; maturing first year.

Habitat
Sandy soils including coastal dunes and ridges near marshes;
often in pure stands.

Range
SE. Virginia south to S. Florida and west to S. and central
Texas; local in SW. Oklahoma and northeastern Mexico; to
300′ (91 m) and in Texas to 2000′ (610 m).

Comments
Live Oak timber was once important for building ships. The
nation's first publicly owned timber lands were purchased as
early as 1799 to preserve these trees, which are called Live
Oak because of the evergreen foliage, for this purpose. The
very broad branches are usually draped with Spanish-moss.

This handsome shade tree is popular in the Southeast, where it attains very large size.

Dahoon
Ilex cassine
50

Evergreen shrub or small tree with rounded, dense crown and abundant, bright red berries.
Height: 30' (9 m). Diameter: 1' (0.3 m).
Leaves: evergreen; alternate; 1½–3½" (4–9 cm) long, ¼–1¼" (0.6–3.2 cm) wide. Oblong or obovate; slightly thick and leathery; usually without teeth or spines; edges often turned under. Shiny dark green and becoming hairless above, light green (and densely hairy when young) beneath.
Bark: dark gray, thin, smooth to rough and warty.
Twigs: slender, densely covered with silky hairs, becoming brown.
Flowers: ³⁄₁₆" (5 mm) wide; with 4 rounded white petals; on short stalks mostly at base of new leaves in spring; male and female on separate plants.
Fruit: ¼" (6 mm) in diameter; berrylike, round, shiny red (sometimes yellow or orange), short-stalked; mealy bitter pulp, 4 narrow, grooved, brown nutlets; maturing in autumn, remaining attached in winter.

Habitat
Wet soils along streams and swamps, sometimes sandy banks or brackish soils.

Range
SE. North Carolina south to S. Florida, and west to S. Louisiana; to 200' (61 m); also Bahamas, Cuba, Puerto Rico and 1 variety in Mexico.

Comments
Also known as Dahoon Holly and Christmas-berry, this species is planted as an ornamental for the evergreen foliage and profuse red fruit used in Christmas decorations. The name Dahoon apparently is of American Indian origin.

Red-osier Dogwood
Cornus stolonifera
51

Large, spreading, thicket-forming shrub, with several stems, clusters of small white flowers, and small whitish fruit; rarely a small tree.
Height: commonly 3–10' (1–3 m), rarely to 15' (4.6 m).
Diameter: 3" (7.5 cm).
Leaves: opposite; 1½–3½" (4–9 cm) long, ⅝–2" (1.5–5 cm) wide. Elliptical or ovate; short- or long-pointed; without teeth; 5–7 long curved sunken veins on each side of midvein. Dull green above, whitish green and covered with fine hairs beneath; turning reddish in autumn.
Bark: gray or brown; smooth or slightly furrowed into flat plates.
Twigs: purplish red, slender, hairy when young, with rings at nodes.
Flowers: ¼" (6 mm) wide; with 4 spreading white petals; many, crowded in upright flattish clusters 1¼–2" (3–5 cm)

wide; in late spring and early summer.
Fruit: ¼–⅜" (6–10 mm) in diameter; whitish, juicy; stone
with 2 seeds; maturing in late summer.

Habitat
Moist soils, especially along streams; forming thickets and in
understory of forests.

Range
Central Alaska east to Labrador and Newfoundland, south to
N. Virginia, and west to California; also northern Mexico; to
5000' (1524 m); to 9000' (2743 m) in the Southwest.

Comments
Red-osier Dogwood is useful for erosion control on stream
banks. The common name recalls the resemblance of the
reddish twigs to those of some willows called osiers, used in
basketry.

Flowering Dogwood
Cornus florida
52, 160, 190, 214

A lovely, small, flowering tree with short trunk and crown of
spreading or nearly horizontal branches.
Height: 30' (9 m). Diameter: 8' (20 cm).
Leaves: opposite; 2½–5" (6–13 cm) long, 1½–2½" (4–6 cm)
wide. Elliptical; edges slightly wavy, appearing not toothed
but with tiny teeth visible under a lens; 6–7 long curved veins
on each side of midvein; short-stalked. Green and nearly
hairless above, paler and covered with fine hairs beneath;
turning bright red above in autumn.
Bark: dark reddish brown; rough, broken into small square
plates.
Twigs: green or reddish, slender, becoming hairless.
Flowers: 3/16" (5 mm) wide; with 4 yellowish-green petals;
many of these tiny flowers tightly crowded in a head ¼" (19
mm) wide, bordered by 4 large, broadly elliptical, white
petal-like bracts (pink in some cultivated varieties) 1½–2"
(4–5 cm) long; in early spring before leaves. The flower heads
(with bracts) 3–4" (7.5–10 cm) across are commonly called
flowers.
Fruit: ⅜–⅝" (10–15 mm) long; berrylike, elliptical, shiny
red; several at end of long stalk; thin mealy bitter pulp; stone
containing 1–2 seeds; maturing in autumn.

Habitat
Both moist and dry soils of valleys and uplands in understory
of hardwood forests; also in old fields and along roadsides.

Range
S. Ontario east to SW. Maine, south to N. Florida, west to
central Texas, and north to central Michigan; to 4000' (1219
m), almost 5000' (1524 m) in southern Appalachians.

Comments
Flowering Dogwood is one of the most beautiful eastern North
American trees with showy early spring flowers, red fruit, and
scarlet autumn foliage. The hard wood is extremely shock-
resistant and useful for making weaving-shuttles. It is also

made into spools, small pulleys, mallet heads, and jeweler's blocks. Indians used the aromatic bark and roots as a remedy for malaria and extracted a red dye from the roots.

Bigleaf Magnolia
Magnolia macrophylla
53

The tree with the largest flowers and the largest leaves of all native North American species (except for tropical palms) and a broad, rounded crown of stout, spreading branches.
Height: 30–40' (9–12 m). Diameter: 1½' (0.5 m).
Leaves: alternate; 15–30" (38–76 cm) long, 6–10" (15–25 cm) wide. Reverse ovate, broadest beyond middle, mostly blunt at tip; notched with 2 rounded lobes at base; not toothed. Bright green above, with silvery hairs beneath. Stout, hairy leafstalks, 3–4" (7.5–10 cm) long.
Bark: light gray; smooth, thin.
Twigs; stout, hairy; with large leaf-scars at nodes and ending in large buds covered with white hairs.
Flowers: 10–12" (25–30 cm) wide; cup-shaped with 6 white petals with spot at base; fragrant; in late spring and early summer.
Fruit: 2½–3" (6–7.5 cm) long; conelike; elliptical or nearly round; rose-red; composed of many separate short-pointed 2-seeded hairy fruits; maturing in autumn.

Habitat
Moist soil of valleys, especially ravines; in understory of hardwood forests.

Range
Central North Carolina south to W. Georgia and west to Louisiana; local in S. Ohio, NE. Arkansas, and SE. South Carolina.

Comments
Planted as an ornamental north to Massachusetts. However, in windy places the giant leaves become torn and unsightly. The "queenliest of all the deciduous magnolias" was named by the French naturalist and explorer André Michaux (1746–1802), who discovered this rare local tree near Charlotte, North Carolina, in 1789.

Umbrella Magnolia
Magnolia tripetala
54

Tree with large leaves, very large flowers, and a broad, open crown of spreading branches; often with sprouts at base.
Height: 30–40' (9–12 m). Diameter: 1' (0.3 m).
Leaves: alternate; 10–20" (25–51 cm) long, 5–10" (13–25 cm) wide. Reverse ovate; broadest beyond middle; not toothed; crowded; short-stalked. Green above, with silky hairs beneath when young.
Bark: light gray; smooth, thin.
Twigs: stout; with ring scars at nodes.
Flowers: 7–10" (18–25 cm) wide; 3 cup-shaped, light green sepals with 6 or 9 shorter white petals; disagreeable odor; at end of twig; in spring.
Fruit: 2½–4" (6–10 cm) long; conelike; oblong; rose-red;

composed of many separate, 2-seeded, short-pointed fruits; maturing in autumn.

Habitat
Moist soils of mountain valleys; in hardwood forests.

Range
S. Pennsylvania south to Georgia, west to SE. Mississippi, north to S. Indiana; local in Arkansas and SE. Oklahoma.

Comments
Fairly common at low altitudes in the Great Smoky Mountains National Park, North Carolina–Tennessee. The arrangement of spreading leaves somewhat resembles the ribs of an umbrella, hence the common name.

Fraser Magnolia
Magnolia fraseri
55

A tree often branched near the base, with an open crown of spreading branches, large leaves, and very large flowers.
Height: 30–70′ (9–21 m). Diameter: 1–2′ (0.3–0.6 m).
Leaves: alternate; crowded; 8–18″ (20–46 cm) long, 5–8″ (13–20 cm) wide. Usually reverse ovate (sometimes ear-shaped); broadest beyond middle, short-pointed at tip, with 2 large pointed lobes at narrow base; not toothed; hairless. Bright green above, pale and whitish beneath.
Bark: light gray; smooth or becoming scaly; thin.
Twigs: brown, stout, with ring scars at nodes.
Flowers: 8–10″ (20–25 cm) wide; 6–9 cream-colored petals; fragrant; solitary at end of twig; in spring.
Fruit: 4–5″ (10–13 cm) long; conelike; oblong; rose-red; composed of many long-pointed hairless 2-seeded fruits that split open in early autumn.

Habitat
Moist soils of mountain valleys in hardwood forests.

Range
W. Virginia and West Virginia south to N. Georgia; at 800–5000′ (244–1524 m).

Comments
Named for John Fraser (1750–1811), the Scottish botanist who introduced many North American plants to Europe. This species has a scattered distribution, but is fairly common in the Great Smoky Mountains National Park. Planted as an ornamental for the large flowers and coarse foliage.

Common Persimmon
Diospyros virginiana
56, 185

Tree with a dense cylindrical or rounded crown, or sometimes a shrub, best known by its sweet, orange fruit in autumn.
Height: 20–70′ (6–21 m). Diameter: 1–2′ (0.3–0.6 m).
Leaves: alternate; 2½–6″ (6–15 cm) long, 1½–3″ (4–7.5 cm) wide. Ovate to elliptical; long-pointed; without teeth; slightly thickened. Shiny dark green above, whitish green and hairless to densely hairy beneath; turning yellow in autumn.
Bark: brown or blackish; thick, deeply furrowed into small square scaly plates.

Twigs: brown to gray, slightly zigzag, often hairy.
Flowers: with bell-shaped, 4-lobed white corolla; fragrant;
scattered and almost stalkless at leaf bases. Male and female on
separate trees in spring. Male, 2–3 together, ⅜" (10 mm)
long. Female, solitary, ⅝" (15 mm) long.
Fruit: ¾–1½" (2–4 cm) in diameter; a rounded or slightly
flat, orange to purplish-brown berry; 4–8 large flat seeds;
maturing in autumn before frost and often remaining attached
into winter; orange pulp becoming soft and juicy at maturity.

Habitat
Moist alluvial soils of valleys and in dry uplands; also at
roadsides and in old fields, clearings, and mixed forests.

Range
S. Connecticut south to S. Florida, west to central Texas, and
north to extreme SE. Iowa; to 3500' (1067 m).

Comments
When ripe, the sweet fruit of Persimmon somewhat recalls the
flavor of dates. Immature fruit contains tannin and is strongly
astringent. Persimmons are consumed fresh and are used to
make puddings, cakes, and beverages. American Indians made
persimmon bread and stored the dried fruit like prunes.
Opossums, raccoons, skunks, deer, and birds also feed upon
the fruit.

Black Tupelo
Nyssa sylvatica
57

Tree with a dense, conical or sometimes flat-topped crown,
many slender, nearly horizontal branches, and glossy foliage
turning scarlet in autumn.
Height: 50–100' (15–30 m). Diameter: 2–3' (0.6–0.9 m).
Leaves: alternate; 2–5" (5–13 cm) long, 1–3" (2.5–7.5 cm)
wide. Elliptical or oblong; not toothed (rarely with a few
teeth); slightly thickened; often crowded on short twigs. Shiny
green above, pale and often hairy beneath; turning bright red
in early autumn.
Bark: gray or dark brown; thick, rough, deeply furrowed into
rectangular or irregular ridges.
Twigs: light brown; slender, often hairy, with some short
spurs.
Flowers: greenish; at end of long stalks at base of new leaves in
early spring; many tiny male flowers in heads ½" (12 mm)
wide; 2–6 female flowers ³⁄₁₆" (5 mm) long; male and female
usually on separate trees.
Fruit: ⅜–½" (10–12 mm) long; berrylike, elliptical, blue-
black; with thin bitter or sour pulp; stone slightly 10- to
12-ridged; maturing in autumn.

Habitat
Moist soils of valleys and uplands in hardwood and pine
forests.

Range
Extreme S. Ontario east to SW. Maine, south to S. Florida,
west to E. Texas, and north to central Michigan; local in

Mexico; to 4000' (1219 m), sometimes higher in southern
Appalachians.

Comments
A handsome ornamental and shade tree, Black Tupelo is also a
honey plant. The juicy fruit is consumed by many birds and
mammals. Swamp Tupelo (var. *biflora*), a variety with
narrower oblong leaves, occurs in swamps in the Coastal Plain
from Delaware to eastern Texas. The fruits are consumed by a
variety of wildlife. Also known as Blackgum.

Cucumbertree
Magnolia acuminata
58

Tree with straight trunk and narrow crown of short, upright
to spreading branches.
Height: 60–80' (18–24 m). Diameter: 2' (0.6 m).
Leaves: alternate; 5–10" (13–25 cm) long, often larger; 3–6"
(7.5–15 cm) wide. Elliptical or ovate; abruptly short-pointed;
edges straight or wavy. Green and becoming hairless above,
paler and often with soft hairs beneath; turning dull yellow or
brown in autumn.
Bark: dark brown; furrowed into narrow scaly forking ridges.
Twigs: stout; with ring scars at nodes; young twigs and buds
densely hairy.
Flowers: 2½–3½" (6–9 cm) wide; bell-shaped, with 6 large
greenish-yellow or bright yellow petals; solitary at end of
twig; in spring.
Fruit: 2½–3" (6–7.5 cm) long; conelike; oblong; dark red;
composed of many pointed fruits that split open, each with 2
seeds that hang down on threads; maturing in late summer.

Habitat
Moist soils of mountain slopes and valleys in mixed forests.

Range
Extreme S. Ontario and W. New York south to NW. Florida,
west to Louisiana, and north to Missouri; at 100–4000' (30–
1219 m).

Comments
Also known as Cucumber Magnolia. The common name refers
to the shape of the fruit, and the Latin species name to the
pointed leaves.

Pawpaw
Asimina triloba
59, 184

Shrub or small tree that forms colonies from root sprouts, with
straight trunk, spreading branches, and large leaves.
Height: 30' (9 m). Diameter: 8" (20 cm).
Leaves: 7–10" (18–25 cm) long, 3–5" (7.5–13 cm) wide.
Alternate; spreading in 2 rows on long twigs; reverse ovate,
broadest beyond middle, short-pointed at tip, tapering to base
and short leafstalk; covered with rust-colored hairs when
young. Green above, paler beneath; turning yellow in
autumn. Bruised foliage has disagreeable odor.
Bark: dark brown, warty, thin.
Twigs: brown; often with rust-colored hairs; ending in small
hairy buds.

Flowers: 1½" (4 cm) wide; 3 triangular green to brown or purple outer petals, hairy with prominent veins; nodding singly on slender stalks; in early spring.
Fruit: 3–5" (7.5–13 cm) long, 1–1½" (2.5–4 cm) in diameter; berrylike; brownish; cylindrical; slightly curved, suggesting a small banana; edible soft yellowish pulp has flavor of custard. Several shiny brown oblong seeds.

Habitat
Moist soils, especially floodplains; in understory of hardwood forests.

Range
S. Ontario and W. New York, south to NW. Florida, west to E. Texas, and north to SE. Nebraska; to 2600' (792 m) in southern Appalachians.

Comments
Pawpaw is the northernmost New World representative of a chiefly tropical family, which includes the popular tropical fruits Annona, Custard-apple, Sugar-apple, and Soursop. The wild fruit was once harvested, but the supply has now decreased greatly due to the clearing of forests. The small crop is generally consumed only by wildlife, such as opossums, squirrels, raccoons, and birds. Attempts have been made to cultivate the Pawpaw as a fruit tree. First recorded by the DeSoto expedition in the lower Mississippi Valley in 1541. The name Pawpaw is from the Arawakan name of Papaya, an unrelated tropical American fruit.

Buttonbush
Cephalanthus occidentalis
60, 163

Spreading, much-branched shrub or sometimes small tree with many branches (often crooked and leaning), irregular crown, balls of white flowers resembling pincushions, and buttonlike balls of fruit.
Height: 20' (6 m). Diameter: 4" (10 cm).
Leaves: opposite 3 at a node (whorled); 2½–6" (6–15 cm) long, 1–3" (2.5–7.5 cm) wide. Ovate or elliptical, pointed at tip, rounded at base; without teeth. Shiny green above, paler and sometimes hairy beneath; at southern limit nearly evergreen.
Bark: gray or brown; becoming deeply furrowed into rough scaly ridges.
Twigs: mostly in 3's; reddish brown, stout, sometimes hairy, with rings at nodes.
Flowers: ⅝" (15 mm) long; with narrow, tubular, white 4-lobed corolla and long threadlike style; fragrant; stalkless; crowded in upright long-stalked white balls of many flowers each, 1–1½" (2.5–4 cm) in diameter; from late spring through summer.
Fruit: ¾–1" (2–2.5 cm) in diameter; compact rough brown balls composed of many small, narrow, dry nutlets ¼" (6 mm) long, each 2-seeded; maturing in autumn.

Habitat
Wet soils bordering streams and lakes.

Range
S. Quebec and SW. Nova Scotia, south to S. Florida, west to Texas, and north to SE. Minnesota; to 3000′ (914 m); in Arizona and California to 5000′ (1524 m); also Mexico, Central America, and Cuba.

Comments
The poisonous foliage of this abundant and widespread species is unpalatable to livestock. The bitter bark has served in home remedies, but its medicinal value is doubtful. Buttonbush is a handsome ornamental suited to wet soils and is also a honey plant. Waterfowl and shorebirds eat the seeds.

Northern Catalpa
Catalpa speciosa
61, 149

Tree with rounded crown of spreading branches; large, heart-shaped leaves; large, showy flowers; and long, beanlike fruit.
Height: 50–80′ (15–24 m). Diameter: 2½′ (0.8 m).
Leaves: 3 at a node (whorled) and opposite; 6–12″ (15–30 cm) long, 4–8″ (10–20 cm) wide; ovate, long-pointed, straight to notched at base; without teeth. Dull green above, paler and covered with soft hairs beneath; turning blackish in autumn. Slender leafstalk 4–6″ (10–15 cm) long.
Bark: brownish gray; smooth, becoming furrowed into scaly plates or ridges.
Twigs: green, turning brown; stout; becoming hairless.
Flowers: 2–2¼″ (5–6 cm) long and wide; with bell-shaped corolla of 5 unequal rounded fringed lobes, white with 2 orange stripes and purple spots and lines inside; in branched upright clusters, 5–8″ (13–20 cm) long and wide; in late spring.
Fruit: 8–18″ (20–46 cm) long, ½–⅝″ (12–15 mm) in diameter; narrow, cylindrical, dark brown capsule; cigarlike, thick-walled, splitting into 2 parts; many flat light brown seeds with 2 papery wings; maturing in autumn, remaining attached in winter.

Habitat
Moist valley soils by streams; naturalized in open areas such as roadsides and clearings.

Range
Original range uncertain; native apparently from SW. Indiana to NE. Arkansas; widely naturalized in southeastern United States; at 200–500′ (61–152 m).

Comments
Northern Catalpa is the northernmost New World example of its tropical family and is hardier than Southern Catalpa, which blooms later and has slightly smaller flowers and narrower, thinner-walled capsules. Both are called Cigartree and Indianbean because of the distinctive fruit.

Southern Catalpa
Catalpa bignonioides
62

Short-trunked tree with broad, rounded crown of spreading branches, large, heart-shaped leaves, large clusters of showy white flowers, and long, beanlike fruit.

Height: 50' (15 m). Diameter: 2' (0.6 m).
Leaves: 3 at a node (whorled) and opposite; 5–10" (13–25 cm) long, 4–7" (10–18 cm) wide. Ovate, abruptly long-pointed at tip, notched at base; without teeth. Dull green above, paler and covered with soft hairs beneath; turning blackish in autumn. With unpleasant odor when crushed. Slender leafstalk 3½–6" (9–15 cm) long.
Bark: brownish gray; scaly.
Twigs: green, turning brown; stout, hairless or nearly so.
Flowers: 1½" (4 cm) long and wide; with bell-shaped corolla of 5 unequal rounded fringed lobes, white with 2 orange stripes and many purple spots and stripes inside; slightly fragrant; in upright branched clusters to 10" (25 cm) long and wide; in late spring.
Fruit: 6–12" (15–30 cm) long, ⁵⁄₁₆–⅜" (8–10 mm) in diameter; narrow, cylindrical, dark brown capsule; cigarlike, thin-walled, splitting into 2 parts; many flat light brown seeds with 2 papery wings; maturing in autumn, remaining attached in winter.

Habitat
Moist soils in open areas such as roadsides and clearings.

Range
Probably native in SW. Georgia, NW. Florida, Alabama, and Mississippi; widely naturalized from southern New England south to Florida, west to Texas, and north to Michigan; at 100–500' (30–152 m).

Comments
Catalpa is the American Indian name, while the scientific name refers to a related vine with flowers of similar shape. Planted as a shade tree and an ornamental for the abundant showy flowers, cigarlike pods, and coarse foliage.

Eastern Redbud
Cercis canadensis
63, 146

Tree with a short trunk, rounded crown of spreading branches, and pink flowers that cover the twigs in spring.
Height: 40' (12 m). Diameter: 8" (20 cm).
Leaves; alternate; 2½–4½" (6–11 cm) long and broad. Heart-shaped, with broad short point; without teeth; with 5–9 main veins; long-stalked. Dull green above, paler and sometimes hairy beneath; turning yellow in autumn.
Bark: dark gray or brown; smooth, becoming furrowed into scaly plates.
Twigs: brown, slender, angled.
Flowers: ½" (12 mm) long; petals slightly unequal; 1 broad upper petal and 2 lateral petals nearly enclosing 2 bottom petals that are joined and shaped like prow of a boat; purplish pink, rarely white; 4–8 flowers in a cluster on slender stalks; in early spring before leaves.
Fruit: 2½–3¼" (6–8 cm) long; flat narrowly oblong pods; pointed at ends; pink, turning blackish; splitting open on 1 edge; falling in late autumn or winter. Several beanlike, flat, elliptical, dark brown seeds.

Habitat
Moist soils of valleys and slopes and in hardwood forests.

Range
New Jersey south to central Florida, west to S. Texas, and north to SE. Nebraska; also northern Mexico; to 2200' (671 m).

Comments
This tree is very showy in early spring, when the leafless twigs are covered with masses of pink flowers. Eastern Redbud is often planted as an ornamental. The flowers can be eaten as a salad, or fried. Also known as the Judas-tree; according to legend, Judas Iscariot hanged himself on the related and similar *Cercis siliquastrum* of western Asia and southern Europe, after which the white flowers turned red with shame or blood.

Quaking Aspen
Populus tremuloides
64

The most widely distributed tree in North America; with a narrow, rounded crown of thin foliage.
Height: 40–70' (12–21 m). Diameter: 1–1½' (0.3–0.5 m).
Leaves: alternate; 1¼–3" (3–7.5 cm) long. Nearly round; abruptly short-pointed; rounded at base; finely saw-toothed; thin. Shiny green above, dull green beneath; turning golden yellow in autumn before shedding. Leafstalks flattened.
Bark: whitish, smooth, thin; on very large trunks becoming dark gray, furrowed, and thick.
Twigs: shiny brown; slender, hairless.
Flowers: catkins 1–2½" (2.5–6 cm) long; brownish; male and female on separate trees; in early spring before leaves.
Fruit: ¼" (6 mm) long; narrowly conical light green capsules in drooping catkins to 4" (10 cm) long; maturing in late spring and splitting in 2 parts. Many tiny cottony seeds; rarely produced in the West, where propagation is by root sprouts.

Habitat
Many soil types, especially sandy and gravelly slopes; often in pure stands and in western mountains in an altitudinal zone below spruce-fir forest.

Range
Across northern North America from Alaska to Newfoundland, south to Virginia, and in Rocky Mountains south to S. Arizona and northern Mexico; from near sea level northward to 6500–10,000' (1981–3048 m) southward.

Comments
The name refers to the leaves, which in the slightest breeze tremble on their flattened leafstalks. The soft smooth bark is sometimes decorated with carved initials and marked by bear claws. A pioneer tree after fires and logging and on abandoned fields, it is short-lived and replaced by conifers. Sometimes planted as an ornamental. Principal uses of the wood include pulpwood, boxes, furniture parts, matches, excelsior, and particle-board. The twigs and foliage are browsed by deer, elk, and moose, as well as by sheep and goats. Beavers,

rabbits, and other mammals eat the bark, foliage, and buds, and grouse and quail feed on the winter buds.

Eastern Cottonwood
Populus deltoides
65, 181, 240

Large tree with a massive trunk often forked into stout branches, and broad, open crown of spreading and slightly drooping branches.
Height: 100' (30 m). Diameter: 3–4' (0.9–1.2 m), often larger.
Leaves: alternate; 3–7" (7.5–18 cm) long, 3–5" (7.5–13 cm) wide. Triangular; long-pointed; usually straight at base; curved, coarse teeth; slightly thickened; shiny green, turning yellow in autumn. Leafstalks long, slender, flattened.
Bark: yellowish green and smooth; becoming light gray, thick, rough, and deeply furrowed.
Twigs: brownish; stout, with large resinous or sticky buds.
Flowers: catkins 2–3½" (5–9 cm) long; brownish; male and female on separate trees; in early spring.
Fruit: ⅜" (10 mm) long; elliptical capsules, light brown; maturing in spring and splitting into 3–4 parts; many on slender stalks in catkin to 8" (20 cm) long; many tiny cottony seeds.

Habitat
Bordering streams and in wet soils in valleys; in pure stands or often with willows. Pioneers on new sandbars and bare floodplains.

Range

Widespread. S. Alberta east to extreme S. Quebec and New Hampshire, south to NW. Florida, west to W. Texas, and north to central Montana; to 1000' (305 m) in east, to 5000' (1524 m) in west.

Comments
One of the largest eastern hardwoods, Eastern Cottonwood is used for boxes and crates, furniture, plywood, woodenware, matches, and pulpwood. It is also planted as a shade tree and for shelterbelts. The common name refers to the abundant cottony seeds; another name, Necklace Poplar, alludes to the resemblance of the long, narrow line of seed capsules to a string of beads. Although short-lived, it is one of the fastest-growing native trees; on favorable sites in the Mississippi Valley, trees average 5' (1.5 m) in height growth annually with as much as 13' (4 m) the first year.

Bigtooth Aspen
Populus grandidentata
66, 222

Medium-sized tree with narrow, rounded crown.
Height: 30–60' (9–18 m). Diameter: 1–1½' (0.3–0.5 m).
Leaves: alternate; 2½–4" (6–10 cm) long, 1¾–3½" (4.5–9 cm) wide. Broadly ovate; short-pointed tip; rounded at base; coarse, curved teeth; with white hairs when young. Dull green above, paler beneath, turning pale yellow in autumn. Leafstalks long, slender, flattened.
Bark: greenish, smooth, thin; becoming dark brown and

furrowed into flat, scaly ridges.
Twigs: brown, slender, hairy when young.
Flowers: catkins 1½–2½" (4–6 cm) long; brownish; male and
female on separate trees; in early spring.
Fruit: ¼" (6 mm) long; narrowly conical capsules; light green;
slightly curved; finely hairy; maturing in spring and splitting
into 2 parts; many tiny cottony seeds.

Habitat
Sandy upland soils, also floodplains of streams, often with
Quaking Aspen.

Range
SE. Manitoba east to Cape Breton Island, south to Virginia,
and west to NE. Missouri; local south to W. North Carolina;
to 2000' (610 m), or to 3000' (914 m) in south.

Comments
Easily distinguishable from Quaking Aspen by the large
curved teeth of leaf edges, mentioned in both common and
scientific names. Like that species, Bigtooth Aspen is a
pioneer tree after fires and logging and on abandoned fields; it
is short-lived and soon replaced by conifers. The foliage, twig
buds, and bark are consumed by wildlife.

Paper Birch
Betula papyrifera
67, 238

One of the most beautiful native trees, with narrow, open
crown of slightly drooping to nearly horizontal branches;
sometimes a shrub.
Height: 50–70' (15–21 m). Diameter: 1–2' (0.3–0.6 m).
Leaves: alternate; 2–4" (5–10 cm) long, 1½–2" (4–5 cm)
wide. Ovate, long-pointed; coarsely and doubly saw-toothed;
usually with 5–9 veins on each side. Dull dark green above,
light yellow-green and nearly hairless beneath; turning light
yellow in autumn.
Bark: chalky to creamy white; smooth, thin, with long
horizontal lines; separating into papery strips to reveal orange
inner bark; becoming brown, furrowed, and scaly at base;
bronze to purplish in varieties.
Twigs: reddish brown, slender, mostly hairless.
Flowers: tiny; in early spring. Male yellowish, with 2 stamens,
many in long drooping catkins near tip of twigs. Female
greenish, in short upright catkins back of tip of same twig.
Cones: 1½–2" (4–5 cm); narrowly cylindrical, brownish,
hanging on slender stalk; with many 2-winged nutlets;
maturing in autumn.

Habitat
Moist upland soils and cutover lands; often in nearly pure
stands.

Range
Transcontinental across North America near northern limit of
trees from NW. Alaska east to Labrador, south to New York,
and west to Oregon; local south to N. Colorado and W. North
Carolina; to 4000' (1219 m), higher in southern mountains.

Comments
Paper Birch is used for specialty products such as ice cream sticks, toothpicks, bobbins, clothespins, spools, broom handles, and toys, as well as pulpwood. Indians made their lightweight birchbark canoes by stretching the stripped bark over frames of Northern White-cedar, sewing it with thread from Tamarack roots, and caulking the seams with pine or Balsam Fir resin. Souvenirs of birch bark should always be taken from a fallen log, since stripping bark from living trees leaves permanent ugly black scars. This tree is also known as Canoe Birch and White Birch.

Yellow Birch
Betula alleghaniensis
68

Large, aromatic tree with broad, rounded crown of drooping branches and slight odor of wintergreen in crushed twigs and foliage.
Height: 70–100′ (21–30 m). Diameter: 2½′ (0.8 m).
Leaves: alternate; 3–5″ (7.5–13 cm) long, 1½–2″ (4–5 cm) wide. Elliptical, short-pointed or rounded at base; sharply and doubly saw-toothed; mostly with 9–11 veins on each side; hairy when young. Dark dull green above, light yellow-green beneath; turning bright yellow in autumn.
Bark: shiny yellowish or silvery gray; separating into papery curly strips; becoming reddish brown and fissured into plates.
Twigs: greenish brown, slender, hairy.
Flowers: tiny; in early spring. Male yellowish, with 2 stamens, many in long drooping catkins near tip of twigs. Female greenish, in short upright catkins back of tip of same twig.
Cones: ¾–1¼″ (2–3 cm) long; oblong; hairy; brownish; upright; nearly stalkless; with many hairy scales and 2-winged nutlets; maturing in autumn.

Habitat
Cool moist uplands including mountain ravines; with hardwoods and conifers.

Range
Extreme SE. Manitoba east to S. Newfoundland, south to extreme NE. Georgia, and west to NE. Iowa; to 2500′ (762 m) in north and 3000–6000′ (914–1829 m) or higher in south.

Comments
Also called Gray Birch and Silver Birch, this is one of the most valuable birches and one of the largest hardwoods in northeastern North America. Yellow Birch when fairly mature is easily recognized by its distinctive bark. Young specimens, which may be mistaken for Sweet Birch, are most readily identified by their hairy twigs and buds and more persistently hairy leaves with mostly unbranched side veins.

River Birch
Betula nigra
69

Often slightly leaning and forked tree with irregular, spreading crown.
Height: 40–80′ (12–24 m). Diameter: 1–2′ (0.3–0.6 m).

Leaves: alternate; 1½–3″ (4–7.5 cm) long, 1–2¼″ (2.5–6 cm) wide. Ovate or nearly 4-sided; coarsely doubly saw-toothed or slightly lobed; usually with 7–9 veins on each side. Shiny dark green above, whitish and usually hairy beneath; turning dull yellow in autumn.
Bark: shiny pinkish brown or silvery gray, separating into papery scales; becoming thick, fissured, and shaggy.
Twigs: reddish brown, slender, hairy.
Flowers: tiny; in early spring. Male yellowish, with 2 stamens, many in long drooping catkins near tip of twigs. Female greenish, in short upright catkins back of tip of same twig.
Cones: 1–1½″ (2.5–4 cm) long; cylindrical, brownish, upright, short-stalked; with many hairy scales and hairy 2-winged nutlets; maturing in late spring or early summer.

Habitat
Wet soil of stream banks, lakes, swamps, and floodplains; with other hardwoods.

Range
SW. Connecticut south to N. Florida, west to E. Texas, and north to SE. Minnesota; local in Massachusetts and S. New Hampshire; to 1000′ (305 m); to 2500′ (762 m) in southern Appalachians.

Comments
Our southernmost birch is the only one at low altitudes in the Southeast. Able to thrive on moist sites, it is useful for erosion control. Also called Red Birch and Black Birch.

Red Mulberry
Morus rubra
70

Medium-sized tree with short trunk, broad rounded crown, and milky sap.
Height: 60′ (18 m). Diameter: 2′ (0.6 m).
Leaves: alternate in 2 rows; 4–7″ (10–18 cm) long, 2½–5″ (6–13 cm) wide. Ovate; abruptly long-pointed; with 3 main veins from often unequal base, coarsely saw-toothed; often with 2 or 3 lobes on young twigs. Dull dark green and rough above, with soft hairs beneath; turning yellow in autumn.
Bark: brown; fissured into scaly plates.
Twigs: brown, slender.
Flowers: tiny, about ⅛″ (3 mm) long; crowded in narrow clusters; male and female on same or separate trees; in spring when leaves appear.
Fruit: 1–1¼″ (2.5–3 cm) long; a cylindrical mulberry; red to dark purple; composed of many tiny beadlike 1-seeded fruits, sweet and juicy, edible; in late spring.

Habitat
Moist soils in hardwood forests.

Range
S. Ontario east to Massachusetts, south to S. Florida, west to central Texas and north to SE. Minnesota; to 2000′ (610 m).

Comments
The wood is used locally for fenceposts, furniture, interior

finish, and agricultural implements. People, domestic animals, and wildlife (especially songbirds) eat the berries. Choctaw Indians wove cloaks from the fibrous inner bark of young mulberry shoots.

White Basswood
Tilia heterophylla
71

Large tree with a dense crown of large leaves with whitish lower surfaces.
Height: 60–80′ (18–24 m). Diameter: 2′ (0.6 m).
Leaves: alternate; 3–7″ (7.5–18 cm) long and almost as wide. Broadly ovate, long-pointed at tip, unequal and nearly straight at base; coarsely saw-toothed, palmately veined; with long, slender leafstalks. Shiny dark green above, with thick coat of white hairs beneath.
Bark: gray; becoming furrowed into scaly ridges.
Twigs: gray or brown, slender, slightly zigzag, hairless.
Flowers: ½–⅝″ (12–15 mm) wide; with 5 yellowish-white petals; fragrant; in long-stalked clusters hanging from middle of leafy greenish bract; in early summer.
Fruit: ⅜″ (10 mm) in diameter; nutlike, round, gray, covered with fine hairs; hard; 1–2 seeds; maturing in late summer.

Habitat
Moist soils of valleys and uplands in hardwood forests.

Range
SW. Pennsylvania south to NW. Florida, and west to N. Arkansas and Missouri; also local north to W. New York; at 200–5000′ (61–1524 m).

Comments
Also called Linden. From some distance the trees can be distinguished by the whitish lower leaf surfaces that are upturned by breezes. Sprouts arise from the base of a tree, sometimes forming a ring around the trunk.

American Basswood
Tilia americana
72, 239

Large tree with long trunk and a dense crown of many small, often drooping branches and large leaves; frequently has 2 or more trunks, and sprouts in a circle from a stump.
Height: 60–100′ (18–30 m). Diameter: 2–3′ (0.6–0.9 m).
Leaves: alternate; 3–6″ (7.5–15 cm) long and almost as wide. Broadly ovate or rounded; long-pointed at tip; notched at base; coarsely saw-toothed; palmately veined; long slender leafstalks. Shiny dark green above, light green and nearly hairless with tufts of hairs in vein angles beneath; turning pale yellow or brown in autumn.
Bark: dark gray; smooth, becoming furrowed into scaly ridges.
Twigs: reddish or green, slender, slightly zigzag, hairless.
Flowers: ½–⅝″ (12–15 mm) wide; with 5 yellowish-white petals; fragrant; in long-stalked clusters hanging from middle of leafy greenish bract; in early summer.
Fruit: ⅜″ (10 mm) in diameter; nutlike, elliptical or rounded, gray, covered with fine hairs; hard; 1–2 seeds; maturing in late summer and autumn, often persisting into winter.

Habitat
Moist soils of valleys and uplands; in hardwood forests.

Range
SE. Manitoba east to SW. New Brunswick and Maine, south to W. North Carolina, and west to NE. Oklahoma; to 3200′ (975 m).

Comments
American Basswood, also called American Linden, is the northernmost basswood species and a handsome shade and street tree. When flowering, the trees are full of bees, hence the nickname Bee-tree; this species is favored by bees over others and produces a strongly flavored honey. The soft, light wood is especially useful for making food boxes, yardsticks, furniture, and pulpwood. Indians made ropes and woven mats from the tough fibrous inner bark.

Green Hawthorn
Crataegus viridis
73

Thicket-forming tree with straight, often fluted, trunk and rounded, dense crown of spreading branches, shiny foliage, showy flowers, and small red to yellow fruit.
Height: 40′ (12 m). Diameter: 1½′ (0.5 m).
Leaves: alternate; 1–2½″ (2.5–6 cm) long, ½–1½″ (1.2–4 cm) wide. Elliptical or nearly 4-angled, short-pointed at tip, gradually narrowed to long-pointed base; finely saw-toothed; sometimes slightly 3-lobed; shiny dark green and becoming hairless above, pale with tufts of hairs in vein angles beneath; often turning scarlet in autumn.
Bark: pale gray with orange-brown inner bark; scaly.
Twigs: gray, hairless, usually without spines.
Flowers: ⅝″ (15 mm) wide; with 5 white petals, about 20 pale yellow stamens, and usually 5 (2–5) styles; many flowers (mostly 8–20), on long slender stalks in branching clusters; in spring.
Fruit: ¼″ (6 mm) in diameter; bright red, orange-red, or yellow; thin juicy pulp; usually 5 nutlets; many, in drooping clusters; maturing in autumn and persisting into winter.

Habitat
Wet or moist soils of valleys and low upland slopes.

Range
Delaware south to N. Florida, west to E. Texas, and north to SW. Indiana; to about 500′ (152 m).

Comments
In 1753 Linnaeus gave this tree its Latin species name, meaning "green"; his decision was based on a specimen with shiny green foliage sent from Virginia.

Downy Hawthorn
Crataegus mollis
74, 155

Handsome tree with tall trunk and compact, rounded crown of spreading branches, large broad hairy leaves, many large flowers, and large scarlet fruit.
Height: 40′ (12 m). Diameter: 1′ (0.3 m).

Leaves: alternate; 3–4" (7.5–10 cm) long and wide. Broadly ovate, short-pointed at tip, rounded or slightly notched at base; doubly saw-toothed; with 4–5 veins on each side ending in shallow pointed lobes; densely covered with white hairs when young. Dark yellow-green above, pale and slightly hairy beneath.
Bark: brown to gray; fissured into scaly plates; becoming thick.
Twigs: covered with white hairs when young; with stout spines, though sometimes nearly thornless.
Flowers: to 1" (2.5 cm) wide; with 5 white petals, 20 light yellow stamens, and 4–5 styles; in broad clusters; in spring.
Fruit: ¾" (19 mm) in diameter; nearly round or short oblong; scarlet or crimson with dark dots; slightly hairy; thick juicy edible pulp; 4–5 nutlets; few, in drooping clusters; maturing in late summer or autumn.

Habitat
Moist soil of valleys and hillsides in open woods.

Range
S. Quebec and Nova Scotia, south to West Virginia and Alabama, west to south-central Texas, and north to SE. North Dakota; to 1500' (457 m) or higher.

Comments
This large hawthorn was once called White Thorn. It was introduced into European gardens as early as 1683.

Eastern Hophornbeam
Ostrya virginiana
75, 167, 176, 234

A tree with a trunk that looks like sinewy muscles and a rounded crown of slender, spreading branches.
Height: 20–50' (6–15 m). Diameter: 1' (0.3 m).
Leaves: alternate; 2–5" (5–13 cm) long, 1–2" (2.5–5 cm) wide. Ovate or elliptical; sharply doubly saw-toothed; with many nearly straight parallel side veins; short, hairy leafstalks. Dull yellow-green and nearly hairless above, paler and hairy chiefly on veins beneath; turning yellow in autumn.
Bark: light brown; thin, finely fissured into long narrow scaly ridges.
Flowers: tiny; in early spring before leaves. Male greenish, in 1–3 drooping, narrowly cylindrical clusters 1½–2½" (4–6 cm) long. Female reddish green, in narrowly cylindrical clusters ½–¾" (12–19 mm) long.
Fruit: 1½–2" (4–5 cm) long, ¾–1" (2–2.5 cm) wide; conelike hanging clusters maturing in later summer; composed of many flattened, small, egg-shaped brown nutlets, each within a swollen, egg-shaped, flattened, light brown cover that is papery and sacklike.

Habitat
Moist soil in understory of upland hardwood forests.

Range
SE. Manitoba east to Cape Breton Island, south to N. Florida, and west to E. Texas; to 4500' (1372 m).

Comments
The common name refers to the resemblance of the fruit clusters to hops, an ingredient of beer. The nutlets and buds are eaten by wildlife such as bobwhites, pheasants, grouse, deer, and rabbits. This species is also called Ironwood for its extremely hard tough wood, which is used for tool handles, small wooden articles, and fenceposts. Although planted as an ornamental, Eastern Hophornbeam is slow growing.

Sweet Birch
Betula lenta
76, 166, 235

Aromatic tree with rounded crown of spreading branches and odor of wintergreen in crushed twigs and foliage.
Height: 50–80′ (15–24 m). Diameter: 1–2½′ (0.3–0.8 m).
Leaves: alternate; 2½–5″ (6–13 cm) long, 1½–3″ (4–7.5 cm) wide. Elliptical, long-pointed, often notched at base; sharply and doubly saw-toothed; mostly with 9–11 veins on each side; becoming nearly hairless. Dull dark green above, light yellow-green beneath; turning bright yellow in autumn.
Bark: shiny, dark brown or blackish, smooth but not papery; on large trunks fissured into scaly plates like Black Cherry.
Twigs: dark brown, slender, hairless.
Flowers: tiny; in early spring. Male yellowish, with 2 stamens, many in long drooping catkins near tip of twigs. Female greenish, in short upright catkins back of tip of same twig.
Cones: ¾–1½″ (2–4 cm) long; oblong, brownish, upright, nearly stalkless; with hairless scales and many 2-winged nutlets; maturing in autumn.

Habitat
Cool, moist uplands; with hardwoods and conifers.

Range
S. Maine southwest to N. Alabama and north to Ohio; local in extreme S. Quebec and SE. Ontario; nearly to sea level in north; at 2000–6000′ (610–1829 m) in southern Appalachians.

Comments
Birch oil, or oil of wintergreen, which was often used to flavor medicines and candy, was once obtained from the bark and wood of young trees. That wasteful process has been replaced by the manufacture of the same oil from wood alcohol and salicylic acid. The trees can be tapped like Sugar Maples in early spring and the fermented sap made into birch beer. Also known as Black Birch and Cherry Birch.

Hackberry
Celtis occidentalis
77, 188

Tree with rounded crown of spreading or slightly drooping branches, often deformed as bushy growths called witches'-brooms.
Height: 50–90′ (15–27 m). Diameter: 1½–3′ (0.5–0.9 m).
Leaves: alternate in 2 rows; 2–5″ (5–13 cm) long, 1½–2½″ (4–6 cm) wide, ovate, long-pointed; usually sharply toothed except toward unequal-sided, rounded base; 3 main veins. Shiny green and smooth (sometimes rough) above, paler and

often hairy on veins beneath; turning yellow in autumn.
Bark: gray or light brown; smooth with corky warts or ridges, becoming scaly.
Twigs: light brown, slender, mostly hairy, slightly zigzag.
Flowers: ⅛" (3 mm) wide; greenish; male and female at base of young leaves in early spring.
Fruit: ¼–⅜" (6–10 mm) in diameter; orange-red to dark purple 1-seeded drupes; dry and sweet; slender-stalked at leaf bases; maturing in autumn.

Habitat
Mainly in river valleys, also on upland slopes and bluffs' in mixed hardwood forests.

Range
Extreme S. Ontario east to New England, south to N. Georgia, west to NW. Oklahoma, north to North Dakota; local in S. Quebec and S. Manitoba; to 5000' (1524 m).

Comments
Used for furniture, athletic goods, boxes and crates, and plywood. The common name apparently was derived from "hagberry," meaning "marsh berry," a name used in Scotland for a cherry. Many birds, including quail, pheasants, woodpeckers, and cedar waxwings, consume the sweetish fruits. Branches of this and other hackberries may become deformed bushy growths called witches'-brooms, which are produced by mites and fungi. The leaves often bear rounded galls caused by tiny jumping plant lice.

Sugarberry
Celtis laevigata
78

Tree with broad, rounded, open crown of spreading or slightly drooping branches.
Height: 80' (24 cm). Diameter: 1½' (0.5 m).
Leaves: alternate in 2 rows 2½–4" (6–10 cm) long, ¾–1¼" (2–3 cm) wide. Broadly lance-shaped, long-pointed, often curved; 2 sides unequal; without teeth, sometimes with a few; 3 main veins from base; thin. Dark green and usually smooth above, paler and usually hairless beneath.
Bark: light gray, thin, smooth, with prominent corky warts.
Twigs: greenish, slender, mostly hairless.
Flowers: ⅛" (3 mm) wide; greenish; male and female at base of young leaves in early spring.
Fruit: ¼" (6 mm) in diameter; orange-red or purple 1-seeded drupes; dry and sweet; slender-stalked at leaf bases.

Habitat
Moist soils, especially clay, on river floodplains; sometimes in pure stands but usually with other hardwoods.

Range
SE. Virginia south to S. Florida, west to central and SW. Texas, and north to central Illinois; also northeastern Mexico; to 2000' (610 m).

Comments
Robins, mockingbirds, and other songbirds eat the sweetish

fruits. Principal uses of the wood are for furniture, athletic goods, and plywood.

Downy Serviceberry
Amelanchier arborea
79, 158, 221

Tree with narrow, rounded crown, or an irregularly branched shrub, with star-shaped, white flowers.
Height: 40' (12 m). Diameter: 1' (0.3 m).
Leaves: alternate; 1½–4" (4–10 cm) long, 1–2" (2.5–5 cm) wide. Ovate or elliptical, pointed at tip, notched at base; finely saw-toothed; with soft hairs when young, especially beneath; with 11–17 straight veins on each side. Dull green above, paler beneath; turning yellow to red in autumn.
Bark: light gray; smooth, becoming furrowed into narrow ridges.
Twigs: red-brown, slender, often covered with white hairs when young.
Flowers: 1¼" (3 cm) wide; with 5 narrow white petals; on slender stalks in terminal clusters; in spring before leaves.
Fruit: ¼–⅜" (6–10 mm) in diameter; like a small apple; purple, edible, nearly dry or juicy and sweet, with several seeds; in early summer.

Habitat
Moist soils in hardwood forests.

Range
S. Newfoundland and Nova Scotia south to NW. Florida, west to Louisiana and E. Oklahoma, and north to Minnesota; to 6000' (1829 m) in southern Appalachians.

Comments
Also called Shadbush. The name Shadbush alludes to the fact that the showy masses of white flowers tend to occur at the same time that shad ascend the rivers in early spring to spawn. An older name is Sarvis. Sometimes planted as an ornamental for the showy clusters of flowers.

Nannyberry
Viburnum lentago
80, 154, 195, 217

Shrub or small tree with short trunk, compact, rounded crown of drooping branches, small white flowers in clusters, and small bluish-black fruit.
Height: 20' (6 m). Diameter: 6" (15 cm).
Leaves: opposite; 2½–4" (6–10 cm) long, 1½–2½" (4–6 cm) wide. Elliptical, long-pointed; finely saw-toothed; with prominent network of veins; broad, often hairy leafstalk. Shiny green above, yellow-green with tiny black dots beneath; turning purplish red and orange in autumn.
Bark: reddish brown or gray; irregularly furrowed into scaly plates; with unpleasant skunklike odor.
Twigs: light green, slender, slightly hairy when young, ending in long-pointed, hairy reddish bud.
Flowers: ¼" (6 mm) wide; with 5 rounded white corolla lobes; slightly fragrant; in branched upright, stalkless clusters of many flowers each, 3–5" (7.5–13 cm) wide; in late spring.
Fruit: ½" (12 mm) long; elliptical or sometimes nearly round,

slightly flat, blue-black with whitish bloom; sweet juicy pulp; somewhat flat stone; drooping on slender reddish stalks; maturing in autumn and remaining attached in winter.

Habitat
Moist soils of valleys and rocky uplands; at forest edges.

Range
SE. Saskatchewan east to New Brunswick and Maine, south to West Virginia, west to Nebraska and NE. Wyoming; local in SW. Virginia; to 2500′ (762 m); to 5000′ (1524 m) in Black Hills.

Comments
When cut, the plants sprout from roots, and old branches will often arch down and take root. Songbirds, gamebirds, and mammals eat the fruit in winter.

Eastern Burningbush
Euonymus atropurpureus
81, 187, 220

Shrub or rarely a small tree with spreading, irregular crown and red or purple capsules suggesting a burning bush.
Height: 20′ (6 m). Diameter: 4″ (10 cm).
Leaves: opposite; 2–4½″ (5–11 cm) long, 1–2″ (2.5–5 cm) wide. Elliptical; abruptly long-pointed at tip; finely saw-toothed. Green above, paler and often with fine hairs beneath; turning light yellow in autumn.
Bark: gray; smooth, becoming slightly fissured.
Twigs: dark purplish brown, slender, sometimes 4-angled or slightly winged.
Flowers: ⅜″ (10 mm) wide; with 4 dark red or purple petals; 7–15 flowers clustered on slender, widely forking stalks; in late spring and early summer.
Fruit: ⅝″ (15 mm) wide; red or purple capsules deeply 4-lobed and 4-celled, each lobe splitting open; smooth; several hanging on slender stalk; maturing in autumn, remaining attached into winter; in each cell, 1–2 rounded light brown seeds with red covering.

Habitat
Moist soils, especially in thickets, valleys, and forest edges.

Range
Extreme S. Ontario to central New York, south to N. Georgia, west to central Texas, and north to SE. North Dakota; to 2000′ (610 m).

Comments
The powdered bark was used by American Indians and pioneers as a purgative. Also called Eastern Wahoo, *Wahoo* being the native term. The Latin species name, meaning "dark purple," refers to the color of the fruit.

Water Tupelo
Nyssa aquatica
82

Large aquatic tree with swollen base, long, straight trunk, narrow, open crown of spreading branches, and large, shiny leaves.
Height: 100′ (30 m). Diameter: 3′ (0.9 m).

Leaves: alternate; 5–8″ (13–20 cm) long, 2–4″ (5–10 cm) wide, sometimes larger. Ovate; often with a few large teeth; slightly thickened; with long hairy leafstalks. Shiny dark green above, paler and hairy beneath.
Bark: dark brown or gray; furrowed into scaly ridges.
Twigs: reddish brown; stout, hairy when young.
Flowers: greenish; on long stalks back of new leaves in early spring; many male flowers ¼″ (6 mm) long, in heads ⅝″ (15 mm) wide; solitary female flowers ⅜″ (10 mm) long; male and female usually on separate trees.
Fruit: 1″ (2.5 cm) long; oblong, berrylike, dark purple; with thin sour pulp; stone with 10 winglike ridges; maturing in early autumn.

Habitat
Swamps and floodplains of streams, close to the water, where submerged a few months each winter and spring; often in pure stands.

Range
SE. Virginia south to N. Florida, west to SE. Texas, and north to S. Illinois; to 500′ (152 m).

Comments
This aquatic tree was named *Nyssa* after one of the ancient Greek water nymphs or goddesses of lakes and rivers. The name Tupelo is from Creek Indian words meaning "swamp tree." The spongy wood of the roots has served locally as a substitute for cork in the floats of fishnets.

American Plum
Prunus americana
83, 151, 186

A thicket-forming shrub or small tree with short trunk, many spreading branches, broad crown, showy large white flowers, and red plums.
Height: 30′ (9 m). Diameter: 1′ (0.3 m).
Leaves: alternate; 2½–4″ (6–10 cm) long, 1¼–1¾″ (3–4.5 cm) wide. Elliptical, long-pointed at tip; sharply and often doubly saw-toothed; slightly thickened. Dull green with slightly sunken veins above, paler and often slightly hairy on veins beneath.
Bark: dark brown; scaly.
Twigs: light brown, slender, hairless; short twigs ending in spine.
Flowers: ¾–1″ (2–2.5 cm) wide; with 5 rounded white petals; in clusters of 2–5 on slender equal stalks; slightly unpleasant odor; in early spring before leaves.
Fruit: a plum ¾–1″ (2–2.5 cm) in diameter; thick red skin; juicy sour edible pulp; large stone; maturing in summer.

Habitat
Moist soils of valleys and low upland slopes.

Range
SE. Saskatchewan east to New Hampshire, south to Florida, west to Oklahoma, and north to Montana; to 3000′ (914 m) in the south and to 6000′ (1829 m) in the southwest.

Comments
The plums are eaten fresh and used in jellies and preserves, and are also consumed by many kinds of birds. Numerous cultivated varieties with improved fruit have been developed. This handsome ornamental, with large flowers and fruit, is also grown for erosion control, spreading by root sprouts.

Pin Cherry
Prunus pensylvanica
84, 152, 189, 218

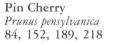

Small tree or shrub with horizontal branches; narrow, rounded, open crown; shiny red twigs; bitter, aromatic bark and foliage; and tiny red cherries.
Height: 30' (9 m). Diameter: 1' (0.3 m).
Leaves: alternate; 2½–4½" (6–11 cm) long, ¾–1¼" (2–3 cm) wide. Broadly lance-shaped, long-pointed; finely and sharply saw-toothed; becoming hairless. Shiny green above, paler beneath; turning bright yellow in autumn. Slender leafstalks often with 2 gland-dots near tip.
Bark: reddish gray, smooth, thin; becoming gray and fissured into scaly plates.
Flowers: ½" (12 mm) wide; with 5 rounded white petals; 3–5 flowers on long equal stalks; in spring with leaves.
Fruit: a cherry ¼" (6 mm) in diameter; red skin; thin sour pulp; large stone; in summer.

Habitat
Moist soil, often in pure stands on burned areas and clearings; with aspens, Paper Birch, and Eastern White Pine.

Range
British Columbia and S. Mackenzie east across Canada to Newfoundland, south to N. Georgia, west to Colorado; to 6000' (1829 m) in southern Appalachians.

Comments
This species is often called Fire Cherry because its seedlings come up after forest fires. The plants grow rapidly and can be used for fuel and pulpwood. It is also a "nurse" tree, providing cover and shade for the establishment of seedlings of the next generation of larger hardwoods. The cherries are made into jelly and are also consumed by wildlife.

American Chestnut
Castanea dentata
85

Formerly a large tree with a massive trunk and a broad, rounded, dense crown; now small sprouts from base of long-dead trees.
Height: 20' (6 m); formerly 60–100' (18–30 m). Diameter: 4" (10 cm); formerly 2–4' (0.6–1.2 m).
Leaves: alternate; 5–9" (13–23 cm) long, 1½–3" (4–7.5 cm) wide. Narrowly oblong, long-pointed; with many straight parallel side veins, each ending in curved tooth; short-stalked. Shiny yellow-green above, paler green below with a few hairs along midvein; turning yellow in autumn.
Bark: dark gray-brown; furrowed into flat ridges; on sprouts smooth.
Twigs: green, slender, hairless.

Flowers: in early summer. Many whitish male flowers ³⁄₁₆″ (5 mm) long, in upright catkins 6–8″ (15–20 cm) long at base of leaf. Few female flowers ³⁄₈″ (10 mm) long, bordered by narrow greenish scales, at base of shorter catkins.
Fruit: 2–2½″ (5–6 cm) in diameter; short-stalked burs covered with many stout branched spines about ½″ (12 mm) long; maturing in autumn and splitting open along 3–4 lines; 2–3 chestnuts ½–¾″ (12–19 mm) long, broadly egg-shaped, becoming shiny dark brown, flattened and pointed; edible.

Habitat
Moist upland soils in mixed forests.

Range
Extreme S. Ontario east to Maine, south to SW. Georgia, west to Mississippi, north to Indiana; to 4000′ (1219 m).

Comments
American Chestnut is gone from the forests, a victim of the chestnut blight caused by an introduced fungus. This disease began in New York City in 1904, spread rapidly, and within 40 years had virtually wiped out this once abundant species. Fortunately, there is no threat of extinction; sprouts continue from roots until killed back by the blight, and cultivated trees grow in western states and other areas where the parasite is absent. Blight-resistant chestnuts such as hybrids between American and Chinese species are being developed for ornament, shade, and wildlife. The wood of this species was once the main domestic source of tannin, and the fruits were an important food for wildlife and a commercial crop.

American Elm
Ulmus americana
86

Large, handsome, graceful tree, often with enlarged buttresses at base, usually forked into many spreading branches, drooping at ends, forming a very broad, rounded, flat-topped or vaselike crown, often wider than high.
Height: 100′ (30 m). Diameter: 4′ (1.2 m), sometimes much larger.
Leaves: alternate in 2 rows; 3–6″ (7.5–15 cm) long, 1–3″ (2.5–7.5 cm) wide. Elliptical, abruptly long-pointed, base rounded with sides unequal; doubly saw-toothed; with many straight parallel side veins; thin. Dark green and usually hairless or slightly rough above, paler and usually with soft hairs beneath; turning bright yellow in autumn.
Bark: light gray; deeply furrowed into broad, forking, scaly ridges.
Twigs: brownish, slender, hairless.
Flowers: ⅛″ (3 mm) wide; greenish; clustered along twigs in early spring.
Fruit: ⅜–½″ (10–12 mm) long; elliptical flat 1-seeded keys (samaras), with wing hairy on edges, deeply notched with points curved inward; long-stalked; maturing in early spring.

Habitat
Moist soils, especially valleys and floodplains; in mixed hardwood forests.

Range
SE. Saskatchewan east to Cape Breton Island, south to central Florida, and west to central Texas; to 2500' (762 m).

Comments
This well-known, once-abundant species, familiar on lawns and city streets, has been ravaged by the Dutch Elm disease, caused by a fungus introduced accidentally about 1930 and spread by European and native elm bark beetles.

Ozark Chinkapin
Castanea ozarkensis
87

Small to medium-sized tree of Ozark region bearing very spiny burs.
Height: 20–50' (6–15 m). Diameter: 4–18" (0.1–0.5 m).
Leaves: alternate; 5–8" (13–20 cm) long, 1½–3" (4–7.5 cm) wide. Narrowly oblong or lance-shaped; with many straight parallel side veins each ending in long straight or curved tooth; leafstalks short, hairless or nearly so. Yellow-green above, paler and with fine whitish hairs or nearly hairless beneath.
Bark: gray-brown; smooth becoming furrowed into scaly plates.
Twigs: gray, slender, hairy when young.
Flowers: in early summer. Many tiny whitish male flowers, in catkins 2–8" (5–20 cm) long at base of leaf. Few female flowers ³⁄₁₆" (5 mm) long at base of smaller catkins.
Fruit: 1–1¼" (2.5–3 cm) in diameter; burs with many long branched hairy spines; maturing in autumn and splitting open. Single rounded to egg-shaped nut, dark brown, edible.

Habitat
Acid soils in dry rocky ridges, slopes, and ravines.

Range
S. Missouri, Arkansas, and E. Oklahoma; at 500–2800' (152–854 m).

Comments
Also known as Ozark Chestnut. This is the only tree species with a natural range limited to the Ozark region, for which it is named. Related to the American Chestnut, the Ozark bears similar but smaller edible chestnuts or chinkapins. The trees are attacked by the same fungus parasite that causes chestnut blight but are less susceptible and not threatened with extinction.

American Beech
Fagus grandifolia
88, 204, 215, 236

Large tree with rounded crown of many long, spreading and horizontal branches, producing edible beechnuts.
Height: 60–80' (18–24 m). Diameter: 1–2½' (0.3–0.8 m).
Leaves: alternate; spreading in 2 rows; 2½–5" (6–13 cm) long, 1–3" (2.5–7.5 cm) wide. Elliptical or ovate, long-pointed at tip; with many straight parallel slightly sunken side veins and coarsely saw-toothed edges; short-stalked. Dull dark blue-green above, light green beneath, becoming hairless or nearly so; turning yellow and brown in fall.

Bark: light gray; smooth, thin.
Twigs: slender, ending in long narrow scaly buds, with short side twigs or spurs.
Flowers: with new leaves in spring. Male flowers small, yellowish with many stamens, crowded in ball ¾–1″ (2–2.5 cm) in diameter, hanging on slender hairy stalk to 2″ (5 cm). Female flowers about ¼″ (6 mm) long, bordered by narrow hairy reddish scales, 2 at end of short stalk.
Fruit: ½–¾″ (12–19 mm) long; short-stalked light brown prickly burs; maturing in autumn and splitting into 4 parts. Usually 2 nuts, about ⅝″ (15 mm) long, 3-angled, shiny brown, known as beechnuts.

Habitat
Moist rich soils of uplands and well-drained lowlands; often in pure stands.

Range
S. Ontario, east to Cape Breton Island, south to N. Florida, west to E. Texas and north to N. Michigan; a variety in mountains of northeastern Mexico; to 3000′ (914 m) elevation in the North, and up to 6000′ (1829 m) in southern Appalachian Mountains.

Comments
American Beech was recognized by the colonists, who already knew the famous, closely related European Beech. American Beech is a handsome shade tree and bears similar edible beechnuts, which are consumed in large quantities by wildlife, especially squirrels, raccoons, chipmunks, bears, other mammals, and game birds. Unlike most trees, beeches retain smooth bark in old age.

American Hornbeam
Carpinus caroliniana
89, 216

Small, shrubby tree with one or more short trunks angled or fluted, long slender, spreading branches, and broad, rounded crown.
Height: 30′ (9 m). Diameter: 1′ (0.3 m).
Leaves: alternate; 2–4½″ (5–11 cm) long, 1–2½″ (2.5–6 cm) wide. Elliptical, long-pointed at tip; sharply doubly saw-toothed; with many nearly straight parallel side veins. Dull dark blue-green above, paler with hairs on veins and vein angles below, turning orange to red in autumn.
Bark: blue-gray; thin, smooth.
Twigs: brown, slender, slightly zigzag.
Flowers: tiny; in early spring before leaves. Male greenish, in drooping catkins 1¼–1½″ (3–4 cm) long. Female reddish green, paired in narrow catkins ½–¾″ (12–19 mm) long.
Fruit: ¼″ (6 mm) long; paired, egg-shaped, hairy greenish nutlets, with leaflike 3-pointed, toothed, greenish scale; in clusters 2–4″ (5–10 cm) long, hanging on slender stalks; maturing in late summer.

Habitat
Moist rich soils, mainly along streams and in ravines; in understory of hardwood forests.

Range
SE. Ontario east to SW. Quebec and central Maine, south to central Florida, west to E. Texas, and north to Minnesota; to 3000' (914 m). Also in Mexico.

Comments
The combination word "hornbeam," originally given to the European Hornbeam (*Carpinus betulus*), refers to the very hard tough wood. The small size of this species limits uses to tool handles and wooden articles. The name beech has been misapplied to this member of the birch family, because of the similar bark. Deer browse the twigs and foliage, and grouse, pheasants, and quail eat the nutlets.

Allegheny Chinkapin
Castanea pumila
90

Shrub-forming thicket or tree with rounded crown, bearing very spiny burs.
Height: 40' (12 m). Diameter: 1' (0.3 m).
Leaves: alternate; 3–6" (7.5–15 cm) long, 1¼–2" (3–5 cm) wide. Oblong or elliptical, short-pointed; with many straight parallel side veins, each ending in short tooth; leafstalks short, hairy. Yellow-green above, with velvety white hairs beneath.
Bark: reddish brown; furrowed into scaly plates.
Twigs: gray, hairy.
Flowers: in early summer. Many tiny whitish male flowers in upright catkins 4–6" (10–15 cm) long at base of leaf. Few female flowers ⅛" (3 mm) long at base of smaller catkins.
Fruit: ¾–1¼" (2–3 cm) in diameter; burs with many branched hairy spines; maturing in autumn and splitting open. Single egg-shaped nut, shiny dark brown with whitish hairs, edible.

Habitat
Dry sandy and rocky uplands; in oak and hickory forests.

Range
New Jersey and S. Pennsylvania south to central Florida, west to E. Texas, and north to SE. Oklahoma, local in S. Ohio; to 4500' (1372 m).

Comments
Captain John Smith published the first record of this nut in 1612: "They [the Indians] have a small fruit growing on little trees, husked like a Chestnut, but the fruit most like a very small acorne. This they call *Checkinquamins,* which they esteem a great daintie."

Black Cherry
Prunus serotina
91, 153

Aromatic tree with tall trunk, oblong crown, abundant small white flowers, and small black cherries; crushed foliage and bark have distinctive cherrylike odor and bitter taste.
Height: 80' (24 m). Diameter: 2' (0.6 m).
Leaves: alternate; 2–5" (5–13 cm) long, 1¼–2" (3–5 cm) wide. Elliptical: 1–2 dark red glands at base; finely saw-toothed with curved or blunt teeth; slightly thickened. Shiny dark green above, light green and often hairy along midvein

beneath; turning yellow or reddish in autumn.
Bark: dark gray; smooth, with horizontal lines; becoming
irregularly fissured and scaly, exposing reddish-brown inner
bark; bitter and aromatic.
Twigs: red-brown, slender, hairless.
Flowers: ⅜″ (10 mm) wide; 5 rounded, white petals; many
flowers along spreading or drooping axis of 4–6″ (10–15 cm)
at end of leafy twig; in late spring.
Fruit: a cherry ⅜″ (10 mm) in diameter; skin dark red turning
blackish; slightly bitter, juicy, edible pulp; elliptical stone;
maturing in late summer.

Habitat
On many sites except very wet or very dry soils; sometimes in
pure stands.

Range
S. Quebec to Nova Scotia, south to central Florida, west to E.
Texas, and north to Minnesota; varieties from central Texas
west to Arizona and south to Mexico; to 5000′ (1524 m) in
southern Appalachians and at 4500–7500′ (1372–2286 m) in
the Southwest.

Comments
This widespread species is the largest and most important
native cherry. The valuable wood is used particularly for
furniture, paneling, professional and scientific instruments,
handles, and toys. Wild cherry syrup, a cough medicine, is
obtained from the bark, and jelly and wine are prepared from
the fruit. One of the first New World trees introduced into
English gardens, it was recorded as early as 1629.

Carolina Silverbell
Halesia carolina
92, 156

Shrub or small tree with irregular, spreading, open crown and
drooping, bell-shaped white flowers; in southern Appalachians
becoming a large tree with straight axis and rounded crown.
Height: 30′ (9 m); in southern Appalachians 80′ (24 m).
Diameter: 1′ (0.3 m); and 2′ (0.6 m) or more in south.
Leaves: alternate; 3–6″ (7.5–15 cm) long, 1½–2½″ (4–6 cm)
wide. Elliptical, abruptly long-pointed; finely saw-toothed.
Dull dark green and becoming hairless above, covered with
white hairs when young and often with tiny star-shaped hairs
on veins beneath; turning yellow in autumn.
Bark: reddish brown; furrowed into loose, broad, scaly ridges.
Twigs: brown, slender, with star-shaped hairs when young.
Flowers: ½–1″ (1.2–2.5 cm) long; with bell-shaped, 4-lobed
white corolla (rarely pink), opening before reaching full size;
in drooping clusters of 2–5 flowers on long stalks on previous
year's twig back of new leaves; in early to midspring.
Fruit: 1¼–2″ (3–5 cm) long; oblong, podlike, with 4 long
broad wings, long-pointed, dark brown, dry; stone containing
1–3 seeds; maturing in late summer and autumn, remaining
closed and attached into winter.

Habitat
Moist soils along streams in understory of hardwood forests.

Range
S. West Virginia south to N. Florida, northwest to S. Illinois; local in Arkansas and SE. Oklahoma; to 5500' (1676 m) in southern Appalachians.

Comments
This tree is common and of largest size in the southern Appalachians, where it is known as Mountain Silverbell. It can be easily seen in the Great Smoky Mountains National Park.

Sourwood
Oxydendrum arboreum
93, 219

Tree with conical or rounded crown of spreading branches, clusters of flowers recalling lily-of-the-valley, and glossy foliage that turns red in autumn.
Height: 50' (15 m). Diameter: 1' (0.3 m).
Leaves: alternate; 4–7" (10–18 cm) long, 1½–2½" (4–6 cm) wide. Elliptical or lance-shaped; finely saw-toothed; with sour taste. Shiny yellow-green above, paler and slightly hairy on veins beneath; turning red in autumn.
Bark: brown or gray; thick; fissured into narrow, scaly ridges.
Twigs: light yellow-green, slender, hairless.
Flowers: buds and young flowers hanging down short-stalked on 1 side of slender axes, with urn-shaped white corolla, ¼" (6 mm) long, slightly 5-lobed; in terminal drooping clusters 4–10" (10–25 cm) long; in midsummer.
Fruit: ⅜" (10 mm) long; a narrowly egg-shaped capsule; gray and covered with fine hairs; upright on curved stalks along drooping axes; 5-celled, splitting along 5 lines; many-seeded; maturing in autumn, remaining attached into winter.

Habitat
Moist soils in valleys and uplands with oaks and pines.

Range
SW. Pennsylvania and SE. Maryland, south to NW. Florida, west to Louisiana, north to S. Indiana; 5000' (1524 m) or slightly higher in southern Appalachians.

Comments
Sourwood is an attractive ornamental throughout the year. Both the genus name, meaning "sour tree," and the common name refer to the acid taste of the foliage, although Sourwood honey is esteemed. Abundant in Great Smoky Mountains National Park.

Slippery Elm
Ulmus rubra
94, 177

Tree with broad, open, flat-topped crown of spreading branches and large rough leaves.
Height: 70' (21 m). Diameter: 2–3' (0.6–0.9 m).
Leaves: alternate; 4–7" (10–18 cm) long, 2–3" (5–7.5 cm) wide. Elliptical, abruptly long-pointed, base rounded with sides very unequal; doubly saw-toothed with many straight parallel side veins; thick. Green to dark green and very rough above, densely covered with soft hairs beneath; turning dull yellow in autumn.

Bark: dark brown; deeply furrowed; inner bark mucilaginous.
Twigs: brownish, stout, hairy.
Flowers: ⅛" (3 mm) wide; greenish; numerous; short-stalked
along twigs in early spring.
Fruit: ½–¾" (12–19 mm) long; nearly round flat 1-seeded
keys (samaras); with light green broad hairless wing, slightly
notched at tip; maturing in spring.

Habitat
Moist soils, especially lower slopes and floodplains, but often
on dry uplands; in hardwood forests.

Range
S. Ontario east to extreme S. Quebec and SW. Maine, south
to NW. Florida, west to central Texas, and north to SE.
North Dakota; to 2000' (610 m).

Comments
The thick, slightly fragrant, edible, gluelike inner bark is
dried and afterwards moistened for use as a cough medicine or
as a poultice. This "slippery" inner bark (found by chewing
through the outer bark of a twig) is helpful in identification.

Witch-hazel
Hamamelis virginiana
95, 165, 203, 237

Slightly aromatic shrub or small tree with a broad, open crown
of spreading branches and small yellow flowers present in
autumn or winter.
Height: 20–30' (6–9 m). Diameter: 4–8" (10–20 cm).
Leaves: alternate; 3–5" (7.5–13 cm) long, 2–3" (5–7.5 cm)
wide. Broadly elliptical, pointed or rounded at tip, blunt to
notched and unequal at base, broadest and wavy-lobed beyond
middle; with 5–7 straight veins on each side; hairy when
young. Dull dark green above, paler below; turning yellow in
autumn.
Bark: light brown; smooth or scaly.
Twigs: slender, zigzag, with gray or rust-colored hairs.
Flowers: 1" (2.5 cm) wide; with 4 bright yellow petals,
threadlike and twisted; few, short-stalked, along leafless twigs
in autumn or winter.
Fruit: ½" (12 mm) long; a hard elliptical capsule ending in 4
sharp curved points, light brown, opening in 2 parts;
maturing in autumn; with 1 or 2 shiny blackish seeds ¼" (6
mm) long; ejected with force by contracting capsule walls.

Habitat
Moist soil in understory of hardwood forests.

Range
S. Ontario east to Nova Scotia, south to central Florida, west
to E. Texas, and north to central Wisconsin; local in
northeastern Mexico; to 5000' (1524 m), sometimes higher in
southern Appalachians.

Comments
The aromatic extract of leaves, twigs, and bark is used in
mildly astringent lotions and toilet water. A myth of
witchcraft held that a forked branch of Witch-hazel could be

used to locate underground water. The foliage and fruits slightly resemble those of the shrub hazel (*Corylus*). Upon drying, the contracting capsule can eject its small seed as far as 30′ (9 m).

Arrowwood
Viburnum dentatum
96, 196

Much-branched shrub with many shoots from base, or sometimes a small tree, with showy clusters of white flowers and blue-black fruit.
Height: 3–10′ (0.9–3 m), rarely 20′ (6 m). Diameter: 3″ (7.5 cm).
Leaves: opposite; 1½–4″ (4–10 cm) long, 1–3½″ (2.5–9 cm) wide. Ovate or rounded, pointed at tip, blunt or notched at base; with many straight sunken side veins ending in large teeth; leafstalks long, slender. Dull green and nearly hairless above, paler and hairy beneath; turning shiny red in autumn.
Bark: gray or reddish brown; smooth.
Twigs: brown, slender, usually hairy, with ringed nodes.
Flowers: ¼″ (6 mm) wide; with 5 rounded white corolla lobes; in branched, upright long-stalked clusters 2–3½″ (5–9 cm) wide, of many flowers each; in spring and early summer.
Fruit: ¼–⅜″ (6–10 mm) long; rounded or elliptical, blue or blue-black, juicy; large flattened stone; maturing in late summer and autumn.

Habitat
Moist to dry soils, especially sandy; forming thickets in open areas, at border and in understory of forest.

Range
Illinois east to Massachusetts, south to Florida, and west to E. Texas; to 4500′ (1372 m) in southern Appalachians.

Comments
Arrowwood is a common, widespread shrub varying in leaf shape, size, and hairiness. In eastern Texas it sometimes becomes a small tree. Indians used the straight young stems as arrow shafts; hence the common name. The fruit is consumed by birds.

Coastal Plain Willow
Salix caroliniana
97

Shrub or small tree with spreading or slightly drooping branches.
Height: 30′ (9 m). Diameter: 1′ (0.3 m).
Leaves: alternate; 2–4″ (5–10 cm) long, ½–¾″ (12–19 mm) wide. Lance-shaped; finely saw-toothed; densely hairy when young. Green above; whitish and nearly hairless beneath. Leafstalks hairy.
Bark: gray to blackish; fairly smooth, furrowed into broad scaly ridges.
Twigs: brown; slender, limber; hairy when young.
Flowers: catkins 3–4″ (7.5–10 cm) long; greenish or yellowish; at ends of leafy twigs in spring.
Fruit: ¼″ (6 mm) long; long-pointed capsules; light reddish brown; maturing in late spring or early summer.

Habitat
Wet soils of stream banks and swamps.

Range
S. Pennsylvania south to S. Florida, west to central Texas, and north to SE. Nebraska; to 2000' (610 m).

Comments
This is the common small tree willow found at low altitudes in the southeastern United States.

Black Willow
Salix nigra
98

Large tree with 1 or more straight and usually leaning trunks, upright branches, and narrow or irregular crown.
Height: 60–100' (18–30 m). Diameter: 1½–2½' (0.5–0.8 m).
Leaves: alternate; 3–5" (7.5–13 cm) long, ⅜–¾" (10–19 mm) wide. Narrowly lance-shaped; often slightly curved to one side; long-pointed; finely saw-toothed; hairless or nearly so. Shiny green above, paler beneath.
Bark: dark brown or blackish; deeply furrowed into scaly, forking ridges.
Twigs: brownish; very slender, easily detached at base.
Flowers: catkins 1–3" (2.5–7.5 cm) long; with yellow hairy scales; at end of leafy twigs in spring.
Fruit: 3/16" (5 mm) long; reddish-brown capsules; hairless; maturing in late spring.

Habitat
Wet soils of banks of streams and lakes, especially floodplains; often in pure stands and with cottonwoods.

Range
S. New Brunswick and Maine south to NW. Florida, west to S. Texas, and north to SE. Minnesota; also from W. Texas west to N. California; local in northern Mexico; to 5000' (1524 m).

Comments
Also called Swamp Willow and Goodding Willow. The largest and most important New World willow with one of the most extensive ranges across the country. In the lower Mississippi Valley it attains commercial timber size, reaching 100–140' (30–42 m) in height and 4' (1.2 m) in diameter. The numerous uses of the wood include millwork, furniture, doors, cabinetwork, boxes, barrels, toys, and pulpwood. In pioneer times the wood of this and other willows was a source of charcoal for gunpowder. Large trees are valuable in binding soil banks, thus preventing soil erosion and flood damage. Mats and poles made from Black Willow trunks and branches provide further protection of riverbanks and levees. Also a shade tree and honey plant.

Eastern Baccharis
Baccharis halimifolia
99

Shrub or small, much-branched, spreading and rounded tree with fruit resembling silvery paintbrushes.
Height: 16' (5 m). Diameter: 4" (10 cm).

Leaves: deciduous (in far Southeast, evergreen); alternate; 1–
2½" (2.5–6 cm) long, ⅜–1¼" (1–3 cm) wide. Elliptical to
obovate; usually a few coarse teeth toward short-pointed tip;
tapering to short-stalked base; slightly thick; hairless or
resinous. Dull gray-green above and beneath; falling late in
autumn.
Bark: dark brown; thin, fissured into forking ridges.
Twigs: green, gray, or brown; slender, angled, hairless or
nearly so.
Flowers: tiny; crowded in greenish bell-shaped heads less than
¼" (6 mm) long; the heads in large upright branching
clusters; in late summer and autumn. Male and female flowers
on separate plants.
Fruit: ½" (12 mm) long and wide; brushlike whitish head
composed of many narrow seeds, each with tuft of whitish
hairs or bristles to ⅜" (10 mm) long; maturing in late
autumn.

Habitat
Moist soils, including salt marshes, borders of streams,
roadside ditches, open woods, and waste places.

Range
Massachusetts south to S. Florida, west to S. Texas, and north
to SE. Oklahoma and Arkansas; to 800' (244 m); also
Bahamas and Cuba.

Comments
Apparently extending its natural range inland from the coastal
plain, Eastern Baccharis is the only native eastern species of
the Composite family that reaches tree size. Baccharis is the
ancient Greek name (derived from the god Bacchus) of a plant
with fragrant roots.

Southern Bayberry
Myrica cerifera
100

Evergreen, aromatic, resinous shrub or small tree with narrow
rounded crown.
Height: 30' (9 m). Diameter: 6" (15 cm).
Leaves: alternate; 1½–3½" (4–9 cm) long, ¼–¾" (6–19
mm) wide; those toward end of twigs often smaller. Reverse
lance-shaped; coarsely saw-toothed beyond middle; slightly
thickened and stiff; aromatic when crushed; short-stalked.
Shiny yellow-green with tiny dark brown gland-dots above,
paler with tiny orange gland-dots and often ˙hairy beneath.
Bark: light gray; smooth, thin.
Flowers: tiny; yellow-green; in narrowly cylindrical clusters ¼–
¾" (6–19 mm) long; at base of leaf. Male and female on
separate trees; in early spring.
Fruit: ⅛" (3 mm) in diameter; 1-seeded drupes; warty; light
green, covered with bluish-white wax; several crowded in a
cluster; maturing in autumn; remaining attached in winter.

Habitat
Moist, sandy soil, in fresh or slightly brackish banks, swamps,
hammocks, flatwoods, pinelands, and upland hardwood
forests.

Range
S. New Jersey south to S. Florida, west to S. Texas, and north to extreme SE. Oklahoma; to about 500' (152 m).

Comments
Also called Candle-berry and Southern Waxmyrtle. One of the very few Puerto Rican trees native also in the United States north of Florida, this popular evergreen ornamental is used for screens, hedges, landscaping, and as a source of honey. Colonists separated the fruit's waxy covering in boiling water to make fragrant-burning candles, a custom still followed in some countries.

Balsam Poplar
Populus balsamifera
101

Large tree with narrow, open crown of upright branches and fragrant, resinous buds with strong balsam odor.
Height: 60–80' (18–24 m). Diameter: 1–3' (0.3–0.9 m).
Leaves: 3–5" (7.5–13 cm) long, 1½–3" (4–7.5 cm) wide. Ovate; pointed at tip; rounded or slightly notched at base; finely wavy-toothed; slightly thickened; hairless or nearly so. Shiny dark green above; whitish, often with rusty veins beneath. Leafstalks slender, round, hairy.
Bark: light brown, smooth; becoming gray, furrowed into flat, scaly ridges.
Twigs: brownish; stout, with large, gummy or sticky buds producing fragrant yellowish resin.
Flowers: catkins 2–3½" (5–9 cm) long; brownish; male and female on separate trees; in early spring.
Fruit: 5/16" (8 mm) long; egg-shaped capsules; pointed; light brown; hairless; maturing in spring and splitting into 2 parts; many tiny, cottony seeds.

Habitat
Moist soils of valleys, mainly stream banks, sandbars, and floodplains, also lower slopes; often in pure stands.

Range
Across northern North America along northern limit of trees from NW. Alaska south to SE. British Columbia and east to Newfoundland, south to Pennsylvania and west to Iowa; local south to Colorado and in eastern mountains to West Virginia; to 5500' (1676 m) in Rocky Mountains.

Comments
The northernmost New World hardwood, Balsam Poplar extends in scattered groves to Alaska's Arctic Slope. Balm-of-Gilead Poplar, an ornamental with broad, open crown and larger, heart-shaped leaves, is a clone or hybrid. Balm-of-Gilead, derived from the resinous buds, has been used in home remedies. Also called Tacamahac and Balm.

Cockspur Hawthorn
Crataegus crus-galli
102

Small, spiny, thicket-forming tree with short, stout trunk and broad, dense crown of spreading and horizontal branches; hairless throughout.
Height: 30' (9 m). Diameter: 1' (0.3 m).

Leaves: alternate; 1–4″ (2.5–10 cm) long, ⅜–2″ (1–5 cm) wide. Spoon-shaped or narrowly elliptical; short-pointed or rounded at tip, widest beyond middle, tapering to narrow base; sharply saw-toothed beyond middle with gland-tipped teeth; slightly thick and leathery. Shiny dark green above, pale with prominent network of veins beneath; turning orange and scarlet in autumn.
Bark: dark gray or brown; scaly, with branched spines.
Twigs: stout; usually with many very long slender brown spines.
Flowers: ½–⅝″ (12–15 mm) wide; with 5 white petals, 10 to sometimes 20 pink or pale yellow stamens, and 2–3 styles; many, in large clusters; in late spring or early summer.
Fruit: ⅜–½″ (10–12 mm) in diameter; rounded; greenish or dull dark red; thin hard pulp; usually 2–3 nutlets; several, in drooping clusters; maturing in late autumn and persisting until spring.

Habitat
Moist soils of valleys and low upland slopes.

Range
S. Ontario and S. Quebec south to N. Florida, west to E. Texas, and north to Iowa; to 2000′ (610 m).

Comments
The common and Latin species names both describe the numerous and extremely long spines, which are used locally as pins. The long spines and shiny dark green spoon-shaped leaves make this one of the most easily recognized hawthorns. Common and widespread, it has been planted for ornament and as a hedge since colonial times.

Blackhaw
Viburnum prunifolium
103

Shrub or small tree with short trunk, spreading, rounded or irregular crown, many showy, small, white flowers, and small, blue-black fruit.
Height: 20′ (6 m). Diameter: 4″ (10 cm).
Leaves: opposite; 1½–3″ (4–7.5 cm) long, ¾–2″ (2–5 cm) wide. Elliptical; finely saw-toothed; slightly thick; hairless or nearly so. Shiny green with network of sunken veins above, dull light green beneath; turning shiny red in autumn.
Bark: gray; rough, furrowed into rectangular plates.
Twigs: gray, slender, stiff, ending in flat, oblong, hairy brown bud.
Flowers: ¼″ (6 mm) wide; with 5 rounded white corolla lobes; in upright flat, stalkless clusters, 2–4″ (5–10 cm) wide; in spring.
Fruit: ½″ (12 mm) long; elliptical, slightly flat, dark blue-black with whitish bloom; thin, slightly sweetish edible pulp; somewhat flat stone; drooping on long slender reddish stalks; maturing in autumn, remaining attached into early winter.

Habitat
Moist soils, especially in valleys, and on slopes; in thickets and at borders of forests.

Range
SW. Connecticut south to Alabama, west to E. Kansas, and north to SE. Wisconsin and SW. Iowa, to 3000' (914 m).

Comments
The fruit is consumed by songbirds, gamebirds, and mammals and can be made into preserves. The astringent bark was formerly used medicinally. The Latin species name refers to the leaves' resemblance to plum leaves.

Yaupon
Ilex vomitoria
104, 191

Evergreen, much-branched, thicket-forming shrub or small tree with rounded, open crown, small shiny leaves, and abundant, round, shiny red berries.
Height: 20' (6 m). Diameter: 6" (15 cm).
Leaves: evergreen; alternate; usually ¾–1¼" (2–3 cm) long, ¼–½" (6–12 mm) wide. Elliptical; blunt at tip; rounded at base; finely wavy-toothed; thick and stiff; short-stalked. Shiny green above, paler beneath.
Bark: red-brown; thin, finely scaly.
Twigs: gray; branching at right angles; slightly angled and hairy when young, becoming rough.
Flowers: ³⁄₁₆" (5 mm) wide; with 4 spreading rounded white petals; on short stalks at base of old leaves; male and female on separate plants.
Fruit: ¼" (6 mm) in diameter; berrylike; shiny red, clustered along twigs, short-stalked; bitter pulp; 4 narrow grooved nutlets; maturing in autumn, often remaining attached in winter.

Habitat
Moist soils, especially along coasts and in valleys, sometimes in sandhills.

Range
SE. Virginia south to central Florida, west to Texas, and north to SE. Oklahoma; to 500' (152 m).

Comments
Yaupon is sometimes grown for ornament and trimmed into hedges. The leaves contain caffeine, and American Indians used them to prepare a tea used to induce vomiting and as a laxative. Tribes from the interior traveled to the coast in large numbers each spring to partake of this tonic. The ornamental twigs with shiny evergreen leaves and numerous red berries are favorite Christmas decorations.

American Holly
Ilex opaca
105, 193

Evergreen tree with narrow, rounded, dense crown of spiny leaves, small white flowers, and bright red berries.
Height: 40–70' (12–21 m). Diameter: 1–2' (0.3–0.6 m).
Leaves: evergreen; alternate; spreading in 2 rows; 2–4" (5–10 cm) long, ¾–1½" (2–4 cm) wide. Elliptical; spiny-pointed and coarsely spiny-toothed; thick, stiff and leathery. Dull green above, yellow-green beneath.
Bark: light gray; thin; smooth or rough and warty.

Twigs: brown or gray; stout, with fine hairs when young.
Flowers: ¼″ (6 mm) wide; with 4 rounded white petals; in short clusters at base of new leaves and along twigs; in spring; male and female on separate trees.
Fruit: ¼–⅜″ (6–10 mm) in diameter; berrylike; bright red (rarely orange or yellow); bitter pulp; 4 brown nutlets; scattered; short-stalked; maturing in autumn, remaining attached in winter.

Habitat
Moist or wet well-drained soils, especially floodplains; in mixed hardwood forests.

Range
E. Massachusetts south to central Florida, west to south-central Texas, and north to SE. Missouri; to 4000′ (1219 m); higher in southern Appalachians.

Comments
The evergreen fruiting branches from wild and planted trees are popular Christmas decorations. Many improved varieties are grown for ornament, shade, and hedges. The whitish, fine-textured wood is especially suited for inlays in cabinetwork. Many kinds of songbirds, gamebirds, and mammals eat the bitter berries of this and other hollies.

Chinkapin Oak
Quercus muehlenbergii
106, 210

Tree with narrow, rounded crown; characteristic of limestone uplands.
Height: 50–80′ (15–24 m). Diameter: 2–3′ (0.6–0.9 m).
Leaves: alternate; 4–6″ (10–15 cm) long, 1½–3″ (4–7.5 cm) wide. Narrowly elliptical to obovate; slightly thickened; pointed at tip; narrowed to base; with many straight, parallel side veins, each ending in curved tooth on wavy edges. Shiny green above, whitish green and covered with tiny hairs beneath; turning brown or red in fall.
Bark: light gray; thin, fissured and scaly.
Acorns: ½–1″ (1.2–2.5 cm) long; egg-shaped, a third or more enclosed by deep thin cup of many overlapping hairy long-pointed gray-brown scales; usually stalkless; maturing first year.

Habitat
Mostly on limestone outcrops in alkaline soils, including dry bluffs and rocky river banks; often with other oaks.

Range
S. Ontario east to W. Vermont, south to NW. Florida, west to central Texas, and north to Iowa; local in SE. New Mexico, Trans-Pecos Texas, and northeastern Mexico; at 400–3000′ (122–914 m).

Comments
The common name refers to the resemblance of the foliage to chinkapins (*Castanea*), while the Latin species name honors Henry Ernst Muehlenberg (1753–1815), a Pennsylvania botanist.

Chestnut Oak
Quercus prinus
107

Large tree with broad, open, irregular crown of chestnutlike foliage.
Height: 60–80' (18–24 m). Diameter: 2–3' (0.6–0.9 m).
Leaves: alternate; 4–8" (10–20 cm) long, 2–4" (5–10 cm) wide. Elliptical or obovate, broadest beyond middle, short-pointed at tip; edges wavy with 10–16 rounded teeth on each side; gradually narrowed to base. Shiny green above, dull gray-green and sparsely hairy beneath; turning yellow in fall.
Bark: gray; becoming thick and deeply furrowed into broad or narrow ridges.
Acorns: ¾–1¼" (2–3 cm) long; egg-shaped, a third or more enclosed by deep, thin cup narrowed at base, composed of short, warty, hairy scales not overlapping; becoming brown; short-stalked; maturing first year.

Habitat
Sandy, gravelly, and rocky dry upland soils, but reaches greatest size on well-drained lowland sites; often in pure stands on dry rocky ridges.

Range
Extreme S. Ontario to SW. Maine, south to Georgia, west to NE. Mississippi, and north to SE. Michigan; at 1500–5000' (457–1524 m).

Comments
Because of its high tannin content, the bark formerly served for tanning leather. The wood is marketed as White Oak. As a shade tree, it is adapted to dry rocky soil.

Overcup Oak
Quercus lyrata
108

Tree with rounded crown of small, often drooping, branches; acorns almost covered by the cup; narrow, deeply lobed leaves.
Height: 60–80' (18–24 m). Diameter: 2–3' (0.6–0.9 m).
Leaves: alternate; 5–8" (13–20 cm) long, 1½–4" (4–10 cm) wide. Narrowly oblong; deeply divided into 7–11 rounded or short-pointed lobes, the longest near short-pointed tip; pointed base. Dark green and slightly shiny above, gray-green and with soft hairs or nearly hairless beneath; turning yellow, brown, or red in fall.
Bark: light gray; furrowed into scaly or slightly shaggy ridges or plates.
Acorns: ½–1" (1.2–2.5 cm) long; nearly round, almost enclosed by large rounded cup of warty gray scales, the upper scales long-pointed; usually stalkless; maturing first year.

Habitat
Wet clay and silty clay soils, mostly on poorly drained floodplains and swamp borders; sometimes in pure stands.

Range
Delaware to NW. Florida, west to E. Texas, and north to S. Illinois; to 500' (152 m), sometimes slightly higher.

Comments
The Latin species name, meaning "lyre-shaped," refers to the leaves.

White Oak
Quercus alba
109, 206

The classic eastern oak, with wide-spreading branches and a rounded crown, the trunk irregularly divided into spreading, often horizontal, stout branches.
Height: 80–100′ (24–30 m) or more. Diameter: 3–4′ (0.9–1.2 m) or more.
Leaves: alternate; 4–9″ (10–23 cm) long, 2–4″ (5–10 cm) wide. Elliptical; 5- to 9-lobed; widest beyond middle and tapering to base; hairless. Bright green above, whitish or gray-green beneath; turning red or brown in fall, often remaining attached in winter.
Bark: light gray; shallowly fissured into long broad scaly plates or ridges, often loose.
Acorns: ⅜–1¼″ (1–3 cm) long; egg-shaped; about ¼ enclosed by shallow cup; becoming light gray; with warty, finely hairy scales; maturing first year.

Habitat
Moist well-drained uplands and lowlands, often in pure stands.

Range
S. Ontario and extreme S. Quebec east to Maine, south to N. Florida, west to E. Texas, and north to east-central Minnesota; to 5500′ (1676 m), or at higher elevations in southern Appalachians.

Comments
The most important lumber tree of the white oak group, its high-grade wood is useful for all purposes. Also called Stave Oak because the wood is outstanding in making tight barrels for whiskey and other liquids. In colonial times the wood was important in shipbuilding. Acorns are a staple in the diet of numerous wild animals, notably wood ducks and blue jays.

Bur Oak
Quercus macrocarpa
110, 205

Tree with very large acorns, stout trunk, and broad, rounded, open crown of stout, often crooked, spreading branches; sometimes a shrub.
Height: 50–80′ (15–24 m). Diameter: 2–4′ (0.6–1.2 m).
Leaves: alternate; 4–10″ (10–25 cm) long, 2–5″ (5–13 cm) wide. Obovate, broadest beyond middle, lower half deeply divided into 2–3 lobes on each side; upper half usually with 5–7 shallow rounded lobes on each side to broad rounded tip. Dark green and slightly shiny above, gray-green and with fine hairs beneath; turning yellow or brown in fall.
Bark: light gray; thick, rough, deeply furrowed into scaly ridges.
Acorns: large; ¾–2″ (2–5 cm) long and wide; broadly elliptical, one half to three quarters enclosed by large deep cup with hairy gray scales, (the upper scales very long-pointed) forming fringelike border; maturing first year.

Habitat
From dry uplands on limestone and gravelly ridges, sandy plains, and loamy slopes to moist floodplains of streams; often in nearly pure stands.

Range
Extreme SE. Saskatchewan east to S. New Brunswick, south to
Tennessee, west to SE Texas and north to North Dakota; local
in Louisiana and Alabama. Usually at 300–2000′ (91–610 m);
to 3000′ (914 m) or above in northwest.

Comments
The acorns of this species, distinguished by very deep fringed
cups, are the largest acorns of all native oaks. The common
name describes the cup of the acorn, which slightly resembles
the spiny bur of Chestnut. Bur Oak is the northernmost New
World oak. In the West, it is a pioneer tree, bordering and
invading the prairie grassland. Planted for shade, ornament,
and shelterbelts.

Post Oak
Quercus stellata
111

Tree with dense, rounded crown and distinctive leaves
suggesting a Maltese cross; sometimes a shrub.
Height: 30–70′ (9–21 m). Diameter: 1–2′ (0.3–0.6 m).
Leaves: alternate; 3¼–6″ (8–15 cm) long, 2–4″ (5–10 cm)
wide. Obovate; with 5–7 deep broad rounded lobes, 2 middle
lobes largest; with short-pointed base and rounded tip;
slightly thickened. Shiny dark green and slightly rough with
scattered hairs above, gray-green with tiny star-shaped hairs
beneath; turning brown in fall.
Bark: light gray; fissured into scaly ridges.
Acorns: ½–1″ (1.2–2.5 cm) long; elliptical, a third to a half
enclosed by deep cup; green becoming brown; usually stalkless
or short-stalked; maturing first year.

Habitat
Sandy, gravelly, and rocky ridges, also moist loamy soils of
floodplains along streams; sometimes in pure stands.

Range
SE. Massachusetts south to central Florida, west to NW.
Texas, and north to SE. Iowa; to 3000′ (914 m).

Comments
The wood is marketed as White Oak and used for railroad
cross-ties, posts, and construction timbers. This species
reaches large size in the lower Mississippi Valley where it is
known as Delta Post Oak. Post Oak and Blackjack Oak form
the Cross Timbers in Texas and Oklahoma, the forest border
of small trees and transition zone to prairie grassland.

Southern Red Oak
Quercus falcata
112

Tree with rounded, open crown of large spreading branches,
and twigs with rust-colored hairs.
Height: 50–80′ (15–24 m). Diameter: 1–2½′ (0.3–0.8 m).
Leaves: alternate; 4–8″ (10–20 cm) long, 2–6″ (5–15 cm)
wide. Elliptical: deeply divided into long narrow end lobe and
1–3 shorter mostly curved lobes on each side, with 1–3
bristle-tipped teeth; sometimes slightly triangular with bell-
shaped base and 3 broad lobes. Shiny green above, with rust-
colored or gray soft hairs beneath; turning brown in fall.

Bark: dark gray; becoming furrowed into broad ridges and plates.
Acorns: ½–⅝″ (12–15 mm) long; elliptical or rounded; becoming brown; ⅓ or more enclosed by cup tapering to broad stalklike base; maturing second year.

Habitat
Dry, sandy loam and clay loam soils of uplands; in mixed forests.

Range
Long Island and New Jersey south to N. Florida, west to E. Texas, and north to S. Missouri; to 2500′ (762 m).

Comments
Often called Spanish Oak, possibly because it commonly occurs in areas of the early Spanish colonies; Southern Red Oak is unlike any oaks native to Spain. The lumber is marketed under the name Red Oak. Cherrybark Oak (var. *pagodifolia*) is a variety with pagoda-shaped leaves having 5–11 broad, shallow lobes, and whitish hairs beneath, and smooth cherrylike bark with short ridges. It is found on well-drained lowland soils from southeastern Virginia to northwestern Florida and eastern Texas.

Black Oak
Quercus velutina
113, 208, 225

Medium-sized to large tree with open, spreading crown.
Height: 50–80′ (15–24 m). Diameter: 1–2½′ (0.3–0.8 m).
Leaves: alternate; 4–9″ (10–23 cm) long, 3–6″ (7.5–15 cm) wide. Elliptical: usually with 7–9 lobes, either shallow or deep and narrow, ending in a few bristle-tipped teeth; slightly thickened. Shiny green above, yellow-green and usually with brown hairs beneath; turning dull red or brown in fall.
Bark: gray and smooth on small trunks; becoming blackish, thick and rough, deeply furrowed into ridges; inner bark yellow or orange, very bitter.
Acorns: ⅝–¾″ (15–19 mm) long; elliptical, one half enclosed by deep thick top-shaped cup narrowed at base, with fringed border of loose rust-brown hairy scales; maturing second year.

Habitat
Dry upland sandy and rocky ridges and slopes, also on clay hillsides; sometimes in pure stands.

Range
Extreme S. Ontario and SW. Maine, south to NW. Florida, west to central Texas, and north to SE. Minnesota; to 5000′ (1524 m).

Comments
Easily distinguishable by the yellow or orange inner bark, formerly a source of tannin, of medicine, and of a yellow dye for cloth. Peeled bark was dried, pounded to powder, and the dye sifted out.

Shumard Oak
Quercus shumardii
114

Large tree with straight axis and broad, rounded, open crown.
Height: 60–90′ (18–27 m). Diameter: 1–2½′ (0.3–0.8 m).
Leaves: alternate; 3–7″ (7.5–18 cm) long, 2½–5″ (6–13 cm)
wide. Elliptical: usually deeply divided nearly to midvein into
5–9 lobes becoming broadest toward tip, with several
spreading bristle-tipped teeth; large rounded sinuses between
lobes, sometimes nearly closed. Slightly shiny dark green and
hairy above, slightly shiny or dull green beneath with tufts of
hairs in vein angles; turning red or brown in fall.
Bark: gray and smooth; becoming dark gray and slightly
furrowed into ridges.
Acorns: ⅝–1⅛″ (1.5–2.8 cm) long; egg-shaped, a quarter to
a third enclosed by shallow cup of tightly overlapping blunt
scales; green becoming brown; usually hairless; maturing
second year.

Habitat
Moist well-drained soils including floodplains along streams,
also on dry ridges and limestone hills.

Range
North Carolina to N. Florida, west to central Texas, and north
to E. Kansas; local north to S. Michigan and S. Pennsylvania;
to 2500′ (762 m).

Comments
A handsome shade tree, Shumard Oak has been suggested as a
substitute for Scarlet Oak, though it is not hardy northward.

Scarlet Oak
Quercus coccinea
115, 207, 224

Large tree with a rounded, open crown of glossy foliage, best
known for its brilliant autumn color.
Height: 60–80′ (18–24 m). Diameter: 1–2½′ (0.3–0.8 m).
Leaves: alternate; 3–7″ (7.5–18 cm) long, 2–5″ (5–13 cm)
wide. Elliptical; deeply divided nearly to midvein into 7
(rarely 9) lobes, broadest toward tip, each lobe ending in
several bristle-tipped teeth; the wide round sinuses between
lobes often forming more than a half-circle; long, slender
stalks. Shiny green above; pale yellow-green, slightly shiny,
and with tufts of hairs in vein angles along midvein beneath;
turning scarlet in fall.
Bark: dark gray, smooth; becoming blackish, thick, rough,
and furrowed into scaly ridges or plates; inner bark reddish.
Acorns: ½–1″ (1.2–2.5 cm) long; egg-shaped; becoming
brown with 2–4 faint rings; ⅓–½ enclosed by thick deep
top-shaped cup of tightly pressed scales, tapering to stalklike
base; maturing second year.

Habitat
Various soils, especially poor and sandy, on upland ridges and
slopes; with other oaks and in mixed forests.

Range
SW. Maine south to Georgia, west to NE. Mississippi, north
to Missouri and Indiana; local in Michigan; to 3000′ (914 m),
locally to 5000′ (1524 m).

Comments
A popular and handsome shade and street tree. A variety of this species, called Red Oak, differs in its shallowly lobed, dull green leaves, and acorns with a shallow cup; it is marketed as lumber. Another variety, Black Oak, is also similar, but has yellow-green leaves with brown hairs beneath and acorns with a deep cup of loose hairy scales.

Pin Oak
Quercus palustris
116

Straight-trunked tree with spreading to horizontal branches, very slender pinlike twigs, and a broadly conical crown.
Height: 50–90′ (15–27 m). Diameter: 1–2½′ (0.3–0.8 m). Leaves: alternate; 3–5″ (7.5–13 cm) long, 2–4″ (5–10 cm) wide. Elliptical; 5–7 deep lobes nearly to midvein with few bristle-tipped teeth and wide rounded sinuses; base short-pointed. Shiny dark green above, light green and slightly shiny with tufts of hair in vein angles along midvein beneath; turning red or brown in fall.
Bark: dark gray; hard; smooth, becoming fissured into short, broad, scaly ridges.
Acorns: ½″ (12 mm) long and broad; nearly round; becoming brown; a quarter to a third enclosed by thin saucer-shaped cup tapering to base; maturing second year.

Habitat
In nearly pure stands on poorly drained, wet sites, including clay soils on level uplands; less common on deep, well-drained bottomland soils.

Range
Extreme S. Ontario to Vermont, south to central North Carolina, west to NE. Oklahoma, and north to S. Iowa; to 1000′ (305 m).

Comments
Named for the many short side twigs or pinlike spurs. A popular, graceful lawn tree with regular compact form and fine-textured foliage, Pin Oak is hardy and easily transplanted because the shallow fibrous root system lacks tap roots.

Blackjack Oak
Quercus marilandica
117, 223

Tree with irregular crown of crooked, spreading branches.
Height: 20–50′ (6–15 m). Diameter: 6–12″ (15–30 cm). Leaves: alternate; 2½–5″ (6–13 cm) long, 2–4″ (5–10 cm) wide. Slightly triangular or broadly obovate, broadest near tip with 3 shallow broad bristle-tipped lobes; gradually narrowed to rounded base; slightly thickened. Shiny yellow-green above, light yellow-green with brownish hairs (especially along veins) beneath; turning brown or yellow in fall.
Bark: blackish; rough, thick, deeply furrowed into broad, nearly square plates.
Acorns: ⅝–¾″ (15–19 mm) long; elliptical, ending in stout point; one third to two thirds enclosed by deep, thick, top-shaped cup of rusty brown, hairy, loosely overlapping scales; short-stalked; maturing second year.

Habitat
Dry sandy and clay soils in upland ridges and slopes with other oaks and with pines.

Range
Long Island and New Jersey south to NW. Florida, west to central and SE. Texas, and north to SE. Iowa; local in S. Michigan; to 3000′ (914 m).

Comments
This species and Post Oak form the Cross Timbers in Texas and Oklahoma, the forest border of small trees and transition zone to prairie grassland. The wood is used for railroad cross-ties, firewood, and charcoal. This tree was first described in 1704 from a specimen in the colony of Maryland, referred to in the Latin species name. Virginia, where earlier plant collections were made, is honored in the species names of Live Oak (*Quercus virginiana*) and several other important trees.

Northern Red Oak
Quercus rubra
118, 209

Large tree with rounded crown of stout, spreading branches. Height: 60–90′ (18–27 m). Diameter: 1–2½′ (0.3–0.8 m). Leaves: alternate; 4–9″ (10–23 cm) long, 3–6″ (7.5–15 cm) wide. Elliptical; usually divided less than halfway to midvein into 7–11 shallow wavy lobes with a few irregular bristle-tipped teeth. Usually dull green above, dull light green beneath with tufts of hairs in angles along midvein; turning brown or dark red in fall.
Bark: dark gray or blackish; rough, furrowed into scaly ridges; inner bark reddish.
Acorns: ⅝–1⅛″ (1.5–2.8 cm) long; egg-shaped, less than a third enclosed by broad cup of reddish-brown, blunt, tightly overlapping scales; maturing second year.

Habitat
Moist, loamy, sandy, rocky, and clay soils; often forming pure stands.

Range
W. Ontario to Cape Breton Island, south to Georgia, west to E. Oklahoma, and north to Minnesota; to 5500′ (1676 m) in south.

Comments
The northernmost eastern oak, it is also the most important lumber species of red oak. Most are used for flooring, furniture, millwork, railroad cross-ties, mine timbers, fenceposts, pilings, and pulpwood. A popular handsome shade and street tree, with good form and dense foliage. One of the most rapid-growing oaks, it transplants easily, is hardy in city conditions, and endures cold.

Silver Maple
Acer saccharinum
119, 179

Large tree with short, stout trunk, few large forks, spreading, open, irregular crown of long, curving branches, and graceful leaves deeply cut toward the midvein.

Height: 50–80′ (15–24 m). Diameter: 3′ (0.9 m).
Leaves: opposite; 4–6″ (10–15 cm) long and nearly as wide.
Broadly ovate, deeply 5-lobed and long-pointed (middle lobe
often 3-lobed); doubly saw-toothed, with 5 main veins from
base; becoming hairless; slender drooping reddish leafstalk.
Dull green above, silvery white beneath; turning pale yellow
in autumn.
Bark: gray; becoming furrowed into long scaly shaggy ridges.
Twigs: light green to brown; long, spreading, and often
slightly drooping; hairless; with slightly unpleasant odor when
crushed.
Flowers: ¼″ (6 mm) long; reddish buds turning greenish
yellow; crowded in nearly stalkless clusters; male and female
in separate clusters; in late winter or very early spring before
leaves.
Fruit: 1½–2½″ (4–6 cm) long including long broad wing;
paired, widely forking keys; light brown, 1-seeded; maturing
in spring.

Habitat
Wet soils of stream banks, floodplains, and swamps; with
other hardwoods.

Range
S. Ontario east to New Brunswick, south to NW. Florida,
west to E. Oklahoma, north to N. Minnesota; to 2000′ (610
m), higher in mountains.

Comments
Its rapid growth makes Silver Maple a popular shade tree;
however, its form is not generally pleasing and its brittle
branches are easily broken in windstorms. Sugar can be
obtained from the sweetish sap, but yield is low.

Red Maple
Acer rubrum
120, 180, 228

Large tree with narrow or rounded, compact crown and red
flowers, fruit, leafstalks, and autumn foliage.
Height: 60–90′ (18–27 m). Diameter: 2½′ (0.8 m).
Leaves: opposite; 2½–4″ (6–10 cm) long and nearly as wide.
Broadly ovate, with 3 shallow short-pointed lobes (sometimes
with 2 smaller lobes near base); irregularly and wavy saw-
toothed, with 5 main veins from base; long red or green
leafstalk. Dull green above, whitish and hairy beneath;
turning red, orange, and yellow in autumn.
Bark: gray; thin, smooth, becoming fissured into long, thin,
scaly ridges.
Twigs: reddish, slender, hairless.
Flowers: ⅛″ (3 mm) long; reddish; crowded in nearly stalkless
clusters along twigs; male and female in separate clusters; in
late winter or very early spring before leaves.
Fruit: ¾–1″ (2–2.5 cm) long including long wing; paired
forking keys; red turning reddish brown; 1-seeded; maturing
in spring.

Habitat
Wet or moist soils of stream banks, valleys, swamps, and

uplands and sometimes on dry ridges; in mixed hardwood forests.

Range
Extreme SE. Manitoba east to E. Newfoundland, south to S. Florida, west to E. Texas; to 6000' (1829 m).

Comments
Red Maple is a handsome shade tree, displaying red in different seasons. Pioneers made ink and cinnamon-brown and black dyes from a bark extract. It has the greatest north-south distribution of all tree species along the East Coast, and is a preferred food of the white-tailed deer.

Sugar Maple
Acer saccharum
121, 227

Large tree with rounded, dense crown and striking, multicolored foliage in autumn.
Height: 70–100' (21–30 m). Diameter: 2–3' (0.6–0.9 m).
Leaves: opposite; 3½–5½" (9–14 cm) long and wide; palmately lobed with 5 deep long-pointed lobes; few narrow long-pointed teeth; 5 main veins from base; leafstalks long and often hairy. Dull dark green above, paler and often hairy on veins beneath; turning deep red, orange, and yellow in autumn.
Bark: light gray; becoming rough and deeply furrowed into narrow scaly ridges.
Twigs: greenish to brown or gray; slender.
Flowers: ³⁄₁₆" (5 mm) long; with bell-shaped, 5-lobed, yellowish-green calyx; male and female in drooping clusters on long slender hairy stalks; with new leaves in early spring.
Fruit: 1–1¼" (2.5–3 cm) long including long wing; paired forking keys; brown, 1-seeded; maturing in autumn.

Habitat
Moist soils of uplands and valleys, sometimes in pure stands.

Range
Extreme SE. Manitoba east to Nova Scotia, south to North Carolina, and west to E. Kansas; local in NW. South Carolina and N. Georgia; to 2500' (762 m) in north and 3000–5500' (914–1676 m) in southern Appalachians.

Comments
Maples, particularly Sugar Maple, are among the leading furniture woods. This species is used also for flooring, boxes and crates, and veneer. Some trees develop special grain patterns, including birdseye maple with dots suggesting the eyes of birds, and curly and fiddleback maple, with wavy annual rings. Such variations in grain are in great demand. The boiled concentrated sap is the commercial source of maple sugar and syrup, a use colonists learned from the Indians. Each tree yields between 5 and 60 gallons of sap per year; about 32 gallons of sap make 1 gallon of syrup or 4½ pounds of sugar.

Sweetgum
Liquidambar styraciflua
122, 182, 226, 230

Large, aromatic tree with straight trunk and conical crown that becomes round and spreading.
Height: 60–100′ (18–30 m). Diameter: 1½–3′ (0.5–0.9 m). Leaves: alternate; 3–6″ (7.5–15 cm) long and wide. Star-shaped or maplelike, with 5, sometimes 7, long-pointed, finely saw-toothed lobes and 5 main veins from notched base; with resinous odor when crushed; leafstalks slender, nearly as long as blades. Shiny dark green above, turning reddish in autumn.
Bark: gray; deeply furrowed into narrow scaly ridges.
Twigs: green to brown, stout, often forming corky wings.
Flowers: tiny; in greenish ball-like clusters in spring; male in several clusters along a stalk; female in drooping cluster on same tree.
Fruit: 1–1¼″ (2.5–3 cm) in diameter; a long-stalked drooping brown ball composed of many individual fruits, each ending in 2 long curved prickly points and each with 1–2 long-winged seeds; maturing in autumn and persistent into winter.

Habitat
Moist soils of valleys and lower slopes; in mixed woodlands. Often a pioneer after logging, clearing, and in old fields.

Range
Extreme SW. Connecticut south to central Florida, west to E. Texas, and north to S. Illinois; also a variety in eastern Mexico; to 3000′ (914 m) in southern Appalachians.

Comments
An important timber tree, Sweetgum is second in production only to oaks among hardwoods. It is a leading furniture wood, used for cabinetwork, veneer, plywood, pulpwood, barrels, and boxes. In pioneer days, a gum was obtained from the trunks by peeling the bark and scraping off the resinlike solid. This gum was used medicinally as well as for chewing gum.

Yellow-poplar
Liriodendron tulipifera
123, 162, 229

One of the tallest and most beautiful eastern hardwoods, with a long, straight trunk, a narrow crown that spreads with age, and large showy flowers resembling tulips or lilies.
Height: 80–120′ (24–37 m). Diameter: 2–3′ (0.6–0.9 m), sometimes much larger.
Leaves: alternate; 3–6″ (7.5–15 cm) long and wide. Blades of unusual shape, with broad tip and base nearly straight like a square, and with 4 or sometimes 6 short-pointed paired lobes; hairless; long-stalked. Shiny dark green above, paler beneath; turning yellow in autumn.
Bark: dark gray; becoming thick and deeply furrowed.
Twigs: brown, stout, hairless, with ring scars at nodes.
Flowers: 1½–2″ (4–5 cm) long and wide; cup-shaped, with 6 rounded green petals (orange at base); solitary and upright at end of leafy twig; in spring.
Fruit: 2½–3″ (6–7.5 cm) long; conelike; light brown; composed of many overlapping 1- or 2-seeded nutlets 1–1½″

(2.5–4 cm) long (including narrow wing); shedding from upright axis in autumn; the axis persistent in winter.

Habitat
Moist well-drained soils, especially valleys and slopes; often in pure stands.

Range
Extreme S. Ontario east to Vermont and Rhode Island, south to N. Florida, west to Louisiana, and north to S. Michigan; to 1000′ (305 m) in north and to 4500′ (1372 m) in southern Appalachians.

Comments
Introduced into Europe from Virginia by the earliest colonists and grown also on the Pacific Coast. Very tall trees with massive trunks existed in the primeval forests but were cut for the valuable soft wood. Pioneers hollowed out a single log to make a long, lightweight canoe.

Sycamore
Platanus occidentalis
124, 183

One of the largest eastern hardwoods, with an enlarged base, massive, straight trunk, and large, spreading, often crooked branches forming a broad open crown.
Height: 60–100′ (18–30 m). Diameter: 2–4′ (0.6–1.2 m), sometimes much larger.
Leaves: alternate; 4–8″ (10–20 cm) long and wide (larger on shoots). Broadly ovate, with 3 or 5 shallow broad short-pointed lobes; wavy edges with scattered large teeth; 5 or 3 main veins from notched base. Bright green above, paler beneath and becoming hairless except on veins; turning brown in autumn. Leafstalk long, stout, covering side bud at enlarged base.
Bark: smooth, whitish and mottled; peeling off in large thin flakes, exposing patches of brown, green, and gray; base of large trunks dark brown, furrowed into broad scaly ridges.
Twigs: greenish, slender, zigzag, with ring scars at nodes.
Flowers: tiny; greenish; in 1–2 ball-like drooping clusters; male and female clusters on separate twigs; in spring.
Fruit: 1″ (2.5 cm) in diameter; usually 1 brown ball hanging on long stalk, composed of many narrow nutlets with hair tufts; maturing in autumn, separating in winter.

Habitat
Wet soils of stream banks, floodplains, and edges of lakes and swamps; dominant in mixed forests.

Range
SW. Maine, south to NW. Florida, west to S. central Texas, north to E. Nebraska; also northeastern Mexico; to 3200′ (975 m).

Comments
Sycamore pioneers on exposed upland sites such as old fields and strip mines. The wood is used for furniture parts, millwork, flooring, and specialty products such as butcher blocks, as well as pulpwood, particleboard, and fiberboard. A

shade tree, Sycamore grows to a larger trunk diameter than any other native hardwood. The present champion's trunk is about 11' (3.4 m) in diameter; an earlier giant's was nearly 15' (4.6 m). The hollow trunks of old, giant trees were homes for chimney swifts in earlier times.

White Mulberry
Morus alba
125

Naturalized small tree with rounded crown of spreading branches, milky sap, and edible mulberries.
Height: 40' (12 m). Diameter: 1' (0.3 m).
Leaves: in 2 rows; 2½–7" (6–18 cm) long, 2–5" (5–13 cm) wide. Broadly ovate but variable in shape; with 3 main veins from rounded or notched base; coarsely toothed; often divided into 3 or 5 lobes; long-stalked. Shiny green above, paler and slightly hairy beneath.
Bark: light brown; smoothish, becoming furrowed into scaly ridges.
Twigs: light brown, slender.
Flowers: tiny; greenish; crowded in short clusters; male and female on same or separate trees in spring.
Fruit: ⅜–¾" (10–19 mm) long; a cylindrical mulberry; purplish, pinkish, or white; composed of many tiny beadlike 1-seeded fruits, sweet and juicy, edible; in late spring.

Habitat
Hardy in cities, drought-resistant, and adapted to dry, warm areas.

Range
Native of China. Widely cultivated across the United States; naturalized in the East and in the Pacific states.

Comments
White Mulberry has been cultivated for centuries, the leaves serving as the main food of silkworms. Introduced long ago in the southeastern United States, where silk production was not successful. It grows rapidly and produces abundant berries that are enjoyed by birds as well as by many people. The trees spread like weeds in cities, where the berries litter sidewalks.

Sassafras
Sassafras albidum
126, 231

Aromatic tree or thicket-forming shrub with variously shaped leaves and narrow, spreading crown of short, stout branches.
Height: 30–60' (9–18 m). Diameter: 1½' (0.5 m), sometimes larger.
Leaves: alternate; 3–5" (7.5–13 cm) long, 1½–4" (4–10 cm) wide. Elliptical, often with 2 mitten-shaped lobes or 3 broad and blunt lobes; not toothed; base short-pointed; long slender leafstalks. Shiny green above, paler and often hairy beneath; turning yellow, orange, or red in autumn.
Bark: gray-brown; becoming thick and deeply furrowed.
Twigs: greenish, slender, sometimes hairy.
Flowers: ⅜" (10 mm) long; yellow-green; several clustered at end of leafless twigs in early spring; male and female usually on separate trees.

Fruit: ⅜″ (10 mm) long; elliptical shiny bluish-black berries; each in red cup on long red stalk, containing 1 shiny brown seed; maturing in autumn.

Habitat
Moist, particularly sandy, soils of uplands and valleys, often in old fields, clearings, and forest openings.

Range
Extreme S. Ontario east to SW. Maine, south to central Florida, west to E. Texas, and north to central Michigan; to 5000′ (1524 m) in southern Appalachians.

Comments
The roots and root bark supply oil of sassafras (used to perfume soap) and sassafras tea, and have been used to flavor root beer. Explorers and colonists thought the aromatic root bark was a panacea for diseases and shipped quantities to Europe. The greenish twigs and leafstalks have a pleasant, spicy, slightly gummy taste. Sassafras apparently is the American Indian name used by the Spanish and French settlers in Florida in the middle of the 16th century. This is the northernmost New World representative of an important family of tropical timbers.

Southeastern Coralbean
Erythrina herbacea
127, 145

A spiny shrub with many slender stems, in south Florida becoming a small tree with crooked trunk, spreading brittle branches, and rounded crown.
Height: 20′ (6 m). Diameter: 8″ (20 cm).
Leaves: alternate; pinnately compound; 6–8″ (15–20 cm) long; with slender stalks, sometimes prickly. 3 leaflets, 1½–3″ (4–7.5 cm) long and almost as wide, sometimes larger; triangular or slightly 3-lobed; not toothed; midvein often prickly beneath; light green.
Bark: light gray; smooth, becoming thick and furrowed; sometimes spiny.
Twigs: light green, stout, brittle, with scattered short curved spines or prickles.
Flowers: 2″ (5 cm) long; very narrow; showy, with dark red tubular calyx and 5 narrow unequal red or scarlet petals; many, in upright long-stalked clusters 8–12″ (20–30 cm) long.
Fruit: 4–8″ (10–20 cm) long; cylindrical pod; dark brown or black, long-pointed at ends, narrowed between seeds; maturing in late summer and opening along 1 edge; several beanlike, shiny red, poisonous seeds.

Habitat
Moist sandy soils.

Range
SE. North Carolina to S. Florida, including Florida Keys, and west to E. and S. Texas; to 500′ (152 m).

Comments
This unusual tropical tree extends its range northward as a

shrub or perennial herb, but is killed back to the ground each winter. It is planted for the showy flowers and seeds, although the brittle branches are subject to damage by windstorms. In Mexico, the toxic seeds have been used for poisoning rats and fish. Although novelties and necklaces can be made from the seeds, they should be kept away from children.

Lime Prickly-ash
Zanthoxylum fagara
128

Evergreen shrub or small tree with spreading rounded crown, often with a leaning trunk; aromatic, spiny, with tiny gland-dots on foliage, flowers, and fruit.
Height: 25' (7.6 m). Diameter: 8" (20 cm).
Leaves: evergreen; alternate; pinnately compound; 3–4" (7.5–10 cm) long; with flat or winged axis. 5–13 leaflets (usually 7–9), ⅜–1" (1–2.5 cm) long; elliptical; wavy-toothed beyond middle; narrowed to base; thick and leathery; stalkless. Shiny green above, paler beneath.
Bark: gray; thin, smooth or warty, becoming scaly.
Twigs: dark gray; slender, zigzag, hairless or nearly so; with paired hooked sharp spines less than ¼" (6 mm) long.
Flowers: ⅛" (3 mm) wide; with 4 yellow-green petals in small clusters to ½" (12 mm) wide, on old twigs; male and female on separate plants; in early spring.
Fruit: 3⁄16" (5 mm) long; podlike, rounded, brown, warty, clustered along twig, 1-seeded; 1–2 from a flower; maturing in autumn and splitting open.

Habitat
Moist soil mostly near coast and on plains.

Range
Central and S. Florida, Florida Keys, and S. Texas; also northern Mexico; to 500' (152 m).

Comments
The powdered bark and leaves have a sharp taste and have been used also as a spice. The crushed foliage has an odor of limes, as the common name suggests.

Black Locust
Robinia pseudoacacia
129, 157

Medium-sized, spiny tree with a forking, often crooked and angled trunk and irregular, open crown of upright branches.
Height: 40–80' (12–24 m). Diameter: 1–2' (0.3–0.6 m).
Leaves: alternate; pinnately compound; 6–12" (15–30 cm) long. 7–19 leaflets 1–1¾" (2.5–4.5 cm) long, ½–¾" (12–19 mm) wide; paired (except at end); elliptical; with tiny bristle tip; without teeth; hairy when young; drooping and folding at night. Dark blue-green above, pale and usually hairless beneath.
Bark: light gray; thick, deeply furrowed into long rough forking ridges.
Twigs: dark brown, with stout paired spines ¼–½" (6–12 mm) long at nodes.
Flowers: ¾" (19 mm) long; petals unequal; 1 broad upper petal and 2 lateral petals nearly enclosing 2 lower petals that

are joined and shaped like prow of a boat; white, with the largest yellow near base; very fragrant; in showy drooping clusters 4–8″ (10–20 cm) long at base of leaves; in late spring.
Fruit: 2–4″ (5–10 cm) long; narrowly oblong flat pod; dark brown; maturing in autumn, remaining attached into winter, splitting open; 3–14 dark brown flattened beanlike seeds.

Habitat
Moist to dry sandy and rocky soils, especially in old fields and other open areas, and in woodlands.

Range
Central Pennsylvania and S. Ohio south to NE. Alabama, and from S. Missouri to E. Oklahoma; naturalized from Maine to California and in southern Canada; from 500′ (152 m) to above 5000′ (1524) in southern Appalachians.

Comments
Black Locust is widely planted for ornament and shelterbelts, and for erosion control particularly on lands strip-mined for coal. Although it grows rapidly and spreads by sprouts like a weed, it is short-lived. Virginia Indians made bows of the wood and apparently planted the trees eastward. British colonists at Jamestown discovered this species in 1607 and named it for its resemblance to the Carob Tree or Old World Locust (*Ceratonia siliqua*). Posts of this durable timber served as cornerposts for the colonists' first homes.

American Mountain-ash
Sorbus americana
130, 194

Small tree with spreading crown or a shrub with many stems, and with showy white flowers, and bright red berries.
Height: 30′ (9 m). Diameter: 8″ (20 cm).
Leaves: alternate; pinnately compound; 6–8″ (15–20 cm) long. 11–17 stalkless, lance-shaped leaflets 1½–4″ (4–10 cm) long, ½–1″ (1.2–2.5 cm) wide; long-pointed; saw-toothed; becoming hairless. Yellow-green above, paler beneath; turning yellow in autumn.
Bark: light gray; smooth or scaly, thin.
Twigs: reddish brown, stout, hairy when young.
Flowers: ¼″ (6 mm) wide; with 5 white rounded petals; numerous flowers, crowded in upright clusters 3–5″ (7.5–13 cm) wide; in late spring.
Fruit: ¼″ (6 mm) in diameter; like small apples; bright red skin; bitter pulp; with few seeds; many, in clusters; maturing in autumn.

Habitat
Moist soils of valleys and slopes; in coniferous forests.

Range
W. Ontario to Newfoundland, south to N. Georgia, and northwest to N. Illinois; to 5000–6000′ (1524–1829 m) in southern Appalachians.

Comments
A handsome ornamental, its showy red fruit persists into

winter. The berries are eaten by birds, especially grouse, grosbeaks, and cedar waxwings. Moose browse the foliage, winter twigs, and fragrant inner bark.

Yellow Buckeye
Aesculus octandra
131, 202

Tree with rounded crown and upright clusters of showy yellow flowers.
Height: 70–90' (21–27 m). Diameter: 2–3' (0.6–0.9 m).
Leaves: opposite; palmately compound; with slender leafstalks 3½–7" (9–18 cm) long. 5–7 leaflets 4–8" (10–20 cm) long, 1½–3" (4–7.5 cm) wide; elliptical to obovate; evenly saw-toothed; short-stalked. Dark green and usually hairless above, yellow-green and often hairy beneath.
Bark: brown to gray; thin, fissured into large scaly plates.
Twigs: light brown; stout, often hairy.
Flowers: 1¼" (3 cm) long; with 4 very unequal yellow petals and 7–8 shorter stamens; in upright branched terminal clusters 4–6" (10–15 cm) long; in spring.
Fruit: 2–3" (5–7.5 cm) in diameter; a pale brown, smooth or slightly pitted capsule, splitting on 2–3 lines; 1–3 large, shiny brown, poisonous seeds; maturing in early autumn.

Habitat
Rich, moist, deep soils from river bottoms to deep mountain valleys or slopes; in mixed forests.

Range
SW. Pennsylvania south to N. Alabama and N. Georgia and north to extreme S. Illinois; at 500–6300' (152–1920 m).

Comments
The largest of the buckeyes, this species is abundant in Great Smoky Mountains National Park. The seeds are poisonous, and young shoots toxic to livestock. American Indians ate the seeds after removing the poison by roasting and soaking.

Shagbark Hickory
Carya ovata
132, 233

Large tree with tall trunk, narrow irregular crown, and distinctive rough shaggy bark.
Height: 70–100' (21–30 m). Diameter: 2½' (0.8 m).
Leaves: alternate; pinnately compound; 8–14" (20–36 cm) long. 5 (rarely 7) elliptical or ovate leaflets, 3–7" (7.5–18 cm) long; stalkless; edges finely saw-toothed and hairy; yellow-green above, paler (and hairy when young) beneath; turning golden brown in autumn.
Bark: light gray; separating into long narrow curved strips loosely attached at middle.
Twigs: brown; stout; ending in large brown hairy buds.
Flowers: tiny; greenish; in early spring before leaves. Male, with 4 stamens, many in slender drooping catkins, 3 hanging from 1 stalk. 2–5 female flowers at tip of same twig.
Fruit: 1¼–2½" (3–6 cm) long; nearly round; flattened at tip; with husk thick, becoming dark brown or blackish and splitting to base. Hickory nut elliptical or rounded, slightly flattened and angled, light brown, with edible seed.

Habitat
Moist soils of valleys and upland slopes in mixed hardwood forests.

Range
Extreme S. Quebec and SW. Maine, south to Georgia, west to SE. Texas, and north to SE. Minnesota; also northeastern Mexico; to 2000′ (610 m) in north and 3000′ (914 m) in southern Appalachians.

Comments
Also known as Scalybark Hickory and Shellbark Hickory. Wild trees and improved cultivated varieties produce commercial hickory nuts. Carolina Hickory (var. *australis*), a variety found in southeastern mountains, has small lance-shaped leaflets and small nuts. The name "hickory" is from *pawcohiccora,* the American Indian word for the oily food removed from pounded kernels steeped in boiling water. This sweet hickory milk was used in cooking corn cakes and hominy. Pioneers made a yellow dye from the inner bark. The nickname "Old Hickory" was given by his backwoods militia to General Andrew Jackson (afterwards our seventh president) because he was "tough as hickory."

Boxelder
Acer negundo
133

Small to medium-sized tree with a short trunk and a broad, rounded crown of light green foliage.
Height: 30–60′ (9–18 m). Diameter: 2½′ (0.8 m).
Leaves: opposite; pinnately compound; 6″ (15 cm) long; with slender axis. 3–7 leaflets sometimes slightly lobed, 2–4″ (5–10 cm) long, 1–1½″ (2.5–4 cm) wide; paired and short-stalked (except at end); ovate or elliptical, long-pointed at tip, short-pointed at base; coarsely saw-toothed, sometimes lobed. Light green and mostly hairless above, paler and varying in hairiness beneath; turning yellow (or sometimes red) in autumn.
Bark: light gray-brown; with many narrow ridges and fissures, becoming deeply furrowed.
Twigs: green, often whitish or purplish; slender, ringed at nodes, mostly hairless.
Flowers: ³⁄₁₆″ (5 mm) long; with very small yellow-green calyx of 5 lobes or sepals; several clustered on slender drooping stalks; male and female on separate trees; before leaves in spring.
Fruit: 1–1½″ (2.5–4 cm) long; paired, slightly forking keys with flat narrow body and long curved wing; pale yellow, 1-seeded; maturing in summer and remaining attached in winter.

Habitat
Wet or moist soils along stream banks and in valleys with various hardwoods; also naturalized in waste places and roadsides.

Range
S. Alberta east to extreme S. Ontario and New York, south to

central Florida, and west to S. Texas; also scattered from New
Mexico to California and naturalized in New England; to
8000' (2438 m) in the Southwest.

Comments
Boxelder is classed with maples having similar paired key
fruits, but is easily distinguishable by the pinnately compound
leaves. Hardy and fast-growing, it is planted for shade and
shelterbelts but is short-lived and easily broken in storms.
Common and widely distributed, it is spreading in the East as
a weed tree. Plains Indians made sugar from the sap. The
common name indicates the resemblance of the foliage to that
of elders (*Sambucus*) and the whitish wood to that of Box
(*Buxus sempervirens*).

White Ash
Fraxinus americana
134, 178, 213

Large tree with straight trunk and dense, conical or rounded
crown of foliage with whitish lower surfaces.
Height: 80' (24 m). Diameter: 2' (0.6 m).
Leaves: opposite; pinnately compound; 8–12" (20–30 cm)
long. Usually 7 (5–9) leaflets 2½–5" (6–13 cm) long, 1¼–
2½" (3–6 cm) wide; paired (except at end); ovate or elliptical;
finely saw-toothed or almost without teeth. Dark green above,
whitish and sometimes hairy beneath; turning purple or
yellow in autumn.
Bark: dark gray; thick, with deep diamond-shaped furrows
and forking ridges.
Twigs: gray or brown, stout, mostly hairless.
Flowers: ¼" (6 mm) long; purplish, without corolla; many in
small clusters before leaves in early spring; male and female on
separate trees.
Fruit: 1–2" (2.5–5 cm) long; brownish key with narrow wing
not extending down cylindrical body; hanging in clusters;
maturing in late summer and autumn.

Habitat
Moist soils of valleys and slopes, especially deep well-drained
loams; in forests with many other hardwoods.

Range
S. Ontario east to Cape Breton Island, south to N. Florida,
west to E. Texas, and north to E. Minnesota; to 2000' (610 m)
in the north; to 5000' (1524 m) in the south.

Comments
The wood of White Ash is particularly suited for making
baseball bats, tennis racquets, hockey sticks, polo mallets,
oars, and playground equipment. A variation of this species
has hairs covering the twigs, leafstalks, and underleaf surfaces;
it has been called Biltmore Ash.

Bitternut Hickory
Carya cordiformis
135

Tree with tall trunk, broad and rounded crown, and bitter
inedible nuts.
Height: 60–80' (18–24 m). Diameter: 1–2' (0.3–0.6 m).
Leaves: alternate; pinnately compound; 6–10" (15–25 cm)

long, with slender hairy axis. 7–9 leaflets, 2–6" (5–15 cm) long; stalkless; lance-shaped; finely saw-toothed. Yellow-green above, light green and slightly hairy beneath; turning yellow in autumn.
Bark: gray or light brown; shallowly furrowed into narrow forking scaly ridges.
Twigs: slender, ending in bright yellow slightly flattened buds.
Flowers: tiny; greenish; in early spring before leaves. Male flowers with 4–5 stamens; many in slender drooping catkins, 3 hanging from 1 stalk. 1–2 female flowers at tip of same twig.
Fruit: ¾–1¼" (2–3 cm) long; nearly round or slightly flattened; short-pointed; husk thin, with tiny yellow scales, and splitting along 4 wings. Nut nearly smooth, thin-shelled, with bitter seed.

Habitat
Moist soil of valleys and in north also on dry upland soil; in mixed hardwood forests.

Range
S. Quebec and SW. New Hampshire, south to NW. Florida, west to E. Texas, and north to Minnesota; to 2000' (610 m).

Comments
Also called Bitternut and Pignut. One of the most widely distributed and most common hickories through eastern United States, and also one of the easiest to identify because of the small bright yellow buds. Rabbits have been observed to eat the bitter seeds which may be unpalatable to most wildlife. Early settlers used oil extracted from the nuts for oil lamps; they also believed it could cure rheumatism.

Pignut Hickory
Carya glabra
136, 199, 232

Tree with irregular, spreading crown and thick-shelled nuts.
Height: 60–80' (18–24 m). Diameter: 1–2' (0.3–0.6 m).
Leaves: alternate; pinnately compound; 6–10" (15–25 cm) long, with slender hairless axis. Usually 5 leaflets, 3–6" (7.5–15 cm) long, largest toward tip; lance-shaped; nearly stalkless; finely saw-toothed; hairless or hairy on veins beneath. Light green, turning yellow in autumn.
Bark: light gray; smooth or becoming furrowed with forking ridges.
Twigs: brown; slender, hairless.
Flowers: tiny; greenish; in early spring before leaves. Male, with 4 stamens, many in slender drooping catkins, 3 hanging from 1 stalk. Female, 2–10 flowers at tip of same twig.
Fruit: 1–2" (2.5–5 cm) long; slightly pear-shaped or rounded; husk thin, becoming dark brown and opening late and splitting usually to middle. Hickory nut usually not angled, thick-shelled, with small sweet or bitter seed.

Habitat
Dry and moist uplands in hardwood forests with oaks and other hickories.

Range
S. Ontario east to southern New England, south to central Florida, west to extreme E. Texas, and north to Illinois; to 4800' (1463 m) in southern Appalachians.

Comments
Also called Smoothbark Hickory and Pignut. One of the most common hickories in the southern Appalachians and an important timber source there, its wood is made into tool handles and skis. It was formerly used for wagon wheels and textile loom picker sticks because it could sustain tremendous vibration. Named in colonial times from the consumption of the small nuts by hogs.

Mockernut Hickory
Carya tomentosa
137

Nut tree with rounded crown and leaves that are very aromatic when crushed.
Height: 50–80' (15–24 m). Diameter: 2' (0.6 m).
Leaves: pinnately compound; 8–20" (20–51 cm) long, with hairy axis; 7 or 9 leaflets, 2–8" (5–20 cm) long; elliptical or lance-shaped; finely saw-toothed; nearly stalkless. Shiny dark yellow-green above, pale and densely hairy and glandular beneath; turning yellow in autumn.
Bark: gray; irregularly furrowed into narrow forking ridges.
Twigs: brown; stout, hairy, ending in large hairy bud.
Flowers: tiny; greenish; in early spring before leaves. Male, with 4–5 stamens; many in slender drooping catkins, 3 hanging from 1 stalk. Female, 2–5 flowers at tip of same twig.
Fruit: 1½–2" (4–5 cm) long; elliptical or pear-shaped; becoming brown; with thick husk splitting to middle or nearly to base. Hickory nut rounded or elliptical, slightly 4-angled, thick-shelled, with edible seed.

Habitat
Moist uplands and less frequently on floodplains; usually with oaks, also pines.

Range
Extreme S. Ontario east to Massachusetts, south to N. Florida, west to E. Texas, and north to SE. Iowa; to 3000' (914 m) in southern Appalachians.

Comments
Hickory wood has a very high fuel value, both as firewood and as charcoal, and is the preferred wood for smoking hams. People must arrive early to gather hickory nuts before they are consumed by squirrels and other wildlife. The Latin species name, meaning "densely covered with soft hairs," describes the undersurfaces of leaflets, a characteristic that makes this tree easily identifiable.

Butternut
Juglans cinerea
138, 200

Tree with short straight trunk, stout branches, broad open crown, and butternut fruit with sticky husk.
Height: 40–70' (12–21 m). Diameter: 1–2' (0.3–0.6 m).

Leaves: alternate; pinnately compound; 15–24″ (38–61 cm) long, with hairy axis, sticky when young, 11–17 leaflets, 2–4½″ (5–11 cm) long; broadly lance-shaped; pointed at tip, unequal and rounded at base; finely saw-toothed; stalkless. Yellow-green and slightly hairy above, paler and covered with soft hairs beneath; turning yellow or brown in autumn.
Bark: light gray; smooth becoming rough and furrowed.
Twigs: brown; stout; with sticky hairs and a hairy fringe above leaf-scars; and with chambered pith.
Flowers: small; greenish; in early spring. Male, with 8–12 stamens; many in catkins. Female, with 2-lobed style; 6–8 at tip of same twig.
Fruit: 1½–2½″ (4–6 cm) long; 3–5 in drooping clusters; narrowly egg-shaped; long-pointed; with 2 ridges, rust-colored sticky hairs, and thick husk. Shell of nut thick, light brown, rough with 8 ridges, containing a very oily edible seed, the butternut.

Habitat
Moist soils of valleys and slopes; also dry rocky soils; in hardwood forests.

Range
S. Quebec east to SW. New Brunswick, south to extreme N. Georgia, west to Missouri and Arkansas, and north to E. Minnesota; to 4800′ (1463 m).

Comments
The edible butternuts soon become rancid, and so must be harvested quickly after maturing. Indians made them into oil for many uses, including ceremonial anointing of the head. They are also eaten by wildlife. The husks of the nuts, which contain a brown stain that colors the fingers, yield a yellow or orange dye. The lumber serves as a cabinet wood.

Pecan
Carya illinoensis
139

Large wild and planted tree with tall trunk, broad rounded crown of massive spreading branches, and familiar pecan nuts.
Height: 100′ (30 m). Diameter: 3′ (0.9 m).
Leaves: alternate; pinnately compound; 12–30″ (30–51 cm) long; 11–17 slightly sickle-shaped leaflets, 2–7″ (5–18 cm) long; long-pointed at tip; finely saw-toothed; short-stalked; hairless or slightly hairy. Yellow-green above, paler beneath; turning yellow in autumn.
Bark: light brown or gray; deeply and irregularly furrowed into narrow forked scaly ridges.
Flowers: tiny; greenish; in early spring before leaves. Male, with 5–6 stamens, many in slender drooping catkins, 3 hanging from 1 stalk. Female, 2–10 flowers at tip of the same twig.
Fruit: 1¼–2″ (3–5 cm) long; oblong; short-pointed at tip, rounded at base; with thin husk becoming dark brown, splitting to base along 4 ridges; 3–10 in cluster. Pecan nut light brown with darker markings, thin-shelled, with edible seed.

Habitat
Moist well-drained loamy soils of river floodplains and valleys; in mixed hardwood forests.

Range
E. Iowa east to Indiana, south to Louisiana, west to S. Texas; to 1600' (488 m); also mountains of Mexico.

Comments
Pecan is one of the most valuable cultivated plants originating in North America. Improved varieties with large, thin-shelled nuts are grown in plantations or orchards in the Southeast; pecans are also harvested locally from wild trees. The wood is used for furniture, flooring, veneer, and charcoal for smoking meats. The word pecan is of Algonquian Indian origin. The Latin species name is from an old term, "Illinois nuts," and refers to the region where traders found wild trees and nuts. Indians may have extended the range by planting. This tree of the Mississippi Valley was unknown to British colonists on the Atlantic coast. Thomas Jefferson planted seeds at Monticello and gave some to George Washington; now these Pecans are the oldest trees in Mount Vernon.

Black Walnut
Juglans nigra
140, 201

Large walnut tree with open, rounded crown of dark green, aromatic foliage.
Height: 70–90' (21–27 m). Diameter: 2–4' (0.6–1.2 m).
Leaves: alternate; pinnately compound; 12–24" (30–61 cm) long. 9–21 leaflets 2½–5" (6–13 cm) long; broadly lance-shaped; finely saw-toothed; long-pointed; stalkless; nearly hairless above, covered with soft hairs beneath. Green or dark green, turning yellow in autumn.
Bark: dark brown; deeply furrowed into scaly ridges.
Twigs: brown, stout, with brown chambered pith.
Flowers: small; greenish; in early spring. Male, with 20–30 stamens, many in catkins. Female, with 2-lobed style, 2–5 at tip of same twig.
Fruit: single or paired, 1½–2½" (4–6 cm) in diameter; thick green or brown husk; irregularly ridged, thick-shelled inner layer covering sweet edible seed.

Habitat
Moist well-drained soils, especially along streams, scattered in mixed forests.

Range
Eastern half of United States except northern border; New York south to NW. Florida, west to central Texas, north to SE. South Dakota; local in southern New England and S. Ontario; to 4000' (1219 m).

Comments
One of the scarcest and most coveted native hardwoods, Black Walnut is used especially for furniture, gunstocks, and veneer. Individual trees fetch high prices, and a few prized trees have even been stolen. Since before Colonial days, Black Walnut

has provided edible nuts and a blackish dye made from the husks. The delicious nuts must be gathered early, before squirrels and other wildlife can consume them. Tomatoes and apples do not survive near mature trees.

Shining Sumac
Rhus copallina
141, 168, 211

Shrub or small tree with a short trunk and open crown of stout, spreading branches.
Height: 25' (7.6 m). Diameter: 6" (15 cm).
Leaves: alternate; pinnately compound; to 12" (30 cm) long; with flat broad-winged axis. 7–17 leaflets (27 in southeastern variety) 1–3¼" (2.5–8 cm) long; lance-shaped; usually without teeth; slightly thickened. Shiny dark green and nearly hairless above, paler and covered with fine hairs beneath; turning dark reddish purple in autumn; stalkless.
Bark: light brown or gray; scaly.
Twigs: brown, stout, slightly zigzag, covered with fine hairs; with watery sap.
Flowers: ⅛" (3 mm) wide; with 5 greenish-white petals; crowded in spreading clusters to 3" (13 cm) wide, with hairy branches; male and female usually on separate plants; in late summer.
Fruit: more than ⅛" (3 mm) in diameter; 1-seeded; crowded in clusters; rounded and slightly flattened, dark red, covered with short sticky red hairs; maturing in autumn, remaining attached in winter.

Habitat
Open uplands, valleys, edges of forests, grasslands, clearings, roadsides, and waste places.

Range
S. Ontario east to SW. Maine, south to Florida, west to central Texas, and north to Wisconsin; to 4500' (1372 m) in the Southeast.

Comments
Shining Sumac is sometimes planted as an ornamental for its shiny leaves and showy fruit. The sour fruit can be nibbled or made into a drink like lemonade. Wildlife eat the fruit, and deer also browse the twigs. It is easily distinguishable from other sumacs by the winged leaf axis and watery sap. This species often forms thickets.

Smooth Sumac
Rhus glabra
142, 197

The most common sumac; a large shrub or sometimes a small tree with open, flattened crown of a few stout, spreading branches and with whitish sap.
Height: 20' (6 m). Diameter: 4" (10 cm).
Leaves: alternate; pinnately compound; 12" (30 cm) long; with slender axis. 11–31 leaflets 2–4" (5–10 cm) long; lance-shaped; saw-toothed; hairless; almost stalkless. Shiny green above, whitish beneath; turning reddish in autumn.
Bark: brown; smooth or becoming scaly.
Twigs: gray, with whitish bloom; few, very stout, hairless.

Flowers: less than ⅛" (3 mm) wide; with 5 whitish petals; crowded in large upright clusters to 8" (20 cm) long, with hairless branches; male and female usually on separate plants; in early summer.
Fruit: more than ⅛" (3 mm) in diameter; rounded, 1-seeded, numerous, crowded in upright clusters; dark red, covered with short sticky red hairs; maturing in late summer, remaining attached in winter.

Habitat
Open uplands including edges of forests, grasslands, clearings, roadsides, and waste places, especially in sandy soils.

Range
E. Saskatchewan east to S. Ontario and Maine, south to NW. Florida, and west to central Texas; also in mountains from S. British Columbia south to SE. Arizona and in northern Mexico; to 4500' (1372 m) in the East; to 7000' (2134 m) in the West.

Comments
The only shrub or tree species native to all 48 contiguous states. One cultivated variety has dissected or bipinnate leaves. Raw young sprouts were eaten by the Indians as salad. The sour fruit, mostly seed, can be chewed to quench thirst or prepared as a drink similar to lemonade. It is also consumed by birds of many kinds and small mammals, mainly in winter.

Staghorn Sumac
Rhus typhina
143, 198, 212

Tall shrub or small tree with irregular, open, flat crown of a few stout, spreading branches; whitish, sticky sap turns black on exposure.
Height: 30' (9 m). Diameter: 8" (20 cm), sometimes larger.
Leaves: alternate; pinnately compound; 12–24" (30–61 cm) long; with stout soft hairy reddish-tinged axis. 11–31 leaflets 2–4" (5–10 cm) long; lance-shaped; often slightly curved; saw-toothed; nearly stalkless. Dark green above, whitish (with reddish hairs when young) beneath; turning bright red with purple and orange in autumn.
Bark: dark brown; thin; smooth or becoming scaly.
Twigs: few, very stout, brittle, dense velvety covering of long, brown hairs.
Flowers: ⅛–³⁄₁₆" (3–5 mm) wide; with greenish petals; crowded in upright clusters to 8" (20 cm) long; branches densely covered with hairs; male and female usually on separate plants; in early summer.
Fruit: ³⁄₁₆" (5 mm) in diameter; rounded, 1-seeded, dark red, covered with long dark red hairs; numerous, crowded in upright clusters; maturing in late summer and autumn, remaining attached in winter.

Habitat
Open uplands, edges of forests, roadsides, and old fields.

Range
S. Ontario east to Nova Scotia, south to NW. South Carolina,

west to Tennessee, and north to Minnesota; to 5000' (1524 m) in the Southeast.

Comments
Staghorn Sumac reaches tree size more often than related species and commonly forms thickets. In winter, the bare, widely forking, stout, hairy twigs resemble velvety deer antlers. Indians made a lemonadelike drink from the crushed fruit of this and related species. Sumac bark and foliage are rich in tannin and were used to tan leather. Grown as an ornamental, especially a variety with dissected leaves, for the autumn foliage and showy fruit.

Cabbage Palmetto
Sabal palmetto
144

Medium-sized, spineless, evergreen palm with stout, unbranched trunk and very large, fan-shaped leaves spreading around top.
Height: 30–50' (9–15 m) or more. Diameter: 1½' (0.5 m).
Leaves: 4–7' (1.2–2.1 m) long and nearly as broad. Folded into many long, narrow segments; long-pointed and drooping; coarse, stiff, and leathery; splitting apart nearly to the stout midrib; with threadlike fibers separating at edges; shiny dark green. Very stout, stiff leafstalks 5–8' (1.5–2.4 m) long; green, ridged above, with long, fibrous, shiny brown sheath at wedge-shaped base, which splits and hangs down with age.
Trunk: gray-brown; rough or ridged.
Flowers: 3/16" (5 mm) long; with deeply 6-lobed whitish corolla; fragrant; nearly stalkless; in curved or drooping, much-branched clusters arising from leaf bases; in early summer.
Fruit: 3/8" (10 mm) in diameter; nearly round berries; shiny black; with thin, sweet, dry flesh; 1-seeded; maturing in autumn.

Habitat
Sandy shores, crowded in groves; inland in hammocks.

Range
Near coast from SE. North Carolina to S. and NW. Florida, including Florida Keys.

Comments
Also called Carolina Palmetto and Cabbage-palm. The trunks are used for wharf pilings, docks, and poles. Brushes and whisk brooms are made from young leafstalk fibers, and baskets and hats from the leaf blades. An ornamental and street tree, it is the northernmost New World palm and one of the hardiest. Formerly, plants were killed in order to eat the large leaf buds as a cabbagelike salad. Their names are from the Spanish *palmito,* meaning "small palm." The fruits are relished by raccoons and robins.

Huisache
Acacia farnesiana
164

Spiny much-branched shrub or small tree with a widely spreading, flattened crown and fragrant, yellow balls of tiny flowers.

Height: 16' (5 m). Diameter: 4" (10 cm).
Leaves: alternate or clustered; bipinnately compound; 2–4" (5–10 cm) long; usually with 3–5 pairs of side axes. 10–20 pairs of leaflets ⅛–¼" (3–6 mm) long; oblong; mostly hairless; stalkless; gray-green.
Bark: grayish brown; thin; smooth or scaly.
Twigs: slightly zigzag, slender, covered with fine hairs when young; with straight slender paired white spines at nodes.
Flowers: 3/16" (5 mm) long; yellow or orange; very fragrant; including many tiny stamens clustered in stalked balls ½" (12 mm) in diameter; mainly in late winter and early spring.
Fruit: 1½–3" (4–7.5 cm) long, ⅜–½" (10–12 mm) in diameter; a cylindrical pod; short-pointed at ends, dark brown or black, haired; maturing in summer, remaining attached, often opening late; many elliptical flattened shiny brown seeds.

Habitat
Sandy and clay soils, especially in open areas, borders of woodlands, and roadsides.

Range
Cultivated and naturalized from Florida west to Texas and S. California; S. Texas and local in S. Arizona; also in Mexico; to 5000' (1524 m).

Comments
In southern Europe this species is extensively planted for the "cassis" flowers, which are a perfume ingredient. After drying in the shade, the flowers can be used in sachets to keep clothes fragrant. The tender foliage and pods are browsed by livestock; it is also a honey plant.

Winterberry
Ilex verticillata
192

A deciduous holly shrub with very small white flowers that grow in the leaf axils.
Flowers: in clusters ¼–½" (6–13 mm) wide, each flower 4- to 6–parted; June–August.
Leaves: 2" (5 cm) long, elliptical, toothed but not spiny.
Fruit: berrylike, showy red, less than ¼" (6 mm) wide, on very short stalks, singly or in small clusters along the branches.
Height: 3–10' (90–300 cm).

Habitat
Swamps, damp thickets, and pond margins.

Range
Ontario to Nova Scotia; south from New England to Georgia; west to Mississippi; north to Tennessee, Missouri, Michigan, and Minnesota.

Comments
Extremely showy in late fall and early winter when covered with their bright red fruit, these shrubs are either male or female—a trait typical of the Holly Family. Birds are readily attracted to them.

BIRDS

A tremendous number of birds—large and small, silent and noisy—find a congenial home in the forests of the East. The attentive visitor will find that a trip into the forests offers many chances to observe birds: inconspicuous and shy towhees, brilliant songsters such as the Cardinal and Wood Thrush, and the imposing, little-known owls. This section covers many of the most typical birds of the eastern forests; learning to identify some of these birds of prey, ground birds, and songbirds will enrich your forest visits.

Eastern Screech-Owl
Otus asio
241

10″ (25 cm). A small, mottled owl with prominent ear tufts; eyes yellow. Both rufous and gray color phases occur, as well as brownish intermediate color phase.

Voice
A tremulous, descending wail; soft purrs and trills.

Habitat
Open deciduous woods, wood lots, suburban areas, lakeshores, old orchards.

Range
Widely distributed from N. Minnesota through SE. Canada to Atlantic Coast, south through Texas and Florida keys to Gulf of Mexico.

Comments
Screech-Owls are fearless in defense of their nests and will often strike an unsuspecting human on the head as he passes nearby at night. When discovered during the day, they often freeze in an upright position, relying on their cryptic coloration to escape detection.

Great Horned Owl
Bubo virginianus
242

25″ (63 cm). Wingspan: 55″ (1.4 m). Varying in color from white to dark brown and gray; mottled and streaked below, setting off the white throat; prominent, widely spaced ear tufts; yellow eyes.

Voice
Series of low, sonorous, far-carrying hoots, *hoo, hoo-hoo, HOO HOO*. Second and third notes shorter than the others.

Habitat
Ubiquitous, frequenting forest, desert, open country, swamps, and even city parks.

Range
Wide ranging, from arctic North America to the Straits of Magellan, but not in the West Indies.

Comments
The largest of American "eared" owls, it is exceeded in size only by the rare Great Gray Owl. The Great Horned Owl preys on a wide variety of creatures including grouse and rabbits as well as beetles, lizards, and frogs. It is one of the first birds to nest, laying its eggs as early as late January.

Long-eared Owl
Asio otus
243

15″ (38 cm). Wingspan: 39″ (1 m). Crow-sized. Long ear tufts close together, heavily mottled brown, chestnut facial disks (flat feathered area surrounding eye).

Voice
Soft low hoots, also whistles, whines, shrieks, and catlike meows. Seldom heard except during breeding time.

Habitat
Deciduous and evergreen forests.

Range
Northern Hemisphere in the temperate zone; in America from Alaska and Canada to the Gulf states and Mexico.

Comments
Although these woodland owls are gregarious in winter, they are so nocturnal and quiet that during the day up to a dozen may inhabit a dense evergreen grove without being detected. They have a tendency to roost near the trunk of a tree, and since they elongate themselves by compressing their feathers, they resemble part of the trunk itself. Only by peering intently upward can one detect the round face and telltale long ear tufts. When protecting their young they put on a spectacular display, lowering their head and fanning their wings over their back in a threatening attitude. A good way to locate an owl roost is to search in pine woods for groups of pellets.

Barred Owl
Strix varia
244

20″ (51 cm). Wingspan: 44″ (1.1 m). A large, stocky owl, gray-brown with cross-barring on the neck and breast and streaks on the belly; no ear-tufts.

Voice
A loud, barking *hoo, hoo, hoo, hoo, hoo, hoo-hooo-aw!;* a variety of other barking calls and screams.

Habitat
Low, wet woods and swamp forest.

Range
East of the Rockies from central Canada to the Gulf of Mexico and in mountains as far south as Honduras.

Comments
This owl is seen only by those who seek it out in its dark retreat, usually a thick grove of trees in lowland forest. There it rests quietly during the day, coming out at night to feed on rodents, birds, frogs, and crayfish. If disturbed, it will fly easily from one grove of trees to another.

Great Gray Owl
Strix nebulosa
245

24–33″ (61–84 cm). Wingspan: 60″ (1.5 m). A huge, dusky gray, earless owl of the north woods, with large facial disks and distinctive black chin spot. Eyes yellow.

Voice
Very deep, booming *whoo's,* repeated 10 times or more, and gradually descending the scale.

Habitat
Boreal coniferous forests and swampy bogs.

Range
Alaska and Interior Canada south to Quebec, Minnesota, Idaho, and northern California. Wanders rarely in winter southward into northern New England and the Great Lakes region.

Comments
Like other owls of the far north, this species hunts during the daytime, often watching for prey from a low perch. Because it spends much of its time in dense conifers, it may be overlooked.

Northern Saw-whet Owl
Aegolius acadicus
246

7″ (17 cm). Very small, earless, yellow-eyed owl; brown above, streaked with white and rufous below.

Voice
Usually silent; in late winter and spring utters a monotonous series of whistles.

Habitat
Low, moist, coniferous woodland; in winter in evergreen thickets in parks, yards, estates; also isolated pines.

Range
S. Alaska, Manitoba, and Nova Scotia south to Connecticut, Maryland, Kansas, New Mexico, California, and southern Mexico. Winters south to Guatemala and the Gulf Coast.

Comments
Saw-whet Owls are almost entirely nocturnal, spending the day roosting quietly in dense foliage. At such times they are extraordinarily tame and may be approached closely or even handled. At night this tiny owl becomes a rapacious hunter, preying on mice and other small rodents.

Ruffed Grouse
Bonasa umbellus
247

16–19″ (40–48 cm). A brown chickenlike bird with a fan-shaped, black-banded tail and black "ruffs" on the sides of the neck.

Voice
Female gives soft henlike clucks. In spring the male often sits on a log and beats the air with its wings, creating a drumming sound that increases rapidly in tempo.

Habitat
Deciduous forests, especially those with scattered clearings; abandoned farmlands and overgrown pastures.

Range
Breeds from Alaska and northern Canada south to the Carolinas, South Dakota, and California, and in the Appalachians to Georgia.

Comments
One of the most highly esteemed gamebirds in North America, Ruffed Grouse are taken annually in large numbers. However, as long as suitable habitat exists, the species seems able to withstand this pressure. Although large numbers of eggs are laid, young grouse have many enemies and few of the young reach maturity. In winter, the grouse grow comb-like rows of bristles on their toes, which serve as snowshoes.

Spruce Grouse
Dendragapus canadensis
248

15–17″ (38–43 cm). Dark, chickenlike bird. Male dusky gray-brown with black throat and white-spotted sides and a chestnut-tipped tail. Female browner, underparts barred with brown.

Voice
Low hooting. Female makes clucking sounds. The drumming of this grouse consists of a noisy whirring and fluttering of the wings either from a log or in the air.

Habitat
Coniferous forests, especially those with a mixture of spruce and pine; edges of bogs.

Range
Alaska, Manitoba, Quebec, and Nova Scotia south to New England, N. New York, and Michigan, across into N. Washington.

Comments
This northern grouse is so extraordinarily tame that it is sometimes referred to as a "fool hen." Humans can come as close as 2 or 3 feet before it retreats. This generally quiet bird is thinly distributed in its habitat and therefore difficult to find. Its principal foods are the needles and buds of evergreens, although insects are eaten in large quantities by young birds. Spruce Grouse are generally found singly or in small family groups, picking their way quietly over the forest floor or sitting in dense conifers. During courtship the male struts boldly, fans its tail, and takes short flights periodically; in these flights, the wingbeats are exaggerated.

Wild Turkey
Meleagris gallopavo
249

Males 48″ (122 cm); females 36″ (91 cm). Similar to the domestic turkey but more slender; tail tipped with chestnut, not white.

Voice
Familiar *gobble* of the domestic bird. Also a number of clucks and yelps.

Habitat
Open woodlands and forests with scattered natural or man-made clearings.

Range
Locally common from Wyoming, Illinois, and New York to Mexico and the Gulf Coast. Formerly more widespread and abundant.

Comments
No bird is more distinctively American than the Wild Turkey. The species was even suggested as our national bird by Benjamin Franklin, who pointed out that the Bald Eagle is principally a carrion feeder. Although well known to the American Indians and widely used by them as food, certain tribes considered these birds stupid and cowardly and did not eat them for fear of acquiring these characteristics. Turkeys

often roost over water because of the added protection that this offers. They are polygamous, and the male gobbles and struts with fanned tail to attract his harem. They are swift runners.

American Woodcock
Scolopax minor
250

11" (28 cm). Quail-sized. Very stocky, with rounded wings and long bill. Rufous below, back mottled and barred with rufous, black, and slaty "dead leaf" patterns. Large bulging eyes.

Voice
Loud, buzzy *beep* similar to the call of a nighthawk and often repeated about every 2 seconds.

Habitat
Moist woodland and thickets near open fields.

Range
Eastern North America from southern Canada to the Gulf states. Winters chiefly in the South.

Comments
The Woodcock is seldom seen, for its protective coloring renders it virtually invisible. When flushed from underfoot, it zigzags off through the brush with a whistling of wings. People fortunate enough to live near woodcock breeding grounds may see these birds perform their courtship flight in early spring each year. In spectacular aerial displays the male spirals up to a considerable height, circles, then plummets down to earth, calling as he descends. Woodcocks subsist chiefly on earthworms, which they extract with their long bills; the tip of the upper mandible is flexible so that they can grasp a worm while probing in mud without opening the bill. Insect larvae are also eaten, and occasionally vegetable matter is consumed.

Chuck-will's-widow
Caprimulgus carolinensis
251

12" (30 cm). Pigeon-sized. Larger than the Whip-poor-will. Buff-brown body, brown throat.

Voice
Chuck-will's-wid-ow, repeated over and over, the *chuck* deep and low, the rest of the call whistled. Also utters a froglike croak when flying.

Habitat
Open woodland and clearings near agricultural country.

Range
Kansas, Indiana, and Long Island south to the Gulf states. Winters chiefly in the West Indies and from Mexico to northern South America.

Comments
The Chuck-will's-widow is nocturnal and rarely seen during the day. When flushed it flies off a short distance, then drops to the ground again. "Chucks" hunt low to the ground, catching flying insects such as moths, beetles, and winged

ants and termites. They have occasionally been reported to take warblers and sparrows.

Whip-poor-will
Caprimulgus vociferus
252

10″ (25 cm). Jay-sized. A leaf-brown, strictly nocturnal bird with a black throat. In flight, male has white outer tail feathers, female's are brown.

Voice
A loud, rhythmic *whip-poor-will,* repeated over and over, at night.

Habitat
Dry open woodland near fields.

Range
Southern Canada to southern United States, and in the mountains as far south as Mexico. Winters from the Gulf of Mexico to Honduras.

Comments
The Whip-poor-will is rarely seen because it sleeps by day on the forest floor, its coloration matching the dead leaves. At night its eyes reflect ruby red in car headlights. It feeds exclusively on moths and other night insects caught on the wing.

Sharp-shinned Hawk
Accipiter striatus
253

10–14″ (25–35 cm). Wingspan: 21″ (0.5 m). Jay-sized. Small, fast-flying hawk with long tail and short, rounded wings. Slate gray above, pale below with fine rust-barring. Has square tail tips.

Voice
Sharp *kick-kick-kick;* also a shrill squeal.

Habitat
Dense coniferous forests, less often in deciduous forests. In migration and winter it may be seen in almost any habitat.

Range
Alaska, Mackenzie, and Newfoundland south to Florida and northern Mexico. Winters north to Montana and New England.

Comments
This species is the commonest of the Accipiters—hawks with short wings and long tail. Sharp-shins are often seen in large numbers migrating along mountain ridges and on the outer beaches. The Sharp-shin preys on small birds such as sparrows and warblers, as well as on small rodents and insects.

Cooper's Hawk
Accipiter cooperii
254

14–20″ (35–51 cm). Wingspan: 28″ (0.7 m). Crow-sized hawk with long tail and short, rounded wings. Slate gray above, finely rust-barred below. Similar to the more common Sharp-shinned Hawk but larger, with tail rounded at tip (tail of Sharp-shin is square).

Voice
Loud *cack-cack-cack-cack*. Also a scream.

Habitat
Deciduous and, less often, coniferous forests, especially where these are interrupted by meadows and clearings.

Range
British Columbia, Ontario, and Nova Scotia south to Florida and Costa Rica. Winters north to southern New England and British Columbia.

Comments
While many people know of the decline of the Peregrine Falcon due to pesticides, few are aware that the once common Cooper's Hawk has suffered a similar fate and is now gone from large areas of the eastern deciduous forest. The larger Northern Goshawk is taking over at the northern limit of this forest, where it borders on spruce and firs. As with many other hawks, the females are larger than the males; some small males are difficult to distinguish from the smaller Sharp-shinned Hawk. Even experienced bird-watchers are often unable to identify hawks in this size range. When Cooper's Hawk is in pursuit of prey its flight is swift and dashing, and its long tail makes it highly maneuverable.

Northern Goshawk
Accipiter gentilis
255

20–26" (51–66 cm). Wingspan: 42" (1.1 m). Larger than a crow. A heavy-bodied hawk with a dark blue-gray back, black crown, pale underparts finely barred with gray, and a conspicuous white eyebrow. Young bird similar but brown above, streaked below.

Voice
Loud *kak-kak-kak-kak* when disturbed.

Habitat
Coniferous forests; also farmland, woodland edges, and open country in the winter.

Range
Alaska, Mackenzie, N. Quebec, and Newfoundland south to New England, Michigan, and New Mexico; also southward in the Appalachians to Maryland. Winters south to Virginia and northern Mexico.

Comments
The Northern Goshawk is an uncommon winter visitor from the North; it is seldom present in large numbers, remaining mostly in the northern coniferous forests unless forced to move south by a periodic decline in the populations of the grouse that are a staple of its diet. The swift flight of a Goshawk chasing a grouse has given the bird the name "Blue Darter." It is fearless in defense of the nest and will boldly attack anyone who ventures too close. It has recently begun extending its range to the south, and now breeds in small numbers in deciduous forests.

Red-shouldered Hawk
Buteo lineatus
256

16–24″ (40–61 cm). Large, long-winged hawk with rust-barred underparts, reddish shoulders, a narrowly banded tail, and a translucent area near the tip of the wing, visible from below. Young birds are streaked below and are best distinguished from young Red-tailed Hawks by their somewhat smaller size; narrower tail; and longer, narrower wings.

Voice
Shrill scream, *kee-yeeer,* with a downward inflection.

Habitat
Deciduous woodlands, especially where there is standing water.

Range
Minnesota and New Brunswick south to the Gulf Coast, and on the Pacific Coast from N. California to Baja California. Winters north to southern New England and the Ohio Valley.

Comments
This hawk generally avoids the upland forests inhabited by the Red-tailed Hawk, and is more often found in lowlands, especially swampy woods and bogs. There it hunts by sitting quietly on a low perch, dropping down to capture snakes and frogs. It also eats insects and small mammals.

Broad-winged Hawk
Buteo platypterus
257

13–15″ (33–38 cm). Wingspan: 33″ (0.8 m). Crow-sized. Adult brown above, barred with rusty below, with broad black-and-white tail bands; immatures similar but streaked below, with tail bands less distinct.

Voice
Thin, unhawklike whistle, *pweeeeee.*

Habitat
Chiefly deciduous woodland.

Range
Breeds from southern Canada south nearly throughout the eastern United States. Winters in tropical South America.

Comments
This hawk is best known for its spectacular migrations; thousands of birds fly by, with single flocks of up to several hundred individuals. During breeding, this hawk is secretive or, rather, unobtrusive. The Broad-winged lives mainly in the woods, beneath the canopy or hidden among the foliage. Often one is made aware of it only through its call. Its food consists mainly of snakes, mice, frogs, and insects. Great numbers migrate along the eastern ridges in mid-September.

Red-tailed Hawk
Buteo jamaicensis
258

18–25″ (46–63 cm). Wingspan: 48″ (1.2 m). Large, stocky hawk with a whitish breast and a rust-colored tail. Young birds are duller, more streaked, and lack the rust-colored tail of the adult; distinguished by their stocky build and broad, rounded wings. This species is quite variable in color; occasional blackish individuals occur but usually retain the rust-colored tail.

Voice
High-pitched descending scream with a hoarse quality.

Habitat
Mainly deciduous forest and adjacent open country.

Range
Alaska and Nova Scotia south to Panama. Winters north to British Columbia and the Maritime Provinces.

Comments
The most common and widespread American member of the genus *Buteo,* which includes the Red-shouldered, Swainson's, and Broad-winged Hawks, among others. Like other hawks of this group, the Red-tailed soars over open country in search of its prey, but just as often perches in a tree at the edge of a meadow, watching for the slightest movement in the grass below. The Red-tail feeds mainly on small rodents.

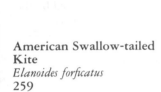

American Swallow-tailed Kite
Elanoides forficatus
259

22–24″ (56–61 cm). Wingspan: 50″ (1.3 m). A graceful bird of prey, with long, pointed wings and deeply forked tail. Head and underparts white, back wings and tail black.

Voice
Shrill squeals or whistles. Also a soft twittering.

Habitat
Swamps, marshes, river bottoms, and glades in open forests.

Range
Breeds mainly on or near the coast from South Carolina to Florida, formerly to Texas; local farther inland in the Gulf states, rare farther north. South to southern South America.

Comments
The Swallow-tail's flight as it rides air currents or swoops rapidly after its prey is graceful, buoyant, and effortless. It spends much of the daylight hours on the wing, rarely perching on some dead tree branch. It feeds extensively on lizards and snakes but snatches much of its food, including dragonflies, right out of the air while aloft. Like a swallow, this Kite skims the water to drink and bathe.

Mississippi Kite
Ictinia mississippiensis
260

12–14″ (30–35 cm). Wingspan: 36″ (0.9 m). Adult gray above and pale gray below with lighter gray head and black tail; immature streaked below, with banded tail. Narrow, pointed wings.

Voice
2 or 3 high clear whistles, but seldom heard.

Habitat
Open woodland and mixed scrub near water.

Range
Southeastern and south-central United States, but extremely local. Winters to southern South America.

Comments
This graceful, buoyant kite is a marvelous flier and spends hours in the air. It is quite gregarious, often seen in flocks and even nesting in loose colonies. Although chiefly insectivorous, feeding largely on grasshoppers and dragonflies, it occasionally takes small snakes and frogs. Its numbers have decreased considerably in recent years.

Wood Stork
Mycteria americana
261

40–44" (102–112 cm). Wingspan: 66" (1.5 m). White with black flight feathers and tail. Head and neck bare, dark gray. Bill long, stout, and slightly curved, black in adults and yellow in immatures. Flies with its neck extended.

Voice
Dull croak. Usually silent except around nest. Young clatter endlessly.

Habitat
On or near the coast, breeding chiefly in cypress swamps; also in mangroves.

Range
Breeds in Florida; wanders to South Carolina and Texas, occasionally farther. Also in South America.

Comments
Often wrongly called "Wood Ibis," this is a true stork. Its naked gray head has earned it the local name "flint head." These birds perch motionless on a bare branch or slowly stalk through marshes in search of food. They are sometimes seen circling high in the air on rising thermal air currents. They nest in enormous colonies numbering up to 10,000 pairs, but in recent years their numbers have declined drastically due to development and draining of their feeding grounds.

Wood Duck
Aix sponsa
262

17–20" (43–51 cm). A beautiful, crested, multicolored small duck. Male patterned in iridescent greens, purples, and blues with a distinctive white chin patch; red, rather long bill; long tail. Female grayish with broad white eye-ring.

Voice
Loud *wooo-eeek*. Also softer *peet* and *cheep* notes.

Habitat
Wooded rivers and ponds; wooded swamps. Visits freshwater marshes in late summer and fall.

Range
British Columbia, Nova Scotia, and Minnesota south to Florida and Texas. Winters north to Washington in the West and New Jersey in the East, rarely farther north. Also breeds in Cuba.

Comments
The Wood Duck's habit of nesting in cavities enables it to breed in areas lacking suitable ground cover. The young leave the nest soon after hatching, jumping from the nesting cavity to the ground. Once in the water, they travel through wooded ponds with their mother.

Common Loon
Gavia immer
263

28–36″ (71–91 cm). Goose-sized. Heavy, long-bodied water bird with thick pointed bill held horizontally. In summer, head and neck black with white collar; back black with white spots. In winter, crown, hind neck, and upperparts grayish; throat and underparts white. When swimming it rides low in the water.

Voice
Wild maniacal laugh, also a mournful yodeled *oo-AH-ho* with middle note higher, and a loud ringing *kee-a-ree, kee-a-ree* with middle note lower. Often calls at night.

Habitat
Forested lakes and rivers; oceans and bays in winter.

Range
Breeds from Aleutian Islands, Alaska, and Northern Canada south to New Hampshire, Montana, and California. Winters south to the Gulf Coast.

Comments
The Loon is known for its call, a far-carrying wail heard on its northern breeding grounds and occasionally during migration. Loons are expert divers and have been caught in nets as far as 200 feet below the surface. Their principal food is fish, but they also eat shellfish, frogs, and aquatic insects. Their feet are located far back on the body, an arrangement that aids them in diving; but on land these birds travel with difficulty, propelling themselves forward on their breasts.

Anhinga
Anhinga anhinga
264

34–36″ (86–91 cm). A blackish bird of southern swamps with a very long, slender neck and long tail. Male's plumage has greenish iridescence; wings silvery gray above. Female's tawny brown neck and breast contrast with black belly.

Voice
Low grunt or harsh grating calls.

Habitat
Freshwater ponds and swamps with thick vegetation, especially cypress.

Range
Atlantic and Gulf coasts from North Carolina to Texas and in the Mississippi Valley north to Arkansas and Tennessee. South to southern South America.

Comments
The Anhinga is also known as the "Snakebird" because its

body is submerged when swimming so that only its head and long, slender neck are visible above the water. Its long, dagger-shaped, serrated bill is ideally suited for catching fish, which it flips into the air and gulps down headfirst. Cormorants and Anhingas lack oil glands with which to preen and so must perch with their wings half-open to dry them in the sun. Unlike cormorants, Anhingas often soar in circles high overhead.

Common Raven
Corvus corax
265

21–27" (53–68 cm). Similar to the Common Crow but larger, with a heavier bill and a wedge-shaped tail. At rest, the throat appears shaggy because of long, lance-shaped feathers. Often soars like a hawk.

Voice
Deep, varied, guttural croaking; a wooden *wonk-wonk*.

Habitat
Coniferous forests and rocky coasts; in the West also in deserts and arid mountains.

Range
Resident from Aleutians, N. Alaska and northern Greenland south to northern New England, the Appalachians, the Dakotas, and, in the mountains, to Nicaragua.

Comments
The Common Raven is common only in wilderness areas, for despite its large size and intelligence it is very sensitive to human persecution and has long since been driven out of settled areas by shooting and poisoning. Ravens are primarily scavengers, and around towns in the North they compete with gulls for garbage. They also raid seabird colonies, consuming many eggs and young. They regularly ride on rising air currents and frequently indulge in aerial displays with mock fighting, tumbling, and other forms of acrobatics.

American Crow
Corvus brachyrhynchos
266

17–21" (43–53 cm). Stocky black bird with a stout bill and a fan-shaped tail.

Voice
Familiar *caw-caw* or *caa-caa*.

Habitat
Woodlands, farmland, and suburban areas.

Range
Breeds from British Columbia and Newfoundland south to Florida, the Gulf Coast, and northern Mexico. Winters north to southern Canada.

Comments
It is impossible to go into the countryside without seeing these birds along highways or flying overhead. Intelligent, wary, virtually omnivorous, and with a high reproductive capacity, the Common Crow is undoubtedly much more

numerous than it was before the arrival of settlers. Crows may gather in roosts of over half a million birds and are so abundant that even an ardent defender of birds might not deny that they are destructive to crops and should be controlled, although they consume enormous amounts of grasshoppers, cutworms, and other harmful insects.

Dark-eyed Junco
Junco hyemalis
267

5–6½″ (13–16 cm). Sparrow-sized. Variable, but generally slate-gray or gray-brown above, with white abdomen sharply demarcated from gray of breast. Shows white along sides of tail in flight. Pink bill. Some birds have buff flanks.

Voice
A slow, musical trill or soft twittering.

Habitat
Coniferous or mixed forests; winters in fields, gardens, city parks, and roadside thickets.

Range
Alaska and Newfoundland south to mountains in Georgia and Mexico. Winters south to the Gulf Coast and northern Mexico.

Comments
Until recently the many geographical forms of this bird were considered separate species, but since they interbreed wherever their ranges meet, they are now considered one species. The eastern form, formerly called the "Slate-colored Junco," is the only one that is usually encountered in the eastern states. Occasionally, however, black-headed, rusty-flanked western birds, "Oregon Juncos," may also be seen, and the "White-winged Junco" from the Black Hills in South Dakota is an accidental winter visitor. Juncos are among the commonest of our winter birds, often visiting feeders.

Black-billed Cuckoo
Coccyzus erythropthalmus
268

12″ (30 cm). Brown above, white below; bill entirely black, wings brown, and trace of white at tips of tail feathers. Narrow red eye-ring.

Voice
A series of *cu-cu-cu-cu* notes in groups of 2 to 5, all on the same pitch.

Habitat
Moist thickets in low, overgrown pastures and orchards; also in thicker undergrowth and in sparse woodland.

Range
Southern Canada to South Carolina, Tennessee, and Kansas. Winters in northwestern South America.

Comments
Like the similar Yellow-billed Cuckoo, this bird is adept at hiding and skulking in dense vegetation, and is more often heard than seen. The loud notes of the Black-billed, repeated

over and over again, are reminiscent of those of grebes and doves, but deeper in tone and more repetitive. When tracked down, they slip away to another location and repeat the call.

White-crowned Pigeon
Columba leucocephala
269

13″ (33 cm). Dark gray with a conspicuous white crown similar to melanistic Rock Dove but with longer tail and blackish, rather than white, wing linings.

Voice
Coo-coo-co-WOOO, with an owl-like quality.

Habitat
Mangroves and occasionally in tropical hardwoods.

Range
Florida Keys and the West Indies; does not winter in Florida but migrates as far as the southern Caribbean Sea.

Comments
In the United States it breeds only in the mangrove swamps of the Florida Keys and, to a lesser extent, among the gumbo-limbo and mahogany trees of the adjacent mainland. Once extensively hunted for food, they became wary. In 1913, protective laws were enacted and their numbers gradually increased. They are great fruit-eaters but also take insects and seeds.

Mourning Dove
Zenaida macroura
270

12″ (30 cm). Soft, sandy buff with a long, pointed tail bordered with white.

Voice
Low, mournful (hence its name) *coo-ah, coo, coo, coo.*

Habitat
Open fields, parks, and lawns with many trees and shrubs.

Range
S. Alaska, British Columbia, Saskatchewan, Ontario, Quebec, and New Brunswick to Panama and the West Indies. Winters north to northern United States.

Comments
This abundant bird has benefited from man's cutting the forest and burning off the grass. It is common in rural areas in all parts of the United States, as well as city parks and, in winter, suburban feeders. In some states it is hunted as a gamebird while in others it is protected as a "songbird." Its species name *macroura* is Greek for "long-tailed."

Pileated Woodpecker
Dryocopus pileatus
271

17″ (43 cm). Crow-sized. Black with white neck stripes, conspicuous white wing linings, and a prominent red crest.

Voice
Call flickerlike, but louder, deeper, and more *cuk-cuk-cuk-cuk-cuk,* rising and then falling in pitch.

Habitat
Dense forest and borders.

Range
Breeds from southern Canada to the Gulf states and the mountains of the western United States.

Comments
Despite its size, this elegant woodpecker is adept at keeping out of sight. Obtaining a close view of one usually requires careful stalking. Although primarily a forest bird, the "Logcock," as this bird is sometimes called, has recently become adapted to civilization and has become relatively numerous even on the outskirts of large cities. Its presence is most easily detected by its loud, ringing call and by its large, characteristically rectangular excavations in trees.

Red-headed Woodpecker
Melanerpes erythrocephalus
272

10″ (25 cm). Jay-sized. Strikingly colored: entire head red, wings and tail bluish-black, white below, large white wing patch on each wing and a white rump, conspicuous in flight. Immature resembles the adult except for its gray head.

Voice
Various chirps, cackles, and squawks. Most often a loud *churr-churr* and *yarrow-yarrow-yarrow*.

Habitat
Open country, farms, rural roads, open parklike woodland, and golf courses.

Range
Saskatchewan, Manitoba, and Quebec south to Florida, the Gulf Coast, and New Mexico. Scarce in northeastern states. Winters in southern South America.

Comments
These woodpeckers are fond of open agricultural country with groves of dead and dying trees, particularly orchards. They often fly-catch, swooping low across a highway or along the shoulder of a road after flying insects. Red-headed Woodpeckers are driven off by aggressive Starlings, which occupy the nest holes, and by the removal of dead trees. Red-headeds store nuts and acorns, hiding them in holes.

Red-bellied Woodpecker
Melanerpes carolinus
273

10″ (25 cm). Robin-sized. Barred black and white above; pale buff below; sexes similar except that male has red crown and nape, female has red nape only. A red patch on the lower abdomen is seldom visible in the field.

Voice
Chuck-chuck-chuck, descending in pitch. Also a loud, oft repeated *churrrr*.

Habitat
Open and swamp woodland; comes into parks during migration and to feeders in winter.

Range

Chiefly southeastern United States west to Texas, ranging north to Minnesota, Michigan, and Connecticut.

Comments

The common woodpecker over much of the South, the Red-bellied is scarcer farther north but has expanded its breeding range in recent years to New York and southern New England. Like most woodpeckers, the "Zebraback" is beneficial, consuming vast numbers of wood-boring beetles as well as grasshoppers, ants, and other insect pests. It also feeds on acorns, beechnuts, and wild fruits.

Yellow-bellied Sapsucker
Sphyrapicus varius
274

8½" (21 cm). A furtive woodpecker mottled with off-white and black; male has red crown and throat; female has only a red crown. Both sexes dull yellowish below. Immatures sooty brown. In all plumages the distinctive mark is a conspicuous white wing stripe, visible both at rest and in flight.

Voice

Mewing notes.

Habitat

Young, open deciduous or mixed forest with clearings; in migration, in parks, yards, gardens.

Range

Alaska and Canada to the mountains of Virginia and California. Winters south to Panama and the West Indies.

Comments

This species, at least on migration, is the quietest of the woodpeckers; aside from a few squeaks and whines, it is mainly silent. It is also the least conspicuous, hitching around to the opposite side of the tree trunk when approached. Sapsuckers get their name from the habit of boring holes into the cambium layer or inner bark, letting the sap exude and run down the trunk. The birds wipe up or suck the oozing sap with their brushlike tongues. They return again and again to the same tree and also consume the insects attracted to it.

Downy Woodpecker
Picoides pubescens
275

6" (15 cm). Sparrow-sized. Black and white, with a small red patch on the nape in males. Similar to the Hairy Woodpecker, but smaller and with a short, stubby bill.

Voice

Dull-sounding *pik*. Also a descending rattle.

Habitat

Wood lots, parks and gardens; suet feeders in winter.

Range

From Alaska and Canada to southern United States.

Comments

This is the smallest, tamest, and most abundant of our eastern woodpeckers. It comes readily to the suet rack in the suburban yard and is a familiar sight in city parks and in roadside shade trees and shrubbery. The Downy is a familiar bird in the assemblages of nuthatches, creepers, kinglets, and chickadees that gather in the woods during the fall migration.

Hairy Woodpecker
Picoides villosus
276

9″ (23 cm). Robin-sized. Black and white with an unspotted white back and long bill; male has red head patch. Like all woodpeckers it has an undulating flight.

Voice
Call note, a sharp, distinctive *peek,* is louder than a Downy's.

Habitat
Deciduous forest; more widespread in winter and migration.

Range
From Alaska and Canada to the Gulf of Mexico, the mountains of Panama, and the Bahamas.

Comments
The Hairy Woodpecker is more a forest bird and is shyer than its smaller relative, the Downy Woodpecker. Thus the two species, found commonly from coast to coast, do not compete with each other. The Hairy Woodpecker is one of the most beneficial birds, saving both forest and fruit trees by destroying many harmful insects such as wood-boring beetles (which it extracts from holes with its barbed tongue). Like other woodpeckers, it hammers on a dead limb as part of its courtship ceremony and to proclaim its territory.

Northern Flicker
Colaptes auratus
277

12″ (30 cm). A large brownish woodpecker. Brown back with dark bars and spots: whitish below with black spots, black crescent on breast; white rump in flight. Eastern birds have red patch on nape (male has a black "mustache") and yellow wing linings.

Voice
Loud, repeated *flicker* or *wicka-wicka-wicka.* Also a loud *kleeer.*

Habitat
Open country with trees; parks and rural estates.

Range
Alaska, Manitoba, and Newfoundland south to S. Florida, the Gulf Coast, and southern Mexico. Also in the West Indies.

Comments
This species includes several very distinct regional forms, which hybridize where they meet. The eastern population was formerly known as the "Yellow-shafted Flicker." Flickers are the only brown-backed woodpeckers in the East. They are the only woodpeckers in North America that commonly feed on the ground, searching for ants and beetle larvae on lawns or even sidewalks. During courtship and to proclaim their territory, flickers hammer on dead limbs or tin roofs.

**Red-cockaded
Woodpecker**
Picoides borealis
278

8″ (20 cm). Cap and nape black; large white cheek patch; back barred black-and-white; white below with black spots on the sides and flanks. Male has small red spot behind eye.

Voice
A nuthatch-like *yank-yank*. Also a rattling scold note.

Habitat
Pine forests, especially yellow and longleaf pines.

Range
Maryland and Kentucky to southeastern United States and west to E. Texas.

Comments
The Red-cockaded Woodpecker is one of the least known of the family. Although widespread in the Southeast, it is local and restricted to pine woods. It is much less noisy and conspicuous than other woodpeckers and therefore seldom noticed. It travels in small flocks, usually in family groups of four to six. It also has the peculiar trait of digging holes in trees adjacent to its nest, allowing pine gum or resin to ooze from the holes. Such signs of pitch reveal its presence.

**Black-backed
Woodpecker**
Picoides arcticus
279

9″ (23 cm). Solid black back, barred flanks, white below; male has yellow crown and female has solid black crown.

Voice
Sharp *kik*. Scolding rattle. It also hammers on dead branches.

Habitat
Coniferous forests in the boreal zone, especially where burned over, logged, or swampy.

Range
Alaska and Canada to the northernmost United States and to the mountains of California in the West.

Comments
This species and the Three-toed Woodpecker are the most northerly of the family. Both are rather tame. The Black-backed, found only in North America, is the more southerly of the two. It is also somewhat more numerous or, rather, less scarce, since these birds are not common anywhere. They visit dead and dying trees, scaling off bits of loose bark with the bill to get at the borers and beetle larvae underneath.

Gray Kingbird
Tyrannus dominicensis
280

9″ (23 cm). A stocky, large-headed, pale gray flycatcher of coastal habitats. Underparts whitish; dusky blackish patch through eye; bill heavy; tail notched, without white.

Voice
Buzzy *pe-CHEER-y* and a harsh note.

Habitat
Coastal, in mangrove thickets, on telephone wires, and in small groves of palms and oaks.

Range
Coastal regions of South Carolina, Georgia, Florida, the West Indies, and smaller islands in the Caribbean. Winters from the Greater Antilles to Colombia, Venezuela, and the Guianas.

Comments
Like other kingbirds, this species is fearless, even chasing hawks and crows. Noisy as well as belligerent, it frequently emits harsh notes as it sits on telephone wires or exposed branches ready to dart after flying insects.

Eastern Wood-Pewee
Contopus virens
281

6½" (16 cm). Dull olive-gray with 2 whitish wing bars, no eye-ring.

Voice
A plaintive *pee-ah-weee* or *pee-weee*, rising on the last note.

Habitat
Forest, open woodland, orchards, and shade trees in parks and along roadsides.

Range
Southeastern Canada to the Gulf of Mexico. Winters from Costa Rica to northwestern South America.

Comments
Wood-Pewees are more often heard than seen because of their dull coloration and because they frequent the dense upper canopy of the forest.

Olive-sided Flycatcher
Contopus borealis
282

7½" (19 cm). Large-billed and heavy-headed; deep olive-drab with dark sides of breast and flanks separated by white down the center of breast; white feather tufts protrude from lower back at base of tail.

Voice
Distinctive and emphatic *quick-three-BEERS*. Call is a loud *pip-pip-pip*.

Habitat
Boreal spruce and fir forests, usually near openings, burns, ponds, and bogs.

Range
Northern portions of Alaska and Canada to the mountains of North Carolina, Arizona, and California. Winters in northwestern South America.

Comments
This flycatcher almost always perches at or very near the tops of tall trees in an exposed position on dead branches. Its old name was *Nuttallornis*, after Thomas Nuttall (1786–1859), an early American ornithologist; *borealis* is Latin for "northern."

Red-eyed Vireo
Vireo olivaceus
283

5½–6½" (14–16 cm). Sparrow-sized. Olive-green above, whitish below, with a narrow white eyebrow bordered above with black. Gray crown; red eye; no wing bars. Warbling Vireo is similar but lacks the gray crown and black border over white eyebrow.

Voice
Series of short, musical, Robinlike phrases endlessly and rapidly repeated.

Habitat
Deciduous forests, and shade trees in residential areas.

Range
Breeds from British Columbia, Ontario, and the Gulf of St. Lawrence south to Florida, S. Texas, Colorado, and Oregon. Winters in South America.

Comments
This vireo is one of the most abundant birds in eastern North America. Its principal habitat, the vast broad leaf forests, supports millions of these birds, often 1 pair per acre. A persistent singer during the breeding season, it utters its endless series of short phrases from dawn till dusk, even on the hottest days when other birds are silent, and may even sing while grappling with the large insects it captures.

Worm-eating Warbler
Helmitheros vermivorus
284

5½" (14 cm). Sparrow-sized. Plain brownish above and below, with conspicuous dark and light crown stripes. Sexes look alike.

Voice
Song a fast, buzzy, insectlike series of *chippy-chippy-chippy* calls.

Habitat
Chiefly dry wooded hillsides.

Range
Breeds from Iowa, Ohio, New York, and Massachusetts south to the southeastern states. Winters in the northern West Indies and from Mexico to Panama.

Comments
The Worm-eating Warbler spends much of its time on or near the ground, quietly searching for its insect prey in the leaf litter and low vegetation. A singing male, however, often perches rather high up in a tree, where its habit of sitting motionless for a long time makes it hard to spot.

White-eyed Vireo
Vireo griseus
285

5" (13 cm). Warbler-sized. Olive-green above and white below with yellow flanks; yellow spectacles; white wing bars. Adult has white eye; immature has dark eye.

Voice
Loud, explosive series of notes: *chip-a-wheeoo-chip* or *quick give me the rain check!*

Habitat
Dense thickets and hillsides with blackberry and briar tangles.

Range
Nebraska, Illinois, Ohio, SE. New York, and central New England south to S. Florida and northeastern Mexico. Winters from the Gulf states to Honduras. Also northern West Indies.

Comments
Although most vireos inhabit tall trees, this species is usually found in thickets, where its presence is most easily detected by its loud and distinctive song. A patient observer can usually get a good look at one by standing quietly and waiting for the bird's curiosity to bring it into view. The Brown-headed Cowbird often lays its eggs in this vireo's nest.

Hooded Warbler
Wilsonia citrina
286

5½" (14 cm). Olive above, yellow below. Male has yellow face and black hood, female similar but lacks hood. Both sexes have white tail spots.

Voice
Clear, ringing, "flirtatious" *tawee-tawee-tawee-tee-o.*

Habitat
Mature, moist forest with luxuriant undergrowth, especially in ravines; also in wooded swamps.

Range
Southern portions of the northern states to the Gulf states. Winters from Mexico to Panama.

Comments
The male is one of the most handsome wood warblers and, unlike many others, has a loud, penetrating, and very melodious song. Even the female, which is much less strikingly patterned and colored, has conspicuous white tail spots and flirts its tail—like the male—by flashing the white tail patches as she moves about. This species usually ranges at a low level, rarely 10 feet above ground.

Kentucky Warbler
Oporornis formosus
287

5½" (14 cm). Sparrow-sized. Sexes similar; olive-green above, bright yellow below; black forecrown, lores (between eyes and base of bill), and sides of throat; bright yellow spectacles. No wing bars.

Voice
Loud, penetrating, rich *tur-dle, tur-dle,* of 5–7 notes.

Habitat
Low, moist, rich woodland with luxuriant undergrowth; often in ravines.

Range
Iowa, Indiana, Pennsylvania, and New Jersey south to southeastern United States. Winters from southern Mexico to northwestern South America.

Comments
Named for the state where it was discovered in 1811 by Alexander Wilson, father of American ornithology, this bird is actually no more common in Kentucky than elsewhere in its range. Usually heard before it is seen, this rather secretive warbler remains hidden, especially in thickly vegetated ravines with streams running through them.

Tennessee Warbler
Vermivora peregrina
288

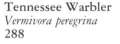

5" (13 cm). In spring, greenish above, white below with a gray cap, white line over eye, black line through eye; in fall, olive above, yellowish below.

Voice
Sharp, staccato *di-dit-di-dit-di-dit-di-dit-dit-dit-dit-dit,* fastest at the end.

Habitat
Open mixed woodlands in the breeding season; in trees and bushes during migration.

Range
Yukon, Manitoba, and Labrador south to Maine, S. Ontario, Wisconsin, and British Columbia. Winters from southern Mexico to northern South America.

Comments
This warbler was first discovered in 1811 by the noted ornithologist Alexander Wilson, who chose its common name because he first saw it in Tennessee. Its numbers fluctuate from year to year: at times it is very numerous with a dozen or more observed in a single tree; in other years few are seen.

Solitary Vireo
Vireo solitarius
289

5–6" (13–15 cm). Sparrow-sized. Olive-green above and white below, with dull yellow flanks. Crown and sides of head slate or bluish gray with bold white "spectacles."

Voice
Rather slow series of sweet, slurred phrases like that of Red-eyed Vireo but slower and more musical.

Habitat
Coniferous and mixed forests.

Range
British Columbia, Manitoba, and Newfoundland south to Connecticut and Michigan, and in the mountains to Georgia and Mexico. Winters from the Carolinas and the Gulf Coast south to Nicaragua.

Comments
This species was formerly called the "Blue-headed Vireo." Handsome and distinctively patterned, it is known to most people as a fairly common migrant, usually arriving somewhat earlier in the spring than other vireos. It is extraordinarily tame and seems to ignore humans near its nest. An incubating bird will even allow itself to be touched. Like other vireos it

moves slowly and deliberately through the trees, peering with head cocked to one side in search of insects.

Yellow-throated Vireo
Vireo flavifrons
290

6″ (15 cm). Sparrow-sized. Bright yellow throat, breast, and "spectacles"; 2 conspicuous white wing bars, olive-green head and back, gray rump, white belly.

Voice
Similar to the song of the Red-eyed and Solitary vireos, but huskier and lower in pitch.

Habitat
Tall deciduous trees at the edge of forests, along streams, roadsides, orchards, parks, and estates.

Range
Minnesota, Ontario, and southern New England south to the Gulf states. Winters from southern Mexico to northern South America.

Comments
This handsome vireo is found mainly in open groves of tall hardwood trees. Its numbers have decreased in recent years because of the spraying of trees with toxic chemicals.

Black-throated Green Warbler
Dendroica virens
291

5″ (13 cm). Crown and upperparts olive green, throat and sides of breast black, face yellow. Female similar but duller.

Voice
Thin, buzzy, lazy *trees, trees, murm' ring' trees;* or faster *zee-zee-zee-zoo-zee.*

Habitat
Open stands of hemlock or pine; in migration in a variety of habitats.

Range
Northwest Territories, Ontario, and Newfoundland south to N. New Jersey, Ohio, Minnesota, and Alberta, and in the mountains to Georgia. Winters from Florida and Texas south to northern South America, and in the West Indies.

Comments
The Black-throated Green is one of the commonest warblers in migration; at this season it feeds at any height above the ground, but where the trees are tall, it spends most of its time among the highest branches. Its distinctive song is one of the easiest of warbler songs to learn.

Pine Warbler
Dendroica pinus
292

5½″ (14 cm). Unstreaked olive above with yellow throat and breast, faint streaking below, white belly, inconspicuous eye-stripe; 2 white wing bars. Female similar but duller.

Voice
Musical, somewhat melancholy trill, soft and sweet.

Habitat
Pine forests.

Range
Southern Canada to the Gulf of Mexico. Winters in southern states, occasionally north to New England, and the northern West Indies.

Comments
No bird is more aptly named: this species nests exclusively in pine trees, spends much of its life there, and only during migration is found in shrubbery or deciduous growth of parks and gardens. It is relatively rare and local inland in the North.

Prairie Warbler
Dendroica discolor
293

5″ (13 cm). Olive above, bright yellow below with black spots and streaks along sides; male has chestnut streaks on back. Wags its tail vigorously.

Voice
Buzzy *zee-zee-zee,* up to 10 rapidly ascending notes.

Habitat
In the North, mixed pine-oak barrens, old pastures, and on hillsides with scattered red cedars; in the South in open scrub; in extreme S. Florida in mangrove swamps.

Range
South Dakota, Wisconsin, Ontario, and central New England south to Oklahoma, the Gulf Coast, and Florida. Winters in S. Florida, the West Indies and Central America.

Comments
This species avoids thick woods and has benefited greatly from the cutting and burning of the forests, which favors the younger seedlings and smaller bushes that sprout after fires. Like the Palm Warbler, it ranges low—about 10 feet.

Yellow-breasted Chat
Icteria virens
294

6½–7½″ (16–19 cm). Larger than a sparrow. Olive-green above with bright yellow breast and white abdomen, stout black bill, black face mask bordered above and below with white; white spectacles. Tail long.

Voice
Series of widely spaced croaks, whistles, and short repeated phrases. Often sings at night. At times it performs a display-flight, flopping awkwardly up and down with legs dangling while singing.

Habitat
Dense thickets and brush, often with thorns; streamside tangles and dry brushy hillsides.

Range
British Columbia, Ontario, and Massachusetts south to Florida, the Gulf Coast, and northern Mexico. Winters in Mexico and Central America.

Comments
This bird is not only large for a warbler but there is doubt about it being a warbler at all. While there is usually no difficulty in distinguishing warblers, tanagers, buntings, and sparrows in North America, these groups merge in the tropics and, as with the chat, no clear-cut distinction is possible.

Canada Warbler
Wilsonia canadensis
295

5" (13 cm). Solid gray above, without wing bars, yellow below with yellow "spectacles"; black-spotted necklace on breast.

Voice
Rapid, jerky warble.

Habitat
Cool, moist woodland that is nearly mature and has much undergrowth.

Range
Southern Canada to northern United States east of the Rockies, and in the eastern mountains to N. Georgia. Winters in northwestern South America.

Comments
This warbler received its name from its discovery in Canada, although it is certainly not confined to Canada, even in the breeding season. It ordinarily ranges at low levels, usually from the ground to six feet up. Like several other warblers it is adept at fly-catching, conspicuously flitting from bush to bush. Flying insects form a great portion of its diet, but it also captures spiders and insect larvae.

Northern Parula
Parula americana
296

4½" (11 cm). A small warbler; blue above with a yellow-green "saddle" on its back; yellow throat and breast and white belly; 2 white wing bars. Male has an orange-brown chest band.

Voice
Single or several rising buzzy notes dropping abruptly at the end; *bzzzzz-zip* or *bz-bz-bz-zip*.

Habitat
Breeds in wet, chiefly coniferous woods, swamps, and along lakes and ponds; more widespread on migration.

Range
Southeastern Canada to the Gulf of Mexico. Winters from S. Florida to the West Indies and from Mexico to Nicaragua.

Comments
This species is almost entirely dependent upon either Spanish moss or beard moss for nest sites. Although breeding mostly in coniferous forests in the North, during migration these birds frequent deciduous trees and shrubs. In such situations they are seen in large numbers in spring along roadsides and in parks, yards, orchards, and gardens as well as woods. Until recently this species was called "Parula Warbler."

Red-breasted Nuthatch
Sitta canadensis
297

4½–4¾" (11–12 cm). Smaller than a sparrow. Often creeps downward headfirst on tree trunks. Upperparts blue-gray, underparts pale rusty. Crown and line through eye black, eyebrow white.

Voice
Tinny *yank-yank*, higher-pitched and more nasal than the call of the White-breasted Nuthatch.

Habitat
Coniferous forests; more widespread in migration and winter.

Range
Alaska, Manitoba, and Newfoundland south to New Jersey, North Carolina, Colorado, and S. California. Winters south to the Gulf Coast and northern Mexico.

Comments
In winter, this species feeds principally on conifer seeds; in years when the seed crop fails in the North, these birds move south in large numbers. Smaller than the White-breasted Nuthatch, they tend to forage on smaller branches and twigs, seeking small insects as well as seeds. Although it accepts suet, it visits feeders less frequently than its relative.

Magnolia Warbler
Dendroica magnolia
298

5" (13 cm). Male is bright yellow below with heavy black streaks, a black facial patch, and a large white wing patch. Female and immature birds are similar but duller. Broad white patches on the sides of tail in all plumages.

Voice
Weeta-weeta-weeteo. Call note *tslip.*

Habitat
Breeds in open stands of young spruce and fir. In migration, this warbler is found almost any place where shrubbery or trees occur.

Range
Central Canada to northeastern United States, and in the mountains south to Virginia. Winters in the West Indies and Middle America.

Comments
This pretty warbler was named by the famous ornithologist Alexander Wilson, who found the first specimen among some magnolia trees in Mississippi in the early 1880s. It actually breeds in conifer trees in the North, but the name has remained. It is one of our most numerous warblers during migrations, and on certain spring days the trees seem to be filled with them. They may also be found feeding near the ground in low bushes.

Yellow-throated Warbler
Dendroica dominica
299

5" (13 cm). Gray, unstreaked upperparts, bright yellow throat, white belly, black-and-white facial pattern, heavy black streaks on sides. Sexes alike.

Voice
Series of clear ringing notes descending in pitch and increasing in speed, rising at the end: *teeew-teeew-teeew-teew-tew-tew-twi.*

Habitat
Forests of pine, cypress, sycamore, and oak, in both swampy places and dry uplands.

Range
S. New Jersey, Ohio, and Illinois south to southeastern United States and west to Missouri and Texas. Winters chiefly in the Gulf states south to the West Indies and Costa Rica.

Comments
This attractive warbler is usually found in live oaks draped with Spanish moss or in longleaf pines. It often creeps over the branches of the trunk like a Black-and-White Warbler. Occasionally it may stray as far north of its usual range as New York and New England.

Kirtland's Warbler
Dendroica kirtlandii
300

6″ (15 cm). A large warbler, gray above with black streaks; yellow below with black streaks on sides; black cheeks with conspicuous white eye-ring. Female similar but duller. Wags its tail.

Voice
Low-pitched, loud, bubbling, and rising at the end.

Habitat
Found only in dense stands of young jack pines.

Range
Breeds only in north-central Michigan. Winters in the Bahamas.

Comments
This warbler is noted for its extremely limited range. During the breeding season it is confined to dense stands of young jack pines that spring up after forest fires. Once such stands reach about 20 feet, the birds abandon them. Even in winter it inhabits low scrub, although not always pines.

Yellow-rumped Warbler
Dendroica coronata
301

5–6″ (13–15 cm). Breeding male dull bluish above, streaked with black; breast and flanks blackish. Rump yellow. 2 white wing bars. Crown and small area at sides of breast yellow. Eastern birds ("Myrtle Warbler") have white throats; western birds ("Audubon's Warbler") have yellow throats. Females, fall males, and young are streaked gray-brown, but always have yellow rump and white spots on tail.

Voice
A thin, buzzy warble; a sharp *chek!*

Habitat
Coniferous and mixed forests; widespread during migration and winter.

Range
N. Alaska, N. Manitoba, and central Quebec south in the West to northern Mexico and in the East to Maine, Massachusetts, N. New York, and Michigan. Winters from southern part of breeding range south to Costa Rica and the West Indies.

Comments
Until recently, the eastern and western populations of the Yellow-rumped Warbler were thought to be two distinct species, respectively the "Myrtle Warbler" and "Audubon's Warbler." However, it has been found that in the narrow zone where the ranges of the two come together, the birds hybridize freely. In the East, the "Myrtle Warbler" is an abundant migrant, and the only warbler that regularly spends the winter in the northern states.

Chestnut-sided Warbler
Dendroica pensylvanica
302

5″ (13 cm). Sexes similar: yellow-green crown; long, thin chestnut line on sides; white underparts, streaked back. Immatures uniform yellow-green above, dull whitish below, with white eye-ring and yellow wing bars.

Voice
Rich and musical with an emphatic ending, sometimes interpreted as *very very pleased to MEET-CHA!*

Habitat
Young, open, second-growth woodland and scrub.

Range
Breeds from southern Canada to east-central United States, south in the Appalachian Mountains. Winters from Nicaragua to Panama.

Comments
This attractive bird was rare in the days of Audubon and Wilson, who seldom saw it and knew little about its habits. It has increased tremendously as abandoned pastures in the northern states have grown up in dense thickets, a vast new habitat unavailable when the land was clothed in virgin forest.

Cape May Warbler
Dendroica tigrina
303

5″ (13 cm). Male in breeding plumage is yellow below with conspicuous chestnut cheek patch, white wing patch, and heavy black streaks on underparts. Female much duller, with greenish-yellow cheeks.

Voice
4 or more high, thin notes without change in pitch or volume: *seet-seet-seet-seet*.

Habitat
Open spruce forests; in migration, in evergreen or deciduous woodlands and often in parks, estates, or suburban yards.

Range
S. Mackenzie, Manitoba, Ontario, and Quebec south to Nova

Scotia, Maine, N. New York, Michigan, and North Dakota.
Winters in S. Florida and the Caribbean region.

Comments
This warbler was first discovered at Cape May, New Jersey,
where it is a common migrant. During migration these birds
show a curious attraction to Norway spruces.

Blackburnian Warbler
Dendroica fusca
304

5" (13 cm). Breeding male black and white with vivid orange
throat and large white wing patch; female is similar but has
yellow throat. Back boldly striped.

Voice
Very thin and wiry, increasing in speed and rising to the limit
of hearing. *Sleet-sleet-sleet-sleet-sleet-sleeeee*. Also *tiddly-tiddly-
tiddly-tiddly* at same speed and pitch.

Habitat
Most numerous in mixed forests of hemlock, spruce, and
various hardwoods, usually ranging high in the trees.

Range
Southeastern Canada to the northeastern United States and
south in the mountains to N. Georgia. Winters chiefly in
northwestern South America.

Comments
Blackburnian Warblers are usually found high in trees, even
during migration, and are not readily noticed in the dense
foliage unless their high-pitched song announces their
presence. At times they may be detected at the ends of
branches, picking at leaves for bugs or caterpillars.

Evening Grosbeak
Coccothraustes vespertinus
305

7½–8½" (19–21 cm). Stocky finch with a very large, pale
greenish or yellowish conical bill. Male has brown head
shading to yellow on lower back, rump, and underparts;
bright yellow forehead and eyebrow; bold white wing patches.
Female similar but grayer.

Voice
Song a series of short, musical whistles; call note a loud,
ringing chirp.

Habitat
Nests in coniferous forests; visits deciduous woodlands and
suburban areas in winter.

Range
British Columbia and Nova Scotia south to northern New
England, Minnesota, Mexico (in mountains), and California.
Winters south to S. California, Texas, and South Carolina.

Comments
This grosbeak formerly bred no farther east than Minnesota,
but more food available at bird feeders may have enabled more
birds to survive the winter, and the species now breeds east to

the Atlantic. Like most of the northern finches, however, these birds are more numerous in some years than in others. In winter they feed in flocks mainly on the seeds of box elder or, at feeders, on sunflower seeds. In spring the outer coating of the bill peels off, exposing the blue-green color beneath.

American Redstart
Setophaga ruticilla
306

4½–5½" (11–14 cm). Male is black with bright orange patches on wings and tail; white belly. Females and young birds dull olive-brown above, white below, with yellow wing and tail patches.

Voice
5 or 6 high-pitched notes or 2-note phrases, ending with an upward or downward inflection: *chewy-chewy-chewy, chew-chew-chew.*

Habitat
Second-growth woodlands; thickets with saplings.

Range
Breeds from SE. Alaska, central Manitoba, central Quebec, and Newfoundland south to Georgia, S. Louisiana, SE. Oklahoma, Colorado, and N. California. Winters from Mexico to South America.

Comments
This is one of the most abundant birds in North America, because its favored habitat—second-growth woodland—covers such vast areas of the continent. The American Redstart has a distinctive habit of dropping down suddenly in pursuit of a flying insect, then fanning its brightly marked tail from side to side. It takes a full year for the males to acquire the black-and-orange adult plumage, so it is not unusual to find what appears to be a female singing and displaying like a male.

American Robin
Turdus migratorius
307

9–11" (23–28 cm). Gray above, brick-red below. Head and tail black in males, dull gray in females. Young birds are spotted below.

Voice
Song is a series of rich caroling notes, rising and falling in pitch: *Cheer-up, cheerily, Cheer-up, cheerily.*

Habitat
Towns, gardens, open woodland, and agricultural land.

Range
Alaska, Manitoba, and Newfoundland south to the Carolinas, Arkansas, and Guatemala; occasionally breeds along the Gulf Coast. Winters north to Newfoundland, S. Ontario, and British Columbia.

Comments
Robins originally nested in forests; the birds that still do so are much shyer than the Robins of the dooryard. Robins breed only rarely in the Deep South, where they prefer large shade

trees on lawns. Although usually considered a harbinger of spring, Robins often winter in the northern states, where they frequent cedar bogs and swamps and are not usually noticed by a casual observer, except when they gather in large roosts, often containing thousands of birds.

Rufous-sided Towhee
Pipilo erythrophthalmus
308

7–9½" (17–24 cm). Male has black head and upperparts, white underparts; bright rufous patches on flanks. Female is similar, but warm brown where male is black.

Voice
Song a cheerful *drink-your-TEA,* second note lower, third note higher. Call a clear *to-wheee?,* also *chewink.*

Habitat
Thickets and brushy woodland edges.

Range
British Columbia, Saskatchewan, and Maine south to Florida, Louisiana, and Guatemala. Winters north to Maryland, Nebraska, and S. British Columbia.

Comments
The name "Towhee," an imitation of this species' call note, was given in 1731 by the naturalist and bird artist Mark Catesby, who encountered the bird in the Carolinas. Few birds show as much geographical variation in voice; the calls of birds in the West bear little resemblance to those in the East. Towhees often feed on the ground, scratching noisily in the dry leaves.

Northern Oriole
Icterus galbula
309

7–8½" (18–12 cm). Eastern male, formerly "Baltimore Oriole," has black head, back, wings, and tail; orange breast, rump, and shoulder patch. Eastern female olive-brown with dull yellow-orange underparts and two dull white wing bars.

Voice
Clear and flutelike whistled single or double notes in short, distinct phrases with much individual variation.

Habitat
Deciduous woodland and shade trees. Before its decline, the American elm was a favorite nesting site for the eastern bird.

Range
Breeds from British Columbia, Saskatchewan, and Nova Scotia south to Georgia, Louisiana, and northern Mexico. Winters from southern Mexico southward.

Comments
Until recently the western populations of this bird ("Bullock's Oriole") were thought to be a separate species from the eastern populations, which were called the "Baltimore Oriole." When trees were planted on the Great Plains, the two forms extended their ranges and met. Despite the differences in their appearance, it was found that they interbreed freely, and most

birds in the central plains are hybrids. Orioles readily accept short pieces of yarn for nesting material and apparently show no color preference.

Bay-breasted Warbler
Dendroica castanea
310

5½" (14 cm). Male in breeding plumage has chestnut cap, throat, and sides, blackish face, and a conspicuous buff patch on side of neck. Upperparts streaked. Females, fall males, and immatures are olive above, with 2 white wing bars, dark legs, and often some trace of chestnut on flanks.

Voice
High, thin *teesi-teesi-teesi-teesi,* without change in pitch or volume.

Habitat
Breeds in open spruce forests. During migration frequents deciduous trees as well.

Range
Southeastern Canada and northeastern United States. Winters in Panama and northwestern South America. Migrates by way of Mexico and Central America on the Atlantic side.

Comments
This warbler, like the Cape May and Tennessee warblers, has increased in numbers in recent years. It is a handsome bird and is eagerly sought by enthusiasts in the spring warbler waves during middle and late May.

Cedar Waxwing
Bombycilla cedrorum
311

6½–8" (16–20 cm). Smaller than a Robin. A sleek, crested, brown bird with a black mask, yellow tips on the tail feathers, hard red waxlike tips on the secondary wing feathers. Almost always seen in flocks.

Voice
Thin lisp, *tseee.*

Habitat
Open woodlands, orchards, and residential areas.

Range
Breeds from British Columbia and Cape Breton Island south to Georgia, Arkansas, and California. Winters from New England and British Columbia to Panama and the Greater Antilles.

Comments
Waxwings spend most of the year in flocks whose movements may be quite erratic. Hundreds will suddenly appear in an area to exploit a crop of berries, only to vanish when that crop is exhausted. Since the young are fed to some extent on small fruits, waxwings tend to nest late in the summer when there is a good supply of berries. Adults store food for the young in their crop, a pouch located in their throat, and may regurgitate as many as thirty choke cherries, one at a time, into the gaping mouths of the young. In summer, insects are

also taken, the birds hawking for them like flycatchers. These social birds have the amusing habit of passing berries or even apple blossoms from one bird to the next down a long row sitting on a branch, until one bird eats the food.

Red Crossbill
Loxia curvirostra
312

5¼–6½" (13–16 cm). Sparrow-sized. Mandibles crossed at tips. Male dusky brick red. Female gray tinged with dull green, brightest on rump.

Voice
Song *chipa-chipa-chipa, chee-chee-chee-chee;* also a *kip-kip-kip.*

Habitat
Coniferous forests; visits ornamental evergreens in winter.

Range
S. Alaska, Manitoba, Quebec, and Newfoundland south in the eastern United States to North Carolina (mountains) and Wisconsin; in the west to northern Nicaragua. Winters south to the Gulf Coast.

Comments
These birds are sporadic visitors in winter, appearing in large numbers, then not appearing for several years. Such winter flocks often travel great distances, and many of the birds that visit New England come all the way from the Rocky Mountains. Crossbills feed exclusively on conifer seeds, the crossed mandibles enabling them to extract the seeds from the cones. Because their chosen food is available in winter, they commonly begin nesting as early as January, but they have been found nesting in every month of the year.

Purple Finch
Carpodacus purpureus
313

5½–6½" (14–16 cm). Sparrow-sized but with a thicker bill. Male dull rosy-red, more raspberry than purple, especially on head and rump. Female and young heavily streaked with dull brown and with bold, pale eyebrow.

Voice
Rich musical warble. Call a distinctive *tick* as it flies.

Habitat
Mixed and coniferous woodlands; ornamental conifers in gardens.

Range
British Columbia, Quebec, and Newfoundland south to New Jersey, Minnesota, and Baja California. Winters from Nova Scotia and British Columbia to Florida, the Gulf Coast, and Texas.

Comments
Purple Finches are quite numerous and conspicuous in spring migration, and for a few weeks each year one can hear the rich, spirited song of the brightly colored males. In winter they visit feeding stations in large numbers, showing a fondness for sunflower seeds.

Pine Grosbeak
Pinicola enucleator
314

8–10" (20–25 cm). Robin-sized. Male dull rose-pink with 2 white wing bars. Female dull gray with yellow-green tinge on head and rump and 2 white wing bars. Conical, stubby bill.

Voice
Soft musical warble or clear whistled *tew-tew-tew*.

Habitat
Coniferous forests; in winter, spreading to mixed woodlands and wherever fruiting trees are found.

Range
Alaska, N. Quebec, and Newfoundland south to northern New England and Manitoba, and in the Rockies to New Mexico. Winters south to Pennsylvania and Kansas.

Comments
Largest of the northern finches, the Pine Grosbeak is less common than siskins or redpolls. When these birds do appear their preference for the seeds and fruit of trees such as mountain ash and cedar makes them more conspicuous than their smaller relatives. They are very tame and slow moving, allowing close approach. On their northern breeding grounds occur mainly in brushy clearings and forest edges.

White-winged Crossbill
Loxia leucoptera
315

6–6½" (15–16 cm). Size of a large sparrow. Mandibles crossed at tips. Male raspberry-pink; females grayer, without pink. Both sexes have 2 white wing bars.

Voice
Song is a series of sweet canarylike warbles and trills. Also a dry, soft trill.

Habitat
Coniferous forests.

Range
Alaska and N. Quebec south to Newfoundland and British Columbia. In winter, south to the Carolinas and Oregon.

Comments
Like the Red Crossbill, these birds use their crossed mandibles to extract seeds from the cones of pines and spruces. Their winter wanderings depend largely on the crop of conifer seeds; in years when seeds are abundant in the northern forests the birds tend to remain there. When the crop fails they come south in large numbers and may often be seen in quiet flocks, clinging to clusters of cones like little parrots.

Rose-breasted Grosbeak
Pheucticus ludovicianus
316

8" (20 cm). Sexes very different; male black and white with a conspicuous rose-red patch on breast and underwings. Female heavily streaked brown on white above and below; prominent white eyebrow.

Voice
Its distinctive call note is a sharp, penetrating, metallic *clink*.

Rich, clear, fluid song, like that of American Robin but softer and more melodious.

Habitat
Moist woodland adjacent to open fields with tall shrubs; also old and overgrown orchards.

Range
Southern Canada to the central United States, and in mountains as far south as N. Georgia. Winters from Mexico to northern South America.

Comments
This handsome grosbeak is one of the most conspicuous birds before the foliage comes into full leaf in early May. It is beneficial to the farmer, consuming many potato beetles and larvae as well as weed seeds, wild fruits, and buds.

Scarlet Tanager
Piranga olivacea
317

7½″ (19 cm). Male in breeding plumage brilliant scarlet with black wings and tail. Female and male in nonbreeding plumage olive-green; male has black wings.

Voice
Call note an emphatic, nasal *chip-bang;* song a burry repetitive warble.

Habitat
Chiefly mature woodland, especially oak and pine.

Range
Breeds from extreme southeastern Canada to the east-central United States. Winters from Colombia to Bolivia.

Comments
The brilliantly colored male Scarlet Tanager gleams in the sunlight but is often difficult to see in thick foliage, especially if it is motionless or moving slowly from branch to branch high up in the tree canopy. Only when perched on a dead tree limb or feeding on the ground during a cold, rainy spell is it conspicuous. During late summer or early autumn some of the males may show a patchwork plumage of red and green as they molt, but the wings and tail remain black.

Summer Tanager
Piranga rubra
318

7–8″ (17–20 cm). Smaller than a Robin. Male solid rose-red with a yellow bill. Female pale olive-green above, dull yellow below. The male Cardinal has a black face, conical red bill, and crest; the male Scarlet Tanager has black wings and tail.

Voice
Distinctive rattling *chick-tucky-TUCK.* Its song is soft and sweet.

Habitat
Open woodlands and shade trees.

Range
Breeds from S. California, Wisconsin, and Delaware south to

the Gulf Coast and northern Mexico. Winters north to southern Mexico.

Comments
Each major forest region of North America has its species of tanager; this one is found in dry oak and mixed forests of the southern states. Despite their bright colors, the males are difficult to detect in the dense foliage. A major part of the diet during the summer consists of flying insects captured in the air. On their breeding grounds Summer Tanagers are most easily located by their calls, which they utter persistently throughout the day.

Northern Cardinal
Cardinalis cardinalis
319

8–9″ (20–23 cm). Male bright red with crest, black face, stout red bill. Female buff-brown tinged with red on crest, wings, and tail.

Voice
Rich *what-cheer, cheer, cheer; purty-purty-purty-purty* or *sweet-sweet-sweet-sweet*. Also a metallic *chip*.

Habitat
Woodland edges, thickets, brushy swamps, and gardens.

Range
Resident from the Dakotas, S. Ontario, and Nova Scotia south to the Gulf Coast, and from S. Texas, Arizona, and S. California southward into Mexico.

Comments
This species, named for the bright red plumage that resembles the red robes worn by Roman Catholic cardinals, has extended its range northeastward into southern Canada in recent decades. Cardinals are aggressive birds, and occupy territories year-round. Both sexes are accomplished songsters and may be heard at any time of year rather than just in the spring when most other birds are singing. Like most members of the finch family, Cardinals feed mainly on seeds, although insects are taken in the breeding season. These birds often come to bird feeders in winter.

Painted Bunting
Passerina ciris
320

5½″ (14 cm). Sparrow-sized. Perhaps our most brilliant bird: male has bright red underparts and rump, green back, purple head, and red eye-ring; female is bright green all over, lighter below.

Voice
Loud, clear, and variable song consisting of a series of high-pitched musical notes. The call is a sharp, metallic *tsick*.

Habitat
Brushy tangles, hedgerows, briar patches, woodland edges, and swampy thickets.

Range
Missouri and North Carolina south to the southeastern states

and west to New Mexico and Oklahoma. Winters from the Gulf states south to the Bahamas and Cuba, and through Mexico to Panama.

Comments
This gaudy finch is one of our most beautiful birds. Its brilliant plumage made it a popular cage bird until it came under federal protection. It is common in parts of the Deep South and raises as many as three broods. The female is one of the few truly green birds in North America.

Ruby-throated Hummingbird
Archilochus colubris
321

3½" (9 cm). Tiny. Metallic green above, white below; male has a brilliant red throat. Needlelike bill.

Voice
Mouselike twittering squeak. In flight they make humming sounds with their wings, which accounts for their name.

Habitat
Suburban gardens, parks, and woodlands.

Range
The only hummingbird breeding east of the Mississippi River. Breeds from southern Canada to the Gulf Coast. Winters chiefly from Mexico to Panama and north to the immediate Gulf states.

Comments
These smallest of all birds are particularly attracted to tubular red flowers such as salvia and trumpet creeper, as well as bee balm, petunia, jewelweed, and thistle. Hummers are also attracted to artificial feeders—red glass tubes filled with a mixture of honey and sugar water. With their remarkable powers of flight they are the only birds that can fly backwards as well as hover in one spot like an insect. They are constantly in motion, perching on twigs or wires only briefly to rest and to survey their surroundings, or when they are at the nest. During courtship the female sits quietly on a perch while the male displays in a pendulum dance, swinging in a wide arc and buzzing loudly with each dip.

Black-throated Blue Warbler
Dendroica caerulescens
322

5" (13 cm). Male blue-gray above, white below, with black face, throat, and sides; female dull olive-green with white eyeline and usually a square white wing patch.

Voice
Buzzy, rising *zwee-zwee-zwee*, sometimes rendered as *please-SQUEEZE-me* or *please-please-SQUEEZE-me*.

Habitat
Mixed deciduous and evergreen forests.

Range
Breeds from southeastern Canada to northeastern United States and in the mountains to N. Georgia. Winters in the Gulf states as well as in the Greater Antilles.

Comments
The male is one of the easier warblers to identify since it retains its strikingly patterned plumage the year-round. These warblers are among the tamest and most trusting of this family. If the observer moves very deliberately, the bird may be approached to within a few feet without taking alarm.

Scrub Jay
Aphelocoma coerulescens
323

11–13" (28–33 cm). Blue Jay-sized. .Wings and tail dull blue, back gray, with dusky mask, and white throat set off by a "necklace" of dull blue marks on the breast. No crest.

Voice
Loud, harsh, and rasping; also has a sweet song of trills and low warbles.

Habitat
In Florida confined to scrub oak.

Range
Breeds from Washington, Wyoming, and Colorado south to Texas and S. Mexico, with a population in central Florida.

Comments
The isolated population of the Scrub Jay in Florida is puzzling, because these birds are separated from their western relatives by more than 1000 miles. Presumably a belt of scrub once extended from the western states across the South and into Florida. Scrub Jays feed entirely on insects, seeds, and nuts, obtained chiefly on the ground. Rather shy for jays, they are often difficult to find even where they are common, except when perching on telephone wires. They soon become tame, however, and learn to come to feeders. Like members of the jay and crow family, they often eat the eggs and young of other birds. They also share a tendency to carry off and hide brightly colored objects.

Blue Jay
Cyanocitta cristata
324

12" (30 cm). Bright blue above with much white and black in the wing and tail; white below; black facial markings; prominent crest.

Voice
Raucous *jay-jay,* harsh cries, and a rich variety of other calls. Also a musical *queedle-queedle.*

Habitat
Chiefly oak forest, but now also city parks and suburban yards, especially where oak trees predominate.

Range
East of the Rockies, from southern Canada to the Gulf of Mexico.

Comments
Although sometimes disliked because they chase smaller birds away from feeders, Blue Jays are among our handsomest birds. They often bury seeds and acorns, and since many are never

retrieved they are, in effect, tree planters. They have a violent dislike of predators, and their raucous screaming makes it easy to locate a hawk or a roosting owl. Although seen throughout the year, Blue Jays are migratory and travel in large loose flocks in both spring and fall.

Blue-gray Gnatcatcher
Polioptila caerulea
325

4½–5″ (11–13 cm). Smaller than a sparrow. Tiny, slender, long-tailed bird, blue-gray above and white below, with white eye-ring and white-bordered black tail.

Voice
Song is a thin, musical warble. Call note is a distinctive *pzzzz* with a nasal quality.

Habitat
Open, moist woodlands and brushy streamside thickets.

Range
Breeds from N. California, Colorado, central Minnesota, S. Ontario, and New Hampshire south to the Bahamas, the Gulf Coast, and Guatemala. Winters north to the Carolinas, the Gulf Coast, and S. California.

Comments
Several species of gnatcatchers are found throughout the warmer parts of the Americas. All of them build exquisite nests, which are exceedingly difficult to find unless the adults are feeding their young; the parents are quite noisy and conspicuous, and seem to ignore intruders. These birds are extremely active, constantly flitting about through the treetops. This species apparently feeds exclusively on insects.

Ruby-crowned Kinglet
Regulus calendula
326

3¾–4½″ (9–11 cm). Tiny. Similar to the Golden-crowned Kinglet but greener, with no face pattern except for a narrow white eye-ring. Males have a tuft of red feathers on the crown, kept concealed unless the bird is aroused.

Voice
Song an excited, musical chattering.

Habitat
Coniferous forests in summer; also deciduous forests and thickets in winter.

Range
Alaska, Manitoba, and Newfoundland south to northern New England, Ontario, New Mexico, and S. California. Winters from S. British Columbia and southern New England to Florida, the Gulf Coast, and Guatemala.

Comments
In the northern states this bird is scarce or absent in winter but is often seen during migration. It frequently sings on its way north, a song surprisingly loud for so tiny a bird. It takes a sharp eye to see the male's red crown patch, which is usually erected for a few seconds at a time when the bird is displaying

aggressively. It has a characteristic habit of nervously flicking its wings.

Acadian Flycatcher
Empidonax virescens
327

6″ (15 cm). Olive-green above, yellowish below. Identified chiefly by voice and habitat.

Voice
Emphatic 2-noted *flee-see* with the second syllable higher in pitch, uttered during breeding and, rarely, on migration.

Habitat
Beech-maple or hemlock forest, usually under the canopy but also in clearings; often in wooded ravines.

Range
The Great Lakes, SE. Pennsylvania, and southern New England south to eastern United States. Winters from Panama to Ecuador and Venezuela.

Comments
The Acadian Flycatcher and its relatives in the genus *Empidonax* are difficult to distinguish, but in much of the South, the Acadian is the only breeding species; between June and August, any *Empidonax* seen in the lowlands south of New Jersey and Missouri can safely be called an Acadian.

Brown-headed Nuthatch
Sitta pusilla
328

4–5″ (10–13 cm). Smaller than a sparrow. Upperparts dull blue-gray, underparts whitish. Crown dull brown, with a whitish spot on the nape.

Voice
Series of high-pitched piping notes, unlike the calls of other eastern nuthatches.

Habitat
Coniferous and mixed forests.

Range
Resident from Delaware, Missouri, and E. Texas south to the Bahamas, Florida, and the Gulf Coast.

Comments
The smallest of our eastern nuthatches, the Brown-headed spends more time among terminal branches and twigs of trees than do the other species. After breeding, these birds gather in flocks of a dozen or more and move through the woods along with woodpeckers and chickadees. They are quite agile and restless, flitting from one cluster of pine needles to another.

Tufted Titmouse
Parus bicolor
329

6″ (15 cm). Sparrow-sized. Gray above and white below, with rust-colored sides; conspicuous gray crest.

Voice
Its commonest call, sung year-round and carrying a

considerable distance, is a whistled series of 4–8 notes
sounding like *Peter-Peter* repeated over and over.

Habitat
Swampy or moist woodland and shade trees in villages and city
parks; in winter, at feeders.

Range
Central portions of Wisconsin, Michigan, and Maine south to
Florida, the Gulf Coast, Texas, and northern Mexico.

Comments
Titmice are social birds and, especially in winter, join with
small mixed flocks of chickadees, nuthatches, kinglets,
creepers, and the smaller woodpeckers. Although a frequent
visitor at feeders, the Tufted Titmouse is not as tame or
confiding as the chickadees. It often clings to the bark of trees
and turns upside down to pick spiders and insects from the
underside of a twig or leaf.

Gray Jay
Perisoreus canadensis
330

10–13″ (25–33 cm). Gray above, whitish below. Forehead
and throat white; nape and stripe through eye dull black.

Voice
Whee-ah, chuck-chuck, also scolds, screams, and whistles.

Habitat
Coniferous forests.

Range
Alaska and Labrador south to northern New England, N. New
York, New Mexico, and N. California. May wander south
in winter to Pennsylvania and the central Great Plains.

Comments
This bird is well known to anyone who has spent time in the
north woods, for like certain other birds of that region it is
very tame and habitually enters camps to take food; hence one
of its many names, "Camp Robber." Gray Jays will eat almost
anything, but in winter they are partial to conifer seeds. They
glue together masses of seeds and buds with their thick saliva
and store them for use when food is scarce.

Northern Shrike
Lanius excubitor
331

9–10½″ (23–26 cm). Robin-sized. Pale gray above, white
below, with faint barring on underparts and a bold black mask
ending at stout, hooked bill. Black tail with white edges.

Voice
Mixture of warbles and harsh tones with a Robinlike quality;
heard especially in late spring.

Habitat
Open woodlands and brushy swamps in summer; open
grasslands with fence posts and scattered trees in winter.

Range
Alaska and the Labrador Peninsula to Quebec, Saskatchewan,

and N. British Columbia. Winters south to Virginia, Texas, and N. California.

Comments
Unusual among songbirds, shrikes prey on small birds and rodents, catching them with the bill and sometimes impaling them on thorns or barbed wire for storage. Like other northern birds that depend on rodent populations, the Northern Shrike's movements are cyclical, becoming more abundant in the South when northern rodent populations are low. At times these birds hunt from an open perch, where they sit motionless until prey appears; at other times they hover in the air ready to pounce on anything that moves.

Carolina Chickadee
Parus carolinensis
332

4–5″ (10–13 cm). Gray above, white below, with black cap and throat, white cheeks. Similar to the more northern Black-capped Chickadee, but feathers of the folded wing usually show less white edging. Best identified by voice and range.

Voice
Chickadee-dee-dee-dee, higher-pitched and faster than the Black-cap's; song a double whistled *see-dee, see-dee,* with a downward inflection, rather than the 2-noted song of the Black-cap.

Habitat
Deciduous woodlands and residential areas.

Range
Resident from central New Jersey, Ohio, Missouri, and Oklahoma south to Florida and Texas.

Comments
So similar are the Carolina and Black-capped Chickadees that Audubon did not realize until 1834 that they were different species—over a century after "the" chickadee had been discovered by Europeans. Like its northern relative, the Carolina Chickadee is a familiar visitor to feeders and is a regular member of the mixed flocks of small birds that roam the winter woods.

Black-capped Chickadee
Parus atricapillus
333

4¾–5¾″ (12–14 cm). Black cap and throat, white cheeks, gray back, dull white underparts. Wing feathers narrowly and indistinctly edged with white.

Voice
Buzzy *chick-a-dee-dee-dee;* clear, whistled *fee-bee,* the second note lower and often doubled.

Habitat
Deciduous and mixed forests, and open woodlands; suburban areas in winter.

Range
Breeds from Alaska and Newfoundland south to N. New Jersey, Missouri, and N. California. Winters south to Maryland and Texas.

Comments
Flocks of this tame and inquisitive bird spend the winter making the rounds of feeders in a neighborhood, often appearing at each feeder with striking regularity. Chickadees form the nucleus of mixed flocks of woodpeckers, nuthatches, creepers, and kinglets that move through the winter woods. Occasionally they move south in very large numbers, many thousands passing through even our largest cities. In spring chickadees disband and move into the woods to nest. They often feed upside down, clinging to the underside of twigs and branches in their search for insect eggs and larvae.

White-breasted Nuthatch
Sitta carolinensis
334

5–6" (13–15 cm). Sparrow-sized. Blue-gray above, underparts and face white, crown black. Usually seen creeping on tree trunks, often downward headfirst.

Voice
Nasal *yank-yank*. Song is a series of low whistled notes.

Habitat
Deciduous and mixed forests.

Range
British Columbia, Ontario, and Nova Scotia south to Florida, the Gulf Coast, and Mexico.

Comments
This nuthatch, common in much of the eastern United States, is generally sedentary, but sometimes in the fall it turns up along the outer beaches, indicating that a migration is taking place. Pairs seem to remain together year-round, for the species may be found in twos even in the dead of winter. Although they often join mixed flocks of chickadees, woodpeckers, and kinglets roaming the winter woods, White-breasted Nuthatches tend to remain in their territories. They are familiar visitors to bird feeders.

Blackpoll Warbler
Dendroica striata
335

5½" (14 cm). Breeding male gray streaked above with black cap, white cheeks and underparts, blackish streaks on sides. Female and nonbreeding male greenish above with streaking. Feet usually flesh-colored.

Voice
Rapid series of high lisping notes all on 1 pitch, increasing and then decreasing in volume; *seet-seet-SEET-SEET-SEET-SEET-seet-seet*.

Habitat
Breeds in coniferous forests. During migration is found chiefly in tall trees.

Range
Alaska and northern Canada to southern Canada and northeastern United States. Migrates through the West Indies and winters in northern South America.

Comments
The Blackpoll is one of the most abundant warblers in the East and has an enormous breeding range in the northern part of the continent. During migration in late May, and again in September and early October, hundreds may be seen in a single day.

Black-and-white Warbler
Mniotilta varia
336

5″ (13 cm). Black and white stripes, including crown. Male has black throat, female's throat white.

Voice
Thin, high-pitched, monotonous *weesy-weesy-weesy-weesy* like a squeaky wheelbarrow.

Habitat
Forests, chiefly deciduous. In migration in parks, gardens, and lawn areas with trees and shrubs.

Range
Breeds from southern Canada to southern United States east of the Rockies. Winters from the southern parts of the Gulf states to northwestern South America.

Comments
This conspicuous warbler arrives in the North early in spring, usually by mid- to late April. It is known for its habit of creeping around tree trunks and along larger branches in search of insect food in crevices in or under the bark; hence its old name, "Black-and-White Creeper." Unlike the Brown Creeper which only moves up a tree, and the nuthatches which only move headfirst down a tree, this warbler does both.

Golden-crowned Kinglet
Regulus satrapa
337

3½–4″ (9–10 cm). Tiny. Olive-green above, paler below, with 2 dull white wing bars. Eyebrow white; crown orange bordered with yellow (adult males) or solid yellow (females and young males), crown patch separated from white eyebrow by a narrow black line.

Voice
Thin, wiry, ascending *ti-ti-ti* followed by a tumbling chatter.

Habitat
Dense, old conifer stands; also in deciduous forests and thickets in winter.

Range
Alaska, Manitoba, and Newfoundland south to Massachusetts and Michigan, and in the mountains to North Carolina, New Mexico, and S. California. Winters south to Florida, the Gulf Coast, and Guatemala.

Comments
These kinglets are best known as winter visitors, often joining mixed flocks of chickadees, woodpeckers, and creepers. They seem to be entirely insectivorous and are adept at finding hibernating insects in twigs and bark.

White-throated Sparrow
Zonotrichia albicollis
338

6–7" (15–17 cm). Upperparts streaked, underparts clear gray. Head has black-and-white stripes; sharply defined white throat patch; dark bill. Females and young birds are duller.

Voice
Song a clear, whistled *Poor Sam Peabody, Peabody, Peabody,* or *Sweet Sweet Canada, Canada, Canada.* The latter rendition is more appropriate, since most of these birds breed in Canada.

Habitat
Brushy undergrowth in coniferous woodland. Winters in brush woodland, pastures, and suburban areas.

Range
Mackenzie, central Quebec, and Newfoundland south to Pennsylvania, Wisconsin, and North Dakota. Winters south to the Gulf Coast and northern Mexico.

Comments
This very common sparrow is known as a winter visitor and a migrant. During the colder months every hedgerow and thicket seems to be filled with White-throats, and on warm days one can readily hear their plaintive song. When evening comes and they gather to roost in dense thickets, their silvery flocking call is almost as evocative as their song.

Pine Siskin
Carduelis pinus
339

4½–5" (11–13 cm). A dark, streaked finch with a notched tail and small patches of yellow in the wings and tail. Usually seen in flocks, which have a distinctive flight pattern: the birds alternately bunch up, then disperse in undulating flight.

Voice
Distinctive rising *bzzzzzt.* Song like a hoarse goldfinch.

Habitat
Coniferous and mixed woodlands, alder thickets, and brushy pastures.

Range
Alaska, Mackenzie, and Quebec south to Nova Scotia and Nebraska, and in the mountains to Pennsylvania.

Comments
This finch's winter visits to the United States occur mainly when the seed crop has failed farther north. In some years large flocks may appear as far south as Florida. Their principal foods are the seeds of hemlocks, alders, birches, and cedars. Like most northern finches, they are also fond of salt, and can be found along highways that have been salted to melt snow.

Fox Sparrow
Passerella iliaca
340

6½–7½" (16–19 cm). A large, heavy sparrow, boldly striped with rich rufous above; underparts white, heavily spotted with rufous. Sides of head gray with rufous stripes. Tail rufous.

Voice
Loud, short, melodious warble.

Habitat
Coniferous forest undergrowth in summer; dense woodland
thickets, weedy pastures, and brushy roadsides in winter.

Range
Breeds from Unalaska Island in the Aleutians, Alaska and N.
Quebec south to New Brunswick, Colorado, S. California.
Winters south to the Gulf Coast and northern Mexico.

Comments
Away from the breeding grounds, Fox Sparrows are most
conspicuous during spring migration, when one frequently
hears their rich, melodious song coming from brushy thickets
and roadsides. They scratch in leaves for food and often make
so much noise that one expects to find a larger animal.

Brown Thrasher
Toxostoma rufum
341

11½" (29 cm). Blue Jay-sized. Rufous-brown above, white
below with dark brown streaks. Curved bill, long tail.

Voice
A variety of musical phrases, each repeated twice. Call is a
sharp *smack!*

Habitat
Thickets, fields with scrub, and woodland borders.

Range
Alberta, Manitoba, Ontario, and northern New England south
to the Gulf Coast and Florida. Winters in the southern part of
the breeding range.

Comments
Brown Thrashers may be confused with thrushes but are
larger, have longer tails, and are streaked, rather than spotted,
below. They belong to the same family as the Mockingbird,
but, unlike that species, are retiring and secretive. Brown
Thrashers often feed on the ground, scattering dead leaves
with their beaks as they search for insects.

Wood Thrush
Hylocichla mustelina
342

8" (20 cm). Robin-sized. Brown above, bright rusty on head,
and white below with large blackish spots.

Voice
A series of rich, melodious, flutelike phrases; a sharp *pit-pit-
pit-pit.*

Habitat
Moist, deciduous woodlands with a thick understory; also
well-planted parks and gardens.

Range
Manitoba, Ontario, and Nova Scotia south to Florida and the
Gulf of Mexico. Winters mainly from Mexico to Panama, but
a few winter in Texas and S. Florida.

Comments
This is the most familiar of our spotted brown thrushes, and

the only one that nests regularly in the vicinity of houses. The Wood Thrush has one of the most beautiful songs of any North American bird; Thoreau wrote of it: "Whenever a man hears it he is young, and Nature is in her spring; wherever he hears it, it is a new world and a free country, and the gates of heaven are not shut against him."

Veery
Catharus fuscescens
343

6½–7¼" (16–18 cm). Smaller than a Robin. Uniform cinnamon-brown above, with faint spotting on the upper breast. Our only spotted thrush with the upperparts cinnamon.

Voice
Rich, downward spiral with an ethereal quality. Call note a descending *whew* with a vibrant tone.

Habitat
Moist deciduous woodlands.

Range
Breeds from British Columbia and Newfoundland south to New Jersey, Indiana, and, in the mountains, to Georgia, New Mexico, and Oregon. Winters in South America.

Comments
The beautiful song of the Veery sounds best at dusk, as it echoes through the deepening gloom of the forest. The bird is rather difficult to see, but it can be lured into view by an imitation of the squeaking of a bird in distress. Its diet consists of insects obtained on the ground and fruit.

Hermit Thrush
Catharus guttatus
344

6½–7½" (16–19 cm). Smaller than a Robin. The only one of our brown, spotted thrushes with dull brown upperparts and a rusty tail. Frequently flicks its tail.

Voice
Series of clear, musical phrases, each on a different pitch, consisting of a piping introductory note and a reedy tremolo. Call note a low *tuck*.

Habitat
Coniferous and mixed forests; deciduous woodlands and thickets in winter.

Range
Alaska, Saskatchewan, and Labrador south to Long Island and Michigan, and in the mountains to Virginia, New Mexico, and S. California. Winters from Washington and southern New England south to Florida and Guatemala.

Comments
Outside the breeding range, this thrush's beautiful song may occasionally be heard late in spring, before the birds head north to nest. The Hermit Thrush is the only one of our spotted thrushes that winters in the northern states, subsisting on berries and buds. During the warm months, however, it feeds largely on insects taken from the ground.

Swainson's Thrush
Catharus ustulatus
345

6½–7¾" (16–19 cm). Uniformly dull olive-brown above, spotted below, with a buff eye-ring and cheek.

Voice
Song a series of reedy spiraling notes inflected upward.

Habitat
Coniferous forests and willow thickets.

Range
Alaska, Manitoba, and Newfoundland south to northern New England, Michigan, and British Columbia, and in the mountains to West Virginia, Colorado, and S. California. Winters in South America.

Comments
This bird is named after the English naturalist William Swainson (1789–1855). Like the Hermit Thrush, it is a furtive, ground-dwelling bird of the northern forests. Its song, while perhaps not as beautiful as that of the Hermit Thrush, is better known to most bird-watchers because the species sings more frequently during migration. It was formerly called the "Olive-backed Thrush."

Ovenbird
Seiurus aurocapillus
346

6" (15 cm). A large warbler, olive-brown above, white below with dark streaks; conspicuous eye-ring; orange-brown crown bordered with black stripes; pinkish legs.

Voice
Loud staccato song—*teacher, teacher, teacher*—with variation in emphasis. Flight song, often uttered at night, is a bubbling and exuberant series of jumbled notes ending with the familiar *teacher, teacher.*

Habitat
Mature, dry forest with little undergrowth.

Range
Breeds from central Canada to the northern Gulf states. Winters from the Gulf of Mexico south to northern South America.

Comments
This warbler gets its name from its peculiar ground nest, which resembles a miniature Dutch oven. The male frequently has more than 1 mate; 1 was known to have 3 mates. Males have been observed feeding the young.

Winter Wren
Troglodytes troglodytes
347

4–4½" (10 cm). A tiny, dark brown bird with a very short tail and a narrow pale eyebrow.

Voice
A high-pitched, varied, and rapid series of musical trills and chatters; call note an explosive *kit!* or *kit-kit!*

Habitat
Dense tangles and thickets in coniferous and mixed forests.

Range
Alaska and Newfoundland south to Connecticut, Michigan, and S. British Columbia, and in the mountains to California and Georgia. Winters south to S. California and the Gulf Coast.

Comments
This wren moves like a mouse, creeping through the low, dense tangle of branches covering the forest floor. Its nest is among the hardest to find; even when an observer has narrowed the search to a few square feet, he must sometimes give up, so cleverly is the nest concealed. Its song, when recorded and played back at half or quarter speed, shows a remarkable blend of halftones and overtones all sung at the same time.

Brown Creeper
Certhia americana
348

5–5¾" (13–14 cm). Smaller than a sparrow. A slender, streaked, brown bird usually seen creeping up tree trunks, using its stiff tail for support.

Voice
High-pitched, lisping *tsee;* song a thin, descending warble.

Habitat
Deciduous and mixed woodlands.

Range
Breeds from Alaska, Ontario, and Newfoundland south to Nicaragua. Winters south to the Gulf Coast and Florida.

Comments
This inconspicuous bird is most often detected by its soft, lisping call as it works its way up a tree trunk, probing the bark for insects. In late winter and spring one may sometimes hear its song—a thin, musical warble. Unlike nuthatches, the Creeper only moves up a tree trunk; having reached the top, it will fly down to the base of another tree and repeat its spiral ascent.

BUTTERFLIES AND MOTHS

Every type of forest in the East is home to at least a few species of butterflies and moths. Some rest, camouflaged, on the bark of a tree, while others flit from flower to flower, sipping nectar. Even the hottest swamps of the South and the coolest mountaintops of the Appalachians offer a home to these delicate creatures. Included in this section are descriptions of some of the most conspicuous butterfly and moth species found in eastern forests.

Luna Moth
Actias luna
349

Wingspan: 3⅛–4½" (80–115 mm). Wings pale green; fore wings have purple front margins, hind wings have long tails. Caterpillar, to 3⅛" (80 mm), is green with a yellow stripe on each side, spiny tubercles, and hair.

Life Cycle
Female lays eggs that hatch into large, conspicuous caterpillars that feed on walnut, hickory, sweetgum, persimmon, and other deciduous trees. Caterpillar pupates in thin, papery cocoon, generally overwintering on ground. 2 well-defined generations a year in most of range. Adults emerge in April and June but do not feed; they mate and begin life cycle again.

Habitat
Deciduous forests.

Range
Eastern half of the United States and southern Canada.

Comments
This beautiful moth is found only in North America. It is now considered an endangered species because many have been killed by pollutants and pesticides.

Veined White
Artogeia napi
350

Wingspan: 1½–1⅝" (32–41 mm). Rounded wings. Above, delicate white. Below, cream-colored to yellowish; hind-wing veins have light to heavy gray-olive or brown scaling; extreme forms also have scales along veins of other wing surfaces. Some summer broods lack dark vein-scaling. Patches of scent scales (1 for male, 2 for female) occasionally appear on fore wing above, often blurred. If fore-wing tips gray, vein-scaling is heavy.

Life Cycle
Pale, vase-shaped egg. Caterpillar forest-green with darker or yellowish back and side stripes.

Flight
April–August in 2 or 3 broods.

Habitat
Deciduous and coniferous woodlands, forest clearings and edges, roadsides, and in cool, moist places.

Range
Alaska to Labrador, south to Arizona, Montana, Lake States, and New York. Absent from S. California and entire Southeast.

Comments
Many lepidopterists have speculated about the Veined White's changed habitat following the introduction of the Cabbage White in 1860. The Cabbage White is reputed to have taken over as the common white of open landscapes, while the Veined White appears to have retreated to the woodlands, where it is better able to compete. But recent studies also

suggest that these habitat changes may be the effect of human land use and not just interspecies competition. Both species have been found to coexist in many marginal places.

Rosy Maple Moth
Dryocampa rubicunda
351

Wingspan: 1⅛–2″ (30–50 mm). Wings and body pale sulfur-yellow; fore wings pastel pink at base and along outer margin. Caterpillar is green with lengthwise white stripes, reddish-brown head, pink below rear abdominal segments, and has short black spines.

Habitat
Deciduous forests, or open brushy areas wherever maples grow.

Range
Eastern United States and southern Canada, west to the Great Plains.

Comments
This moth's caterpillars, called "Green-striped Maple Worms," are sometimes so abundant that they strip trees of all foliage.

Florida White
Appias drusilla
352

Wingspan: 1⅝–2⅜″ (41–60 mm). Male all white on both surfaces except for black along margin of fore wing's leading edge. Female variable, may be off-white or have dark-bordered fore wing and pale orange hind wing, with fore wing below orange at base and hind wing below pale orange. Both sexes have drawn out, rather pointed fore wing (especially male) concave on outer margin, and silky sheen to inner portion of wings above and hind wing below.

Life Cycle
White eggs turn yellow before hatching; deposited in groups of 2 or 3. Caterpillar, to 1¼″ (33 mm), dark green, gray and white-lined on sides, stippled with fine yellow and black hair. Chrysalis pale gray-green with reddish spots and some black and white markings.

Flight
At least 2 broods annually; virtually year-round in southern part of range.

Habitat
Shaded hardwood hammocks, evergreen river forests, and open areas with flowers.

Range
Resident in S. Texas and S. Florida, rarely emigrating northward as far as Nebraska and New York.

Comments
The Florida White is one of the few North American butterflies that prefers shaded thicket interiors to glades or open sunny spaces. However, it will go into the sun to take nectar from yellow composite flowers.

Falcate Orangetip
Anthocharis midea
353

Wingspan: 1⅜–1½" (35–38 mm). Male white above with bright orange patch near tip of fore wing and black fore-wing cell spot. Female white, with black fore-wing cell spot, lacks orange patch on fore wing but occasionally has pale orange flush at fore-wing tip. Both sexes checked around the edges with black and hooked at tip of fore wing. Below, marbled loosely over hind wing with bright chartreuse or greenish brown.

Life Cycle
Eggs greenish yellow to pale orange, elongated. Grown caterpillar, to ⅞" (22 mm), moss-green, striated with blue, green, and yellow, with orange back stripes and white side stripes. Chrysalis looks like green thorn, thickened in middle.

Flight
April–May; 2 weeks in any locality.

Habitat
Eastern deciduous forests or mixed oak-pine woods or pine barrens; especially glades, roads, rocky sites, and low, moist woods near streams.

Range
S. Wisconsin and central Massachusetts south to Kansas; central Texas and N. Louisiana along coast to Georgia.

Comments
The unmistakable Falcate Orangetip is a familiar spring butterfly in the eastern United States. The name "falcate" refers to the hooked tip of the fore wing. Population levels of this butterfly fluctuate from year to year, and can easily drop to near zero when woodlands are developed. For many years, butterfly seekers have visited West Rock, a protected state park outside New Haven, Connecticut, in the early spring to find the Falcate Orangetip. It appears even on cool and semicloudy days, perhaps an adaptation to the brevity and unpredictability of its early season.

Gypsy Moth
Lymantria dispar
354

Wingspan, male: ¾" (20 mm); female: 1⅛–2¾" (28–70 mm). Male's fore wings brownish gray with brown irregular lines more or less parallel to outer margin; hind wings dark around outer margin. Female's wings yellowish white with narrow wavy lines paralleling outer margin and with series of dark brown dots around outer margin of hind wing. Male has feathery antennae and slender, conical abdomen. Female has threadlike antennae and bulbous abdomen. Caterpillar is gray with long dark hair along sides and 5 pairs of blue tubercles and 6 pairs of red tubercles on its back.

Life Cycle
Female deposits masses of 400–1000 eggs on tree trunks, buildings, or other protected spots in June–July. Eggs overwinter, hatching in spring as young tree leaves are expanding. Emerging caterpillars pass through 5–6 molt stages, feeding voraciously on foliage of more than 500 species

of deciduous and evergreen trees and shrubs. Caterpillar larvae mature by midsummer and spin flimsy cocoons, in which they pupate for 10–14 days. Males emerge July–August with strong flights but emerging females are flightless. Females emit a scent that attracts males. After mating the cycle begins again. 1 generation a year.

Habitat
Deciduous, coniferous, or mixed forests.

Range
Northeastern United States and extreme southern portions of Canada; recently introduced in many other parts of the United States.

Comments
In 1869 this species was accidentally carried to Massachusetts from Europe. Their caterpillars have become major pests of forest and shade trees. They denuded millions of acres of trees in the early 1970s and are advancing westward at a rate of 5–15 miles a year.

Spotted Tiger Moth
Halisidota maculata
355

Wingspan: 1⅜–2″ (35–50 mm). Fore wings beige with brown mottling and spots. Hind wings translucent yellowish. Caterpillar is yellowish white in the North and mostly black in the South with long pencils of white hair on thorax and abdomen; head black.

Life Cycle
Caterpillars emerge in spring and eat foliage of poplar, maple, and other deciduous trees. Cocoon is spun of silk mixed with hairs shed during spinning process. Pupa overwinters; adults emerge by following midsummer, and females lay eggs.

Habitat
Deciduous forests and woods.

Range
Quebec to North Carolina, west to California.

Comments
The Hickory Tiger (*H. caryae*), same size, has silver-spotted fore wings and occurs east of the Rocky Mountains in the northern United States and southern Canada, to Texas and Arizona.

Pepper-and-salt Skipper
Amblyscirtes hegon
356

Wingspan: ⅞–1″ (22–25 mm). Black above with vaguely greenish cast; faint, light fore-wing spots and moderately developed white, curved fore-wing spot band. Below, putty-gray with understated light spots; greenish cast over hind wing. Checkered fringes.

Life Cycle
Caterpillar light green with green back stripes, yellow side stripes, and brown head. Chrysalis straw-colored with greenish tinge.

Flight
1 brood, perhaps 2; May–August.

Habitat
Forest edges, clearings and glades, coniferous and mixed woods, boggy stream banks, and hayfields.

Range
South-central and southeastern Canada to Iowa and Georgia; possibly Texas and Mississippi.

Comments
Unlike most roadside skippers, this species prefers northern and Appalachian woodlands.

White-marked Tussock Moth
Orgyia leucostigma
357

Wingspan, male: 1⅛–1¼″ (28–33 mm); female wingless, body ½–⅝″ (12–16 mm). Male's wings dark gray with tan and black mottling; antennae feathery. Female is gray-brown and has threadlike antennae and very broad abdomen, which is conspicuous until eggs are laid. Caterpillar, to 1¼″ (33 mm), has a bright red head, pale brown body with yellow and black stripes, and pencils of black hair and white tufts on abdomen.

Life Cycle
Female lays single large egg mass encased in foamy white secretion that forms protective covering. Eggs overwinter. In spring, caterpillars emerge to feed on foliage of many deciduous trees and shrubs. Caterpillars pupate in cocoons spun of silk and body hair on bark, tree branches, or other support. There are 2 or more generations each year, depending on local climatic conditions.

Habitat
Deciduous and mixed forests.

Range
East of the Rocky Mountains.

Comments
The female moth dies soon after laying a single mass of eggs, which overwinter. Caterpillars pupate in cocoons spun of silk and hair on bark, tree branches, or other supports. There are 2 or more generations a year. A number of closely similar species occur in the United States and Canada. At times the populations of any of these may become so large locally that these pests severely defoliate host trees.

Promethea Moth
Callosamia promethea
358

Wingspan: 2¾–4″ (70–100 mm). Sexes dissimilar. Male's body, legs, and wings largely brownish black with faint spots (or no spots), rather obscure pale crossband, reddish tip enclosing prominent eyespot, and tan outer margin with wavy dark brown lines and spots. Female's body and wings reddish brown with markings similar to those of male but much more prominent and contrasting. Caterpillar, to 3″ (75 mm), is bluish green with 2 pairs of red tubercles on thorax, 6 rows of

small black tubercles on thorax and abdomen, 1 yellow
tubercle on abdomen, yellow rear and legs, and a yellowish-
green head; sometimes entire body appears frosted.

Life Cycle
Female lays eggs that hatch into large, conspicuous
caterpillars. Prefers wild cherry, tuliptree, sweetgum, laurels,
and a great variety of other deciduous trees. Caterpillars spin
large brown silken cocoons on plant stems or branches near
ground, incorporating leaves. Pupae overwinter; adults emerge
late spring to early summer, mate, and begin cycle again.

Habitat
Deciduous woods and open areas.

Range
Southeastern Canada and the eastern half of the United States,
west to the Great Plains.

Comments
Male moths may fly in the late afternoon like butterflies, but
females fly only at night. They were once considered to be a
possible source of raw silk, but finding cheap labor to unreel
the cocoons proved impossible in North America.

Carolina Satyr
Hermeuptychia sosybius
359

Wingspan: 1⅛–1⅝" (28–41 mm). Wings rounded. Above,
dark brown with eyespots minute or absent. Below, brown
frosted with white scales, crossed by darker brown lines and,
just inside hind-wing margin, a row of 6 small eyespots with
light rims and bluish pupils, second and fifth largest.

Life Cycle
Egg green, rounded. Caterpillar light green with dark green
stripes and fine, yellowish pile. Chrysalis curved, olive.

Flight
Successive broods in Florida; year-round. 2 broods farther
north; spring–late summer.

Habitat
Deciduous woodlands with standing water, pinelands, and
shady meadows; more common at lower altitudes.

Range
Southeast, from New Jersey to Florida and around Gulf to
Texas, north in Mississippi Valley at least to Kentucky.

Comments
One of the smallest satyrs in North America, it is abundant
and widespread in the Southeast, where luxuriant growth
provides moisture, shade, and grasses. Unlike most satyrs, the
Carolina visits flowers frequently.

Polyphemus Moth
Antheraea polyphemus
360

Wingspan: 3½–5½" (90–140 mm). Wings brownish yellow
or ocher with a black and white irregular line parallel to the
paler outer border. Fore wings have eyespot edged in yellow.

Hind wings have larger eyespot edged in yellow and surrounded by black and blue. Caterpillar, to 3½" (90 mm), is plump, bright green, with yellow bands, and has red and silver tubercles.

Life Cycle
Female lays eggs after flying in summer. Eggs hatch into green caterpillars that feed on numerous deciduous tree and shrub leaves, such as oak, hickory, maple, and birch. Caterpillar spins dense cocoon, usually wrapped in a leaf that, in autumn, falls to the ground, where insect passes winter in pupal stage. Adults take flight in July. 2 generations are produced each year in the South, 1 in the North.

Habitat
Deciduous forests.

Range
East of the Rocky Mountains from Canada to Mexico.

Comments
Because of the conspicuous eyespot on each hind wing, this moth is named after Polyphemus, the one-eyed giant of Greek myths. At night adults often fly to artificial lights. The fully grown caterpillars spin tough egg-shaped cocoons, which may remain attached to branches, but usually fall with the leaves in late autumn. There are 2 generations a year in the South; 1 in the North.

Little Wood Satyr
Megisto cymela
361

Wingspan: 1¾–1⅞" (44–48 mm). Wings rounded. Above, dull brown; below, dull brown to tan, crossed by darker brown lines. Each wing, both above and below, has 2 prominent black eyespots with yellow rims and 2 light pupils; smaller eyespots may be clustered around large ones; margins are rimmed with brown lines. Populations in southern Florida have violet-gray upper side.

Life Cycle
Egg pale yellowish green. Caterpillar brown, stippled with minute white tubercles; overwinters partially grown. Chrysalis rounded and curved at rear toward point of attachment, usually on a sedge stem.

Flight
1 brood in North; April until midsummer, beginning as late as June in Wisconsin. 2 broods in far southern part of range; March–October.

Habitat
Deciduous woods with glades and ponds, pinelands, nearby thickets and groves, salt bays and brackish streamsides, hammocks, plantations, and clearings.

Range
Saskatchewan, Dakotas, NE. Colorado, Texas, and northeastern Mexico east throughout southern Canada and eastern United States.

Comments
Despite its name, the Little Wood Satyr is larger than most of the other small satyrs formerly grouped together in the genus *Euptychia*. It is highly adaptable to moderate environmental change, requiring only that some woods, brush, grass, and moisture remain to provide shelter and food. With a fairly long flight period and prolific reproduction, the Little Wood Satyr can be enormously abundant under the right conditions. The adult expertly negotiates tall grass and thick shrubbery with its dancing, slow-motion flight.

Large Wood Nymph
Cercyonis pegala
362

Wingspan: 2–2⅞″ (52–73 mm). Variable. Above, light cocoa-brown to deep chocolate-brown (very pale in northern Great Basin). Below, paler and heavily striated with darker scales. Normally fore wing above and below has 1 or 2 small to very large black eyespots, often yellow-rimmed, with small white or large blue pupil; eyespots may lie in a vague or discrete broad band of bright or dark yellow. Hind wing above may have small eyespots; hind wing below may have 1 or 2 small eyespots or a full row of 6 eyespots. Hind wing below usually divided into darker inner and lighter outer portion by single zigzagged, dark line. Female normally larger, paler, with bigger eyespots.

Life Cycle
Egg lemon-yellow, keg-shaped, and ribbed. Caterpillar grass-green, with 4 lengthwise yellow lines, fine, fuzzy pile, and 2 reddish tails; overwinters shortly after hatching. Chrysalis green, rather plump.

Flight
1 brood; generally June–August or September, varying with locality.

Habitat
Open oak, pine, and other woodlands; meadows, fields, and along slow watercourses with long, overhanging grasses; marshes, prairie groves, thickets, and roadsides.

Range
Central Canada to central California, Texas and central Florida. Absent from Pacific Northwest Coast and much of Gulf region.

Comments
The Large Wood Nymph occupies much of North America; it is the largest wood nymph and the only one east of the Mississippi. Extremely variable, this butterfly has been given dozens of names. Today, all are considered a single species. As they perch on tree trunks or boughs to bask or drink sap, Large Wood Nymphs blend beautifully with the bark. When disturbed or seeking mates, they fly erratically through tall grasses, with little speed but great skill and endurance. Western wood nymphs visit such flowers as alfalfa and spiraea, while eastern populations seem to favor rotting fruit.

Palmetto Skipper
Euphyes arpa
363

Wingspan: 1⅜–1¼″ (35–44 mm). Long, triangular wings. Male tawny-orange on inner two thirds above, crossed on fore wing by dark patch of scent scales, brown beyond; female dark brown with square apricot-colored spots across fore-wing disk above. Both sexes orange beneath on leading edge and tip of fore wing and on hind wing; basal third of fore wing black. Head and collar golden.

Life Cycle
Caterpillar light green with black collar, black and white head, and yellow stripes; lives in cylinder of leaves.

Flight
Successive broods; March–December.

Habitat
Coastal stands of saw palmetto.

Range
Coastal plain of Mississippi, Alabama, Florida, and Georgia.

Comments
The Palmetto Skipper was first described from a painting done in Georgia by John Abbot, an early 19th-century naturalist; however, it is now a very uncommon insect in Georgia.

Hobomok Skipper
Poanes hobomok
364

Wingspan: 1–1⅜″ (25–35 mm). Above, male yellow-orange with dark borders, black cell spot; female tawny-orange, brown fore-wing base. Below, fore wing yellower than above in both sexes; tips and outer margins dark and may be bordered with violet; hind wing violet-edged, broadly on female, narrowly on male, with brown base and broad, curved, yellow spot band or broad, yellow disk; bright spots on male, dull on female. Dark female form dark brown above, with white spots and small fore-wing cell spot.

Life Cycle
Caterpillar dark green or brown with rows of tiny black spines; caterpillar or chrysalis may overwinter.

Flight
1 extended brood; May–September, although flight period in a single area usually more restricted.

Habitat
Deciduous woods and adjacent roads, valley bottoms, and moist gullies; hedgerows, fields, and meadows.

Range
Saskatchewan to Maritime Provinces, south to Georgia, Arkansas, New Mexico, north to Dakota Black Hills.

Comments
The Hobomok Skipper is a fairly common butterfly over much of its broad range, which overlaps extensively with that of the Zabulon Skipper.

Leonardus Skipper
Hesperia leonardus
365

Wingspan: ⅞–1⅜" (22–35 mm). Above, dark brown; male has broad dark border, tawny-orange toward base, and large patch of scent scales; female all dark brown except for tawny-orange bands on each wing. Below, fore wing orange at base, brown along margin, yellow across disk; hind wing rust-colored on male, chestnut on female, both with offset whitish spots in limited band.

Life Cycle
Young caterpillar overwinters; mature caterpillar maroon with green highlights.

Flight
1 brood; August–September.

Habitat
Fields, meadows, and nearby roads, pine-oak barrens, and oak openings.

Range
Ontario and Nova Scotia to Carolinas, Missouri, Alabama, and Louisiana.

Comments
The Leonardus Skipper can be quite abundant in the Adirondacks after most others are gone.

Hackberry Butterfly
Asterocampa celtis
366

Wingspan: 1¾–2¼" (41–57 mm). Complexly and variably marked above with brown, black, and purplish gray. Typical male brown to grayish brown above; female lighter, tawnier. Above, both have dark fore-wing tips with white spots, 1 black, broad eyespot, usually without pupil, on fore-wing, and, just inside hind-wing margin, a row of black eyespots, which sometimes have white pupils; fore-wing cell has 1 dark bar and 2 dark spots. Below, eyespots repeated, amid purplish gray-brown bars, spots, and chevrons and whiter patches. Male's wings narrow, concave and elongated at tip; female's broader, rounder. Green sheen to wings when fresh.

Life Cycle
Egg pale yellow to white. Caterpillar, 1¼" (32 mm), rather sluglike, bright grass-green with yellow and chartreuse lengthwise stripes, 2 tails projecting from rear and small, branched horns on head. Chrysalis, to ⅞" (22 mm), bluish green, sharply horned and razor-backed.

Flight
1 brood in North; June–August. 3 broods southward; March–October.

Habitat
In vicinity of hackberry trees in deciduous woodlands along roads, trails, and margins; also in suburbs and city parks.

Range
S. Ontario and North and South Dakota east to Massachusetts, south to N. Florida and E. Texas.

Comments
Populations of Hackberry Butterflies have recently been
divided into 3 main species groups: those related to the
Hackberry Butterfly; to the Empress Leilia (*A. leilia*); and to
the Tawny Emperor (*A. clyton*). The Hackberry Butterfly's
closest relatives are the Empress Antonia (*A.
antonia*) and the
Empress Alicia (*A. celtis* form "alicia"), but the latter may
actually be a population of the Hackberry Butterfly that occurs
along the Gulf. To confuse matters further, the name Empress
Alicia has also been applied to a different eastern Florida
population of the Hackberry Butterfly.

Red Admiral
Vanessa atalanta
367

Wingspan: 1¾–2¼" (44–57 mm). Fore-wing tip extended,
clipped. Above, black with orange-red to vermilion bars across
fore wing and on hind-wing border. Below, mottled black,
brown, and blue with pink bar on fore wing. White spots at
fore-wing tip above and below, bright blue patch on lower
hind-wing angle above and below.

Life Cycle
Egg greenish, barrel-shaped. Caterpillar, to 1¼" (32 mm),
patterned light and dark from shiny black and yellow to
brown and tan; warty and spiny. Chrysalis brown, gold-
flecked; has dull short tubercles on thorax and curved
abdomen. Adults and chrysalises overwinter in mild areas.

Flight
2 broods in most of range; generally April or May–October,
year-round in far South.

Habitat
Forest margins and glades, rivers, shorelines; also barnyards,
gardens, parks, roads; meadows, fields, and savannahs; open
woods and clearings.

Range
Subarctic Canada to Central America; naturalized in Hawaii.

Comments
Unmistakable and unforgettable, the Red Admiral will alight
on a person's shoulder day after day in a garden. This species
emigrates north in the spring, and there is some evidence of a
dispersed return flight in the fall. If the season is mild,
occasional individuals may pass a winter in the North;
however, Red Admirals are not usually year-round residents in
freezing climates. In midsummer it is not unusual to see them
chasing each other or Painted Ladies just before a
thunderstorm or at dusk. During the full sunshine hours, they
are more likely to be found quietly drinking from flowers or
fruit.

Spicebush Swallowtail
Pterourus troilus
368

Wingspan: 3½–4½" (89–114 mm). Both sexes black-brown
above with cream-white to cream-yellow spots around fore-
wing outer margin; hind wing above black at base, with 1

bright orange spot on leading edge, 1 on trailing edge. Male hind wing above is broadly clouded with diffuse but brilliant blue-green between spots. Series of sharply defined, pale blue-green crescents runs around outer curve of wing. Female bluer above than male; hind wing has broad cloud of dark green and blue scales and lime-green crescents. Below, hind wing of both sexes has 2 curved rows of bright orange-red spots (1 around margin, 1 parallel but midwing), enclosing area heavily spotted with blue. 1 rounded black tail on the hind wing.

Life Cycle
Pale green egg. Caterpillar, to 1⅝" (41 mm), is dark green with 2 pairs of yellowish eyespots on front and rear of hump. Winter chrysalis, to 1¼" (32 mm), smooth, bark-colored, swollen about wing cases; summer chrysalis may be green.

Flight
Spring–early autumn; dates and number of broods vary, depending on latitude.

Habitat
Woods, forest edges, and pine barrens; also meadows, fields, rights-of-way, along streams, and in gardens.

Range
Eastern North America below southern Canada, becoming more rare westerly; absent from prairies except where wooded; in the west only rarely reaching High Plains or Rocky Mountains.

Comments
A grand and beautiful butterfly, the Spicebush Swallowtail takes nectar from joe-pye Weed, jewelweed, and honeysuckle. Like black female Tigers, it mimics the Pipevine Swallowtail.

Mourning Cloak
Nymphalis antiopa
369

Wingspan: 2⅞–3⅜" (73–86 mm). Large. Wing margins ragged. Dark with pale margins. Above, rich brownish maroon, iridescent at close range, with ragged, cream-yellow band, bordered inwardly by brilliant blue spots all along both wings. Below, striated, ash-black with row of blue-green to blue-gray chevrons just inside dirty yellow border.

Life Cycle
Egg pale, becoming black before hatching; laid in groups resembling small berries on or around a twig. Caterpillar, to 2" (51 mm), velvety black with white speckles, a row of red spots on back, and several rows of branched black bristles; has rust-colored legs. Feeds in groups. Chrysalis, to ⅞" (28 mm), tan to gray, with 2 head horns, a "beak," and several thorny tubercles down the body; hangs upside down.

Flight
Number of broods varies with latitude and altitude; year-round, most common in spring, late summer, and early autumn.

Habitat
Watercourses, sunny glades, forest borders, parks, gardens, open woodlands, and groves.

Range
Much of Northern Hemisphere south to northern South America where sufficient moisture occurs, except for high Arctic and subtropical regions.

Comments
Absolutely unique, the Mourning Cloak camouflages itself perfectly against dark bark at rest, then flaps instantly into flight at the approach of any predator, emitting an audible "click." Few butterflies show such a great contrast between the drab underside and colorful upper side. In summer, adults may be attracted with fruit for closer observation.

Tiger Swallowtail
Pterourus glaucus
370

Wingspan: 3⅛–5½" (79–140 mm). Males and some females above and below are yellow with black tiger-stripes across wings and black borders spotted with yellow. Long, black tail on each hind wing. Hind wing above and below usually has row of blue patches inside margin, with orange spot above and sometimes much orange below, running through yellow. Dark-form females are black above with border-spotting of yellow, blue, and orange (blue sometimes becomes cloud on hind wing), below brown-black with shadowy "tiger" pattern. Yellow spots along outer edge of fore wing below are separate in all but northernmost populations. Most have orange uppermost spot on outer margin of hind wing above and below and orange spot on trailing edge. Alaskan, Canadian, and northeastern butterflies smaller and paler than eastern populations.

Life Cycle
Very large yellow-green, globular egg. Young caterpillar brown and white, resembling bird droppings; mature caterpillar, to 2" (51 mm), is green, swollen in front, with big orange and black eyespots and band between third and fourth segments. Mottled green or brown sticklike chrysalis, to 1¼" (32 mm), overwinters.

Flight
1–3 broods; spring–autumn, actual dates vary with latitude.

Habitat
Broadleaf woodland glades, gardens, parks, orchards, and along roads and rivers.

Range
Central Alaska and Canada to Atlantic; southeast of Rockies to Gulf of Mexico. Rarer at northern and southern edges of range.

Comments
This species is the most widely distributed Tiger Swallowtail, and one of the most common and conspicuous butterflies of

the East. Feeding in groups, adults take nectar from a wide range of flowers. The black female form has evolved to mimic the distasteful Pipevine Swallowtail; its presence in the population reflects the abundance of the species it mimics.

Zebra Longwing
Heliconius charitonius
371

Wingspan: 3–3⅜″ (76–86 mm). Wings long and narrow. Jet-black above, banded with lemon-yellow (sometimes pale yellow). Beneath similar; bases of wings have crimson spots.

Life Cycle
Egg yellow, resembling miniature ear of corn. Caterpillar, to 1⅝″ (41 mm), white; 6 dark-patched rows of black, branched spines. Mottled brown chrysalis, to 1⅛″ (28 mm), has metallic spots on sides; spiny.

Flight
Multiple broods; year-round in Florida, except when colder weather occurs.

Habitat
Hammocks, thick woods, and forest edges.

Range
Resident from Texas to South Carolina, south through West Indies and Latin America.

Comments
The Zebra's usual flight is slow, feeble, and wafting, although it is able to dart quickly to shelter. Zebra Longwings roost communally at night, assembling at dusk. Hammocks and thickets throughout Everglades National Park are good places to see gatherings of these butterflies.

Palamedes Swallowtail
Pterourus palamedes
372

Wingspan: 3⅛–5½″ (79–140 mm). Very large with rounded wings. Blackish brown above, rimmed by yellow spots and crossed midwing by yellow band, which is broken on fore wing but is entire on hind wing, where it ends in bright blue spot. Below, fore wing has 2 rows of yellow border-spots; hind wing has orange spots enclosing row of blue and gold to olive clouds and long, straight yellow bar parallel to abdomen down inner third of hind wing below.

Life Cycle
Yellowish-green egg. Grass-green caterpillar, to 2″ (51 mm), has double set of rimmed orange eyespots with black pupils. Possibly overwinters as a caterpillar as well as a chrysalis, unusual for group. Chrysalis, to 1⅝″ (41 mm), slightly mottled, greenish.

Flight
April–August in mid-range; February–December in up to 3 broods in Florida.

Habitat
Subtropical wetlands, coastal swamps, and humid woods with standing water.

Range
Resident from S. Maryland to S. Florida, throughout
Southwest, around Gulf to S. Texas and northern Mexico.
North in Mississippi Valley to Missouri.

Comments
This butterfly is the signature swallowtail of the great swamps
—the Everglades, Big Cypress, Great Dismal, Okefenokee,
and Okeechobee. The adults take nectar from pickerelweed
and are reported to roost communally in oaks and palmettos.

Hammock Skipper
Polygonus leo
373

Wingspan: 1¾–2″ (44–51 mm). Long-winged; hind wing
curved into a stumpy lobe. Warm brown above, with several
square, glassy white spots on fore-wing disk, smaller pair near
tip. Below, fore-wing tip and hind wing frosty violet with
brown bands; hind wing has 1 small brown dot near base.
Purple in sun.

Life Cycle
Caterpillar yellowish green with yellow stripes and patches
along its sides.

Flight
Several broods in Florida; year-round. Fewer broods from
Texas westward; mainly late summer and fall.

Habitat
Shady glades in hardwood hammocks.

Range
S. California, Arizona, W. Texas, S. New Mexico, Florida
south to Argentina; also West Indies.

Comments
The Hammock Skipper's name derives from its strict habitat
preference in Florida, where it is common.

Florida Purplewing
Eunica tatila
374

Wingspan: 1⅝–2″ (41–51 mm). Fore-wing tip concavely
indented at tip. Dark brown above, inner two thirds heavily
overlaid with iridescent purple scales. Fore-wing tips have 7
prominent white spots and bars. Mottled dark and dull brown
below. Hind wing has eyespots above and below.

Life Cycle
Unknown.

Flight
Several broods; any month.

Habitat
Dense coastal hardwood hammocks.

Range
Central America and Antilles north to S. Florida.

Comments
Purplewings haunt the undeveloped Florida hardwood

hammocks. Their undersides are camouflaged against the tree bark on which they perch. The purple iridescence shows only in direct sunshine; they look brown in the shade. Sometimes purplewings take to the ground to drink from fruit or mud, or wander out to the edges of hammocks or along roadsides.

Spring Azure
Celastrina ladon
375

Wingspan: ¾–1¼″ (19–32 mm). Spring brood deep silvery violet-blue above, female has coal-black fore-wing border; below, slate-gray, black checkered border, and variable black hind-wing interior spotting with marginal spotting small and fading toward fore wing. Summer brood blanched violet-blue above, with pale white basal half to fore wing and most of hind wing; female black-bordered and much whiter; below, washed-out pale white with faint markings.

Life Cycle
Egg pea-green; laid in flowers and buds. Caterpillar highly variable; usually cream-colored, daubed rosy, checkered on dusky back and green side slashes. Plump, golden-brown chrysalis overwinters.

Flight
Multiple broods on East Coast; March to mid-April, May–June, mid-July to August. Fewer northward, perhaps more to South; 1–2 broods in West.

Habitat
Open deciduous woods, roadsides, and brushy areas from sea level through mountains; clearings, glades, and many other places in and near woodlands.

Range
Alaska east across Canada, and south through entire United States to Mexico and Panama in mountains.

Comments
Widespread and common in early spring, Spring Azures signal the return of warm weather. This species presents a complex set of identities to entomologists; only recently was the Sooty Azure recognized as a separate species. Genetic and biological evidence suggests several distinct butterflies still remain within the broad definition of the Spring Azure. A darker, bluer first brood that is highly variable in form produces chrysalises that may overwinter or emerge the same year. Chrysalises from the first of the paler, single form, late spring and summer broods will hatch several weeks later, with the last ones of late summer overwintering. The caterpillars of different broods feed on different plants depending upon what is flowering at the time.

Banded Hairstreak
Satyrium calanus
376

Wingspan: 1–1¼″ (25–32 mm). Above, jet-black with sooty cast. Below, male warm brownish black; female slate-colored; fore-wing midband consists of thin rectangles, continuous although sometimes twisted, broken slightly if at all; band

and other dashes white-outlined on outer edges. Blue patch near tail; orange on either side may extend along margins.

Life Cycle
Egg overwinters. Caterpillar yellowish green or brownish, with duller broad transverse side stripes and deep brown wide band along back. Hairy, mottled brown chrysalis holds fast with tight silken girdle.

Flight
1 brood; late June–early July.

Habitat
Deciduous forests eastward; woodland clearings, edges, roadsides.

Range
E. Saskatchewan, S. Wyoming, and SE. Utah south to Gulf, east to Atlantic.

Comments
This most common of dark eastern hairstreaks clings to low leaves and shrubs bathed in sunbeams and engages all newcomers in territorial tussles. Sometimes half a dozen may chase around together before settling. They can be found on their favorite nectar plants, such as milkweed, dogbane, daisies, and sumac. Banded Hairstreaks and their allies are some of the most variable butterflies; certain identifications often can be made only by experts. The Banded Hairstreak may actually prove to be a group of sibling species; southern populations may be distinct. Formerly called *S. falacer*.

Big Poplar Sphinx
Pachysphinx modesta
377

Wingspan: 3½–5½" (90–140 mm). Fore wings with alternating bands colored mouse-gray to velvet-brown. Hind wings suffused with red tinge; blue-gray in wing base. Caterpillar, to 4" (100 mm), is bluish green with small yellowish-white dots, oblique white lines on sides, and short tail horn.

Life Cycle
Female lays eggs that hatch into caterpillars that feed on foliage of deciduous trees, especially poplars and willows. A light cocoon is spun and pupa overwinters among leaves on ground. Adults take flight May–August, mate, and begin new life cycle.

Habitat
Deciduous and mixed forests.

Range
Coast to coast in southern Canada, south to Gulf in the East; in the West, south to Colorado in the Rockies.

Comments
This moth has one of the greatest wingspans of all North American sphinx moths. Adults are rapid fliers and feed on nectar.

Hickory Hairstreak
Satyrium caryaevorus
378

Wingspan: 1–1¼" (25–32 mm). Above, brown-black with slate-colored cast. Below, cool soot-gray to slate, overlaid with distinctly bluish cast when fresh. Fore-wing midband white-outlined on both inner and outer edges, broken with branches strongly offset, inflated near top (especially in male). Small orange-red area, large blue hind-wing spot below near tail.

Life Cycle
Grass-green caterpillar has straight dark green band on back, dark green side marks. Sparsely hairy chrysalis mottled brown.

Flight
1 brood; June–July.

Habitat
Mixed forest zone south of boreal forests; deciduous woods, roadsides, and edges of fields.

Range
Minnesota and Quebec south through Iowa and Connecticut to Kentucky and W. Pennsylvania; rarely farther south.

Comments
Easily overlooked, Hickory Hairstreaks are difficult to spot among hordes of Banded Hairstreaks, although they too are sporadically very abundant. The Northeast was inundated with this butterfly in the early 1960s, and again in 1980. It is not known whether Hickory Hairstreaks expand their range after long retractive periods or undergo explosive local booms. This species seeks nectar from dogwood, milkweed, Queen Anne's lace, and many other flowers.

INSECTS AND SPIDERS

By far the most numerous animals on earth, insects and spiders are also fascinating. Some have carved out a niche for themselves as tiny predators in an immense landscape; others inhabit the inner recesses of fallen logs or make a home on the underside of leaves. Included in this section are descriptions of some of the most conspicuous and abundant insects and spiders in eastern forests.

Eastern Eyed Click Beetle
Alaus oculatus
379

1–1¾″ (25–45 mm). Elongate. Shiny black with small, white dotlike scales on back. Upper part of thorax has 2 large, velvety black eyespots surrounded by a dense ring of white scales. Elytra have thin lengthwise ridges with speckled depressions in between.

Habitat
Deciduous and mixed woods, especially around rotting timber.

Range
East of the Rocky Mountains, except in the Southeast.

Life Cycle
Eggs are laid in soil. Larvae grow slowly and pupate in unlined cells below the ground or within rotting wood. Adults are numerous from spring to September.

Comments
Adults sometimes rest on trunks of orchard trees, particularly on pruned trees. The related Blind Click Beetle (*A. myops*), 1–1½″ (25–38 mm), occurs in the Southeast; it is reddish brown to black and has vague whitish-gray eyespots. The Arizona Eyed Click Beetle (*A. lusciosus*), 1¾″ (45 mm), has circular eyespots and yellowish-white scales on its body.

Common Black Ground Beetles
Pterostichus spp.
380

½–⅝″ (13–16 mm). Elongate. Shiny black. Antennae, legs, and downturned sides of elytra reddish brown. Head narrows behind eyes. Elytra have rounded forward corners, lengthwise grooves.

Habitat
Beneath stones, boards, and logs in gardens, moist woods, and sometimes fields planted with forage or grain.

Range
Throughout North America.

Life Cycle
Eggs are left singly in upper soil mid- to late summer. Larvae overwinter and feed in early spring before pupating. Adults emerge July–September.

Comments
This is one of the few genera of ground beetles found coast to coast.

Black-horned Pine Borer
Callidium antennatum
381

⅜–½″ (11–14 mm). Flattened. Bright bluish black or purplish. Antennae shorter than elytra, which have low lengthwise ridges and fine pits. Femora swollen. Larva is yellowish white, legless.

Habitat
Coniferous forests and lumberyards.

Range
Throughout North America.

Life Cycle
Eggs are laid on bark of dying or felled trees that have not been stripped of bark. Larvae bore between the bark and wood, eating out extensive passageways. They pupate beneath bark, emerging as adults May–July. 1 generation a year.

Comments
This borer appears to favor felled trees that have been seasoned for one winter.

Horned Fungus Beetle
Bolitotherus cornutus
382

⅜–½″ (8–12 mm). Oblong, rough. Dull black to dark brown. Clubbed antennae arise far apart. Male has 2 hornlike projections on upper part of thorax that extend forward beyond head and 1 forked horn on middle of head; female has only tubercles on upper part of thorax.

Habitat
Woods.

Range
Eastern United States and adjacent Canada.

Life Cycle
Eggs are deposited in or on fungi. Larvae pupate within woody fungi or in nearby soil. Adults are active June–August.

Comments
If disturbed, adults feign death and remain motionless, resembling fragments of rotted wood.

Elephant Stag Beetle
Lucanus elephus
383

Male 1¾–2⅜″ (45–60 mm) including jaws; female 1⅛–1⅜″ (30–35 mm). Elongate, somewhat flat. Shiny reddish brown with blackish antennae and legs. Male's head is wider than front portion of thorax and bears a crest above eyes. Male's antlerlike jaws, as long as head and front portion of thorax combined, have small teeth along inner edge, and are forked at end. Female's head much narrower than thorax; jaws are barely longer than head.

Habitat
Woods.

Range
Virginia and North Carolina west to Oklahoma, northeast to Illinois.

Life Cycle
Eggs are laid in crevices of wet decaying wood. Larvae pupate in earthen cells near food source. Adults emerge July–August and live 2 or more years. 1 generation a year.

Comments
Males are formidable in self-defense, but these insects have difficulty righting themselves if overturned. They sometimes fly to lights at night.

Bark Beetles
Scolytus spp.
384

⅛–¼" (3–5 mm). Shiny reddish brown, dark brown, or black. Cylindrical, rounded sharply at front of thorax and behind elytra. Concave below at rear of abdomen. Male's abdomen usually has blunt spines below, pointing to rear. Elytra grooved, pitted. Antennae clubbed.

Habitat
Deciduous and mixed forests.

Range
Throughout North America.

Life Cycle
In early spring female cuts holes for eggs in bark of dying or dead trees and deposits each egg in separate side tunnel of inner bark, hollowed parallel to grain. Larvae bore deeper, overwinter, and pupate in second summer. Adults emerge late summer or fall.

Comments
These beetles do major damage to trees. The European Elm Bark Beetle (*S. multistriatus*), ⅛" (3 mm), is shiny reddish brown and the male has 1 blunt spine below its abdomen. It carries the fungus that causes Dutch elm disease, and ranges east of the Mississippi and farther west. The Hickory Bark Beetle (*S. quadrispinosus*), ⅛–¼" (3–5 mm), is black or dark brown and the male has 4 side spines beneath its abdomen. It attacks hickory trees throughout the eastern United States.

Divergent Metallic Wood Borer
Dicerca divaricata
385

⅝–⅞" (16–21 mm). Cylindrical. Pale brown or gray with bronze highlights above, shiny coppery below. Elytra have scattered, raised smooth areas; tips of elytra usually diverge.

Habitat
Forests and orchards.

Range
Newfoundland to Georgia, west to California, north to Alaska.

Life Cycle
Eggs are laid on bark. Larvae feed on inner wood and pupate in tunnels close to bark. Adults active May–August.

Comments
These larvae damage coniferous timber trees and many orchard trees. They are generally unnoticed on ash, birch, elm, ironwood, and maple trees.

Twig Pruners
Elaphidionoides spp.
386

⅜–⅝" (9–17 mm). Slender, almost cylindrical. Brown except thick shiny base of antennae dark reddish brown. Body covered by patches of fine, short grayish-yellow hair. Male's antennae are longer than body, female's slightly shorter.

Habitat
Deciduous forests.

Range
Eastern United States and Canada.

Life Cycle
Eggs are laid on twigs, into which larvae tunnel. Later, larvae cut through twigs, causing them to break off. Pupation occurs in twigs or in soil.

Comments
Species differ noticeably in the coarseness of spines at the tips of the elytra and in the shape of the upper part of the thorax (pronotum). The Spiny Twig Pruner (*E. mucronatus*) has a cylindrical pronotum and coarse spines. Its larvae feed on dead hardwoods in the East. The southeastern Gray Twig Pruner (*E. villòsus*), ½–¾" (12–18 mm), has a barrel-shaped front portion of thorax, and its larvae eat twigs of living hardwoods, pruning off new growth.

Slender Checkered Beetles
Cymatodera spp.
387

¼–⅜" (5–11 mm). Slender with long slender legs and threadlike antennae. Earth-brown or slightly paler, covered with spiny yellow hair. Generally unmarked, but elytra pitted shallowly in lengthwise rows.

Habitat
Woods with oaks.

Range
Throughout North America; individual species of *Cymatodera* have localized ranges.

Life Cycle
Female actively hunts on foliage and twigs of oaks for gall wasps, then lays eggs close to the site of gall wasp eggs, sometimes attacking gall wasps. After a few weeks, beetle larvae hatch, invade developing galls (swellings in plant tissue), feed on wasp larvae, eventually killing hosts and ending development of galls. Beetle larvae usually pupate in galls. Larvae, pupae, or adults overwinter. Adults emerge in summer.

Comments
These beetles help reduce the number of gall-formers on oak trees and are considered to be highly beneficial.

Red Flat Bark Beetle
Cucujus clavipes
388

⅜–½" (10–14 mm). Elongate, sides almost parallel, constricted between front portion of thorax and elytral bases. Bright yellowish red with black antennae and eyes; elytra dull red below. Elytra extremely flat, sometimes slightly concave. Larva is brownish yellow.

Habitat
Woods under bark of ash and popular, especially of recently felled trees.

Range
Throughout eastern North America.

Life Cycle
Eggs are laid under bark, where larvae seek prey. Fully grown larvae construct circular pupal cells from small particles of the decaying bark and wood, where they overwinter. Adults are active March–December.

Comments
This species is much larger and more brightly colored than most others.

Oak Timberworm Beetle
Arrhenodes minutus
389

¼–1⅛″ (7–30 mm). Cylindrical, elongate. Front portion of thorax pear-shaped. Dark brownish red; elytra with yellowish streaks or spots and with lengthwise grooves. Female has long slender beak with minute jaws at tip; male has pincerlike flattened jaws, toothed on inner surface. Antennae with 10–11 segments arise in front of eyes. Femora stout, particularly fore pair.

Habitat
Deciduous forests, beneath bark of dying or dead beech, oak, poplar, and maple trees.

Range
Eastern North America

Life Cycle
Female uses beak and jaws to cut a cylindrical hole through bark into wood, while male stands nearby to help free female if beak gets stuck. Eggs are laid in hole, then female uses hairy antennae to brush off beak. Larvae bore galleries in solid wood and pupate under bark, where adults overwinter. Adults active May–September.

Comments
Adults can be found under loose bark at any season.

Cylindrical Hardwood Borer
Neoclytus acuminatus
390

¼–¾″ (6–18 mm). Elongate, cylindrical. Reddish brown. Elytra parallel-sided, crossed by 4 narrow yellow bands interspersed with dark brown. Antennae are longer than head and front portion of thorax combined.

Habitat
Forests, woods, and adjacent clearings.

Range
Eastern United States and Canada.

Life Cycle
Eggs are laid on bark of living or dead trees. Larvae tunnel inward, later pupate close to bark. Adults emerge during first warm days of spring.

Comments
Adults are common on clustered flowers. If approached, they scramble quickly, drop off, or fly away.

American Carrion Beetle
Silpha americana
391

⅝–⅞" (17–22 mm). Broadly oval, gently convex above. Upper part of thorax is ivory to yellowish with black center. Elytra brownish black with 3 raised ridges connected by numerous dark cross-ridges. Head antennae, legs, and underside are black.

Habitat
Wherever carrion is found.

Range
East of the Rocky Mountains in the United States and southern Canada.

Life Cycle
Eggs are laid singly on or near carrion. Larvae hatch in few days, feed under the carcass or in its cavities, and pupate in a cell excavated in soil nearby. Adults emerge May–July.

Comments
This beetle flies actively on warm days, locates carrion by scent, alights, and crawls quickly out of sight.

Pennsylvania Firefly
Photuris pennsylvanicus
392

⅜–⅝" (9-15 mm). Elongate, flattened. Head visible from above; eyes large, widely separated. Antennae threadlike. Head and upper part of thorax are dull yellowish, latter with a black spot surrounded by reddish ring. Elytra are brown or gray and have yellow bands along sides near midline and a narrow pale stripe down middle. Both sexes have flashing green light. Larva is spindle-shaped with light organ below abdomen at rear.

Habitat
Meadows and open woods.

Range
Atlantic Coast to Texas, north to Manitoba.

Life Cycle
Eggs are concealed singly among rotting wood and humid debris on ground. Larvae hatch in spring. Fully grown larvae overwinter in pupal chambers just below soil surface and pupate in spring. Adults emerge early to late summer.

Comments
Eggs, larvae, and pupae are all luminous. This firefly flashes its light every 2 or 3 seconds while in flight.

Pine and Spruce Engraver Beetles
Ips spp.
393

⅛–¼" (4–6 mm). Cylindrical. Black, brown, or reddish brown, sometimes with fine yellow hair. Head concealed from above by upper part of thorax, but flattened club of antennae project. Front tibiae widen toward tip, with several fine teeth on outer surface. Tip of elytra deeply cut and edged with coarse teeth.

Habitat
Coniferous forests.

Range
Throughout North America; individual species more localized.

Life Cycle
Adults cut cylindrical tunnels through bark to feeding area, then expand brood galleries, where eggs are laid. Larvae excavate galleries further in a pattern resembling an engraving when bark is peeled away. Larvae pupate inside the galleries. Adults emerge in summer.

Comments
Spending most of their time in galleries, adults come into the open on warm sunny days, when they fly off and disperse widely. Their tunnels provide openings for fungus, which often hastens the death of a tree already in decline.

Goldsmith Beetle
Cotalpa lanigera
394

¾–1″ (20–26 mm). Heavy, egg-shaped. Head, thorax, and triangular shield where elytra meet thorax are yellow to greenish with a metallic luster. Elytra are yellow to beige. Underside is covered with long, dense, woolly hair.

Habitat
Woods and adjacent fields.

Range
New England to Florida, west to Mississippi River basin, north to Ontario.

Life Cycle
Eggs are scattered on soil below trees. Larvae burrow to reach food, pupate in earthen cells at end of first or second year. Adults emerge May–July.

Comments
This brilliantly colored beetle is the celebrated "gold bug" of Edgar Allan Poe's short story.

Dogwood Calligrapha
Calligrapha philadelphica
395

⅜″ (8-10 mm). Oval, hemispherical. Head and thorax dark metallic olive-green; elytra ivory-white marked with variable dark green stripes and spots. Antennae, legs, and mouthparts dark reddish brown.

Habitat
Woods, parks, and forest edges.

Range
Atlantic Coast in Canada down the Appalachians to Georgia, west to the Mississippi River basin, north to Nebraska.

Life Cycle
Eggs are attached to leaves and branches. Larvae feed on leaves, drop to soil to pupate, overwinter in soil as pupae or young adults. Beetles fly actively May–August.

Comments
At the slightest disturbance these beetles drop to the ground and become almost impossible to see.

Eastern Black Oak Acorn Weevil
Curculio baculi
396

¼" (6–7 mm). Egg-shaped, constricted between front portion of thorax and elytra. Grayish to reddish brown with short, pale gray scales; very long, curved beak.

Habitat
Deciduous forests.

Range
New York to Alabama, northwest to Nebraska.

Life Cycle
Female bores small hole in acorn, lays 1 or more eggs in separate pockets in hole, and seals opening with a fecal pellet that resembles a white dot on outside of dry acorn. Larvae feed and pupate inside. Adults are active during summer months. 1 generation annually, corresponding to acorn crop.

Comments
Many weevils are major agricultural pests, although a few species have been used for biological control of weeds. The Eastern Black Oak Acorn Weevil can be easily recognized by its long beak.

Florida Hunting Wasp
Palmodes dimidiatus
397

¾–⅞" (18–22 mm). Head, thorax, and legs blue-black. Abdominal segments 2, 3, and front of 4 brownish red; segment 3 has a dark middle blotch above; rest of abdomen blue-black, including 1-segmented "waist" between thorax and abdomen. Wings blackish to blue-black.

Habitat
Fields and woods.

Range
Throughout North America, except the Northwest.

Life Cycle
Female excavates a short burrow ending in a somewhat expanded single chamber and then temporarily closes entrance. Female hunts prey and brings anesthetized victim to burrow, then opens entrance and stuffs prey inside. Female lays 1 egg and then reseals entrance.

Comments
Like all other members of the large, diverse sphecid wasp family, the Florida Hunting Wasp can sting painfully.

Giant Ichneumons
Megarhyssa spp.
398

Male 1–1½" (25–38 mm), female 1⅜–3" (35–75 mm) with egg-laying organ at tip of abdomen 2–4⅜" (50–110 mm). Body pale to dark brown with extensive yellow V-shaped markings bordered with black on sides of abdomen. Female has more brown spots on yellow legs than male. Wings smoky.

Habitat
Deciduous and mixed forests with dead and dying broad-leaved trees and logs.

Range
Throughout North America, except plains and deserts.

Life Cycle
Mated female flies from tree to tree, pressing its long antennae against the bark to detect vibrations made by horntail larvae in wood. Female curls egg-laying organ up over abdomen, curving it down to enter bark at right angle. Sharp tips cut progressively deeper until they reach larval tunnels. Female inserts a very slender egg into each tunnel. Each larva attacks horntail host, which dies when ichneumon larva is grown.

Comments
Best known is the Eastern Giant Ichneumon (*M. macrurus macrurus*), which has extensive brown markings on its wings and ranges from Florida to Mexico. A northern subspecies, the Lunar Giant Ichneumon (*M. m. icterosticta*), has clear wings and occurs from Quebec and Nova Scotia to Georgia, west to South Dakota and Texas. The Western Giant Ichneumon (*M. nortoni*) is black with red and yellow spots and mostly yellow legs. It is found mainly in mountains from California to Alaska, also in Colorado, Utah, and Nevada, and in the East, in Georgia. Its larvae are internal parasites of siricid horntails in coniferous trees.

Tree-hole Mosquito
Aedes triseriatus
399

¼–⅜" (5–8 mm). Brown to black with many silvery-white and dark brown scales in streaks and patches on head and thorax. Abdomen appears to have dark and light bands; blue-black scales above, patches of white scales along sides. Hind femora yellowish near body, dark toward tips; white spots on knee joints. Wings have brown scales.

Habitat
Mature forests, in tree holes.

Range
Quebec to Florida, west to Texas, north to British Columbia.

Life Cycle
Eggs are deposited in water, accumulated in tree holes, tubs, cans and other containers. Larvae are present in most months in the South. Many overlapping generations a year.

Comments
Of all mosquitoes that breed in tree holes, this is the most widely distributed.

Pigeon Horntail
Tremex columba
400

1–1½" (25–38 mm). Cylindrical. Dark red to black, abdomen marked with yellowish crossbands. Wings dusky to yellowish. Female has blunt egg-laying organ one-fourth as long as body, yellowish. Both sexes have horny, spearlike plate at tip of abdomen.

Habitat
Hardwood and mixed forests.

Range
Eastern North America.

Life Cycle
Female uses egg-laying organ at tip of abdomen to bore
through bark into wood, depositing 1 slender egg in each
hole. Eggs are covered with fungal spores from a special
pocket in female's abdomen. As embryos prepare to hatch,
fungi begin to grow and soften wood. Larvae tunnel into
infected wood, making cylindrical passageways into side
branches. They feed for up to two years, then pupate under
bark in cocoons made of silk and wood chips. Adults are active
in fall.

Comments
After depositing the last egg, the female often dies without
removing its ovipositor from the wood. The dead female
becomes food for some insectivorous animal. Some ichneumon
species, which parasitize and kill horntail larvae, are helpful in
biological control of Pigeon Horntails. There are about 22
Tremex species worldwide but only 1 in North America.

Yellow Jackets
Vespula spp.
401

½–⅝″ (12–16 mm). Body stout, slightly wider than head.
Abdomen narrow where attached to thorax with short "waist."
First antennal segment black (yellow in western species);
subsequent segments black. Head, thorax, and abdomen black
and yellow or white. Wings smoky.

Habitat
Meadows and edges of forested land, usually nesting in ground
or at ground level in stumps and fallen logs.

Range
Throughout North America; various species more localized.

Life Cycle
In spring mated female constructs small nest and daily brings
food to larvae until first brood matures; females serve as
workers, extending nest and tending young. In late summer
males develop from unfertilized eggs and mate. When cold
weather begins, all die except mated females, which
overwinter among litter and in soil.

Comments
Yellow jackets can be pests at picnics, and they will carry off
bits of food. Females sting repeatedly at the least provocation.
If the nest can be found and its opening covered at night with
a transparent bowl set firmly into the ground, adults will be
confused by their inability to escape and seek food in daylight;
they will not dig a new escape hole and will soon starve.

Cicada Killer
Sphecius speciosus
402

1⅛–1⅝″ (30–40 mm). Short "waist" between thorax and
abdomen. Black, marked with yellow across thorax, on sides
above, and on first 3 abdominal segments. Legs yellowish;
middle tibiae have 2 spurs at tip. Wings dusky.

Habitat
Forest edges and city parks.

Range
Throughout North America.

Life Cycle
Several females work together to build nest of branching tunnels in light clay to sandy soil, making 2 or 3 cells at end. Front legs are used for digging, hind legs for kicking out dirt. Nest entrance is usually left open, while females hunt cicadas one at a time. Each victim is stung and carried back to nest. 1–2 cicadas are placed in each cell; 1 egg is laid on last one. Adults are seen July–August.

Comments
Because of its large size, this common wasp is sometimes called the "Giant Cicada Killer."

Giant Hornet
Vespa crabro germana
403

¾–1⅛″ (18–30 mm). Short "waist" between thorax and abdomen. Head, antennae, thorax, legs, and first abdominal segment reddish brown. Back of head and sides of thorax sometimes have yellow stripe. Rest of abdomen bright yellow with dark crossbands and small spots. Wings amber.

Habitat
Forests and towns.

Range
S. Massachusetts to Georgia, west to Indiana.

Life Cycle
A covered, tan-colored paper nest is built in a hollow tree, under porch floor, or in an outbuilding. First generation is all female workers, which feed later generations. In late summer unfertilized eggs produce males that mate and then die.

Comments
Introduced to America in the mid-1800s, this hornet is common locally around the western limits of its range. It defends its nest from intruders but otherwise avoids confrontations when possible.

Honey Bee
Apis mellifera
404

Male drone ⅝″ (15–17 mm); queen ¾″ (18–20 mm); sterile female worker ⅜–⅝″ (10–15 mm). Drone more robust with largest compound eyes; queen elongate with smallest compound eyes and larger abdomen; worker smallest. All mostly reddish brown and black with paler, usually orange-yellow rings on abdomen. Head, antennae, legs almost black with short, pale erect hair densest on thorax, least on abdomen. Wings translucent. Pollen collecting basket on hind tibia.

Habitat
Hives in hollow trees. Workers visit flowers of many kinds in meadows, open woods, and gardens.

Range
Worldwide.

Life Cycle
Complex social behavior centers on maintaining queen for full life-span, usually 2 or 3 years, sometimes up to 5. Queen lays eggs at intervals, producing a colony of 60,000–80,000 workers, which collect, produce, and distribute honey and maintain hive. Workers feed royal jelly to queen continuously and to all larvae for first 3 days; then only queen larvae continue eating royal jelly while other larvae are fed bee bread, a mixture of honey and pollen. By passing food mixed with saliva to one another, members of hive have chemical bond. New queens are produced in late spring and early summer; old queen then departs with a swarm of workers to found new colony. About a day later the first new queen emerges, kills other new queens, and sets out for a few days of orientation flights. In 3–16 days queen again leaves hive to mate, sometimes mating with several drones before returning to hive. Drones die after mating; unmated drones are denied food and die.

Comments
Settlers brought the Honey Bee to North America in the 17th century. Today these bees are used to pollinate crops and produce honey. They are frequently seen swarming around tree limbs. Honey Bees are distinguished from bumble bees and bees in other families mostly by wing venation.

Red-tailed Bumble Bee
Bombus ternarius
405

Male drone ⅜–½″ (9–14 mm); workers ⅜–½″ (9–14 mm); spring queen ½–¾″ (14–18 mm). Robust, hairy. Thorax yellow on sides with broad black band between the wings. Abdominal segments above: 2–3 red; 1 and 4 yellow; 5–6 black. Wings smoky. Pollen-collecting baskets on hind tibiae.

Habitat
Woods and open fields.

Range
Nova Scotia south to Georgia; also Michigan, Kansas, Montana, and British Columbia.

Life Cycle
In early spring queen enters opening in soil to build storage cells for honey and brood cells. Small workers develop first, visit flowers for nectar, and construct new brood cells. With warmer weather larger adults develop. Only young mated females overwinter.

Comments
Unlike the Honey Bee worker, a bumble bee can sting many times.

Black Flies
Simulium spp.
406

$\frac{1}{16}-\frac{1}{8}''$ (2–4 mm). Humpbacked, head pointing downward. Grayish brown to shiny black. Antennae thick, often with many segments. Wings smoky to clear; veins near front margin heavy, others delicate.

Habitat
Near running water in forests, mountains, and tundra.

Range
Labrador south to Georgia, west to California and Mexico, north to Alaska.

Life Cycle
Eggs are laid on stones or leaves at the edge of rapidly flowing streams, or on the water surface itself. Larvae tumble into water. Fully grown larvae pupate in cocoons that coat rocks in water, resembling moss. Adults burst out, rise on a bubble of trapped air, and fly away in late spring and early summer.

Comments
Biting adults are the bane of the North Country and mountain resorts, particularly early in the season. Some species transmit waterfowl malaria, which accounts for up to half of the deaths of ducks, geese, swans, and turkeys.

Deer Flies
Chrysops spp.
407

$\frac{3}{8}-\frac{5}{8}''$ (9-15 mm). Body somewhat flattened, head smaller than that of horse fly. Black with yellow-green markings on thorax and most of abdomen. Antennae cylindrical. Eyes bright green or gold with zigzag or other patterns. Hind tibiae have 2 spurs at tip. Wings have distinctive brownish-black pattern. Larva is yellowish white or greenish with brown rings.

Habitat
Deciduous and mixed forests, meadows, roadsides, and suburbs near water.

Range
Throughout North America.

Life Cycle
Shiny black eggs are laid in clusters on leaves of emergent plants just above water. Fully grown larvae pupate in mud at edge of water. Adults emerge May–August.

Comments
A deer fly circles over its intended victim before settling, then immediately bites. Some transmit bacteria that cause tularemia in rabbits, hares, and occasionally people. The most common species, the Callidus Deer Fly *(C. callidus)*, has black on its thorax and V-shaped black marks on abdominal segments 2, 3, and 4. It pesters animals and people during June and July, from Maine to Florida, west to Texas, north to British Columbia.

Mason Bees
Osmia spp.
408

⅜–½" (10–14 mm). Black with long black hair on thorax and sides of head. Tongue long; jaws prominent, sharp. Female has pollen-collecting brush below abdominal segments 2–3. Legs black. Wings clear to brownish.

Habitat
Meadows and forest edges.

Range
Throughout North America; every state and Canadian province has a dozen or more distinct species, each showing more limited distribution.

Life Cycle
Female constructs small nest cells of clay, individually or in clusters, that are attached to twigs or stones or built into cavities of wood. Each cell is provisioned with pollen and nectar, then 1 egg is laid inside. Larvae spin tough cocoons before pupating. Adults are seen April–June. 1 generation a year.

Comments
Mason bees convert clay into a cementlike material. Some species include plant fragments in their nest construction. Others build inside empty snail shells, and still others line each nest with snips of flower petals.

Oak Lace Bug
Corythuca arcuata
409

⅛" (3–4 mm). Prominent hood on front of upper part of thorax, usually covering head. Body pale, crossed by 2 dark bands; black below. Antennae and legs yellow. Wings clear.

Habitat
Oak forests and isolated trees.

Range
Wherever oaks grow in North America.

Life Cycle
Female forces eggs into leaf tissues close to central vein and coats them with hard, resinlike secretion. Nymphs pierce leaf cells from below, then deposit fecal pellets, which adhere to leaf, giving it peppered appearance. Adults overwinter beneath ground litter, fly and mate on warm spring days. Usually 1 generation a year, more in the South.

Comments
Nymphs cling to leaves and remain motionless if approached, but adults drop off or fly away. The similar Alder Lace Bug *(C. pergandei)*, ⅛" (3 mm), feeds on hazel and birch as well as alder in most of the United States and eastern Canada. The Goldenrod Lace Bug *(C. marmorata)*, ⅛" (3–4 mm), is yellowish white above, speckled with brown, and has 4 narrow brown lines across the fore wings. It is common on plants of the daisy family, including asters, horticultural chrysanthemums, and goldenrod, and sometimes invades greenhouses.

Black Pine Sawyer
Monochamus scutellatus
410

⅝–1″ (15–25 mm). Upper part of thorax has prominent spine in middle of each side. Elytra elongate, rounded at tip. Black but appearing bronze because of gray and brown hair. Antennae have scarlike area on outer end of first segment; male's are bare and nearly twice length of body; female's hairy, shorter. Larva is white with brown head.

Habitat
Coniferous forests.

Range
Eastern North America.

Life Cycle
Female cuts deep pits in bark and lays 1–6 eggs inside each. Larvae bore U-shaped tunnels, packing wastes behind them, and almost reach their starting point, where they pupate. Adults chew their way to freedom. Cycle takes 1–4 years, depending on conditions.

Comments
The sound of gnawing larvae can be heard by pressing an ear against the bark of infested trees. This beetle does considerable damage to recently felled trees and those scorched by fire. The Spotted Sawyer *(M. maculosus)*, ⅝–1″ (15–25 mm), is dark brown and has irregular bluish spots on its elytra. It attacks pines from Colorado and New Mexico to California, north to British Columbia. The larger Northeastern Sawyer *(M. notatus)*, ½–1⅛″ (12–28 mm), is brown with black spots, white flecks, and silver-gray hair on its elytra. It attacks pines, spruces, and firs. The Eastern Sawyer *(M. titillator)*, ¾–1⅛″ (20–28 mm), is brown and mottled gray with brown and black hair. It feeds on pines from Quebec to Georgia.

Fungus Gnats
Mycetophila spp.
411

⅛–¼″ (3–6 mm). Slender, mosquitolike. Brownish to grayish yellow, sometimes streaked and ringed with dark brown. Thorax hairy. Legs blackish, long, slender; bases of legs greatly elongated. Wings smoky.

Habitat
Moist dark woodlands and shaded valleys; indoors in potted houseplants.

Range
Throughout North America.

Life Cycle
Eggs are laid on or in food materials, where larvae feed. They pupate near surface of food. Adults emerge in summer outdoors, or in any season indoors.

Comments
Mosquitolike adults flit close to wet areas. The many species can only be distinguished by a specialist on the basis of details of wing venation, body bristles, and genitalia.

Buffalo Treehoppers
Stictocephala spp.
412

⅜" (9 mm). Bright green to yellowish above, yellowish below. Wings clear, tapering toward end of abdomen. Upper part of thorax projects forward at each side to short stout point, suggesting horns of buffalo or bison, hence the common name.

Habitat
Woods, orchards, crop fields, and meadows.

Range
Throughout the United States and southern Canada.

Life Cycle
Pairs of smooth white eggs are pressed into crescent-shaped slits cut in bark of young stems. Eggs overwinter, hatch in spring. Nymphs mature in about 6 weeks.

Comments
This is the best-known and most widely distributed treehopper. The genus is represented by almost a dozen species, each having minute distinguishing features and some differences in food and habitat. Formerly assigned to genus *Ceresa*.

True Katydid
Pterophylla camellifolia
413

1¾–2⅛" (45–55 mm). Leaf-green. Fore wings convex, oval, crossed by many conspicuous veins between front margin and longitudinal vein. Head pointed at front. Side plates of front portion of thorax about as long as high.

Habitat
Woodlands and forests.

Range
Massachusetts to Florida, west to Texas and Kansas, northeast to Ontario.

Sound
Both sexes make sounds. The most common call is the loud 2-part *katy-DID;* less often is the 3-part *katy-DIDN'T.*

Life Cycle
Eggs are laid on bark and young stems in fall, overwinter, and hatch in spring. 1 generation a year.

Comments
Nymphs are seldom seen near the ground, but adults perch on low shrubs, sometimes along roadways and forest margins. This katydid is known as the True Katydid because it was the first species to have its call transcribed. It can be heard easily when chirping from treetops to ground level.

Black-horned Tree Cricket
Oecanthus nigricornis
414

½" (13 mm). Pale greenish yellow to very dark green, almost black. Antennae with a few black or brownish marks on first segment, rest of antennae black. Legs mostly black. Male's fore wings paddle-shaped.

Habitat
Deciduous woods and forests.

Range
Nova Scotia to North Carolina and Tennessee, west to
California, north to Oregon.

Sound
A continuous trill. Pitch higher in warmer weather.

Life Cycle
Female selects and nudges male until it stops singing. Female
then nibbles on secretion from gland on male's back while
they mate. Eggs inserted in bark overwinter and hatch in
spring. Nymphs mature by midsummer.

Comments
These crickets sometimes damage slender stems of grapevines,
rose bushes, and fruit trees by incising rows of egg pits in
their bark. The various species of tree crickets are
distinguished mostly by the form and spotting of the first 2
antennal segments.

Dogday Harvestfly
Tibicen canicularis
415

1⅛–1¼″ (27–33 mm). Wingspan: to 3¼″ (82 mm). Black
with green markings. Wings clear green along rear half of
fore-wing margin.

Habitat
Coniferous and mixed woods.

Range
Northeastern United States and adjacent Canada.

Sound
A powerful call that sounds like a circular saw cutting through
a board.

Life Cycle
Nymphs take 3 years before maturing to adult. A new
generation hatches each summer in the same area.

Comments
Since this cicada disappears from mixed forests soon after all
the pines are eradicated, it probably feeds on pine roots. It is
seen during the hot "dog days" of summer, hence its common
name.

Periodical Cicadas
Magicicada spp.
416

1⅛″ (27–30 mm). Wingspan: to 3″ (77 mm). Stout. Black to
brownish. Eyes bulging, dark red. Wings membranous with
orange tinge and orange along basal half of fore-wing front
margin. Legs reddish. Undersurface of abdomen primarily
reddish brown to yellow.

Habitat
Deciduous and mixed forests; also found in adjacent grasslands
and pastures.

Range
Mostly east of the Mississippi River, from the Great Lakes to
the Gulf of Mexico.

Sound
An intense whining, rising and falling in pitch.

Life Cycle
Mated female uses egg-laying organ to slit tree branch lengthwise, then wedges a series of eggs into the fresh crevice. Nymphs burrow into soil to reach tree roots, where they feed and grow very slowly, requiring 13–17 years to complete development. Each nymph crawls to nearest upright support, splits its skin, and transforms into an adult. The simultaneous appearance of thousands of cicadas during a few weeks overwhelms predators, permitting the great majority to mate undisturbed.

Comments
Unlike cicadas of other genera, Periodical Cicadas emerge in a single locality only once every 13 or 17 years. Each synchronized population is called a brood. Some are large and occupy major areas of the United States, while others are small and cover less than 100 square miles. Only 14 broods of 17-year cicadas and 5 of 13-year cicadas are known to exist today. Broods that are separated by 4 years tend to overlap in geographic distribution, whereas those separated by only 1 year border each other geographically, without any overlap.

Carolina Mantid
Stagmomantis carolina
417

2⅜″ (60 mm) including wings. Head and thorax almost as long as rest of the body. Antennae about half as long as middle legs. Pale green to brownish gray, often inconspicuous on vegetation. Wings extend to about middle of abdomen.

Habitat
Meadows and gardens, on herbs, low shrubs, and flower heads, including goldenrod.

Range
Virginia to Florida, west to Mexico and California, northeast to Indiana.

Life Cycle
Masses of 30–80 elongate eggs, packed in parallel rows, overwinter attached to plant stem. They are coated with a tan frothy material that dries like a hard meringue. Nymphs appear in spring and begin ambushing prey.

Comments
This voracious predator can make two separate strikes with its forelegs in a fraction of a second, often before a fly can spread its wings and escape. The adult female often captures and devours parts of her mate even as he continues to transfer sperm.

Northern Walkingstick
Diapheromera femorata
418

Male 3″ (75 mm), female 3¾″ (95 mm). Very elongated, wingless. Male brown, female greenish brown. Antennae two-thirds length of body. Tail projections with 1 segment, often resemble palps at tip of abdomen.

Habitat
Deciduous woods and forests.

Range
Atlantic Coast to N. Florida, west to New Mexico, north to Alberta.

Life Cycle
Female drops eggs singly. Eggs overwinter among ground litter and hatch in spring, when nymphs push open domelike ends of the eggs. Nymphs crawl up woody vegetation at night to reach edible foliage.

Comments
The Northern Walkingstick's resemblance to slender twigs camouflages it from predatory birds during the day. When many females are dropping eggs, the sound is like the pitter-patter of light rain.

Oyster Shell Scale
Lepidosaphes ulmi
419

Female scale ⅛″ (3 mm) long, less than ⅙″ (1 mm) wide. Male scale smaller. Both pale to dark brown, often S-curved, tapering to a point. Scale suggests shape of an oyster shell crossed by several grooves.

Habitat
Woods, orchards, and lawns

Range
Nova Scotia to Georgia mountains, west to California, north to British Columbia.

Life Cycle
40–100 oval white eggs overwinter under female's scale, which still clings to bark after female has died from frost. Whitish nymphs disperse for 2–48 hours in spring. They pierce bark to feed, develop scales, and mature by mid-July. Usually 2 generations a year.

Comments
The Oyster Shell Scale was introduced long ago from Europe. It has now spread to more than 100 different American plants.

American Tent Caterpillar Moth
Malacosoma americanum
420

Wingspan: 1⅛–1⅝″ (30–41 mm). Dark brown, bluish, or blackish, with 2 oblique whitish lines nearly parallel to outer margins of fore wings. Males smaller than females, both hairy and robust with feathery antennae. Caterpillar, about 2″, marked by white stripe down back, bordered by reddish brown. Blue and white spots on both sides of body.

Habitat
Woodlands, orchards, and towns.

Range
Throughout the United States and Canada east of the Rocky Mountains.

Life Cycle
Females deposit eggs in brown masses that form hard, varnishlike rings around limbs of deciduous trees, where eggs overwinter. In early spring larvae emerge and crawl to nearby crotch in tree where they spin a communal webbed nest or tent. Caterpillars leave tent to feed on nearby foliage, returning to tent to rest. After 4–6 weeks, caterpillars disperse to pupate in tough, white cocoons composed of silk mixed with a yellowish powder. After 2–3 weeks the adults emerge, May–July, and mate. 1 generation each year.

Comments
Both wild and cultivated trees of cherry, plum, apple, hawthorn, and others are sometimes completely defoliated over thousands of acres during periodic outbreaks.

Eastern Daddy-long-legs
Leiobunum spp.
421

¼–⅜″ (6–8 mm). Long thin legs. Yellowish to greenish brown with blackish stripe along midline above and on each side. Legs pale to dark. Each pedipalp ends in a microscopic claw.

Habitat
Open areas on foliage and tree trunks, or on shady walls outside buildings.

Range
East of the Rocky Mountains.

Life Cycle
Female uses slender egg-laying organ to insert eggs individually as far as possible into soil, where they overwinter, hatching in spring. Adults most common in autumn.

Comments
Sometimes daddy-long-legs cluster in tree holes with their legs intertangled, as though seeking insulation from the winter cold. In areas where frost is frequent, few adults survive until spring. The different species are distinguishable only on the basis of inconspicuous features.

Golden-silk Spider
Nephila clavipes
422

Male ⅛″ (4 mm), female ⅞–1″ (22–25 mm). Female's cephalothorax pale gray with 3 black spots on each side; legs dark with brownish bands and conspicuous tufts of black hair on first and last pairs of legs. Female's abdomen brownish green, spotted with white in irregular pattern. Male's body color drabber; legs also have tufts of black hair. In both sexes abdomen is 2½–3 times as long as it is broad.

Habitat
Shaded woodlands and swamps.

Range
Southeastern United States.

Life Cycle
Web strong, slightly inclined orb with notchlike support

lines; may measure 2–3′ (1 m) across. Female attaches elongated egg mass to undersurface of leaf and then rests nearby. Spiderlings disperse, each to make web elsewhere. At first, they build only two-thirds of a web, leaving the top somewhat irregular across from principal support line.

Comments
During the day the spider hangs head downward from the underside of the web near the meshlike center or hub. The spider repairs the webbing each day, replacing half but never the whole web at one time.

Eastern Wood Ticks
Dermacentor spp.
423

⅛″ (3–4 mm). Male's body pale gray with reddish-brown spots and legs. Female's body reddish brown with small shield of black-speckled gray near head. Legs brown; head often orange above.

Habitat
Woodlands and shrubbery beside trails.

Range
Eastern North America.

Life Cycle
Tick clings to plants while extending forelegs to seize passing host. Tick climbs on prey for a meal, dropping off after fully engorged. If not yet mature, tick molts and repeats process. Mature female, if mated before last major meal, drops many eggs, producing 6-legged larvae.

Comments
This tick can transfer disease organisms from one host to the next. After a walk through a field, it is wise to inspect clothing and hair for ticks. Then the ticks should be removed and burned or drowned in alcohol.

Wandering Spiders
Ctenus spp.
424

Male ¼–⅞″ (5–21 mm), female ⅜–1″ (8–25 mm). Cephalothorax yellowish to orangish brown. Legs orangish brown to brown, palest close to body. Abdomen grayish yellow to black. Body sparsely coated with fine down.

Habitat
Woods, on the ground or on foliage; also in caves.

Range
Alabama and Mississippi; S. Texas and northeastern Mexico.

Life Cycle
Egg mass is concealed among litter or attached to undersurface of a leaf. Apparently they mature at any time of year and overwinter at any stage. This spider hunts in litter, among mosses, or under logs almost like a small wolf spider.

Comments
Most members of this genus are tropical and are transported into North America on plants and fruit. Identification is based

on differences in the genitalia, spines on the legs, teeth on the chelicerae, and color patterning.

Forest Wolf Spider
Lycosa gulosa
425

Male ⅜" (10–11 mm), female ⅜–½" (10–13 mm). Dark brown with grayish-yellow stripe along middle of cephalothorax and narrow grayish-yellow stripe on each side. Male's abdomen has 2 incomplete black stripes on front third. Pedipalps large, hairy.

Habitat
Woods, among litter.

Range
Maine to Georgia, west to Utah, north to S. Manitoba.

Life Cycle
Female drags eggs in a spherical sac until they hatch. Spiderlings ride on female until able to fend for themselves.

Comments
This spider hides among litter by day, hunts at night. It makes no nest or silken shelter, although it secures a dragline before leaping upon potential prey. The light of a flashlight is reflected from its silvery eyes, making this wolf spider easy to find at night.

Metaphid Jumping Spiders
Metaphidippus spp.
426

Male ⅛–¼" (3–5 mm), female ⅛–¼" (3–6 mm). Brown to yellow. Body and legs somewhat grayish due to covering of dense hair. Male usually has white band on sides of abdomen. Both sexes have spots, bands, and chevrons.

Habitat
Meadows and woods, on foliage, tree bark, fence posts, and tall grasses.

Range
Throughout North America; individual species more restricted.

Life Cycle
After mating, female constructs cocoon for eggs, attaches it to twigs, and stays close by. Spiderlings disperse rapidly.

Comments
These spiders run freely, producing an anchor line when they leap on potential prey or walk about on the ground.

WILDFLOWERS

From March to October, the eastern forests put on a brilliant display of color as thousands of wildflowers burst into bloom. Some of these, such as violets, are common and easily recognized; others, like orchids, are unusual and offer the visitor a special kind of delight. In this section, you will find descriptions of some of the East's most typical and beautiful wildflowers.

Wild Sarsaparilla
Aralia nudicaulis
427

The leafless flower stem, topped with clusters of greenish-white flowers, is beneath a large, umbrellalike leaf.
Flowers: hemispherical clusters 1½–2" (3.8–5 cm) wide; flowers with highly reflexed, tiny petals, 5 green stamens; July–August.
Leaves: single, long-stalked, 8–15" (20–38 cm) tall; rising above the flower stalk in 3 branching parts, each with 3 to 5 ovate, finely toothed leaflets.
Fruit: purple-black berries, in clusters.
Height: 8–15" (20–38 cm).

Habitat
Upland woods.

Range
Across Canada; south to Georgia; west through Tennessee and Illinois to Missouri.

Comments
The aromatic rhizomes of this plant are used as a substitute for sarsaparilla. The species name, from the Latin *nudus* ("naked") and *cauli* ("stalk"), refers to the leafless flowerstalk. Devil's walking-stick (*A. spinosa*), a small tree or large shrub, has leaves and stems covered with spines.

White Baneberry
Actaea pachypoda
428, 501

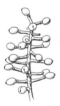

An erect stem bears large, highly divided leaves and, at the top, a dense, oblong cluster of many small white flowers.
Flowers: about ¼" (6 mm) wide; petals 4–10, narrow, stamens numerous; pistil 1; May–June.
Leaves: leaflets to 4" (10 cm) long, toothed, ovate.
Fruit: clustered shiny white berries, each with a black dot, on thick red stalks.
Height: 1–2' (30–60 cm).

Habitat
Rich woods and thickets.

Range
Manitoba to Nova Scotia; south through New England to Georgia; west to Alabama, Louisiana, and Oklahoma.

Comments
This plant is sometimes called Doll's Eyes because the shiny white fruits resemble the china eyes once used in dolls. A red-fruited form of this species is distinguished from the otherwise similar Red Baneberry (*A. rubra*) by its thick floral stalk.

Red Baneberry
Actaea rubra
429, 504

A bushy plant with large, highly divided leaves and a short, thick, rounded cluster of small white flowers.
Flowers: about ¼" (6 mm) wide; petals fall as flower opens leaving the numerous stamens; May–July.
Leaves: 9–27 ovate, sharply-toothed leaflets, each about 2½" (6.3 cm) long.
Fruit: clustered red berries on slender stalks.
Height: 1–2' (20–60 cm).

Habitat
Woods and thickets.

Range
Newfoundland and Nova Scotia; south through New England to West Virginia; west to Mississippi River.

Comments
When in flower the clustered stamens give this plant a feathery appearance. The showy fruits are poisonous, as are those of White Baneberry (*A. pachypoda*).

Foamflower
Tiarella cordifolia
430

Small, white flowers are in a feathery, somewhat elongated, terminal cluster.
Flowers: ¼" (6 mm) wide; sepals 5; petals 5, clawed; stamens 10, protruding, anthers reddish or yellow; pistils 2, of unequal size; April–June.
Leaves: 2–4" (5–10 cm) long; basal, stalked, lobed and sharply toothed, somewhat maplelike, usually hairy.
Fruit: pair of capsules, each of which splits open along 1 side.
Height: 6–12" (15–30 cm).

Habitat
Rich woods.

Range
Ontario to Nova Scotia; south through New England to upland North Carolina; west to Tennessee; north to Michigan.

Comments
This attractive wildflower, which spreads by underground stems, forms colonies and makes excellent ground cover for shady, wooded sites. The tiny flowers and fine textures of the stamens resemble foam.

Devil's Bit
Chamaelirium luteum
431

A wandlike stem, often drooping at the tip, arises from a basal cluster of leaves and has a densely packed, elongated terminal cluster of tiny white flowers.
Flowers: about ⅛" (3 mm) long, with very narrow segments (petals 3 and sepals 3); male and female flowers on separate plants, with female cluster shorter, more slender; May–July.
Leaves: basal ones 3–8" (8–20 cm) long, spatulate to ovate; stem leaves smaller, narrower.
Fruit: 3-part, dry, elliptic capsule.
Height: 1–4' (30–120 cm); male plant shorter.

Habitat
Wet meadows, rich woods and thickets.

Range
S. Ontario, Massachusetts, and New York; south to Florida; west to Arkansas; north to Illinois, Michigan, and Ohio.

Comments
"Fairy Wand" is a most descriptive alternate name for this

interesting plant. On the plants with all-male flowers, the yellow stamens create the more creamy color of the male flower spike. The plant can be readily cultivated.

False Solomon's Seal
Smilacina racemosa
432

An arching stem bears at its tip a pyramidal cluster of many small white flowers.
Flowers: ⅛" (3 mm) long; petals 3; sepals 3, petal-like; stamens 6; May–July.
Leaves: 3–6" (7.5–15 cm) long; alternate, elliptic, hairy beneath and along margins, conspicuously parallel-veined.
Fruit: berry; at first green speckled with red, finally translucent, ruby red.
Height: 1–3' (30–90 cm).

Habitat
Woods and clearings.

Range
Quebec and Nova Scotia; south through New England to Virginia, Georgia, and Missouri.

Comments
The feathery, creamy-white masses of flowers borne at the end of the stem distinguish this species from the true solomon's seals (*Polygonatum* spp.), which have pendulous, axillary, bell-like flowers. The rhizome lacks the seal-like pattern of the true solomon's seals, but exhibits circular stem scars.

Poison Ivy
Rhus radicans
433

Upright, climbing, or trailing shrub that bears small yellowish-white flower clusters; old stems, covered with fibrous roots, look hairy.
Flowers: ⅛" (3 mm) wide, in loose clusters 1–3" (2.5–7.5 cm) long at lower leaf axils; May–July.
Leaves: compound, divided into 3 glossy or dull green leaflets, each 2–4" (5–10 cm) long.
Fruit: to ¼" (6 mm) wide, clustered, white, berrylike; August–November, persisting through winter.
Height: vine.

Habitat
Open woods, thickets, fence rows, roadsides, and waste places.

Range
Throughout.

Comments
All parts of this plant contain volatile oil that can cause severe skin inflammation, itching, and blistering on direct contact or if borne by sooty smoke. Washing thoroughly with soap or swabbing with alcohol immediately on exposure removes the oil irritant. Poison Ivy is extremely variable in form, occurring as a ground cover along roadsides, an erect shrub (especially in sandy coastal areas), or a large vine on trees. Red fall foliage is especially conspicuous.

Early Meadow Rue
Thalictrum dioicum
434

Drooping, greenish-white flowers are in long-stalked terminal and axillary clusters on a smooth, leafy stem.
Flowers: about ¼" (6 mm) long; petals absent. Male and female flowers on separate plants; the male flowers with numerous long, yellow, showy stamens protruding from the 4–5 petal-like sepals; female flowers with a few elongated, purplish pistils; April–May.
Leaves: on long stalks, divided into 3–4 roundish, lobed segments ½–2" (1.3–5 cm) wide, pale beneath.
Fruit: ovoid, 1-seeded, strongly ribbed.
Height: 8–30" (20–75 cm).

Habitat
Rich moist woods, ravines.

Range
Ontario to Quebec; south to Georgia; west to Missouri; north to North Dakota and Minnesota.

Comments
The species name alludes to the fact that the male and female flowers are on separate plants, and is derived from a Greek word meaning "two households."

Goldthread
Coptis groenlandica
435

A small plant with solitary white flowers and lustrous, evergreen basal leaves rising from a threadlike, yellow underground stem.
Flowers: ½" (1.3 cm) wide; sepals 5–7, white, petal-like; petals very small, clublike; stamens numerous; pistils several; May–July.
Leaves: 1–2" (2.5–5 cm) wide, all basal, palmately divided into 3 leaflets with scalloped, toothed margins.
Fruit: dry pod, splitting open along 1 side.
Height: 3–6" (7.5–15 cm).

Habitat
Cool woods, swamps, and bogs.

Range
Manitoba to Greenland, Labrador, Newfoundland, and Nova Scotia; south through New England and New Jersey to the mountains of North Carolina; west to Tennessee, Ohio, Indiana, and Iowa.

Comments
The common name refers to the golden-yellow underground stem that both Indians and colonists chewed to treat mouth sores. (Hence another common name for the plant, Canker-root.) It was also made into a tea for use as an eyewash.

Mountain-laurel
Kalmia latifolia
436, 484

A large evergreen shrub with showy clusters of deep pink buds and pinkish-white flowers on sticky stalks.
Flowers: ¾–1" (2–2.5 cm) wide; corolla with 5 united lobes, each having 2 pockets with 1 stamen tucked into each; late May–mid-July.

Leaves: 2–4″ (5–10 cm) long; mostly alternate, ovate-lanceolate or elliptic, pointed at each end, shiny green with yellow-green petiole, leathery.
Fruit: dry brown capsule.
Height: 3–15′ (90–450 cm).

Habitat
Open hardwood forests.

Range
New England and New York south to Florida; west to Louisiana; north to Indiana.

Comments
As the flowers mature, the stamens may pop out of the petal pouches or they may be dislodged as an insect enters the flower, spraying the pollen onto its back. Mountain Laurel is relatively tolerant of fire; when stem-killed to the ground, it grows back vigorously. It is often very long-lived.

Great Laurel
Rhododendron maximum
437

A large evergreen shrub with clusters of pinkish-white, cup-shaped flowers on glandular and sticky stalks.
Flowers: 1½–2″ (3.8–5 cm) wide, with 5 blunt corolla lobes; June–July.
Leaves: 4–8″ (10–20 cm) long; leathery, smooth, elliptic-oblong, pointed at base and tip, dark green above, often paler and closely hairy below.
Fruit: smooth brown capsule.
Height: 5–35′ (1.5–10.5 m).

Habitat
Damp woods and forested wetlands.

Range
Maine south to Georgia and Alabama; north to Ohio and S. Pennsylvania; most common from Pennsylvania southward.

Comments
This tall, straggly shrub often forms impenetrable thickets on moist slopes or in swamps. It is frequently used as an ornamental for its showy flowers and handsome foliage. The leaves droop in frost and may curl under lengthwise; the colder the temperature, the tighter the roll.

Highbush Blueberry
Vaccinium corymbosum
438, 510

A multistemmed shrub with green, or often red, twigs and terminal clusters of small, urn-shaped white flowers.
Flowers: ¼–½″ (6–13 mm) long; corolla 5-toothed; May–June.
Leaves: 1½–3″ (3.8–7.5 cm) long; elliptic, entire, smooth above but usually somewhat hairy beneath.
Fruit: blue berry, with whitish bloom; June–August.
Height: 5–15′ (1.5–4.5 m).

Habitat
Swamps or dry upland woods.

Range
Quebec to Nova Scotia; south to Georgia; west to Alabama; north to Wisconsin.

Comments
Our cultivated blueberries have been derived from this tall-growing shrub. It is often found in wet areas, but closely related growths occur in dry sites. The berries, twigs, and foliage are eaten by wildlife. Food value and spectacular red fall foliage make these shrubs excellent for landscaping.

Mayapple
Podophyllum peltatum
439

Solitary, nodding flower borne in the crotch between a pair of large, deeply lobed leaves.
Flowers: 2″ (5 cm) wide, with 6–9 waxy white petals; April–June.
Leaves: to 1′ (30 cm) wide.
Fruit: large, fleshy, lemonlike berry.
Height: 12–18″ (30–45 cm).

Habitat
Rich woods and damp, shady clearings.

Range
S. Ontario and W. Quebec; south to Florida; west to Texas; north to Minnesota.

Comments
The common name refers to the May blooming of this plant's flowers, which resemble apple blossoms. Although the leaves, roots, and seeds are poisonous if ingested in large quantities, the ripe golden-yellow fruits are edible. The alternate popular name, Mandrake, rightly belongs to an unrelated Old World plant with a similar root.

Bloodroot
Sanguinaria canadensis
440

On a smooth stalk a solitary white flower, with a golden-orange center, grows beside a lobed basal leaf that often curls around the stalk. Roots and stem with acrid red-orange juice.
Flowers: to 1½″ (3.8 cm) wide; petals 8–10, separate, the alternate ones slightly narrower; sepals 2, falling as flower opens; stamens golden, numerous, surrounding single pistil; March–May.
Leaves: 4–7″ (10–17.5 cm) long, bluish green, palmately scalloped into 5–9 lobes.
Fruit: 2-parted capsule, pointed at both ends.
Height: to 10″ (25 cm).

Habitat
Rich woodlands and along streams.

Range
Across Canada to Nova Scotia; south from New England to Florida; west to E. Texas; north to Manitoba.

Comments
This fragile spring flower develops and rises from the center of

its curled leaf, opening in full sun, and closing at night. Like most members of the poppy family, it lasts for a relatively short time.

Wood Anemone
Anemone quinquefolia
441

A low, delicate plant with a whorl of 3 stalked, deeply cut leaves and a solitary, stalked white flower.
Flowers: 1" (2.5 cm) wide; sepals 4–9, white, often pink on the reverse side, petal-like; petals absent; pistils and stamens numerous; April–June.
Leaves: palmately divided into 3 or 5 sharply toothed segments, each about 1¼" (3.1 cm) long; basal leaves similar.
Fruit: seedlike, hairy, in a globose cluster.
Height: 4–8" (10–20 cm).

Habitat
Open woods, clearings, thickets.

Range
Quebec to New York; south to North Carolina; locally in Ohio and Kentucky.

Comments
This is an early spring wildflower that often forms sizable stands on woodland borders. Usually slender-stalked, they tremble in the breeze, and have been called Wind Flowers.

Sweet White Violet
Viola blanda
442

A fragrant, white violet with leaves and flowers on separate, reddish stalks rising from underground stem. Runners present.
Flowers: about ½" (1.3 cm) wide; petals 5, the upper ones bent backward and twisted; lower petal purple-veined; April–May.
Leaves: up to 2½" (6.3 cm) wide; ovate with heart-shaped bases, dark green, shiny, sharp-pointed.
Fruit: purplish, ovoid seed capsule.
Height: 3–5" (7.5–12.5 cm).

Habitat
Rich woods.

Range
Quebec south through New England to Maryland and upland to Georgia; west to Tennessee, Ohio, Indiana, Illinois, Wisconsin, and Minnesota.

Comments
Very similar to the Northern White Violet (*V. pallens*), but the latter grows in wet woods and beside brooks, has a greenish seed capsule, and does not have the reddish stems.

Starflower
Trientalis borealis
443

Fragile white flowers are on delicate stalks arising from a whorl of 5–9 leaves.
Flowers: about ½" (1.3 cm) wide; petals usually 7; stamens usually 7, with golden anthers; May–August.

Leaves: 1¾–4″ (4.5–10 cm) long, lanceolate; small scale leaf present near middle of stem below whorled leaves.
Fruit: 5-valved capsule.
Height: 4–8″ (10–20 cm).

Habitat
Cool woodlands, peaty slopes, ascending to subalpine regions.

Range
Saskatchewan to Labrador, Newfoundland, and Nova Scotia; south through New England to Virginia; west to West Virginia, Ohio, Indiana, Illinois, and Minnesota.

Comments
The backgrounds of shiny green leaves against which these pure white, starlike flowers are set accentuates the allusion to a star.

Partridgeberry
Mitchella repens
444, 508

A trailing, evergreen herb with white, fragrant, tubular flowers in pairs.
Flowers: ½–⅔″ (1.3–1.6 cm) long; corolla funnel-form with 4 spreading lobes, fringed on the inside. Flowers are either staminate (male) or pistillate (female); June–July.
Leaves: ½–¾″ (1.3–2 cm) long, opposite, roundish, shiny, green, with white veins.
Fruit: ovaries of the paired flowers fuse to form a red, edible, berrylike fruit.
Height: creeper, with stem 4–12″ (10–30 cm).

Habitat
Dry or moist woods.

Range
Throughout.

Comments
A most attractive woodland creeper with highly ornamental foliage, it can be used as a groundcover under acid-loving shrubs and in terraria in the winter. The common name implies that the scarlet fruits are relished by partridges, but they do not appear to be of much importance to wildlife.

Bunchberry
Cornus canadensis
445, 506

Erect stems from a creeping rootstock have at their summits 4 white, petal-like bracts above a whorl of leaves.
Flowers: set of bracts (the "flower"), about 1½″ (3.8 cm) wide, surround a globose cluster of tiny yellowish-green flowers; May–July.
Leaves: 1½–3″ (3.8–7.5 cm) long; ovate, pointed, with veins curved into an arc. 1 or 2 pairs of reduced, scalelike leaves present on stem below whorled main leaves.
Fruit: tight cluster of bright red berrylike drupes.
Height: 3–8″ (7.5–20 cm).

Habitat
Cool woods and damp openings.

Range
Across southern Canada to Labrador and southern Greenland;
south to Maryland; west through West Virginia, Ohio, and
Illinois to South Dakota; north to Minnesota.

Comments
This showy wildflower and the Northern Dwarf Cornel
(*C. suecica*) of the northern forests are the only herbs in the
dogwood group, the other members being trees or shrubs.
C. suecica occurs in Canada, south to the St. Lawrence River
and east to Nova Scotia. It has small purple flowers
surrounded by 4 bracts.

Large-flowered Trillium
Trillium grandiflorum
446

The large, solitary, waxy-white flower (turning pink with age)
is on an erect stalk above a whorl of 3 broad leaves.
Flowers 2–4″ (5–10 cm) wide; petals 3, large, wavy-edged;
sepals 3, green; stamens 6, with yellow anthers; April–June.
Leaves–3–6″ (7.5–15 cm) long; broadly ovate to diamond-
shaped, pointed.
Fruit: red berry.
Height: 8–18″ (20–45 cm).

Habitat
Rich woods, thickets; usually basic or neutral soils.

Range
Ontario, Quebec, W. Maine, and New Hampshire; south to
Georgia; west to Arkansas; north to Minnesota.

Comments
This largest and most showy trillium is frequently cultivated
in wildflower gardens. The underground rootstalks were once
gathered and chewed by Indians for a variety of medicinal
purposes. The plants have also been picked and eaten as
cooked greens. Because the plants arise from the rootstalk, this
practice may be fatal to the plant; the rootstalks often die if
the leaves are removed.

Painted Trillium
Trillium undulatum
447

The erect, stalked flower has an inverted, pink V at the base of
each white, wavy-edged petal.
Flowers: 2–2½″ (5–6.3 cm) wide; sepals 3, green; petals 3,
white and pink; stamens 6, pink-tipped; April–June.
Leaves: 2½–5″ (6.3–12.5 cm) long, in a whorl of 3, stalked,
ovate, tapering to a point, bluish-green, waxy.
Fruit: shiny red berry.
Height: 8–20″ (20–50 cm.)

Habitat
Moist, acid woods and swamps.

Range
Manitoba to Nova Scotia and Quebec; south to New England,
New Jersey, Pennsylvania, West Virginia, and, in the
mountains, to Georgia and Tennessee; west to Michigan and
Wisconsin.

Comments
This attractive woodland trillium is easily recognized
by the splash of pink in the center of the white flower.

Showy Orchis
Orchis spectabilis
448

A short floral stalk with 2–15 white and deep lavender flowers
at the top rises from between 2 large, glossy green leaves.
Flowers: 1″ (2.5 cm) long; 2 lateral petals and 3 sepals fused
together, forming a purple or pink hood over a white spurred
lower lip petal; flowers borne in axils of bracts; April–June.
Leaves: 2½–8″ (6.3–20 cm) long, ovate or elliptic, sheathe
the stem.
Height: 5–12″ (12.5–30 cm).

Habitat
Rich, damp woods and swamp margins.

Range
New Brunswick to New England; south to Georgia; west to
Alabama; north to Tennessee, Missouri, NE. Kansas,
Nebraska, Minnesota, and Ontario.

Comments
The long spur of this beautiful, fragrant orchid of rich woods
provides a syrup very rich in sugar. A rare northern species,
Small Round-leaved Orchis (*O. rotundifolia*), has a single leaf
and purple spots on a white lip.

Indian Pipe
Monotropa uniflora
449

A white, saprophytic plant with a thick, translucent stem
covered with scaly bracts and terminated by a solitary nodding
flower.
Flowers: ½–1″ (1.3–2.5 cm) long; white or salmon-pink;
petals 4–5; stamens 10–12; single pistil; June–September.
Leaves: reduced to scales.
Fruit: ovoid capsule, becoming enlarged and erect as seeds
mature.
Height: 3–9″ (7.5–22.5 cm).

Habitat
Woodland humus.

Range
Throughout.

Comments
This non-green, waxy plant gets its nourishment from decayed
organic material through a symbiotic relationship with a
fungus that is associated with the roots. The plant turns black
as the fruit ripens or when it is picked and dried.

Dutchman's Breeches
Dicentra cucullaria
450

Clusters of fragrant, white, pantaloon-shaped flowers are on a
leafless stalk and overtop the divided, feathery basal leaves.
Flowers: ¾″ (2 cm) long; petals 4, the 2 outer ones with
inflated spurs forming a V; April–May.
Leaves: 3–6″ (7.5–15 cm) long, compound, long-stalked,

grayish green above, paler beneath, with deeply cut leaflets.
Fruit: oblong to linear capsule, opening to base into 2 parts
when mature.
Height: 4–12″ (10–30 cm).

Habitat
Rich woods.

Range
Nova Scotia and Quebec; south through the mountains from
New England to Georgia; west to Alabama and Missouri.

Comments
The generic name of this delicate spring flower derives from
the Greek for "two-spurred." The flowers are pollinated by
early bumblebees, whose proboscis is long enough to tap the
nectar. Honeybees, with a shorter proboscis, can gather only
the pollen with their front feet.

Shinleaf
Pyrola elliptica
451

Greenish-white, waxy, fragrant flowers are in an elongated
cluster on a stalk that rises above evergreen basal leaves.
Flowers: about ⅔″ (16 mm) wide; petals 5, thin, encircling 10
stamens with yellow anthers; pistil 1, with distinctly curved
protruding style; June–August.
Leaves: up to 2¾″ (7 cm) long, dark olive-green, broadly
elliptic or oblong; stalk red.
Fruit: 5-chambered capsule.
Height: 5–10″ (12.5–25 cm).

Habitat
Dry or moist woods.

Range
Newfoundland, Nova Scotia, and New England to
Pennsylvania; west to West Virginia, Ohio, Indiana, N.
Illinois, Iowa, and South Dakota.

Comments
One of the commonest of several species of *Pyrola*. Members of
the genus contain a drug closely related to aspirin; the leaves
have been used on bruises and wounds to reduce pain. Such a
leaf plaster has been referred to as a shin plaster, hence the
common name of this plant.

Canada Mayflower
Maianthemum canadense
452

The short, often zigzag stem has a small dense cluster of tiny
white star-shaped flowers at its top and 1–3 ovate leaves.
Flowers: about ⅙″ (4 mm) long; petals 2; petal-like sepals 2;
stamens 4; May–June.
Leaves: 1–3″ (2.5–7.5 cm) long; heart-shaped at base.
Fruit: berries, initially green, but turning a speckled, dull red
in late summer and red in fall.
Height: 2–6″ (5–15 cm).

Habitat
Upland woods, clearings.

Range
Manitoba to Labrador, Newfoundland, and Nova Scotia; south to New England, Pennsylvania, Delaware; in Appalachian mountains, extends as far south as to Georgia and Tennessee; west to Iowa.

Comments
This common forest herb spreads by rhizomes and frequently forms carpetlike colonies. An unusual member of the lily family, it has only 2 petals, 2 sepals, and 4 stamens instead of the usual 3-3-6 pattern.

Spotted Wintergreen
Chimaphila maculata
453

Nodding, fragrant, waxy, white or pinkish flowers are in small clusters at the top of a stem with whorled evergreen leaves mottled with white.
Flowers: about ⅔″ (16 mm) wide; petals 5; stamens 10; pistil knobby; June–August.
Leaves: ¾–2¾″ (2–7 cm) long, lanceolate, striped with white along midvein.
Fruit: brown capsule, persisting through the winter.
Height: 3–9″ (7.5–22.5 cm).

Habitat
Dry woods.

Range
S. Ontario to S. New Hampshire; south to Georgia; west to Alabama, Tennessee, NE. Illinois, and Michigan.

Comments
This is a conspicuous plant in both winter and summer because of its white and green mottled leaves. It appears to increase both vegetatively and by seedling reproduction following light wildfires. A slightly taller relative, Pipsissewa (*C. umbellata*), has shiny, dark green leaves that lack mottling.

Indian Cucumber Root
Medeola virginiana
454

Several nodding, yellowish-green flowers emerge from the center of a whorl of 3 leaves at the top of a slender, woolly, unbranched stem, on stalks that sometimes bend down below the leaves.
Flowers: ½″ (1.3 cm) long; 3 recurved petals and 3 recurved petal-like sepals; stamens, 6, reddish; ovary with 3 long, brownish, recurved stigmas; May–June.
Leaves: in 2 whorls; those atop stem are 1–3″ (2.5–7.5 cm) long; midway down the stem is another whorl of 6–10 leaves, 2½–5″ (6.3–12.5 cm) long. All ovate to lanceolate.
Fruit: dark bluish-purple berry.
Height: 1–2½′ (30–75 cm).

Habitat
Moist woodlands.

Range
Ontario, Quebec, and Nova Scotia; south to Florida; west to Alabama and Louisiana; north to Minnesota.

Comments
The root is white, has a brittle texture, and tastes and smells somewhat like a cucumber. Once used by Indians for food, today the plant is scarce. Birds are attracted to the fruit. At the time the berries turn bluish purple, the cluster of leaves below them turns red at the lower half.

Bluebead Lily
Clintonia borealis
455, 509

The stalk rises from a basal set of shiny, bright green, oblong leaves and has at its summit 3–6 yellowish-green, drooping, bell-like flowers.
Flowers: ¾–1″ (2–2.5 cm) long; sepals 3, petal-like; petals 3; stamens 6; May–August.
Leaves: 5–8″ (12.5–20 cm).
Fruit: shiny, oval, pure blue berry ½″ (1.3 cm) in diameter.
Height: 6–15″ (15–38 cm).

Habitat
Moist woods, acid soils.

Range
Labrador to northern New England; south to mountains of Georgia and Tennessee; north to Michigan, Wisconsin, and Minnesota.

Comments
The clusters of beautiful fruits are noted for their extraordinary true-blue color. The berries are somewhat poisonous. A less common species, White Clintonia (*C. umbellulata*), has erect white flowers and black berries.

Jack-in-the-pulpit
Arisaema triphyllum
456, 503

Distinctive "Jack-in-the-pulpit" formation grows beneath large leaves.
Flowers: curving ridged hood (the spathe or "pulpit"), green or purplish brown, often streaked or mottled, envelops an erect club (the spadix or "Jack") 2–3″ (5–7.5 cm) long. Spadix bears tiny separate male and female flowers at the base; April–June.
Leaves: 1 or 2, long-stemmed, 3-parted, veined, dull green.
Fruit: cluster of shiny red berries on spadix, late summer–fall.
Height: 1–3′ (30–90 cm).

Habitat
Damp woods and swamps.

Range
S. Quebec and New Brunswick; south through Appalachians and coastal plain to Florida; west to Louisiana and E. Texas.

Comments
Because of needlelike calcium oxalate crystals in the underground tuber, this plant is peppery to the taste and causes a strong burning reaction if eaten raw. This unpleasant property can be eliminated by cooking, and American Indians gathered the fleshy taproots (corms) as a vegetable—hence the alternate common name, Indian Turnip.

Dutchman's Pipe
Aristolochia durior
457

A tall climbing vine with a pipe-shaped or S-shaped, brownish-purple flowers.
Flowers: 2″ (5 cm) long; calyx flares into 3 short lobes; April–June.
Leaves: large, untoothed, heart-shaped, green underside, 6–15″ (15–38 cm).
Height: vine.

Habitat
Rich, moist woods and stream banks.

Range
SW. Pennsylvania and West Virginia; south to uplands of Georgia and Alabama.

Comments
A characteristic plant of the southern Appalachian hardwood forests, Dutchman's Pipe is often cultivated eastward to New Jersey and north to New England. Flowers of this family were once used as an aid in childbirth, since they were thought to resemble a human fetus.

Spanish Moss
Tillandsia usneoides
458

Cascading masses of slender stems covered with gray scales, with a solitary flower at the end of short axillary branches.
Flowers: ½–¾″ (1.3–2 cm) long, with 3 short, narrow, pale green petals that fade to yellow; short bracts; April–June.
Leaves: 1–2″ (2.5–5 cm) long, threadlike, covered with scales.
Height: epiphyte.

Habitat
Hangs from live oak and other tree branches and from telephone wires.

Range
Primarily coastal, Virginia south to Florida; west to Texas.

Comments
Spanish Moss is an air plant (epiphyte), not a parasite; it photosynthesizes its own energy from the sun. The scales help the plant absorb water and nutrients, most of which come from minerals leached from the foliage of the host tree.

Wild Ginger
Asarum canadense
459

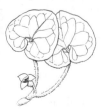

Growing at ground level in the crotch between 2 leafstalks is a single darkish red-brown to green-brown flower.
Flowers: 1½″ (3.8 cm) wide, cup-shaped, with 3 pointed lobes; April–May.
Leaves: a pair; large, hairy, heart-shaped, each 3–6″ (7.5–15 cm) wide, overshadowing the flower.
Height: 6–12″ (15–30 cm).

Habitat
Rich woods.

Range
Quebec to New Brunswick; south to South Carolina; west through Kentucky to Missouri; north to Minnesota.

Comments
The root of this spring flower has a strong gingerlike odor and, when cooked with sugar, can substitute for ginger.

Purple Trillium
Trillium erectum
460

The solitary, nodding flower, with an unpleasant odor, rises on a stalk above a whorl of 3 ovate, diamond-shaped leaves.
Flowers: about 2½" (6.3 cm) wide; petals 3, maroon or reddish brown; sepals 3, green; stamens 6; April–June.
Leaves: to 7" (17.5 cm) long; dark green, net-veined (not parallel-veined as is typical of most members of this family).
Fruit: oval reddish berry.
Height: 8–16" (20–40 cm).

Habitat
Rich woods.

Range
Ontario, Quebec, and Nova Scotia; south to New England, Delaware, Pennsylvania, West Virginia, and, in the mountains, to Georgia; west to Tennessee; north to Michigan.

Comments
This is one of the most common eastern trilliums. Its foul smell attracts carrion flies that act as pollinators. Early herbalists used this ill-scented plant to treat gangrene. The floral parts and leaves of these perennials are arranged in 3s or multiples of 3, typical of the lily family.

Flame Azalea
Rhododendron calendulaceum
461

A deciduous shrub with terminal clusters of orange, red, or yellow flowers that are tubular and vase-shaped.
Flowers: 1½–2" (3.8–5 cm) wide, with 5 corolla lobes exceeded by 5 long stamens and style; corolla tube glandular and sticky; flowers not fragrant; May–June.
Leaves: 2–4" (5–10 cm) long, ovate.
Fruit: hairy capsule.
Height: to 15' (4.5 m).

Habitat
Dry open woods and mountain balds.

Range
SW. Pennsylvania south through mountains to Georgia and Alabama; west to West Virginia and SE. Ohio.

Comments
This beautiful southern azalea forms striking displays on some of the grassy balds of the southern Appalachians. A wide variation of color forms occurs, from all shades of yellow to orange and scarlet. Flowers appear before or with new leaves.

Wood Lily
Lilium philadelphicum
462

An erect stem bears whorled leaves and 1–5 upward-opening, orange flowers with purplish-brown spots.
Flowers: 2" (5 cm) wide; 6-segmented, with 3 petals and 3 petal-like sepals, each tapering to a stalked base with spaces

between the stalks; stamens 6; June–August.
Leaves: 1–4″ (2.5–10 cm) long; lanceolate, usually in whorls of 3–8.
Fruit: an oblong capsule, 1–2″ (2.5–5 cm) long.
Height: 1–3′ (30–90 cm).

Habitat
Dry woods and thickets.

Range
S. Ontario and Quebec; south to Maine, southern New England, Delaware, Maryland, West Virginia, and, in the mountains, to North Carolina and Kentucky.

Comments
This bulbous Lily, one of our truly showy woodland species, is usually found in relatively dry sites. The bulbs were gathered for food by Indians. The Southern Red Lily (*L. catesbaei*) has alternate, lanceolate leaves pressed against the stem, and the Orange Lily (*L. bulbiferum*) has sepals and petals downy within and bulblets in the axils of the upper leaves.

Trout Lily
Erythonium americanum
463

A pair of brownish-mottled leaves sheath the base of a stalk that bears a solitary nodding flower, yellow inside, bronzy outside.
Flowers: 1″ (2.5 cm) wide; petals 3 and petal-like sepals 3, all curved backwards; stamens 6, with brownish or yellow anthers; March–June.
Leaves: 2–8″ (5–20 cm) long, elliptic.
Fruit: ovoid capsule.
Height: 4–10″ (10–25 cm).

Habitat
Rich woods and meadows.

Range
Ontario to New Brunswick and Nova Scotia; south through New England to Georgia; west to Tennessee, Arkansas, Oklahoma; north to Minnesota.

Comments
Another widely used name for this species is Dogtooth Violet, which refers to the toothlike shape of the white underground bulb. The name "Trout Lily" (a more suitable name, since the flower is not a violet) refers to the similarity between the leaf markings and those of the brown or brook trout.

Woodland Sunflower
Helianthus strumosus
464

Yellow flower heads on branches from a smooth or slightly rough main stem.
Flowers: 2½–3½″ (6.3–9 cm) wide, with 9–15 ray flowers surrounding yellow disk flowers; August–September.
Leaves: 3–8″ (7.5–20 cm) long, mostly opposite, ovate to broadly lanceolate, shallow-toothed or with a smooth margin; rough above, pale to whitish and somewhat hairy underneath.
Height: 3–7′ (90–210 cm).

Habitat
Woods, thickets, and clearings.

Range
Quebec; New England south to Georgia; west to Oklahoma; north to North Dakota.

Comments
This is one of approximately 20 species of sunflowers with yellow disk flowers that bloom in our range.

Sessile Bellwort
Uvularia sessilifolia
465

The 1 or 2 creamy-yellow, drooping flowers are at the top of an angled stem having unstalked leaves.
Flowers: about 1″ (2.5 cm) long; narrowly bell-shaped; sepals 3, petal-like; petals 3; stamens 6; April–June.
Leaves: 1¾–3″ (4.5–7.5 cm) long; oblong, light green above, whitish below.
Fruit: 3-angled capsule similar to a beechnut.
Height: 6–12″ (15–30 cm).

Habitat
Woods, thickets.

Range
New Brunswick, Nova Scotia, and New England; south to Georgia; west to Alabama, Missouri, and North Dakota.

Comments
This common woodland wildflower has a near relative, Perfoliate Bellwort (*U. perfoliata*), whose stem appears to pierce the leaves. The interior surface of the flowers is roughened with small glands. At one time these plants were thought to cure throat diseases because the flowers resemble the uvula, the lobe at the back of the throat.

Downy False Foxglove
Aureolaria virginica
466

At the top of a downy stem is a terminal cluster of funnel-shaped, yellow flowers, with each flower solitary in the axils of opposite bracts.
Flowers: 1″ (2.5 cm) wide; corolla with 5 flaring lobes, stamens 4; June–August.
Leaves: 2½–5″ (6.3–12.5 cm) long; opposite, downy, lanceolate to ovate; the lower ones pinnately lobed, upper leaves with fewer lobes or none.
Height: 1–5′ (30–150 cm).

Habitat
Dry open woods.

Range
New Hampshire south to N. Florida; west to Louisiana; north to Michigan.

Comments
Like the very similar Smooth False Foxglove (*A. laevigata*), this plant is partly parasitic on the roots of oaks.

Spicebush
Lindera benzoin
467

A deciduous shrub with dense clusters of tiny, pale yellow flowers that bloom before the leaves from globose buds along the twigs.
Flowers: ⅛" (3 mm) wide; sepals and petals all alike, 6. Male and female flowers occur on separate plants; March–April.
Leaves: 2–5½" (5–13.8 cm) long; dark green, oblong, smooth, untoothed, and have an aromatic, spicy fragrance when crushed.
Fruit: ovoid, shiny, red, berrylike drupes.
Height: 6–17' (1.8–5.1 m).

Habitat
Swamps and wet woods.

Range
Maine south to Florida; west to Texas; north to Missouri, Iowa, and Ontario.

Comments
In the North this plant is thought of as the "forsythia of the wilds" because its early spring flowering gives a subtle yellow tinge to many lowland woods where it is common. A tea can be made from the aromatic leaves and twigs.

Yellow Lady's Slipper
Cypripedium calceolus
468

Borne terminally on a leafy stalk are 1 or 2 fragrant flowers with an inflated, yellow, pouch-shaped lower "lip" petal.
Flowers: lip about 2" (5 cm) long; side petals 2, spirally twisted, greenish yellow to brownish purple; sepals 2, greenish yellow, lanceolate, 1 above and 1 below lip; April–August.
Leaves: up to 8" (20 cm) long, usually 3–5, oval to elliptic, with pronounced parallel veins.
Height: 4–28" (10–70 cm).

Habitat
Bogs, swamps, and rich woods.

Range
Newfoundland, south to mountains of Georgia; west to Texas and Arkansas.

Comments
These plants form a highly variable population. Other varieties are recognized, among them Small Yellow Lady's Slipper (var. *parviflorum*), once considered a separate species, which has very fragrant flowers and is found mostly in limestone wetlands, only rarely as far south as the Appalachian mountains. The species name derives from Latin and means "a little shoe."

Pinesap
Monotropa hypopitys
469

A saprophytic, red, pink, lavender, or yellow plant with several vaselike, nodding flowers on a downy, scaly stem; stem and flower same color.
Flowers: about ½" (1.3 cm) long; petals 4 on lateral flowers, 5 on terminal one; June–November.

Leaves: reduced to scales up to ½" (1 cm) long; clasp the stem, more numerous toward base of plant.
Fruit: erect, ovoid capsule.
Height: 4–16" (10–40 cm).

Habitat
Upland woods, usually in acid soil.

Range
Throughout.

Comments
The plant pictured here is an autumn-flowering one, characterized by the red color. Early-flowering plants are genetically different forms and are yellow. Like its single-flowered relative, Indian Pipe (*M. uniflora*), this plant is a saprophyte; it does not carry on photosynthesis but obtains its nourishment from fungi associated with roots, often those of oaks or pines. Sweet Pinesap (*Monotropsis odorata*), closely related and similar, occurs in the southern mountains and Piedmont.

Pink Lady's Slipper
Cypripedium acaule
470

A leafless stalk bears 1 flower (rarely 2) with a distinctive pink, inflated, slipperlike lower "lip" petal, veined with red and with a fissure down the front.
Flowers: lip about 2½" (6.3 cm) long; sepals and side petals greenish brown, spreading; petals lanceolate, narrower than sepals; April–July.
Leaves: to 8" (20 cm) long, in 2's, basal, oval, ribbed, dark green above, silvery-hairy beneath.
Fruit: erect capsule, to 1¾" (4.5 cm) long.
Height: 6–15" (15–37.5 cm).

Habitat
Dry forests, especially pine woods; often in humus mats covering rock outcrops; occasionally in moist woods.

Range
Saskatchewan to Newfoundland and Nova Scotia; south to South Carolina and Georgia; west to Alabama and Tennessee; north to Minnesota.

Comments
This is one of the largest native orchids and is found both in low, sandy woods and in higher, rocky woods of mountains. At times several hundred of these striking flowers grow in a small area. Nevertheless, like other woodland wildflowers it should not be picked. Also called Pink Moccasin-flower.

Calypso
Calypso bulbosa
471

A single, showy pendant flower with an inflated, slipperlike lower "lip" petal.
Flowers: 1½–2" (3.8–5 cm) long; lip petal white blotched with purple, bearded with yellow hairs, and with 2 hornlike points at the toe; 5 purplish-pink, narrow parts (sepals and petals) are above the lip; May–July.

Leaves: about 3″ (7.5 cm) long, solitary, basal, ovate, margin wavy; it withers after plant flowers and is replaced by an overwintering leaf.
Height: 3–8″ (7.5–20 cm).

Habitat
Cool, damp, mossy woods, mainly coniferous.

Range
Across Canada; south to New England and N. New York; west to Michigan and Minnesota.

Comments
This short perennial rises from a small tuber and is the only species in this genus found in the northern latitudes. Named for the nymph in Homer's *Odyssey*, it is also called the Fairy Slipper.

Twinflower
Linnaea borealis
472

A low, delicate evergreen plant with trailing stems having short, upright branches, each terminated by 2 pinkish-white, nodding, bell-shaped flowers. Stems hairy.
Flowers: ½″ (1.3 cm) long; corolla 5-lobed, hairy inside; June–August.
Leaves: about ½″ (1 cm) wide and ½–1″ (1.3–2.5 cm) long; opposite, rounded, light green, with toothed edges; low on flower stalks.
Height: creeper, with flowering branches 3–6″ (7.5–15 cm) high.

Habitat
Cool woods and bogs.

Range
Alaska to Greenland; south to New England, Maryland, and West Virginia; west to Ohio, Indiana, and South Dakota.

Comments
A beautiful trailing plant of the North, this is the American variety of a European plant. It was named after Carolus Linnaeus (1707–1778), the father of modern botany, who was so fond of the flower he had his portrait painted with it.

Sand Myrtle
Leiophyllum buxifolium
473

A low, upright, widely branching evergreen shrub with crowded, leathery leaves and small pink or pinkish-white flowers in dense, bracted clusters.
Flowers: about ¼″ (6 mm) wide; sepals and petals 5; stamens 10; April–June.
Leaves: ⅓–1″ (8–25 mm) long; opposite or alternate, oval to oblong, smooth, shining.
Height: 4–20″ (10–50 cm).

Habitat
Rocky or sandy woods and bluffs.

Range
New Jersey, North and South Carolina, E. Kentucky.

Comments
The genus name is from the Greek *leios* ("smooth") and *phyllon* ("leaf"). The species name also refers to the leaves, similar to those of Box (*Buxus*).

Wild Columbine
Aquilegia canadensis
474

A nodding, red and yellow flower with upward spurred petals alternating with spreading, colored sepals and numerous yellow stamens hanging below the petals.
Flowers: 1–2″ (2.5–5 cm) long; sepals 5, red; petals 5, the blade yellow and the hollow spur red; stamens forming a column; April–July.
Leaves: 4–6″ (10–15 cm) wide, compound, long-stalked, divided into 9–27 light green, 3-lobed leaflets.
Fruit: beaked, dry pod, splitting open along inner side.
Height: 1–2′ (30–60 cm).

Habitat
Rocky, wooded or open slopes.

Range
Ontario to Quebec; south throughout New England to Georgia; west to Tennessee and Wisconsin.

Comments
This beautiful woodland wildflower has showy, drooping, bell-like flowers equipped with distinctly backward-pointing tubes, similar to the garden Columbines. These tubes, or spurs, contain nectar that attracts long-tongued insects especially adapted for reaching the sweet secretion. European Columbine (*A. vulgaris*), with blue, violet, pink, or white short-spurred flowers, was introduced from Europe and has now become well established in many parts of our range.

Fringed Polygala
Polygala paucifolia
475

A low plant, flowering from prostrate underground stems and rootstocks, with pink flowers tinged with purple in the axils of clustered upper leaves.
Flowers: ¾″ (2 cm) long; sepals 5, the 2 lateral ones winglike; petals 3, forming a tube with a delicate, finely fringed yellow or pink crest; May–June.
Leaves: upper ones ¾–1½″ (2–3.8 cm) long; oval, crowded at top of stem; lower ones reduced, bractlike.
Height: 3–7″ (7.5–17.5 cm).

Habitat
Rich, moist woods.

Range
Manitoba to New Brunswick; south through New England, and inland to Virginia and the mountains of Georgia; west to Tennessee, N. Illinois, Minnesota, and Manitoba.

Comments
This exquisite Orchid-like wildflower resembles a tailless, tiny airplane. It was thought that, if eaten by nursing mothers or fed to cows, milkworts would increase milk production.

Shooting Star
Dodecatheon meadia
476

Nodding flowers with strongly backward-pointing petals are in flat-topped clusters.
Flowers: 1" (2.5 cm) long; petals 5, rose, lilac, or white; stamens 5, yellow, protruding; April–June.
Leaves: up to 6" (15 cm) long, basal, dark green, lanceolate with reddish bases.
Height: 8–20" (20–50 cm).

Habitat
Open woods, meadows, and prairies.

Range
Pennsylvania to Georgia; west to E. Texas; north to Wisconsin.

Comments
The Shooting Star is often cultivated. Bees, the chief pollinators, must force their tongues between the united stamens to reach the stigma of the pistil. The plant was far more abundant during the days of the prairie settlers.

Wild Bleeding Heart
Dicentra eximia
477

Several deep pink to red, drooping, heart-shaped flowers are strung along a leafless stem.
Flowers: ¾" (2 cm) long; petals 4, in 2 pairs; rounded outer petals form "heart" while inner petals form "drop of blood"; May–August.
Leaves: to 10" (25 cm) long, all basal, pinnately compound, finely cut.
Height: 10–18" (25–45 cm).

Habitat
Rocky woods and cliffs.

Range
New York south to Georgia; west to West Virginia and Tennessee.

Comments
This native perennial resembles the more showy Asian species of Bleeding Heart (*D. spectabilis*), which is often cultivated in eastern gardens. Typical of rocky woods and ledges, this species is common southward along the mountains.

Lousewort
Pedicularis canadensis
478

A hairy plant with tubular, 2-lipped flowers, all red, all yellow, or yellow and red in a short, dense, terminal cluster.
Flowers: ¾" (2 cm) long; petals united, the upper lip arched, with 2 small teeth, the lower lip shorter, 3-lobed, spreading; stamens 4, 2 long and 2 short, attached to upper lip. Leaflike bracts present beneath flowers; April–June.
Leaves: 3–5" (7.5–12.5 cm) long, mostly basal, oblong-lanceolate, deeply divided into toothed lobes.
Height: 6–18" (15–45 cm).

Habitat
Woods and clearings.

Range
Manitoba to Quebec; south through central Maine to Florida; west to Mississippi, Louisiana, and Texas; north to Minnesota.

Comments
Also known as Wood Betony, these low, semi-parasitic plants get some of their nourishment from the roots of other plants. The genus name and the common name both refer to the misconception once held by farmers that cattle and sheep became infested with lice when grazing on the plants.

Wood Sage
Teucrium canadense
479

A terminal, spikelike cluster of lavender-pink flowers on a downy, square stem.
Flowers: ¾" (2 cm) long; corolla appears 1-lipped (actually 2) with 5 lobes, the lower lobe long and flattened, the lateral and upper lobes short; projecting stamens 4; June–September.
Leaves: 2–4" (5–10 cm) long; opposite, lanceolate, toothed, with undersurfaces densely hairy.
Height: 1–3' (30–90 cm).

Habitat
Thickets, woods, and shores.

Range
E. New Brunswick and Nova Scotia south along the coast to Florida and Texas; up Mississippi River; west to Oklahoma.

Comments
The alternate name, Germander, was derived from a Greek name for ground oak, *chamaidrys*. Two smaller, bushier species have been introduced from Europe into our range: *T. scordonia*, also called Wood Sage, has yellow flowers; Cut-leaved Germander (*T. botrys*) is an annual with purplish flowers.

Fireweed
Epilobium angustifolium
480

A terminal, spikelike cluster of deep pink flowers and narrow willowlike leaves on a tall stem.
Flowers: 1" (2.5 cm) wide; petals 4, spreading; stamens 8; and a 4-parted stigma at the end of the style; July–September.
Leaves: up to 8" (20 cm) long, lanceolate to linear.
Fruit: capsule up to 3" (7.5 cm) long; splits open to reveal white, silky down aiding in seed dispersal.
Height: 2–6' (60–180 cm).

Habitat
Recently cleared woodlands, especially burned over areas.

Range
Throughout Canada; south to Maryland and in the mountains of North Carolina and Tennessee; west to N. Ohio, central Indiana, and South Dakota.

Comments
This is a showy, post-fire invader and a spectacular sight in mass. The seeds are dispersed far and wide by long white hairs. 9 other native species with small flowers occur in the East.

Large Purple Fringed Orchid
Habenaria fimbriata
481

The deeply fringed, fragrant, lavender flowers are in a many-flowered, elongated cluster on a leafy stem.
Flowers: 1" (2.5 cm) long; upper sepal and 2 lateral petals, erect; lateral sepals ovate, spreading; lower "lip" petal with 3 fan-shaped, fringed lobes and backward-pointing spur; sepal and petals similarly colored; June–August.
Leaves: lower ones to 8" (20 cm) long, ovate to lanceolate, sheathing the stem; upper ones small, lanceolate.
Height: 2–4' (60–120 cm).

Habitat
Cool moist woods, wet meadows, and swamp margins.

Range
Newfoundland to New England; south to Maryland and West Virginia; in the mountains to North Carolina and Tennessee; northwest to Wisconsin and Ontario.

Comments
These Fringed Orchids are pollinated by moths. The pollen masses bear a sticky disc that protrudes below the anther. As the moth extends its tongue into the spur of the lip petal and then out again, it pulls the pollen mass from the anther and carries it to another flower where cross-pollination occurs.

Pinxter Flower
Rhododendron nudiflorum
482

A deciduous shrub with terminal clusters of pink, tubular, vase-shaped, slightly fragrant flowers.
Flowers: 1½–2" (3.8–5 cm) wide; 5 corolla lobes exceeded by 5 long, curved stamens and 1 style; May–June.
Leaves: 2–4" (5–10 cm) long; thin, oblong, pointed at both ends, clustered in pseudowhorls near ends of twigs; hairy only on midrib beneath.
Fruit: slender, erect, hairy capsule.
Height: 2–6' (60–180 cm).

Habitat
Upland woods and thickets; borders of swamps and bogs.

Range
Massachusetts to South Carolina, Tennessee, and S. Ohio.

Comments
This much-branched shrub, also called Pink Azalea, is especially showy in flower. It is relatively tolerant of dry sites and can be transplanted into wild shrub gardens. The flowers often appear before its leaves are fully expanded.

Wild Bergamot
Monarda fistulosa
483

A dense, rounded cluster of lavender tubular flowers is at the top of a square stem.
Flowers: 1" (2.5 cm) long; corolla with hairy 2-lobed upper lip, broader 3-lobed lower lip, stamens 2, projecting; bracts under flower cluster often pink-tinged; June–September.
Leaves: about 2½" (6.3 cm) long; gray-green, opposite, lanceolate, coarsely toothed.
Height: 2–4' (60–120 cm).

Habitat
Dry fields, thickets, borders; common in calcareous regions.

Range
Quebec and western New England; south to Maryland, upland to Georgia and Alabama; west to Louisiana and E. Texas.

Comments
A showy perennial, frequently in cultivation, its aromatic leaves can be used to make mint tea. Long ago, oil from the leaves was used to treat respiratory ailments.

Purple-flowering Raspberry
Rubus odoratus
485

This erect, shrubby, thornless plant has rose-lavender flowers in loose clusters; new branches have bristly hairs.
Flowers: 1–2″ (2.5–5 cm) wide; 5 roselike petals; many stamens and pistils; June–September.
Leaves: 4–10″ (10–25 cm) wide, large, maple-like, 3–5 lobed, heart-shaped at base.
Fruit: red, broad, shallow; raspberry-like when mature.
Height: 3–6′ (90–180 cm).

Habitat
Rocky woods, thickets.

Range
S. Ontario to Nova Scotia; south through New England to Georgia; west to Tennessee; north to Michigan.

Comments
Baked-apple Berry (*R. chamaemorus*) is a dwarf form only 12″ (30 cm) tall, with a solitary white flower, an amber-colored berry, and smaller leaves. It is found on mountaintops in New England and northward into Canada. All other species in our range have compound leaves and usually spiny stems.

Trailing Arbutus
Epigaea repens
486

A trailing evergreen plant with sweet-scented pink or white flowers in terminal and axillary clusters on hairy stems.
Flowers: about ½″ (1.3 cm) wide; corolla tubular, hairy within, flaring into 5 lobes, each as long as the corolla tube; February–May.
Leaves: ¾–3″ (2–7.5 cm) long; leathery, oval, with hairy margins.
Fruit: capsule splitting open into 5 parts, exposing whitish pulp covered with tiny seeds.
Height: creeper.

Habitat
Sandy or rocky woods, especially on acid soil.

Range
Quebec and Nova Scotia; south from New England and New York to Florida; west to Mississippi and Ohio.

Comments
For this favorite wildflower with an exquisite fragrance, one must search among the fallen leaves in early spring. It favors

exposed sites where the plants are not smothered by leaf litter.
Abrupt environmental disturbances, such as lumbering and
grazing, may account for its present scarcity.

Round-lobed Hepatica
Hepatica americana
487

A low plant with round-lobed basal leaves and several hairy
stalks bearing solitary, pinkish, lavender, or white flowers.
Flowers: ½–1″ (1.3–2.5 cm) wide; sepals 5–9, petal-like;
petals lacking; stamens numerous; pistils several. Three green
sepal-like, broadly oval to elliptic bracts surround flower;
March–June.
Leaves: 2–2½″ (5–6.3 cm) wide, basal, with 3 rounded lobes.
Fruit: several, hairy, seedlike.
Height: 4–6″ (10–15 cm).

Habitat
Dry rocky woods.

Range
Manitoba to Nova Scotia; south to N. Florida; west to
Alabama; north to Missouri and Minnesota.

Comments
This is an early spring wildflower, usually with lavender
flowers and 3-lobed leaves that persist throughout the winter.
The Sharp-lobed Hepatica (*H. acutiloba*) has more pointed leaf
lobes and bracts. The genus name refers to the 3-lobed leaf
that supposedly resembles the liver.

Common Wood Sorrel
Oxalis montana
488

A low-growing plant with Cloverlike foliage and several white
or pink flowers, with only 1 flower per stalk.
Flowers: ¾″ (2 cm) wide; petals 5, notched, with deep pink
veins; stamens 10; pistil 1; May–July.
Leaves: basal, divided into 3 heart-shaped leaflets, each about
½″ (1.3 cm) wide; slightly sour taste, close at night.
Height: 3–6″ (7.5–15 cm).

Habitat
Rich, damp woods.

Range
Newfoundland and Nova Scotia; south to central and W. New
England; west to Pennsylvania and in the mountains to North
Carolina and Tennessee; west to Ohio, Michigan, Wisconsin,
Minnesota, and Manitoba.

Comments
This dainty flower of the mountains and cool, moist woodland
glens is especially common in New England and westward to
the lake states. It is difficult to grow in gardens.

Spring Beauty
Claytonia virginica
489

A low plant with loose clusters of pink or whitish flowers,
striped with dark pink.
Flowers: ½–¾″ (1.3–2 cm) wide; sepals 2; petals 5; stamens
5 with pink anthers; March–May.

Leaves: 2–8" (5–20 cm) long, usually a single pair, opposite, dark green, linear, tapering; present midway up stem.
Fruit: small capsule enclosed by the 2 sepals.
Height: 6–12" (15–30 cm).

Habitat
Moist woods, thickets, and clearings.

Range
Ontario to Quebec and southern New England; south to Georgia; west to Louisiana and Texas; north to Minnesota.

Comments
This most attractive spring perennial is spectacular in large patches. It grows from an underground tuber like a small potato; this has a sweet, chestnutlike flavor. Indians and colonists used these tubers for food.

Bluets
Houstonia caerulea
490

A low plant with erect, slender stems bearing pale blue flowers with golden-yellow centers.
Flowers: about ½" (1.3 cm) wide; corolla tubular, with 4 flattish lobes. Flowers pistillate (female) or staminate (male); April–June.
Leaves: basal ones to ½" (1.3 cm) long, oblong, in tufts; stem leaves tiny, opposite.
Height: 3–6" (7.5–15 cm).

Habitat
Grassy slopes and fields, thickets, and lawns on acid soils.

Range
Ontario to Nova Scotia; south to Georgia; west to Alabama; north to Wisconsin.

Comments
This lovely, delicate flowering plant is often found in striking patches of light blue. The Star Violet (*H. minima*), to 4" (10 cm) high, has a tiny purple flower and occurs in fields and open woods westward to Kansas, Arkansas, and Texas.

Bird-foot Violet
Viola pedata
491

This smooth plant has deep blue-violet flowers and deeply-cut leaves on separate stalks.
Flowers: often 1½" (3.8 cm) wide, larger than most violets; petals 5, beardless, the lower one whitish, veined with violet, grooved and spurred; stamens 5, with orange anthers conspicuous in throat of flower; March–June.
Leaves: 1–2" (2.5–5 cm) long, fan-shaped, with linear, toothed segments.
Height: 4–10" (10–25 cm).

Habitat
Dry, sandy fields; wood openings.

Range
Throughout most of eastern North America; west to E. Kansas and Oklahoma.

Comments
A most beautiful violet of dry, upland sites, its showy, light violet-blue flowers, distinctive "bird's-foot"-shaped leaves make it easy to identify. Bird-foot Violet is pollinated by bees and butterflies. The bicolored form of this species, with its 2 upper petals a deep violet and the lower 3 a lilac shade, has been considered the most beautiful violet in the world.

Common Blue Violet
Viola papilionacea
492

This smooth, low plant has flowers and leaves on separate stalks.
Flowers: ½–¾" (1.3–2 cm) wide; blue to white, or white with purple veins; petals 5, the lower one longer and spurred, the 2 lateral ones bearded; March–June.
Leaves: to 5" (12.5 cm) wide; heart-shaped with scalloped margins.
Fruit: 3-valved capsule.
Height: 3–8" (7.5–20 cm).

Habitat
Damp woods, moist meadows, roadsides.

Range
Throughout eastern North America.

Comments
In addition to the normal flowers there are often flowers near the ground that fail to open, but their whitish fruit produces vast quantities of seeds. Violet leaves are high in vitamins A and C and can be used in salads or cooked as greens. The flowers can be made into candies and jellies.

Spring Larkspur
Delphinium tricorne
493

An open cluster of blue or violet spurred flowers is at the top of a simple, fleshy stem that has deeply cleft leaves.
Flowers: ¾" (2 cm) wide; sepals 5, petal-like, the upper one prolonged into a slightly bent, backward-projecting spur about ½" (1.3 cm) long; petals 4, very small, the upper ones enclosed in the calyx spur; April–May.
Leaves: 2–4" (5–10 cm) wide; deeply palmately cut into narrow lobes.
Fruit: seedpod that separates into 3 widely-diverging parts, the dried ends curling upward like horns.
Height: 4–24" (10–60 cm).

Habitat
Rich woods.

Range
Pennsylvania south to Georgia; west to Arkansas, Oklahoma, and Nebraska; north to Minnesota.

Comments
The species name refers to the 3-horned fruits. The flower structure is similar to that of the Rocket Larkspur (*D. ajacis*), which is often cultivated in gardens. Larkspurs contain a harmful alkaloid that frequently poisons grazing cattle.

Passionflower
Passiflora incarnata
494

A climbing or trailing vine with large, strikingly fringed flowers.
Flowers: 1½–2½" (3.8–6.3 cm) wide; 5 outer sepals and 5 petals form a whitish or bluish, wheel-like backdrop, upon which rests a fringe of 2–3 circles of purple and pinkish threadlike segments; stamens 5, drooping, suspended around 3-styled pistil; June–September.
Leaves: 3–5" (7.5–12.5 cm) wide, palmately 3-lobed; 2 conspicuous glands on petiole near blade; tendrils present.
Fruit: yellow berry, 2–3" (5–7.5 cm) long.
Height: vine.

Habitat
Sandy thickets and open areas.

Range
SW. Pennsylvania to Maryland; south to Florida; west to Texas; north to Oklahoma, Missouri, Illinois, Indiana, and Ohio.

Comments
This unusual flower is widely distributed in the South, especially from Florida to Texas. The name relates to the resemblance of the floral parts to aspects of the crucifixion story. The 10 petal-like parts represent the disciples, excluding Peter and Judas; the 5 stamens the wounds Jesus received; the knoblike stigmas the nails; the fringe the crown of thorns. Yellow Passionflower (*P. lutea*), a small yellow-flowered species, occurs in many parts of the Southeast.

Crested Dwarf Iris
Iris cristata
495

A single, violet-blue flower (occasionally 2), with 6 spreading petal-like parts, is at the top of a short, slender stalk.
Flowers: about 2½" (6.3 cm) wide; 3 broad, down-curved petal-like sepals and 3 narrower, arching petals. Sepals "bearded"–crested with yellow or white ridges, streaked with purple; styles 3, curving over the sepals, 2-lobed; stamens 3, hidden under the styles; April–May.
Leaves: 4–7" (10–17.5 cm) at flowering time, longer later, ½–1" (1.3–2.5 cm) wide; flat, lanceolate, sheath the stem.
Fruit: sharply 3-sided capsule.
Height: 4–9" (10–22.5 cm).

Habitat
Wooded hillsides and ravines.

Range
Maryland south to Georgia; west to Mississippi, Arkansas, Oklahoma, Missouri, and Indiana.

Comments
This is a low, bearded Iris of southern and midwestern wooded uplands. The Dwarf Iris (*I. verna*) is very fragrant, has non-bearded sepals, narrower leaves less than ½" (1.3 cm) wide, and occurs on peaty soils and pine barrens from Maryland south.

Fringed Phacelia
Phacelia fimbriata
496

A branching plant with 1-sided, coiled clusters of light blue, lavender, or white flowers with deeply fringed petals.
Flowers: ½" (1.3 cm) wide; corolla somewhat bell-shaped, with 5-spreading, fringed lobes; May–June.
Leaves: about 2" (5 cm) long; pinnately cut into 5–11 triangular-to-oblong lobes; the upper leaves unstalked, lower ones stalked.
Height: 8–16" (20–40 cm).

Habitat
Upland woods.

Range
Virginia to Alabama.

Comments
The strikingly fringed petals are especially beautiful under a hand lens. They characterize this spring wildflower of the Great Smoky Mountains, where it can occur in abundance.

Virginia Bluebells
Mertensia virginica
497

Erect plant with smooth gray-green foliage; nodding clusters of pink buds open into light blue trumpet-shaped flowers.
Flowers: about 1" (2.5 cm) long; corolla 5-lobed; March–June.
Leaves: basal leaves 2–8" (5–20 cm) long; stem leaves smaller, alternate, oval, untoothed.
Height: 8–24" (20–60 cm).

Habitat
Moist woods; rarely, meadows; especially on floodplains.

Range
S. Ontario; W. New York south to N. North Carolina and Alabama; west to Arkansas and E. Kansas; north to Minnesota.

Comments
When it grows in masses, this species—also called Virginia Cowslip—makes a spectacular show. A smaller, trailing, rosy-pink-flowered species, Sea Lungwort (*M. maritima*), occurs on beaches from Newfoundland to Massachusetts.

Harebell
Campanula rotundifolia
498

Blue, bell-like flowers borne singly or in clusters on nodding threadlike stalks.
Flowers: ¾" (2 cm) long, 5-lobed; with 3-part stigma, not protruding beyond petals, and 5 lavender stamens; June–September.
Leaves: stem leaves to 3" (7.5 cm) long, numerous, narrow; basal leaves, when present, broadly ovate.
Fruit: nodding capsule.
Height: 6–20" (15–50 cm).

Habitat
Rocky banks and slopes, meadows, and shores.

Range
Northern Canada through Northeast and Midwest to Texas.

Comments
The characteristics of this perennial vary considerably, depending on habitat conditions. Among other common species are the Southern Harebell (*C. divaricata*), with wider leaves and smaller, white or pale lavender flowers, typical of wet, grassy meadows. The common garden Bellflower (*C. rapunculoides*), which frequently escapes from cultivation, has lanceolate or heart-shaped leaves.

Mistletoe
Phoradendron serotinum
499

Semiparasitic shrub with short, interrupted, axillary clusters of tiny yellow flowers on smooth, green, jointed stems.
Flowers: about ⅛" (3 mm) wide; petals lacking; calyx 3-lobed; male and female flowers on different plants; September–October.
Leaves: ¾ to 5" (2–12.5 cm) long, opposite, ovate to lanceolate, thick, leathery.
Fruit: white, berrylike, less than ¼" (6 mm) in diameter.
Height: 1' (30 cm).

Habitat
Parasitic on branches of deciduous trees exposed to sun.

Range
New Jersey and Pennsylvania south to Florida and west to West Virginia, Ohio, Indiana, Illinois, Missouri, Kansas, and E. Texas.

Comments
This is the common Mistletoe hung at Christmastime. The fruits are covered with a sticky substance poisonous to man, but relished by such birds as cedar waxwings and bluebirds. The birds spread the seeds through their droppings and by wiping their beaks on branches, where a new plant may become established.

Winterberry
Ilex verticillata
500, 505

A deciduous holly shrub with very small white flowers that grow in the leaf axils.
Flowers: in clusters ¼–½" (6–13 mm) wide, each flower 4- to 6-parted; June–August.
Leaves: 2" (5 cm) long, elliptical, toothed but not spiny.
Fruit: berrylike, showy red, less than ¼" (6 mm) wide, on very short stalks, singly or in clusters along the branches.
Height: 3–10' (90–300 cm).

Habitat
Swamps, damp thickets, and pond margins.

Range
Ontario to Nova Scotia; south from New England to Georgia; west to Mississippi; north to Tennessee, Missouri, Michigan, and Minnesota.

Comments
Extremely showy in late fall and early winter when covered with their bright red fruit, these shrubs are either male or

female—a trait typical of the holly family. Birds are readily attracted to Winterberry. Since this shrub grows in both wet and dry sites, it is an adaptable naturalizer.

Winged Sumac
Rhus copallina
502

A shrub or small tree with hairy twigs, milky sap, and small greenish flowers.
Flowers: clusters to 6″ (15 cm) long, dense pyramidal, terminal; July–September.
Leaves: hairy, pinnately compound, with winged midrib between untoothed shiny leaflets 3″ (7.5 cm) long.
Fruit: berrylike, reddish brown, covered with short hairs.
Height: 3–30′ (90–900 cm).

Habitat
Dry woods and clearings.

Range
New York south to Florida; west to Texas; north to Kansas and Wisconsin.

Comments
Like the Smooth (*R. glabra*) and Staghorn Sumac (*R. typhina*), this plant is cropped by deer and moose. The fruits are rich in vitamin A and, though apparently not much relished by birds, are a good food source in winter when other fruits are scarce.

Bearberry
Arctostaphylos uva-ursi
507

Low, trailing evergreen shrub with terminal clusters of white or pale pink, bell-shaped flowers.
Flowers: about ⅕″ (5 mm) long; petals 5, fused; May–July.
Leaves: ½–1½″ (1.3–3.8 cm) long; spatulate or wedge-shaped, smooth, leathery, green on both sides.
Fruit: red, berrylike.
Height: creeper; flowering branches 6–12″ (15–30 cm) high.

Habitat
Exposed rocky and sandy sites.

Range
Arctic regions south to Virginia; west to Indiana and N. Illinois.

Comments
This ground-trailing shrub has the papery, reddish, exfoliating bark typical of woody plants in northern climes. It is frequently seen as a ground cover in sandy areas of the Northeast, especially the New Jersey Pine Barrens. It is very common on Cape Cod, where it covers vast areas in open, sandy, pine-studded communities. It is a hardy shrub for landscaping rocky or sandy sites. An astringent tea, sometimes used as a laxative, can be made by steeping the dried leaves in boiling water. The fruit is edible but mealy and tasteless; it is much favored by birds and other wildlife. The genus name, from the Greek *arctos* ("bear") and *staphyle* ("bunch of grapes"), and the species name, meaning "bear's grape" in Latin, both refer to the fruit.

REPTILES AND AMPHIBIANS

The eastern forests harbor a wide array of handsome and colorful reptiles and amphibians. They provide shelter and food for many species, from the dreaded venomous Copperheads, which prey on small mammals, to the brightly colored newts and salamanders of cooler, moister areas, and the musical choruses of treefrogs. This section provides descriptions of some of the most frequently seen of these animals.

Painted Turtle
Chrysemys picta
511

4–9⅞" (10.2–25.1 cm). Carapace olive or black; oval, smooth, flattened, and unkeeled; plate seams bordered with olive, yellow, or red. Red bars or crescents on marginal plates. Plastron yellow, unpatterned or intricately marked. Yellow and red stripes on neck, legs, and tail. Distinctly notched upper jaw.

Habitat
Slow-moving shallow streams, rivers, and lakes. Likes soft bottoms with vegetation and half-submerged logs.

Range
British Columbia to Nova Scotia, south to Georgia, west to Louisiana, north to Oklahoma, and northwest to Oregon. Isolated populations in the Southwest.

Comments
This is the most widespread turtle in North America. It is fond of basking and often dozens can be observed on a single log. Young turtles are basically carnivorous, but become herbivorous as they mature.

Eastern Box Turtle
Terrapene carolina
512

4–8½" (10–21.6 cm). Terrestrial. Movable plastron hinge allows lower shell to close tightly against carapace. Carapace high-domed and keeled; variable in color and pattern. Plastron often as long as carapace; tan to dark brown, yellow, orange, or olive; patternless or with some dark blotching. Males usually have red eyes and depression in rear portion of plastron; females have yellowish-brown eyes.

Habitat
Moist forested areas; wet meadows, pastures, floodplains.

Range
S. Maine south to Florida Keys and west to Michigan, S. Illinois, Missouri, and E. Kansas, Oklahoma, and Texas. Isolated population in extreme SE. Wisconsin.

Comments
Box Turtles are usually seen early in the day, or after rain. They are fond of earthworms, wild strawberries, and · mushrooms poisonous to man—which habit has killed many a human who has eaten this turtle's flesh. New York Indians ate Box Turtle meat, used the shells for ceremonial rattles, and buried turtles with the dead. A few specimens are known to have lived more than 100 years. If habitat conditions remain constant, a Box Turtle may spend its life in an area scarcely larger than a football field.

Wood Turtle
Clemmys insculpta
513

5–9" (12.7–23 cm). Formed by concentric growth ridges, each large carapace plate looks like an irregular pyramid. Upper shell brown and keeled, appears sculptured and rough. Plastron yellow, with black blotches usually present along outer margins of plates; hingeless. Skin of neck and forelegs often reddish orange. Male has concave plastron and thick tail.

Habitat
Cool streams in deciduous woodlands, red-maple swamps, marshy meadows, and farm country.

Range
Nova Scotia south to N. Virginia and discontinuously west through S. Quebec and the Great Lakes region to NE. Iowa.

Comments
"Ole redlegs" is reputedly an intelligent turtle. An excellent climber, it can surmount 6-foot (1.8 m) chain-link fences. After spring downpours, it is often seen searching for worms in freshly plowed fields. It was once taken for food and now suffers from overcollection and habitat loss.

Five-lined Skink
Eumeces fasciatus
514

5–8¹/₁₆″ (12.7–20.5 cm). Black or brown with 5 broad light stripes, including stripe at juncture of back and sides. Stripes fade with age; adults may be uniform brown. Tail blue to gray. Wide lengthwise row of scales under tail. Breeding males usually have red-orange head. Juveniles have brilliant striping, bright blue tail.

Habitat
Humid woodlands with decaying leaf litter, stumps, logs. May be seen in gardens and around houses.

Range
Southern New England to N. Florida, west to E. Texas, north to Kansas, Wisconsin, and S. Ontario.

Comments
Diurnal. The Five-lined Skink is terrestrial; it climbs only to bask on stumps or the lower reaches of tree trunks. It feeds on insects and their larvae, spiders, earthworms, crustaceans, lizards, even small mice.

Coal Skink
Eumeces anthracinus
515

5–7″ (13–17.8 cm). Brown, with 4 light stripes extending from neck onto tail. Dark band on side, more than 2 scale rows wide, separates pair of light side stripes. Upper light stripe follows edge where third and fourth scale rows meet, counting from middle of back. No stripes on head. Male sometimes has reddish color on head. Young have blue tail.

Habitat
Damp wooded areas with abundant leaf litter or loose stones.

Range
Scattered populations; W. New York through Appalachians to Gulf Coast, Louisiana and Missouri west to central Kansas, Oklahoma, and Texas.

Comments
Diurnal. Coal Skinks readily dive into water to avoid capture. When this happens, they can usually be located by turning over stream-bed rocks, under which they tend to hide.

Mole Skink
Eumeces egregius
516

3½–6½" (8.9–16.5 cm). Relatively long-bodied brownish skink with 4 light stripes on head and body. Upper 2 stripes confined to second scale rows counting from middle of back. Legs tiny; 5 toes. Ear opening partly closed. Tail reddish or blue. Breeding male has reddish chin and belly.

Habitat
Sandy soils of coastal dunes; inland sandhill scrub and turkey-oak. Also, under rocks and tidal wrack on beaches.

Range
Coastal plain of Georgia, Alabama, and Florida.

Comments
Diurnal. Adapted for tunneling and digging, as its name implies, this species successfully preys on burrowing or secretive insects, spiders, and small crustaceans.

Ground Skink
Scincella lateralis
517

3–5⅛" (7.6–13.0 cm). Long-tailed; brown, with black stripes at juncture of back and sides; no stripes on back. Small legs, 5 toes. Transparent window in movable lower eyelid enables animal to see when eyelid is closed to keep out dirt.

Habitat
Humid forests, hardwood hammocks, and forested grasslands, generally where leaf litter is abundant.

Range
New Jersey south through Florida, west to central Texas, north to Nebraska and Missouri.

Comments
Diurnal. The Ground Skink's food consists of insects and spiders. Occasional specimens have been observed to bite off their own tails and eat them.

Broadheaded Skink
Eumeces laticeps
518

6½–12¾" (16.5–32.4 cm). Large and brown, with wide head and 5 broad light stripes, including stripe at juncture of back and sides. Stripes fade with age; adult males uniform brown with red-orange head. Tail blue to brown; wide lengthwise row of scales under tail. Juveniles black with brilliant striping, bright blue tail.

Habitat
Moist wooded areas; also open areas where low shelter is provided by leafy debris or piles of rubble.

Range
SE. Pennsylvania to central Florida, along the Gulf Coast to E. Texas, north to Kansas and Illinois.

Comments
Diurnal. This lizard is often found hunting insects high in trees. It has been observed shaking the nests of paper wasps to dislodge pupae, which it eats, apparently impervious to stings.

Green Anole
Anolis carolinensis
519

5–8″ (12.7–20.3 cm). A slender lizard with expandable pink throatfan, large toe pads. Snout long, wedge-shaped. Usually green, but in seconds can change to brown or intermediate colors. Tail round.

Habitat
Tree-dwelling. Encountered on vertical surfaces like fence posts and walls; but favors tree trunks, shrubs, vines, tall grasses, palm fronds.

Range
S. Virginia to the Florida Keys, west to central Texas and Oklahoma.

Comments
Diurnal, but easily collected by night with the aid of a light; moisture on the skin makes these anoles shine as though they were covered with reflecting yellow paint. Adults prefer shaded perches. Juveniles prefer sunnier locations closer to the ground. Basking anoles are typically brown; fighting males turn green with a black patch behind the eyes. They slowly stalk their prey: flies, beetles, moths, spiders, and even small crabs.

Rough Green Snake
Opheodrys aestivus
520

20–45⅝″ (51–115.9 cm). Slender tree-dwelling snake; uniform pea-green with a long, tapering tail. Belly white to yellowish green. Hatchlings greenish gray. Scales keeled. Scale in front of anus divided.

Habitat
Vines, bushes, and trees near water; sea level to 5000′ (1500 m).

Range
S. New Jersey west to E. Kansas, south to Florida Keys west through Texas into E. Mexico.

Comments
A graceful, mild-tempered tree-dweller. Abroad during the day, it moves slowly through vegetation in search of grasshoppers, crickets, caterpillars, and spiders. Swims well and may take to water when disturbed.

Racer
Coluber constrictor
521

34–77″ (86.4–195.5 cm). Large, slender, agile, and fast-moving. Adults uniformly black, blue, brown, or greenish above; white, yellow, or dark gray below. Young typically gray and conspicuously marked with dark spots on sides and dark gray, brown, or reddish-brown blotches down midline of back. Scales smooth. Scale in front of anus divided.

Habitat
Abandoned fields, grassland, sparse brushy areas along prairie land, open woodland, mountain meadows, rocky wooded hillsides, grassy-bordered streams, and pine flatwoods; sea level to about 7000′ (2150 m).

Range
S. British Columbia and extreme S. Ontario; every state in continental United States, except Alaska; scattered populations through eastern Mexico to northern Guatemala.

Comments
Diurnal. Racers may be encountered in most any terrestrial situation except atop high mountains and in the hottest deserts. They are often observed streaking across roads. Although agile and a good climber, the Racer spends most of its time on the ground. When hunting, it holds its head high and moves swiftly through cover.

Pine Woods Snake
Rhadinaea flavilata
522

10–15⅞″ (25.4–40.2 cm). Tiny golden-brown or reddish-brown snake with white to yellow belly. Upper lip scales yellowish, some with dark specks. Top of head darker than body; dark stripe runs from snout through eye to corner of mouth. Faint narrow back and side stripes may be present. Scales smooth. Scale in front of anus divided.

Habitat
Low marshy areas, damp pine flatwoods and hammocks, and coastal islands.

Range
Coastal plain, North Carolina, to S. Florida and west to E. Louisiana.

Comments
The secretive "yellow-lipped snake" is most often seen during spring months when the water table is high. It often burrows into the centers of damp rotting pine logs and stumps or under forest litter or loose soil. Although harmless to man, the Pine Woods Snake's saliva is mildly toxic to its prey—frogs and lizards.

Coachwhip
Masticophis flagellum
523

36–102″ (91.4–259 cm). Large, lithe, long-tailed and fast-moving. Eastern form: head and neck region dark brown to almost black, gradually fading to light brown toward rear. Occasionally all black. No pale side stripes. Western races generally yellow, tan, brown, gray, or pinkish; essentially patternless or with dark crossbars on neck. Scales smooth. Scale in front of anus divided.

Habitat
Dry, relatively open situations; pine and palmetto flatwoods, rocky hillsides, grassland prairies, desert scrub, thorn forest, and chaparral; sea level to about 7000′ (2150 m).

Range
SE. North Carolina, SW. Tennessee, extreme SW. Illinois, extreme SW. Nebraska, E. Colorado, north-central New Mexico, SW. Utah, west-central and S. Nevada, and central California, south through Florida, Texas, and California to central Mexico.

Comments

The Coachwhip is perhaps our fastest snake. It prowls about during the day in search of grasshoppers, cicadas, lizards, snakes, and small rodents. When pursued, it may take to a tree or disappear into a mammal burrow. If cornered, it coils, vibrates its tail, and strikes repeatedly—often at an enemy's face. Contrary to popular belief, it does not chase down an adversary and whip it to death. Record longevity is 16 years, 7 months.

Rat Snake
Elaphe obsoleta
524

34–101″ (86.4–256.5 cm). Long, powerful constrictor with 3 different adult color patterns predominating: plain, striped, and blotched. Plain is black, often with white showing between scales. Striped is red, orange, yellow, brown, or gray with 4 dark stripes. Blotched is light gray, yellow, or brown with dark brown, gray, or black blotches down back. Belly uniformly white, yellow, orange, or gray, often with dark mottling or checks. Belly scales flat in middle, ends angled up sharply. Underside of tail not striped. If present, dark stripe through eye does not reach neck. All young vividly blotched. Scales weakly keeled. Scale in front of anus divided.

Habitat

Hardwood forest, wooded canyons, swamps, rocky timbered upland, farmland, old fields, barnyards; from wet to arid situations; sea level to 4400′ (1350 m).

Range

E. Ontario and S. Vermont south to Florida Keys, west to W. Texas and adjacent Mexico, north to SW. Minnesota, and S. Michigan.

Comments

The Rat Snake is active during the day in spring and fall but becomes nocturnal in summer. A skillful climber, it ascends trees or rafters of abandoned buildings in search of birds, eggs, and mice. It also eats other small mammals and lizards. Hawks may home in on a nest-raiding Rat Snake when it is being heckled by other birds. In northern areas the Rat Snake often shares winter dens with Timber Rattlesnakes and Copperheads. It has lived 20 years and more in captivity.

Common Kingsnake
Lampropeltis getulus
525

36–82″ (91.4–208.3 cm). A large, chocolate-brown to black kingsnake with a highly variable back and belly pattern. Light-centered scales may form distinct crossbands, "chain links," lengthwise stripes, blotches, or speckles on the back. Belly ranges from plain white to heavily blotched with dark pigment to plain black. Scales smooth. Scale in front of anus undivided.

Habitat

Diverse: New Jersey Pine Barrens to Florida Everglades; dry, rocky, wooded hillsides to river swamps, coastal marshes, and prairie; sea level to 6900′ (2100 m).

Range
S. New Jersey to S. Florida, west to SW. Oregon and S. California, south to S. Baja California and Zacatecas, Mexico.

Comments
Active during the day, especially early in the morning or near dusk, this species becomes nocturnal in summer. It is primarily terrestrial, occasionally climbing into shrubs. A strong constrictor, it eats snakes—including rattlesnakes and Copperheads—as well as lizards, mice, birds, and eggs.

Common Garter Snake
Thamnophis sirtalis
526, 527

18–51⅛" (45.7–131.1 cm). Most widely distributed snake in North America. Coloration highly variable, but back and side stripes usually well defined. Red blotches or a double row of alternating black spots often present between stripes. Scales keeled. Scale in front of anus undivided.

Habitat
Near water—wet meadows, marshes, prairie swales, irrigation and drainage ditches, damp woodland, farms, parks; sea level to 8000' (2450 m).

Range
Atlantic to Pacific coasts, except desert regions of Southwest.

Comments
The most frequently encountered snake in many parts of its range, the Common Garter Snake is active during the day and most often seen amid moist vegetation, where it searches for frogs, toads, salamanders, and earthworms. Occasionally it takes small fish and mice. This species is able to tolerate cold weather and may be active all year in the southerly part of its range.

Eastern Diamondback
Rattlesnake ⊗
Crotalus adamanteus
528

36–96" (91.4–244 cm). Our largest rattler. Heavy-bodied with large head sharply distinct from neck. Back patterned with dark diamonds with light centers and prominently bordered by a row of cream to yellow scales. Prominent light diagonal lines on side of head. Vertical light lines on snout. Scales keeled.

Habitat
Sandhill or longleaf pine and turkey oak country, dry pine flatwoods, abandoned farmland; sea level to 500' (150 m).

Range
Lower coastal plain, SE. North Carolina to Florida Keys, west to S. Mississippi, and extreme E. Louisiana.

Comments
Give it a wide berth; this is the most dangerous snake in North America! Its venom is highly destructive to blood tissue. Stumpholes, gopher tortoise burrows, and dense patches of saw palmetto often serve as retreats.

Timber Rattlesnake ⊗
Crotalus horridus
529

35–74½" (88.9–189.2 cm). Northern forms range from yellow through brown or gray to black, with dark back and side blotches on front of body and blotches fused to form crossbands on rear of body. Head unmarked. Southern forms yellowish gray, brownish gray or pinkish gray, with tan or reddish-brown back stripe dividing chevronlike crossbands; dark stripe behind eye. Both forms have black tail. Scales keeled.

Habitat
Remote wooded hillsides with rock outcrops in the North; unsettled swampy areas, cane thickets, and floodplains in the South; sea level to 6600′ (2000 m).

Range
Extreme SW. Maine south to N. Florida, west into SE. Minnesota and central Texas.

Comments
Active April to October; in the daytime in spring and fall, at night during the summer. In northern areas, Timber Rattlesnakes congregate in large numbers about rocky den sites and may overwinter with Rat Snakes and Copperheads. They are often encountered coiled up waiting for prey— squirrels, mice, chipmunks, and small birds—remaining motionless when approached. Record longevity exceeds 30 years. Until recently, southern populations were recognized as *C. h. atricaudatus,* the Canebrake Rattlesnake.

Copperhead ⊗
Agkistrodon contortrix
530

22–53" (55.9–134.6 cm). Stout-bodied; copper, orange, or pink-tinged, with bold chestnut or reddish-brown crossbands constricted on midline of back. Top of head unmarked. Heat-sensitive facial pit, for locating prey, between eye and nostril. Scales weakly keeled. Scale in front of anus undivided.

Habitat
Wooded hillsides with rock outcrops above streams or ponds; edges of swamps and periodically flooded areas in coastal plain; near canyon springs and dense cane stands along Rio Grande; sea level to 5000′ (1500 m).

Range
SW. Massachusetts west to extreme SE. Nebraska south to Florida panhandle and south-central and W. Texas.

Comments
The Copperhead basks during the day in spring and fall, becoming nocturnal as the days grow warmer. Favored summer retreats are stonewalls, piles of debris near abandoned farms, sawdust heaps, and rotting logs, and large flat stones near streams. It feeds on small rodents, lizards, frogs, large caterpillars, and cicadas. The young twitch their yellow-tipped tail to lure prey. In fall, Copperheads return to their den site, often a rock outcrop on a hillside with a southern or eastern exposure. Copperhead bites are painful, but rarely pose a serious threat to life.

Corn Snake
Elaphe guttata
531

24–72" (61–182.9 cm). Long and slender; orange or brownish yellow to light gray, with large black-edged red, brown, olive-brown, or dark gray blotches down middle of back. 2 alternating rows of smaller blotches on each side, extending onto edges of belly scales. Large squarish black marks on belly, becoming stripes under tail. Dark spear-point mark on top of head, and dark stripe extending from eye onto neck. Belly scales flat in middle, with ends angled up sharply. Scales smooth or weakly keeled. Scale in front of anus divided.

Habitat
Wooded groves, rocky hillsides, meadowland; along watercourses, around springs, woodlots, barnyards, and abandoned houses. Sea level to about 6000' (1850 m).

Range
S. New Jersey south through Florida and S. Tennessee to Texas, Mexico, and E. New Mexico, SE. Colorado, SE. Nebraska to SW. Illinois.

Comments
The Corn Snake is primarily nocturnal, but is often active in early evening. It readily climbs trees and enters abandoned houses and barns in search of prey: mice, rats, birds, and bats. The name Corn Snake probably originated not from an association with barns and corncribs but from the similarity of the belly markings to the checkered patterns of kernels on Indian corn. It is one of the most beautiful snakes in our range. Captive longevity is 21¾ years.

Pigmy Rattlesnake ⊗
Sistrurus miliarius
532

15–30⅞" (38–78.5 cm). Small rattler; slender tail is tipped with a tiny rattle. Gray to reddish, with brown to black blotches along midline of back; 1–3 rows of spots on sides. Narrow reddish back stripe sometimes present. Reddish-brown to black bar extends from eye to rear of jaw; usually bordered below with white line. Top of head has 9 enlarged scales. Scales keeled. Scale in front of anus undivided.

Habitat
Everglades prairie, palmetto-pine flatwoods, sandhills, mixed pine-hardwood forest, borders of cypress ponds, and vicinity of lakes and marshes.

Range
E. North Carolina to Florida Keys, west to E. Oklahoma and E. Texas.

Comments
This species is called "ground rattler" in parts of its range. The tiny rattle makes a buzzing sound audible for only a few feet. The Pigmy Rattlesnake is usually encountered in the summer, quietly sunning itself or crossing a road late in the day. Some are pugnacious and strike with little provocation, while others appear lethargic. They eat lizards, small snakes, mice, and occasionally insects.

Milk Snake
Lampropeltis triangulum
533

14–78¼″ (35.6–199 cm). Gray or tan marked with a light Y-shaped or V-shaped patch on neck and chocolate-brown to reddish-brown, black-bordered blotches down back and sides. Or colorfully ringed and blotched with red (or orange), black, and yellow (or white). Light neck collar followed by black-bordered red bands separated by light rings. Light rings widen near belly. Scales smooth. Scale in front of anus undivided.

Habitat
Diverse situations: damp coastal bottomland, open deciduous woodlands, tropical hardwoods, and farmlands; sea level to about 6000′ (1800 m).

Range
SE. Maine, SW. Quebec, SE. and south-central Ontario, S. Wisconsin, and central and SE. Minnesota south through most of the United States east of the Rocky Mountains.

Comments
Usually found under rotting logs or stumps or damp trash, the Milk Snake is secretive and seldom seen in the open except at night. It eats small rodents, birds, lizards, and snakes— including venomous species. In the North, it is often mistaken for the Copperhead; in the South, for the Eastern Coral Snake. Its common name is based on the mistaken belief that it milks cows.

Eastern Coral Snake ⊗
Micrurus fulvius
534

22–47½″ (55.9–120.7 cm). Body encircled by wide red and black rings separated by narrow yellow rings. Head uniformly black from tip of blunt snout to just behind eyes. Red rings usually spotted with black. Scales smooth and shiny. Scale in front of anus divided.

Habitat
Moist, densely vegetated hammocks near ponds or streams in hardwood forests; pine flatwoods; rocky hillsides and canyons.

Range
SE. North Carolina to S. Florida and Key Largo, west to S. Texas and Mexico.

Comments
Do not confuse this venomous species with its harmless mimics—the Scarlet Snake and Scarlet Kingsnake. The Eastern Coral Snake is usually seen under rotting logs or leaves or moving on the surface in early morning or late afternoon.

Green Treefrog
Hyla cinerea
535

1¼–2½″ (3.2–6.4 cm). Bright green, yellow, or greenish gray. Has sharply defined light stripe along upper jaw and side of body; side stripe occasionally absent. Sometimes has tiny, black-edged gold spots on back. Large toe pads.

Voice
Cowbell-like when heard at a distance. Nearer, sound is *quank, quank.*

Habitat
Vegetation near permanent water.

Range
Delaware south along the coastal plain into Florida and the Keys, west to S. Texas, and north through central Arkansas and W. Tennessee to Illinois.

Comments
Green Treefrogs congregate in large choruses of several hundred. A typical treefrog, this species prefers to walk rather than jump. When fleeing a predator in the trees it takes gangly leaps into space.

Carpenter Frog
Rana virgatipes
536

1⅝–2⅝″ (4.1–6.7 cm). Small, brown; 4 distinct yellowish stripes down back but no folds at juncture of back and sides. Underside cream to yellow, with random dark spotting. Webbing does not reach tip of longest toe.

Voice
A rhythmic hammering sound; chorus sounds like carpenters at work.

Habitat
Sphagnum bogs and sphagnum fringes of lakes and ponds. Also found in tea-colored, slow-moving water with abundant emergent vegetation.

Range
Coastal plain from the Pine Barrens of New Jersey to S. Georgia.

Comments
Nocturnal. This frog is often seen wholly out of the water but is never far from the edge. When frightened, it leaps into water and hides beneath vegetation, swimming only a short distance before it breaks the surface for a quick look at the pursuer.

Southern Leopard Frog
Rana sphenocephala
537

2–5″ (5.1–12.7 cm). Slender and narrow-headed; green to brown, with large dark spots between light-colored ridges at juncture of back and sides; ridges continuous to groin. Light stripe along upper jaw; typically, a light spot in center of eardrum.

Voice
Series of short throaty croaks.

Habitat
Any freshwater location. Wanders among moist vegetation in the summer, returns to freshwater ponds and streams and brackish marshes rest of year.

Range
From S. New York to the Florida Keys, west to Texas and E. Oklahoma, north to east-central Kansas.

Comments
This is the most ubiquitous frog of the eastern states. It is primarily nocturnal. To elude a predator—such as a raccoon or water bird—this frog dives into the water, makes a sharp turn while still submerged, and surfaces amid vegetation at the water's edge; meanwhile the predator continues to search in the direction of the original dive.

Pine Woods Treefrog
Hyla femoralis
538

1–1¾" (2.5–4.4 cm). Gray to reddish brown, usually with dark blotches; yellow to white spots on dark rear surface of thigh visible only when leg is extended. Has large toe pads.

Voice
A series of measured notes, like the tapping together of wooden dowels. Chorus sounds like an office of industrious typists. Solitary males call from high in treetops.

Habitat
Pine flatwoods near ponds and marshes.

Range
Coastal plain from SE. Virginia to S. Florida (except the Everglades) and west along the Gulf Coast to Louisiana. Some isolated populations in central Alabama.

Comments
Nocturnal. It is difficult to observe because of its treetop habitat and its mottled appearance, which blends well with pine tree bark. It is most easily located when it calls in early evening.

Fowler's Toad
Bufo woodhousei fowleri
539

2½–5" (6–12.7 cm). Large toad with back blotched, chest unspotted. Prominent bony ridges on head touch elongate parotoid glands. Yellow to green to brown.

Voice
Like the bleat of a sheep with a cold.

Habitat
Sandy areas near marshes, irrigation ditches, backyards, and temporary rain pools.

Range
Lake Michigan east through most of Pennsylvania to SE. New York and southern New England, south to the Gulf Coast (excluding coastal South Carolina, Georgia, and most of Florida), west to E. Texas and north to Missouri and S. Illinois.

Comments
Fowler's is a subspecies of Woodhouse's Toad, which is widespread through most of the United States. Primarily nocturnal, this is the toad commonly seen at night catching insects beneath lights. Occasionally it is active during the day, but more frequently remains in its burrow or hides in vegetation.

Cope's Gray Treefrog and Common Gray Treefrog
Hyla chrysoscelis and *Hyla versicolor*
540

1¼–2⅜" (3.2–6 cm). Skin rough; greenish or brownish to gray, with several large dark blotches on back. Dark-edged light spot beneath eye. Undersurfaces of thighs bright yellow-orange. Large toe pads.

Voice
A hearty, resonating trill, usually heard in spring and early summer.

Habitat
Trees and shrubs growing in or near permanent water.

Range
From S. Ontario and Maine to N. Florida west to central Texas, north through Oklahoma to Manitoba.

Comments
The 2 species of Gray Treefrog are identical in appearance, and since their ranges overlap extensively, they cannot be distinguished in the field. However, Cope's Treefrog has a faster trill and only half as many chromosomes as the Common.

Southern Chorus Frog
Pseudacris nigrita
541

¾–1¼" (1.9–3.2 cm). Rough warty skin; light tan or gray, with 3 longitudinal rows of black spots, which may be fused into stripes. Black stripe runs through eye. Small round toe tips.

Voice
A rasping trill.

Habitat
Among damp leaf litter in woodlands; wet or moist grassy meadows, ponds, and sinkholes.

Range
The coastal plain from E. North Carolina through Florida to S. Mississippi.

Comments
This species is primarily nocturnal, but is occasionally found foraging during daylight. The tiny toe pads limit its climbing ability. It burrows into the banks of ponds and ditches.

Wood Frog
Rana sylvatica
542

1⅜–3¼" (3.5–8.3 cm). Pink, tan, or dark brown, with prominent dark mask ending abruptly behind eardrum. Light stripe on upper jaw; sometimes light line down middle of back. Ridges at juncture of back and sides prominent. Dark blotch on chest near base of each front leg. Belly white, may have dark mottling. Toes not fully webbed; male has swollen "thumbs."

Voice
A series of short raspy quacks.

Habitat
Moist woodlands in eastern areas; open grasslands in western; tundra in the Far North.

Range
Widespread throughout northern North America.

Comments
The Wood Frog is the only North American frog found north
of the Arctic Circle. It is primarily diurnal.

Pickerel Frog
Rana palustris
543

1¾–3⁷⁄₁₆″ (4.4–8.7 cm). Smooth-skinned, tan, with parallel
rows of dark squarish blotches running down back. Jaw has
light stripe. Folds at juncture of back and sides yellow. Belly
and undersurfaces of hind legs bright yellow to orange.

Voice
A steady low croak. May call in a rolling snore while under
water.

Habitat
Slow-moving water and other damp areas, preferably with
low, dense vegetation; stream, swamps, and meadows.

Range
Throughout the eastern states except the extreme Southeast.

Comments
Nocturnal. An irritating skin secretion makes this frog
unappetizing to some predators. The secretion will kill other
frogs kept in the same collecting container or terrarium.

American Toad
Bufo americanus
544

2–4⅜″ (5.1–11.1 cm). Large, with elongate parotoid glands
not touching prominent bony ridges on head. Brown to brick-
red to olive, with various patterns in lighter colors. Spots
brownish, warts brown to orange-red. Light stripe down
middle of back may be present. Belly usually spotted. Male
has dark throat.

Voice
A pleasant musical trill lasting up to 30 seconds.

Habitat
Common wherever there are abundant insects and moisture.

Range
In Canada from SE. Manitoba to James Bay and Labrador,
south in the East through Maritime Provinces, New England,
and the Appalachian Mountains; west from central Georgia to
E. Oklahoma and Kansas; north through Wisconsin into
Canada.

Comments
The American Toad is primarily nocturnal. It is a prodigious
insect eater.

Southern Toad
Bufo terrestris
545

1⅝–4½″ (4.1–11.3 cm). A large plump toad with high,
conspicuously knobby, bony ridges on head and prominent
parotoids. Brown, reddish, or black; some dark spotting may

surround warts. Occasional light stripe down middle of back. Male has dark throat.

Voice
A high-pitched, musical trill, piercing at close range. Males call when in or near the water.

Habitat
Widely distributed. Abundant in open scrub oak where the soil is sandy and easily burrowed.

Range
Coastal plain from SE. Virginia to Louisiana.

Comments
The Southern Toad is nocturnal, spending the day inside its burrow. It is often found in suburban areas, near houses and mowed lawns, where it feeds on insects drawn to night-lights.

Spring Peeper
Hyla crucifer
546

¾–1⅜" (1.9–3.5 cm). Tan to brown to gray, with characteristic dark X on back. Large toe pads.

Voice
A high-pitched ascending whistle, sometimes with a short trill. Chorus sounds like the jingle of bells.

Habitat
Wooded areas in or near permanent or temporarily flooded ponds and swamps.

Range
Manitoba to the Maritime Provinces, south through central Florida, west to E. Texas, and north into central Wisconsin.

Comments
Nocturnal. The Spring Peeper is one of the most familiar frogs in the East. Its chorus is among the first signs of spring. Peepers hibernate under logs and loose bark.

Eastern Newt
Notophthalmus viridescens
547, 550

2⅝–5½" (6.5–14 cm). Aquatic and terrestrial forms. Aquatic adult yellowish brown or olive-green to dark brown above, yellow below; back and belly both peppered with small black spots. Land-dwelling form is orange-red to reddish brown; varies in size from 1⅜–3⅜" (3.5–8.6 cm).

Habitat
Ponds and lakes with dense submerged vegetation, quiet stretches or backwaters of streams, swamps, ditches, and neighboring damp woodlands.

Range
Nova Scotia to Florida and west to SW. Ontario and Texas.

Comments
Adult newts are often seen foraging in shallow water. They prey voraciously on worms, insects, small crustaceans and mollusks, amphibian eggs, and larvae. Searching for eggs,

they visit the spawning beds of fish. Newts secrete toxic substances through the skin and so are avoided by fish and other predators. Terrestrial individuals can be found on the forest floor after a shower. A hungry one may consume 2000 springtails.

Mountain Dusky Salamander
Desmognathus ochrophaeus
548

2¾–4⅜″ (7–11.1 cm). Varies greatly in color and pattern. Pale line from eye to angle of jaw. Tail rounded; half of total length. Northern forms: gray, brown, olive, yellow, or orange; have wide, straight-edged, dark-bordered stripe marked with V shapes down back and tail. Southern forms: dark margins of stripe usually wavy, but vary from nearly straight to zigzagged; dark bars cross stripe. 14 grooves on sides.

Habitat
Uplands from 600–6500′ (183–1981 m). At low elevations, stays close to streams, springs, and seepage areas. At higher elevations, favors cool, moist floors of spruce-fir forests.

Range
West of Hudson River in New York to NE. Georgia; also NE. Alabama.

Comments
Entire populations of the Mountain Dusky Salamander may congregate around springheads and seepages during winter. These sites also provide brooding areas for females and an aquatic habitat for larvae. It is also seen on wet cliff faces. It eats small flies, beetles, mites. Salamanders from areas near the Great Smokies may have reddish cheek patches, mimicking the Appalachian Woodland Salamander.

Appalachian Woodland Salamander
Plethodon jordani
549

3¼–7¼″ (8.3–18.4 cm). Highly variable throughout range. Many are black above, gray below, unmarked or with small white spots on sides and cheeks. Others have heavy brassy flecking on upper surfaces. In Great Smokies most have bright red cheek patches; in the Nantahala Mountains, red legs. No red on back, except for an occasional spot in young; no back stripe. Chin light. 16 grooves on sides.

Habitat
Humid, heavily forested slopes, with moss-covered logs and slabs of rock; most populations live at higher elevations; 700–6400′ (213–1951 m).

Range
Southern Appalachians; SW. Virginia south through E. Tennessee and W. North Carolina into NE. Georgia and NW. South Carolina.

Comments
This salamander is well known for its extensive geographical variation. Early herpetologists thought the various color forms were different species or subspecies. Occasionally this species

hybridizes with the closely related Slimy Salamander. Active April to November, it is usually seen well away from water, under rotting logs, flat stones, or at night at the entrance of small burrow holes. The cheek patches and leg markings are mimicked by the Imitator Salamander. When moved 500' from its retreat, this salamander can find its way home.

**Eastern Tiger
Salamander**
Ambystoma tigrinum tigrinum
551

6–13⅜" (15.2–40 cm). World's largest land-dwelling salamander. Stoutly built, with broad head and small eyes. Body dark with olive spots. Tubercles on soles of feet. 11–14 (usually 12–13) grooves on sides.

Habitat
Varied: pine barrens, mountain forests, and damp meadows where ground is easily burrowed; also in mammal and invertebrate burrows; sea level to 8000' (2400 m).

Range
East Coast; also central Ohio to NW. Minnesota and south to Gulf of Mexico.

Comments
These salamanders are often seen at night after heavy rains, especially during breeding season; they live beneath debris near water or in crayfish or mammal burrows. They are voracious consumers of earthworms, large insects, small mice, and amphibians. Several other subspecies of the Tiger Salamander occur in North America, mainly in the West. They have varied color patterns and ranges.

Marbled Salamander
Ambystoma opacum
552

3½–5" (8.9–12.7 cm). Chunky; dark gray to black above, with bold white or silvery crossbands. Belly black. 11–12 grooves on sides. Recently transformed juveniles are dark gray to brown, with light flecks. Male brighter than female.

Habitat
Woodlands, from low swampy areas to relatively dry hillsides.

Range
S. New Hampshire to N. Florida, west to E. Texas, north to lakes Michigan and Erie.

Comments
The nesting female typically curls herself around the eggs while waiting for rain to fill the nest cavity. The larvae usually hatch a few days after inundation. If autumn rains are scant, eggs may not hatch until spring.

MUSHROOMS

The damp, shady forest floor provides exactly the right sort of habitat for many kinds of mushrooms. Some of these grow on the ground, while others spring to life on fallen tree trunks and branches. Some species are quite inconspicuous; others lend a touch of unexpected color—bright reds and oranges—to somber areas. This section provides descriptions of some of the most familiar and conspicuous mushrooms that grow in our eastern forests.

Destroying Angel ⊗
Amanita virosa
553

Cap 2–5" (5–12.5 cm) wide; stalk 3–8" (7.5–20 cm) tall.
Cap white, convex to almost flat, usually with central knob,
which may darken. Somewhat sticky in humid weather. No
striations at cap margin, or very obscure striations. Gills
white, close, free (or just slightly attached to stalk). Stalk
white, somewhat hairy, with skirtlike white ring above (from
partial veil), and saclike white volva (sheathing cup) beneath
(from universal veil).

Season and Habitat
June–November. On the ground under hardwoods, or in
mixed woods. Also in grassy areas near trees.

Range
Throughout North America, but much more common in East.

Comments
Deadly poisonous. Unfortunately this very dangerous
mushroom is attractive and similar in some respects to a few
common edible species; it is best not to pick any mushroom
that looks like this. Always check carefully for the volva,
which may break apart in the soil or become detached from
the stalk. This extremely toxic mushroom is in a complex of
species that includes the infamous Death Cap (*Amanita
phalloides*), which has greenish tones in the cap. Keep in mind
the warning implicit in the common name, Destroying Angel.

Tacky Green Russula
Russula aeruginea
554

Cap 2–2⅜" (5–8.5 cm) wide; stalk 1⅝–2⅜" (4–6 cm) tall.
Cap yellow-green to olive-gray, usually with a sunken center;
sticky in humid weather; smooth, with lined or roughened
margin. Gills attached, close, yellowish white. Stalk dry, just
about smooth, yellowish white.

Season and Habitat
July–September. In deciduous and coniferous woods,
particularly under oak, aspen, and lodgepole pine.

Range
Widespread in North America.

Comments
Although it is edible, this mushroom cannot be recommended
for the table, since other similar species have not been
thoroughly tested for edibility.

Slimy Gomphidius
Gomphidius glutinosus
555

Cap 1–4" (2.5–10 cm) wide; stalk 2–4" (5–10 cm) tall. Cap
purple-gray to brownish gray, with darker spots, smooth and
slimy. Gills close to somewhat distant, running down stalk;
white at first but eventually turning a dark smoky gray from
maturing spores. Stalk tapers to base; white above, yellow
beneath, with a slimy partial veil usually darkened by spores.

Season and Habitat
June–November. On the ground under conifers, primarily
spruce.

Range
Across northern United States; also in coniferous forests in southern mountains.

Comments
This species usually occurs in abundance.

Fawn Mushroom
Pluteus cervinus
556

Cap 1¼–4¾" (3–12 cm) wide; stalk 2–4" (5–10 cm) tall. Cap dark brown to gray-brown, smooth with a few hairs at center, usually wrinkled, a bit sticky in humid weather. Gills free, close, white becoming pink. Stalk white, sometimes darker, with a few fibers present.

Season and Habitat
May–October in the East. Decaying wood, stumps, sawdust, buried wood.

Range
Widespread in North America.

Comments
This common species is edible, but only young mushrooms are good. Immature gills are white, but turn pink with age.

Brick Tops
Naematoloma sublateritium
557

Cap 1⅝–4" (4–10 cm) wide; stalk 2–4" (5–10 cm) tall. Cap light to dark brick-red with a paler margin. Gills attached to stalk, close; whitish at first but eventually becoming purplish gray from mature spores. Stalk off-white with thin zone of fibrils on upper part (the remains of a cobwebby veil).

Season and Habitat
Typically in autumn: August–November. Stumps and logs of deciduous trees.

Range
Eastern North America.

Comments
This is a good edible that grows in clusters, but it may be mistaken for the poisonous Sulfur Tuft (*Naematoloma fasciculare*), which has a yellowish cap and greenish-yellow immature gills.

Orange Mycena
Mycena leaiana
558

Cap ⅜–2" (1–5 cm) wide; stalk 1¼–2¾" (3–7 cm) tall. Cap reddish orange to orange-yellow, shiny and sticky. Gills attached, close to crowded, with reddish-orange edges. Stalk yellow to orange.

Season and Habitat
June–September. In clusters on deciduous wood, in particular on beech.

Range
North-central and northeastern United States, south to North Carolina.

Comments
This beautiful mushroom may appear even when many other species do not. Its edibility is unknown.

Jack O'Lantern ⊗
Omphalotus illudens
559

Cap 3–8″ (7.5–20 cm) wide; stalk 3–8″ (7.5–20 cm) tall. Cap orange to orange-yellow, usually with small central knob; smooth but streaked with flat hairs. Gills close, yellow-orange, running down stalk. Stalk dry, smooth, yellow to light orange.

Season and Habitat
July–November. Clustered at the base of hardwood stumps or buried roots, most frequently oak.

Range
Eastern North America.

Comments
This poisonous species is sometimes mistaken for the edible Chanterelle (*Cantharellus cibarius*). The gills of *Omphalotus illudens* glow in the dark, emitting an eerie greenish light and explaining its common name. Formerly called *Omphalotus olearius*.

Chanterelle
Cantharellus cibarius
560

Cap 1–4″ (2.5–10 cm) wide; stalk 1–3″ (2.5–7.5 cm) tall. Cap is yellow to orange-yellow, and slightly hairy or smooth. Gill-like blunt ridges, with much cross-veining, run down the pale stalk. The entire mushroom is funnel-shaped.

Season and Habitat
July and August in Northeast, June–September in Southeast. Mixed woods, or under conifers or oaks.

Range
Distributed widely throughout North America.

Comments
This beautiful mushroom is highly regarded and widely sought as a choice edible. It usually emits an apricot fragrance. The Jack O'Lantern (*Omphalotus illudens*), a similar and poisonous species, has gills; the gills are not cross-veined.

Two-colored Bolete
Boletus bicolor
561

Cap 2–6″ (5–15 cm) wide; stalk 2–4″ (5–10 cm) tall. Cap rose-red to pinkish with paler margin, dry. Tiny pores on undersurface of cap, yellow. Stalk mostly red, yellow at top.

Season and Habitat
June–October. Primarily under oaks.

Range
Northeast states south to Georgia, west to Michigan.

Comments
This esteemed edible is often abundant in oak woods. When it is sliced open, the yellow interior slowly turns blue.

King Bolete
Boletus edulis
562

Cap 3¼–10" (8–25 cm) wide; stalk 4–10" (10–25 cm) tall. Cap reddish brown (varying to lighter or darker), bun-shaped; sticky in humid weather. Pore-bearing undersurface is white at first, maturing to greenish yellow. Stalk stout, usually bulbous, pale, with fine, white network on upper part.

Season and Habitat
June–October. Under conifers, and under birch and aspen.

Range
Widespread throughout North America.

Comments
A choice edible, the King Bolete has a nutty flavor. It occurs in several variations. One bitter-tasting look-alike species has a pinkish undersurface.

Dotted-stalk Suillus
Suillus granulatus
563

Cap 2–6" (5–15 cm) wide; stalk 1⅝–3¼" (4–8 cm) tall. Cap buff, mottled with cinnamon, smooth, sticky when wet, sometimes slimy. Pores small, pale yellow, sometimes bruising brown. Stalk yellow above, cinnamon below, covered with reddish or brownish dots.

Season and Habitat
June–November. Under various conifers.

Range
Along East Coast as far south as North Carolina; also in West.

Comments
The Dotted-stalk Suillus is a good edible and one of many look-alikes. The beginning mushroom hunter should never gather and eat these mushrooms on his own, however.

Old Man of the Woods
Strobilomyces floccopus
564

Cap 1⅝–6" (4–15 cm) wide; stalk 2–4¾" (5–12 cm) tall. Cap covered with gray-brown to gray-black scales, with bits of cobwebby material (partial veil) hanging from margin. Pore surface white at first, becoming gray; stains darker when rubbed. Stalk somewhat scaly or shaggy; dark gray, with ring zone from partial veil not always discernible.

Season and Habitat
July–October. Under hardwoods, conifers, or in mixed woods.

Range
Throughout eastern and midwestern states.

Comments
Although this mushroom is common and edible, it is not really excellent eating.

Scaly Tooth
Hydnum imbricatum
565

Cap 2–8" (5–20 cm) wide; stalk 1⅝–4" (4–10 cm) tall. Cap light to dark brown, covered with coarse, raised scales; dry. Undersurface of cap covered with light brown spines that become darker with age. Stalk pale brown, dry, smooth.

Season and Habitat
June–October. In coniferous, deciduous, and mixed woods.

Range
Widely distributed throughout North America.

Comments
The flavor of this common edible is variable, but even at its best, it is not particularly good.

Thick-maze Oak Polypore
Daedalea quercina
566

Cap 2–6" (5–15 cm) wide; no stalk. Cap whitish when young, maturing to ash-gray, with fine hairs; margin thick. Undersurface white to brownish; pores elongated to suggest a labyrinth, and occasionally gill-like.

Season and Habitat
All year. Primarily oak stumps and logs.

Range
Northeastern and north-central United States.

Comments
This species somewhat resembles the Thin-maze Flat Polypore (*Daedaleopsis confragosa*), which usually grows on birch or willow rather than oak trees. The genus names of both species recall Daedalus, who is credited with the design of the Minotaur's labyrinth in Greek legend.

Half-free Morel
Morchella semilibera
567

Cap ⅜–1⅛" (1–4 cm) wide at freely hanging base, ⅜–1⅛" (1–4 cm) high; stalk 3¼–4" (8–10 cm) tall. Cap conical with brown ridges around oval, yellow-brown pits. Lower half of cap free; upper half attached to pale, grainy, ribbed stalk.

Season and Habitat
Early spring. Damp ground in open deciduous woods.

Range
Eastern North America west to Iowa.

Comments
The Half-free Morel is one of a group of grossly similar species, none of which is easy to see against the mottled background of the springtime forest floor. A good edible species.

Netted Stinkhorn
Dictyophora duplicata
568

Head 1¼–1⅝" (3–4 cm) wide, 2" (5 cm) high; stalk 4–5" (10–12.5 cm) tall. Head initially covered with greenish slime, which obscures deep pits and chambers beneath. A small porelike opening is at tip of head. A netted veil hangs from lower margin of head. Stalk white with white or pink volva (cup). A cordlike structure (rhizomorph) is present at base of stalk. Odor strongly disagreeable.

Season and Habitat
June–October. Near deciduous trees and stumps.

Range
Generally throughout eastern North America and parts of southern Canada.

Comments
The Netted Stinkhorn is one of several related mushrooms that utilize insects as primary agents of spore dispersal. Insects are attracted to this mushroom by its fetid odor; they remove the dark green slime, which bears the spores.

Devil's Urn
Urnula craterium
569

Cup 1¼–3¼" (3–8 cm) wide, 1⅝–2⅜" (4–6 cm) high; stalk 1¼–1⅝" (3–4 cm) tall. Cup closed at first, opening to suggest a tiny urn with notched rim; inner surface dark brown to black, outer surface similar. Jellylike when young, maturing to tough and leathery texture. Stalk dark, with black hairs at base.

Season and Habitat
Early spring. Clustered on fallen hardwood, primarily oak.

Range
Widely distributed in eastern United States.

Comments
One of the earliest mushrooms to appear in spring, the Devil's Urn is easily overlooked because of its dark coloration.

Stalked Scarlet Cup
Sarcoscypha occidentalis
570

Cup ¼–⅝" (0.5–1.5 cm) wide; stalk ⅜–1¼" (1–3 cm) tall. Cup with scarlet inner surface and whitish outer surface; both surfaces smooth. Stalk white and cylindrical.

Season and Habitat
May–September, but common in spring. Hardwood debris in wet areas.

Range
Generally throughout the eastern United States.

Comments
This small reddish cup on a white stalk is as delightful as any wildflower in the spring woods.

Beefsteak Polypore
Fistulina hepatica
571

Cap 3–10" (7.5–25 cm) wide; stalk 2–4" (5–10 cm) long, occasionally absent. Cap blood-red to reddish orange, minutely roughened; virtually flat; moist to juicy. Pores on undersurface formed by closely stacked, individual, open-ended tubes; whitish at first, becoming red-brown. Stalk lateral, colored same as cap.

Season and Habitat
July–October. Decaying trunks and stumps of oak, or on base of living oak.

Range
Widely distributed but most common in East.

Comments
The separate tubes on the undersurface make this an odd polypore. It is a good edible and avidly sought by many pothunters.

Violet Toothed Polypore
Trichaptum biformis
572

Cap ⅜–3″ (1–7.5 cm) wide; no stalk. Cap semicircular, white to brownish with violet margin; zoned, hairy. Pores on undersurface with toothlike extensions; white to brown but usually with violet hue.

Season and Habitat
May–December, but lasting for several years. Decaying deciduous trees; also rarely on coniferous wood.

Range
Widespread throughout North America.

Comments
This species is one of the most common polypores in the United States. Fallen logs and the standing trunks of dead trees may be festooned with overlapping violet caps.

Common Fiber Vase
Thelephora terrestris
573

Fan-shaped caps 1–2″ (2.5–5 cm) wide, typically overlapped in rosettes to 4¾″ (12 cm) wide; stalk short or absent. Cap hairy to scaly, brown, with pale and usually tattered margin. Undersurface brownish, wrinkled, and pimply. Texture leathery.

Season and Habitat
All year. Sandy soil under pines; also on stumps and very young trees.

Range
Northern North America, and south in Appalachians to Georgia.

Comments
Like some other mushrooms in our range, this species can be an enemy of the tree seedlings on which it sometimes grows.

Common Split Gill
Schizophyllum commune
574

Cap ⅜–1⅝″ (1–4 cm) wide; no stalk. Cap fan-shaped, varying to saucer-shaped; white to gray; dry, densely hairy, with lobed margin. Undersurface with gill-like radiating structures split lengthwise; hairy; white, gray, or pinkish.

Season and Habitat
All year. Hardwood stumps, logs, and sticks.

Range
Northeastern United States west to North Dakota and south to Tennessee.

Comments
In dry weather the split "gills" of this species curl back and inward, straightening again with the return of moisture.

Coral Slime
Ceratiomyxa fruticulosa
575

Mushroom (called a spore column) ¹⁄₆₄–¹⁄₃₂″ (0.5–1 mm) wide, ¹⁄₃₂–³⁄₈″ (0.1–1 cm) tall. Normally white, but also yellow or yellowish green, growing in tight masses usually reaching several inches across, suggesting an undersea coral; usually accompanied by smaller unconnected masses that look like tiny bushes. Entire fingerlike structure develops from watery, translucent globules that emerge from the substrate.

Season and Habitat
June–October. On decaying wood. Very infrequently on dead leaves and debris.

Range
Widely distributed in North America.

Comments
The Coral Slime is the most common member of the group called slime molds (Myxomycetes). These are bizarre organisms that seem animal-like in the initial jellylike stage and plantlike in the final, spore-bearing stage pictured here. This species (like its few allies) bears external spores; all other slime molds produce spores internally. The Coral Slime is commonly seen as a white patch on decaying logs; using a magnifying glass will help to reveal its structure.

Crown-tipped Coral
Clavicorona pyxidata
576

Mushroom ³⁄₄–2³⁄₈″ (2–6 cm) wide, 2–5″ (5–12.5 cm) high; stalk very short but present, ¹⁄₁₆–¹⁄₈″ (1.5–3 mm) thick. Mushroom yellow at first, becoming yellowish brown, whitish tan, or pink-tinged, and darkening with age. Repeatedly branched into slender, equal, upright clusters, each branch terminating in a yellow, crownlike tip. Stalk whitish to brownish pink.

Season and Habitat
June–September. Decaying wood, especially poplar, aspen, and willow.

Range
Widely distributed throughout North America.

Comments
Mushrooms of this type resemble undersea coral, which gave rise to the common name for the group. Most coral mushrooms grow on the ground, so the wood habitat is a good clue to identification of this species. It is edible but somewhat peppery tasting.

MAMMALS

The forests are teeming with life, yet some of the most interesting animals can be shy and hard to observe. The visitor who learns to wait and watch—quietly, and with patience—will be rewarded by the sight of a deer, Beaver, fox, or other animal that lives in the forests of the East. This section includes descriptions of many typical mammals of the forests, from the tiny shrews and mice of the forest floor to the formidable Black Bear.

Pygmy Shrew
Microsorex hoyi
577

3⅛–3⅞" (7.8–9.8 cm) long. Tiniest mammal in North America, weighing no more than a dime. Brownish to grayish above; pale or silvery below.

Habitat
Deep woods, open and brushy fields; sphagnum-moss bogs.

Range
Alaska, most of Canada, and northern United States.

Comments
The Pygmy Shrew is one of the rarest North American mammals, and little is known of its behavior in the field. It forages among dead plant matter, probably feeding on insects and insect larvae, and other invertebrates.

Short-tailed Shrew
Blarina brevicauda
578

3¾–5" (9.6–12.7 cm) long. Largest shrew in North America. Solid gray above and below. Short tail.

Habitat
Woods and wet areas in warmer and drier parts of range.

Range
Southeastern Canada to northeastern United States south to Nebraska, Missouri, Kentucky, and Alabama. Isolated populations in NE. North Carolina and west-central Florida.

Comments
One of the most common North American mammals, this shrew is also one of the most ferocious. It bites its victim in the throat and face, paralyzing it almost instantly with a poison in its saliva. The venomous saliva is not dangerous to man, but a bite may be painful for several days.

White-footed Mouse
Peromyscus leucopus
579

6⅛–8⅛" (15.6–20.5 cm) long. Grayish to dull orange-brown above; white below. Tail similarly bicolored, nearly one-half total length. Large ears, ½" (13–14 mm) long.

Tracks
In dust, hindprint ⅝" long, with 5 toes, printing; foreprint ¼" long and wide, with 4 toes printing; straddle, 1⅜"; foreprints print behind and between hindprints.

Habitat
Wooded and brushy areas.

Range
Eastern United States.

Comments
White-footed Mice are active year-round, though they may remain in their nests during extremely cold weather; a few may hibernate. They construct nests in any concealed location.

Deer Mouse
Peromyscus maniculatus
580

4¾–8¾″ (11.9–22.2 cm) long. Grayish to reddish brown above; white below; tail distinctly bicolored and short-haired.

Tracks
Usually a 4-print pattern is seen in snow, with foreprints showing 4 toes, hindprints 5. 1½–1¾″ wide, with individual prints from ¼″ to ⅝″ long.

Habitat
Prairies; brushy areas; woodlands.

Range
Mexico to S. Yukon and Northwest Territories; in the East, Hudson Bay to Pennsylvania, the southern Appalachians, central Arkansas, and central Texas.

Comments
These mice feed on seeds and nuts, small fruits and berries, insects, centipedes, and the subterranean fungus *Endogone*. Seeds and small nuts are routinely stored in protected areas.

Cotton Mouse
Peromyscus gossypinus
581

6–8⅛″ (15.2–20.5 cm) long. Reddish brown above; white below. Tail short-haired, usually bicolored.

Habitat
Woodlands; swamps; brushlands; rocky areas; beaches.

Range
Southeastern United States: from E. Texas and SE. Oklahoma east to SE. Virginia, E. North Carolina, E. South Carolina, Georgia, and Florida.

Comments
Skillful climbers, Cotton Mice run up trees like Gray Squirrels and are fairly strong swimmers, both useful adaptations for the southern swamps where they are most abundant.

Eastern Woodrat
Neotoma floridana
582

12¼–17⅜″ (31–44.4 cm) long. Grayish brown above; white or grayish below. Bicolored tail less than half total length.

Habitat
Rocky cliffs, caves, tumbled boulders in the North; Osage-orange and other hedges and wooded low areas in the South.

Range
Much of southeastern United States from mid-peninsular Florida north to Pennsylvania and S. New York (excluding coastal area from New Jersey to North Carolina and west to N. Georgia); west to SW. South Dakota, west-central Nebraska, E. Colorado, most of Kansas, E. Oklahoma, and E. Texas.

Comments
The Eastern Woodrat usually constructs its stick house in a protected location. When built in a cave, the house may be open at the top. Young woodrats cling tenaciously to their mother's teats; if alarmed, she often drags the whole litter with her as she flees.

Woodland Vole
Microtus pinetorum
583

4⅛–5¾" (10.5–14.5 cm) long. Reddish brown above with short soft fur; grayish, washed with buff below. Tail short, reddish brown, about the length of hind foot.

Habitat
Deciduous woodlands with thick leaf mold or thick herbaceous ground cover; sometimes parklike grassy areas.

Range
Eastern United States west to central Iowa and central Texas; north to central New England and central Wisconsin; in southern states except for most coastal areas.

Comments
The Woodland Vole spends most of its time in tunnel systems one to several inches below the surface. It usually constructs these burrows itself, digging with forefeet and incisors and pushing back the dirt with the hind feet. It is somewhat colonial, although colonies sometimes disband and disappear for no apparent reason.

Woodland Jumping Mouse
Napaeozapus insignis
584

8–10" (20.4–25.6 cm) long. Brightly colored: orange sides with scattered dark hairs; brownish back; white underparts. Long tail with white tip. Forefeet small.

Habitat
Coniferous and hardwood forests in cool moist environments.

Range
Southeastern Canada from Manitoba to E. Labrador, south to E. West Virginia and northwest to NE. Minnesota; also in the Alleghenies to NE. Georgia.

Comments
The Woodland Jumping Mouse consumes the subterranean fungus *Endogone,* which forms about a third of its diet, providing water as well as food; this consumption also benefits the fungus, because excretion of the fungal spores aids in their dispersal, and the mouse's digestive juices are probably essential for their germination.

Eastern Chipmunk
Tamias striatus
585

8½–11¾" (21.5–29.9 cm) long. Reddish brown above; belly white. 1 white stripe on sides (bordered by 2 black stripes); stripes end up at rump. Dark center stripe down back; light facial stripes above and below eyes. Tail brown on tip, edged with black. Prominent ears. Large internal cheek pouches.

Tracks
In mud, hindprint 1⅞" long, foreprint considerably smaller; straddle 1¾–3½"; stride 7–15", with hindprints closer together and printing ahead of foreprints.

Breeding
Mates in early spring; 3–5 young born in May; litter in late July–August, probably by first-year females not breeding in early spring.

Habitat
Open woodland; forest edges; brushy areas; bushes and stone walls in cemeteries and around houses.

Range
Southeastern Canada and northeastern United States west to North Dakota and E. Oklahoma, and south to Virginia, NW. South Carolina, and Mississippi.

Comments
Essentially a ground species, this pert chipmunk does not hesitate to climb large oak trees when acorns are ripe. It is single-minded in its food gathering, making trips from tree to storage burrow almost continuously.

Red Squirrel
Tamiasciurus hudsonicus
586

10⅝–15¼″ (27–38.5 cm) long. Smallest tree squirrel in its range. Rust-red to grayish red above, brightest on sides; white or grayish white below. Tail similar to back color but outlined with broad black band edged with white. In summer, coat is duller and a black line separates reddish back from whitish belly. In winter, large ear tufts.

Tracks
In mud, hindprint about 1½″ long, with 5 toes printing; foreprints half as long, with 4 toes printing. In rapid bounds, front tracks appear between hind; in slow bounds, front tracks slightly behind hind. Straddle 4″.

Habitat
Often abundant in any kind of forest; natural coniferous forest, pine plantations, mixed forest, or hardwood; often around buildings.

Range
Throughout much of Canada and Alaska; in northeastern United States south to Iowa, N. Illinois, N. Indiana, N. Ohio, N. Virginia, and south through the Alleghenies; also through Rocky Mountain states.

Comments
In conifer forests the Red Squirrel feeds heavily on pine seeds and leaves piles of cone remnants everywhere. In the fall, it cuts green pine cones and buries them in damp earth, sometimes up to a bushel per cache.

Fox Squirrel
Sciurus niger
587

17⅞–27½″ (45.4–69.8 cm) long. Largest tree squirrel. 3 color phases: in northeastern part of range, gray above, yellowish below; in western part, bright rust; in South, black, often with white blaze on face and white tail tip. Large bushy tail with yellow-tipped hairs. In South Carolina, typically black with white ears and nose.

Habitat
Woods, particularly oak hickory; in the South, live oak and mixed forests, cypress and mangrove swamps, and piney areas.

Range
Eastern United States except for New England, most of New Jersey, extreme W. New York, NE. Pennsylvania; west to the Dakotas, NE. Colorado, and E. Texas.

Comments
The Fox Squirrel is most active in morning and late afternoon burying nuts, which in winter it will locate by its keen sense of smell, even under snow.

Gray Squirrel
Sciurus carolinensis
588

16⅞–19¾" (43–50 cm) long. Gray above, with buff underfur showing especially on head, shoulders, back, and feet; underparts paler gray. Black phase common in northern parts of range. Flattened tail bushy, gray with silvery-tipped hairs.

Tracks
Foreprints, round, 1" long, hindprints, more triangular, 2¼" long. On ground when bounding: paired hindprints slightly ahead of paired foreprints; sometimes foreprints between rear parts of hindprints, often directly behind them, leaving tracks like exclamation points (!!); bounding stride from a few inches to over 3'. On snow, foreprints 1½–1¾", hindprints nearly 3", with claws usually showing.

Habitat
Hardwood or mixed forests with nut trees, especially oak-hickory forests.

Range
Eastern United States west to S. Manitoba, E. North Dakota, most of Iowa, E. Kansas, E. Oklahoma, and E. Texas.

Comments
Especially active in morning and evening, the Gray Squirrel is abroad all year, even digging through snow to retrieve buried nuts. It does not remember where it buried nuts but can smell them under a foot of snow.

Southern Flying Squirrel
Glaucomys volans
589, 590

8¼–10" (21.1–25.3 cm) long. Smallest tree squirrel. Very silky coat grayish brown above, white below. Flattened gray-brown tail. Loose fold of skin between front and hind legs. Large black eyes.

Tracks
Similar to those of the Red Squirrel, but slightly smaller.

Habitat
Various forests such as beech-maple, oak-hickory, live oak.

Range
Eastern United States (except for northern New England and tip of Florida) west to Minnesota, E. Kansas, and E. Texas.

Comments
The Southern and Northern flying squirrels are the smallest tree squirrels, the only nocturnal ones, and the most

carnivorous of the group. It does not truly fly, but glides through the air, up to 80 yards from the top of one tree down to the trunk of another, with legs outstretched and the fold of skin spread between foreleg and hind leg acting as a combination parachute and sail (or glider wing).

Northern Flying Squirrel
Glaucomys sabrinus
591

10⅜–14½″ (26.3–36.8 cm) long. Small. Very soft fur, rich brown above, white below. A loose fold of skin between forelegs and hind legs. Large black eyes.

Habitat
Coniferous forests, mixed forests; sometimes in hardwoods where old or dead trees have numerous woodpecker-type nesting holes, especially in stumps 6–20′ high.

Range
E. Alaska, S. Yukon, S. Northwest Territories, southern tier of Canadian provinces, Labrador. In eastern United States to Minnesota, Wisconsin, Michigan, New England, and New York, and through Appalachian Mountains; south in western United States through California, Idaho, Montana, Utah, and N. Wyoming.

Comments
This squirrel is quite common, but because it is nocturnal, it is seldom seen. It spreads its legs and stretches its flight skin in gliding from tree to tree, pulling upright at the last instant to land gently.

Snowshoe Hare
Lepus americanus
592

15–20½″ (38.2–52 cm) long. In summer, dark brown, with tail dark above and dusky to white below; in winter, white, sometimes mottled with brown. In the Adirondack Mountains there are some black (melanistic) hares that remain black all year. Moderately long ears, black-tipped. Large hind feet, with soles well furred, especially in winter.

Tracks
When slow hopping, the 4 prints are bunched together, with hindprints outermost, alongside, or slightly in front of smaller foreprints; length about 10″ when hopping; 24″ when leaping.

Habitat
Northern forests.

Range
Alaska and most of Canada south to N. Minnesota, N. Michigan, N. New Jersey, and south through the Alleghenies, in the East; to N. California and N. New Mexico in the West.

Comments
The molt by which these hares (and other species displaying winter coloration) change coats is governed by lengthening or shortening periods of daylight. As daylight diminishes in autumn, the hare begins to grow a white-tipped winter coat, at first patchy—excellent camouflage against patchy snow—

and by the time large expanses of ground are blanketed, the hare has turned white to match. When daylight lengthens in spring, the winter coat is gradually replaced with brown.

New England Cottontail
Sylvilagus transitionalis
593

14¼–19″ (36.3–48.3 cm) long. Brownish, heavily sprinkled with black. Black patch between ears. Never a white spot on forehead. Short ears, with outer edge bordered by a broad black stripe.

Habitat
Woods or brushlands.

Range
New England through the Alleghenies to NE. Alabama.

Comments
The habits of this rabbit are very similar to those of the Eastern Cottontail, but it is much more secretive and rarely ventures from cover. Its home range is about half to three quarters of an acre. In recent years, its numbers have been declining and its range shrinking, probably because of loss of habitat and the introduction of other rabbit species.

Eastern Cottontail
Sylvilagus floridanus
594

14¾–18¼″ (4.9–6.8 cm) long. Grayish brown above, interspersed with some black; forehead often has white spot. Distinct rust-colored nape. Short tail cottony white below. Whitish feet. Long ears.

Tracks
In clusters of 4; foreprints almost round, about 1″ wide, slightly longer hindprints oblong, about 3–4″ long, depending on size and speed of rabbit. When sitting or standing: 2 foreprints side by side just ahead of 2 more widely spaced hindprints. When moving: one foreprint slightly ahead of the other; hindprints ahead of foreprints, as forefeet are fulcrums for hops. Straddle 4–5″; stride variable with speed.

Habitat
Brushy areas, old fields, woods, cultivated areas; especially thickets and brush piles.

Range
Eastern United States except for New England, west through North Dakota, Kansas, Texas, N. New Mexico, and into Arizona.

Comments
The most common rabbit in North America, the Eastern Cottontail breeds from February through September and usually produces 3–4 litters per year of 1–9 young (usually 4–5), which are nursed at dawn and dusk. Within hours of giving birth the female mates again. If no young were lost, a single pair, together with their offspring, could produce 350,000 rabbits in 5 years. However, this rabbit's death rate vies with its birth rate; few rabbits live more than one year.

Woodchuck
Marmota monax
595

16½–32¼" (41.8–82 cm) long. Large. Grizzled brown (or reddish to blackish); uniformly colored. Prominent bushy tail. Small ears. Short legs. Feet dark brown or black.

Habitat
Pastures, meadows, old fields, and woods.

Range
In the East, southern Canada south to Virginia and N. Alabama. In the West, east-central Alaska, British Columbia, most of S. Canada, N. Idaho, E. Kansas, and NE. North Dakota.

Comments
Also known as the Groundhog and Marmot. The sun-loving Woodchuck is active by day, especially in early morning and late afternoon. Green vegetation such as grasses, clover, alfalfa, and plantain forms its diet. Woodchucks are beneficial in moderate numbers, for their defecation inside the burrow, in a special excrement chamber separate from the nesting chamber, fertilizes the earth.

Hoary Bat
Lasiurus cinereus
596

4–6" (10.2–15.2 cm) long. Largest bat in the East. Light brown above with tips of fur heavily frosted white; throat buff. Ears short and rounded, with black, naked rims.

Habitat
Hangs from evergreen branches.

Range
Throughout continental United States except for peninsular Florida; also found in southern Canada.

Comments
Although it is the most widely distributed bat in the United States, the Hoary occurs only in small numbers and is rarely seen. It emerges late in the evening and eats mostly moths.

Beaver
Castor canadensis
597

35½–46" (90–117 cm) long. Very large rodent. Dark brown. Large black scaly tail, horizontally flattened, paddle-shaped. Large hind feet, black, webbed, with inner 2 nails cleft. Small eyes and ears.

Tracks
Distinctive when not obliterated by wide drag mark of tail. Usually only 3 or 4 of the 5 toes print, leaving wide, splay-toed track 3" long. Webbed hind feet leave fan-shaped track often more than 5" wide at widest part, at least twice as long as forefeet; webbing usually shows in soft mud.

Habitat
Rivers, streams, marshes, lakes, and ponds.

Range
Most of Canada and United States, except for most of Florida, much of Nevada, and S. California.

Comments
Active throughout the year, the Beaver is primarily nocturnal. Beavers living along a river generally make burrows with an underwater entrance in the riverbank; those in streams, lakes, and ponds usually build dams that incorporate a lodge, which has one or more underwater entrances and living quarters in a hollow near the top; wood chips on the floor absorb excess moisture and a vent admits fresh air.

Nine-banded Armadillo
Dasypus novemcinctus
598

24¼–31½" (61.5–80 cm) long. The only North American mammal armored with heavy, bony plates. Scaly-looking plates cover head, body, and tail. Between wide front and back plates, a midsection of 9 (sometimes fewer) narrow, jointed armor bands permit the body to curl. Head small. Underparts and upright ears are soft. Sparsely haired body is brown, tan, or sometimes yellowish but, depending on where it burrows, may be stained dark, even black, by earth or mud.

Tracks
Foreprint about 1¾" long, 1½" wide; hindprint over 2" long, 1½" wide. In sand or dust, blurred and appear almost hooflike. In soft earth or mud, occasionally all the long toes show more or less clearly; forefoot has 4 toes, the middle ones closely spaced, the outer spread wide and much shorter; hind foot has 5 toes more evenly spread, the 3 middle ones long, the outer ones short, with no separation from heel pad.

Habitat
Abundant in sandy soils; in clay, where digging is more difficult; along streams where soil is moist and flaky.

Range
Southeastern United States where in recent years it has rapidly expanded its range: most of Florida and parts of Georgia west to SE. Kansas, Oklahoma, and Texas.

Comments
The Spanish conquistadores first encountered this strange creature and named it the "little man in armor." It spends most waking hours digging for food and building burrows, grunting almost constantly. The Nine-banded Armadillo does not hibernate and cannot survive prolonged below-freezing weather. It goes about its business with a steady, stiff-legged jog, but when approached, escapes by running away or rolling into a ball to protect its vulnerable belly; it can also burrow underground with amazing speed.

Marten
Martes americana
599

19¼–26⅞" (49–68.2 cm) long. Weasel-like. Brownish, varying from dark brown to blond, with paler head and underparts, darker legs, orange or buff throat patch. Long, bushy tail; pointed snout; small ears.

Tracks
1½–1⅞" wide, showing all 5 toes; straddle 2½–3", to 6" in

snow; walking stride 9″ for males, 6″ for females; more than doubles when running.

Breeding
Mates midsummer; delayed implantation; 2–4 young born blind, naked, around April in leaf nest.

Habitat
Forests, particularly coniferous ones.

Range
Most of Canada; in the East, to northern New England and N. New York; in the West, south to N. California through Rocky Mountains.

Comments
Martens are active in early morning, late afternoon, and on overcast days, traversing a home range of 5–15 square miles. They spend much of their time in trees. They pounce on prey; the Red Squirrel is favored, but flying squirrels, rabbits, mice, and birds are also taken. The varied diet also includes carrion, eggs, berries, conifer seeds, and honey.

Virginia Opossum
Didelphis virginiana
600

25⅜–40″ (64.5–101.7 cm) long. House-cat size. Grizzled white above; long white hairs cover black-tipped fur below. In some areas, individuals may appear brownish or blackish. Long, naked prehensile tail. Head, throat, and cheeks whitish; ears large, naked, black with pinkish tips. Legs short; first toe of hind foot opposable (thumblike) and lacks nail. Females with fur-lined abdominal pouch.

Tracks
In mud, hindprint approximately 2″ wide, with 5 toes printing: large thumblike toe slanted inward or backward, 3 middle toes close together, and remaining toe separate; foreprint slightly smaller, with 5 toes printing in starlike fashion. Hind- and foreprints parallel and close together; straddle 4″; walking stride 7″

Habitat
Open woods, brushy wastelands, and farmlands.

Range
Most of eastern United States, except Maine, N. Michigan, and N. Minnesota. Extends southwest to Colorado and most of Texas. Also SE. Arizona and the coastal areas of California, Oregon, Washington, and S. British Columbia.

Comments
Nocturnal and solitary. When threatened, the Opossum sometimes rolls over, shuts its eyes, and allows its tongue to loll, feigning death, or "playing possum," for some time. More often, it tries to bluff its attacker by hissing, salivating, and opening its mouth wide to show all of its 50 teeth. The Virginia Opossum is the only North American marsupial, or pouched mammal.

Long-tailed Weasel
Mustela frenata
601

11–21¾″ (28–55 cm) long. Brown above, white below. Tail brown with black tip; feet brownish. During winter in northern latitudes, entirely white except for black nose, eyes, and tail tip. Males almost twice as large as females.

Tracks
Hindprints ¾″ wide, 1″ long or more, usually with only 4 of the 5 toes printing; foreprints slightly wider, but approximately half as long. Hind feet usually placed in or near foreprints, but prints are sometimes side by side, more often with 1 slightly ahead; straddle 3″. Stride varies as weasels run and bound, often alternating long and short leaps; when carrying prey or stalking, 12″; when running, 20″.

Breeding
Mates in midsummer; 4–9 young born blind, nearly naked, in early May in abandoned dens of other small mammals; disperse at 7–8 weeks, when males are already larger than mother. Females mate in first year, males not until second season.

Habitat
Varied; forested, brushy, and open areas, including farmlands, preferably near water.

Range
S. British Columbia, Alberta, Manitoba, and Saskatchewan south through most of United States except SE. California and much of Arizona.

Comments
Weasels are wholly carnivorous, preying mainly on mice but also taking rabbits, chipmunks, shrews, rats, and birds, including poultry. They attack prey several times their size, climb 15–20′ up a tree after a squirrel, and occasionally go on killing sprees. Their killing instinct is triggered by the smell of blood; even an injured sibling will be killed and eaten.

Ermine
Mustela erminea
602, 604

7½–13½″ (19–34.4 cm) long. Elongated body, dark brown above, white below. Tail brown with black tip; feet white. In winter, throughout northern range, white with black tail tip, nose, and eyes. Males almost twice as large as females.

Tracks
Similar to Long-tailed Weasel's but usually smaller.

Breeding
Mates in July; 4–9 young born blind, with fine hair, in spring in some protected area, such as under a log, a rock pile, or tree stump; eyes open at 35 days.

Habitat
Varied: open woodlands, grasslands, wetlands, farmlands.

Range
Most of Canada south to N. Iowa, Michigan, Pennsylvania, and Maryland in East; to N. California, W. Colorado, and N. New Mexico in West.

Comments
Though the Ermine hunts mainly on the ground, it can climb trees and occasionally even pursues prey into water. After a rapid dash, it pounces on its victim with all four feet, biting through the neck near the base of the skull. Mice are its main food, but it also eats shrews, baby rabbits, and birds.

Fisher
Martes pennanti
603

31⅛–40¾" (79–103.3 cm) long. Long, thin body; dark brown above and below with grayish cast on head. Bushy tail; broad head with pointed snout; small ears.

Tracks
Similar to Marten's but larger; wider than long, with claws showing; 2" wide on dirt, more than 2½" on snow.

Breeding
Mates March–April, right after giving birth in a rock crevice or hollow tree; delayed implantation, with gestation of nearly a year; 1–5 young born blind the following spring.

Habitat
Mature forests.

Range
Southern tier of Canadian provinces south in the East to northern New England and New York; in the west, south to N. California and in the Rocky Mountains to Utah.

Comments
Although primarily nocturnal like most mustelids, the Fisher is sometimes abroad by day. A good climber and swimmer, it travels well-established trails or fallen logs, and moves between trees, from branch to branch. Snowshoe Hares and Porcupines are its main prey.

Striped Skunk
Mephitis mephitis
605

20½–31½" (52.2–80 cm) long. Black with 2 broad white stripes on back meeting in cap on head and shoulders; thin white stripe down center of face. Bushy black tail, often with white tip or fringe. Coloration varies from mostly black to mostly white. Males larger than females.

Tracks
Show 5 toes when clear, sometimes claws. Hindprints 1¼–2" long, less wide, broadest at front, more flat-footed; foreprints 1–1¾" long, slightly wider; stride 4–6".

Breeding
Mates in late winter; in mid-May, 4–7 young born blind, with very fine hair clearly marked with black-and-white pattern; weaned at 6–7 weeks when scent has developed.

Habitat
Grassy plains, woodlands, deserts, suburbs.

Range
Most of United States, southern tier of Canadian provinces.

Comments
Whereas most mammals have evolved coloration that blends with their environment, the Striped Skunk is boldly colored, advertising to potential enemies that it is not to be bothered. Its anal glands hold fetid, oily, yellowish musk, enough for five or six jets of spray—though one is usually enough.

Eastern Spotted Skunk
Spilogale putorius
606

13½–22¼" (34.3–56.3 cm) long. Small. Black with horizontal white stripes on neck and shoulders, irregular vertical stripes and elongated spots on sides. Tail with white tip; white spots on top of head, between eyes.

Tracks
Like Striped Skunk's but smaller. Hindprint 1¼" long; heel pad shows more definite lobing. Unlike other skunks, stride very irregular.

Breeding
Mates in late winter; 4–5 young born in spring, blind, furred, and achieve adult coloration in early summer.

Habitat
Mixed woodlands and open areas, scrub, and farmlands.

Range
In the Midwest and Southeast, Minnesota and South Dakota south to Texas and Louisiana; in the East, S. Illinois and south-central Pennsylvania south to Mississippi, W. South Carolina and Florida; also in extreme northern Mexico.

Comments
The Spotted Skunk's spraying behavior is unique: if a predator refuses to retreat when it raises its tail, the skunk turns its back, stands on its forefeet, raises its tail again, spreads its hind feet, and sprays, often for a distance of 12'.

Raccoon
Procyon lotor
607

23¾–37⅞" (60.3–95 cm) long. Reddish brown above, with much black; grayish below. Distinguished by a bushy tail with 4–6 alternating black and brown or brownish-gray rings and a black mask outlined in white. Ears relatively small.

Tracks
Hindprint 3¼–4¼" long, much longer than wide; resembles a miniature human footprint with abnormally long toes. Foreprint much shorter, 3", almost as wide as long; claws show on all 5 toes. Tracks are large for animal's size because Raccoon is flat-footed, like bears and men. Stride 6–20", averaging 14".

Breeding
Though Raccoons are sedentary, males travel miles in search of mates. Female accepts only 1 male per season, usually in February in the North, December in the South. He remains in her den a week or more, then seeks another mate. Lethargic during pregnancy, the female prefers to make a leaf nest in

large hollow trees but may also use such protected places as culverts, caves, rock clefts, Woodchuck dens, or under wind-thrown trees. Litter of 1–7 young, average 4–5, born April–May, weighing about 2 oz at birth, open eyes at about 3 weeks, clamber about den mouth at 7–8 weeks, are weaned by late summer.

Habitat
Various, but most common along wooded streams.

Range
Southern edge of southern provinces of Canada; most of United States except for portions of the Rocky Mountain states, central Nevada, and Utah.

Comments
Native only to the Americas, the Raccoon is nocturnal and solitary except when breeding or caring for its young. Omnivorous, it eats grapes, nuts, grubs, crickets, grasshoppers, voles, deer mice, squirrels, other small mammals, birds' eggs, and nestlings.

Wolverine
Gulo gulo
608

31½–44¼" (80–112.5 cm) long. Bulky, somewhat bearlike. Dark brown, with broad yellowish bands from shoulders back over hips and meeting at base of tail; light patches in front of ears. Males larger than females.

Tracks
If perfect, all 5 toes and semiretractile claws print; small toe often does not print. Foreprint 4½–7" long, varying with size of animal or condition of snow, and about as wide; heel pad often showing 2 lobes, a wide lobe in front of smaller round lobe, which does not always register; hindprint similar to foreprint; stride extremely variable; straddle 7–8".

Breeding
Mates April–September; implantation delayed until January; 2–5 young born early spring in some protected area, such as a thicket, or a rock crevice; remain with mother 2 years.

Habitat
Forests; tundras.

Range
Northern Canada south in West to NW. Washington. Spotty distribution in southeastern United States.

Comments
Perhaps the most powerful mammal for its size, the ferocious Wolverine is capable of driving even a bear or Cougar from its kill. It prefers carrion but eats anything it can kill or find, including Moose or Elk slowed down in heavy snow, Beavers, deer, Porcupines, birds, squirrels, eggs, roots, and berries. It trails Caribou herds, eating the remains of wolf kills; follows trap lines, eating bait, trapped animals, and cached food; and raids cabins, marking everything it cannot eat with musk and sometimes urine and droppings.

Black Bear
Ursus americanus
609

4½–6¼' (137–188 cm) long. In the East, nearly black. Snout tan or grizzled; in profile straight or slightly convex. Males much larger than females.

Tracks
Broad footprints 4" long, 5" wide turning in slightly at the front and showing 5 toes on fore and hind feet. Hindprints 7–9" long, 5" wide. Individually, prints (especially hindprints) look as if made by a flat-footed man in moccasins, except that large toe is outermost, smallest toe innermost and occasionally fails to register.

Breeding
Mates June–early July; 1 litter of 1–5 (usually twins or triplets) born January–early February, generally every other year. Sows mate during their third year, with most producing 1 cub the first winter, 2 on subsequent breedings.

Habitat
In the East, primarily forests and swamps.

Range
Most of Canada, Alaska, south on West Coast through N. California, in Rocky Mountain states to Mexico, N. Minnesota, Wisconsin, and Michigan; in New England, New York, and Pennsylvania south through Appalachians; in Southeast, most of Florida, and S. Louisiana.

Comments
This uniquely American bear, although primarily nocturnal, may be seen at any time, day or night, ranging in a home area of 8–10 square miles, sometimes as many as 15. It is solitary except briefly during mating season and when congregating to feed at dumps. Its walk is clumsy, but in its bounding trot it attains surprising speed, with bursts up to 30 mph.

Gray Wolf
Canis lupus
610

39½–80⅝" (100–205 cm) long. Usually grizzled gray but shows great variation in color, ranging from white to black. Long, bushy tail with black tip. Nose pad 1" (2.5 cm) wide. Males larger than females.

Tracks
Similar to domestic dog's but larger. Foreprint 4¼–5" long; hindprint slightly smaller. Walking stride 30"; sometimes hind feet come down in forefeet prints.

Breeding
Mates February–March; 5–14 young, averaging 7, born April–June in den in an enlarged chamber without nesting material; at 1 month pups emerge to play near den entrance guarded by an adult.

Habitat
Open tundra; forests.

Range
Once most of North America, but now only Alaska, Canada,

N. Washington, N. Idaho, N. Montana, Isle Royale National Park in Lake Superior, and NE. Minnesota.

Comments
A social animal, the Gray Wolf mates for life and lives in packs of 2–15, usually 4–7, formed primarily of family members and relatives. The strongest male is normally the leader; all members of the pack help to care for the young. Usually hunting at night, the Gray Wolf—also called the Timber Wolf—feeds primarily on large mammals such as Moose, Caribou, and deer.

Gray Fox
Urocyon cinereoargenteus
611

31½–44¼″ (80–113 cm) long. Grizzled gray above, reddish below and on back of head; throat white. Tail with black "mane" on top and black tip; feet rusty-colored. Large ears.

Tracks
When in straight line, similar to those of a very large domestic cat, except that nonretractile claws may show. Similar to Red Fox's, but often smaller with larger toes and more sharply defined because of less hair around pads. Foreprint about 1½″ long; hindprint as long, slightly narrower; 4 toes with claws.

Breeding
Mates February–March; 2–7 young, average 3–4, born in March or April; weaned at 3 months, hunting for themselves at 4 months, when they weigh about 7 lb.

Habitat
Varied, but associated much more with wooded and brushy habitats than are Red Foxes.

Range
Eastern United States west to E. North and South Dakota, Nebraska, Kansas, Oklahoma, most of Texas, New Mexico, Arizona, and California, north through Colorado, S. Utah, S. Nevada, and W. Oregon.

Comments
Although primarily nocturnal, the Gray Fox is sometimes seen foraging by day in brush, thick foliage, or timber. The only American canid with tree climbing ability, it occasionally forages in trees and frequently takes refuge in them, especially in leaning or thickly branched ones. Favored den sites include woodlands and among boulders on the slopes of rocky ridges.

Red Fox
Vulpes vulpes
612

35⅜–40⅜″ (90–103 cm) long. Small, doglike. Rusty reddish above; white underparts, chin, and throat. Long, bushy tail with white tip. Prominent pointed ears. Back of ear, lower legs, feet black. Elliptical pupils. Color variations include a black phase (almost completely black), a silver phase (black with silver-tipped hairs), a cross phase (reddish brown with a dark cross across shoulders), and intermediate phases, all with white-tipped tail.

Tracks
Foreprint about 2¼" long, hindprint slightly smaller, narrower, more pointed; both show 4 toe prints. Often blurred in winter; sometimes brushed out by tail in heavy snow.

Breeding
Mates January–early March. After 51–53 days gestation, 1–10 kits, average 4–8, born March–May in maternity den. When about 1 month old, they play above ground and feed on what is brought them by their parents.

Habitat
Varied: mixed cultivated and wooded areas, brushlands.

Range
Most of Canada and United States except for much of West Coast; NW. Texas and Southeast (coastal North Carolina to peninsular Florida); Southwest (S. California, N. Nevada, Arizona); S. Alberta and SW. Saskatchewan to SW. Oklahoma.

Comments
Even when fairly common, the Red Fox may be difficult to observe, as it is shy, nervous, and primarily nocturnal (though it may be abroad near dawn or dusk or on dark days). Omnivorous, it eats whatever is available.

Bobcat
Felis rufus
613

28–49⅜" (71–125 cm) long. Tawny (grayer in winter), with indistinct black spotting. Short, stubby tail with 2 or 3 black bars and black tip above; pale or white below. Upper legs have dark or black horizontal bars. Face has thin, often broken black lines radiating onto broad cheek ruff. Ears slightly tufted. Males larger than females.

Tracks
Fore- and hindprints about same size, 2" long, slightly longer than wide, with 4 toes, no claw marks. If clearly outlined, heel pad distinguishes from canine print: dog's is lobed only at rear; Bobcat's is lobed at rear and concave at front, giving print scalloped front and rear edges.

Breeding
Mates in spring. Litter of 1–7 young, usually 2–3, born late April–early May in maternity den of leaves or other dry vegetation in hollow log, rock shelter, under fallen tree, or other protected place.

Habitat
Primarily scrubby country and broken forests, but adapts to swamps, farmlands, and arid lands if rocky or brushy.

Range
Spottily distributed from coast to coast from southern Canada into Mexico. Probably most plentiful in Far West, from Idaho, Utah, and Nevada to Pacific and from Washington to Baja California. Scarce or absent in most of central and lower Midwest.

Comments
Found only in North America, where it is the most common wildcat, the Bobcat gets its common name from its stubby, or "bobbed," tail. It "lies up" by day in a rock cleft, thicket, or other hiding place. The Bobcat spends less time in trees than the Lynx but is also an expert climber. Sometimes it rests on a boulder or a low tree branch, waiting to pounce on small game that passes; its mottled fur provides excellent camouflage.

Lynx
Felis lynx
614

29⅛–41⅞" (74–107 cm) long. Buff or tawny with mixed blackish hairs; underparts cinnamon-brownish. Short tail tipped with black. Long black ear tufts. Large, pale cheek ruffs, whitish with black barring, forming a double-pointed beard at throat. Feet very large and well furred. Males larger than females.

Tracks
Foreprint 3–4¼" long, almost as wide; hindprint slightly smaller; both with 4 toes, no claws showing. Because of well-furred paws, prints are much larger and rounder than Bobcat's and especially large when toe pads spread and blur in powdery snow. Straddle usually less than 7", almost as narrow as Bobcat's. Normally short stride 14–16".

Breeding
Mates mid-March–early April; usually 1 litter of 2 young born May–July. Kittens remain with mother through first winter.

Habitat
Deep forest.

Range
In the East, northern New England and extreme N. New York; in the Midwest, N. Michigan and N. Wisconsin. Much of Canada and Alaska south into much of Washington, N. Oregon, N. Idaho, and extreme NW. Montana. Also Rocky Mountain areas of Wyoming and N. Colorado.

Comments
By day the Lynx rests under a ledge, the roots of a fallen tree, or a low branch. It frequently, and expertly, climbs trees and sometimes rests in them, waiting to leap down on passing prey. The long ear tufts serve as sensitive antennae, enhancing hearing. Large, thickly furred feet permit silent stalking and speed through soft snow, in which some prey may flounder, though not the Snowshoe Hare, the Lynx's chief prey.

Wild Boar
Sus scrofa
615

4½–6' (132–182 cm) long. Usually black, sometimes brown or gray, often with grizzled or frost-tipped guard hairs. Pureblooded Wild Boars have coat of long, bristly hairs thickening into erect mane on neck and shoulders, upper spine, sometimes onto jaw; dense undercoat in winter. Hybrids much more variable in color, frequently less hairy.

Tail moderately long, never coiled. Head long, shaggy, with flexible snout disc like that of domestic swine. Upper tusks (modified canines) usually 3–5″ but up to 9″ long, curl out and up along sides of mouth; lower canines smaller, turn out slightly, rising outside mouth.

Tracks
Cloven but more rounded and splayed than deer tracks, 2½″ long; hindprints often half-covering foreprints. Front dewclaws low, long, and pointed, in soft earth almost always print as crescents outside and behind main print; hind dewclaws print as dots; stride 18″.

Breeding
Mating peaks in December; gestation 16 weeks; litter of 3–14 young, usually 4–5, born April in small, grass-lined depression that sow has hollowed in pile of grass and branches in secluded thicket; piglets at birth 6–8″ long, brown, with 9–10 pale longitudinal body stripes that disappear within 6 months; follow sow at 1 week; weaned at 3 months; disperse the following spring; sexually mature at 1½ years.

Habitat
Variable: densely forested mountainous terrain, brushlands, dry ridges, and swamps.

Range
Chiefly W. North Carolina; E. Tennessee (especially Nantahala and Cherokee national forests); Santa Cruz Island (off California); Monterey and San Luis Obispo counties, California. Small numbers, primarily in preserves, in New Hampshire, Vermont, Pennsylvania, perhaps other states. Small feral hogs in Florida; hybrids or feral hogs in Alabama, Arizona, Arkansas, Georgia, Louisiana, Mississippi, Missouri, Oklahoma, Oregon, South Carolina, and Texas.

Comments
Especially active at dawn and dusk, Wild Boars are fast runners and good swimmers. Sows and their young forage in family groups, usually of about half a dozen animals, but sometimes join other groups in herds up to 50. Except during breeding season, mature males are solitary or band in small groups.

White-tailed Deer
Odocoileus virginianus
616

4½–6¾′ (134–206 cm) long. Tan or reddish brown above in summer; grayish brown in winter. Belly, throat, nose band, eye ring, and inside of ears white. Tail brown, edged with white above, often with dark stripe down center, white below. Black spots on sides of chin. Bucks' antlers with main beam forward and several unbranched tines behind; a small brow tine. Antler spread to 3′ (90 cm). Does normally lack antlers. Fawns spotted.

Tracks
Like narrow split hearts, pointed end forward, about 2–3″ long; dewclaws may print twin dots behind main prints in

snow or soft mud. In shallow snow (1″ deep), buck may drag its feet, leaving drag marks ahead of prints; in deeper snow, both bucks and does drag feet. Straddle 5–6″ wide. Stride, when walking, 1′; when running, 6′ or more, and hindprints sometimes register ahead of foreprints; when leaping, 20′.

Habitat
Farmlands, brushy areas, and woods.

Range
Southern half of southern tier of Canadian provinces; most of United States except most of California, Nevada, Utah, N. Arizona, SW. Colorado, and NW. New Mexico.

Comments
Although primarily nocturnal, deer may be active at any time, grazing on green plants, including aquatic ones in the summer; eating acorns, beechnuts, and other nuts and corn in the fall; and in winter, browsing on woody vegetation, including the twigs and buds of viburnum, birch, maple, and many conifers. Once nearly exterminated in much of the Northeast and Midwest, Whitetails are now more abundant than ever, owing to hunting restrictions and the decline in numbers of their predators. They have become the most plentiful game animal in eastern North America.

Moose
Alces alces
617

6¾–9′ (206–279 cm) long. Largest deer in the world. Horse-size. Long, dark brown hair. High, humped shoulders; long, pale legs; stubby tail. Huge pendulous muzzle; large dewlap under chin; large ears. Males much larger than females, with massive palmate antlers, broadly flattened. Antler spread usually 4–5′ (120–150 cm); record of 81″ (206 cm).

Tracks
Cloven prints usually more than 5″ long and pointed. Lobes somewhat splayed in snow, mud, or when running. Dewclaws often print behind main prints in snow, mud, or when running, lengthening print to 10″. Stride, 3½–5½′ when walking, more than 8′ when trotting or running.

Habitat
Spruce forest, swamps, and aspen and willow thickets.

Range
Most of Canada; in the East south to Maine, Minnesota, and Isle Royale in Lake Superior; in the West, Alaska, N. British Columbia and southeast through Rocky Mountains to NE. Utah and NW. Colorado.

Comments
Moose are solitary in summer, but several may gather near streams and lakes to feed on willows and aquatic vegetation, including the leaves of water lilies. When black flies and mosquitoes torment them, Moose may nearly submerge themselves or roll in a wallow to acquire a protective coating of mud. Migrating up and down mountain slopes seasonally,

they may herd in winter, packing down snow, which facilitates movement; then they browse on woody plants, including the twigs, buds, and bark of willow, balsam, aspen, dogwood, birch, cherry, maple, and viburnum.

Caribou
Rangifer tarandus
618

4½–6¾' (137–210 cm) long. Coloration variable; generally brown shaggy fur with whitish neck and mane; belly, rump, underside of tail white. Nearly white on Arctic islands; more brownish on tundra, taiga, and forest. Fawns unspotted. Large snout; short, furry ears; short, well-furred tail. Foot pads large and soft in summer, shrunken in winter; rounded hooves. Males and most females with antlers. Bulls' antlers are branched, semipalmated, and have flattened brow tines, 20–62" (52–158 cm) long. Cows' antlers small and spindly, 9–20" (23–50 cm) long. Antler spread to 60" (153 cm).

Tracks
Widely separated crescents, 5" wide, slightly shorter, almost always followed by dewclaw marks; on thin, crusted snow, only round outlines of hooves may print; hindprints usually overlap foreprints, leaving double impressions 8" long.

Habitat
Tundra, taiga; farther south where lichens abound in coniferous forests in mountains.

Range
Alaska and much of Canada south through British Columbia to E. Washington and N. Idaho; also N. Alberta and northern two-thirds of Saskatchewan and Manitoba; in the East, south to Lake Superior and east to Newfoundland.

Comments
The Caribou of North America, now considered to be the same species as the Reindeer of Europe and Asia, is among the most migratory of all mammals. These gregarious animals usually form homogeneous bands of bulls, cows with calves, or yearlings, but may gather in groups of 10–100,000 of both sexes and all ages in late winter before the spring migration, after calving, and before the fall migration and rutting. Especially active in mornings and evenings, in summer Caribou feed on mushrooms and many green plants, twigs of birches and willows, and fruit; dropped antlers are avidly eaten by Caribou and rodents. In winter, lichens are the chief food. They can run at speeds of nearly 50 mph but cannot maintain such a pace for very long. In summer, to avoid heat and insects, they often lie on snowbanks and on the north side of hills; in winter they sun on frozen lakes. Their spongy foot pads provide traction and good weight distribution on boggy summer tundra; in winter, when the pads have shrunk, hardened, and are covered with tufts of hair, the hoof rim bites into ice or crusted snow to prevent slipping.

PART IV   APPENDICES

GLOSSARY

Abdomen In insects, the hindmost of the three subdivisions of the body; in spiders, the hindmost of the two subdivisions of the body.

Accidental A bird species that has appeared in a given area a very few times only and whose normal range is in another area.

Achene A small, dry, hard fruit that does not open and contains one seed.

Aestivation Dormancy during a hot, dry season.

Allelopathy An inhibiting or harmful influence of one plant species on another through the secretion of toxic substances.

Alternate Arising singly along the stem.

Annual Having a life cycle completed in one year or season.

Anther The saclike part of a stamen, containing pollen.

Association A group of organisms typically found together in a particular environment.

Auriculars Feathers covering a bird's ear opening and the area immediately around it; often distinctively colored. Also called ear coverts.

Axil The angle formed by the upper side of a leaf and the stem from which it grows.

Bald A shrubby or grassy area without trees on a mountain summit.

Bench The wave-cut shore of a river or sea.

Biomass The total weight of all living organisms in a particular area.

Bipinnate With leaflets arranged on side branches off a main axis; twice-pinnate; bipinnately compound.

Bloom A whitish, powdery coating found on certain fruits and leaves.

Boreal Northern; pertaining to the cool, moist coniferous forest region of North America that stretches from Alaska to Newfoundland.

Bract A modified and often scalelike leaf, usually located at the base of a flower, a fruit, or a cluster of flowers or fruits.

Broad-leaved Having wide leaves (as distinct from coniferous); pertaining to deciduous trees.

Brood A generation of butterflies hatched from the eggs laid by females of a single generation; members of a brood fly during the same general period.

Calyx Collective term for the sepals of a flower; the calyx is usually green.

Cambium In woody plants, the sheath of embryonic cells, between wood and bark, that divides to form new tissue.

Canopy The uppermost level of a forest community, usually formed by the tallest trees.

Capsule A dry, thin-walled fruit containing two or more seeds and splitting along natural grooved lines at maturity.

Carapace The upper part of a turtle's shell.

Caste In social insects, a specialized form of adult with a distinct role in the colony.

Catkin A compact and often drooping cluster of reduced, stalkless, and usually unisexual flowers.

Cell The area of a butterfly's wing that is entirely enclosed by veins; also called discal cell.

Cephalothorax The first subdivision of a spider's body, combining the head and the thorax.

Climax The plants and animals in a given community that will persist in that community so long as conditions remain stable.

Cloaca In certain vertebrates, such as reptiles, the chamber into which the digestive, urinary, and reproductive systems empty, opening to the outside through the anus.

Colonnade A row of trees, often with stiltlike roots, remaining after the decay and disappearance of nurse logs.

Community In a particular area, all plant and animal organisms living in close association and interacting.

Compound eye One of the paired visual organs consisting of several or many light-sensitive units, or ommatidia, usually clustered in a radiating array with exposed lenses fitting together.

Conifer A cone-bearing tree of the pine family.

Corolla Collective term for the petals of a flower.

Coverts In birds, small feathers that overlie or cover the bases of the large flight feathers of the wings and tail, or that cover an area or structure (e.g., ear coverts).

Creeper Technically, a trailing shoot that takes root at the nodes; used here to denote any trailing, prostrate plant.

Crepuscular Active at twilight.

Cutin An impermeable, varnishlike covering on the epidermis of plants.

Deciduous Shedding leaves seasonally, and leafless for part of the year.

Dewclaw A functionless digit or "toe," usually on the upper part of a mammal's foot; on deer, it is located above the true hoof.

Disk The central portion of a butterfly's wing, tangential to the costal and trailing margins.

Diurnal Active during the daytime hours.

Dominant Species of plant or animal most abundant in a community or exercising the greatest influence on the environment.

Drone One of a caste of social bees, consisting only of reproductive males.

Drupe A stone fruit; a fleshy fruit with the single seed enveloped by a hard covering (stone).

Duff Decaying organic matter on the forest floor.

Ecosystem A system of ecologically linked animals and plants that have evolved together in a certain environment. The elements of an ecosystem are mutually dependent.

Ecotone The transition area between two communities; ecotones contain species from each area as well as organisms unique to it.

Elytron The thickened forewing of beetles, serving as protective covers for the hind wings.

Entire Smooth-edged, not lobed or toothed.

Epiphyte A plant growing on another plant but deriving little or no nutrition from it; also called an air plant.

Esker Long, narrow, sinuous ridge of sand, gravel, and boulders deposited by a stream on, within, or beneath a glacier.

Exotic Not native to a given area; also, an introduced plant.

Eyespots Spots resembling eyes on winged insects, such as butterflies and moths.

Femur The third segment of an insect's leg, between trochanter and tibia.

Flight feathers In birds, the long, well-developed feathers of the wings and tail, used during flight. The flight feathers of the wings are divided into primaries, secondaries, and tertials.

Follicle A dry, one-celled fruit, splitting at maturity along a single grooved line.

Fungus A plant that lacks chlorophyll and reproduces by means of spores.

Gravid Bearing eggs or developing young; pregnant.

Graywacke Dark-colored sandstone conglomerate.

Habitat The place or community where a plant or animal naturally grows and lives.

Hardwood A broad-leaved tree (angiosperm), as opposed to a conifer. The wood may be hard or soft.

Head A crowded cluster of flowers on very short stalks, or without stalks, as in the sunflower family.

Herb A plant with soft, not woody, stems that dies to the ground in winter.

Herbaceous Herblike, with little or no woody tissue, and dying, or dying down, at the end of a growing season.

Host plant The food plant of a caterpillar.

Hybrids The offspring of two different varieties, races, species, or genera.

Inflorescence A flower cluster on a plant; especially the arrangement of flowers on a plant.

Intergrades Animals of related and adjoining subspecies that may resemble either form or exhibit a combination of their characteristics.

Introduced Intentionally or accidentally established in an area by man, and not native; exotic or foreign.

Involucre A whorl or circle of bracts beneath a flower or flower cluster.

Key A dry, one-seeded fruit with a wing.

Lanceolate Shaped like a lance, several times longer than wide, pointed at the tip and broadest near the base.

Larva A post-hatching immature stage that differs in appearance from the adult and must metamorphose before assuming adult characters.

Leaflet One of the leaflike parts of a compound leaf.

Lichen Any of a large number of small plants made up of an alga and a fungus growing symbiotically on various solid surfaces, such as rocks.

Litter Surface layer of forest floor, consisting of slightly decomposed organic matter.

Loam A rich soil of clay, silt, sand, and humus (organic matter).

Lobed Indented on the margins, with the indentations not reaching to the center or base.

Lore In birds, the space between the eye and the base of the bill, sometimes distinctively colored.

Margin The edge of the wing.

Molt The periodic loss and replacement of feathers; most species have regular patterns and schedules of molt.

Moraine A formation of boulders, gravel, sand, clay, etc., deposited directly by a glacier.

Motte A small clump or grove of trees.

Nitrogen fixation Conversion by plants of atmospheric nitrogen into a usable form (nitrates) by certain soil bacteria in their nodules.

Node The place on the stem where leaves or branches are attached.

Nurse log A fallen log or snag on which sprouts or seedlings of a tree begin to grow.

Oblanceolate Reverse lanceolate; shaped like a lance, several times longer than wide, broadest near the tip and pointed at the base.

Obligate Bound to a certain restricted condition of life.

Obovate Reverse ovate; oval, with the broader end at the tip.

Opposite leaves Occurring in pairs at a node, with one leaf on either side of the stem.

Ovary The swollen base of a pistil, within which seeds develop.

Ovate leaf Egg-shaped, pointed at the top, technically broader near the base.

Overwinter To go through a period of dormancy during the cold season.

Palmate Having three or more divisions or lobes, looking like the outspread fingers of a hand.

Palp A sensory structure associated with an insect's mouthparts.

Parasite A plant or animal living in or on another plant or animal, and deriving its nutrition from the host organism to the detriment of the host.

Parotoid gland A large glandular structure on each side of the neck or behind the eyes of toads and some salamanders.

Parthenogenesis Reproduction by the development of an unfertilized egg; some animals produce only one sex and reproduce by means of unfertilized eggs.

Pedicel The stalk of an individual flower.

Pedipalp One of the second pair of appendages of the cephalothorax of a spider, usually leglike in a female but enlarged at the tip in a male as a special organ for transferring sperm; used by both sexes for guiding prey to the mouth.

Peduncle The main flowerstalk or stem holding an inflorescence.

Perennial Living more than two years; also, any plant that uses the same root system to produce new growth.

Petal Of a flower, the basic unit of the corolla; flat, usually broad, and brightly colored.

Petiole The stalklike part of a leaf, attaching it to the stem.

Pheromones Sex-attractant scent molecules produced by the scent scales, or androconia, of some insects and other animals.

Phloem The vascular tissue in a plant that conducts food material.

Pinnate leaf A compound leaf with leaflets along the sides of a common central stalk, much like a feather.

Pioneer species A plant or animal that begins a new cycle of life in a barren area; pioneers prepare the way for, and eventually are replaced by, different species.

Pistil The female organ of a flower, consisting of an ovary, style, and stigma.

Pistillate flower A female flower, having one or more pistils but no functional stamens.

Plastron The lower part of a turtle's shell.

Pod A dry, one-celled fruit, splitting along natural grooved lines, with thicker walls than a capsule.

Podzol Any of an infertile group of soils typical of conifer and mixed forests in cool, moist environments. Often covered by a mat of undecayed litter.

Pollen Spores formed in the anthers of a flower that produce the male cells.

Pome A fruit with fleshy outer tissue and a papery-walled, inner chamber containing the seeds.

Prehensile Adapted for grasping or wrapping around; said of the toes, claws, and tails of certain animals.

Primaries The outermost and longest flight feathers on a bird's wing. Primaries vary in number from 9 to 11 per wing, but always occur in a fixed number in any particular species.

Proboscis A prolonged set of mouthparts adapted for reaching into or piercing a food source.

Pupation In insects, the transformation from caterpillar to chrysalis or from larva to adult.

Race A distinctive geographical population, equivalent to a subspecies or variety.

Raceme A long flower cluster on which individual flowers each bloom on a small stalk all along a common, larger, central stalk.

Ray flower The bilaterally symmetrical flowers around the edge of the head in many members of the sunflower family; each ray flower resembles a single petal.

Regular flower With petals and/or sepals arranged around the center, like the spokes of a wheel; always radially symmetrical.

Reproductive In social insects, a member of the caste capable of reproduction; reproductives usually gain wings for brief mating flights, as occurs in termites and ants.

Respiration The process in which a plant receives oxygen through air or water, breaks it down and uses it (oxidation), and excretes the waste products, especially carbon dioxide.

Rhizome A horizontal underground stem, distinguished from roots by the presence of nodes, often enlarged by food storage.

Rosette A crowded cluster of leaves; usually basal, circular, and appearing to grow directly out of the ground.

Saprophyte A plant lacking chlorophyll and living on dead organic matter.

Scale One of millions of shinglelike plates covering the wings of butterflies.

Scent scales Specialized scales that produce and disperse sex attractants; also called androconia.

Schist Metamorphic rock, such as mica, with foliate layers that break in parallel planes.

Scrub Stunted vegetation growing in sand or infertile soil.

Secondaries In birds, the large flight feathers located in a series along the rear edge of the wing, immediately inward from the primaries.

Sepal A basic unit of the calyx, usually green, but sometimes colored and resembling a petal.

Seral Part of the series of stages in a community from the initial (pioneer) stage to the climax. Each stage is marked by the presence or absence of particular plants and animals.

Serotinous Late or delayed in developing, and opened by fire; said of the cones of certain pines.

Serpentine Metamorphic rock, typically dull green mottled with red, but often other colors.

Sessile leaf A leaf that lacks a petiole, the blade being attached directly to the stem.

Sheath A more or less tubular structure surrounding a part, as the lower portion of a leaf surrounding the stem.

Simple eye A light-sensitive organ consisting of a convex lens bulging from the surface of the head, concentrating and guiding light rays to a cup-shaped cluster of photoreceptor cells. Also called an ocellus.

Simple leaf A leaf with a single blade, not compound or composed of leaflets.

Spadix A dense spike of tiny flowers, usually enclosed in a spathe, as in members of the arum family.

Spathe A bract or pair of bracts, often large, enclosing the flowers.

Spike An elongated flower cluster, each flower of which is without a stalk.

Spur A stout, spinelike projection, usually movable, such as is present commonly toward the end of the tibia.

Stamen One of the male structures of a flower, consisting of a threadlike filament and a pollen-bearing anther.

Staminate flower A male flower, that is, one with anthers and without pistils.

Stigma The tip of a pistil, usually enlarged, that receives the pollen.

Stipules Small appendages, often leaflike, on either side of some petioles at the base.

Stolon A stem growing along or under the ground; a runner.

Style The narrow part of the pistil, connecting ovary and stigma.

Subspecies A more or less distinct geographic population of a species that is able to interbreed with other members of the species.

Succession An orderly sequence of plant and animal communities, one group replacing another, ending in a climax community, or final stage. The climax is sometimes never reached because of repeated disturbances, such as fire.

Symbiosis An intimate biological relationship between two species. Symbiosis may take the form of parasitism, where one organism lives at the expense of the other; commensalism, where the presence of one neither helps nor damages the other; and mutualism, where both gain from the relationship.

Taproot The main root of a tree or plant, growing vertically downward, from which smaller, lateral roots extend.

Tarsus In butterflies, the foot section of the leg; it has hooks at the end for clinging; in birds, the lower, usually featherless, part of the leg.

Thorax The subdivision of the body between head and abdomen, consisting of 3 segments (the prothorax, mesothorax, and metathorax) and bearing whatever legs and wings are present.

Timberline A limit, created by climatological, topographical, or environmental factors, beyond which trees do not grow.

Transition zone An area between two communities that has plants and animals from each community; an ecotone.

Transpiration Loss of water by evaporation from leaves and other parts of plants.

Tubercle A raised, wartlike knob.

Turgor The usual state of distension in plant cells, essential for their functioning.

Type Tree species growing together in an association; forest types are defined by the trees actually growing on a site.

Umbel A flower cluster in which the individual flower stalks grow from the same point, like the ribs of an umbrella.

Understory The lower foliage layer in a forest, shaded by the canopy. Also the middle- and lower-level plants beneath the canopy, including shrubs, flowers, and seedlings.

Venation The pattern of veins on a wing.

Vent The anus; the opening of the cloaca to the outside of the body.

Virgin forest Woodland that exists in its primeval state.

Viviparous reproduction Giving birth to active young that have developed with no identifiable egg stage within the mother.

Vocal sac An expandable pouch on the throat of male frogs and toads that becomes filled with air and acts as a resonating chamber when they vocalize during courtship; the sac collapses at the end of the call.

Whorl A circle of three or more leaves, branches, or pedicels at a node.

Wing bar A conspicuous, crosswise wing mark.

Wing stripe A conspicuous mark running along the opened wing.

Worker One of a caste of social insects, usually incapable of reproduction, that procures and distributes food or provides defense for the colony.

BIBLIOGRAPHY

Barnett, Lincoln.
The Ancient Adirondacks.
New York: Time-Life Books, 1974.

Braun, E. Lucy.
Deciduous Forests of Eastern North America.
Philadelphia: Blakiston, 1950.

Brooks, Maurice.
The Appalachians.
Boston: Houghton Mifflin Company, 1965.

Carr, Archie.
The Everglades.
New York: Time-Life Books, 1974.

Daniel, Glenda and Jerry Sullivan.
A Sierra Club Naturalist's Guide to the North Woods.
San Francisco: Sierra, 1981.

Flader, Susan, ed.
The Great Lakes Forest.
Minneapolis: University of Minnesota Press, 1983.

Forman, Richard T. T., ed.
Pine Barrens: Ecosystem and Landscape.
New York: Academic Press, 1979.

George, Jean Craighead.
Everglades Wildguide.
U.S. Department of the Interior, National Park Service, Office of Publications, Natural History Series, 1972.

McCormick, Jack.
The Living Forest.
New York: Harper & Brothers, 1959.

Peattie, Donald C.
A Natural History of Trees of Eastern and Central North America.
Boston: Houghton Mifflin Company, 1966.

Rhodes, Richard.
The Ozarks.
New York: Time-Life Books, 1974.

Tanner, Ogden.
New England Wilds.
New York: Time-Life Books, 1974.

Watson, Geraldine.
Big Thicket Plant Ecology.
Saratoga, Texas: Big Thicket Museum Publication Series, No. 5, 1979.
Great Smoky Mountains.
Washington D.C.: Handbook 112, Division of Publications, National Park Service, U.S. Department of the Interior, 1981.

CREDITS

Photo Credits
The numbers in parentheses are plate numbers. Some
photographers have pictures under agency names as well as
their own.

Harry Ahles (509)
David H. Ahrenholz (364 right)

Alabama Society of Ornithology
Charles W. Brasfield (281)

Ruth Allen (443, 446, 458 right)

Amwest
Y. Momatiuk (392)

Animals Animals
Tom Brakefield (518) B. Kent (513) Zig Leszczynski (526,
529, 531, 539, 545, 546, 548) B. MacDonald (421)
Raymond A. Mendez (223) C. Perkins (425) Perry Slocum
(519) Stouffer Productions Ltd. (592)

William Aplin (164)
Ron Austing (250, 253, 254, 285, 289, 310, 317, 321–323,
325, 456)
Stephen F. Bailey (269)
Arthur S. Bailie (556)
David E. Baker (286, 291)
Roger Barbour (581, 583)
Harley Barnhart (559, 563)
Bob Barrett (312)
John Behler (512)
Michael Beug (555)
Les Blacklock (227, 470 left, 472)
J. Harry Boulet, Jr. (428, 476)
Tom Brakefield (601)
Richard W. Brown (67 left)
Richard T. Bryant (14)
Jean T. Buermeyer (436, 465)
Sonja Bullaty (5, 15, 477, 496)
Sonja Bullaty and Angelo Lomeo (1st frontispiece, 2nd
frontispiece, 3rd frontispiece, 5th frontispiece, 13, 19 left and
right, 20 right, 22 right, 23 left and right, 24 left and right,
25 left and right, 26 left and right, 27 right, 28 right, 29 left
and right, 30 left and right, 31 left and right, 32 left and
right, 34 left and right, 35 left and right, 36 left and right,
37 left and right, 38 left and right, 39 left and right, 40 left
and right, 43 left and right, 44 left and right, 45 left and
right, 46 left and right, 47 left and right, 48 left and right,
49 left and right, 50 left and right, 51 left and right, 52 left
and right, 53 left and right, 54 left and right, 55 left and
right, 56 left and right, 57 left and right, 58 left and right,
59 left and right, 60 left and right, 61 left and right, 62 left
and right, 63 left and right, 65 left and right, 66 left, 67
right, 68 right, 69 right, 71 left and right, 72 left and right,
73 left and right, 74 left and right, 75 left and right, 76 left
and right, 77 left and right, 78 left and right, 79 right, 80

left and right, 82 left and right, 83 left and right, 84 left and right, 85 left and right, 86 left and right, 87 left and right, 89 right, 90 left and right, 91 left and right, 92 left and right, 93 left and right, 94 left, 95 left and right, 98 left and right, 99 left and right, 100 left and right, 102 left and right, 103 left and right, 104 left and right, 105 left and right, 106 left and right, 107 left and right, 108 left and right, 109 left, 110 left and right, 111 left and right, 112 left and right, 113 left and right, 114 left and right, 115 left and right, 116 left and right, 117 left and right, 118 left and right, 119 left and right, 120 left and right, 121 left and right, 122 left and right, 123 left and right, 124 right, 125 left, 126 left, 129 left and right, 130 left and right, 131 left and right, 132 left and right, 134 left and right, 135 left and right, 136 left and right, 137 left and right, 138 left and right, 139 left and right, 140 left and right, 141 left and right, 142 left and right, 143 left and right, 144 left, 146– 150, 155, 156, 160–162, 182, 206, 212, 214, 219, 221, 230–232, 237, 238)
Ken Carmichael (255, 279)
Robert P. Carr (33 left and right, 394, 413)
David Cavagnaro (4, 64 left, 133 left)
Scooter Cheatham (81 left and right, 96 left and right, 127 left and right, 128 left and right)
Herbert Clarke (270, 294, 345)

Click/Chicago
James P. Rowan (8) Phil and Judy Sublett (1) Tom J. Ulrich (609)

Bruce Coleman, Inc.
Fred J. Alsop (244) Robert Carr (378) E. R. Degginger (402) D. Overcash (418) Hans Reinhard (615) Stouffer Productions (589) Larry West (379, 442)

Stephen Collins (196, 435, 506, 507, 510)

Cornell Laboratory of Ornithology
Betty D. Cottrille (300) J. H. Dick (278) John S. Dunning (284, 320) Michael Hopiak (268, 290, 342) C. B. Moore (568, 574) Gary Shackleford (327) Perry Slocum (251)

Helen Cruickshank (280)
James A. Cunningham (452 left and right)
Thase Daniel (292)
Kent and Donna Dannen (70 right, 198)
Harry Darrow (350, 353 left and right, 362, 363, 369 left and right, 373, 374 left, 403, 409, 416, 423)
Thomas Davies (376)
Edward R. Degginger (16, 18, 94 right, 144 right, 170, 173, 226, 358, 360, 368, 371 right and left, 400, 401, 474, 485, 547, 549, 577, 605, 614)
David M. Dennis (7, 12)
Jack Dermid (6, 20 left, 41 left, 261, 271, 494, 517, 522, 523, 550)
Larry Ditto (265)
Georges Dremeaux (306)

Robert Duncan (366 left)
Wilbur H. Duncan (42 right, 97 right)

DRK Photo
Stephen J. Krasemann (480) Wayne Lankinen (257, 313)

Robert L. Eikum (41 right, 145)
Lang Elliott (274)
Harry Ellis (415, 430, 431 left and right, 439, 441, 453 left and right, 501, 503)
Harry Engels (617)
Chuck Farber (364 left)
Mary Ferguson (450)
William E. Ferguson (395, 410)
Kenneth W. Fink (307, 594)
Richard B. Fischer (432)
Jeff Foott (245, 602)
John H. Gerard (433)
Jeff Gnass (2)
Lois Theodora Grady (21 right, 28 left)
Farrell Grehan (166)
William D. Griffin (267)
Annie Griffiths (3)
Raymond P. Guries (64 right, 154)
Pamela J. Harper (69 left, 70 left, 125 right, 133 right, 153, 157, 159, 163, 176, 191, 211, 224)
James Hawkings (305)

Grant Heilman Photography (169, 194)
Walter H. Hodge (124 left, 151, 158, 185) Alan Pitcairn (458 left)

Cecil B. Hoisington/Vermont Institute of Natural Science (455)
Michael Hopiak (283, 337)
Gord James (288)
Isidor Jeklin (252, 302, 341)
Charles C. Johnson (21 left, 466, 479, 488, 504)
Emily Johnson (561)
J. Eric Juterbock (541, 552)
Steven C. Kaufman (248)
J. James Kielbaso (22 left)
Dwight R. Kuhn (398)
Wayne Lankinen (247, 258, 263, 297, 311, 314, 315, 324, 338, 339)
Mary Lecroy (464)
Donald J. Leopold (27 left, 79 left)
Clarence E. Lewis (109 right, 213, 217, 228)
© Angelo Lomeo (Cover)
William B. Love (525, 534)
John A. Lynch (68 left, 152, 216, 218, 222, 225, 229, 233–235, 239, 240, 420, 462, 467 right)
John MacGregor (449, 454, 457, 459, 528, 535, 584, 606)
Thomas W. Martin (293, 298, 301, 304, 309, 316, 334, 335, 575)

Virginia Mayfield (273, 308, 340)
Joe McDonald (259, 578)
Ann McGrath (427)
Robert K. McIlvin (487)
Sturgis McKeever (357)
Anthony Mercieca (262, 318, 319, 344, 613)
Robert W. Mitchell (349, 382, 389, 391, 404, 417, 424)
C. Allan Morgan (242, 387)

National Audubon Society Collection/Photo Researchers, Inc.
A. Ambler (502) J. Arlington (532) William Bacon III (608)
N. Beck, Jr. (385) C. Belinky (192, 505) Ken Brate (434,
451 left and right, 588, 598) L. Broman (493) S. Collins
(508, 515, 533) Stephen Dalton (384) Marjorie Dezell (355)
Phil Dotson (607) Bill Dyer (296) M. Gadomski (437, 543)
P. Grace (171) W. Harlow (175, 181) H. Hoffman (499)
H. Hungerford (445) William J. Jahoda (354) Russ Kinne
(172, 183, 220, 593, 600) Stephen J. Krasemann (591)
Thomas W. Martin (303) Sturgis McKeever (527, 537, 590)
P. McLaughlin (469) I. Oakes (490) R. Parker (187) O. S.
Pettingill (586) G. Porter (536, 540, 544) Noble Proctor
(438, 467 left) Louis Quitt (429) William Ray (256) Leonard
Lee Rue III (511, 524) D. Rust (448) C. Schwartz (514)
R. Simmons (396) Alvin E. Staffan (177–179, 208–210)
Dan Sudia (348) P. Taylor (180) Mary Thacher (195, 500)
V. Weinland (66 right) Helen Williams (603)

John and Vikki Neyhart (375)
William A. Niering (482)
J. Oldenettel (264)
Arthur Panzer (243, 246)
C. W. Perkins (498)
Robert Perron (4th frontispiece)
Rod Planck (343, 346)
Betty Randall (101 left and right, 383)
John P. Ratti (277)
Susan Rayfield (168, 473)
J. V. Remsen (260)
Laura Riley (272)
Samuel Ristich (557, 572)
Edward S. Ross (380, 381, 390, 397, 406, 408, 412, 419)
Leonard Lee Rue III (266, 275, 440, 599, 616, 618)
Kit Scates (560, 565, 566, 573)
Werner W. Schutz (444)
Secrest Arboretum (165)
John Shaw (333, 351, 356, 359, 370, 377, 386, 405, 407,
422 left and right, 463)
Ervio Sian (330)
Robert S. Simmons (516, 520, 521, 530, 538, 542)
Richard Singer (367 left)
Arnold Small (299)
Arlo I. Smith (174)
John J. Smith (88 right, 126 right)
William Smith (554)
Joy Spurr (564)

Tom Stack and Associates
G. Brady (475) Harry Ellis (553, 569, 571) M. Gadomski
(481) Rick McIntyre (610) A. Nelson (483) C. Summers (604)

Alvin E. Staffan (89 left, 167, 184, 186, 188–190, 193,
197, 199–205, 207, 236, 241, 276, 287, 295, 329, 332,
336, 414, 447, 460 461, 468, 478, 484, 486, 491, 492,
495, 582, 585, 587, 597, 611, 612)
Lynn M. Stone (9)
Dan Sudia (328)
Rick Sullivan and Diana Rogers (42 left, 97 left)
Arthur Swoger (579)
Barbara Tagawa (567, 576)
Ian C. Tait (347)
Leo J. Tanghe (570)
Bill Thomas (10, 11, 17)
F. S. Todd (249)
Paul Tuskes (374 right)
Merlin D. Tuttle (596 left and right)
Tom J. Ulrich (609)

Valan Photos
Albert Kuhnigk (367 right)

William Vandivert (580, 595)
C. Wallis (471)
Richard G. Weber (399)
Larry West (88 left, 352, 365, 366 right, 388, 393, 426,
470 right, 497)
Klinton M. Wigren (215)
Jack Wilburn (331)
D. Dee Wilder (411)
E. N. Woodbury (361, 372)
Greg Wright (562)
Eleanor Yarrow (558)
Robert Zappalorti (551)
Dale and Marian Zimmerman (282, 326)
Jack Zucker (489)

Illustrations
The drawings of wildflowers were principally executed by
Bobbi Angell; the tree silhouettes, by Dolores R.
Santoliquido. The following artists also contributed to this
guide: Daniel Allen, Robin Jess, Steven Phillips, and Wendy
B. Zomlefer. Dot Barlowe contributed the drawings of
mammal tracks.

THE AUDUBON SOCIETY

The National Audubon Society is among the oldest and largest private conservation organizations in the world. With over 525,000 members and more than 500 local chapters across the country, the Society works in behalf of our natural heritage through environmental education and conservation action. It protects wildlife in more than seventy sanctuaries from coast to coast. It also operates outdoor education centers and ecology workshops and publishes the prizewinning AUDUBON magazine, AMERICAN BIRDS magazine, newsletters, films, and other educational materials. For further information regarding membership in the Society, write to the National Audubon Society, 950 Third Avenue, New York, New York 10022.

CHANTICLEER STAFF

Publisher: Paul Steiner
Editor-in-Chief: Gudrun Buettner
Executive Editor: Susan Costello
Managing Editor: Jane Opper
Series Editor: Mary Beth Brewer
Text Editor: Ann Whitman
Associate Editor: Marian Appellof
Assistant Editors: David Allen, Constance Mersel
Production Manager: Helga Lose
Production: Amy Roche, Frank Grazioli
Art Director: Carol Nehring
Art Associate: Ayn Svoboda
Picture Library: Edward Douglas, Dana Pomfret
Maps and Symbols: Paul Singer
Natural History Consultant: John Farrand, Jr.
Design: Massimo Vignelli